PERSONALITY

Theories, Research, and Applications

Lewis R. Aiken

Pepperdine University

PRENTICE HALL
Englewood Cliffs, New Jersey 07632

Library of Congress Cataloging-in-Publication Data

Aiken, Lewis R., (date)
   Personality : theories, research, and applications / Lewis R. Aiken.
     p.   cm.
   Includes bibliographical references and indexes.
   ISBN 0–13–658733–X
   1. Personality. I. Title.
BF698.A3364 1993
155.2—dc20

                                92–30073
                                      CIP

Acquisitions editor: Susan Finnemore Brennan
Editorial assistant: Jenny Katsaros
Editorial/production supervision: Mary McDonald
Interior design: Peggy Gordon
Copy editor: Peter K. Reinhart
Cover design: Anne Ricigliano
Prepress buyer: Kelly Behr
Manufacturing buyer: Mary Ann Gloriande

Printed in the United States of America
10 9 8 7 6 5 4 3 2 1

ISBN 0-13-658733-X

Prentice-Hall International (UK) Limited, *London*
Prentice-Hall of Australia Pty. Limited, *Sydney*
Prentice-Hall Canada Inc., *Toronto*
Prentice-Hall Hispanoamericana, S.A., *Mexico*
Prentice-Hall of India Private Limited, *New Delhi*
Prentice-Hall of Japan, Inc., *Tokyo*
Simon & Schuster Asia Pte. Ltd., *Singapore*
Editora Prentice-Hall do Brasil, Ltda., *Rio de Janeiro*

Dedicated to
Ralph Mason Dreger,
my first psychology teacher
and lifelong mentor.

The older one gets the more one realizes how saturated life is in mystery, and the biggest mystery of all, it often seems to me, is the mystery of the human personality.

Susan Howatch, *Scandalous Risks*

Contents

7. Phenomenological Theories   166

8. Behavioral and Social Learning Theories   199

PART III.   BIOLOGICAL AND SOCIOCULTURAL INFLUENCES

9. Biological Foundations of Personality   232

◇◇◇

Preface

As used in this text, the term *personality* refers to the organized totality of the qualities, traits, and behaviors that characterize a person's individuality and by which, together with his or her physical attributes, the person is recognized as unique. This definition is abstract rather than operational, and broad rather than narrow. Although one may quibble with the objectivity and precision of the definition, it is adequate to describe the subject matter of this textbook. In short, the text is concerned with the description, causes, and consequences of individual *uniqueness* in behavior and thought processes. The theme of the book is that human personality is a unique combination of cognitive and affective characteristics, describable in terms of a typical, fairly consistent, organized pattern of behavior.

The topics of personality assessment, theories, research methods and findings, and practical applications of personality studies are all covered in some detail in this textbook. The figures, tables, Activities and Applications, and other study aids included in the text should make it attractive to students and professors in courses on personality at the undergraduate level. The book contains interesting, informative material, presented with sufficient clarity so it can be read with enjoyment and scholarly benefit by psychology majors and others who elect to take a course in the subject.

In addition to the central concepts of dispositional, psychodynamic, phenomenological, behavioristic, and cognitive theories of personality, research pertaining to these theories and other concepts concerned with individual differences in psychological functioning are considered. An entire section is devoted to the topic of personality and health (physical and mental), and another chapter considers recent applications of personality research and theory in educational, business and industrial, legal, and political contexts. Continuing, but not unresolvable, issues in personality study (e.g., traits versus situations, hereditary versus environmental determinants, idiographic versus nomothetic approaches, and clinical versus statistical assessment and prediction) and criticisms of practices stemming from personality theory, research, and measurement also receive ample attention.

The prerequisites for understanding the material in this book are not extensive. Obviously, the student should be a good reader. In addition, one or two previous courses in psychology will help prepare one for the theories, concepts, and methods considered in the text. Although a small amount of statistical material is included in Chapters 2 and 4, a formal course in statistics is not a prerequisite for understanding this book. A brief introduction to factor analysis has been included as Appendix B.

As with any textbook, the preparation of this volume was a cooperative effort. I am especially grateful to the reviewers for their constructive criticisms and suggestions and to the copy editor, Peter Reinhart, and the production editor, Mary McDonald. Whatever success may have resulted from my efforts should be shared with those individuals who tried to make this a better book. It goes without saying, however, that the final responsibility for errors of omission and commission, which I trust are minimal, belongs only to the author.

Lewis R. Aiken

A special supplement offer for professors who use *Personality: Theories, Research, and Applications* by Lewis R. Aiken:

Students in courses concerned with personality, personality theories, and personality assessment need experience in performing the course-related tasks described in the Activities and Applications sections in this text. While teaching the Personality and Personality Assessment courses at Pepperdine University, Lewis Aiken has developed a software package that fits these needs. The twenty computer programs, written in BASICA for IBM-PC's and compatible computers, are designed to provide users with experience in taking various personality assessment instruments and in designing their own tests and questionnaires. Also, one program will be helpful in reviewing the definitions of important concepts found in the text and identifying the names of theorists and/or researchers and their contributions to the psychology of personality. The programs are informative and interesting to use and should serve as a useful supplement to other course activities.

Here are the programs in this software package:

1. Administering and Scoring an Objective Personality Test
2. Altruism Inventory
3. College Course Evaluation Inventory
4. Constructing an Objective Personality Test
5. Dot Pattern Test
6. Educational Values Inventory
7. Five-Factor Inventory
8. Learning to Associate Names with Terms
9. Levels of Aspiration and Performance
10. Likability Inventory—Construction
11. Likability Inventory—Administration and Scoring
12. Prisoner's Dilemma Game
13. Projective Line Drawings
14. Ranking Adjectives for Your Real and Ideal Selves
15. Rating Your Professor's Personality
16. Sentence Completion Test
17. Sociability, Activity, and Emotionality Scales
18. Sports Success Inventory
19. Women's Rights and Images Questionnaires
20. Word Association Test

To obtain a detailed description of each program or to obtain the software for use with *Personality: Theories, Research, and Applications* in your classroom, please contact your local Prentice Hall representative or write to:

Psychology Editor
Prentice Hall
113 Sylvan Avenue, Route 9W
Englewood Cliffs, NJ 07632

CHAPTER 1

Introduction and Historical Foundations

CHAPTER OUTLINE

"Genes Appear to Influence Shyness, Aggressiveness"
"Personality and the X Chromosome"
"The Addictive Personality"
"Presidential Personalities"
"Altruism: Inborn or Taught?"
"The Character of Personality"

These headlines represent just a sample of stories concerned with personality and its correlates that appear daily in newspapers and magazines throughout the world. Other articles deal with the interactions between personality and place of residence, birth order, exercise, sports, diet, pets, eye color and eye signs, blood type, breathing, color preferences, speech patterns, the use of time, and the (heavenly) stars. Motion pictures, plays, novels, short stories, and popular songs [1] also attest to the importance of personality in achieving health, happiness, and material and romantic success. Professional journals in psychology, psychiatry, education, cultural anthropology, and many other fields also publish reports of empirical research concerned with the relationships of personality to heredity, health, physical characteristics, occupational success, and behavior.

Many popular and professional writings on personality can be explained as understandable responses to the question of "What makes people tick?" Efforts to discover the truth about ourselves and how we function are laudable, but there are also entertaining and practical aspects to reports concerning personality. Sometimes the reports or stories are designed merely to titillate or satisfy the human appetite for the bizarre or outrageous rather than to inform or teach. On the other hand, the reader may learn something useful from stories about the personalities of anorexics, sex deviates, or other people with problems, and may even be able to apply such information to his or her own personal decision making. The findings of research on personality also assist in the very pragmatic concerns of selecting employees or students and in the diagnosis and treatment of personality disorders.

Meaning and Measurement

People are both similar and different. There may be more similarities than differences among people, but the differences definitely count. Even identical twins, who originate from the same fertilized egg and hence share the same hereditary characteristics, differ in significant ways. This is true whether they are reared in the same or different environments. Despite the fact that human beings are unique, everyone is like everyone else in certain ways. We have different biological and experiential backgrounds, but we still share certain physical and mental qualities that distinguish us as human beings rather than other animals, plants, or inanimate matter. Thus people are both unique and similar; they possess a combination of physical, mental, and behavioral characteristics that identify them as human and endow them with individual personalities.

The ancient Greeks and Romans had no word for *personality* in the modern sense. The word is derived, however, from the Greek *persona,* or mask, associated with a role played by an actor in a play. The notion that personality is synonymous with *character* has the same theatrical origins as *persona.* The dictionary definition of character as "the aggregate of features and traits that form the individual nature of a person" might also serve as a definition of personality.

Rather than relating it specifically to character, *personality* may also be defined as "the public, social stimulus, or organized behavioral characteristics of a person that are visible to other people and make an impression on them." Another definition of personality stresses the private, central, inner core of an individual. Included within this private core are motives, attitudes, interests, beliefs, fantasies, cognitive styles, and other mental processes.

Some definitions of personality emphasize its "person quality," personal existence, or identity features. An extreme example is the view that *personality* is a mysterious charisma possessed only by Hollywood stars and other celebrities, so-called "personalities" who may have no other talents than decorating themselves and behaving in a friendly fashion. Other meanings of personality have been associated with specific disciplines or professions. Among these are selfhood, ideal of perfection, and supreme value (philosophy); the individual members of the Trinity (theology); and a person having legal status (law) (Hunt, 1986).

According to a global, or omnibus, definition, personality is an organized composite of qualities or characteristics—the sum total of the physical, mental, emotional, and social qualities of a person. This is the way in which the term is employed in this book; as such, it is essentially synonymous with the psychology of the individual (Murray, 1938). More specifically, the term *personality* refers to a unique composite of inborn and acquired mental abilities, attitudes, temperaments, and other individual differences in thoughts, feelings, and actions. This collectivity of cognitive and affective characteristics, as it exists in a particular human being, is associated with a fairly consistent pattern of behavior.

The use of such a broad definition implies that the study of personality encompasses a wide range of variables. Among these variables are not only affective characteristics such as emotion, temperament, character, and stylistic traits, but also cognitive variables such as achievement, intelligence, and specific aptitudes, as well as various psychomotor abilities or physical skills and mannerisms. This book focuses on individual differences in affective characteristics, which encompass the traditional, albeit somewhat limited, conception of personality variables. Reference is also made to cognitive and psychomotor variables, but they are not discussed at length. For a more complete description of cognitive and psychomotor abilities the student should consult *Assessment of Intellectual Functioning* (Aiken, 1987) and *Psychological Testing and Assessment (7th ed.)* (Aiken, 1991b) or similar volumes on psychological testing in general or cognitive and affective assessment in particular. Measurement is basic to the conceptualization and manipulation of any psychological variable, but in addition to personality measurement, we shall be concerned with theories of personality structure and dynamics, research on personality, and practical findings stemming from the study of personality.

Historical Foundations

The history of personality study goes back to a time when people first became aware of individual differences in thinking and acting. Some of these differences were ascribed to totems, signs, or symbols under which people were born.

Although there are no written records of the earliest behavioral observations, the *Epic of Gilgamesh* (circa 2000 B.C.) and the Bible contain citations indicating an awareness of differences in personality. For example, in Judges 7:3–7:7, God says to Gideon:

> "You have too many men for me to deliver Midian into their hands. In order that Israel may not boast against me that her own strength has saved her, announce now to the people, 'Anyone who trembles with fear may turn back and leave Mount Gilead.' " So twenty-two thousand men left, while ten thousand remained.
>
> But the Lord said to Gideon, "There are still too many men. Take them down to the water, and I will sift them for you there. If I say, 'This one shall go with you,' he shall go; but if I say, 'This one shall not go with you,' he shall not go."
>
> So Gideon took the men down to the water. There the Lord told him, "Separate those who lap the water with their tongues like a dog from those who kneel down to drink." Three hundred men lapped with their hands to their mouths. All the rest got down on their knees to drink.
>
> The Lord said to Gideon, "With the three hundred men that lapped I will save you and give the Midianites into your hands. Let all the other men go, each to his own place." And the Lord said unto Gideon, "By the three hundred men that lapped will I save you, and deliver the Midianites into thine hand: and let all the other people go every man unto his place."

God presumably surmised that the men who lapped like dogs while drinking were more alert or wary and hence would prove to be just as effective as a larger fighting force.[2]

Ancient Greece and Rome

Efforts to analyze and assess human personality can also be seen in the writings of the ancient Greeks and Romans. The Greek physician Hippocrates (460–377 B.C.), arguing that natural rather than supernatural forces are the causes of disease, proposed that there are four "humors" in the human body—blood, black bile, yellow bile, and phlegm. Around A.D. 200, Galen, a Roman physician who subscribed to Hippocrates' humoral theory, concluded from his observations that there are four types of temperament corresponding to an overabundance of each of the four humors. These four temperament types are sanguine, melancholic, choleric, and phlegmatic. An individual with a *sanguine* temperament, who purportedly had an excess of blood, was characterized as forceful, direct, and courageous. An individual with a *melancholic* temperament, who was generally brooding, moody, and withdrawing, was said to have a predominance of black bile. A person with a *choleric* temperament, who presumably had an excess of yellow bile, was characterized as irritable, bitter, and resentful. And a person characterized as habitually weak, fragile, and indecisive, was described as a *phlegmatic* personality having an overabundance of phlegm in the body.

The ancient Greeks were greatly interested in human characteristics and wrote extensively on the subject. Famous philosophers such as Plato (427–347 B.C.) and Aristotle (384–322 B.C.), for example, had much to say on the subject of individual differences. Plato's distinction between the rational and irrational in man and his analyses of conflict (as opposed to "harmony") and repression presumably influenced psychoanalytic theorizing 22 centuries later. The doctrine of the soul, which was formulated initially by the Pythagoreans, was also developed by Plato and Aristotle. To these philosophers there were three kinds of souls: *nutritive souls* are characteristic of plants, *sensing souls* are characteristic of animals, and *rational souls* are characteristic of humans. Aristotle viewed the soul as a spirit moving in the body, a "perfect unity toward which bodily functions are directed."

We also owe the word *psychology* to the ancient Greeks, *psyche* being the Greek word for soul, and *logos,* the word for knowledge or study of. Hardly anyone today, however (and certainly no psychologist!), would define psychology as "the study of the soul." In fact, it is doubtful that many psychologists could be found who would subscribe to the nineteenth-century definition of psychology as "the study of the mind." For this reason, it has been quipped that psychology first lost its soul and then lost its mind.

Of particular interest to personality assessment are the 30 descriptions or sketches provided by the Greek writer Theophrastus (372–287 B.C.). These descriptive sketches, like the humoral theory of Hippocrates and Galen, were overgeneralizations based on observations of human behavior. Examples of the character types described by Theophrastus were the Flatterer, the Garrulous Man (a chatterbox), the Liar, the Penurious Man (a miser), the Surly Man (a bad-tempered person), and the Tasteless Man (an unrefined person). Excerpts from two of these sketches, describing the dominant characteristics and typical style of action of certain types of individual, are given in Report 1–1. Theophrastus presented no scientific evidence for the existence of such character types, although his sketches are entertaining and perhaps thought provoking.

The Middle Ages and Renaissance

A number of other events that have contributed to the scientific study of personality are listed in Table 1–1. Despite a widespread interest in individual differences, little genuine progress in the scientific analysis of personality was made until fairly recent times. Descriptive characterizations were provided by playwrights and novelists such as William Shakespeare, Miguel de Cervantes (*Don Quixote*), and Charles Dickens. Adjectives such as quixotic, malapropistic,

REPORT 1–1

Sample Descriptions of the Characters of Theophrastus

The Garrulous Man

The Garrulous man is one that will sit down close beside somebody he does not know, and begin talk with a eulogy of his own life, and then relate a dream he had the night before, and after that tell dish by dish what he had for supper. As he warms up to his work he will remark that we are by no means the men we were, and the price of wheat has gone down, and there's a ship of strangers in town. . . . Next he will surmise that the crops would be all the better for some more rain, and tell him what he is going to grow on his farm next year, adding that it is difficult to make both ends meet . . . and "I vomited yesterday" and "What day is it today?" . . . And if you let him go on he will never stop. (Edmonds, 1929, pp. 48–49)

The Penurious Man

A Penurious man is one who goes to a debtor to ask for his half-obol interest before the end of the month. At a dinner where expenses are shared, he counts the number of cups each person drinks, and he makes a smaller libation to Artemis than anyone. If someone has made a good bargain on his account and presents him with the bill he says it is too much. When his servant breaks a pot or a plate, he deducts the value from his food. If his wife drops a copper, he moves furnitures, beds, chests and hunts in the curtains. If he has something to sell he puts such a price on it that the buyer has no profit. He forbids his wife to lend anything—neither salt nor lampwick nor cinnamon nor marjoram nor meal nor garlands nor cakes for sacrifices. . . . To sum up, the coffers of the penurious men are moldy and the keys rust; they wear cloaks which hardly reach the thigh; a very little oil-bottle supplies them for anointing; they have hair cut short and do not put on their shoes until midday; and when they take their cloak to the fuller they urge him to use plenty of earth so that it will not be spotted so soon. (Quoted by Allport, 1937 p. 57)

and Falstaffian, which were coined from characters in well-known tales and dramas, have become a part of the English language. The characterizations of these famous writers, are, however, like those of Theophrastus, stereotypes or overgeneralizations. It was not until the late nineteenth century that the scientific exploration and measurement of human personality began in earnest.

The study of individuality and personality was held back by the same social and religious forces that restricted progress in art and science until the Renaissance. The Middle Ages, which lasted approximately from the fall of the Roman Empire (A.D. 476) until the fifteenth century, was, for most people, a time of unquestioning faith and a struggle to survive and do one's duty. Augustine and

TABLE 1–1 Events in the History of Personality Study

400 B.C.	Hippocrates relates personality characteristics to body types.
4th century B.C.	Theophrastus describes 30 personality types or characters.
2nd century A.D.	Galen relates Hippocrates' theory of body humors to temperament.
Circa 1800	Franz Gall and Johann Spurzheim found pseudoscience of phrenology, relating bumps on the skull to personality.
1884	Francis Galton describes methods for the measurement of character, including word association and behavior-sampling techniques.
1900	*The Interpretation of Dreams*, by Sigmund Freud, is published.
1905	Carl Jung uses word association tests to detect and analyze mental complexes. First practical intelligence test, the Binet-Simon Scale, by Alfred Binet and Théodore Simon, published.
1906	Heymans and Wiersma develop a list of symptoms indicative of psychopathology.
1907	Emil Kraepelin's classification of mental disorders published in his book *Clinical Psychiatry*.
1910	Kent Rosanoff word lists published.
1919	Robert Woodworth's Personal Data Sheet, the first standardized personality inventory, based on the Heymans-Wiersma symptoms list, used in U.S. military selection. Pressey X-O Test published.
1920	Hermann Rorschach's Inkblot Test published. Watson/Rayner study of conditioned fear of white rat in Little Albert.
1920s	Kurt Lewin and others begin experimental study of personality.
1925	Ernst Kretschmer describes his observations on the relationships of body build to personality and mental disorder.
1926	Florence Goodenough's Draw-a-Man Test published.
1928	Hartshorne and May studies of character reported.
1935	Thematic Apperception Test (TAT) developed by Murray and Morgan. Louis Thurstone develops centroid method of factor analysis. Kurt Lewin publishes *A Dynamic Theory of Personality*.
1936	Ross Stagner's *Psychology of Personality* published.
1937	Gordon Allport's *Personality: A Psychological Interpretation* published.
1938	Henry Murray's *Explorations in Personality*, describing theoretical foundations of the Thematic Apperception Test, published. Bender Visual-Motor Gestalt Test for assessing personality and brain damage published.
1939	*Frustration and Aggression*, by Dollard, Doob, Miller, Mowrer, and Sears, published.
1940	J. P. Guilford applies factor analysis to the construction of a personality inventory.
1942	Sheldon and Stevens report their research on the relationships of body build to temperament.
1943	Minnesota Multiphasic Personality Inventory, by Starke Hathaway and Fred McKinley, published.
1950	Dollard and Miller's *Personality and Psychotherapy* published. *The Authoritarian Personality* by Adorno, Frenkel-Brunswik, Levinson, and Sanford published.
1951	Rogers' *Client-Centered Therapy* published.
1952	*Diagnostic and Statistical Manual I* published by the American Psychiatric Association.
1953	Q-sort technique devised by William Stephenson. Whiting and Child's *Child-Training and Personality* published.

TABLE 1–1   Events in the History of Personality Study (Continued)

1954	Paul Meehl's *Clinical Versus Statistical Prediction* published. Rogers and Dymond's *Psychotherapy and Personality Change* published.
1955	George Kelly's *Psychology of Personal Constructs* published.
1961	David McClelland's *The Achieving Society* published.
1968	Walter Mischel's *Personality and Assessment* published.
1970–1990	Increasing use of computers in designing, administering, scoring, analyzing, and interpreting personality assessment procedures and instruments.
1972	Holland's Self-Directed Search, a measure of interests and personality, published.
1975–1980	Growth of behavioral assessment techniques.
1980	*Diagnostic and Statistical Manual III* published by the American Psychiatric Association.
1987	California Psychological Inventory–Revised published.
1989	MMPI–II published.

other theologians emphasized turning inward and introspective reflection, while materialism and science were considered enemies of the church. Owing to a combination of social and economic forces, the influence of the Catholic Church began to diminish during the fifteenth century. As a consequence, supernatural views and a preoccupation with death, demons, and the hereafter gave way to more temporal, earthly concerns.

The Renaissance, which lasted from the fourteenth to the seventeenth century A.D., together with the subsequent period of Enlightenment during the eighteenth century, witnessed a return to the ancient Hellenistic perspective on the value and worth of the individual. According to this ideal, people are capable of influencing their temporal situation and circumstances. Freed from the constraints of intolerance and censorship, they can use their abilities to understand the world and themselves, and thereby improve the human condition.

Traditional church doctrine had held that life is a battleground between the forces of good and evil. People were considered to be basically evil, born in sin with only a hope and not a guarantee of salvation and a better life after death. In contrast, many philosophers during the Enlightenment and the succeeding Age of Romanticism maintained that human beings are not bad by nature. The French philosopher Jean-Jacques Rousseau (1712–1778) maintained that people are born in a state of goodness and that naturalness is virtuous. Rousseau, who believed that it is society which makes people bad, argued for a return to the natural state of the "noble savage." This point of view influenced a number of modern humanistic psychologists, who saw the human struggle as an attempt to realize the good or growth potential within oneself. On the other hand, the view that people are born in neither a state of goodness nor evil, that each person's mind is a "blank tablet" (*tabula rasa*) at birth, was favored by John Locke, Voltaire, and certain other philosophers. The writings of these empiricistic philosophers influenced the conceptions of many developmental and experimental psychologists during the twentieth century.

Pseudoscience and Personality Study

Most people are curious about what makes them "tick" and how they will turn out. Before the modern era, people often relied on oracles, soothsayers, and other fortune tellers to diagnose their character and foretell their futures. For example, the Oracle at Delphi's advice to "Know thyself" was widely quoted and believed. Unfortunately, much of the "knowledge" of the time, as well as the pseudosciences which perpetuated it, was based on false assumptions and biased observations. Pseudosciences such as astrology, numerology, palmistry, graphology, phrenology, and physiognomy, the majority of which have ancient origins, are still believed by many people today. Astrology, numerology, and palmistry were more concerned with forecasting the future or fate of individuals than with analyzing personality and character, but inasmuch as personality affects one's future, these pseudosciences form a part of the history of personality study.

Astrology. Among the oldest pseudosciences is astrology, which is based on the notion that the relative positions of the sun, the moon, and the planets at a specific point in time, such as a person's birth date, affect one's fortune. Each of the twelve signs of the *zodiac*, or constellations (Aries, Libra, Scorpio, etc.) of heavenly bodies, is supposedly associated with certain aspects of character, temperament, and aptitude (see Table 1–2). Given the exact time and place of a person's birth,[3] an astrologer can prepare an individualized chart, or *horoscope*, of the planetary positions associated with that person. From this information, astrologers claim to be able to predict the person's future and advise him or her on decisions and possible actions.

TABLE 1–2 Personality Characteristics Allegedly Related to the Zodiac

Constellation	Planet	Birth Date	Personality Characteristics
Capricorn	Saturn	12/21–1/20	Ambition, caution, work
Aquarius	Uranus	1/21–2/19	Humane, unconventional, high and low spirits
Pisces	Neptune	2/20–3/20	Inspiration, easily influenced, dreaming
Aries	Mars	3/21–4/20	Impulsiveness, adventure, disputes
Taurus	Venus	4/21–5/21	Endurance, obstination, labor
Gemini	Mercury	5/22–6/21	Skill, versatility, good relationships
Cancer	Moon	6/22–7/23	Appreciates home life, imagination, indecision
Leo	Sun	7/24–8/23	Generality, pride, desire for power
Virgo	Mercury	8/24–9/23	Analytical, studious, modest
Libra	Venus	9/24–10/23	Justice, artistic sense, sensitivity
Scorpio	Mars	10/24–11/22	Critical sense, secrecy, fights
Sagittarius	Jupiter	11/23–12/20	Idealism, open-mindedness, mobility

See M. Gauquelin, *Cosmic influences on human behavior* (London: Garnstone Press, 1973).

Numerology. Like astrology, *cartomancy* (which uses playing cards), *geomancy* (which employs figures or lines), and dream symbolism, numerology has been used for centuries to foretell the futures of individuals and the outcomes of various enterprises. In numerology, as pioneered by the Greek mathematician Pythagoras, various operations are performed on numbers, the results of which are interpreted and predictions made. Examples of numbers possessing special meanings are 13 (an unlucky number), 3 (perfection, the Holy Trinity), 7 (a lucky number, harmony), and 666 (the Beast in the Book of Revelations).

Palmistry. Similar in some respects to astrology, and equally old, is *palmistry*, or chiromancy. Palmists claim to be able to analyze the character and foretell the destiny of a person by analyzing the features of his or her hand. Special attention is given to the seven mounts (Jupiter, Saturn, Apollo or the Sun, Mercury, Mars, the Moon, and Venus) located at the bases of the thumb and fingers and on the sides of the hand. The following descriptions are examples of characteristics said to be associated with the development of the respective mount:

> Jupiter—ambition, concern for honor, interest in religion; overdevelopment reveals pride and superstition.
> Mars—high development indicates bravery and a martial character; low development suggests cowardice.
> Saturn—related to luck and wisdom.
> Apollo (the sun)—related to intelligence.
> Venus—related to amorousness.

In addition to the seven mounts, palmists study the relative length and depth of the head, heart, life, and fortune lines of the hand: A short or broken life line points to an early death or serious illness. The head line is associated with intelligence; the heart line relates to affection; and the line of fortune predicts success and failure.

Phrenology. Related to palmistry, but focusing on the head instead of the hand, is *phrenology*. Few people today seriously believe in phrenology, but it was viewed more seriously by Thomas Jefferson, Edgar Allan Poe, and certain other learned men during the nineteenth century. As developed by Franz Gall (1758–1828) and his student Johann Spurzheim (1776–1832), phrenology is a pseudoscience in which abstract mental qualities such as acquisitiveness, agreeableness, artistic talent, courage, greed, and pride are associated with the development of over three dozen "organs" of the brain. Phrenologists believed that overdevelopment of one or more of these brain "organs" results in a protuberance (bump) on the skull over the corresponding area (see Figure 1–2). If this belief is true, then personality or character should be interpretable by fingering the skull to analyze the configuration of bumps. It was believed by a number of nineteenth-century physicians that it might even be possible to diagnose mental disorders in this manner.

A description from O. L. Fowler's *Practical Phrenology* (1890, p.1) reveals

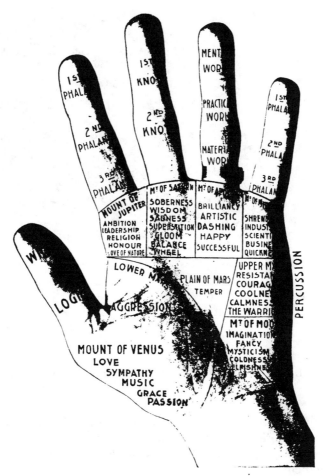

FIGURE 1–1   Benham's system of hand-zone nomenclature. (From *The Book of Palmistry* by Fred Gettings. Copyright 1974, Triune Books, London, England.)

how a pseudoscience like phrenology may appear to be quite scientific in its methods:

> Like all other exact sciences, large portions of it was discovered and brought to its present stage of perfection, entirely by induction . . . by an observation and a classification of facts. . . . The following is the method adopted by Dr. Gall in the discovering of competitiveness. . . . After collecting a promiscuous company of ordinary persons from the streets, he assertained from them which were cowardly and which courageous. He then placed the former by themselves, and proceeded to examine and compare the respective developments of the different portions of their heads, until he assertained that not withstanding the great diversity of shape in other parts, yet the heads of the courageous ones all displayed a fullness and thickness just behind the top of the ear, and that the heads of the cowardly were all thin and depressed in that particular region. This discovery . . . was then applied to innumerable other subjects, until its correctness was fully established.

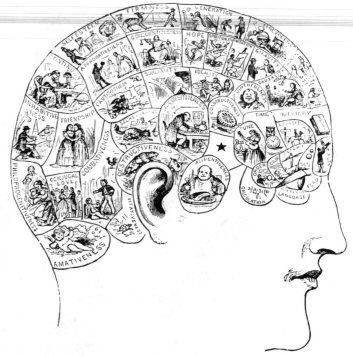

FIGURE 1–2   Phrenologists' chart of brain functions. (Courtesy of Bettman Archive.)

By the end of the nineteenth century, the research of Pierre Flourens, Paul Broca, and other neurophysiologists had disproved the notion that specific brain areas are associated with the complex functions described by Gall and Spurzheim.

Physiognomy. Another pseudoscience that attempts to determine temperament and character from external bodily features, especially the face, is *physiognomy.* Remnants of physiognomy exist in contemporary personality assessment, for example, in the requirement that a personal photograph be submitted with an employment application, and in the Szondi Test. The Szondi Test consists of six sets of photographs, with eight pictures per set, of mental patients having different psychiatric diagnoses (catatonia, depression, hysteria, mania, etc.). In taking the test, examinees select from each set the two pictures that they like most and the two that they like least. The basic assumption underlying the test is that the facial features of the mental patients depicted in the 12 selected and 12 unselected photographs have special meanings for the examinee. The needs and personality of the examinee are interpreted as being similar to those of the patients in the photographs they like most and dissimilar to those of the photographs they like least.

Physiognomy should not be confused with the analysis of meanings or messages communicated by facial expressions such as smiling and crying (e.g., Ekman & Friesen, 1984). Physiognomy is concerned with determining personal characteristics from the form or features of the body, especially the face. The analysis of facial expressions, however, is a more scientifically accepted and valid effort to understand the meanings and origins of nonverbal behavior.

Graphology. For hundreds of years, and by studying hundreds of books written on the subject, people have tried, without notable success, to assess individual personality by analyzing handwriting samples. The pseudoscience of *graphology* as a respected discipline did not emerge, however, until the nineteenth century in continental Europe. Some *graphologists* attempt to interpret handwriting intuitively on the basis of overall impressions, whereas others are more analytic in stressing certain signs or clues such as the way the writer dots *i*'s or slants letters. To be fair, graphology is not viewed as having quite the same degree of quackery as astrology or phrenology, and it continues to have many proponents. For example, certain business organizations use the services of graphologists in employee selection. Unfortunately, the claims of these proponents are more often than not just as wrong as those of the phrenologists.

It makes sense that handwriting, which is a type of stylistic behavior, could reflect personality characteristics to some extent. Graphologists are, however, not noted for the validity of their analyses. Even attempts to analyze handwriting by means of computers have failed to demonstrate that graphology is a valid method of personality assessment (Rothenberg, 1990). One problem in using handwriting as a diagnostic test is inconsistency: A person's handwriting is affected by alcohol, drugs, aging, disease, and many other factors (E. L. Kelly, 1987). After reviewing the scientific literature on graphology, the conclusion that "graphological predictions would seem to play a role akin to that played by placebos in medicine: not completely ineffective, but for reasons other than those that make the real thing effective" (Ben-Shakhar, Bar-Hillel, Bilu, Ben-Abba, and Flug, 1986, pp. 652–653) appears justified.

The Beginnings of Personality Study

After the French Revolution of 1789, a more humane attitude toward the mentally ill developed through the influence of Philippe Pinel (1745–1826), who instituted reforms in mental hospitals throughout France. The emphasis of early nineteenth-century psychiatry was on the *organic* basis of mental illness, which was a marked improvement over the older belief that the mentally ill are possessed of demons that must be exorcised by incantations, beatings, burnings, and other rituals. However, many later nineteenth-century and twentieth-century psychiatrists emphasized *functional* causes of mental illnesses, viewing them as faulty habit patterns acquired by experience. As a consequence, psychological approaches such as reeducation, psychotherapy, and hypnosis, rather than medicine or surgery, were recommended as treatments for mental illness. Jean-Martin Charcot (1825–1893) and Pierre Janet (1859–1947) were psychiatric pioneers in the development of the concept of functional causes of mental illness and the use of hypnosis for treating certain mental disorders. In addition to treating these disorders, French psychiatrists and psychologists developed methods of diagnosing them, including various observational and testing techniques.

The most famous successor to Charcot and Janet was Sigmund Freud, who, like Rousseau, considered civilized society to be the villain in man's struggle to express his true nature. Unlike Rousseau, Freud believed that the nature of mankind is not necessarily good. Freud perceived a newborn child as bent on the satisfaction of its sexual and aggressive needs, with never a care for the concerns or conveniences of others. He realized that social rules, regulations, and other restraints on the expression of the true nature of children are necessary, but by imposing these restraints on children civilization dooms mankind to eternal neurosis and discontent.

By the end of the nineteenth century, psychology had been formally christened a science, and the scientific study of behavior and mental life was well under way. Despite the disinterest of experimental psychology's founding father, Wilhelm Wundt (1832–1920), in the study of individual differences in motivation, emotion, intelligence, thought, and personality, certain psychologists began conducting research on these topics.

Sir Francis Galton (1822–1911), whose primary research interest was the measurement of mental abilities, proposed to measure emotions by recording changes in heartbeat and pulse rate and to assess good temper, optimism, and other so-called "character traits." Among the methods described by Galton for measuring these variables were the behavior sampling technique of observing people in contrived social situations. Galton was also the first scientist to advocate the use of the *word association technique* for studying personality. In this technique, the examinee is told to respond to each of a series of words with the first word that comes to mind. The word association technique was also employed several years later by Emil Kraepelin and Carl Jung, who used it to identify and analyze mental complexes. The extensive observations and descriptions of mental disorders provided by Emil Kraepelin, Richard von Krafft-Ebing, and other psychiatrists during the late nineteenth and early twentieth centuries also provided a framework for later research on personality and the development of psychodiagnostic instruments such as the Rorschach Inkblot Test and the Minnesota Multiphasic Personality Inventory.

Another psychologist whose primary claim to fame came from the measurement of intelligence, but who was also interested in personality assessment, was Alfred Binet (1857–1911). Prior to his work on intelligence testing, Binet had devised methods for studying the personality characteristics of eminent persons. Among these techniques were responses to inkblots, stories told about pictures (fantasy life), and the analysis of handwriting samples. In one study, seven graphologists were asked to analyze handwriting samples obtained from 37 highly successful men and 37 less successful men. In contrast to the findings of more recent research on graphology, Binet concluded that the diagnostic conclusions drawn by his graphologists were fairly accurate (Rothenberg, 1990).

Into the Twentieth Century

The first personality inventory, the Woodworth Personal Data Sheet (Woodworth, 1920), was constructed near the end of World War I. This paper-and-pencil, single-score inventory was a kind of standardized psychiatric interview designed to screen U.S. Army recruits for emotional disorders and hence determine their fitness for military duty.

Other noteworthy events in the history of personality assessment were the publication of Rorschach's Inkblot Test (1921), Murray's Thematic Apperception Test (1938), and Hathaway and McKinley's Minnesota Multiphasic Personality Inventory (1943). All three instruments remain popular to this day. Also related to personality assessment is the extensive work during the late 1920s and succeeding years on the measurement of interests, attitudes, and values by E. K. Strong, L. L. Thurstone, and other psychologists.

Experimental research by Kurt Lewin and his coworkers on conflict, frustration, and aspiration level also showed how personality could be studied and assessed scientifically. Lewin (1935) and Goldstein (1939) were pioneers in the application of gestalt theory to personality, including such formulations as the phenomenal field, self-concept, and self-actualization. In the behavioristic camp, research on the frustration-aggression hypothesis was conducted by John Dollard and his associates (Dollard, Doob, Miller, Mowrer, & Sears, 1939). Several psychoanalytic concepts were scientifically investigated by Robert Sears (1943), and efforts to interpret psychoanalytic concepts in terms of learning theory were also made by Dollard and Miller (1950).

During the 1950s, noteworthy research related to personality was conducted by Adorno, Frenkel-Brunswik, Levinson, and Sanford (1950) on the *authoritarian personality,* by J. W. M. Whiting and Child (1953) on cultural differences in child rearing and personality, by Herman Witkin and his colleagues (Witkin, Lewis, Hertzman, Machover, Meissner, & Wapner, 1954) on personality differences between field-dependent and field-independent people, and by Harry Harlow (1958) on tactile stimulation and love in rhesus monkeys. The 1960s were marked by David McClelland's (1961) research on *achievement motivation,* Donn Byrne's (1961) research on repression-sensitization, and Julian Rotter's (1966) studies of locus of control.

The growth of clinical and counseling psychology, educational and school psychology, and industrial and organizational psychology after World War II, coupled with the development of more sophisticated psychometric procedures and instrumentation, stimulated even greater interest in personality assessment, research, and theory. The first edition of the most renowned book on personality theories was published in 1957 (Hall & Lindzey, 1957).

Scientific Theories

Together with measurement and research, science proceeds by thoughtful, speculative analyses of events. In psychology, as in other disciplines, such analyses often take the form of theories. A psychological *theory* is a systematic, organized set of ideas about why people or other organisms behave in the ways that they do. A good theory serves as a condensed description of some phenomenon—a kind of scientific shorthand that encapsulates and explains the results of numerous data observations. Furthermore, by means of an interlocking set of assumptions combined with deductive and inductive reasoning, a good theory enables the scientist to make predictions about future events. These predictions can then be confirmed or disconfirmed by further research.

A good theory is *parsimonious,* in that its concepts are few in number; it is *precise,* in that it makes accurate predictions; it is *testable,* in that it can be confirmed or disconfirmed; and it is *heuristic,* in that it can assist in the formulation of interesting scientific questions and stimulate suggestions concerning their answers. A good theory of personality, in particular, summarizes available data concerning the origins, development, dynamics, and disorders of personality in an accurate, efficient, and fruitful manner, and it can be applied in a variety of ways to answer questions and solve practical problems concerning human behavior.

In a rather informal sense, everyone develops "theories" as to why people behave in certain ways. Often our very survival depends upon the accuracy of these theories. For example, if we know that people in general (or a certain person in particular) are apt to respond aggressively to certain actions on our part, we are more likely to control our tendencies to engage in such actions around those individuals. But Everyperson's theories are rarely very systematic or based on detailed observations, and predictions made from them are not very accurate. Unfortunately, much the same assertion can be made about certain theories of personality devised by professors and practitioners of psychology.

More modern theories of personality, beginning with the psychodynamic theories of Freud and his associates and coming on down to the social learning and cognitive behavioral theories of Bandura and Mischel, are described in detail in Section II of this book. Although the structure and inner workings of these theories, as well as the predictions made from them, are not as impressive as those of theories in the physical sciences, personality theories have served as guides to research and practice. Psychoanalytic theory, in particular, has stimulated a great deal of research designed to test certain theoretical propositions such as those stemming from the concepts of psychological stages of development, the dynamics of repression, and the operations of anxiety and the ego defense mechanisms.

Fields of Psychology

Historically, two fields of psychology—psychometrics and abnormal psychology—were the parents of the study of personality. The Darwinian emphasis on differences between and within species stimulated an interest in the development of measures of individual differences, and hence the field of psychometrics. As with the second parent of personality study (abnormal psychology and its cousin clinical psychology), developments in the field of psychometrics began in the late nineteenth century.

During the twentieth century, a number of other disciplines, some fairly young and others much older, have contributed to the growth of personality study. Among these disciplines are biology, sociology, cultural anthropology, and criminology, as well as developmental psychology, social psychology, physiological psychology, and personnel psychology. Research on other topics, such as learning, motivation, perception, attitudes, and interests, has also contributed to the understanding of personality. Thus personality study, like psychology in general, is a composite discipline, interacting with and borrowing from many other fields in addition to developing concepts and methods of its own. This multifaceted character of personality study requires that the student have at least some acquaintance with a variety of social and biological science fields, and, depending on how extensively one wishes to pursue the study of personality, a fair knowledge of research methods and statistics as well. Be assured, however, that this is an introductory text, and we shall try not to go too far or too fast. When we reach a point at which the topic becomes too technical or too specialized for an introductory course, we shall provide references for further study by those who choose to pursue it.

The Current Scene

Although "personality" is only one of many chapter titles in a typical introductory psychology textbook, it is an important topic, taking its place as one of several bridges between the study of individual differences and the study of social phenomena. The study of personality is not usually classified as a profession in and of itself, but is listed as one of several specialties falling under psychological measurement, clinical psychology, social psychology, and other fields of psychology. The relationship of personality study to psychological measurement is the focus of the activities of the Society for Personality Assessment, and its relationship to social psychology is the interest of Division 8 of the American Psychological Association: the Society of Personality and Social Psychology.

Certainly, as revealed by the list of periodicals in Table 1–3, professional interest in theories, assessment, research, and applications of personality study is fairly widespread. Some of these periodicals are clinical in their orientation, whereas others focus on assessment, research, and applications in other areas. Likewise, some of the journals take an objective, empiricistic approach to personality study, while others lean toward subjective, or impressionistic, data collection and analysis.

As with the dozens of periodicals concerned with personality study, textbooks on the subject vary markedly in their approaches. Some bend over backward to be objective, empirical, and positivistic; others have a more subjective or phenomenological orientation. The great majority of books on personality, at least for undergraduate courses, attempt to remain as objective as possible. However, much of the data concerned with the dynamics of personality is subjective and less than perfectly reliable.

TABLE 1–3   Professional Journals Concerned with Personality Study

Advances in Personality Assessment
Behavior Genetics
British Journal of Projective Psychology and Personality Study
Character and Personality
Child Personality and Psychopathology: Current Topics
European Journal of Personality
Imagination, Cognition, and Personality
Individual Psychology
Journal of Abnormal Child Psychology
Journal of Abnormal Psychology
Journal of Child Psychology and Psychiatry
Journal of Clinical Child Psychology
Journal of Clinical Psychology
Journal of Cross-Cultural Psychology
Journal of Experimental Research in Personality
The Journal of Multivariate Experimental Personality
Journal of Personality
Journal of Personality and Clinical Studies
Journal of Personality and Social Psychology
Journal of Personality and Social Systems
Journal of Personality Assessment
Journal of Personality Disorders
Journal of Projective Techniques and Personality Assessment
Journal of Psychohistory
Journal of Psychopathology and Behavioral Assessment
Journal of Research in Personality
Journal of Social and Personal Relationships
Journal of Social Behavior and Personality
Personality
Personality and Individual Differences
Personality and Psychopathology
Personality and Social Psychology
Personality Monographs
Personality, Psychopathology, and Psychotherapy
Personality Study and Group Behavior
Perspectives in Personality
Progress in Experimental Personality Research
Psychoanalytic Psychology
Psychoanalytic Quarterly
Psychoanalytic Review
Psychoanalytic Study of the Child
Review of Personality and Social Psychology
Sex Roles: A Journal of Research
Social Behavior and Personality

This text emphasizes the scientific method in personality study, but the term "scientific" is used in a broad sense. The student will find not only descriptions and conclusions of carefully conducted experiments, but also the results of observational and correlational studies and even discussions of fairly speculative theories and subjective interpretations of data. The author believes that to do otherwise—that is, to deal only with experimentally verified results—would detract from the human interest and richness of personality study. For this reason, some of the statements are made to provoke further thinking, discussion, and reformulation. In any event, the cautious reader should be able to differentiate between hypotheses and facts, between objective observation and interpretation, and between speculation and reality.

In working your way through this book, you should be aware of several continuing issues or questions in personality study. One question is "Where does personality come from—heredity, environment (physical and sociocultural), or some dynamic interaction between heredity and environment?" A second question, not entirely unrelated to the first, is "How stable is personality, and how and why does it develop and change?" A third question is concerned with the variables or constructs which we choose to assess and with which we talk about personality—types, traits, motives, expectations, person-situation interactions, and so on. A fourth question deals with the relationships of personality variables to behavior or performance—in educational, occupational, clinical, and social contexts. A complete understanding of human personality also requires an explanation of why it goes wrong, that is, why people develop disorders of personality, behavior, mood, thought, and the like. Finally, we need to know how to cope with people who have personality problems and what types of therapeutic efforts are most successful.

Finding answers to these questions can be facilitated by the development of good theories, assessment techniques, and research investigations, topics with which we shall be concerned from now until the end of the text. Throughout the text, the preceding questions and the themes of theory, assessment, research, and applications will be stressed repeatedly. Although this is not specifically a "how to do it" book on personality, the author will not be displeased if the student comes away from reading it with a feeling that something of practical value, as well as scholarly and interesting information, has been obtained.

Summary

The study of personality is concerned with the description, analysis, and prediction of individual uniqueness in organized patterns of behavioral and mental functioning. Personality study consists of assessment, theory, research, and applications. Although attempts to understand human personality are as old as humankind, efforts to apply scientific methods to the study of personality did not begin until the late nineteenth century. These efforts have been assisted greatly by the construction of personality assessment procedures and devices and the development of various personality theories and research methods for studying human behavior.

Although research and other developments directed toward understanding personality have been far from systematic and have not resulted in an impressive body of substantiated fact, progress has been made. Indications of this progress are a clearer understanding of the (1) biological and sociocultural origins of personality, (2) reasons for stability and change in personality, (3) the structure and dynamics of personality, and (4) the causes of personality disorders and methods of treating them.

Key Concepts

Astrology   Pseudoscience of interpreting an individual's personality and future circumstances from his or her birth date and the relative positions of the moon and planets.

Authoritarian personality   A tendency to view the world in terms of a strict hierarchy in which a person higher on the hierarchy demands cooperation and deference from those lower on the hierarchy.

Graphology   Analysis of handwriting to ascertain the character or personality of the writer.

Humoral theory   Theory of Hippocrates and Galen linking personality to an excess of one of the four "humors" in the body. The four humors and the corresponding personality types are yellow bile–choleric, black bile–melancholic, blood–sanguine, and phlegm–phlegmatic.

Numerology   Analysis of numbers, such as those designating the year of one's birth, to determine their presumed influence on one's life and future.

Palmistry   Art or practice of telling fortunes and interpreting character from the lines and configurations of the palm of the hand.

Personality   Sum total of all the qualities, traits, and behaviors that characterize a person's individuality and by which, together with his or her physical attributes, the person is recognized as unique.

Phrenology   Discredited theory and practice of Gall and Spurzheim relating affective and cognitive characteristics to the configuration (bumps) of the skull.

Physiognomy   Pseudoscience which maintains that the personal characteristics of an individual are revealed by the form or features of the body, and especially the face.

Psychohistory   Biography, such as Erikson's *Young Man Luther* (1958) or *Gandhi's Truth* (1969), usually written from a psychodynamic (psychoanalytic) point of view.

Theory   A set of assumptions or propositions set forth to explain available information and to predict new facts concerning some phenomenon. Theories are typically conjectural rather than being established fact, and they are usually fairly broad in scope.

Word association technique   Reading a list of words aloud to a person who has been directed to respond to each one with the first word that comes to mind. The word association technique was introduced by Francis Galton and first used for clinical diagnostic purposes by Carl Jung.

Activities and Applications

1. Construct a list of terms derived from the names of characters in plays, novels, and other literary sources that refer to personality characteristics. The characters in Shakespeare's plays (Hamlet, Falstaff, Othello, Shylock, etc.) and Dickens' novels (e.g., Uriah Heep, Mr. Micawber, the Artful Dodger) are a good place to start.

2. Certain periods in history have been associated with particular forms of behavior or thinking—for example, Victorian or Edwardian. List as many such periods and the modal behaviors associated with each as you can.

3. A colleague and I (Aiken & Zweigenhaft, 1978) found that, in a sample of Iranian men and women, the signatures of women were smaller than those of men, and the signatures of people of higher social status were larger than the signatures of people of lower social status. Collect signatures from a sample of five men and five women students and five men and five women professors. Obtain a measure of signature size by multiplying the length times the height of the signature. Do the signatures of the ten women differ in size or in other features from those of the ten men? Do the signatures of the ten students (lower social status) differ in size or in other features from those of the ten professors (higher social status)? With what other demographic or personality variables would you expect signature size and style to be related? How would you test your hypotheses? Consult a book on graphology to stimulate your thinking on this matter.

4. Many popular historical novelists (e.g., Jean M. Auel, James Michener) attempt to capture the personalities and times of people who lived hundreds or even thousands of years ago. Is it really possible for a writer living in the twentieth century to mentally "project" himself or herself into another era and understand the personalities and behaviors of people who lived long ago, people who were subject to environmental conditions and circumstances different from those existing today? Or is all historical writing, and especially that having a psychological flavor (*psychohistory*), very much a matter of writing from one's own temporal perspective, and hence "projecting" one's own personality onto historical characters, even when one attempts to be objective?

5. The ancient Greeks believed that the physical world is composed of four elements—earth, air, fire, and water. The four humors of Hippocrates corresponded to these four elements. Influenced by the ancient Greek preference for things in "fours," certain early mental philosophers divided the human mind into four functions: aesthesia (feeling or sensation), bulia (volition or will), gnosis (knowing or cognition), and thymia (emotion or affect). The prefixes *hypo* (a deficiency of), *hyper* (an excess of), and *para* (a distortion of or beyond) were then attached to each of these four terms to describe certain personality patterns or disorders. Thus "hypobulia" referred to a deficiency of will power, "hyperthymia" to excessive emotionality, and paragnosis (later corrupted to "paranoia") to a distortion of cognition. Construct and interpret the remaining nine terms. Then see if you can find any other English words with ancient Greek or Latin stems that are descriptive of personality, emotions, or mental abilities.

6. Defend graphology and physiology as legitimate areas of research and application in personality study.

7. Survey the students in one of your classes to determine how many of them believe in astrology. Use the following question:

What do you think of the predictions made by astrologers?
____ I strongly believe in them.
____ I believe in them.
____ I don't know whether to believe or disbelieve in them.
____ I disbelieve in them.
____ I strongly disbelieve in them.

Did you note any differences in the characteristics of the students who believe (or strongly believe) and those who disbelieve (or strongly disbelieve) in astrology? Some possible characteristics that might be related to a belief in astrology are sex, grade-point average, classification (freshman, sophomore, junior, senior), and college major. Suppose that you do find some significant differences between the characteristics of people who believe and those who do not believe in astrology. What can you make of these differences? Be careful not to overgeneralize, and do not conclude that two things are causally related merely because they are related. There may be a third variable lurking in the background!

8. Certain adjectives and certain nouns are likely to go together in English to describe the behavioral or personality characteristics of certain individuals. Consider the following matching test item:

Directions: On each of the line segments in the Adjective column, write the letter corresponding to the associated word in the Noun column.

Adjective	*Noun*
____ 1. brown	a. arm
____ 2. disarming	b. eyes
____ 3. fast	c. face
____ 4. glad	d. forehead
____ 5. golden	e. gaze
____ 6. high	f. hand
____ 7. intense	g. lips
____ 8. poker	h. nose
____ 9. sensuous	i. palms
____ 10. shifty	j. shuffle
____ 11. silver	l. smirk
____ 12. strong	k. smile
____ 13. sweaty	m. tongue
	n. voice

After you have made your matches, indicate which adjective-noun combinations are indications or signs of deception (lying). Can you think of any other adjective-noun combinations that describe other behaviors or personality characteristics?

Key: 1-h, 2-k, 3-j, 4-f, 5-n, 6-d, 7-e, 8-c, 9-k, 10-b, 11-m, 12-a, 13-i. The following pairs are suggestive of deception: 1-h, 2-k, 3-j, 4-f, 8-c, 10-b, 11-m, 12-a, 13-i. Why do you think there are so many?

9. Ever since people have walked the earth, they have depended on other animals for their very existence. Recognition of the importance of animals—for food, for clothing, for transportation, for various household objects, for companionship, and even as objects of worship—is seen in the drawings, paintings, and carvings of animal images from prehistoric times to the modern era. Early humans undoubtedly spent a great deal of time watching animals and wondering what they were thinking and what spirits possessed them. Animals were also thought to have personalities, and some of these same personality characteristics, perhaps through reincarnation, were seen in humans. For example, consider the following animals: (1) eagle, (2) fox, (3) lion, (4) mule, (5) owl, (6) peacock, (7) pig, (8) rabbit, (9) sheep, (10) skunk, (11) snake, (12) vulture, (13) wolf. Can you associate one or more of the following "personality characteristics" with each of these animals: wise, blindly following, stubborn, courageous (brave), timid, sly, flirtations, devouring, gluttonous, sharp-eyed, disreputable (untrustworthy), proud, mean? Can you think of any other animals that are associated with a particular personality trait?

Suggested Readings

Aiken, L. R. (1989). *Assessment of personality* (pp. 3–16). Needham Heights, MA: Allyn & Bacon.

Allport, G. W. (1937). *Personality: A psychological interpretation.* New York: Holt.

Ben-Shakhar, G., Bar-Hillel, M., Bilu, Y., Ben-Abba, E., & Flug, A. (1986). Can graphology predict occupational success? Two empirical studies and some methodological ruminations. *Journal of Applied Psychology, 71,* 645–653.

DuBois, P. H. (1970). *The history of psychological testing.* Boston: Allyn & Bacon.

Gauquelin, M. (1973). *Cosmic influences on human behavior.* London: Garnstone Press.

Leahey, T. (1987). *History of psychology: Main currents in psychological thought* (2nd ed.). Englewood Cliffs, NJ: Prentice-Hall.

Murray, H. (1938). *Explorations in personality.* New York: Oxford University Press.

Pervin, L. A. (1990). A brief history of modern personality theory. In L. A. Pervin (Ed.), *Handbook of personality theory and research* (pp. 21–65). New York: Guilford Press.

Snyder, C. R. (1974). Why horoscopes are true: The effects of specificity on acceptance of astrological interpretation. *Journal of Clinical Psychology, 30,* 557–580.

Notes

1 As is often the case in popular fiction and music, a stanza of a ballad of yesteryear appears to equate personality with physical attractiveness or sex appeal:
   When Madame Pompadour
   Was on the ballroom floor,
   Said all the gentlemen, "Obviously,
   The Madame has the cutest . . . personality."

2 Even older than the water-lapping test of Judges is the test in Genesis as to whether Adam and Eve would eat of the tree of knowledge of good and evil, a test that they obviously failed.

3 Perhaps having its origins in astrological beliefs is the following "Days of Birth" poem of unknown authorship:
   Monday's child is fair of face,
   Tuesday's child is full of grace,
   Wednesday's child is full of woe,
   Thursday's child has far to go,
   Friday's child is loving and giving,
   Saturday's child works for its living,
   And a child that's born on the Sabbath day
   Is fair and wise and good and gay.

CHAPTER 2

Personality Research Concepts and Methods

CHAPTER OUTLINE

Since the late nineteenth century, when psychology was christened a science, psychologists have been busy formulating concepts and research methods to make their profession more scientific. Greater success has accompanied these efforts in such branches of psychology as the laboratory-based, "tough-minded" fields of perception and learning than in perhaps more "tender-minded" fields such as personality and social psychology.

A survey of research on personality conducted during the past century is as impressive for its lack of organization and steady progress as for anything else. Although cooperation among psychological researchers has been lacking in other fields of psychology, this lack has been especially noticeable in personality study. All too often the personality theorist or researcher has elected to go his or her own way without paying sufficient attention to the ideas or findings of other psychologists. Consequently, the number of tried-and-true facts regarding human personality, as well as predictions made from these facts, has not been overwhelming. Be that as it may, the body of published research on personality is interesting, not only for the findings but also for the multitude of ingenious approaches used by psychological researchers in attempting to understand something as subjective and elusive as human personality.

Discussions of personality research are sprinkled throughout the text, but this chapter considers some of the concepts of psychological science in general and the methods employed by psychologists to establish a foundation for a science of personality in particular. These methods, ranging from simple observation to complex experimentation, are not unique to personality research; they have been applied in many areas of psychology and in other disciplines as well. However, the focus here is on the scientific analysis of personality.

Variables, Definitions, and Reasoning

Like all scientific enterprises, personality study begins with *variables*—events or measurable phenomena that can change or take on more than one value. Some of the most common personality variables are listed in Table 2–1. Scientists are particularly interested in variables that change in value as a function of other variables; the former are called *dependent variables,* and the latter are *independent variables.* Thus we say that dependent variable Y varies as a function of independent variable X. For example, level of aggression (a dependent variable) varies as a function of interference or frustration (an independent variable).

Intervening Variables and Moderator Variables

In addition to independent and dependent variables, there are *intervening variables,* which come between independent and dependent variables and hence affect the relationship between them. Thus the relationship between grade-point average (a dependent variable) and aptitude test score (an independent variable) may vary with motivational level (an intervening variable). A special kind of intervening variable is a *moderator variable,* which affects or "moderates" the relationship between an independent and a dependent variable. Examples of moderator variables that have been shown to influence the relationship between aptitude and achievement are gender and compulsiveness. Certain studies have found that the correlation between aptitude and achievement is higher for girls than for boys and lower for more compulsive than for less compulsive students. Since higher correlation implies more accurate prediction of the dependent variable by the independent variable, the old saying that women are less predictable than men may be questioned—at least as far as forecasting achievement from aptitude is concerned!

In all fields of science, certain variables receive the most attention. Such variables are often referred to as the major theoretical concepts or constructs of the science. The phenomena studied by the science are described and explained in terms of these basic dimensions or abstractions. Some of the constructs that have been investigated in personality research are in Table 2–1.

Constructs such as those in Table 2–1 are not easily defined, but in order to obtain a high degree of agreement on the meaning of a construct, it should be defined operationally. An *operational definition* tells what to do or what procedure to follow in order to experience the construct of interest; that is, it defines a construct by describing the operations to be used in order to understand the meaning of the construct. Thus an operational definition of the construct "anxiety" may be a precise description of the behavior of a person who is in an "anxious" state and the process by which he or she came to be in that state. The meaning of "anxiety" and other operationally defined constructs consists of the operations employed in manipulating the construct and the method by which it is

TABLE 2–1 Illustrative Personality Concepts (Constructs)

Achievement motive	Learned helplessness
Affiliation motive	Level of aspiration
Aggression	Leveling-sharpening
Altruism	Locus of control
Anxiety	Machiavellianism
Attachment	Masculinity-femininity (gender identity)
Attributional style	Obedience to authority
Authoritarianism	Power motive
Competence motivation	Reflective/impulsive
Compulsivity	Repression-sensitization
Conflict	Risk taking
Depression	Self
Dominance-submission	Self-actualization
Empathy	Self-concept
Field independence/dependence	Self-efficacy
Frustration tolerance	Self-monitoring
Hardiness	Sensation seeking
Hostility	Stress
Introversion-extroversion	Type A (versus Type B) behavior

measured. In this way, psychological constructs are tied to behavioral processes rather than being "free floating" with no anchor and no commonly accepted meaning.

Operational definitions are indicative of the efforts of psychologists to be as publicly meaningful and efficient in their science making as they can. Efforts are made to formulate the simplest, clearest descriptions and explanations of behavior. The need for such a "principle of parsimony" was recognized long ago by William of Occam (1280–1349), and it is sometimes referred to as "Occam's razor." Operational definitions are a kind of Occam's razor of particular importance to psychological science. Such definitions help to make concepts or constructs less ambiguous and fuzzy, to improve communication among researchers, and to develop a workable understanding of human and animal behavior.

Data and Scientific Reasoning

The basic information collected by any science is referred to as *data,* and the procedures by which data are obtained are known as *methods.* Whatever the method may be, data are obtained for a purpose. In some instances, the purpose is spelled out in terms of a hypothesis. The psychological researcher then collects data to determine whether the hypothesis is correct or incorrect. Some psychologists develop complex *theories* or *models* of behavior to guide their research. Words such as *theory* and *model,* as used by psychologists, refer to systems of ideas about why people or animals behave in certain ways. As noted in Chapter 1, in order to be useful, a psychological theory of model must not only explain data or facts that are already known, it must also be able to predict future events or outcomes. However, not all psychological research begins with an explicit theory; a researcher may simply decide to collect some data to see whether anything interesting happens. He or she may have no specific hypothesis, but rather may be looking for anything intriguing or orderly in the data. This "shotgun" approach sometimes leads to serendipitous findings or hypotheses that can be tested by future research, but it may also lead to blind alleys. "Garbage in, garbage out" is as true of the fate of poorly constructed scientific propositions as it is of the results of processing meaningless data by a computer. Regardless of whether the researcher is following an explicit hypothesis or theory, he or she will have some method of collecting and recording the results of an investigation.

Objectivity and Empiricism

Psychological scientists pride themselves on being objective and empirical. The fact that they are *objective* means that they try to keep their own beliefs and opinions from influencing what they observe and record. They go to great lengths to be objective—using automated equipment or obtaining independent observations of an event from other researchers. Psychological scientists are also *empirical* in that they are more influenced by facts than by authority, hearsay, or speculation. They are not averse to "armchair speculation," however, if such speculation leads to a reasonable explanation or clarification that is consistent with what is already known.

Deduction and Induction

The methods by which scientific discoveries are made and scientific laws are formulated involve both deductive and inductive reasoning. *Deductive reasoning* is reasoning from a general law or principle in order to deduce a particular conclusion or prediction. Deduction is the kind of reasoning that occurs in the formal logic of a syllogism (e.g., "All men are mortal; Socrates was a man; therefore, Socrates was mortal"). The theorems of geometry, for example, are "deduced" or proved by deduction. *Inductive reasoning,* on the other hand, is reasoning from the particular to the general. A general law is "induced" or inferred as a consequence of observing many events or happenings having something in common or behaving in the same way under similar circumstances. A frequently cited example of inductive reasoning is the formulation of the law of gravity by the physicist Sir Isaac Newton. Newton observed many instances of falling bodies (not merely the popular caricature of one apple falling on his head!) before arriving at the concept of universal gravitation. In science, inductive reasoning is more widely used than deductive reasoning, because in most instances scientists are not aware of the general laws of nature but are trying to discover and state those laws.

Probability

A useful tool of inductive reasoning is *probability,* a concept that has been applied extensively in psychological research and practice. Although the mathematical theory of probability is quite complex, some understanding of probability is needed in order to appreciate how research findings are analyzed by statistical methods. In predicting that an event will occur, the psychologist is seldom absolutely certain that his or her prediction will be verified. Obviously, many variables can intervene to influence any predicted outcome. Therefore, the psychologist may state that the occurrence of a given event is probable, or likely, as opposed to improbable or unlikely.

Probability is expressed as a numerical index between .00 and 1.00. If the probability of occurrence of a given event is close to .00, then the event is very unlikely to occur. If the probability of occurrence of the event is close to 1.00, the event is almost certain to occur (1.00 is absolute certainty). If the probability of occurrence of an event is .50, the event is as likely as not to occur. If the probability of occurrence of an event is between .50 and 1.00, the event is more likely to occur than not to occur. And if the probability is between .00 and .50, the event is less likely to occur than not to.

Measurement, Reliability, and Validity

Measurement, the assignment of numbers to events, is one of the foundations of science. A look at the history of science reveals that advances in measurement have driven scientific breakthroughs, that is, that scientific discoveries were preceded by the formulation or invention of new techniques of measuring natural phenomena.

Almost any effort to describe and classify natural phenomena involves measurement of some sort, albeit sometimes a rather crude level of measurement. Measurements in psychology and other behavioral or social sciences are admittedly not as precise as those in natural sciences such as physics, but they are useful in summarizing data on human behavior and drawing inferences from those data. The quantification of observations provides a more objective basis for making intra- and interindividual comparisons, which are critical to an understanding of differences both within and between individuals.

Measurement Error, Reliability, and Validity

All measurement involves a certain amount of error, but one reason why science has progressed is that scientists have continually sought new ways of improving the accuracy of their measurements. Early interest in human variability was kindled by men who noted that there were differences among measurements of the same thing made by different observers—the so-called *personal equation*.

Although physical science can make extremely precise measurements, psychological measurements are frequently very crude. It is certainly true that psychology has made progress during the past century in the accuracy of measurements made in research and assessment, but the great majority of these measurements are still only approximations. Some of the inaccuracy is due to the vagueness and uncertainty about what is being measured. For example, different psychologists do not necessarily agree on how "intelligence" or "anxiety," both of which are widely used constructs "measured" by psychological tests, should be defined or measured.

A lack of adequate measuring devices has impeded the progress of psychological science, as a similar lack handicapped the physical and biological sciences during their early years. Whatever psychologists may do to improve their measuring instruments, at least two characteristics must be possessed by any good measuring instrument. These characteristics are *reliability* and *validity*.

Reliability. A measuring device is said to be *reliable* if it measures anything consistently, that is, if the measure of an object or event under one set of conditions is very nearly equal to the measure of the object or event under a different set of conditions. In most instances, the values or measures obtained under one set of conditions, say at time A, are not precisely equal to those obtained under another set of conditions, say at time B, but the differences may be small enough to be tolerable. In any event, a numerical index of the reliability of a measuring instrument may be obtained by computing the correlation between (1) a set of measures obtained on one occasion with those obtained on another occasion or (2) a set of measures obtained from one form of the instrument with those obtained from another form of the instrument. Procedure 1 is referred to as *test-retest reliability,* and procedure 2 as *alternate-forms* or *parallel-forms reliability.* A variation on procedure 2 is that in which two separate scores are computed from a single administration of a test or other psychometric instrument. One score is based on responses to one-half of the items, and the other score is based on responses to the remaining half of the items. The correlation between the two sets of scores is then determined and "corrected" to yield a *split-half* or *internal consistency reliability coefficient.* Procedures 1 and 2 may also be combined to produce an estimate of reliability based on scores obtained on two forms of a test administered at two different times. Further descriptions of the various kinds of reliability are given in Table 2–2.

Assigning ratings to personal characteristics or behavior, or scoring performance on some task or test frequently entails making subjective judgments. In order to determine whether or not these judgments possess adequate reliability, an index of agreement between the ratings or scores assigned by different judges is made. Such an index is known as an *interscorer* or *interrater reliability coefficient.* Another method is to have many judges score the responses of one person or to have many judges score the responses of many people. The results of the former approach can be quantified as an *intraclass coefficient,* the results in the latter case

TABLE 2–2   Types of Reliability

Alternate-forms (parallel-forms) reliability: An index of reliability determined by correlating the scores of a group of people on one form of a psychometric instrument with their scores on another (parallel) form of the instrument.

Concordance reliability: Several raters or scorers make numerical judgments of a characteristic or behavior shown by a large sample of people. Then a *coefficient of concordance,* an index of agreement among the judgments of the scorers or raters, is computed.

Internal consistency reliability: The extent to which the items comprising a test or other psychometric instrument measure the same construct. The reliability of a test computed by the Spearman-Brown, Kuder-Richardson, or Cronbach alpha formulas is a measure of the test's internal consistency.

Interrater (interscorer) reliability: Two scorers assign a numerical rating or score to a sample of people. Then the correlation between the two sets of numbers is computed.

Intraclass reliability: Several raters or scorers make a numerical judgment of a characteristic or behavior of a person. Then an *intraclass coefficient,* an index of agreement among the numbers assigned by the various judges, among the scores is computed.

Split-half reliability: An estimate of reliability determined by applying the Spearman-Brown formula for $m = 2$ to the correlation between two halves of the same test, such as the odd-numbered items and the even-numbered items.

Test-retest reliability: A method of assessing the reliability of a test or other psychometric instrument by administering it to the same group of people on two different occasions and computing the correlation between their scores on the two occasions.

---

as a *coefficient of concordance*. Procedures for calculating these coefficients can be found in statistics or psychometrics textbooks (e.g., Nunnally, 1978).

Validity. The validity of a measuring instrument is the extent to which the instrument measures what it was designed to measure. Thus a paper-and-pencil test designed to measure "hostility" is not a valid measure of "hostility" if the scores are affected more by reading comprehension than by hostility. A valid instrument is always valid for a specific purpose; it may be a valid measure of one construct but not of another construct. The validity of many psychological instruments is determined by computing the correlation between measures (scores) obtained on the instrument and measures obtained on some criterion of behavior or performance; the closer the correlation coefficient is to $+1.00$, the greater the validity of the instrument. The validity of a test of "academic motivation," for example, may be determined by finding, for a representative group of students, the correlation between their scores on the test and their grade-point averages. If the correlation coefficient is fairly high, one may say that the validity of the test for predicting grade-point average is high. The concept of validity is a complex one, and there are different kinds of validity—content validity, criterion-related validity, and construct validity. Definitions and explanations of these different kinds of validity are given in Table 2–3.

Scientific Methods

The term *scientific method* may remind the reader of a series of steps learned in grade school—steps presented as a prescription for the scientific method. Perhaps there were five steps somewhat like the following: (1) a problem arises; (2)

TABLE 2–3 **Types of Validity**

Concurrent validity: The extent to which the scores obtained by a group of individuals on a particular psychometric instrument are related to their simultaneously determined scores on another measure (a criterion) of the same characteristic that the instrument is supposed to measure.

Content validity: A psychometric instrument is said to have content validity if a group of experts on the material with which the instrument is concerned agree that the instrument measures what it was designed to measure.

Construct validity: The extent to which scores on a psychometric instrument designed to measure a certain characteristic are related to measures of behavior in situations in which the characteristic is supposed to be an important determinant of behavior.

Face validity: The extent to which the appearance or content of the materials (items and the like) on a test or other psychometric instrument are such that the instrument appears to be a good measure of what it is supposed to measure.

Predictive validity: The extent to which scores on a psychometric instrument are predictive of performance on some criterion measure assessed at a later time; usually expressed as a correlation between the instrument (predictor variable) and the criterion variable.

facts and other information pertaining to the problem are collected; (3) a hypothesis or theory based on the available information is proposed; (4) an experiment is planned and conducted; and (5) conclusions based on the results of the experiment are formulated. This time-honored sequence certainly describes one of the methods of science, that of experimentation. There are, however, at least four fundamental "scientific methods": observation, survey, correlation, and experiment. The most basic of these is observation, because scientists usually observe before they do anything else. But experimentation is the method of choice in science because scientific hypotheses can be tested and questions of cause and effect answered more rigorously by means of experiments than by any other research method.

Observation

When using the method of observation, one simply takes note of events or occurrences in the environment and makes a record of what is observed. These observations may be controlled or uncontrolled. In *controlled observation,* the researcher arranges a situation to determine how people (or animals) react in that situation. Thus a researcher may be interested in observing, by means of a television monitor or one-way vision screen, the interaction between members of a small discussion group. By remaining unseen, the researcher attempts to minimize the effects of his or her own behavior on the behaviors of the discussants.

Perhaps more common in psychology is *uncontrolled observation,* in which the researcher merely observes behavior "on the wing" without exercising any control over the situation. Making observations in a naturally occurring situation, as in observing the behavior of children on a playground or pedestrians passing a street corner, is referred to as *naturalistic observation.*

Clinical Method. Much of what is known about human personality has been obtained from observations made by clinical psychologists and psychiatrists of their clients or patients. This approach is known as the *clinical method.* It should be obvious, however, that in the clinical method an observer can have a marked effect on the behavior of the person being observed. Not only does the therapist-observer affect the patient's behavior, but the patient also affects the therapist's behavior. Because of the dynamic interaction between patient and therapist, clinical observations are seldom completely objective.

Case Study. Related to the clinical method is the *case study,* which consists of obtaining and analyzing a biographical description of a person's behavior and circumstances during a part or all of his or her lifetime. A case study of an individual is almost always a necessary preliminary to more intensive clinical investigation. A case study may be conducted in a clinical or educational context to determine the cause(s) of a specific problem of behavioral or mental functioning. Details of the individual's background and characteristics are obtained both from the individual herself (himself) and significant other persons; follow-up data are also collected over a period of time. Information on all of the following may be obtained: (1) the family (persons in home, home attitudes); (2) the culture (cultural group, cultural deviation and conflict); (3) medical examinations and history (health and disorder, physical development, physical conditions especially related to adjustment, sex development); (4) developmental history (prenatal period and birth, early developmental signs, intellectual development, speech development, emotional development, social development); (5) educational history (school progress, educational achievement, school adjustment, educational aspirations and plans); (6) economic history (in the case of older children and adults, occupation, occupational history, vocational plans and ambitions); (7) legal history (delinquencies, arrests); and (8) the person's life (life routines, interests, hobbies, recreations, fantasy life, sex, social adjustments).

When a case study is conducted to determine the cause(s) of a specific psychological problem, hypotheses or conclusions pertaining to causation may be formulated and specific recommendations made concerning treatment—psychotherapy, drugs or other medical treatment, special education, and so on. A follow-up assessment to evaluate the effectiveness of the prescribed treatment program should also be conducted after an appropriate time interval.

Despite its yield of potentially useful information for forming an overall picture as well as an in-depth understanding of the individual, a clinical case study has some notable weaknesses. These include the retrospective nature of the data (memory is seldom completely accurate), the fact that the person conducting the study is frequently biased in selecting and evaluating certain kinds of data or measurements, and the extent to which the findings are generalizable across situations or circumstances encountered by the individual. Employing a variety of measures in a systematic sample of situations and being aware of the likelihood of bias in selection and evaluation can help reduce but not entirely eliminate misinterpretations and overgeneralizations.

Developmental Approach. The *developmental approach* is related to the clinical and case-study methods. In this method the investigator records the physical and behavioral development of one or more persons over a period of years. In situations where it is impossible to obtain accurate records of the development of the same individuals over the specified time period (the *longitudinal developmental approach*), the investigator may use the *cross-sectional developmental approach*. The latter consists of drawing conclusions about development from a study of the records of different groups of people at different ages (see Figure 2–1).

Sampling

The term *survey* is applied to observations made or data collected on characteristics of a subset of individuals (a *sample*) selected from a larger target *population*. One of several sampling plans may be employed, but the person who is conducting the survey usually prefers a procedure that will ensure that the sample is

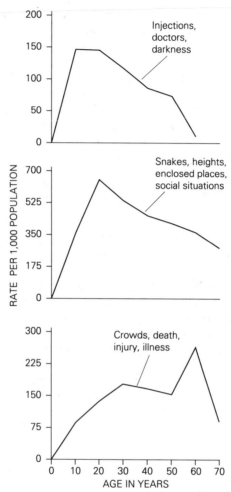

FIGURE 2–1 Changes in fears with chronological age (adapted from Agras, Sylvester, & Oliveau, 1969).

representative of the population. In other words, the sample should be like the population in all important respects. Unfortunately, this ideal can seldom be achieved in actual practice.

A variety of procedures may be used by a researcher to select subjects for a survey, for an experiment, or for standardizing an assessment instrument. In *simple random sampling,* every individual in the population has an equal chance of being selected for the sample. *Stratified random sampling* is more likely than simple random sampling to yield a sample that is representative of a specified population (the *target population*). The population is divided into several levels on the basis of some significant variable, such as sex or socioeconomic status, and a random sample of people from each level is selected. The size of the sample selected from each group or level of the stratification variable is proportional to the number of people in the total population who are members of that group. Similarly, in *area sampling* the population is divided into areas or blocks on the basis of geography, and a random sample of individuals is selected from each block.

Not all samples that are selected for a survey research project are random. For various reasons (cost, inconvenience, etc.) it may be impossible to obtain a random sample of the target population. Consequently a researcher may employ a systematic but nonrandom procedure of sampling names from a directory (*sampling from lists*) or selecting a certain number of people from those who are available until a specified number of individuals in each of several categories (e.g., men and women) has been obtained (*quota sampling*). Finally, the researcher may simply ask for volunteers and conduct his or her study or standardize a measuring instrument on those who volunteer. Such a procedure, however, is not likely to yield a sample that is representative of the target population, and hence generalization of the research findings to that population is likely to be invalid.

Whatever the situation may be in which behavioral observation or assessments are made, the observers or assessors should always be objective. That is, they must be careful not to let their biases and expectations distort what they observe. One way to minimize the effects of bias and other personal factors is to make an immediate record of what is observed and a separate record of the observer's interpretation of the event. For example, recording that "George was angry at Betsy" simply because he pulled her hair is an interpretation rather than an observation. It would be better to note what actually occurred and report this information separately from the interpretation placed on the event. "Observation: George pulled Betsy's hair. Interpretation: He pulled her hair because he was angry at her."

Correlation

The method of *correlation* is used extensively in psychological research, particularly whenever it is impossible or undesirable to conduct experiments. In determining the direction and magnitude of correlation between two variables, we are concerned with the extent to which the variables change together or covary. If it is found that variables X and Y are significantly correlated, then it is known that changes in variable X will be accompanied by changes in variable Y. Since correlation implies prediction, a significant correlation between X and Y will lead to a demonstrable improvement in the prediction of Y from X (or X from Y). The direction and accuracy of the prediction depend on the algebraic sign and magnitude of the *coefficient of correlation* (r), an index number ranging from -1.00 to $+1.00$. When r is high positive (between .50 and 1.00), then the two variables (X and Y) will change (increase or decrease) in the same direction: High scores on X will tend to be accompanied by high scores on Y, and low scores on X will tend to be accompanied by low scores on Y. When r is high negative (between

$-.50$ and -1.00), then X and Y will increase or decrease in opposite directions: High scores on X will tend to be accompanied by low scores on Y, and low scores on X will tend to be accompanied by high scores on Y. Whether the value of r is high positive or high negative, a person's score on variable Y can be predicted from his or her score on variable X better than chance. But when the correlation between any two variables is close to .00, the prediction of scores on one variable from scores on the other variable is little or no better than chance.

The fact that two variables are significantly correlated does not mean that changes in one variable *cause* changes in the other variable. For example, although certain measures of hostility and the incidence of coronary heart disease are significantly correlated, it is not safe to conclude from this finding alone that hostility is a cause of heart disease. It may be that both hostility and coronary heart disease are caused by some yet unspecified third variable, such as heredity or diet.

Experimentation

When two variables are found to be highly correlated, the researcher does not know which variable, if either, is a cause and which is an effect of changes in the other variable. Although the method of correlation enables researchers to make predictions from one variable to the other, it is limited in its ability to explain or interpret. When a psychologist finds that two variables are significantly related, he or she frequently does not know why. In contrast, the *method of experiment* enables one to answer cause-effect questions and hence has greater explanatory value than the method of correlation.

Experimental questions may be very informal, such as "What will happen if I do thus and so?" Or they may be formulated as statements of complex hypotheses such as "Performance varies as a curvilinear function of motivation." In any case, the experimenter is interested in what leads to what, that is, what effect is produced by introducing some change in a situation. In order to make certain that the observed effect is produced by intended actions and not by some other unobserved or uncontrolled change in the situation (some *extraneous variable*), the experimenter must take precautions. These precautions are known as *controls,* and basically an experiment is controlled objective observation. These observations may take place in the laboratory or in the field, a more natural context. Laboratory experiments typically have greater *internal validity;* that is, the results are freer from the effects of extraneous variables. On the other hand, field experiments may have greater *external validity,* or generalizability, because they are conducted in a more real-world context.

Sometimes an extraneous variable is made part of the research design; that is, it becomes a second independent variable. For example, a personality characteristic such as trait anxiety, which might be viewed as an extraneous variable in a study of the effects of psychological stress on behavior, can be included as part of a research design in which the effects on specified behaviors of stress and trait anxiety in various combinations are studied. In this case, not only can the relationships of stress to the specified behaviors and the relationships of anxiety to those behaviors be determined, but the interaction of stress and anxiety in their combined effects on behavior can also be evaluated. Such *interaction effects* are often the most interesting findings of psychological experiments.

Although it is difficult to achieve perfect control in psychological experiments, there are several standard procedures for minimizing the effects of extraneous variables on the outcome of an experimental investigation. One of these procedures is to use many *subjects* (people or animals subjected to the experimental condition) in the *experimental group*. This procedure is especially important when differences among individuals in physical or psychological characteristics other than those of primary interest to the experimenter can influence the results of the experiment. Because individuals selected as subjects for an experiment may differ greatly with respect to such variables, special procedures are necessary in the selection of subjects. Usually, a large number of subjects are employed with the hope that extraneous individual differences will cancel each other out. In addition, using a large number of subjects rather than a few makes the results of the experiment more generalizable to individuals other than those particular subjects. Of course, the experimenter expects the research findings to apply to a larger population of subjects similar to those in the sample and not just to the limited sample of subjects on whom the experiment was conducted.

Another way to control for the effects of extraneous variables is to use a *control group* of subjects. In the simplest kind of psychological experiment, the procedure is to divide the available sample of subjects into two groups. One of these groups is the control group, and the other is the experimental group. Ideally, this division results in the individuals in the control group being matched, person for person, with those in the experimental group on all variables except the one whose effects are being investigated (the independent variable). Because such matching is nearly impossible to achieve in actual practice, the available subjects are usually assigned to the two groups at random.

The use of a control group is particularly important in psychological experiments, because the very fact of being in an experiment may produce changes in subjects' behavior above and beyond those caused by the experimental condition. Just as the attention or TLC (tender loving care) of medical personnel may have a greater effect than medicines or other treatments in curing an illness, being treated as "special" by a prestigious experimenter, regardless of what he or she does, may cause subjects to react differently than they would otherwise. These reactions or effects in the control group, are, depending on the context and the specific effect, referred to as placebo effects, Hawthorne effects, or John Henry effects. A *placebo effect* occurs when patients or subjects in an experiment show improvement or change even though an inert substance (a *placebo*) has been administered to them. A *Hawthorne effect* occurs when the behavior of participants in an experiment is influenced by their knowledge that they are being experimented upon. A *John Henry effect* occurs when the subjects in a control group are aware that they are being compared with subjects in an experimental group, and hence, because they are competitive or ego-involved, they perform better than they ordinarily would. Effects such as these must be taken into account when evaluating the influence of the independent variable(s) on the dependent variable(s). Furthermore, the effects of a specified treatment on the experimental group are not necessarily due exclusively to the independent variable. The subjects or participants in an experiment frequently have preconceptions, correct or incorrect, about what is going on in the experiment and what is expected of them. These speculations, assumptions, or expectations, which are known as *demand characteristics* (Orne, 1962), may be even more important than the manipulated, independent variable in determining how subjects react or behave in an experimental context.

Another problem occurs in an experiment when subjects or experimenters are aware of the kind of treatment specific subjects are getting. For example, in an experiment involving the effects of a specified drug, if the subjects know they are receiving a real drug rather than a placebo, they may behave differently than they would otherwise. If the experimenter knows which subjects are getting the drug, he or she may treat those subjects differently or evaluate the changes in their behavior differently than if the subjects were known to be part of the control (placebo) group. For this reason, a *single-blind procedure,* in which the subjects do not know what drug (if any) they are receiving, or, better still, a *double-blind procedure,* in which neither the subjects nor the experimenters know which subjects are receiving the drug and which the placebo, is advisable.

A Little Statistics

In popular usage, *statistics* are counts or other numbers obtained from observations made on objects or events. The number of these events may vary from a singular case, as when one refers to the "statistics" of a certain beauty contestant or to the vital statistics (number of births, deaths, marriages, divorces, etc.) amassed annually by a government agency on its citizens. These numbers are known as *descriptive statistics,* because they describe certain characteristics or states of people or things. A bit more complicated than simple counts or frequencies are statistical measures of central tendency (arithmetic mean, median, mode), variability (range, variance, standard deviation), and correlation (correlation coefficient). Other useful descriptive statistics, especially in psychological assessment, are standard scores (z scores) and percentile ranks. Procedures for computing these measures may be found in any elementary statistics book (e.g., Pagano, 1990).

Descriptive statistics are quite helpful in summarizing certain features of a set of data and making comparisons between different data sets, but *inferential statistical procedures* are even more useful in research. These procedures, which are based on the theory of probability, enable a researcher to collect a sample of data and make inferences about the characteristics of a larger population of which the sample is a part. Of course, the researcher never knows the true mean, standard deviation, or other *parameters* of the population of which the sample is a part, and in inferring those population parameters on the basis of sample statistics he or she may be grossly in error.

To make the process of statistical inference more objective and accurate, as well as to provide methods for estimating how much researchers are in error when they use sample statistics to estimate population parameters, statisticians follow a logical decision process. In this process, the researcher begins by setting up a kind of straw man known as a *null hypothesis*. The precise form in which the null hypothesis is stated varies with the particular inferential procedure, but a common approach in psychological research is a null hypothesis that states that there is no difference between the means on the dependent variable of two or more treatment groups. The researcher also states an *alternative hypothesis,* which is the opposite of the null hypothesis. By computing various ratios (*t* ratio, *F* ratio, etc.) the researcher decides whether or not to reject the null hypothesis. If the null hypothesis is rejected, then the alternative hypothesis that the means of the treatment groups are not equal is accepted.

In conducting tests of statistical hypotheses, what is being estimated is the probability that chance factors alone can account for any observed difference between the obtained results and the results that would be expected if the null hypothesis were true. Because statistical tests are based on probabilities, mistakes can be made in deciding whether or not to reject the null hypothesis. One kind of error made in statistical inference is known as a *Type I error,* which occurs when a true null hypothesis is rejected. The probability of a Type I error is called *alpha*—the significance level of the statistical test. A second kind of error, understandably referred to as a *Type II error,* consists of not rejecting a false null hypothesis. The probability of a Type II error is called *beta,* the value of which depends on a number of factors. For a more conservative test of the null hypothesis, in which case we want to be very sure that when we reject the null hypothesis it is false, we will set alpha equal to .01. If we are somewhat less concerned about making a Type I error, we select an alpha value of .05 rather than .01.

Although the probability of a Type I error is specified by the researcher and hence under his or her direct control, the probability of a Type II error is not. In general, Type I and Type II errors vary in opposite directions. A consequence of making alpha large is to make beta small, and vice versa. Beta may also be reduced by using a large sample size and selecting a statistical procedure with greater power to reject a false null hypothesis.

Today statistical methods are being applied everywhere. High-speed computers have made the computations of statistics based on hundreds of cases faster than our ability to interpret the results. Unfortunately, sometimes the results of these computations are not very meaningful because the data on which they were based are unreliable and unrepresentative of any population, or just plain uninteresting and unimportant. Usually, in such cases, the researcher has not done his or her homework and has failed to devote a sufficient amount of time to thinking about the research problem or question before launching into a haphazard process of data collection.

It is not enough for psychological researchers to be proficient in statistical methods, computer programming and operation, and the use of other research tools and techniques. They must also be good thinkers, that is, people who reserve judgment and do not let their own blind spots or desires interfere with the quest for truth. Last but by no means least, researchers must be ethical, painstakingly and sensitively weighing the possible negative effects of a research study on the participants against the potential theoretical or practical benefits of an investigation. All sorts of ethical guidelines for conducting research with humans and animals have been published, but the "Ethical Principles of Psychologists" remains the principal ethical creed to which psychological researchers should subscribe. The preamble to the proposed revision of the APA ethics code is given in Report 2–1. The principles of this revised ethics code include compe-

◆◇◆

REPORT 2–1

Preamble to Proposed Revision of the APA Ethical Principles of Psychologists

Psychologists work to develop a valid and reliable body of scientific knowledge based on research. They may apply that knowledge to human behavior in a variety of contexts. In doing so, they perform many roles, such as researcher, educator, diagnostician, therapist, supervisor, consultant, administrator, social interventionist, and expert witness, for example. Their goal is to broaden knowledge of behavior and, where appropriate, to apply it pragmatically to improve the condition of both society and the individual. Psychologists afford appropriate respect to the importance of freedom of inquiry and expression in research, teaching, and publication. They also strive to help the public in developing informed judgments and choices concerning human behavior. This Ethics Code provides a common set of values upon which psychologists build their professional and scientific work.

This Code is intended to provide both the general principles and the decision rules to cover most situations encountered by psychologists. It has as its primary goal the welfare and protection of the individuals and groups with whom psychologists work and of society. It is the individual responsibility of each psychologist to aspire to the highest possible standards of conduct. Psychologists respect and protect human and civil rights, and do not knowingly participate in nor condone unfair discriminatory practices.

The development of a dynamic set of ethical standards for a psychologist's work-related conduct requires a personal commitment to a lifelong effort to act ethically, to encourage ethical behavior by students, supervisees, employees, and colleagues as appropriate, and to consult with others as needed concerning ethical problems. Each psychologist supplements, but does not violate, the Ethics Code's values and rules on the basis of guidance drawn from personal values, culture, and experience.

◆◇◆

I, _____, voluntarily give my consent to serve as a participant in the research study titled:

_____

I have received a satisfactory explanation of the general purpose of the study, as well as
a description of what I shall be asked to do and the conditions to which I shall be exposed. I
realize that it may not be possible for the researcher to explain all aspects of the study to me until
it has been completed. In return for my service in the study, I will receive:

_____

It is my understanding that the researcher is responsible for any risks that I may sustain in
this study. I have been informed of the following risks or potentially unpleasant experiences:

_____

_____

I further understand that I may terminate my participation in this study at any time, and that any
data obtained will be kept confidential.

_____   _____
Signature of Participant   Researcher Prints Name Here

_____   _____
Date   Signature of Researcher

FIGURE 2–2   Form for informed consent to participate in psychological research study.

tence, integrity, professional and scientific responsibility, respect for people's
rights and dignity, concern for the welfare of others, and social responsibility
(American Psychological Association, 1992).

Of particular importance among the ethical principles of psychologists is
the need for researchers to obtain the *informed consent* of subjects prior to their
participation in an investigation. The requirement of informed consent can be
met by explaining the purposes of the investigation to the subjects, what they will
be asked to do, and any possible dangers to which they will be exposed. To make
the subject's participation legal, a form such as that in Figure 2–2 should be
completed and signed by both the subject (or his or her legal representative) and
the researcher.

Summary

As in other fields of science, research in psychology is concerned with the
relationships between independent and dependent variables. The independent
variables in psychological research are stimuli of various kinds, and the dependent variables are usually behavioral or organismic changes. Intervening variables that come between independent and dependent variables, moderator
variables that affect the relationship between an independent and a dependent
variable, and extraneous variables that introduce error into the interpretation of
changes in the dependent variable, are also important. Whenever possible,
research variables should be defined operationally; that is, they should be
described in terms of the procedures or operations required to experience and
manipulate them.

All measuring instruments should be reliable and valid. Reliability refers to the extent to which an instrument measures anything consistently. Validity refers to the extent to which an instrument measures what it was designed to measure. Another important concept is that of probability, the chances (.00 to 1.00) that when one event or circumstance occurs, a second event or circumstance is likely to occur.

Experimentation is the method of choice in scientific research, but observational, survey, and correlational methods have also contributed to knowledge in psychology and other fields. It is only by means of experiments, however, that cause-effect relationships can be established. Personality variables have not been used as extensively in experimental research as in controlled observational or correlational studies, but sometimes measures of personality have served as control or concomitant variables in experiments on behavioral changes.

When conducting an experiment, it is important to be aware of placebo effects, Hawthorne effects, and other changes in the dependent variable that are not produced directly by the independent variable(s). Such effects can be controlled by a double-blind procedure, random assignment of subjects to groups, and other precautions. Expectancy effects and demand characteristics should also be considered in designing experiments and evaluating research results.

Descriptive statistics such as the mean, median, and standard deviation are computed to describe the characteristics of a sample of data. Inferential statistics are used to make inferences from samples to populations. Inferential statistical methods begin with a null hypothesis, an alternative hypothesis, and a specified level of significance. The level of significance, alpha, is the probability of a Type I error—rejecting the null hypothesis when it is true; beta is the probability of a Type II error—retaining the null hypothesis when it is false. Alpha is set by the researcher; beta is determined by the sample size, the magnitude of the true effect of the independent variable on the dependent variable, and the ability (power) of the statistical test to detect that effect.

Conducting research in psychology, and research on personality in particular, is not only a matter of having a well-thought-out research project and the technical competence to conduct the project and analyze the results. Researchers must also be cognizant of their ethical responsibilities of obtaining the informed consent of the participants and weighing the potential benefit of the research to society against the discomfort that it may cause the participants.

Key Concepts

Correlation   The degree of relationship between two variables, signified by an index number (a *correlation coefficient*) ranging from -1.00 (a perfect negative relationship) to $+1.00$ (a perfect positive relationship).

Experiment   A scientific procedure, involving control of extraneous variables, to determine the effect of an independent variable on a dependent variable.

Measurement The assignment of numbers to events. Measurements may be made on scales ranging in their refinement or accuracy from nominal through ordinal and interval to ratio scales.

Null hypothesis The "straw man" in a scientific procedure, which states that there is no significant difference between the obtained results and the results expected by chance. The null hypothesis may be rejected or not rejected; if rejected, then the alternative hypothesis is accepted.

Observation method Observing people in a controlled or uncontrolled situation and making a formal or informal record of their behavior. Observation is basic to all science.

Operational definition A definition that tells what to do, that is, what procedure or measurement operation to employ, in order to experience the variable being defined.

Probability The likelihood or chance that a certain event will occur, as indicated by an index number ranging from .00 (complete certainty that the event will not occur) to 1.00 (complete certainty that the event will occur).

Reliability Consistency or repeatability of measurement; relative freedom from errors of measurement. Reliability coefficients vary from .00 (complete unreliability) to 1.00 (complete reliability).

Scientific reasoning Applying both deductive and inductive thinking in an effort to predict, understand, and explain some phenomenon. *Deductive (syllogistic) reasoning* is reasoning from the general to the particular; *inductive reasoning* is reasoning from the particular to the general.

Statistics Mathematical procedures used to summarize sample data (*descriptive statistics*) and to estimate or make inferences concerning population parameters (*inferential statistics*).

Theory A system of assumptions, definitions, and postulates designed to explain some phenomenon and make predictions concerning its occurrence or nonoccurrence. Good theories are parsimonious, precise, and fruitful in their explanations.

Validity The extent to which an assessment instrument measures what it was designed to measure. Validity can be assessed in several ways: by an analysis of the instrument's content (*content validity*), by relating scores on the test to a criterion (*predictive* and *concurrent validity*), and by a more thorough study of the extent to which the test is a measure of a certain psychological construct (*construct validity*).

Activities and Applications

1. Locate a personality research article in a professional journal in the library. Read the article, and answer the following questions:

a. What was the purpose of the research investigation; that is, what research question(s) was (were) asked, and/or what hypothesis was tested?

b. What scientific (research) method was used to answer the research question?

c. How were the results analyzed, and how did the analysis turn out?

e. What criticisms do you have of this investigation?

2. Interview a personality researcher at your college or university, or at a neighboring institution, and ask him or her the following questions:

a. Why did you decide to become a personality researcher?

b. What kinds of research investigations have you conducted thus far?

c. What kinds of research studies do you plan to conduct in the future?

d. Is the field of personality psychology a good career for a student like me?

3. Identify the independent and dependent variable(s) in each of the following examples:

a. Two groups of athletes, starters and nonstarters, were administered a sensation-seeking inventory to determine whether their mean scores on this personality variable were significantly different.

b. Students at a private university were compared with students at a public university on their attitudes toward war.

c. A group of children was followed up over a period of 10 years to determine what changes occurred in their personalities as they grew older.

d. One group of children was shown a violent film, and a second group was shown a nonviolent comedy. The two groups of children were compared on the aggressiveness of their play after viewing the films.

4. Make a list of five topics concerned with personality that you would like to study more. What sources would you use to obtain information on these topics?

5. Explain the following statement, and tell why it is true:

Reliability is a necessary but not a sufficient condition for validity.

6. What is wrong with the following statement?

The relationship between sociability and grade-point average is significantly negative. Therefore, if you are very sociable you'll probably do poorly in school work.

7. What type of correlation (positive, negative, zero) is described by each of the following?

a. As X decreases, Y decreases.

b. As X increases, Y increases.

c. As X increases, Y decreases.

d. As X decreases, Y increases.

e. As *X* increases, *Y* remains unchanged.

f. As *X* decreases, *Y* remains unchanged.

Suggested Readings

Aiken, L. R. (1991). *Psychological testing and assessment* (7th ed.) (Chapters 1 and 4). Needham Heights, MA: Allyn & Bacon.

Craik, K. H. (1986). Personality research methods: An historical perspective. *Journal of Personality, 54*(1), 18–51.

Ethical principles of psychologists (Amended June 2, 1990). (1990). *American Psychologist, 45*, 390–395.

Miller, S. A. (1987). *Developmental research methods.* Englewood Cliffs, NJ: Prentice-Hall.

Ozer, D. J. (1989). Construct validity in personality assessment. In D. M. Buss & N. Cantor (Eds.), *Personality psychology: Recent trends and emerging directions* (pp. 224–234). New York: Springer-Verlag.

Pagano, R. R. (1990). *Understanding statistics in the behavioral sciences* (3rd ed.). St. Paul, MN: West.

Shaughnessy, J. J., & Zechmeister, E. B. (1990). *Research methods in psychology* (2nd ed.) (Chapters 2, 3, 5). New York: McGraw-Hill.

Strohmer, D. C., et al. (1988). Personal hypothesis testing: The role of consistency and self schema. *Journal of Counseling Psychology, 35*, 56–65.

CHAPTER 3

Personality Assessment

CHAPTER OUTLINE

Research and practice in psychology depend on the availability of effective assessment procedures, whether these procedures are formal or informal, structured or unstructured. The selection or development of a test or other technique for assessing characteristics of behavior and personality begins with the questions of why people think and act in certain ways and what they are likely to do or be like in the future. These diagnostic and prognostic questions may be posed in a variety of settings:

1 In mental health settings as an aid in diagnosis, treatment, and residential placement.
2 In educational settings as an aid in formulating proper remediation measures.
3 In legal settings as an aid in court evaluations, such as sanity hearings, as well as assisting the judicial branch in planning rehabilitation measures.
4 In medical settings as an aid in hospital consultation to various clinics in evaluating the psychological aspects of illness.
5 In psychotherapeutic settings as an aid in planning and evaluating psychotherapy and chemotherapy, and in offering referring therapists better initial understanding of the client's dynamics and important focal issues.
6 As research and teaching tools for the study of human personality, particularly with special populations, for example, prisoners and juvenile delinquents.
7 In various evaluations required by law, such as cases involving federal compensation. (Petzelt & Craddick, 1978)

The general goals of personality assessment—to provide a valid description of the personality and behavior of persons and to make accurate predictions of their future actions—are the same regardless of the setting. However, the specific goals—to determine the presence or absence of certain characteristics, symptoms, or conditions, and to make recommendations for specific treatments—vary with the person and the situation.

Personality assessment procedures and instruments include observations, interviews, biographical questionnaires, checklists, rating scales, mental ability tests, personality inventories, projective techniques, and even perceptual/motor and psychophysiological measures. The specific assessment instruments may be published or unpublished, standardized or nonstandardized, and objective or subjective. Understandably, the reliability of objective, standardized instruments tends to be greater than that of subjective, nonstandardized instruments. However, the validities of commercially available personality assessment instruments are not always as high as they should be.

The validity of a test or other psychometric instrument can vary substantially with the situation in which it is administered, and it is often necessary to construct special assessment devices for specific situations and purposes. Depending on the purposes of the assessment, the assessor may need to administer several tests and procedures. It is essential, however, not to overwhelm the examinee with tests that add little or nothing to an understanding of his or her personality and behavioral functioning or the nature of any psychological problems.

The selection or construction of a personality assessment instrument depends on the specific purposes of the assessment, in addition to the characteristics of the person to be assessed (chronological age, sex, education, social class, temperament, estimated mental abilities, etc.) and the skill and theoretical orientation of the assessor. Theoretical orientations, or theories of personality, are discussed at length in Chapters 4 through 8. Every psychological examiner has some set of ideas or theoretical framework that serves as a guide in collecting and interpreting data pertaining to personality. Whether that orientation is psychodynamic, psychometric, behavioristic, or some other, instrument selection and data analysis are accomplished more effectively with respect to a set of explicit assumptions about human behavior and the nature of personality. Adherents to a psychodynamic theory place greater emphasis on the subjective judgment of the assessor in data collection and interpretation, whereas assessors with a psychometric orientation emphasize the administration and interpretation of rating scales and personality inventories. Finally, behaviorally oriented assessors focus on the determination of antecedent and consequent events that elicit and control behavior.

Rather than sticking strictly to a single theory or model of personality, many psychodiagnosticians prefer an eclectic or omnibus approach in which constructs from several theories are combined into a workable scheme. In conducting a case study of a person, these assessors are likely to follow Sundberg's (1977) recommendations:

1 Begin by surveying the person's overall life situation and problems; then obtain more details in areas of particular relevance to the assessment.
2 Be sensitive to the social, cultural, and ethnic background, as well as the age and sex, of the examinee.
3 Use more objective, rather than subjective, assessment techniques and data.
4 Obtain not merely *more* information, but the *right kind* of information pertaining to the specific purposes of the assessment.
5 Avoid overspeculation in interpreting results and making behavioral predictions; be especially careful in predicting behaviors of low probability.
6 Compare your findings and interpretations with those of other assessors if possible, and keep a record of your agreements and disagreements, successes and failures.
7 Report your findings clearly, in a form and style that can be understood by the persons for whom they are intended.

The report of a psychological assessment may follow an outline such as that in Figure 3–1. The writer of a psychological assessment report needs to keep clearly in mind the referral questions and any other questions concerning the diagnostic and prognostic implications of the assessment findings. Before transmitting the report to the proper authorities, and in fact even before administering any tests or conducting other assessment procedures, the examiner should obtain the informed consent of the person or his/her legal representative. As indicated by Standard 16.3 of the *Standards for Educational and Psychological Testing* (American Educational Research Association et al., 1985), unless otherwise required by law, the examinee's informed consent or that of his/her legal representative is needed to release assessment results by name of the examinee to

---

Name of Examinee: _____ Sex: _____
Birth Date: _____ Age: _____ Education: _____
Referred by: _____
Place of Examination: _____ Date of Exam: _____
Examined by: _____ Date of Report: _____
Tests Administered: _____

Reason for Referral. State briefly why the examinee was referred for psychological testing. What was the purpose of the referral, and what person or facility made it?

Observations and Interview Findings. Briefly describe the appearance and behavior of the examinee during the examination. Give the examinee's own story, as well as that of other observers if available. Describe the examinee's physical and psychological history and characteristics, educational and employment situation. In the case of children in particular, information on the home and family (social status, characteristics of parents, siblings, etc.) is also important to obtain. Serious sensory or psychomotor handicaps, as well as the presence of emotional disorder, should also be noted.

Results and Interpretations. Give a detailed description of the results of the tests and any other instruments administered and how they should be interpreted. If the examiner is interpreting the results according to a particular theory of personality, make certain that the reader understands the language and assumptions of the theory. Be as specific and individualized as possible in interpreting the results. Describe the examinee's characteristics, his or her approach to the tasks, level of motivation and emotionality, and any other factors that might have affected the results.

Conclusions and Recommendations. Briefly describe the conclusions (descriptive, dynamic, diagnostic) stemming from the observational, interview, and standardized or unstandardized test data. What recommendations are warranted by the results? Include appropriate interpretative cautions, but don't "hedge" or deal in generalities. Among the recommendations that might be made are additional psychological assessments (be specific), neurological or other medical examinations, counseling or psychotherapy, special class placement and training, vocational rehabilitation, and institutionalization. If a handicap or disability exists, is it remediable?

_____
Name and Signature of Examiner

FIGURE 3–1 Format of a psychological assessment report.

any other person or institution. That consent may be obtained in a signed form such as the one in Figure 3–2.

In addition to obtaining the informed consent of examinees or their legal representatives, psychological examiners must be keenly aware of limitations in the assessment instruments that they plan to administer as well as limitations in their own skills in administering and interpreting the results of those instruments. Considerable training is needed to administer and interpret psychological assessment instruments, and in most states a psychological examiner is required by law to be licensed or certified to conduct formal personality assessments. Improper practices, which represent a violation of the ethical code of the American Psychological Association (APA) as well a violation of legal statutes, can lead to a warning, termination of membership in the APA, revocation of the practitioner's right to practice psychology in that state, and other penalties.

Informed Consent for a Psychological Examination

I, _____, voluntarily give my consent to serve as a participant in a psychological examination conducted by _____. I have received a clear and complete explanation of the general nature and purposes of the examination and the specific reasons why I am being examined. I have also been informed of the kinds of tests and other procedures to be administered and how the results will be used.

I realize that it may not be possible for the examiner to explain all aspects of the examination to me until it has been completed. It is also my understanding that I may terminate my participation in the examination at any time without penalty. I further understand that I will be informed of the results and that they will be reported to no one else without my permission. At this time, I request that a copy of the results of this examination be sent to:

_____

_____

_____   _____
Signature of Examinee   Examiner Prints Name Here

_____   _____
Date   Signature of Examiner

FIGURE 3–2   Form for obtaining informed consent for a psychological examination.

Observations and Interviews

Whether they are employed for research or assessment purposes, observations and interviews are the most common techniques for obtaining information on behavior and personality. The popularity of observational and interviewing methods is a consequence of several factors, including their directness as measures of behavioral and mental functioning, their immediate availability and adaptability to various contexts, and the richness of the data provided by them. Observing what people do and what they say, either informally or in a formal, controlled observational or interview setting can provide a wealth of data on characteristic responses or styles of reacting to other people and to the nonhuman environment.

Observations

Behavioral observations made for personality assessment purposes may be controlled or uncontrolled. More planning and preparation, of what to observe and how to record the data, go into *controlled observation*. An example of controlled observation for purposes of personality assessment is *situational testing*, in which several people are asked to discuss an issue or solve a specified problem while observers inconspicuously note, record, and rate the behaviors of the group members.

Uncontrolled observation is more open or unstructured, but typically less reliable and less free from observer bias than controlled observation. On the other hand, uncontrolled observations can yield a great deal of interesting information and suggest potentially explanatory hypotheses concerning human behavior. In both controlled and uncontrolled observation the observers try to make their presence as unobtrusive as possible, so they will have a minimal effect on what is being observed.

Certain scientists, such as cultural anthropologists, believe that in order to keep individuals who are being observed from behaving unnaturally—that is, feeling as if they were "on stage" and hence tempted to play a role—observers must try to immerse themselves into the group being observed and become part of it. This method, referred to as *participant observation,* is not always successful, but when it is the resulting data are often more meaningful and realistic than data obtained by other means.

Selecting and Training Observers. It is virtually impossible for observers to separate themselves completely from their own background and personality, but certain individuals approach the observational task more objectively and perceptively than others. To some extent, people can be trained to make and record observations accurately, to differentiate between what is observed and how it is interpreted and to be aware of the effects of personal biases and other factors on what is observed. But certain people appear to be equipped by nature or prior experience with greater interpersonal perceptivity, empathy, and objectivity. Certain novelists, such as Henry James, are renowned for their observational acumen. In a short story entitled "Four Meetings," James describes Miss Caroline Spencer (Fadiman, 1945, pp. 3–4 passim) thusly:

> I saw her but four times, though I remember them vividly. She made an impression on me. Close upon thirty, by every presumption, she was made almost like a little girl and had the complexion of a child. She was artistic, I suspected. Her eyes were perhaps too round and too inveterately surprised, but her lips had a certain mild decision, and her teeth, when she showed them, were charming.

Somewhat less poetic is the following description from a psychological examination report:

> Michael is an attractive child, with long, straight brown hair and freckles. He seemed a little anxious during the examination: he squirmed around in his chair, but not excessively. He tended to give up easily on more difficult tasks, and manifested other signs of a low frustration tolerance (deep sighs, a reluctance to attempt some tasks). However, he was fairly cooperative during the examination and seemed mildly interested in the test materials. He was generally attentive and energetic, but showed signs of fatigue toward the end of the examination. Throughout the examination, he answered questions briefly in a slow, sparing, somewhat uncertain manner. He did not speak except when spoken to, and did not smile during the entire time.

Self-Observation. It would seem that if people find it hard to be objective and unbiased in observing others, they would experience even greater difficulty in making valid observations of themselves. Nevertheless, psychotherapists and other psychologists have had notable successes in training individuals to make objective, systematic self-observations (e.g., Thoreson & Mahoney, 1974).

The process of self-observation may involve keeping a continuous written record of one's thoughts, feelings, and actions. A mass of data of this sort can be found in diaries, autobiographies, letters, drawings, and other personal documents. As revealed in Gordon Allport's (1965) book *Letters from Jenny*, a *content analysis* of such data may yield important insights into the personality and behavior of the self-observer and reporter.

Nonverbal Behavior. In the words of Sigmund Freud (1905a, p. 94), "He that has eyes to see and ears to hear may convince himself that no mortal can keep a secret. If his lips are silent, he chatters with his fingertips; betrayal oozes out of him at every pore." Freud was referring to nonverbal behavior, which some psychologists and language experts believe to be more revealing and less deceptive than words. A variety of instruments and procedures, such as the Profile of Nonverbal Sensitivity (PONS) (Rosenthal, Hall, DiMatteo, Rogers, & Archer, 1979) and the Facial Action Coding System (FACS) (Ekman & Friesen, 1984), have been designed to assess nonverbal behavior and one's sensitivity to nonverbal messages. These instruments are, however, not widely used, and observations of nonverbal behavior continue to be a more or less informal in clinical and other assessment contexts.

Observations for Behavior Modification. Based on learning theory and research, *behavior modification* consists of a set of techniques designed to modify personally debilitating or socially inappropriate behaviors (phobias, substance abuse, enuresis, chronic anxiety or pain, eating disorders, etc.). Careful observations of the specific *target behaviors,* in addition to the antecedents and consequences of such behaviors, form an important part of behavior modification. Depending on the problem and the context in which it occurs, these observations may be made by parents, teachers, nurses, psychiatric aides, and the patients themselves. In making self-observations (*self-monitoring*), the patient observes and tabulates instances of specific behaviors, a process which may, in itself, result in a decline in the frequency of those behaviors.

Interviews

An interview is a "face-to-face verbal interchange in which one person, the interviewer, attempts to elicit information or expressions of opinion or belief from another person or persons" (Maccoby & Maccoby, 1954, p. 449). As such, it is a special kind of observation that focuses not only on what the individual says in response to a series of questions asked by an interviewer, but also how he or she says it. The content of the interviewee's verbal responses is of primary impor-

TABLE 3–1   General Outline for Assessment Interview

1. *Identifying data:* name, age, sex, education, ethnic group, nationality, address, date of birth, marital status, date of interview, etc.
2. *Purpose of interview:* employment, psychiatric intake, psychodiagnostic, problem solving or "troubleshooting," performance evaluation, termination or exit, etc.
3. *Physical appearance:* clothing, grooming, physical description (attractiveness, unusual features, etc.), obvious or apparent physical disorders or disabilities.
4. *Behavior:* attitudes and emotions (cooperative, outgoing or reserved, friendly or hostile, defensive, etc.); motoric behavior (active versus passive, posture, gait, carriage); level of intellectual functioning (bright, average, retarded—estimated from vocabulary, immediate and long-term memory, judgment, abstract thinking); signs of mental disorder (distorted thought processes—bizarre constructions, thought blocking, etc.; distorted perceptions—delusions, hallucinations, disorientation in time or space, etc.; inappropriate or extreme emotional reactions—depression, mania; unusual mannerisms, postures, or facial expressions).
5. *Family:* parents, siblings, other family members; sociocultural group; attitudes toward family members.
6. *Medical history:* present health, health history, physical problems.
7. *Developmental history:* physical, intellectual, language, emotional, and social development; irregularities or problems of development.
8. *Education and training:* schools attended, performance level, adjustment to school, plans for further education and training.
9. *Employment:* nature and number of jobs or positions held, military service (rank and duties), job performance levels, job problems.
10. *Legal problems:* arrests and convictions, nature of misdemeanors or felonies.
11. *Sexual and marital history:* sexual activities and problems, marriages, marital problems, separations and divorces, children.
12. *Interests and attitudes:* hobbies, recreational activities, social activities and attitudes toward others, level of self-acceptance and satisfaction, aspirations or goals.
13. *Current problems:* details of current problems and plans for solving them.

tance, but the body postures and poise, gestures, eye movements, and the quality and pattern of speech may also provide significant data.

When conducted by a skilled interviewer, an interview, which is one of the most popular of all psychological assessment techniques in clinical and employment contexts, can provide a great deal of information on what an individual does in certain situations and how he or she feels about specific persons and things. The particular approach—structured or unstructured, direct or indirect—varies with the purposes of the interview. In any case, interviewing requires patience and sensitivity. It is rarely a one-way, master-slave situation, but, rather, a reciprocally interactive situation shaped by the personalities of both participants—interviewer and interviewee.

Table 3–1 provides a general outline for a psychological assessment interview. This outline is suggestive rather than definitive, and the particular areas or topics that are covered will vary with the purposes of the interview, the particular situation, and the characteristics of the participants. Questions pertaining to certain areas, such as identifying data, education, training, and employment, may be answered fairly quickly, but proper coverage of other areas takes more time.

An interview usually begins with a warm-up, get-acquainted period in which the interviewer asks a few nonthreatening lead-in questions. In a fairly structured interview, the interviewer may then simply go down a list of questions to be answered briefly one after another. On the other hand, in a more unstructured, clinical interview, the interviewer may deviate from a strict list of questions and let the interviewee talk at length when a topic of potential significance comes up.

The recommendations listed in Table 3–2 concerning the interviewer's behavior apply to all interviews, but especially to clinical interviews conducted for psychodiagnostic or intake purposes in a mental health setting. These recommendations are generally applicable, but the specific techniques employed will vary with the theoretical orientation (behavioral, dispositional, psychodynamic, client-centered, etc.) of the clinical interviewer. As with other types of personality assessment, in conducting an interview one should have a sense of what he or she is searching for and where one wants to go in the interview. In addition to being more open-ended or unstructured than others, some interviewers are more eclectic, adhering less to a specific theoretical orientation and applying a combination of techniques.

Computer-Based Interviewing. Many structured forms for clinical or psychiatric interviews in particular have been devised, and some of these forms and other interviewing procedures have been programmed for administration, scoring, and interpretation by computer. Examples are the Psychological/Psychiatric Status Interview (from Slosson Educational Publications, Inc.) and the Diagnostic Interview for Children and Adolescents (from Multi-Health Systems, Inc.). Computer-based interviews often have higher reliabilities than interpersonal interviews, and most interviewees do not object to being questioned by a computer. There are, however, certain difficulties with computer-based interviews, including the facts that they are fairly expensive, inappropriate in certain cases, and typically limited to obtaining structured, verbal information.

TABLE 3–2   Recommendations for Conducting a Psychological Interview

1. Assure the interviewee of the confidentiality of the interview.
2. Convey a feeling of interest and warmth (rapport).
3. Try to put the interviewee at ease.
4. Try to "get in touch" with how the interviewee feels (empathy).
5. Be courteous, patient, and accepting.
6. Encourage the interviewee to express his or her thoughts and feelings freely.
7. Adjust the questions to the cultural and educational background of the interviewee.
8. Avoid psychological or psychiatric jargon.
9. Avoid leading questions.
10. Share personal information and experiences with the interviewee (self-disclosure) if appropriate and timed accurately.
11. Use humor sparingly, and only if appropriate and not insulting.
12. Listen without overreacting emotionally.
13. Attend not only to what is said but also to how it is said.
14. Take notes or make a recording as inconspicuously as possible.

Stress Interviewing. The purpose of stress interviewing is to determine the ability of an interviewee to cope or solve problems under emotionally stressful conditions. Stress interviewing may be used when time is limited or it is very difficult to elicit information from the interviewee, but it is certainly not recommended for inexperienced interviewers. Reminiscent as it is of a police interrogation session, stress interviewing demands a great deal of professional competence and may easily get out of control in inexperienced hands.

Reliability and Validity of Observations and Interviews. The reliability of observational or interview data is not determined in the same manner as that of psychological tests and questionnaires. In addition to having two or more persons observe or interview the same individuals, the results of observations and interviews can be scored or evaluated separately by two or more persons and the evaluations compared in some way. As described in Chapter 2, this method is known as *interscorer* or *interrater reliability* and is usually summarized as a correlation between two or more sets of observational or interview data. Unfortunately, the resulting reliability coefficients are usually not very high. Different observers or interviewers often form different impressions of the same person, and two interviewers may behave differently and hence elicit different responses from the same interviewee. Although the interscorer reliabilities of structured and semistructured interviews are higher than those of unstructured interviews, they rarely exceed .80 (Bradley & Caldwell, 1977; Disbrow, Doerr, & Caulfield, 1977).

Many of the reliability problems of interviews are related to the characteristics and behavior of the interviewer, whose manner determines to a great extent what the interviewee will say and do. Interviewers also tend to give more weight to first impressions and to be influenced more by unfavorable than by favorable information about a person. Impressions are influenced by the neatness, posture, and other nonverbal behaviors of the interviewee as much as by his or her answers and other verbal behaviors. Among the errors to which observers and interviewers are subject are the *halo effect* of making judgments on the basis of general impressions and the *contrast error* of letting the evaluations of one interviewee be affected by the evaluations made of a preceding interviewee. Audio- or videotape recordings of interviews for later playback and evaluation can improve both the reliability and validity of interviews, but it is generally recognized that the validity of interviewing as a diagnostic and selection technique is overrated.

Checklists and Rating Scales

The mass of data provided by observations and interviews is frequently recorded and summarized in a checklist or rating scale format. In the case of objective observations, especially, the observer notes the frequency and intensity of specified behavioral acts on a checklist or rating form.

Checklists

As applied to the assessment of personality, a *checklist* is a list of words, phrases, or statements that describes certain personal characteristics or behaviors of the person being evaluated. The checker, who may be either the person himself or someone else, indicates with a check mark or another indicator which items on the list are descriptive of the person.

Checklists are relatively simple to construct and fairly reliable. The so-called frequency response set—the tendency of some individuals to check more items than other individuals, no matter whom they are evaluating—must be handled in some way. Still, the flexibility and efficiency of checklists usually outweigh this difficulty if the checklist is not the only instrument administered in a personality or behavioral assessment. One great advantage of a checklist is that it can be administered repeatedly to evaluate changes over time as a function of experience or intervention procedures. For example, the behavioral checklist in Figure 3–3 has been administered to determine changes in the performance anxiety of patients over eight time periods, when a behavioral modification procedure (systematic desensitization) was being applied.

	Time Period							
Behavior Observed	1	2	3	4	5	6	7	8
1. Paces								
2. Sways								
3. Shuffles feet								
4. Knees tremble								
5. Extraneous arm and hand movement (swings, scratches, toys, etc.)								
6. Arms rigid								
7. Hands restrained (in pockets, behind back, clasped)								
8. Hand tremors								
9. No eye contact								
10. Face muscles tense (drawn, tics, grimaces)								
11. Face "deadpan"								
12. Face pale								
13. Face flushed (blushes)								
14. Moistens lips								
15. Swallows								
16. Clears throat								
17. Breathes heavily								
18. Perspires (face, hands, armpits)								
19. Voice quivers								
20. Speech blocks or stammers								

FIGURE 3–3   Behavioral checklist for performance anxiety. (Adapted from *Insight vs. Desensitization in Psychotherapy* by Gordon L. Paul, with the permission of the publishers, Stanford University Press. © 1966 by the Board of Trustees of the Leland Stanford Junior University.)

Many checklists are available commercially, one of the most popular of which is the Mooney Problem Check List (from the Psychological Corporation). The four separate forms of the Mooney (Junior High School, High School, College, Adult) each consist of a list of 210–330 problem statements in eight categories: health and physical development; home and family; boy and girl relations; morals and religion; courtship and marriage; economic security; school or occupation; social and recreational. In filling out the Mooney, respondents are asked to underline the problems of some concern and circle the problems of most concern to them. The examiner summarizes the problems in each category for later discussion with the examinee.

Also widely administered are several published checklists of adjectives referring to personal characteristics. Examples of these instruments are the Adjective Check List (from Consulting Psychologists Press) and the Multiple Affect Adjective Check List (from the Educational and Industrial Testing Service). The Adjective Check List consists of 300 alphabetically arranged adjectives from "absentminded" to "zany"; respondents are asked to check those adjectives that are self-descriptive. The responses can be scored on the 37 scales or areas listed in Table 3–3. The numbers in the last column of the table are converted T scores, based on a mean of 50 and a standard deviation of 10, of a particular person.

An interpretation of the T scores in Table 3–3 is given in Report 3–1. Note that this report also contains descriptive background information, which is referred to in interpreting the person's checklist scores. In this case, as in the great majority of psychological case studies, the scores yielded by a particular test or other assessment tool are not analyzed "blindly," but rather against a background of information obtained from a variety of sources. The more that the various sources of information support or substantiate each other, the greater confidence one can place in the validity of the psychological interpretation, diagnosis, and prognosis.

Rating Scales

In mental health, educational, and employment contexts, rating scales are comparable in popularity to checklists. Introduced into scientific investigation by Francis Galton during the late nineteenth century, ratings of self and others have become commonplace in psychological research and practice.

A checklist is actually a dichotomous rating scale—one with two categories (checked versus not checked). On a bona fide rating scale, however, the response dichotomy of the checklist is extended to five or seven scaled categories. The rater is instructed to check or otherwise indicate the category in which the ratee should be placed on the behavior or characteristic in question. This straightforward extension of a checklist typically results in greater precision of measurement and somewhat higher reliability. Rating scales are, however, generally considered to be less precise than personality inventories and more superficial than projective techniques in what they measure.

TABLE 3–3   Scales and Illustrative *T* Scores on the Adjective Check List

Scale Name and Designation	T Scores for Report 3–1
Modus operandi	
1. Total number of adjectives checked (No. Ckd)	37
2. Number of favorable adjectives checked (Fav)	62
3. Number of unfavorable adjectives checked (Unfav)	59
4. Communality (Com)	68
Need scales	
5. Achievement (Ach)	57
6. Dominance (Dom)	50
7. Endurance (End)	53
8. Order (Ord)	57
9. Intraception (Int)	57
10. Nurturance (Nur)	44
11. Affiliation (Aff)	53
12. Heterosexuality (Het)	46
13. Exhibition (Exh)	44
14. Autonomy (Aut)	49
15. Aggression (Agg)	58
16. Change (Cha)	58
17. Succorance (Suc)	41
18. Abasement (Aba)	56
19. Deference (Def)	49
Topical scales	
20. Counseling Readiness (Crs)	55
21. Self-control (S-Cn)	48
22. Self-confidence (S-Cfd)	59
23. Personal Adjustment (P-Adj)	53
24. Ideal Self (Iss)	64
25. Creative Personality (Cps)	63
26. Military Leadership (Mls)	52
27. Masculine Attributes (Mas)	54
28. Feminine Attributes (Fem)	69
Transactional analysis	
29. Critical Parent (CP)	62
30. Nurturing Parent (NP)	48
31. Adult (A)	56
32. Free Child (FC)	46
33. Adapted Child (AC)	41
Origence-intellectence	
34. High Origence, Low Intellectence (A-1)	47
35. High Origence, High Intellectence (A-2)	64
36. Low Origence, Low Intellectence (A-3)	44
37. Low Origence, High Intellectence (A-4)	63

REPORT 3–1

Case Description Accompanying Adjective Check List Scores in Table 3–3

This 19-year-old undergraduate student majoring in biology maintained an A – grade average and planned to go to graduate school. She was brought up in a close-knit, large family, and had warm feelings about her parents and her childhood. Before college, she had always lived in small towns or semirural areas. Coming to an urban college required quite an adjustment, but she liked the excitement and stimulation of city life. She retained her religious beliefs and regularly attended church. She viewed herself as a political and economic conservative. Her life-history interviewer described her the following way:

> She is an intelligent, vivacious, attractive young woman, enthusiastic about her life at the University. Although she views herself as introverted, her behavior is more extraverted; she was talkative, outgoing, candid, and not hesitant to assume a leadership role. Her parents were strict, expected the children to assume responsibilities, and placed a high value on academic achievement. She described her mother as a demanding, extremely shy woman who participated in social activities from a sense of duty. She said her father was somewhat intimidating, but affectionate; she feels closer to him now than she did when she was growing up. Being at school—away from home and the relative isolation of that environment—is very exciting.

Scores on her ACL profile are in agreement with the case-history data and staff evaluations. Moderate elevations occur on the scales for Achievement, Self-Confidence, and Personality Adjustment, and scores of 60 or greater on the scales for Ideal Self, Creative Personality, and A-2 (high origence, high intellectence). The ACL profile also revealed scores of 60 or greater on the scales for Favorable, Communality, Femininity, Critical Parent and A-4 (low origence, high intellectence). Although the staff rating of 54 on Femininity was above average for the sample of 80 students included in this project, it is not as high as the score of 69 on her self-descriptive ACL. Because she had scores greater than 50 on *both* Masculinity and Femininity, she is in the androgynous cell in the interaction diagram between the two scales. The profile also reveals elevated scores on *both* Favorable and Unfavorable, which suggests she is more complex, internally differentiated, and less repressive than her peers.

One of the most common types of rating scale is a *numerical scale*, on which ratings of a particular person on a given variable are indicated by a single-digit number. Typically the numbers range from 1, representing the smallest amount of the variable, to 5 or 7, representing the greatest amount. For example, on a scale of "sociability" a rating of 1 or 2 would designate "very unsociable" or "unsociable," and a rating of 4 or 5, "sociable" or "very sociable."

Also widely employed are *graphic rating scales,* consisting of a series of descriptive (graphic) categories arranged on a continuum. The following is an example of a graphic rating scale:

Will this person benefit from psychological counseling?

| |_____|_____|_____|_____| |

Will not	Will obtain	Will obtain	Will obtain	Will benefit
benefit at all	minimum	some benefit	above-average	greatly
	benefit		benefit	

On this item and a series of other items on a graphic rating instrument, the rater marks the point on the line indicating his or her judgment of the ratee's standing on the designated variable.

Other traditional rating techniques are standard rating scales and semantic differential scales. On a *standard rating scale,* the rater compares the ratee with a set of standards. For example, ratings on "cooperativeness" might be made by comparing the ratee with five preselected individuals known by the rater and varying on a continuum from least to most cooperative.

On a *semantic differential scale* the respondent rates concepts rather than people. These concepts (e.g., father, mother, sickness, sin, hatred, love) are rated on a set of seven-point bipolar adjectival scales, for example:

MOTHER

Bad	|_____|_____|_____|_____|_____|_____|	Good
Weak	|_____|_____|_____|_____|_____|_____|	Strong
Slow	|_____|_____|_____|_____|_____|_____|	Fast

After all concepts have been rated on approximately ten such scales, the concepts are scored on several semantic (connotative meaning) dimensions and the scores compared. The rater's *semantic space* may then be constructed by plotting his or her concept scores on these dimensions. Both intra- and interindividual comparisons of semantic spaces arrived at in this way may then be made (Osgood, Suci, & Tannenbaum, 1957). For example, in order to obtain insight into the dynamics of a multiple personality, one might compare the semantic spaces of the two or more personalities.

Despite their convenience and low cost, ratings are subject to various kinds of errors. Among these are constant errors, the halo effect, the contrast error, and the proximity error. Constant errors include the *leniency* or *generosity error* of assigning a higher rating than deserved and the *severity error* of assigning lower ratings than justified. Another common rating error, the *halo effect,* consists of overgeneralizing by letting ratings on one or two traits affect the ratings on all other characteristics. A *contrast error* occurs when the rater lets the evaluation (favorable or unfavorable) of a preceding ratee affect the ratings assigned to a subsequent ratee. Finally, the *proximity error* refers to the tendency to assign similar ratings to items that are positioned near each other on the printed pages of a rating instrument.

Like observations and interviews, ratings can be made more accurate by carefully selecting and training raters who are interested in the rating task, thoroughly familiar with what they are supposed to rate, and alert to biases in rating. Ratings may also be improved by means of various methodological procedures, such as combining the ratings of several raters, arranging the scales in an easily understood and usable format, and paying careful attention to the design of rating items. Behaviorally anchored and forced-choice scales, in particular, represent efforts to make ratings more objective and reliable. On a *behaviorally anchored rating scale,* the terminology is more descriptive of actual behavior than it is on traditional scales.

The items on a *forced-choice rating scale* consist of two to four statements equated for social desirability. Here is an example of a four-statement forced-choice item designed to evaluate supervisors:

> Assumes responsibility easily.
> Doesn't know how or when to delegate.
> Has many constructive suggestions to offer.
> Doesn't listen to others' suggestions.

Respondents are asked to indicate which statement is most descriptive and which is least descriptive of the person being rated. Obviously, the first and third statements of the example are positive and the second and fourth are negative things to say about a person. The highest rating is earned when the most positive statement is said to be most descriptive and the most negative statement is said to be least descriptive of the ratee. But which of the two positive statements is *more* positive, and which of the two negative statements is *more* negative is presumably not apparent to the rater. Consequently, the tendency to assign a more socially desirable rating than justified is controlled for by the fixed-choice format. Unfortunately, raters often find the forced-choice format awkward and prefer a simpler numerical or graphic rating scale.

Personality Inventories

A *personality inventory,* a self-report questionnaire consisting of a set of statements concerning personal characteristics and behaviors, is a kind of self-rating scale. The items on a personality inventory, however, are generally longer and deal with a wider range of variables than those on a rating scale. The response format on a personality inventory is also usually different from the ordered categories of a rating scale. Typically there are two or three response categories, such as "Yes," "No," and "Cannot say," on a personality inventory, compared with the five to seven ordered categories on a numerical or graphic rating scale.

The design, standardization, and validation of widely used inventories such as the Minnesota Multiphasic Personality Inventory and the Sixteen Personality

Factor Questionnaire is a more painstaking process than the development of a rating scale. Many rating scales and personality inventories were designed in mental health settings, but the former have been constructed and administered just as often in employment contexts and are more likely to be special-purpose, home-grown instruments.

Content-Validated and Theory-Based Inventories

Since the introduction of the Woodworth Personal Data Sheet, a single-score questionnaire constructed during World War I for screening military personnel, the design of personality inventories has become more psychometrically sophisticated. Following the Woodworth was the multiscore Bernreuter Personality Inventory, which yielded six different scores. Similar content-validated inventories, based on reasoning, knowledge of test construction procedures, and some theory, are the California Psychological Inventory, the Omnibus Personality Inventory, the Jesness Inventory of Adolescent Personality, and the Edwards Personal Preference Schedule (EPPS) (from the Psychological Corporation). The EPPS is unique among these inventories in that it has a forced-choice response format to control for the *social desirability response set,* the tendency for examinees to select the more socially desirable response. Items on the EPPS consist of pairs of statements presumably equated on social desirability; the examinee selects the statement in each pair that is more characteristic or self-descriptive. The 15 need scales on which the EPPS is scored are listed under "Need scales" in Table 3–3. Although the forced-choice format of the EPPS does control to some extent for the social desirability response set, and although the instrument has been used extensively in personality research studies, many examinees have found its response format awkward and difficult.

Two other content-validated personality inventories that have been used extensively in research are the Myers-Briggs Type Indicator (from Consulting Psychologists Press) and the Jenkins Activity Survey (JAS) (from the Psychological Corporation). Based on Carl Jung's theory of personality types, the Myers-Briggs Type Indicator is a forced-choice inventory with two options per item. It is scored on four bipolar scales: Introversion-Extroversion, Sensing-Intuition, Thinking-Feeling, and Judging-Perceptive (Figure 3–4). Sixteen personality types are described from the combinations of these four scores, an example being the ENFP and ISTJ types. The predominant modes of the ENFP type are Extroversion, Intuition, Feeling, and Perceptive, whereas the ISTJ type is characterized by the Introversion, Sensing, Thinking, and Judging modes.

The Jenkins Activity Survey (JAS) was designed to detect a behavior pattern associated with symptoms of coronary heart disease. This *Type A* pattern assessed by the JAS is described as aggressive, ambitious, extremely competitive, preoccupied with achievement, impatient, restless, and having chronic feelings of being challenged and under pressure. People with the contrasting *Type B* behavior pattern, who are less prone than Type A's to heart disease, are described as more relaxed, easygoing, and patient people who speak and act more slowly and evenly (Jenkins, Zyzanski, & Rosenman, 1979).

There are no "right" and "wrong" answers to these questions. Your answers will help show how you like to look at things and how you like to go about deciding things. Knowing your own preferences and learning about other people's can help you understand where your special strengths are, what kinds of work you might enjoy, and how people with different preferences can relate to each other and be valuable to society.

Part I: Which Answer Comes Closer to Telling How You Usually Feel or Act?

4. Do you prefer to
   (A) arrange dates, parties, etc., well in advance, or
   (B) be free to do whatever looks like fun when the time comes?

21. Do you usually
    (A) value sentiment more than logic, or
    (B) value logic more than sentiment?

Part II: Which Word in Each Pair Appeals to You More?

Think about what the words mean, not how they look or sound.

39. (A) systematic
    (B) casual

64. (A) quick
    (B) careful

Part III: Which Answer Comes Closer to Telling How You Usually Feel or Act?

79. Are you
    (A) easy to get to know, or
    (B) hard to get to know?

84. When you start a big project that is due in a week, do you
    (A) take time to list the separate things to be done and the order of doing them, or
    (B) plunge in?

FIGURE 3–4 Sample Items for the Myers-Briggs Type Indicator–Form G. (Reproduced by special permission of the Publisher, Consulting Psychologists Press, Inc., Palo Alto, CA 94303 from Myers-Briggs Type Indicator by Katarine C. Briggs and Isabel Briggs Myers. Copyright 1977 by Peter Briggs Myers and Katherine D. Myers. All rights reserved. Further reproduction is prohibited without the Publisher's written consent. Myers-Briggs Type Indicator and MBTI are registered trademarks of Consulting Psychologists Press, Inc.)

Factor-Analyzed Inventories

Factor analysis, which consists of a set of mathematical procedures for analyzing a matrix of correlations among tests or other measures to determine what factors (constructs) explain the correlations, is discussed in Appendix B. These procedures, which began with Charles Spearman and have been applied by many psychologists to research and development in cognitive and affective assessment and theory, have contributed to the construction of several noteworthy personality inventories. Among these instruments are the Thurstone Temperament Schedule, the Guilford-Zimmerman Temperament Survey, the Sixteen Personality Factor Questionnaire, and the Eysenck Personality Inventory. A narrative score report for one of these inventories, the Sixteen Personality Factor Questionnaire (16 PF) (from the Institute for Personality and Ability Testing), is shown in Figure 3–5. As indicated in this computer-generated report, the 16 PF is scored on 16 bipolar

(Text continues on page 66)

This report is intended to be used in conjunction with professional judgment. The statements it contains should be viewed as hypotheses to be validated against other sources of data.   All information in this report should be treated confidentially and responsibly.

NAME-John Sample   June 29, 1990
ID NUMBER-   AGE-29; SEX-M

VALIDITY SCALES

SCORES			1 2 3 4 5 6 7 8 9 10		
Raw	Sten				
1	2			Faking good is very low.	
5	8			Faking bad is high.	

16 PF   PROFILE

SCORES				LEFT MEANING	1 2 3 4 5 6 7 8 9 10	RIGHT MEANING	%
Raw	Sten						
	U	C					
8	4	4	A	Cool, Reserved		Warm, Easygoing	23
10	8	8	B	Concrete Thinking		Abstract Thinking	89
10	2	3	C	Easily Upset		Calm, Stable	11
22	10	10	E	Not Assertive		Dominant	99
21	9	9	F	Sober, Serious		Enthusiastic	96
11	4	4	G	Expedient		Conscientious	23
19	7	7	H	Shy, Timid		Venturesome	77
9	6	6	I	Tough-Minded		Sensitive	60
11	8	8	L	Trusting		Suspicious	89
16	7	7	M	Practical		Imaginative	77
4	2	2	N	Forthright		Shrewd	4
15	8	7	O	Self-Assured		Self-Doubting	77
15	9	9	Q1	Conservative		Experimenting	96
14	8	8	Q2	Group-Oriented		Self-Sufficient	89
12	5	5	Q3	Undisciplined		Self-Disciplined	40
14	7	6	Q4	Relaxed		Tense, Driven	60

average

Note: "U" indicates uncorrected sten scores. "C" indicates sten scores corrected for distortion (if appropriate). The interpretation will proceed on the basis of corrected scores. This report was processed using male adult (GP) norms for Form A.

SECOND-ORDER FACTORS   **COMPOSITE SCORES**

Extraversion..average (5.9)   Adjustment....above average (6.5)
Anxiety.......above average (7.1)   Leadership....average (5.6)
Tough Poise...average (4.9)   Creativity....very high (9.0)
Independence..extremely high (10.0)
Control.......below average (4.2)   Profile Pattern Code = 2323

FIGURE 3–5   Narrative score report for the Sixteen Personality Factor Questionnaire (16 PF). (Copyright © 1967, 1970, 1971, 1986 by the Institute for Personality and Ability Testing, Inc., P.O. Box 188, Champaign, Illinois. All rights reserved. "16 PF" is a trademark of IPAT, Inc.

Name: John Sample   -2-   June 29, 1990

PERSONAL COUNSELING OBSERVATIONS

Adequacy of adjustment is above average (6.5).
Effectiveness of behavior controls is below average (4.2).

INTERVENTION CONSIDERATIONS

The influence of a controlled environment may help. Suggestions include:
A graded series of success experiences to improve self-confidence.
A structured, active program to reduce anxiety.

PRIMARY PERSONALITY CHARACTERISTICS OF SPECIAL INTEREST

Capacity for abstract skills is high.
Involvement in problems may evoke some emotional upset and instability.
In interpersonal relationships, he leads, dominates, or is stubborn.
His style of expression is often lively, optimistic, and enthusiastic.
He tends to project inner tension by blaming others, and becomes jealous or suspicious easily.
In his dealings with others, he is emotionally natural and unpretentious, though somewhat naive.
He is experimenting, has an inquiring mind, likes new ideas, and tends to disparage traditional solutions to problems.
Being self-sufficient, he prefers tackling things resourcefully, alone.

BROAD INFLUENCE PATTERNS

His attention is directed about equally toward the outer environment and toward inner thoughts and feelings. Extraversion is average (5.9).
At the present time, he sees himself as somewhat more anxious than most people. His anxiety score is above average (7.1).
In comparison with those who tend to approach problems coolly and dispassionately or those who emphasize the emotional relationships involved, he is average (4.9).
His life-style is independent and self-directed, leading to active attempts to achieve control of the environment. In this respect, he is extremely high (10.0).
He tends to be very expedient and to pursue his own wishes rather than the expectations of others. Thus, he may lack restraint and may fail at times to meet his responsibilities. This tendency is above average (6.8).

FIGURE 3–5 (Continued)

factors, in addition to several second-order factors and composite scores. Although fairly popular and based on sound psychometric procedures, because of their brevity many of the 16 PF scales have only low to moderate reliabilities. More sparse than the 16 PF in the number of personality factors assessed is the Eysenck Personality Inventory, which yields scores on Neuroticism (N), Extraversion (E), and Psychoticism (P).

Criterion-Keyed Inventories

By far the most popular of all personality inventories is the Minnesota Multiphasic Personality Inventory (MMPI) (from National Computer Systems). Developed by S. R. Hathaway and J. C. McKinley during World War II as a kind of streamlined psychiatric interview, the original version of the MMPI consists of 550 statements to be answered "Yes," "No," or "Cannot say." The number of items was increased to 567 in MMPI-2, the revised version. Responses to these statements, which are concerned with attitudes, emotions, motor disturbances, psychosomatic symptoms, and other reported feelings and behaviors indicative of psychiatric problems, are scored on nine "clinical" scales, four "validity" scales, a Social Introversion scale, and numerous supplementary scales. In evaluating an MMPI-2 profile, such as the one in Figure 3–6, scores on the validity scales (?, L, F, K) are inspected first to determine whether the profile is a valid one and should be interpreted further. Next the pattern of scores on the clinical scales is examined, *T* scores above 65 being particularly significant. Psychiatric patients generally score high on scale 2 (a measure of depression) and scale 7 (a measure of anxiety or tension). High scores on scales 1, 2, and 3 are referred to as the "neurotic triad," and high scores on scales 6, 7, 8, and 9 as the "psychotic tetrad," because high scores on these groups of scales are frequently associated with psychoneuroses or psychoses, respectively. As seen in Report 3–2, being able to produce a meaningful interpretation of a profile of scores on the MMPI or MMPI-2 requires a great deal of experience and skill.

The MMPI is referred to as a criterion-keyed inventory because scores on specific items and scales were validated against psychiatric diagnoses of people in the original standardization groups. Another criterion-keyed inventory, a kind of "normal" offspring of the MMPI, is the California Psychological Inventory (CPI) (from Consulting Psychologists Press). The revised version of the CPI consists of 462 true-false statements emphasizing more positive, normal aspects of personality than the items on the MMPI. The CPI can be scored on 25 scales classified into five groups. The scales may also be grouped into three conceptual categories of measures: (1) folk concept measures; (2) special-purpose scales, indexes, and regression equations; (3) a theoretical model containing three major themes—role, character, and competence. Scoring the CPI is a complex procedure, and familiarity with both this instrument and the MMPI requires a great deal of training and experience.

Examples of other criterion-keyed inventories of personality that are not administered as frequently as the MMPI and the CPI are the Personality Inventory for Children, the Millon Clinical Multiaxial Inventory, and the Jackson

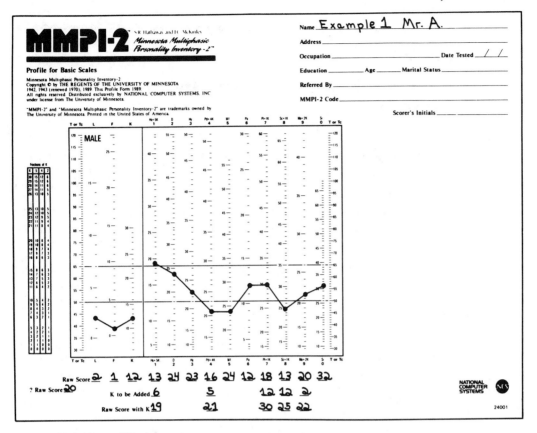

Mr. A. 60-year-old businessman.
Code: 12-670 39/845 /LK:F

FIGURE 3–6 Sample profile of scores on MMPI-2. Reproduced by permission. See Report 3–2. (Source: Minnesota Multiphasic Personality Inventory–2. Copyright © by the Regents of the University of Minnesota, 1942, 1943, 1951, 1967 (renewed 1970), 1989. This manual 1989. Reproduced by permission of the publisher.)

Personality Inventory. The factor-analytic and other psychometric procedures employed in designing and standardizing the last two instruments were particularly sophisticated.

Projective Techniques

The tendency to fake or bias responses to rating scales and personality inventories is a chronic problem having no completely satisfactory solution. Carefully constructed inventories, such as the MMPI, are equipped with special validity scales designed to detect tendencies to "fake good" or "fake bad" and failure to understand the test directions. In addition, many inventories pose rather penetrating questions, countering the allegation that such questionnaires measure

Interpretive Report on MMPI-2 Profile in Figure 3–5

Mr. A was seen in a medical outpatient service complaining of a variety of abdominal pains and distress. He is a sixty-year-old businessman, white, married, with two years of college. Little evidence could be found for an organic basis for his complaints, and he was referred for psychological assessment.

The profile he obtained on the MMPI-2 is shown in Figure 3–6; the code is:12-*670 39/845/LK:*F. All the traditional validity indicators are below the mean and suggest that he was very cooperative with the test. There is no evidence of defensiveness or of intention to distort his self-presentation on the inventory. His L and K scores fell in the ranges that raise the possibility that he was deliberately faking a poor adjustment, but his score on the F scale does not indicate that this is true. The correlates of these validity indicators suggest that this man is open, conventional, likely to display his problems, but is not in the midst of a serious emotional crisis.

On scale 1, his highest clinical score, he earned a T score of 66. A score in the high range on this scale suggests that he is rather self-centered and demanding, pessimistic and defeatist in his view of the future, and is likely to over-react to any real problems. It is likely Mr. A will have numerous physical complaints that will shift to different places on his body.

His second highest score is on scale 2 and it falls in the moderate range. This score also suggests that he is pessimistic and discouraged about the future. He is dissatisfied with himself or the world, is worrying and moody. His temperament is introverted, but he is a responsible and modest individual.

Three other scores fall within the moderate range: scales 6, 7, and 0. These scores also characterize Mr. A as responsible, hard-working, and reserved.

Individuals with 12/21 profiles show an exaggerated reaction to physical disorders, are prone to fatigue, and are often shy, irritable, seclusive, and depressed. Visceral pain, over-concern with bodily functions, and lack of insight are prominent features.

The scale-by-scale analysis of this man's profile highlights some hypochondriacal and depressive trends in an introverted, moody, and hard-working man. The code type characteristics are present but only to a moderate degree, as would be expected for profile elevations of this magnitude.

These characterizations are clearly borne out in the background information about Mr. A. He was married at the age of 25 to his present wife; there have been no marital difficulties. However, Mrs. A has recently quit her job, which resulted in a loss in the family income. They have one child, a son age 25, who is living away from home.

Mr. A has consulted his family physician very frequently in the last year and has made three visits to a Veterans Administration outpatient clinic in the last few months. In addition to his abdominal symptoms, Mr. A has had problems sleeping, complains of chronic fatigue, a loss of interest in sex, and recurring fears of death. He has also lost considerable weight and has had difficulty concentrating in his work. Sedatives have not been helpful. The present diagnostic impression is that Mr. A is suffering from dysthymia (moderate depression) with hypochondriacal features.

only superficial aspects of personality. Be that as it may, devotees of projective techniques maintain that the problems with more objectively scored, paper-and-pencil inventories and scales is that respondents often do not know the truth about themselves, and even if they do know the truth they will not necessarily reveal it on a personality inventory. In contrast to the alleged superficiality of personality inventories, projective techniques are said to probe deeper, unconscious layers of personality.

A projective technique is a relatively unstructured personality assessment device consisting of inkblots, ambiguous pictures, incomplete sentences, or other vague stimuli. Depending on the particular technique, examinees must associate, complete, rearrange, or construct something. They may respond to the test materials by producing a verbal association, indicating what they perceive in the materials (what they could be), making up stories about the materials, or completing, constructing, or rearranging the materials in some way. Because the test materials are fairly unstructured, whatever structure is imposed on them by the examinee is interpreted as a "projection" of his or her own needs, conflicts, fears, or other personal problems or characteristics. Interpretations of responses to most projective techniques are based on, but not limited to, psychodynamic theory and its concepts of unconscious dynamic forces and conflicts that affect conscious thoughts and behavior.

Word Associations and Sentence Completions

One of the simplest types of projectives is a word association test, in which the examinee is instructed to respond to each word in a list with the first word that comes to mind. The words may refer to significant persons in the examinee's life (mother, father, etc.), sources of potential problems (sex, interpersonal conflicts, strong emotions, etc.), or actions that the examinee may have committed but has not admitted. Unusual associations and slow responding are considered noteworthy and suggestive of a possible problem or conflict pertaining to the word.

Also fairly simple to construct are sentence completion tests such as the one shown in Figure 3–7. Examinees are asked to complete each sentence to express their real feelings. As with word association tests, responses to incomplete sentences are usually interpreted rather subjectively. The interpreter looks for

Directions: Finish these sentences to show your real feelings.

1. I like _____ .
2. The best time _____ .
3. My mother _____ .
4. I feel _____ .
5. I can't _____ .
6. Other children _____ .
7. I need _____ .
8. My father _____ .
9. This school _____ .
10. I want _____ .
11. I don't like _____ .
12. I am very _____ .
13. My teacher _____ .
14. I worry about _____ .
15. I am sorry that _____ .

FIGURE 3–7 A sentence completion test for children.

unusual or particularly revealing completions, and also takes into account the time to respond. Efforts to make the scoring of both word association and sentence completion tasks more objective are represented by some of the standardized instruments of these types. Examples are the Kent-Rosanoff Free Association Test, the Forer Structured Sentence Completion Test (from Western Psychological Services), and the Rotter Incomplete Sentences Blank (from the Psychological Corporation).

Inkblots

Perhaps the most widely used of all projective techniques is the Rorschach Inkblot Test. The Rorschach consists of ten 5½-by-9½-inch bilaterally symmetrical cards, five of which are black and white and five colored. The cards are presented one at a time to the examinee, who is asked to indicate what he or she sees in the blot—that is, what it might be. For example, when shown the inkblot in Figure 3–8, one young woman responded:

> I see in the background two facelike figures pointing toward each other as if they are talking. It also resembles the pelvis of a skeleton. In the middle there is a cute little bat; the upper half looks like a mouse.

FIGURE 3–8   An inkblot similar to those on the Rorschach Inkblot Test.

After responding to all ten cards, the examinee is questioned further to determine what features of the blots (shape, color, shading, texture, movement, etc.) determined the responses and to elicit any further reactions to the inkblots. The responses may then be scored and interpreted according to any number of schemes, the one proposed by Exner (1978, 1986) perhaps being the most common. Scoring involves determining the number of responses in each of several categories (location, determinant, content, popularity/originality) and computing certain ratios of the number of responses of various kinds.

Since the Rorschach first appeared in 1921, thousands of research articles concerning this test have been published. Although many studies have found that it lacks adequate reliability and validity, the Rorschach remains a favorite assessment instrument of clinical psychologists and psychiatrists. Other inkblot tests, such as the Holtzman Inkblot Technique, are sounder instruments from a psychometric viewpoint, but they have not succeeded in displacing the Rorschach as a popular tool in the clinical psychologist's battery of tests.

Picture Stories

Second in popularity to the Rorschach among projective techniques is the Thematic Apperception Test (from the Psychological Corporation). The TAT consists of four overlapping sets of 19 cards containing black-and-white pictures of people in ambiguous situations, plus one blank card. The examinee is asked to tell a five-minute story about each picture, including what's going on now, what led up to it, and how it will probably turn out.

Most TAT examiners prefer to interpret the stories subjectively, or impressionistically, searching for common themes and the principal feelings or attitudes expressed in the stories. The needs of the "hero" of the story, the environmental forces (*press*) impinging upon him or her, and the hero's successes and failures

are given particular attention. It is possible to score the stories more systematically or objectively (Bellak, 1986) rather than impressionistically, but this is rarely
done.

The TAT was published originally in the 1930s (Murray, 1938), and many
of the pictures have become dated. In addition, the pictures are not considered
appropriate for special groups, such as young children, minorities, and the
elderly. Over the years several modifications of the TAT, or completely new
picture story tests, have been designed. Despite the care with which many of these
instruments were constructed and standardized, the TAT remains the leader
among picture story projectives.

In addition to the paper-and-pencil checklists, rating scales and inventories,
and the wide variety of projective techniques, several other approaches to the
assessment of personality have been devised. These "objective measures of
personality" were not designed originally to assess personality, but are the
products of research in perception, psychophysiology, and cognition. Among
these instruments are Witkin's (Witkin, Dyk, Faterson, Goodenough, & Karp,
1962; Witkin & Goodenough, 1977) tests of field independence/dependence
(Body Adjustment Test, Rod and Frame Test, Embedded Figures Test) (see
Figure 3–9), Cattell and Schuerger's Objective-Analytic Batteries (Institute for
Personality and Ability Testing), Kagan's Matching Familiar Figures Test
(Kagan, Rosman, Day, Albert, & Phillips, 1964), as well as the polygraph (Kubis,

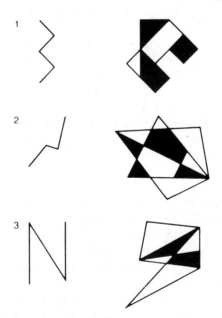

FIGURE 3–9 Sample Embedded Figures Test item. People who have difficulty locating
the figures at the left in the complex patterns at the right may be characterized as field
dependent. (Adapted from Witkin et al., 1977. Copyright 1977 by the American
Educational Research Association. Reprinted by permission of the publisher.)

1962) and the voice-stress analyzer (Holden, 1975). None of these measures, however, can be considered serious contenders to personality inventories and projective techniques.

Summary

Procedures and instruments for assessing personality include observations, interviews, checklists, rating scales, personality inventories, and certain measures of perceptual, cognitive, and physiological functioning. The most basic of all personality assessment methods is observation—uncontrolled, naturalistic, and controlled. Related to observations are interviews, both structured and unstructured, which focus on the content and style of the interviewee's answers to questions asked by the interviewer. Observations and interviews form an integral part of case studies conducted for screening, psychodiagnostic, and prognostic purposes in clinical settings.

Used as a part of the observational and interview processes, or as ends in themselves, are checklists and rating scales. A checklist consists of a set of adjectives or other descriptive words or phrases; the respondent checks the items that are descriptive or characteristic of his (her) personality and behavior. A rating scale is an extension of a checklist on which the rater, who may also be the ratee, judges and indicates the ratee's position or standing on an ordered multipoint scale with respect to some behavior or personality variable.

More psychometrically sophisticated than a checklist or rating scale is a personality inventory, consisting of a series of statements to be endorsed ("Yes," "True"), not endorsed ("No," "False"), or omitted ("Cannot say"), or in some other way responded to by the examinee as descriptive or not descriptive of him (her). Personality inventories, such as the MMPI, were developed originally in clinical or psychiatric settings, but have been extended to the appraisal of "normal" personality in educational, employment, military, government, and other contexts.

Advocates of projective techniques maintain that personality inventories are superficial measures that can be consciously or unconsciously faked. Proponents of personality inventories point to empirical findings showing that, because their scoring is subjective, projective techniques typically have low reliabilities and validities. In any event, both types of instruments have strong adherents; many clinicians administer both personality inventories and projective techniques. Among the most commonly administered projectives are word association tests, sentence completion tests, inkblot tests, and picture story tests. The most popular of all projective techniques is the Rorschach Inkblot Test, followed by the Thematic Apperception Test.

Measures of perceptual/cognitive styles, such as tests of field independence/dependence and reflectivity/impulsivity, as well as physiological measures of various sorts (polygraph or lie detector, voice-stress analyzer, etc.), may also provide insights concerning human personality.

Key Concepts

Checklist   List of words, phrases, or statements descriptive of personal characteristics; respondents endorse (check) those items characteristic of themselves (self-ratings) or other people (other-ratings).

Content analysis   Method of studying and analyzing written (or oral) communications in a systematic, objective, and quantitative manner to assess certain psychological variables.

Factor analysis   A mathematical procedure for analyzing a matrix of correlations among measurements to determine what factors (constructs) are sufficient to explain the correlations.

Halo effect   Rating a person high on one characteristic merely because he or she rates high on other characteristics.

Interview   Systematic procedure for obtaining information by asking questions and, in general, verbally interacting with a person.

Nonverbal behavior   Any behavior in which the respondent does not make word sounds or signs. Nonverbal behavior serving a communicative function includes movements of large (*macrokinesics*) and small (*microkinesics*) body parts, interpersonal distance or territoriality (*proxemics*), tone and rate of voice sounds (*paralinguistics*), and communications imparted by culturally prescribed matters relating to time, dress, memberships, and the like (*culturics*).

Personality inventory   A self-report inventory or questionnaire consisting of statements concerned with personal characteristics and behaviors. On a true-false inventory, the respondent indicates whether or not each test item or statement is self-descriptive; on a multiple-choice or forced-choice inventory, the respondent selects the statements that are self-descriptive.

Rating scale   Psychometric instrument for making ratings of the characteristics or behavior of people on some multipoint scale. The graphic rating scale is the most popular, but numerical rating scales, standard rating scales, semantic differential scales, and behaviorally anchored scales are also employed.

Response sets (styles)   Tendencies for individuals to respond in relatively fixed or stereotyped ways in situations where there are two or more response choices, such as on personality inventories. Tendencies to guess, to answer true (acquiescence), and to give socially desirable answers are among the response sets that have been investigated.

Sentence completion test   A personality (projective) test consisting of a series of incomplete sentences that the examinee is instructed to complete as quickly as possible to express his or her true feelings.

Situation(al) test   A performance test in which the examinee is placed in a realistic but contrived situation and directed to accomplish a specified goal. Situation tests are sometimes employed to assess personality characteristics such as honesty and frustration tolerance.

Word association test   A list of words read aloud to an examinee, who has been instructed to respond to each one with the first word that comes to mind. Introduced as a clinical tool by Carl Jung in his investigation of complexes, word association tests are often used in the analysis of personality.

Activities and Applications

1. Select a person in one of your classes as a subject for observation, preferably someone whom you do not know and toward whom you have neutral feelings. Observe the person over a period of three or four class meetings, inconspicuously recording what he or she does and says. Try to be as objective as possible, looking for consistent, typical behaviors, and noting responses that occur infrequently. At the end of the observation period, summarize your observations. Without having access to any other information about this person (what other students say about the person, how well he or she does in college, etc.), how would you describe his or her characteristic behaviors and personality?

2. Have each of several people draw a picture of a person on a clean sheet of paper. Then have them turn the sheet over and draw a picture of a person of the opposite sex on the other side of the paper. Collect the drawings and tell the participants that you are going to have the drawings interpreted by an expert personality analyst and that you will give them the interpretations later. Some time later, present the following personality description (Forer, 1949) to each of the participants:

> You have a strong need for other people to like you and for them to admire you. You have a tendency to be critical of yourself. You have a great deal of unused capacity which you have not turned to your advantage. While you have some personality weaknesses, you are generally able to compensate for them. Your sexual adjustment has presented some problems for you. Disciplined and controlled on the outside, you tend to be worrisome and insecure inside. At times you have serious doubts as to whether you have made the right decision or done the right thing. You prefer a certain amount of change and variety and become dissatisfied when hemmed in by restrictions and limitations. You pride yourself on being an independent thinker and do not accept others' opinions without satisfactory proof. You have found it unwise to be too frank in revealing yourself to others. At times you are extroverted, affable, social, while at other times you are introverted, wary, reserved. Some of your aspirations tend to be pretty unrealistic.

Be sure to scramble the sentences in the interpretation so the order will be different for different people. Ask each person to read the description and tell you whether it is (a) a highly accurate description, (b) an accurate description, (c) a somewhat accurate and somewhat inaccurate description, (d) an inaccurate description, or (e) a very inaccurate description of his or her personality. Tabulate the results, interpret them as well as you can, and report them to your course instructor. After the exercise has been completed, you should tell the participants that you have deceived them, and hope that they react to the deception with good humor!

3. Construct a ten-item self-concept inventory using a Likert-type format (SA = Strongly Agree, A = Agree, U = Undecided, D = Disagree, SD = Strongly Disagree). Write five of the statements in the positive direction (positive self-concept) and five in the negative direction (negative self-concept), mixing up positive and negative statements in the final form. An example of a "positive" statement is "I believe that I can accomplish almost anything that I decide to do." An example of a "negative" statement is "There are times when I have serious doubts about my abilities." Administer the self-concept inventory to several students, and compute their total scores according to the following key:

Positive self-concept items: SA = 4 A = 3 U = 2 D = 1 SD = 0
Negative self-concept items: SA = 0 A = 1 U = 2 D = 3 SD = 4

Compute the mean, median, range, and standard deviation of the total scores. On the basis of these results, what can you say about the average self-concept of these students, and the range of individual differences in self-concept in this group?

4. Construct a checklist of 30 adjectives pertaining to personality (e.g., angry, anxious, sociable, etc.), and administer it to a dozen acquaintances of yours. Ask each person to check the adjectives that are descriptive of his or her personality. Tabulate and compare the number of people who checked each adjective.

5. Construct 12 incomplete sentences concerning potential interpersonal problems for college students. Type your incomplete sentences on a sheet of paper and make a dozen or so copies. Ask each student to fill in each blank (complete each sentence) as quickly as possible with the word or words that express his or her true feelings. After collecting the completed sentences, try your hand at interpreting them in terms of what you know about the student and what they seem to imply about his or her personality.

6. Make an inkblot picture by placing a drop of black ink in the middle of a clean sheet of paper, folding the sheet in half, creasing the sheet in the middle where the ink is, and pressing it flat. If you are careful, on unfolding the sheet you should have an interesting, symmetrical ink blot. You may wish to make several inkblots in this way. Finally, administer your "inkblot test" to several friends. Ask them to tell you what they see in the blot (what it might be, where it is, and what feature of the blot made them think of that). Record the responses of each person to each blot, and then see if you can interpret the responses to reveal something interesting or informative about the individual's personality.

7. Look through several popular magazines and either cut out or photocopy five pictures of people in ambiguous situations. That is, it should not be immediately obvious what the people in the pictures are doing or thinking. Present your pictures, one at a time, to several people, and ask them to tell a story about each picture. Tell them that they should include in their stories (a) what is going on now, (b) what led up to it (what happened before), and (c) how it will turn out. Try your hand at interpreting the story in terms of common themes, the actions and feelings of the main characters, the pressures and frustrations occurring in the story, whether the story is generally pleasant or unpleasant, and whether the ending is upbeat or downbeat (comedic or tragic). Are there common elements in all the stories? What can you tell from these stories about the personality, attitudes, and feelings of the storyteller?

Suggested Readings

Aiken, L. R. (1988). *Assessment of personality* (chaps. 4–5). Newton, MA: Allyn & Bacon.

Burisch, M. (1986). Methods of personality inventory development—a comparative analysis. In A. Angleitner & J. S. Wiggins (Eds.), *Personality assessment via questionnaires* (pp. 109–123). New York: Springer.

Briggs, S. R. (1989). The optimal level of measurement for personality constructs. In

D. M. Buss & N. Cantor (Eds.), *Personality psychology: Recent trends and emerging directions* (pp. 246–260). New York: Springer.

Erdberg, P. (1990). Rorschach assessment. In G. Goldstein & M. Hersen (Eds.), *Handbook of psychological assessment* (2nd ed., pp. 387–399). New York: Pergamon.

Hogan, R., & Nicholson, R. A. (1988). The meaning of personality test scores. *American Psychologist, 43,* 621–626.

Keller, L. S., Butcher, J. N., & Slutske, W. S. (1990). Objective personality assessment. In G. Goldstein & M. Hersen (Eds.), *Handbook of psychological assessment* (2nd ed., pp. 345–386). New York: Pergamon.

Newmark, C. S. (Ed.). (1989). *Major psychological assessment instruments* (Vol. 2, chaps. 1–6). Needam, Heights, MA: Allyn & Bacon.

Robinson, J. P., Shaver, P. R., & Wrightsman, L. S. (1991). *Measures of personality and social psychological attitudes.* San Diego: Academic Press.

Rorer, L. B. (1990). Personality assessment: A conceptual survey. In L. A. Pervin (Ed.), *Handbook of personality theory and research* (pp. 693–720). New York: Guilford Press.

Wiggins, J. S., & Pincus, A. L. (1992). Personality structure and assessment. In M. R. Rosenzweig & L. W. Porter (Eds.), *Annual Review of Psychology, 43.* Palo Alto, CA: Annual Reviews, Inc.

CHAPTER 4

Dispositional Theories of Personality

CHAPTER OUTLINE

Type Theories
Gordon Allport: The First Trait Theorist
Two Representative Factor Theories of Personality
    Eysenck's Supertraits
    Cattell's Multifactor Theory
    The Big Five Factors
Traits versus Situations
    Attribution Theory and Aggregation
    Consistency as a Trait
    Interaction and Template Matching
Illustrative Research on Dispositional Theories
    Achievement Motive
    Affiliation Motive
    Field Independence and Dependence
Summary
Key Concepts
Activities and Applications
Suggested Readings
Notes

Description and explanation that lead to valid predictions are the hallmarks of a good theory. An effective theory should not only provide accurate descriptions of the features or characteristics of the phenomenon of interest, but it should also explain the causes of the phenomenon, or the conditions under which it occurs and changes. A useful theory of personality should not only describe the differences and similarities in the ways that people perceive, think, and act—the "what" of personality; it should provide explanations to account for such differences and similarities—the "why" of personality.

The personality theories discussed in this chapter fulfill, to some extent, the requirement of accurate description, but for the most part they are weak on explanation. These *dispositional,* or *type* and *trait,* theories represent ways of categorizing and defining human tendencies to perceive, think, and behave in certain fairly consistent ways across time and situations. The behavioral predictions made by type and trait theories possess some accuracy, but the theories run the risk of circular reasoning when they attempt to serve as explanations of the causes of people's behavior. Thus one may say that, because Johnny is outgoing, friendly, and sociable, a boy who enjoys team sports and being the center of attention, he is high in extroversion. But having said this, it is not fair to turn the statement around and conclude that Johnny is outgoing, friendly, sociable, and so on because he is an extrovert. Still, this is precisely what certain dispositional theorists have attempted to do with trait and type concepts.

Although it is possible to adopt a fairly atheoretical, empirical approach in conducting research on personality, even psychologists such as B. F. Skinner, who had no great love for theories, made some assumptions or had some preconceptions concerning the nature and expected outcomes of their research. At the other extreme from Skinner and other radical behaviorists, who have avoided psychological theories, is the extreme rationalist who attempts to develop an intricate, all-encompassing explanatory model of human motives and actions. Unfortunately, such grandiose theories are frequently based on a minimum of actual observations of the objects and events of concern. Somewhere in the middle are personality psychologists who use theories in an *eclectic* way, hopefully selecting the most useful aspects of different conceptualizations.

Almost everyone has some "theory" as to why people behave in certain ways. Like the descriptions of novelists, playwrights, and poets, these implicit theories of human nature and behavior typically consist of stereotypes or other overgeneralizations. Nevertheless, they do provide rough guides as to what can be expected of people and how we should act toward them. Such theories shape our impressions and descriptions of people and influence how we treat our fellow human beings. It is obviously important to formulate explanations about why people do the things they do and expectations of what they may do next. The comfort and sometimes the very survival of a person depend on the ability to understand and predict the behavior of other people and adjust to their idiosyncrasies and actions.

Psychologists realize that everyone is different from other people in many respects, and that human behavior is very complex and sometimes inconsistent.

Consequently, the professional personality theorist is usually cautious in accepting the truth and the explanatory power of commonsense theories. The individuality and intraindividual complexity of human behavior and mental life appear so overwhelming that some psychologists have abandoned efforts to discover general principles or laws to explain the seeming vagaries of human nature. These psychologists have dismissed the *nomothetic approach*—a search for general laws of behavior and personality—as unrealistic and inadequate to the task of understanding the individual. Rather, they advocate an *idiographic approach* of viewing each person as a lawful, integrated system worthy of analysis in his or her own right. Gordon Allport (1937), the psychologist who first described the idiographic/nomothetic distinction in personality assessment, recognized the usefulness of the nomothetic approach but warned of its shortcomings:

> Each single life is lawful, for it reveals its own orderly and necessary process of growth. . . . Most studies of personality are comparative . . . and these tools are valuable. The danger is that they may lead to a dismemberment of personality in such a way that each fragment is related to corresponding fragments in other people, and not to the personal system within which they are embedded. . . . Psychology is truly itself only when it can deal with individuality. . . . The truth is that psychology is *assigned* the task of being curious about human persons, and persons exist only in concrete and unique patterns. (Allport, 1961, pp. 572–573)

Rather than personality inventories and other norm-based instruments, Allport advocated the use of personal records (biographies, diaries, etc.), case studies, observations, and other nonstandardized procedures as more individualized assessment procedures.

Among the major questions with which personality theorists have wrestled is the explanation of motivation. What drives people to behave in certain ways, and to what extent is this behavior based on nature (heredity) rather than nurture (environment)? Certain personality theorists appear to be more concerned with the structure rather than the dynamics of personality, but almost all recognize that accounting for human motivation—what makes people do the things that they do—is an important function of a psychological theory. Another concern is the question of how personality develops and changes as a result of social and nonsocial experiences, both during childhood and later. A third question is concerned with how the different characteristics or facets of personality are integrated or organized to produce unique patterns of perceiving, thinking, and acting. Not all personality theorists have attempted to answer these questions, or other relevant questions, in the same ways. There are many differences among theories of personality, differences that often seem to reflect the theorist's own personality as much as the actual nature of human behavior and mental life.

One important difference among personality theories is the relative emphasis placed on heredity and environment as molders of behavior. Another difference is the extent to which the internal, personal characteristics of the individual rather than external, situational variables are the major determinants of human actions. As these and other points of dispute among personality theorists indicate, there is no comprehensive theory of personality that is supported by all psychologists. On the contrary, theories and research findings in the field of personality are constantly developing and changing. Despite their shortcomings, such theories have contributed to our understanding of inter- and intraindividual differences in behavior and cognition.

Type Theories

As seen in the discussion of Theophrastus's "characters" in Chapter 1, one of the oldest approaches to personality is the notion of fixed categories or types of people. An ancient example of a type theory of personality is Hippocrates' and Galen's doctrine of the four body "humors," described on pages 4–5 of Chapter 1. This theory is now only of historical interest (however, see Figure 4–3), but remnants of it exist in language. For example, it is sometimes heard that a person is in a "good humor" or a "bad humor." And better-educated writers or teachers may refer to a person as sanguine, melancholic, phlegmatic, or choleric. Modern scientific findings of relationships between hormone secretions and behavior may also owe a historical debt to Hippocrates and Galen.

On somewhat firmer ground than humoral theory, but still quite shaky, are the body-type theories of Lombroso, Kretschmer, and Sheldon. Like humoral theory, the notion that physique is related to personality is very old. In Shakespeare's *Julius Caesar* (act 1, scene 2), Caesar observes:

> Let me have men about me that are fat,
> Sleek-headed men, and such as sleep a-nights.
> Yond Cassius has a lean and hungry look;
> He thinks too much; such men are dangerous.
> Would he were fatter! . . . He reads much;
> He is a great observer, and he looks
> Quite through the deeds of men: He loves no plays,
> As dost thou Antony; he hears no music;
> Seldom he smiles; and smiles in such a sort
> As if he mock'd himself, and scorn'd his spirit
> That could be mov'd to smile at anything.
> Such as he be never at heart's ease
> Whiles they behold a greater than themselves;
> And therefore are they very dangerous.

Perhaps more scientifically based than the descriptions of playwrights and novelists were the writings of the criminologist Cesare Lombroso (1836–1909). Lombroso maintained that the physical characteristics of criminals are different from those of other people. Viewing criminals as being at a lower stage of biological development, Lombroso noted that they had large jaws, receding foreheads, and other primitive physical traits. The presence of these atavistic traits was interpreted by Lombroso as demonstrating that criminals are "born" to be what they become. However, the fact that many criminals did not possess the characteristics listed by Lombroso made it easy to attack his conception of inborn criminality.

Another body typologist was Ernst Kretschmer (1888–1964). After making extensive measurements of the physiques of mental patients and others, Kretschmer formulated the first scientific theory relating body build to personality (see Figure 4–1). On the basis of his observations, Kretschmer concluded that a tall, thin, lanky, angular body build (*asthenic* or *leptosomic* physique) is associated with withdrawing or introverted tendencies (*schizoid* temperament), and that such individuals are more likely than others to develop symptoms of schizophrenia. A second type, a rotund, stocky body build (*pyknic* physique), was found to be associated with emotional instability (*cycloid* temperament). Persons of this type were more likely than others to develop bipolar (*manic-depressive*) disorder. A third body build, *athletic* individuals with broad shoulders and slim hips, was as likely to develop manic-depressive psychosis as they were schizophrenia. Physiques that failed to fit into any of these three categories were referred to as *dysplastic*. Because of its low validity, efforts to apply Kretschmer's somatotypology in practical situations were soon discontinued.

Related to Kretschmer's theory is the somatotypology of William Sheldon and S. S. Stevens (1940, 1942). The Sheldon and Stevens somatotype system classifies human physiques into three components according to their degree of *endomorphy* (fatness), *mesomorphy* (muscularity), and *ectomorphy* (thinness) on a scale of 1 to 7. Thus, an extreme endomorph is a 7–1–1, an extreme mesomorph a 1–7–1, and an extreme ectomorphy a 1–1–7. The degree of each component is determined by measurements taken from photographs of the person in various orientations (see Figure 4–2).

An excess of any one of the three somatotype components in the Sheldon-Stevens system was found to be related to the temperament types of viscerotonia, somatotonia, and cerebrotonia. An individual's standing on each of the temperament dimensions, also scored on a 7-point scale, was determined from a series of ratings. Ratings on 20 trait dimensions were made on the basis of observations and questionnaire responses. *Viscerotonics* are characterized as sociable, friendly, and loving of comfort and eating. *Somatotonics* are assertive, dominating, noisy, and callous, have a youthful orientation, and love physical adventure, and exercise. *Cerebrotonics* are restrained, quick-reacting, introversive, and hypersensitive to pain; they also have difficulty sleeping and are oriented toward later periods of life. Moderate to high correlations have been found between ratings on endomorphy and viscerotonia, mesomorphy and somatotonia, and ectomorphy and cerebrotonia.

Body-type theories are interesting, but, because of the many exceptions to the hypothesized relationships between body build and personality, their scientific status is not very impressive. In addition, various interpretations have been given to the correlations between physique and personality. Contemporary psychologists also object to typologies because they place people in categories and

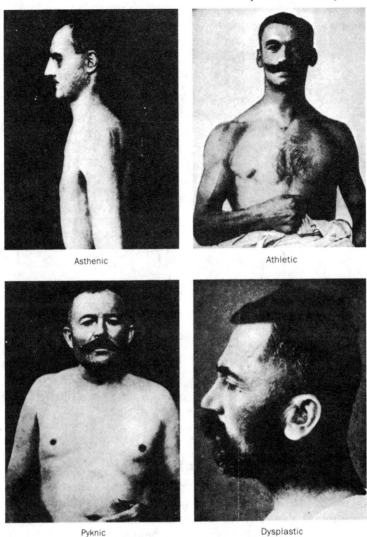

Asthenic   Athletic

Pyknic   Dysplastic

FIGURE 4–1 Kretschmer's four body types. (Source: *Physique and Character: An Investigation of the Nature of Constitution and of the Theory of Temperament* [2nd ed.] by E. Kretschmer, 1936, New York: Harcourt, Brace & Company.)

assign labels to them. Labeling overemphasizes internal causation of behavior, and it may also encourage a self-fulfilling prophecy in which people become what they are labeled as being. Thus people who are labeled as "introverts" may be left alone by would-be friends, causing them to become even more socially isolated. Similarly, "extroverts" may become more outgoing or sociable because other people expect them to behave in this manner.[1]

Sheldon's somatotypes

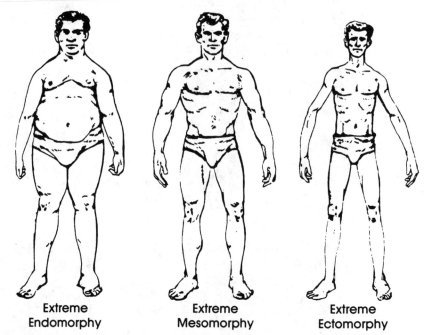

Extreme
Endomorphy

Extreme
Mesomorphy

Extreme
Ectomorphy

FIGURE 4–2 Sheldon's somatotypes. (From *Elements of Psychology*, second edition, by David Krech, Richard Crutchfield, and Norman Livson. Copyright © 1969 by Alfred A. Knopf, Inc. Reprinted by permission of publisher.)

Gordon Allport: The First Trait Theorist

Narrower than the concept of personality *type* is that of a personality *trait*, or predisposition to respond in a particular way to persons, objects, or situations. Unlike a "type," which is more apt to be thought of as an "all-or-none" tendency or propensity, a trait is on a continuum such that different people possess different amounts of it.

The first and one of the most prominent trait theorists was Gordon Allport (1897–1967). In 1936, Allport and H. S. Odbert began by listing 17,953 words in the English language that refer to characteristics of personality and reducing them to a smaller list of trait names (Allport & Odbert, 1936). A *trait* was defined as a "neuropsychic structure having the capacity to render many stimuli functionally equivalent, and to initiate and guide equivalent (meaningfully consistent) forms of adaptive and expressive behavior" (Allport, 1961, p. 347). Allport visualized human personality as consisting of the dynamic organization of those traits that determine an individual's unique adjustment to the environment.

According to Allport, there are, in order of their pervasiveness across different situations, *cardinal traits* (e.g., authoritarianism, humanitarianism, Machiavellianism or power striving, sadism, narcissism or self-love), *central traits* (e.g., affectionateness, assertiveness, distractibility, honesty, kindness, reliability, sociability), and *secondary traits* (e.g., food preferences or musical preferences). A cardinal trait is a disposition or theme so dominant in a person's life that it is expressed in almost all of his or her behavior, whereas a central trait is a tendency to behave in a particular way in various situations. Most people have few cardinal traits, more central traits, and even more secondary traits. Central traits are less general or pervasive than cardinal traits, whereas secondary traits are more situation-specific and affect behavior less than central traits.

In terms of the extent to which traits are general or shared among different people, Allport differentiated among *common traits* (e.g., aggression), *individual traits,* and *personal dispositions.* Although common traits and individual traits can be measured by standardized assessment instruments, personal dispositions are identifiable only by careful study of a person.

As seen in the book *Letters from Jenny* (Allport, 1965), Allport believed strongly in the *idiographic approach* to personality study. He maintained that every person is a unique, lawful, integrated system in his or her own right, and that the personality researcher should seek to understand that uniqueness by an in-depth study of the individual personality. Another important principle in Allport's theorizing is that of the *functional autonomy of motives.* According to this principle, in which he took issue with the psychoanalytic doctrine of the perpetuation of childhood motives in adulthood, Allport maintained that many adult motives have only a historical, not a dynamic, connection with motives in earlier life. Thus a sailor who, as a young man, earned his living from the sea, may desire to return to the sea as an old man, not because he still needs to earn his living from it, but because of a motive which has become functionally independent of its original source. Allport maintained that simply because adult behavior resembles childhood behavior, the two are not necessarily propelled by the same motives.[2]

Two Representative Factor Theories of Personality

Before discussing factor theories of personality, it may be helpful to consider some details of the statistical methods on which these theories are based. A brief introduction to factor analysis is given in Appendix B, and the student may wish to read that material before proceeding with this chapter. However, a familiarity with the statistical procedures of factor analysis is not essential for an understanding of the two representative factor theories discussed in this section.

A number of psychometricians, such as L. L. Thurstone and J. P. Guilford, have employed factor-analytic techniques to define a set of variables that could be measured by personality inventories and rating scales. Certain psychologists, however, have gone beyond the use of factor analysis as a convenient tool for identifying personality variables to be assessed with questionnaires and have applied it as a technique for revealing the structure of personality and its relationships to other variables.

Eysenck's Supertraits

The most parsimonious of the trait-factor theories of personality is that of Hans J. Eysenck, a German expatriate who has lived in England since the 1930s. Eysenck conceptualized human personality in terms of three factors, or *supertraits*. The first two of these supertraits are *introversion versus extroversion* and *emotional stability versus emotional instability (neuroticism)*. As depicted in the circular diagram of Figure 4–3, rather than being dichotomous types, introversion and extroversion are conceived of as a continuous dimension.

Introversion/Extroversion. Introverts and extroverts are described by Eysenck and Eysenck (1975) as follows:

> The typical introvert is a quiet, retiring sort of person, introspective, fond of books rather then people; he is reserved and distant except to intimate friends. He tends to plan ahead, "looks before he leaps," and mistrusts the impulse of the moment. He

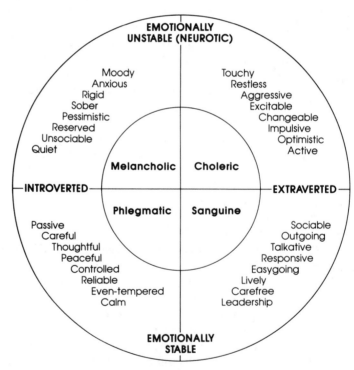

FIGURE 4–3   A two-dimensional classification of personality. (From *Personality and Individual Differences* by H. J. Eysenck and M. W. Eysenck, 1958, New York: Plenum Publishing. Reprinted by permission of the publisher.)

does not like excitement, takes matters of everyday life with proper seriousness, and likes a well-ordered mode of life. He keeps his feelings under close control, seldom behaves in an aggressive manner, and does not lose his temper easily. He is reliable, somewhat pessimistic, and places greater value on ethical standards.

The typical extrovert is sociable, likes parties, has many friends, needs to have people to talk to, and does not like reading or studying by himself. He craves excitement, takes chances, often sticks his neck out, acts on the spur of the moment, and is generally an impulsive individual. He is fond of practical jokes, always has a ready answer, and generally likes change; he is carefree, easygoing, optimistic, and "likes to laugh and be merry." He prefers to keep moving and doing things, tends to be aggressive and loses his temper quickly; altogether his feelings are not kept under control, and he is not always a reliable person. (p. 5)

In Eysenck's schema, the introversion-extroversion dimension is at the highest level of a hierarchy. Under this supertrait are three subordinate levels—the trait level, the habitual response level, and the specific response level—in order of decreasing generality.

In addition to paper-and-pencil questionnaires such as the Maudsley Personality Inventory and the Eysenck Personality Inventory, Eysenck devised a number of objective tests to differentiate between introverts and extraverts. One of these is the famous "lemondrop test," in which a standard amount of lemon juice is placed on the examinee's tongue. In comparison with extroverts, introverts tend to secrete a greater amount of saliva in response to the lemon juice.

Many other perceptual and physiological variables are related to the introversion-extroversion dimension. Bakan (1957) and Claridge (1960) found that introverts were more vigilant than extraverts in a watch-keeping (vigilance) situation, and Harkins and Green (1975) found that introverts do better at signal-detection tasks than extroverts. Other research findings are that persons with higher introversion scores take fewer involuntary rest pauses in performing a monotonous tapping task (Eysenck, 1967) and are less tolerant of pain but more tolerant of sensory deprivation (Petrie, 1967; Lynn & Eysenck, 1961) than extroverts. Extroverts, however, are more readily conditioned than introverts to stimuli associated with sexual arousal (Kantorwitz, 1978). In general, it can be concluded that, compared with extroverts, introverts are more vigilant, more sensitive to pain, more cautious, and more easily disrupted by stimulation.

These findings are consistent with Eysenck's (1967) hypothesis that introversion is associated with a higher level of central nervous system arousal than extroversion. Introverts, who presumably inherit a more sensitive and highly aroused nervous system than extroverts, are more strongly affected by reward and punishment than extroverts. In short, introverts are more alert, less distractible, and more attentive to the task at hand. Extraverts, on the other hand, appear to have a greater need for external stimulation, and they seek out sensations more than introverts. Extroverts are also more likely to engage in impulsive acts, such as starting on a trip without appropriate planning, and to say they would like to try parachute jumping (Farley & Farley, 1967). Certain occupations, such as that of fireman or salvage diver, appear to attract extroversive individuals who enjoy thrilling, stimulating experiences.

Emotional Stability and Instability. On one pole of Eysenck's second bipolar personality dimension—emotionally unstable (neurotic) versus emotionally stable—are anxious, moody, restless, touchy, emotionally responsive individuals, who have difficulty returning to a normal state after a stressful experience (Eysenck & Eysenck, 1968). At the other pole are calm, careful, even-tempered, emotionally stable individuals.

Psychoticism. After spending many years researching the personality dimensions of introversion/extroversion and emotional stability/instability, Eysenck added a third supertrait to his personality theory. High scorers on this dimension, which was labeled *psychoticism,* are described as "egocentric, aggressive, impulsive, impersonal, cold, lacking in empathy and concern for others, and generally unconcerned about the rights and welfare of other people" (Eysenck, 1982, p. 11).

As depicted in Figure 4–3, a person may score high on both extroversion and neuroticism, may score low on both supertraits, or may possess any combination of scores on these two dimensions. This is also the case when the psychoticism dimension is added to the other two supertraits. Certain combinations of scores are, however, associated with specific psychiatric diagnoses or other categories. Patients who have been diagnosed as psychoneurotic tend to score high on neuroticism and low on extroversion, whereas antisocial persons and criminals usually score high on all three supertraits (Eysenck, 1982).

Inheritance of the Supertraits. In addition to studying the relationships among scores on measures of the three supertraits and other psychological and physiological variables, Eysenck amassed an impressive array of evidence in support of the hypothesis that these personality traits are to a large extent inherited. According to Eysenck, something like two-thirds of the variability of scores on these supertraits can be accounted for by genetic factors and only one-third by environmental or experiential variables. The differences in cortical arousal and other aspects of nervous system functioning resulting in the differences in the behaviors of introverts and extroverts are considered to be due in large measure to heredity.

Cattell's Multifactor Theory

A genuine tour de force among factor theories of personality is represented by the work of Raymond B. Cattell, an Englishman who immigrated to the United States, where he has spent most of his professional life. Beginning in somewhat the same fashion as Allport and Odbert (1936), Cattell (1950) listed 4,500 trait names and reduced them to 200 by grouping together traits having the same or almost the same meaning. Next he obtained ratings of large samples of individuals on these traits and subjected the resulting scores to factor analysis. The 36 *surface traits* derived in this manner were initially reduced to 12 *source traits,* which Cattell believed to be the basic organizing factors of personality and to which he assigned rather esoteric labels. According to Cattell, surface traits are easily observed in a person's behavior, but source traits can be discovered only by factor analysis. The 12 source traits, plus four additional traits, are measured by the 16 Personality Factor Questionnaire (see Figure 3–4). The 16 traits are

A	Cool, reserved versus warm, easygoing
B	Concrete thinking versus abstract thinking
C	Easily upset versus calm, stable
D	Not assertive versus dominant
E	Sober, serious versus enthusiastic
F	Expedient versus conscientious
G	Shy, timid versus venturesome
H	Tough-minded versus sensitive
I	Trusting versus suspicious
J	Practical versus imaginative
K	Forthright versus shrewd
L	Self-assured versus self-doubting
Q₁	Conservative versus experimenting
Q₂	Group-oriented versus self-sufficient
Q₃	Undisciplined versus self-disciplined
Q₄	Relaxed versus tense, driven

Some of the source traits were described as *environmental-mold traits,* which Cattell believed to be formed by the environment, whereas other source traits, called *constitutional traits,* were conceived of as being determined by hereditary factors. A second differentiation was between *general* and *specific* source traits; the former influence behavior in many more situations than the latter. In addition to classifying traits as surface versus source, constitutional versus environmental-mold, and general versus specific, Cattell distinguished between common versus unique traits and dynamic versus ability versus temperament traits. Like Allport, Cattell saw *common traits* as characterizing all people, and *unique traits,* which are Allport's *individual traits,* as peculiar to the individual. The distinction between dynamic traits, ability traits, and temperament traits is a reflection of a conception of personality that encompasses affective and cognitive variables. *Dynamic traits* motivate the person toward a goal, *ability traits* determine the ability to achieve the goal, and *temperament traits* pertain to the emotional aspects of goal-directed activity.

With respect to the methodology of research on personality, Cattell (1965) distinguished between L-data, obtained from life history reports and records; Q-data, from questionnaires; and OT-data, from performance on objective tests. Cattell hoped that these three separate sources of data would reveal similar personality factors, and to some extent that hope has been realized. Similar factors were found with Q-data and L-data, although certain factors were unique to each source.

The 16 Personality Factor Questionnaire and related questionnaires have been by far the most successful of Cattell's commercial enterprises. In recent years, however, he has turned his attention more to OT-data involving some 500 short tests (e.g., finger maze test, arm-shoulder movement tempo, letter comparisons). A number of these tests have been standardized and published as the

Objective-Analytic Batteries (Institute for Personality and Ability Testing). The tests were designed to measure the following source traits:

Ego Standards (competitiveness)
Independence (perceptual accuracy and the capacity for intense, self-directed concentration)
Evasiveness (self-serving manipulation of social norms)
Exuberance (spontaneity and rapidity of thinking)
Capacity to Mobilize versus Regression
Anxiety; Realism versus Tensidia (the latter term referring to a tense, inflexible dissociation from reality)
Asthenia versus Self-assurance (overconformity versus egoistic self-assertion)
Exvia versus Invia (extroversion versus introversion)
Discouragement versus Sanguineness (pessimism versus optimism)

These ten tests consist of a variety of perceptual, cognitive, and behavioral tasks which, on the surface, seem more like aptitude variables than personality measures. Included are tasks of perceptual-motor rigidity, picture perception, endurance of difficulty, criticalness of judgment, humor appreciation, musical preferences, and the like.

Concerning his analysis of dynamic traits, Cattell concluded that human motivation is comprised of *attitudes, sentiments,* and *ergs.* Attitudes, or readinesses to act, are the starting point of Cattell's *dynamic lattice model* of personality (see Figure 4–4). Attitudes are subsidiary to sentiments, which in turn are subsidiary to ergs. Ergs, which are biologically based needs or drives, are satisfied by means of attitudes and sentiments. For example, a person's interest in plays and films (attitude level) may stem from an involvement with photography (sentiment level), which in turn may satisfy various needs (sex, gregariousness, curiosity) at the ergic level. Other examples of ergs are security and self-assertion. Examples of sentiments, which are environmentally determined motives, are motives concerning career or occupation, religion, and one's self-concept.

Although Cattell believes strongly in the influence of heredity on personality, he recognizes that personality traits are not all-encompassing or invariably transsituational in their manifestations. In a particular situation a person may experience a transitory state of anxiety, depression, curiosity, or fatigue that may belie his or her typical behavior. The mood of a person and the role that is played may also change with the situation. Thus a particular situation may bring out ergs or sentiments that are not typical of the person but are more appropriate in the particular situational context.

Like Eysenck, Cattell has conducted extensive research on his theory, including studies of personality changes from age four through adulthood, the relative importance of heredity and environment in personality, cross-cultural differences in personality, and the personality characteristics of leaders (Cattell, 1965). Despite the magnitude of these efforts and the popularity of the 16 PF questionnaire, American psychologists have not been especially favorable toward Cattell's system or theory. Part of the reason for this reaction is undoubtedly a

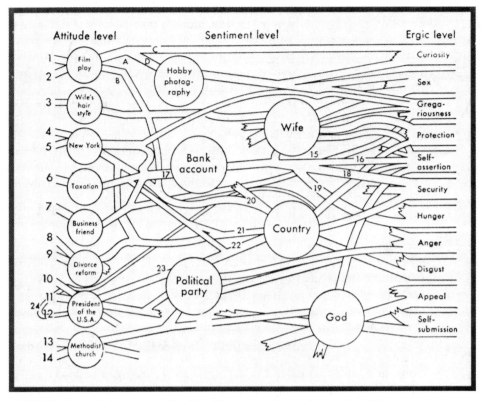

FIGURE 4–4 A dynamic lattice. The illustration shows the relationships among attitudes, sentiments, and ergs for a particular personality. (From *Personality: A Systematic, Theoretical, and Factual Study* (p. 158) by R. B. Cattell, 1950, New York: McGraw-Hill. Reprinted with permission.)

lingering suspicion that the procedures of factor analysis do not actually reveal much about how human personality develops and changes. Then, too, there is a reluctance to consider the extracted personality factors as anything other than hypothetical constructs or convenient fictions rather than psychological entities.

Many psychologists do not believe that factor analysis, regardless of its mathematical sophistication, reveals true dimensions of personality in any substantive sense. Rather, by disclosing internal consistencies and differences among test items and scales, factor analysis merely helps to clarify the relationships among personality constructs or variables.

The Big Five Factors

Despite the criticisms of factor analysis, there is fairly widespread agreement among psychometric psychologists that a large number of personality inventories measure at least the introversion/extroversion and emotional stability/instability factors defined by Eysenck. Furthermore, there is substantial support for a five-factor model of personality. These five factors are labeled as extroversion or surgency, agreeableness, conscientiousness, emotional stability, and culture by Goldberg (1980), and as neuroticism, extraversion, openness, agreeableness, and conscientiousness by Costa and McCrae (1986).

The factor of *neuroticism* is defined by bipolar adjectives such as worrying versus calm, insecure versus secure, and self-pitying versus self-satisfied. High scorers on the neuroticism factor feel generally anxious, cope poorly with stress, have unrealistic self-assessments, and readily experience many negative emotions. The factor of *extroversion* is described by bipolar adjectives such as sociable versus retiring, fun-loving versus sober, and affectionate versus reserved. Extroverts are active, assertive, cheerful, optimistic people who enjoy social gatherings—the opposite of introverts. The factor of *openness* is described in bipolar terms such as imaginative versus down-to-earth, preference for variety versus preference for routine, and independent versus conforming. High scorers on the openness factor feel emotions keenly, are intellectually sensitive, and are attuned to external sights and sounds and internal experiences. Low scorers on openness are conventional, down-to-earth people who have narrow interests and low aesthetic appreciation. The factor of *agreeableness* is described by bipolar adjectives such as softhearted versus ruthless, trusting versus suspicious, and helpful versus uncooperative. High scorers on the agreeableness factor are eager to help other people and expect to be treated similarly; low scorers are cynical, suspicious, and uncooperative. The factor of *conscientiousness* is described by bipolar adjectives such as well-organized versus disorganized, careful versus careless, and self-disciplined versus weak-willed. High scorers on the conscientiousness factor are persistent, consistent, reliable, and frequently puritanical in attitudes; low scorers are aimless, lax, and unreliable.

A great deal of research has been stimulated by the "big five factor theory" (e.g., McCrae & Costa, 1987; Peabody, 1987). The five factors appear to be highly consistent across different situations and different groups of people.

Traits versus Situations

A traditional assumption of trait theories of personality is that behavior is influenced to a great extent by traits that manifest themselves in a consistent way across different situations. Trait theorists have not denied that environment (the specific situation) is also important in determining behavior, but they have concentrated on personality traits and their measurement. Despite the professional and popular focus on personality traits, the fact that the situation is frequently more important than personal characteristics in determining specific behavior was clearly demonstrated many years ago by the results of Hartshorne and May's (1928) studies of character in children.

Four decades later, in a book that took personality research and theorizing by storm, Walter Mischel (1968) summarized evidence demonstrating that, although the behavioral correlates of cognitive abilities are fairly consistent across different situations, personal-social behavior is highly dependent on the specific situation in which it occurs. Consequently, Mischel concluded that inferences regarding personality dynamics or traits are less useful than knowledge of situational variables in predicting behavior. He further argued that assessments of generalized traits of personality are not particularly useful because such traits so often fail to show cross-situational generality.

> Global traits and states are excessively crude, gross units to encompass adequately the extraordinary complexity and subtlety of the discriminations that people constantly make. Traditional trait-state conceptions of man have depicted him as victimized by his infantile history, as possessed by unchanging rigid trait attributes, and as driven inexorably by unconscious irrational forces. This conceptualization of man, besides being philosphically unappetizing, is contradicted by massive experimental data. The traditional trait-state conceptualizations of personality, while often paying lip service to man's complexity and to the uniqueness of each person, in fact lead to a grossly oversimplified view that misses both the richness and the uniqueness of individual lives. A more adequate conceptualization must take full account of man's extraordinary adaptiveness and capacities for discrimination, awareness, and self-regulation; it must also recognize that men can and do reconceptualize themselves and change, and that an understanding of how humans can constructively modify their behavior in systematic ways is the core of a truly dynamic personality psychology. (Mischel, 1968, p. 301)

Rather than analyzing personality into a complex of traits or factors, Mischel (1986) proposed a social learning approach which stresses the fact that people learn to make different responses in different situations and that the accuracy with which a person's behavior in a specific situation can be predicted must take into account his or her learning history in similar situations.

It is widely recognized that social norms, roles, and other group-related conditions exert powerful effects on people and often override temperament or style as determiners of action and thought. In fact, highly structured situations in which the norms of constraints are quite strong exert an especially powerful effect on individual behavior. On the other hand, more flexible situations in which the norms of behavior are not so fixed or apparent provide a greater opportunity for the manifestation of a wide range of personality traits. In certain ("strong") situations, the features of the situations themselves are more important in determining how people will react; in other ("weak") situations, personal characteristics are more influential (Monson, Hesley, & Chernick, 1982).

As long as a social situation is fairly constant and the expected behaviors and sanctions are quite apparent, people tend to submerge their idiosyncrasies or individualities and adjust their behavior and thinking to the expectations and reward-punishment schedules provided by others in that situation. It has been amply demonstrated by research in social psychology and by candid television programs that when in Rome all kinds of people "do as the Romans do." Acceptance of this truism does not imply, however, that individual personality has no influence on behavior.

Attribution Theory and Aggregation

In support of Mischel's position, research on *attribution theory* has revealed a tendency for people to overestimate the importance of traits and to underestimate the importance of situations in determining behavior, a phenomenon referred to as the *fundamental attributional error*. But people also have a greater tendency to attribute their own behavior to variables in the specific situation and to attribute the behaviors of other people to personality traits (Jones & Nisbett, 1972). One possible explanation for this tendency is that people understand themselves better than they understand others and more accurately perceive external circumstances as the principal determinant of their own behavior.

Also related to the trait/situation debate is Epstein's (1979) demonstration that aggregating (summing) behavioral measures across different times and situations increases both the reliability and validity of those measures. Several studies have found that aggregation procedures increase the correlations between measures of traits and behavior and thereby improve predictions of behavior (Cheek, 1982; Rushton, Brainerd, & Pressley, 1983). The increased predictability is, however, greater when behavior is aggregated across time than when it is aggregated across situations. In actuality, recent studies have shown that measures of personality traits are fairly stable, even over rather long periods of time (Conley, 1985; Rowe, 1987).

Consistency as a Trait

A number of investigators (e.g., Bem & Allen, 1974; Block, 1977; Underwood & Moore, 1981) have found that the consistency of traits across situations is itself an individual difference variable of which the individual is aware. In an investigation by Bem and Allen (1974) people who believed themselves to be fairly consistent in friendliness and conscientiousness tended to be so, whereas those who perceived themselves as being less consistent tended to be just that. In another study, Bem and Funder (1978) maintained that a person will behave similarly in two or more situations if he or she perceives the situations as similar. Situations, like people, may be conceptualized as having "personalities," and as long as the characteristics of a situation are congruent with those of the person, the latter is likely to behave as expected in that situation. Unexpected or inconsistent behavior, according to Bem and Funder, is the consequence of a person-situation mismatch. However, the mismatch need not be on all personal characteristics, but only on certain prototypic variables that are important or salient to the individual and the situation. Not all traits are equally relevant for describing behavior; some traits characterize certain people and other traits characterize other people.

Interaction and Template Matching

As Mischel and other psychologists recognize, a person's behavior in a specific situation is caused by a multitude of factors, including personal characteristics and the nature of the situation in which the behavior occurs. More generally, it is the interaction between personality and the situation that determines behavior. Thus it can be argued that efforts at developing effective measures of personality would be more successful if the developers would begin by providing a conceptual model of how personality dispositions and situational characteristics interact and then constructed measures of both sets of variables to make possible a true "interactional assessment" (McReynolds, 1979). One proposal for understanding the person-situation interaction is Bem and Funder's (1978) *template-matching technique*. These writers conceptualize a situation template as a pattern of behavior characterizing the way in which person "I" is ideally expected to behave in the situation. Then the extent to which person "J" behaves in the same way in that situation depends on the match between the personality characteristics of J and those of I. An extension of the interactionist approach is the recognition that trait-situation interactions are actually reciprocal or *transactional* events. Thus a sequence of behavior in a particular situation is the result of the way in which the situation is perceived, which determines how the individual behaves. That very behavior, in turn, influences the situation and determines the way in which it reacts to the presence of the individual, and so on in a sequence of reciprocal interactions or dynamic transactions.

Illustrative Research on Dispositional Theories

Material concerned with research and applications of dispositional theories of personality is included in several other chapters of this book. With some exceptions, studies concerned with dispositional theories have been principally correlational or quasi-experimental in nature. For example, the relationships between measures of particular characteristics or traits (anxiety, authoritarianism, sensation seeking, hardiness, Type A personality, etc.) and measures of behavior of psychophysiological functioning have been investigated in numerous studies. Rather than being true experiments, these studies are concerned with the utility of measures of particular personality traits in predicting behavior and other aspects of individual functioning. As such, they actually constitute investigations of the predictive or construct validity of the measuring instrument and are only indirectly concerned with cause and effect. Likewise, the theoretical concepts of Allport, Eysenck, and Cattell have been applied in designing numerous psychometric instruments, but little systematic research has been conducted to test specific predictions made from the theories.

Illustrative of the type of research that has been conducted on dispositional theories of personality are David McClelland's studies of the motives for achievement, affiliation, and power. Examples of research on the first two motives will be described here, although research on the power motivation (McClelland, 1975) is also of interest.

Achievement Motive

The *achievement motive*, defined as a psychosocial motive to accomplish, excel, or attain higher goals, is one of the psychogenic needs proposed by Henry Murray (1938). David McClelland and his associates (McClelland, Atkinson, Clark, &

Lowell, 1953) developed a method for measuring the strength of the achievement motive in a given person from the stories created by the person in response to a set of pictures of people in ambiguous situations. The stories were then scored to provide a measure of the strength of the achievement motive, which was correlated with a number of other variables. Among the findings of these studies are the following (McClelland et al., 1953; Winterbottom, 1953; Atkinson & Litwin, 1960):

1 College students with low achievement motivation perceive their parents as being friendly and helpful, whereas students with high achievement motivation perceive their parents as relatively distant.
2 Students with high achievement motivation perceive themselves as more independent of authority, and, in actuality, they are less conforming than students with low achievement motivation to group opinion on tests of social suggestion.
3 Achievement motivation is positively correlated with the age at which independence training is begun in boys. Boys who are encouraged or forced to be more independent at an early age tend to become more motivated to achieve.
4 Students who are highly motivated to achieve, but who are not made anxious by tests, prefer tasks that are moderately challenging. In contrast, students who have low achievement motivation and who are made anxious by tests select less challenging tasks.
5 The vigor of the economic development of a nation is highly correlated with the value placed on achievement in the stories (folktales) of the nation. An upsurge in a nation's economy is preceded by an increase in the number of achievement themes in the literature of that nation.

Affiliation Motive

Forming friendships and associations, loving, greeting, joining, and living with others, cooperating and conversing socially with others—all of these activities are indicative of a need to be with others of one's kind, a need that is exhibited especially by humans and other higher mammals. An experiment that illustrates the operation of the need for affiliation was conducted by Stanley Schachter (1959). College girls were divided into two groups: Girls in group 1 were shown a formidable apparatus, and the experimenter announced that they would be exposed to an intense and painful, but not actually harmful, electric shock. In contrast, the girls in group 2 saw no apparatus and were assured that the shock would be quite mild and merely tickle. After receiving the instructions, the girls in both groups were given the choice of waiting alone or together until the start of the experiment. Nearly two-thirds of the subjects in group 1 ("high-anxiety" group) chose to wait together, whereas only one-third of those in group 2 ("low-anxiety" group) made that same choice. Apparently, the threat of painful electric shock aroused the affiliative needs of the majority of students in the first group.

An additional finding of experiments of this sort is that a significantly greater proportion of students in the "high-anxiety" group who were firstborn children chose to wait together rather than alone. On the other hand, a greater percentage of later-born students in the "high-anxiety" group chose to wait alone. The difference between first- and later-borns did not occur in the "low-anxiety" condition. The experimenter interpreted the greater need for affiliation shown by the firstborns than by the later-borns as due to the greater amount of attention and comfort that had been given to the firstborns as children.

Field Independence and Dependence

Another series of investigations concerned with a dispositional "minitheory" of personality was conducted by Hermann Witkin and his colleagues (Witkin et al., 1962; Witkin & Goodenough, 1977). Three tests—the Body Adjustment Test, the Rod and Frame Test, and the Embedded Figures Test—were used in these studies to classify individuals according to their degree of field independence or field dependence. On the Body Adjustment Test, the examinee was seated in a tilted chair located in a tilted room and told to adjust the chair to the true vertical position. On the Rod and Frame Test, the examinee was seated before a luminous rod affixed to a luminous square frame in a completely darkened room and instructed to adjust the rod to the true vertical when the rod and frame have been tilted in opposite directions. Several trials were given on both the Body Adjustment Test and the Rod and Frame Test. On the Embedded Figures Test, the rapidity with which the examinee was able to locate simple figures within each of a series of complex forms was measured (see Figure 3–8). According to Witkin, these three tests, which have substantial positive correlations with each other, measure much the same thing: field independence versus field dependence, or the ability to differentiate aspects or parts of a complex, confusing whole. Scores on all three tests may be combined into a single index; people who score high on this index are referred to as *field independents,* and people who score low as *field dependents.*

Of particular interest is the fact that field independents have different personalities from field dependents. Witkin's description of a highly field-independent person is that of a secure, independent, controlled, more psychologically mature, self-accepting individual. Such a person is active in dealing with the environment, tends to use intellectualization (artificially separating emotional content from intellectual content) as a defense mechanism, and is more aware of his or her inner experiences (Witkin et al., 1962). In contrast, a typical field-dependent person tends to be tense, less secure, psychologically immature, passive, less attuned to his inner experiences, and less self-insightful. Field independents also tend to have greater feelings of inferiority and a low evaluation of the physical self, and they are more likely to use primitive defense mechanisms such as repression and denial.

College major, sex, and sociocultural factors have also been found to be related to field independence and dependence. Field-independent individuals tend to do better in engineering, the sciences, and mathematics—subjects requiring high analytic ability, whereas field-dependent individuals tend to do better in counseling, social sciences, teaching, and other people-oriented professions (Witkin, 1973). With respect to sex and sociocultural differences, boys are usually more field independent than girls, and members of hunting and foraging cultures are more field independent than those in sedentary, agricultural societies (Witkin & Berry, 1975). Field-dependent individuals are also more attentive than field-independent individuals to facial and other nonverbal social cues (Witkin & Goodenough, 1977).

With respect to intrafamilial factors, significant relationships between the field independence scores of mothers and sons and fathers and daughters have been reported (Kagan & Kogan, 1970). The parents of field-independent children tend to be less restrictive and less authoritarian than those of field-dependent children. Compared with typical Anglo-American parents, Mexican-American parents tend to be more authoritarian and family-centered in the treatment of their children, discouraging independent and assertive behavior. These differences are believed to contribute to the greater field dependence of Mexican-American children (Witkin et al., 1973; Ramirez & Casteneda, 1974).

Summary

The conceptualization of human personality in terms of types or traits is consistent with historical and contemporary popular psychology. In our efforts to understand our fellow humans, it is efficient, if frequently inaccurate, to depict or categorize them in terms of a stereotypic set of traits or even in terms of highly overgeneralized types. Type and trait theories have been fostered by novelists, playwrights, and other creative artists whose stock in trade is the description and analysis of human character and personality. Consequently, it is not surprising that the body-type theories of Kretschmer, Lombroso, and Sheldon or the trait theories of Allport, Eysenck, and Cattell have had a great deal of popular and professional appeal. Science thrives on parsimonious descriptions of concepts and methods, and type and trait theories are nothing if not parsimonious.

Modern type theorists were antedated by humoral theorists, phrenologists, physiognomists, and others who formulated seemingly plausible (at the time!) theories of relationships between physical characteristics and personality. The somatotypologies (body-type theories) of Kretschmer and Sheldon were based on more careful observation and measurement. Sheldon's endomorph, mesomorph, and ectomorph somatotypes and their relationships to the viscerotonic, somatotonic, and cerebrotonic temperament types, in particular, are viewed as interesting concepts, although they are overgeneralized and merely descriptive rather than explanatory. Typologies are, of course, still with us, as seen, for example, in the 16 personality types measured by the Myers-Briggs Type Indicator and the Type A and Type B measures of the Jenkins Activity Survey.

Although scores on many personality inventories and scales are expressed in terms of trait variables, the most systematic approaches to characterizing personality in terms of a set of traits are seen in the writings of Gordon Allport, Hans Eysenck, and Raymond Cattell. All three of these theorists view personality traits as hierarchically organized. For Allport, cardinal traits are at the top of the hierarchy, with central traits in the middle and secondary traits at the bottom. In Eysenck's hierarchy, there are three subordinate levels (trait, habitual response, specific response) under the supertraits. Cattell's system is also partially hierarchical, as seen in his distinctions between surface and source traits and between general and specific source traits.

The theories of Eysenck and Cattell are based on the results of factor analysis, with Eysenck's factors being much more parsimonious than Cattell's. Eysenck has attempted to account for much of the variability in human behavior in terms of three supertraits: introversion/extroversion, neuroticism, and psychoticism. Research by Eysenck and others has concentrated in particular on correlates and causes of the first of these supertraits.

Cattell's conception of personality includes not only temperament traits but also ability traits and dynamic (motivational) traits. Other distinctions made by Cattell include surface versus source traits, general versus specific traits, constitutional versus environmental-mold traits, and common versus unique traits. The various kinds of traits are identified by three different sources of data: Q (questionnaire) data, L (life history) data, and OT (objective test) data. Similar, but not identical, factors have been obtained from these three methodologies.

As seen in his dynamic lattice model, Cattell has also made progress in analyzing human motivation into a hierarchy consisting of ergs at the top, sentiments at a middle level, and attitudes at the bottom. He has also conducted and stimulated numerous studies concerned with the hereditary basis of personality traits, in addition to the longitudinal development and cross-cultural variability of traits.

Recent research offers support for a "big five" theory of personality, consisting of the factors of neuroticism, extroversion, openness, agreeableness, and conscientiousness. However, debate over the relative importance of traits and situations as determinants of behavior, although not as heated as it was in the 1970s, continues. Although most human behavior is fairly consistent across situations, the degree of behavioral consistency varies with the individual and the situation. Some people are more consistent than others, and, regardless of individual differences in traits, some situations are more powerful than other situations in eliciting conformity. A successful resolution of the conflict between trait and situation theorists demands a more sophisticated theory that conceptualizes behavior in situations as due to the dynamic interaction, or transaction, between the characteristics of the individual and the nature of the situation in which that individual is placed.

McClelland and his colleagues found that persons with higher achievement motivation received relatively early independence training. These investigators also reported that the strength of the achievement motive varies with social class, culture, and religion. McClelland proposed a psychological theory of history which maintains that the economic development of a nation depends on the overall level of achievement motivation among its people.

Hermann Witkin and his associates used data from three perceptual tests—the Body Adjustment Test, the Rod and Frame Test, and the Embedded Figures Test—to assess a person's ability to separate or differentiate an object from its background. These tests are measures of the perceptual dimension of field independence/field dependence. High scorers on field independence are characterized as more secure, independent, controlled, psychologically mature, and self-accepting than low scorers. High scorers on field dependence are more tense, insecure, psychologically immature, passive, less attuned to inner experience, and less self-insightful than low scorers on this variable. A number of other personality and sociocultural variables have also been found to be related to the field-independence/field-dependence dimension.

Key Concepts

Attribution   Process of interpreting the cause of a person's behavior to forces within (*internal attribution*) or outside (*external attribution*) the person. The *fundamental attribution error* is the tendency to attribute one's own behavior to situational influences but to attribute the behavior of other people to dispositional causes.

Cardinal trait   According to G. W. Allport, a disposition or theme so dominant in a person's life that it is expressed in almost all of his or her behavior (e.g., power striving, self-love).

Functional autonomy of motives   Gordon Allport's term for the persistence of a behavior pattern long after the original impetus for the behavior has disappeared.

Idiographic approach   Approach to personality assessment and research in which the individual is viewed as a lawful, integrated system in his or her own right. See *Nomothetic approach.*

Introversion-extroversion   Dimension of personality, first formulated by Carl Jung, characterized by the degree to which an individual is oriented inwardly toward the self (*introversion*) or outwardly toward the external world (*extroversion*).

Neuroticism-stability   In Hans Eysenck's conceptualization of personality, the dimension ranging from extreme moodiness to even-temperedness.

Nomothetic approach   A search for general laws of behavior and personality that apply to all individuals. See *Idiographic approach.*

Somatotype   Classification of body build (physique) in W. H. Sheldon's three-component system (endomorphy, mesomorphy, ectomorphy).

Source traits   R. B. Cattell's term for organizing structures or dimensions of personality that underlie and determine surface traits.

Surface traits   Publicly manifested characteristics of personality; observable expressions of source traits.

Trait theory   Personality theory that conceptualizes human personality as consisting of a combination of traits. *Traits* are cognitive, affective, or psychomotor characteristics possessed in different amounts by different people.

Type   A larger dimension of personality than *trait;* a combination of traits characterizing a particular kind of personality, e.g., Type A or Type B.

Activities and Applications

1. It has been argued that stereotypes are overgeneralized characteristics in which all people of a certain group (sex, ethnic background, nationality, etc.) are "tarred with the same brush." Be that as it may, the tendency to categorize all members of a group on the basis of a few physical features, attitudes, or behavior patterns possessed by only a minority of people in the group is an illustration of the all-too-human tendency to simplify our experiences and make our perceptions and actions more efficient. What are the pros and cons, the advantages and disadvantages, of such stereotypes, and how common are they?

2. Regardless of its value in personality study, what evidence and arguments can you cite in support of somatotyping as a valid procedure in anthropology, medicine, and criminal justice?

3. The relationships between body build and personality noted by Kretschmer, Sheldon, and other researchers do not *prove* that physique is a direct cause of temperament or other aspects of personality, or vice versa. Correlation implies prediction but not causation. However, the results of investigations that have found significant correlations between body build and personality must be explained. With these correlations in mind, in what ways might body build influence personality development? In what ways might personality influence body build? Could the relationships between physical characteristics and personality be dynamic, reciprocal, and interactive? If you agree, explain how these relationships might occur.

4. Distinguish between type and trait theories of personality in terms of their validity, comprehensiveness, and generalizability.

5. Describe the similarities and differences among the trait theories of Gordon Allport, Raymond Cattell, and Hans Eysenck. Read a brief biography of each of these three psychologists and see if you can relate the nature of the theory to the theorist's own personality. Brief biographies of these three men may be found in Feist (1990), Hall and Lindzey (1985), and Hergenhahn (1990).

6. Take the following "personality inventory" yourself; then make multiple copies and administer it to several other people.

Directions: For each statement, circle the number that indicates how true the statement is of you.

How true is this of you?

	Hardly at All				A Lot
1. I make friends easily.	1	2	3	4	5
2. I tend to be shy.	1	2	3	4	5
3. I like to be with others.	1	2	3	4	5
4. I like to be independent of people.	1	2	3	4	5
5. I usually prefer to do things alone.	1	2	3	4	5
6. I am always on the go.	1	2	3	4	5
7. I like to be off and running as soon as I wake up in the morning.	1	2	3	4	5
8. I like to keep busy all of the time.	1	2	3	4	5
9. I am very energetic.	1	2	3	4	5
10. I prefer quiet, inactive pastimes to more accurate ones.	1	2	3	4	5
11. I tend to cry easily.	1	2	3	4	5
12. I am easily frightened.	1	2	3	4	5
13. I tend to be somewhat emotional.	1	2	3	4	5
14. I get upset easily.	1	2	3	4	5
15. I tend to be easily irritated.	1	2	3	4	5

From L. Willerman, *Individual and Group Differences*. New York: Harper's College Press, 1975. Reprinted with permission.

Scoring: For all items except numbers 2, 4, 5, and 10 the score is simply the number circled; for items 2, 4, 5, and 10, reverse the numbers before scoring (1 = 5, 2 = 4, 3 = 3, 4 = 2, 5 = 1). Add the scores on items 1–5 to yield an index of "Sociability," the scores on items 6–10 to yield an index of "Activity Level," and the scores on items 11–15 to yield an "Emotionality" index. Interpret your scores and those of other people to whom you administer the inventory with respect to the following average ranges within which 68 percent of samples of female and male students at the University of Texas at Austin scored on the three scales:

	Average Range for Females	*Average Range for Males*
Sociability	15–20	13–19
Activity level	13–20	13–19
Emotionality	11–18	9–16

Scores outside these ranges can be interpreted as "high" or "low" on the particular characteristic. Why is it important for you to be cautious in your interpretations of scores on this inventory?

7. What are the criteria of an effective theory of personality? That is, what should it attempt to explain and how should it be validated?

8. Most departments of psychology keep on file specimen sets of standardized tests, including personality assessment instruments. A typical specimen set includes a test booklet, an answer sheet, scoring keys, a manual, and perhaps other interpretative materials. If available, select one of the following personality inventories, examine the inventory, the manual, and other accompanying materials, and prepare a critical review according to the following outline. When you have completed your review, consult the *Mental Measurements Yearbook* (Conoley & Kramer, 1989 and previous volumes) and *Test Critiques* (Keyser & Sweetland, 1984–1988) for a professional review of your test. Compare your review with the published review.

A-S Reaction Study
Early School Personality Questionnaire
Edwards Personal Preference Schedule
Eysenck Personality Inventory
Eysenck Personality Questionnaire
Guilford-Zimmerman Temperament Survey
High School Personality Questionnaire
IPAT Anxiety Scale Questionnaire
Jenkins Activity Survey
Maudsley Personality Inventory
Myers-Briggs Type Indicator
Neuroticism Scale Questionnaire
Objective-Analytic Batteries
Sixteen Personality Factor Questionnaire
Study of Values

Format for Reviewing a Psychometric Instrument

Content. List the title, author, publisher, date and place of publication, forms available, type of instrument, and cost. Give a brief description of the sections of the instrument, the kinds of items of which it is composed, and the characteristics or variables the instrument is supposed to measure. Indicate how the items or parts of the instrument were selected and whether the construction procedure and theory on which it is based are clearly described in the manual.

Administration and Scoring. Describe any special instructions, whether the administration is timed, and if so the time limits. Give details concerning scoring: as a whole, by sections or parts, and so on. Indicate whether the directions for administration and scoring are clear.

Norms. Describe the groups (composition, size, and so on) on which the instrument was standardized and how the samples were selected (systematic, stratified random, and so on). What kinds of norms are reported in the manual or technical supplements? Does the standardization appear to be adequate for the recommended uses of the instrument?

Reliability. Describe the kinds of reliability information reported in the manual (internal consistency, parallel forms, test-retest, and so on). Are the nature and sizes of the samples on which the reliability information is reported adequate with respect to the stated uses of the instrument?

Validity. Summarize the available information on the validity (content, predictive, concurrent, construct) of the instrument given in the manual. Is the validity information satisfactory in terms of the stated purposes of the instrument?

Summary Comments. Give a summary statement of the design and content of the instrument, and comment briefly on the adequacy of the instrument as a measure of what it was designed to measure. Does the manual give satisfactory descriptions of the design, content, norms, reliability, and validity of the instrument? What further information and data are needed to improve the instrument and its uses?

Suggested Readings

Allport, G. W. (1961). *Pattern and growth in personality*. New York: Holt, Rinehart & Winston.

Buss, A. H., & Finn, S. E. (1988). Classification of personality traits. *Journal of Personality and Social Psychology, 52,* 432–444.

Cattell, R. B. (1990). Advances in Cattellian personality theory. In L. A. Pervin (Ed.), *Handbook of personality theory and research* (pp. 101–110). New York: Guilford Press.

Digman, J. M. (1990). Personality structure: Emergence of the five-factor model. In M. R. Rosenzweig & L. W. Porter (Eds.), *Annual Review of Psychology* (pp. 417–440). Palo Alto, CA: Annual Reviews.

Eysenck, H. J. (1982). Personality. In H. J. Eysenck (Ed.), *Personality, genetics, and behavior: Selected papers* (pp. 49–109). New York: Praeger.

Funder, D. C. (1991). Global traits: A neo-Allportian approach to personality. *Psychological Science, 2*(1), 31–39.

Jung, C. G. (1923). *Psychological types*. London: Routledge & Kegan Paul.

Kenrick, D. T., & Funder, D. C. (1988). Profiting from controversy: Lessons from the person-situation debate. *American Psychologist, 43,* 23–34.

Mischel, W. (1990). Personality dispositions revisited and revised: A view after three decades. In L. A. Pervin (Ed.), *Handbook of personality theory and research* (pp. 111–134). New York: Guilford Press.

Weiner, B. (1990). Attribution in personality theory. In L. A. Pervin (Ed.), *Handbook of personality theory and research* (pp. 465–485). New York: Guilford Press.

Zuroff, D. C. (1986). Was Gordon Allport a trait theorist? *Journal of Personality and Social Psychology, 51,* 993–1000.

Notes

1 As seen in the Myers-Briggs Type Indicator and the Jenkins Activity Survey, the concept of "personality types" is still very much alive. The Myers-Briggs Type Indicator, a personality inventory consisting of 166 or 126 two-choice items, is scored on four bipolar scales (Introversion-Extroversion, Sensing-Intuition, Thinking-Feeling, Judging-Perception). Combinations of scores on these four two-part categories result in 16 possible personality types. The Jenkins Activity Survey, which is described in detail in Chapter 11, is a questionnaire that is scored in terms of two personality types (A and B) and four subtypes (A1, A2, B3, and B4).

2 The direction of Allport's theorizing was shaped to some extent by an encounter with the father of psychoanalysis, Sigmund Freud. As a young man, while traveling through Europe, Allport decided to stop by Vienna and seek an appointment with the great man. On meeting with Freud, perhaps made uncomfortable by the latter's silence, Allport decided to "break the ice" by describing an incident involving a small boy with a

dirt phobia and his perfectionistic mother whom he had observed on the train. After Allport had finished relating the story, much to his chagrin Freud responded with, "And was that little boy you?" Apparently this experience turned Allport against the depth interpretations of psychoanalysis for life and prompted him to seek another theoretical orientation. Whether or not Freud was correct in the analysis inherent in his question has been the topic of whimsical speculation among certain psychologists.

CHAPTER 5

Psychodynamic Theories I: Freud and Jung

CHAPTER OUTLINE

It has been said that historically there were three cataclysmic assaults on the human sense of self-importance or specialness. Before the Copernican revolution of the sixteenth century, it was generally believed that the earth was the center of the universe and hence that the creature whom God had given dominion over the earth was only a little lower than the angels. Although war, famine, pestilence, and disease took their toll of lives and taxed human feelings of security, there was comfort and pride in the belief that eternal peace and happiness awaited the faithful in a heavenly afterlife.

The replacement of the Ptolmaic geocentric (earth-centered) theory with the Copernican heliocentric (sun-centered) theory, which relegated the earth to the status of a planet revolving around the sun, was damaging enough to the human psyche, but two events that occurred four centuries later dealt even harder blows to human superiority. One of these events was the publication in 1859 of Darwin's *Origin of Species* and the associated theory that human beings, like other animals, evolved from lower life forms. The "monkey theory" (to use its popular name) that humans were descended from an apelike creature, if correct, meant that people are essentially animals and in no way divine.

The third blow to human uniqueness and status also occurred in the nineteenth century, with the doctrine of the unconscious. Now not only were humans displaced from the center of the universe and descended from lower animal forms, but, according to the doctrine of the unconscious mind, they were not even aware of themselves and what motivates their actions. Thus people, like unthinking beasts, became creatures that were not unique or independent from other life forms, could hope for nothing beyond this temporal existence, and were victims of their own unconscious, uncontrolled, incomprehensible animal urges. The triple-barreled assault by the Copernican heliocentric theory, the Darwinian theory of evolution, and the Freudian theory of the unconscious contributed to what would be characterized as the Age of Anxiety in the twentieth century.

This chapter and the next are concerned with the theories of Sigmund Freud, Carl Jung, Alfred Adler, and other psychodynamic theorists. Psychodynamic theories focus on motivation, the internal forces that drive and shape behavior. All psychodynamic theorists have been influenced by Freud's psychoanalysis, which has been called one of the great intellectual movements of our time. Certainly on any list of ten individuals who most influenced twentieth-century thinking would appear the name of Sigmund Freud (1856–1939), the father of psychoanalysis. Freud, who was barely five feet seven inches in height, was a true intellectual giant of our time. Wide-ranging in his interests and abilities, he had an important influence not only on psychology and psychiatry, but also on sociology, anthropology, art, literature, history, and many other areas of knowledge and culture. The Freudian influence and legacy have not been uniformly positive, and some have viewed it more as a source of evil than of good. Furthermore, psychoanalytic theorizing has not always been correct and psychoanalytic practice not always effective. Nevertheless, Freud was a highly creative thinker who made people view themselves from a new perspective and led them to question old myths and ways of dealing with human problems and aspirations.

The Beginnings of Psychoanalysis

The term *psychoanalysis* is singular, but it actually refers to a plurarity. Not only is psychoanalysis a theory of personality, it is also a method of psychotherapy and a methodology for research on human personality and mental disorders. Both the theory and methodology devised by Freud were derivatives of the therapy. The theoretical concepts and explanations were modified continuously during Freud's lifetime as a result of his clinical observations and readings. Throughout much of his professional career, Freud saw patients downstairs during the day and recorded his thoughts and experiences upstairs at night in his home at Bergasse 19 in Vienna. These activities and the resulting books and papers were not always viewed favorably by the conservative medical and intellectual community of late nineteenth- and early twentieth-century Vienna. The theory of infantile sexuality, in particular, caused a storm of protest in Viennese medical society and undoubtedly affected Freud's professional advancement and acceptance. Some of this criticism was probably exacerbated by the fact that Freud was a Jew attempting to compete in a fundamentally anti-Semitic society. In Freud's own words, spoken near the end of his life (Simpson, 1987):

> I started . . . as a neurologist, trying to bring relief to my neurotic patients. I discovered some important new facts about the unconscious . . . the role of instinctual urges, and so on. Out of these findings grew a new science, psychoanalysis, a part of psychology, and a new method of treatment of the neuroses. I had to pay heavily for this bit of good luck. People did not believe in my facts and thought my theories unsavory. Resistance was strong and unrelenting. In the end, I succeeded. . . . But the struggle is not yet over.

Studies in Hysteria

As indicated in the quotation, Freud's initial research was in neurology, which he pursued after being appointed to the medical faculty of the University of Vienna in 1873. For approximately ten years he worked as a neurologist, making contributions to medical understanding of the connections between the spinal cord and the cerebellum, the roots of the acoustic nerve, and the corresponding structures in the sensory nuclei of the cranial nerves and the sensory ganglia of the spinal cord (Jones, 1990). He also conducted research during these early years on methods of staining neural tissue and the uses of cocaine. However, his inquiring mind and ambition led Freud to collaborate with Josef Breuer, a Viennese physician who was treating a young female patient (Bertha Papenhausen, alias Anna O.) suffering from hysteria. *Hysteria,* a disorder which had been known since Hippocrates' time, is characterized by a loss of sensation or a paralysis in certain body parts. Freud and Breuer discovered that when Anna talked about her physical symptoms and feelings, she felt better, and the symptoms diminished or disappeared. Unfortunately, the previous symptoms were often replaced by other physical problems.

During this early stage of his career, Freud also studied with Jean-Martin Charcot and Hippolyte Bernheim, two French physicians who were applying hypnosis to the treatment of hysteria. Medical usage of hypnosis had begun in the eighteenth century, when the Austrian physician Franz Mesmer demonstrated to Parisian audiences that the symptoms of certain mental disorders can be produced and eliminated by the use of magnets applied to the body of a person, a process which he called *animal magnetism*. Because of Mesmer's overdramatic, "hocus pocus" style, *mesmerism,* or *hypnotism* as it was later named, did not become popular among physicians of the time. However, in the last quarter of the nineteenth century, Charcot, Bernheim, Ambroise-Auguste Liébault, Pierre Janet, and a few other French psychiatrists revived medical interest in hypnotism by demonstrating that the anesthesias and paralyses of hysteria can be removed by this method. These demonstrations were important, because they suggested that there is a psychological or psychodynamic basis for certain mental disorders.

Although he used it for a while in his treatment of hysterics, Freud soon abandoned hypnosis in favor of "the talking cure," which he called *free association.* Free association consists of a patient's saying anything that comes into his or her mind, holding back nothing. While concentrating on a particular symptom, the patient attempts to remember anything that might throw light on the origin of the symptom. To Freud, free association served not only the cathartic function of relieving the patient of anxiety but also yielded insights—both to the analyst and the patient—concerning the causes of the latter's illness. By achieving insight into the origins or causes of such symptoms, they would reportedly diminish and not be replaced by other pathological symptoms.

Another therapeutic concept that was recognized and described by Freud in his work with hysterics was *transference,* a psychological phenomenon in which the patient transfers unconscious feelings for a parent or some other significant person onto the analyst. The patient behaves toward the analyst as if the latter were that significant other person; the patient relives and reexpresses the feelings and conflicts that were experienced with respect to that person. In the early stages of therapy, the transference is usually positive—characterized by friendly, even amorous feelings toward the analyst. But as therapy progresses, more negative, hostile feelings begin to surface. Freud felt that both positive and negative transference are normal and essential processes for the progress of psychoanalytic therapy.

A book, *Studies in Hysteria,* summarizing their work with Anna O. and several other cases, and describing the concepts of the unconscious, free association, and transference, was published by Freud and Breuer in 1895. This book, which was to be followed by nearly two dozen other volumes by Freud over a 45-year period (see Table 5–1) marks the formal beginning of psychoanalysis as a method of psychotherapy and a theory of personality. In *Studies in Hysteria,* Freud and Breuer concluded that psychoneurotic problems are caused by uncon-

TABLE 5–1   Books by Sigmund Freud

1895	*Studies in Hysteria* (with Josef Breuer)
1900	*The Interpretation of Dreams*
1901	*The Psychopathology of Everyday Life*
1905	*Three Essays on Sexuality*
	Jokes and Their Relation to the Unconscious
1913	*Totem and Taboo*
1915	*A General Introduction to Psychoanalysis*
1917	*Introductory Lectures on Psychoanalysis*
1920	*Beyond the Pleasure Principle*
1921	*Group Psychology and the Analysis of the Ego*
1922	*Reflections*
1923	*The Ego and the Id*
1925	*Inhibitions, Symptoms, and Anxiety*
	Autobiography
1926	*The Problem of Anxiety*
1927	*The Future of an Illusion*
1930	*Civilization and Its Discontents*
1933	*New Introductory Lectures on Psychoanalysis*
1936	*The Ego and the Mechanisms of Defense*
1939	*Moses and Monotheism*

scious sexual conflicts. This was a bold conclusion during a time when neurologists were still attempting to treat hysteria by means of electrotherapy. Soon after the publication of their book, however, Breuer broke with Freud and the latter continued his psychoanalytic researches alone in his only laboratory—the clinical consulting room in his Vienna home. The break with Breuer, as with the later alienations from Fliess and Jung, became characteristic of a strong personality such as Freud's. Freud felt protective of his theories, and especially the theories concerning the roles of the unconscious and the sex instinct, which he considered the cornerstones of psychoanalysis.

Theory of Sexual Energy

In addition to being a doctor who treated patients, Freud was an intellectual and a scientist whose principal interest was in developing a theory of the mind based on natural science. Influenced by his teachers Theodor H. Meynert and Ernst von Brücke, and through them by the great German scientist and physician H.L.F. von Helmholtz, Freud came to believe that psychological events, like physical events, are determined and hence explicable in causal terms (the concept of *psychic determinism*). His psychological model of the mind was a kind of "hydraulic theory" consisting of psychological counterparts of pressures, control devices, and other mechanical structures. The *psychic energy* on which this "hydraulic theory" operated was believed to remain constant throughout a person's lifetime and obeyed the principle of the conservation of energy. Psychic energy, also referred to as *libido,* was principally sexual in nature and could be directed toward thinking about objects or events. The investment of psychic energy in thinking about need-satisfying objects and processes was referred to as *cathexis,* and the divestment of this energy from those thoughts was called *anticathexis.*

Since society will not permit the uncontrolled expression of sexual energy, Freud postulated that it becomes temporarily repressed, or held back from awareness in the unconscious mind. However, failure of expression of the libido results in *psychic conflict,* anxiety, and various neurotic symptoms. Illustrative of such symptoms are the hysterical anesthesias and paralyses of Anna O. and Dora, the obsessive-compulsive behavior of "The Rat Man," and the paranoid ideation of Judge Schreber. These were four of the 12 cases analyzed in detail in Freud's writings.

Of particular significance in early psychoanalytic theorizing was the notion of seduction. Many of the patients whom Freud saw during the 1880s and 1890s reported having been sexually seduced by a parent or other relative, a claim that Freud first accepted as authentic and later discounted. Freud, who himself was always a devoted husband to his wife and a devoted father to his six children, initially found a patient's confession that one or more of his (her) parents had attempted or achieved seduction of the child as startling, although it did seem to account for the early sexual awakening and preoccupations of these patients. For whatever reasons—counterarguments and counterevidence or social and professional pressure—Freud subsequently dismissed the notion that the reported seductions had actually occurred, and reinterpreted them as fantasy or wish fulfillment. He made the fantasy ideation of childhood seduction a part of his theorizing on the role of sexuality in neuroses, and maintained in later years that thinking of the reported seductions as imaginary rather than real was the beginning of the science, therapy, and profession of psychoanalysis.

According to Masson (1984), in light of our current knowledge of the occurrence of incest in families of all social classes, Freud may have been too hasty in discounting the claims of his patients that successful or unsuccessful attempts had been made to seduce them when they were children. It is possible that many of the reported seductions or attempted seductions actually happened.

Interpretation of Dreams

In addition to the existence of the unconscious and childhood sexuality, Freud felt that one of his most important contributions was the understanding of dreams. In fact, *The Interpretation of Dreams* (Freud, 1900) is considered by many authorities to be Freud's most original work. Freud viewed dreams as protectors of sleep; by dreaming, the person is able to remain asleep rather than being awakened by every external or internal distraction. Although a dream can be precipitated by an environmental stimulus (e.g., a noise or the wind blowing across one's body) or an experience that occurred during the preceding day, the content of the dream is fashioned from memories that go back as far as early childhood.

Freud believed that every dream is an attempt on the part of the dreamer to fulfill a desire or need, frequently of a sexual or aggressive nature. Because the desire is too painful or guilt inducing to be consciously acknowledged, it becomes repressed into the unconscious (Freud, 1933). Hence for the psychoanalyst dreams are the "royal road to the unconscious." The nature of the desire or wish that a dream is attempting to fulfill cannot be directly ascertained from the *manifest content*—that is, the aspects of the dream of which the dreamer is aware. To understand that wish and the meaning of the dream, the *latent content* must be deciphered by the *method of amplification*—that is, having the dreamer "free associate" to the manifest content, indicating and elaborating on what he or she is reminded of in recalling each part of the dream. The meaning of the dream may also be clarified by considering other facts about the dreamer's personal history and the nature of his or her psychological problem. Typically, it is the patient rather than the analyst who contributes most to the interpretation of the dream; the analyst serves primarily as a facilitator in extracting the appropriate interpretation from the patient.

The reason why a dream must be interpreted is that the nature of the wishes or desires in the latent content are distorted by a mental "censoring" process known as the *dreamwork*. The dreamwork involves *condensation*, in which a dream image represents several ideas at the same time; *displacement*, in which an unacceptable thought is replaced by a symbolically equivalent but acceptable thought; and other processes (distortion, symbolism, secondary elaboration, etc.) that distort of camouflage the real meaning of the dream. The following are among the sexual symbols to be found in dreams:

> Bullets, fire, guns, hoses, knives, snakes, sticks, umbrellas: *male sex organs*
> Bottles, boxes, caves, closets, ovens, ships, tunnels: *female sex organs*
> Apples, cantaloupes, grapefruit, peaches: *breasts*
> Climbing a flight of stairs, crossing a bridge, entering a room, flying in an airplane, riding in an elevator, train traveling through a tunnel: *sexual intercourse*

During sleep, when the "censor" is less on guard or not as alert as when the individual is awake, much significant material gets by the censor in disguised form and becomes an integral part of the manifest content of the dream

Report 5–1 is an example of a dream and Freud's interpretation of it. Note that the dream is formed from a combination of events that occurred during the previous day and earlier experiences of the dreamer. Much of the content of the dream is symbolic or distorted, and the analyst's task is to get past the overt, manifest content and try to understand the latent content, or real meaning of the dream.

Along with free association, the *analysis of transference* and the *analysis of resistance* (analyzing behaviors that indicate resistance to the progress of psychoanalytic therapy), dream analysis became one of the major techniques of psychoanalytic therapy. A skilled dream interpreter is sometimes able to obtain valuable information about the meaning of the dream with respect to the patient's conflicts and other problems.

REPORT 5–1

A Man's Dream and the Accompanying Freudian Interpretation

He sees two boys tussling with each other; they are cooper's boys, as he concludes from the tools which are lying about; one of the boys has thrown the other down; the prostrate boy is wearing ear-rings with blue stones. He runs towards the assailant with lifted cane, in order to chastise him. The boy takes refuge behind a woman, as though she were his mother, who is standing against a wooden fence. She is the wife of a day-laborer, and she turns her back to the man who is dreaming. Finally she turns around and stares at him with a horrible look, so that he runs away in terror; the red flesh of the lower lid seems to stand out from her eyes.

This dream has made abundant use of trivial occurrences from the previous day, in the course of which he actually saw two boys in the street, one of whom threw the other down. When he walked up to them in order to settle the quarrel, both of them took to their heels. Cooper's boys—this is explained only by a subsequent dream, in the analysis of which he used the proverbial expression: "*To Knock the bottom out of the barrel.*" Ear-rings with blue stones, according to his observation, are worn chiefly by *prostitutes*. This suggests a familiar doggerel rhyme about two boys: "The other boy was called Marie": that is, he was a girl. The woman standing by the fence: after the scene with the two boys he went for a walk along the bank of the Danube and taking advantage of being alone, urinated *against a wooden fence*. A little farther on a respectably dressed, elderly lady smiled at him very pleasantly, and wanted to hand him her card with her address.

Since, in the dream, the woman stood as he had stood while urinating, there is an allusion to a woman urinating, and this explains the "horrible look" and the prominence of the red flesh, which can only refer to the genitals gaping in a squatting posture; seen in childhood, they had appeared in later recollection as "*proud flesh,*" as a "*wound.*" The dream unites two occasions upon which, as a little boy, the dreamer was enabled to see the genitals of little girls, once by throwing the little girl down, and once while the child was *urinating;* and, as is shown by another association, he had retained in his memory the punishment administered or threatened by his father on account of these manifestations of sexual curiosity.

Source: From *The Interpretation of Dreams* (pp. 102–103) by S. Freud (Trans. A. A. Brill), 1900/1950, New York: Modern Library.

Psychoanalysis and Everyday Life

Although *The Interpretation of Dreams* was Freud's most original and monumental book, *The Psychopathology of Everyday Life* (Freud, 1901) was his most popular. In this little book, Freud extended the growing science of psychoanalysis to phenomena that occur in everyday life: slips of the tongue, slips of the pen, misplacing objects, and forgetting appointments and names. Consistent with his belief in psychic determinism, Freud maintained that even the simplest, seemingly accidental, aspects of human behavior require a causal rather than a chance explanation. He explained apparently innocent little mixups and other mistakes in speaking and writing, which are sometimes amusing and sometimes embarrassing, as not accidental but rather as due to the partial failure of repression. In everyday life, people sometimes repress—that is, unconsciously forget—the name of a person who has angered or embarrassed them or the details of a frightening experience. Repression is seldom complete or clear-cut, but a partial failure of repression may lead one to mispronounce the name of a former friend, such as Finley Tucker or Virginia Duda, from whom one has become estranged. Mistakes of this sort may also occur in writing, as when one begins a letter to a current lover with the name of an old flame or addresses a letter to a fair-weather friend named Robert Roper with "Dear Rabid Raper." Obviously, such "mistakes" may on occasion be consciously intended rather than unconsciously motivated.

Other examples of the psychopathology of everyday life are to be found in jokes, which Freud believed, like dreams and slips of the tongue and pen, were motivated by repressed sexual and aggressive desires. Telling a joke relieves the tension caused by repressed impulses. The accomplished humorist knows how to build up tension in the audience in telling a joke, finally releasing the pent-up tension with the punch line.

To many people the funniest jokes or sayings are those that deal with taboo topics such as sex and aggression. An exception occurs when the person deals with such material every day, as when porno stars or flesh peddlers find sex jokes patently unfunny and morticians fail to appreciate "mortuary humor." In any event, the purpose of both dreams and jokes is to permit the indirect expression of socially (and perhaps personally) unacceptable impulses. It has been said that what one finds humorous often provides a clue to what is repressed in the unconscious mind.

Expansion and Development of Psychoanalysis

By 1902, Freud had gathered around him a small group of followers (Alfred Adler, Max Kahane, Rudolf Reitler, Wilhelm Stekel), who formed what was known as the Wednesday Psychological Circle. By 1908 the Wednesday Circle had grown to 22 members, a group which developed into the Vienna Psychoanalytic Society and by 1910 into the International Psychoanalytic Association. Several members of the group, on the invitation of G. Stanley Hall, the president of Clark University, traveled to America in 1909 (see Figure 5–1). The personal appearances and lectures of Freud and his colleagues during that tour mark the beginnings of psychoanalysis in the United States, a country whose intellectual and social climate proved to be more hospitable than Europe to the new science.

FIGURE 5–1 Photograph taken during the visit of Freud and Jung to Clark University, 1909. Top row, from left to right: A. A. Brill, Ernest Jones (Freud's biographer), and Sandor Ferenczi. Bottom row, from left to right: Sigmund Freud, G. Stanley Hall (the president of Clark University), and Carl Jung. (Courtesy of Bettman Archive.)

At the meetings of the Wednesday Circle and subsequently the Vienna Psychoanalytic Society and the International Psychoanalytic Association, Freud would sit smoking one of his 20 cigars for that day, expound on his latest bit of theory or insight, and listen to other members do likewise. During these early years, the psychoanalytic blueprint of human personality was taking shape, and Freud was presenting his conception of the three-part theory to his colleagues.

A general picture of human personality as envisioned by Freud is shown in Figure 5–2. In addition to the *unconscious,* those drives and experiences of which we are not directly aware, and the *conscious,* those that we are aware of at any given moment, there is the *preconscious,* consisting of memories of which we are not presently aware but which can with effort be brought into conscious awareness. In addition to this three-part division in terms of levels of consciousness, Freud visualized three personality components or processes—id, ego, and super-ego. In Freud's own words, "in the beginning there was *id*" the unconscious

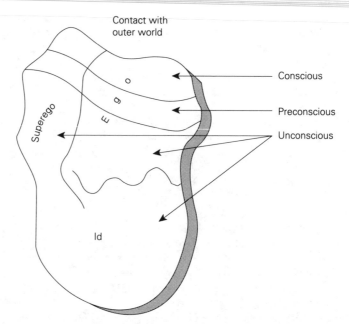

FIGURE 5–2   Freud's conception of the human mind. (From *The Structure and Meaning of Psychoanalysis* by W. Healy et al. Copyright 1930 and renewed 1958 by Alfred A. Knopf, Inc. Reprinted by permission of the publisher.)

reservoir of instinctive urges of sexual and aggression, the untamed animal nature of man. However, the id cannot express these urges with impunity in an orderly world, so out of id energy there develops a mediator or compromiser—the *ego*. The id operates under the *pleasure principle*, according to which the desire for pleasure is foremost and alone activates individual behavior. The ego, on the other hand, operates under the *reality principle*, according to which the consequences of one's behavior are considered before acting. A third component of personality, the *superego*, develops later when the child begins to internalize the prohibitions and sanctions of parents, teachers, and other important persons. The superego, consisting of the *ego ideal* (what the person would like to be) and the *conscience*, acts according to the *moral principle*. As shown in Figure 5–2, the id is totally unconscious, whereas the ego and superego are partly conscious, partly preconscious, and partly unconscious.

Freud viewed human personality as a kind of battleground where the id, ego, and superego struggle for supremacy. The id runs into conflict with both the ego and the superego, producing *neurotic anxiety* in the former case and *moral anxiety* in the latter. The fear that one's id impulses will get out of hand and lead to punishment produces neurotic anxiety; moral anxiety consists of the guilt that one feels when a moral code has been violated or is about to be violated by the person. Finally, conflict between the ego and the external world generates *reality anxiety*, the fear that is felt when genuine, objective danger is present.

In some ways, the often fragile ego has the most difficult task of all in this conception of personality. It must act as an executive mediator between the relentless struggle of the id and superego for control without constantly antagonizing the external world—that is, other people. The id says "Now!," the superego says "Never!," but the ego must say "Later" or "In some socially acceptable way" to the expression of the id's desires. Although id impulses and the conflict of id with superego and ego usually take place in the unconscious mind, they are expressed in thoughts and behavior in various disguised forms. The expression of unconscious drives and conflicts can occur in dreams, under hypnosis, by having patients say whatever comes into their minds (free association), or by using a variety of other techniques (e.g., projective tests). In its role as a mediator between the id and superego and in its dealings with the external world, the ego must think, solve problems, make decisions, and control the actions of the person. To match the *primary process* images—the fanciful and wish-related images that the id conjures up in an effort to satisfy its needs—with the demands of the real world, the ego tries to arrange a compromise. The process by which the ego achieves such a compromise matching between id impulses with objects and events in the real world is known as *reality testing,* which in Freudian terminology is a *secondary process.*

Defense Mechanisms

In his early theorizing, Freud viewed anxiety as the result of repression, the release of unexpressed libido. As the ego gained in importance in his thinking, Freud reversed the sequence that "repression produces anxiety" to "anxiety produces repression" (Freud, 1926). Anxiety, resulting from conflict between the ego and the id or the ego and the superego, was now seen as leading to the exclusion of unpleasant, painful memories from consciousness. Thus repression became the forerunner of all other defense mechanisms.

Freud distinguished between *repression* and *suppression,* the latter being a conscious, voluntary pushing of unacceptable desires and impulses out of consciousness. Repression, on the other hand, is an involuntary, unconscious way of protecting the ego from anxiety. Freud pointed to clinical evidence, which has subsequently been substantiated to some degree by experimental evidence, that people tend to remember pleasant experiences longer than unpleasant ones, as the concept of repression implies.

According to Freud's later thinking, repression is the primary defense mechanism. Repression serves to keep sexual and aggressive drives below the level of conscious awareness, and the use of other mechanisms is necessitated by a partial failure of repression. An alternative explanation is that repression is itself not a defense mechanism but that defense mechanisms serve the function of keeping anxiety-arousing material repressed. Whether one accepts the former or the latter explanation of repression, defense mechanisms do protect the individual from thoughts and realizations that threaten the ego or sense of self-esteem. Among these mechanisms are denial, rationalization, identification, compensation, displacement, sublimation, reaction formation, projection, fantasy, and regression.

Denial. One of the simplest defense mechanisms, and quite similar to suppression, is *denial,* simply refusing to accept or acknowledge anxiety-arousing information. Unlike repression, in which an experience is obliterated from consciousness, in denial the person selectively attends to and reinterprets an experience. He or she simply refuses to recognize or accept anxiety-arousing information or events. The terms *redefinition* and *reappraisal* are synonyms for denial.

Rationalization. When individuals provide socially acceptable reasons for inadequate behavior or for actions determined by socially unacceptable impulses, they are using the defense mechanism of *rationalization.* Rationalization is one of the most common mechanisms, and it is characterized as finding "good," socially acceptable, and ego-cushioning reasons for one's behavior. The student who continually fails examinations because "the teachers don't explain the material well" or "I didn't feel well" and the "sour-grapes" attitude of "I didn't want the old prize anyway; it's not so hot" are examples of rationalization. The "sweet-lemon" philosophy that "things couldn't be better" even when they are actually pretty bad is a related mechanism.

Identification. When an individual matches his or her behavior to that of another person or tries to be like someone else by copying what that person does, the individual is said to *identify* with the other person. Identification with parents and other people is, of course, important for a child's development; the child learns how to act and perform by copying the behavior of someone else. Adolescents typically have idols with whom they identify, but the idols tend to change rather frequently. Thus identification is useful in promoting a person's social development, and it is considered a defense mechanism only when one's individuality is consistently sacrificed by identifying with others in order to keep from feeling anxious. In certain cases of extreme identification, a pattern known as *vicarious living* develops. Here the person literally tries to "take on" the personality of another by copying that person's behavior in every way. In this instance, because one's own identity is sacrificed for that of another person, the mechanism of identification is clearly maladaptive.

Another example of "identification gone wrong" is identification with the aggressor. As reported by survivors of Nazi concentration camps, some prisoners actually became convinced that their captors were right and consequently cooperated with them in controlling other prisoners. A similar tendency to agree with the captors' views, the so-called *Stockholm syndrome,* has occurred in hostages held by terrorists or other criminals (Skurnik, 1988).

Displacement. In displacement, an unwanted thought or feeling is redirected from its original source to another object, person, or situation. For example, a feeling of hostility or aggression may be transferred from a threatening, powerful person to a weaker person or object. A love-smitten adolescent whose overtures have been rejected may beat the wall with his fist, or a husband may tongue-lash or physically abuse his wife after being bawled out by his boss. A chain reaction is often associated with displaced aggression. For example, the captain berates the lieutenant; the lieutenant then reprimands the sergeant; the sergeant, in turn, curses the private; and finally, the private kicks the dog. Displacement does need not invariably involve aggression; sexual feelings may also be displaced or redirected. When the results of displacement are advantageous to civilization, the process is referred to as *sublimation.*

Sublimation. In *sublimation,* basic drives such as those of sex and aggression are channeled into socially approved activities. Although there is some question as to whether clear-cut sublimation actually occurs, some frequently cited examples are writing romantic poetry to sublimate the sex drive, taking care of other people's children as a sublimation of the urge to have children of one's own, or becoming active in certain sports or occupations (butcher, surgeon) to sublimate aggressive impulses. Freud considered sublimation to be one of the most adaptive defense mechanisms, in that it resulted in something advantageous to human civilization.

Reaction Formation. In *reaction formation,* the individual behaves in a manner directly opposite to an unconscious wish or impulse, for example, being kind instead of cruel. Illustrations of dramatic changes suggestive of reaction formation may be found in literature, such as the minister in Somerset Maugham's short story "Rain" who was attracted to the prostitute. Extreme protests or moral outrage may also be manifestations of reaction formation, as in motion picture or book critics who see moral turpitude in almost every film they see or every book they read.

Projection. Projection consists of attributing one's unacceptable desires and impulses to other people. Thus a person who unrealistically views others as being against him or "having it in for him" is projecting. This common mechanism is self-reinforcing, in that a person who believes others are "out to get" him will tend to behave aggressively toward them and as a result provoke counteraggression. In this way, overuse of the projection mechanism creates the kind of world that the projecting person believes to exist. Chronic use of projection is potentially a very serious matter, being particularly characteristic of paranoid disorders.

Fantasy. Fantasy behavior is daydreaming and imagining; the thoughts of fantasy are the results of motives and emotions rather than reason. In fantasy, the individual vicariously satisfies desires, fulfills wishes, and creates his or her own private, nonfrustrating world. Although fantasy is very common in normal people, and though it may help to cushion the shock of disappointment and even assist in planning for the future, excessive use of fantasy is a feature of certain kinds of schizophrenia.

Regression. Regression occurs when conflict or frustration results in the repetition of behavior that is more appropriate for an earlier stage of development. Sometimes a frustrated child or even a mature adult will regress, or revert, to behavior that is more suitable to an earlier developmental stage. Examples of regression are the five-year-old who starts behaving like a two-year-old when a new baby is born in the family, or an adult who cries, bites his fingernails, sucks his thumb, or throws a temper tantrum when denied a desirable object or outcome.

Psychosexual Stages

Freud conceived of the developing personality as progressing through a series of *psychosexual stages.* At each of these stages, a different body area is the center of libidinal stimulation and gratification. During the first or *oral stage,* which lasts from birth until 1½ years, pleasure comes from stimulation of the mouth and lips as in sucking and eating. During the second or *anal stage,* lasting from about age 1½ to age 3 years, the primary area of gratification is the anus, and the child achieves satisfaction from retaining and eliminating feces. It is during the anal stage that *negativism* is most pronounced. Negativism, often associated with early toilet training, is defiant behavior in which the child refuses to do what he or she is asked or ordered to do. During the *phallic stage* of development, which occurs between ages three and six years, the body area of primary interest is the genitalia. It is during the phallic stage that the *Oedipus complex* occurs. This complex, which Freud thought to be universal, is characterized by the boy's immature sexual feelings for his mother and hostility toward his father. Freud maintained that fear of castration, the so-called *castration complex,* leads to the destruction of the Oedipus complex. Now the boy relinquishes his incestuous desires and settles for identification with his father, that is, being like his father but not attempting to take his place.

Parallel to the Oedipus complex in the boy is the *Electra complex* in the girl, earmarked by hatred of the mother and love of the father. Significant in Freud's psychology of women is the discovery by the little girl that she lacks a penis; observing that the boy has a penis leads to *penis envy* in the girl. Penis envy in girls is the psychoanalytic counterpart of castration anxiety in boys. To Freud, the Electra complex and the problem of penis envy in the girl are resolved when she identifies with her mother.

During the *latency period,* which extends from age six to prepuberty, there is, according to Freud, a reduction in the intensity of the sexual urge. At the onset of puberty, the child who has successfully learned the lessons and resolved the problems of the previous stages enters the *genital stage* of psychosexual development. During this stage, the individual usually attains mature sexual union with a member of the opposite sex.

Freud believed that many individual differences in adult personality and character are caused by failure to progress from one stage of psychosexual development to the next. He used the term *fixation* to refer to the process by which an individual remains emotionally stuck at a given psychosexual stage, with the libidinal energies of the person becoming permanently attached to that stage. In addition, traumatic experiences or psychological stress may result in a partial *regression* or return to behavior patterns that are typical of an earlier developmental stage. For example, overeating, overtalkativeness, thumb sucking, nail biting, and smoking in older children and adults are possible signs of fixation at or regression to the oral stage of development. An argumentative, sarcastic, hostile adult may owe his or her personality to fixation at the aggressive phase of the oral stage, during which satisfaction was obtained by biting and chewing. Excessive dependency, greediness, and passivity are also viewed as indicators of oral fixation.

Fixation at the anal stage is characterized by three *p*'s: parsimony, petulance, and pedantry. Anal personalities are compulsive, orderly, excessively conforming, stingy, and stubborn. To Freud, such characteristics are symbolic equivalents of the withholding of feces during early childhood. Thus the miserly collector who is preoccupied with details and the compulsive Mr. Clean may have experienced difficulties with toilet training and hence remain emotionally fixated at the second year of life. Fixation can also occur at other stages of psychosexual development, leaving an indelible imprint on adult character and personality.

Civilization and Religion

As noted previously, Freud had wide-ranging interests that went beyond psychology and psychiatry and penetrated to the very heart of Western civilization. A natural scientist and an atheist, he viewed religion and other features of civilized behavior as efforts by organized society to control the expression of individual sexual and aggressive impulses. Freud's analysis of history and the role of religion in that history are to be found in several books (*Totem and Taboo, The Future of an Illusion, Civilization and Its Discontents, Moses and Monotheism*) written over a quarter of a century. The views presented in these books attack not only the Judeo-Christian religious tradition but all religions as illusory explanations of human behavior and the human condition. For example, a case is made in *Moses and Monotheism* for Moses having been an Egyptian prince who exploited the one-god concept of the Pharaoh Akhnaton to gain personal power through leadership of the captive Israelites. Furthermore, Freud interpreted the real or symbolic crucifixion of Christ ("the eldest son") as an atonement for the killing of the prehistoric father by his sons, a kind of racial Oedipal drama with a twist. Like his friend and collaborator Carl Jung, Freud believed in the Lamarckian theory of the inheritance of acquired characteristics and speculated that the ancient Oedipal drama has been imprinted in the minds of the members of subsequent generations and reenacted in their development.

Until his death in 1939, Freud was continually revising his conceptions of personality and applying his ideas to other areas of human endeavor. Prior to World War I, he had considered the sexual instinct (*Eros*) to be the basic motivator of human behavior. But the mass killings in the war led him to postulate a death instinct (*Thanatos*), which went *Beyond the Pleasure Principle* in affecting human behavior and personality.

Freud loved Vienna, and it was with great reluctance that he moved from Austria to England during the late 1930s. Nazism rejected psychoanalysis as a decadent Jewish science and burned Freud's books, along with those of other famous classical and modern authors. As with many other ideas and movements spawned on the European continent, the future of psychoanalysis became associated with the United States and the United Kingdom.

Despite the efforts of his followers to attain it for him, Freud never won the Nobel Prize. He was, however, awarded the Goethe prize for literature. This was perhaps his most cherished honor and one well-deserved by an accomplished author who just happened to be a neurologist, a psychologist, and an amateur archaeologist as well.

Research and Evaluation

Freud's psychoanalytic theory was based on his clinical observations of approximately 100 patients and discussions of these cases with his friends and colleagues. Among the most famous cases were those of Anna O. and Dora (hysteria), the Rat Man (obsessive-compulsive neurosis), Judge Schreber (paranoid schizophrenia), and Little Hans (phobia). By observing the behavior of patients during psychoanalytic treatment sessions, Freud noted consistencies and deduced logical connections in what they said. By analyzing the resistances, transferences, and dreams of the patient, Freud was able to deduce hypotheses and eventually conclusions pertaining to the underlying dynamics of the patient's problems and explanations for the symptoms of the particular disorder.

Subsequent systematic research by Luborsky (1970), employing the *symptom-context method* and the *core conflictual relationship theme method,* has provided support for certain principles derived by Freud from the clinical case approach. In the symptom-context method, the researcher analyzes tape recordings of therapy sessions to determine whether there is a significant relationship between occurrences of a symptom and events transpiring in the therapeutic context. In the core conflictual relationship theme method, expert judges rate the transcripts of therapy sessions to determine the presence and nature of transference. Judges rate the patient's feelings toward another person, the responses of that person, and the responses of the patient to determine the theme or core conflict that characterizes the transferences relationship.

Also providing some confirmation for a Freudian concept is the research of Silverman and his coworkers (Silverman, 1976; Silverman & Fishel, 1981; Silverman & Weinberger, 1985; Weinberger & Silverman, 1987). Their main research procedure was to present certain stimulus materials subliminally—that is, below the threshold of conscious awareness for 90 percent or more of the subjects—by means of an instrument known as a tachistoscope. Consistent with Freud's interpretation of depression as inwardly turned aggression, Silverman (1976) found that subliminally presented aggressive images made depressed people even more depressed. Also, consistent with the psychoanalytic notion that stutterers equate stuttering with defecation, when stutterers were exposed to subliminally presented pictures of a dog defecating, their stuttering increased (Silverman, Klinger, Lustbader, Farrell, & Martin, 1972). Furthermore, studies of *perceptual defense*—failing to report seeing emotionally arousing stimuli (such as the words *whore, bitch,* and *raped*) when presented subliminally (although there is a galvanic skin response to these stimuli)—have been interpreted as confirmation of the phenomena of unconscious motivation and unconscious perception (McGinnies, 1949; Maddi, 1980).

Although many early psychoanalysts maintained that Freudian theory stands or falls on the authenticity of the Oedipus complex, anthropological research findings concerning its universality have been mixed and variously interpreted (e.g., Malinowski, 1927/1955; Spiro, 1982). In a laboratory study conducted by Silverman, Bronstein, and Mendelsohn (1976), indirect evidence was found for the existence of the Oedipus complex. Male college students participating in the study were exposed to one of three subliminal messages: "BEATING DAD IS WRONG"; "BEATING DAD IS OK"; "PEOPLE ARE WALKING." In a subsequent dart-throwing tournament, the students who were exposed to the first message, which was designed to arouse Oedipal conflicts, scored lowest; students exposed to the second message scored highest; and students exposed to the third (neutral) message scored in between. Although these findings were interpreted as evidence for the Oedipus complex, they have been criticized and have not been uniformly replicated.

Other Freudian concepts that have been subjected to research tests include the notion of psychosexual stages of development and the importance of family dynamics for moral development. With respect to oral, anal, and phallic character types, there is evidence in support of such characterizations (e.g., Tribich & Messer, 1974; Fisher & Greenberg, 1977; Kline, 1972) but little support for the existence of psychosexual developmental stages per se. Certainly child-rearing procedures influence personality development (e.g., Hunt, 1979), but apparently not in the way envisioned by Freud.

The results of various investigations have also supported the existence of repression and other mechanisms of defense (see Maddi, 1972; Masling, 1983), but the role of penis envy in female psychology and the notion that males are more moral than females because males have resolved the Oedipus complex has not held up under research scrutiny.

Despite its ambiguities and the fuzziness of many of its concepts, which make empirical testing difficult, Freudian theory has obviously served to generate a great deal of research. In general, it can be said that such research has tended to support Freud's ideas concerning unconscious motivation, conflict, and certain aspects of dream functioning and analysis, as well as the dynamics of psychotherapy. But many of Freud's ideas concerning the importance of childhood sexuality and its role in personality development have failed to be confirmed.

Freudian theory has been criticized for being pessimistic with respect to human nature, for equating happiness with freedom from tension, for overemphasizing the role of biological influences (i.e., sexual and aggressive instincts) and unconscious factors in determining behavior, and for being inconsistent and in large measure untestable. As is true of many great personages, not everything that Freud said or believed is true. Nevertheless, he did penetrate further into the human psyche than anyone before him, and he made observers and students of human behavior aware of the complexity of personality. No thinker can completely divorce himself from his or her own time and culture, and many of Freud's insights concerning the unconscious, the role of sexual repression in shaping neuroses, and the existence of childhood sexuality were affected by the conservative Victorian era in which he lived and worked. However, Freudian theory is not necessarily less applicable in the late twentieth century than it was in the late nineteenth. Human psychology is not *that* unstable, but it does change with time and culture. Freud's greatest contribution, and his legacy, lies not in the specific ideas he presented, which were constantly undergoing revision during his lifetime, but rather in the enormous influence that he exerted on a generation of psychologists and thinkers in other disciplines concerned with human development and motivation.

Carl Jung and Analytic Psychology

Carl Gustaf Jung (1875–1961), the son of a poor pastor in the Swiss Reformed Church, was expected to follow in his father's footsteps and enter the ministry. Indeed, Carl Jung did maintain a lifelong interest in religion, but, rather than being attracted to the traditional religious life-style of his father and other family members, he found philosophy and psychiatry more appealing. After receiving his medical degree Jung became interested in spiritualism and the occult through the influence of a cousin who was a medium. Jung wrote his doctoral dissertation on this topic, and remained intrigued with mysticism until his death in 1961.

One of Jung's postdoctoral mentors was Eugen Bleuler, a famous psychiatric researcher who had coined the term *schizophrenia* for the mental disorder that had previously been known as dementia praecox. It was during this period of Jung's life that he began applying the word association technique, which Francis Galton and Wilhelm Wundt had pioneered some years before, in clinical contexts. Jung discovered that patients' verbal associations to various words were sometimes peculiar, illogical, and, because they contained sexual or other "immoral" content, often embarrassing to the respondent. To Jung, these verbal associations provided information concerning the operation of unconscious conflicts or *complexes*.

After reading Sigmund Freud's *Interpretation of Dreams*, Jung began a correspondence with Freud and eventually visited him in Vienna. The two men soon became friends and intellectual comrades, maintaining a close professional collaboration from 1907 to 1912. After their trip to America in 1909, Freud began grooming Jung to be his successor in the worldwide psychoanalytic movement. Jung received Freud's unqualified endorsement for the presidency of the International Psychoanalytical Association, a post which Jung assumed in 1911. But within a year or so it became apparent that the two men were going in different theoretical directions. In particular, Jung disagreed with Freud's emphasis on the sexual instinct as being the prime mover and shaper of human personality and behavior. By 1913 the disagreements between the two men culminated in a severing of their personal and professional relationship. Jung subsequently went through a three-year period of withdrawal and extended soul-searching, giving free reign to the introspective interests of his earlier years and experiencing something akin to a mental breakdown. In retrospect, it is clear that this was a period of intense creativity for Jung and a preparation for the path that he was to follow for the rest of his long professional career.

Personality Components

Certain of Jung's theoretical ideas bear the imprint of his association with Freud, but they are "Freudian" with a difference. For example, Jung's concepts of the *libido*, the *ego*, and the *unconscious* are similar to Freud's. But unlike Freud's notion of the libido as being sexual energy, the Jungian libido is a more general life energy. The Jungian ego, the conscious "I" or "me" of personality, is essentially identical to the Freudian ego, but the Jungian unconscious is divided into two parts: the personal unconscious and the collective unconscious. The *personal unconscious*, which is essentially the same as the Freudian *unconscious*, consists of memories of experiences in the individual's own lifetime that he or she has either repressed or forgotten. More complex than the personal unconscious is the *collective unconscious*, a part of the mind that is shared with all humanity, a storehouse of inherited, archaic molds (*archetypes*) and propensities from the evolutionary past. To quote Jung, the collective unconscious is "the depository of ancestral experience from untold millions of years, the echo of prehistoric world events to which each century adds an infinitesimally small amount of variation and differentiation" (Jung, 1928, p. 162).

The many different *archetypes* within the collective unconscious are inherited universal predispositions to respond to certain features of the world. Some of the archetypes, as they are revealed in dreams, fairy-tales, fantasies, delusions, myths, and religion, are birth, death, rebirth, power, magic, unity, the hero, the child, fire, water, the earth mother, the shadow, God, the demon, the old wise man, and the animal. Among the archetypes studied most intensively by Jung are the persona, the anima, the animus, the shadow, and the self. The *persona* is the mask that an individual shows to the outside world, the externally presented "me" or social self. Consistent with Jung's *principle of opposites* are the *anima,* which is the female component of the male psyche, and the *animus,* the male component of the female psyche. According to Jung, attaining a balance between anima and animus is a major goal of personality development.

Similar to the Freudian *id* is the archetype of the *shadow*—the primeval, animal nature of humanity. The demonic nature of the individual, or evil personified, is found in the shadow. The composite of all parts of the personality—ego, personal unconscious, and collective unconscious—constitutes the *self.* Symbolized by the *mandala* or circle (see Figure 5–3), the self represents the human effort to achieve unity or wholeness, an integration of the personality. The self unites opposing forces or propensities, such as the anima and the animus, or introversion and extroversion.

Like Freud, Jung saw human personality as the result of an internal struggle. But Jung's conception of the self reveals a more optimistic viewpoint than Freud's concerning the future of the individual and humanity in general. To Freud, personality was a battleground of continuing conflict between id, ego, and superego, and true harmony or peace between the conflicting forces was unlikely if not impossible to attain. Jung's *self,* with its striving for harmony, set the stage for later humanistic, or "third force," theories that are at odds with Freudian psychoanalysis concerning the goals and potentialities of human nature.

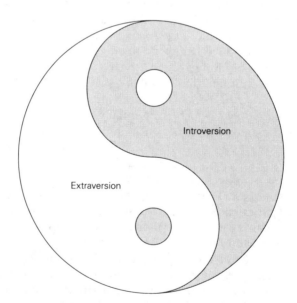

FIGURE 5–3 The unity of the self, the yin and yang of personality. (Figure from *Theories of Personality,* second edition, by Jess Feist. Copyright © 1990 by Holt, Rinehart and Winston, Inc. Reprinted by permission of the publisher.)

Orientations and Functions

From a more dynamic point of view, Jung maintained that the individual self could relate to the world by means of two orientations or attitudes: *introversion* (inwardly, toward the subjective world) or *extroversion* (outwardly, toward the external world of people and things). Complementing these two attitudes are four *functions* of thought: thinking, feeling, sensing, and intuiting. The first two are *rational functions,* and the last two are *irrational functions. Sensing,* which is concerned with detecting objects or things through sensory data, is the opposite of *intuiting,* which provides hunches or guesses about what something is when sensory data are not available. Likewise, *thinking* reveals what objects are, and *feeling* determines the worth of specific objects to a person.

Jung conceived of eight personality *types* resulting from the various combinations of the two attitudes and the four functions. These personality types are not separate or distinct, but are possessed in varying degrees by everyone. The eight types are the *thinking introvert,* the *thinking extrovert,* the *feeling introvert,* the *feeling extrovert,* the *sensing introvert,* the *sensing extrovert,* the *intuiting introvert,* and the *intuiting extrovert.* These types constitute the theoretical basis of the Myers-Briggs Type Indicator, a personality inventory that was described in Chapter 3 (see pages 62–63). The results of research using the Myers-Briggs Type Indicator are fairly consistent with Jung's theory of psychological types. Stricker and Ross (1964), for example, found that introverted types tend to enter technical and scientific fields, sensation types tend to enter practical fields, and feeling types tend to enter the helping professions.

Personality Development

Unlike Freud's conception of psychosexual developmental stages and their critical influences on adult character and personality, Jung's theory does not place much emphasis on stages in personality development. Jung discussed childhood (birth to adolescence), young adulthood (adolescence to middle age), middle age (age 40 to later years), and some of the lessons and tasks that must be mastered at these times, but the role of stage-specific conflicts and the associated notions of fixation and regression form no part of Jung's analytic psychology. Rather, he elaborated on the importance of *individuation,* in which, over time, people develop different degrees of introversion and extroversion and varying tendencies toward the four functions (sensing, intuiting, thinking, and feeling). Through the process of individuation, the person becomes aware of and gives expression to his or her attitudes, functions, and archetypes. The goal or aim of individuation is to attain a state of mental harmony, or *self-actualization,* a concept which was developed by later humanistic theorists.

Jung considered middle and later life as particularly important for the development of philosophical and spiritual values, a time when the search for the meaning of life becomes more focused. It is noteworthy that, in contrast to Freud's pessimism regarding the effectiveness of psychotherapy with older adults, Jung was a pioneer in applying psychotherapeutic techniques to the treatment of middle-aged and elderly people with psychological problems.

Jungian Therapy

As practiced by Jung, psychotherapy was an eclectic enterprise consisting of a variety of approaches and techniques. Eugen Bleuler, Sigmund Freud, and Alfred Adler all influenced Jung and his approach to psychotherapy, but Jung viewed what he had learned from these men in terms of a series of developmental stages. The first stage stemmed from Bleuler's emphasis on confession of a pathogenic secret and a resulting cathartic release of tension. The second stage, which involves interpretation, explanation, and insight, Jung attributed to Freud. The third stage, which emphasizes educating the patient as a social being, is due to Adler. The fourth and final stage, which was uniquely Jungian, involves a transformation of the patient to attain self-realization—an understanding of the inner self.

Jung employed both Freudian and Adlerian therapeutic techniques and concepts in the treatment of neurotics, especially those who were in the first half of life and experiencing sexual or power conflicts. However, in treating the loss of meaning, aimlessness, and fear of death in older patients, Jung focused on helping them to find a new philosophical orientation. Jung viewed the goal of psychotherapy with the mature person as helping him or her to find meaning and to attain balance and wholeness.

In any event, the overall aim of Jungian psychotherapy is to help the patient work toward self-realization. Among the techniques that may be useful in this regard are discussion, dream analysis, understanding the doctor-patient relationships (transference and countertransference), and encouraging the patient to experiment with his or her life. Jung noted, "My aim is to bring about a psychic state in which my patient begins to experiment with his own nature—a state of fluidity, change, and growth where nothing is externally fixed and hopelessly petrified" (Jung, 1931/1954, p. 46). In a sense, Jungian psychotherapy is an existential "I-thou" relationship in which two unique personalities make contact, and as a consequence both are transformed.

Evaluation of Jung

In many ways, Jung was a mystic, more in sympathy with the primitive shaman than the modern scientist. His fairly loose collection of theoretical ideas, and the acceptance of seemingly unscientific notions (e.g., teleology, entropy, the inheritance of acquired characteristics) contributed to making Jung's writings and psychotherapeutic procedures less popular than those of Freud, especially to the more pragmatic, empirically based community of American psychologists and psychiatrists. In addition to being mystical, Jungian theory has been criticized for its lack of clarity as well as its inconsistency and internal contradictions.

On the more positive side, Jung's writings have been a source of inspiration to anthropologists, artists, historians, and theologians. His notion of the collective unconscious, in particular, has served as the focal point of several novels, plays, and films. Furthermore, Jung's more optimistic viewpoint, together with the concepts of the self, self-actualization, and striving for psychic harmony, have influenced humanistic psychologists.

Although the number of Jungian analysts, throughout the world and especially in the United Kingdom, is substantial, compared with Freudian psychoanalysis Jung's analytic psychology has had relatively few adherents. As we shall see in the next chapter, it is principally Freudian, not Jungian, theory that has been revised and extended by twentieth-century psychiatrists and psychologists. Perhaps Freud was a stronger personality and a better organizer than Jung, or perhaps Freud's concepts are easier to understand and apply. On the other hand, the ascendancy of Freudian psychology may have been due simply to Freud's having had the good luck of getting there first, and consequently always being viewed as the teacher or mentor, with Jung being seen as the student or disciple. For whatever reasons, Freudian psychoanalysis has had a greater influence than Jungian analytic psychology, not only on psychology and psychiatry, but on social science and twentieth-century Western culture in general.

Summary

Advances in biological science during the late nineteenth century created an intellectual climate in Europe for the beginnings of a science of mind. Neurology, psychiatry, and psychology all contributed to these developments, and it was in this milieu that Sigmund Freud became interested in psychological explanations for disorders that previously had been treated by physical means. Freud's work with Breuer, Charcot, and other psychiatrists led to his clinical researches on hysteria, the unconscious, and a psychodynamic conception of the human mind. Using the clinical case study method, Freud formulated psychoanalytic theories of mental disorders such as hysteria, obsessive-compulsive neurosis, paranoid disorders, and phobias. Through the use of the methods of free association, dream analysis, the analysis of transference, and the analysis of resistance with psychoneurotic patients, he made progress in understanding unconscious motivation, repression, the structure of personality, and defense mechanisms.

Freud's three-part theory of personality structure includes the id, the ego, and the superego. The id is the reservoir of instinctive urges of sex and aggression and acts according to the pleasure principle. The ego is the "I" or "me," the conscious self of personality, which acts according to the reality principle. The superego, which consists of the conscience and the ego ideal, acts according to the moral principle. Conflicts between these three components of personality, coupled with the conflict between the ego and the external world, give rise to anxiety and subsequently to defense mechanisms, neuroses, and other mental problems.

Ego defense mechanisms are automatic, unconsciously prompted techniques for coping with intrapsychic conflict and anxiety. The most common defense mechanisms are denial, rationalization, identification, displacement, sublimation, reaction formation, projection, fantasy, and regression.

Dreams, which Freud considered the "royal road to the unconscience," have a manifest and a latent content. Dreams are attempts at wish fulfillment, but through various dreamwork processes the real (latent) meaning of the dream is consciously expressed in distorted form. The manifest content of a dream must be interpreted by the analyst and the analysand (the "patient") to yield information on the nature of the underlying wish and the roots of the analysand's problem. Insights into the functioning of personality can also be obtained by analyzing slips of the tongue, slips of the pen, jokes, selective forgetting, and other psychopathological clues in everyday behavior.

From its rather humble beginnings in Freud's Vienna home, during the first decade of this century psychoanalysis began to grow into an international movement with a worldwide influence on psychiatry, psychology, and other cultural disciplines. This growth did not, however, occur without controversy. Particularly controversial were Freud's notions of the primacy of the sexual instinct, the existence of infantile sexuality, and psychosexual stages of development. These psychosexual stages, through which Freud maintained all children pass on their way to sexual maturity, are the oral stage, the anal stage, the phallic stage, the latency stage, and the genital stage. Failure to resolve the conflicts and problems at a given stage can result in fixation at that stage or regression to an earlier stage. Freud maintained that the problems encountered during the various stages of psychosexual development place an indelible stamp on adult character and personality.

Freud was not content to be only a psychiatrist whose activities were limited to the consulting room and the psychoanalytic couch. His interests and influence spanned a wide range of disciplines, including archaeology, history, art, and religion. His views on religion, as enunciated in several books, are among his most speculative and controversial. Also, after World War I he went beyond the notion of the primacy of the sexual instinct (Eros) and included its polar opposite, aggression (Thanatos), as a second powerful instinct in shaping human personality.

Freud continually revised and extended his ideas during his own lifetime, a process that was continued by his students and followers. One of those students was Carl Jung, a Swiss psychiatrist who initially was a close collaborator of Freud. But Jung took issue with Freud on the primacy of the sex instinct and certain other theoretical matters, and the two men parted company in 1913. Jung subsequently developed his own analytic psychology, which was similar in some respects to Freudian psychoanalysis but more complex and mystical. In Jung's theory, the self consists of the conscious ego, the personal unconscious, and the collective unconscious. The collective unconscious, which is the (inherited) part of the unconscious mind containing ideas and images (archetypes) common to all people, is Jung's most controversial concept. Among the archetypes that Jung studied most closely are the persona (or public mask of personality), the anima (female side of male personality), the animus (male side of female personality), the shadow (similar to Freud's id), and the self. To Jung, mental harmony, or self-actualization, demands a satisfactory compromise between the various polar opposites in human nature.

Jung also differentiated between two orientations or attitudes (introversion and extroversion) and four functions (sensing, thinking, feeling, and intuiting), which in combination result in eight personality types. Also important in Jungian psychology is the concept of individuation, a developmental process in which the individual becomes aware of and gives expression to certain attitudes, functions, and archetypes.

Jung's analytic psychology has not been as well-received and consequently not as influential as Freudian psychoanalysis. Critics find Jung's ideas unclear, inconsistent, self-contradictory, and too mystical. However, his writings have influenced novelists, artists, historians, theologians, and film makers. Furthermore, Jungian psychotherapy continues to be practiced by a number of psychiatrists and psychologists throughout the world. Finally, Jung's optimistic conception of human nature and destiny, and in particular his concepts of the self and self-actualization, influenced humanistic theorists of a later generation.

Key Concepts

Archetype   In C. G. Jung's theory of personality, a collectively inherited, conscious idea, thought pattern, or image that is present in everyone.

Collective unconscious   According to Jung's analytical theory of personality, that part of the unconscious mind that contains material common to all people in a given culture. See *personal unconscious.*

Defense mechanisms   In psychodynamic theory, psychological techniques that defend the ego against anxiety, guilt, and a loss of self-esteem resulting from awareness of certain impulses or realities.

Dream analysis   In psychoanalysis, analyzing the manifest content of a dream to reveal the underlying latent content, including the patient's unconscious wishes and conflicts. The term *dreamwork* refers to various techniques, including condensation, displacement, distortion, and symbolism, used in a dream to disguise its real meaning.

Ego   In psychoanalytic theory, the executive, reality-oriented aspect of personality, which acts as a mediator between the id and superego.

Free association   In psychoanalytic therapy, the uncensored, uninhibited expression of ideas or feelings by the patient.

Id   In the psychoanalytic three-part theory of personality, the reservoir of instinctive impulses and strivings. The id, or "animal nature" of humans, is concerned only with immediate gratification of the pleasure and destructive impulses.

Oedipus complex   A composite of sexual feelings toward the mother and dislike of the father in a 3- to 6-year old boy, viewed by Freud as a universal phenomenon. The comparable situation in a girl, disliking the mother and loving the father, is referred to as the Electra complex.

Persona   In Carl Jung's analytical theory, the external or public personality that the individual presents to others to satisfy environmental demands, and not the real, inner personality.

Personal unconscious   In Carl Jung's theory of personality, that part of the unconscious mind that is unique to the individual. The individual is not immediately aware of his (her) personal unconscious, but can easily become so.

Psychoanalysis   As developed by Sigmund Freud, psychoanalysis is (1) a theory of personality concerned with the interaction between the conscious and unconscious; (2) a psychotherapeutic method for dealing with personality problems; and (3) a research method for studying personality.

Psychosexual stages   Sequence of stages in sexual development (oral, anal, phallic, latency, genital) characterized by a focus on different erogenous zones.

Shadow   In Jungian theory, the archetype representing the evil side of human nature.

Superego   In psychoanalytic theory, the part of the personality that acts according to the moral, idealistic principle, incorporating parental (societal) prohibitions and sanctions.

Unconscious   In psychoanalytic theory, that part of the personality that is below the level of conscious awareness and is brought into consciousness only in disguised form.

Activities and Applications

1. For a week, on awakening each morning, before you do anything else so they are still fresh in your mind, write out a description of the dreams that you had the night before. At the end of the week, read through the dreams and look for common themes in them. Taking a Freudian approach, try to analyze the manifest content of the dreams in terms of (a) the needs or desires that the dream is attempting to fulfill; (b) whether there are any symbols in the dreams and what they might mean; (c) what significance particular persons or other characters in the dream have for you; and (d) how the dream ends—happy, sad, uncertain, etc. Try free associating to the various elements of the dream. What do the characters and events in the dream remind you of—anything that has happened or occurred to you recently? What events in the day before or the recent past do you think triggered the dream? Can you see anything in the dream that is attempting to tell you something about the future, and your future in particular? Ask several friends to tell you about their dreams; treat them the same way as you did yours.

2. What defense mechanisms do you typically employ when your ego is threatened—rationalization, projection, fantasy, sublimation, displacement, etc.? Are these mechanisms generally effective in reducing your anxiety? Describe several instances when you engaged in psychologically defensive behavior.

3. What evidence can you cite from your personal experience showing that you have an unconscious mind? Can you remember any occasions on which you were "beside yourself" or acted irrationally without knowing why? Have unwanted or bizarre thoughts ever entered your mind? What other signs of your unconscious have you experienced?

4. Ask several friends whether they have ever made any "slips of the tongue," "slips of the pen," or other potentially embarrassing mistakes containing a sexual or aggressive component. Compare them with similar experiences that you have had.

5. Hold a pen or pencil in your hand on a piece of paper, and while you are reading or concentrating on something else just let your hand relax and do what it wants to do with the pencil. After approximately 30 minutes, look at the sheet of paper and see if you have written anything legible. If so, what do you think the "automatic writing" means?

6. Have you ever participated in a séance involving a ouija board? If so, describe the experience and whether the words that were spelled out could have been a reflection of the unconscious desires or conflicts of one or more of the participants.

7. If you own or can obtain a tape recorder, try talking into it for 30 minutes to an hour, simply saying anything that comes into your mind. Let your thoughts wander freely, saying whatever you feel like saying. After a while, play back the tape. What were your reactions to what you said? What do you think a psychoanalyst would say about it?

8. Do you believe in motivated forgetting, that is, that people sometimes forget the name of a person, an appointment, or some other fact or experience because recalling it would be too anxiety-arousing? Can you remember any personal experiences in which you forgot the name of someone who "gave you a bad time" or caused anxiety or embarrassment to you? Can you remember being late for a stressful appointment because you unconsciously wanted to miss it?

9. Construct a list of 25 words pertaining to matters of interest to people in your age group (e.g., college, grades, graduation, failure, sex, marriage, religion, mother, father, career, health) and administer it to a dozen acquaintances. Tell each person that you are going to read a list of words out loud, and that after each word is read the person should respond with the first word that comes to mind. Record the response time, in seconds, and the association given to each word. Summarize the results in terms of the number of responses of a particular kind given to each stimulus word, average response times, and insights provided into the personalities of the respondents.

10. In the book *Jokes and Their Relation to the Unconscious* (London: Hogarth Press, 1905b/1960), Freud analyzes the sources of many jokes as being unconscious sexual and aggressive wishes. Consider the jokes or humorous stories that you have heard or read. How many of them fit in the categories of sexual or aggressive jokes? Freud also argued that humorous stories or anecdotes build up tension which is released by the punch line, a kind of "delight of the ego," so to speak. Other researchers have noted that humorous stories are frequently funny because they describe incongruities. For example, it is not incongruous, and hence not funny, when a person dressed in a bathing suit falls into the water, but it is incongruous, and hence funny, when a person dressed in a tuxedo takes a dip. Comment on this assertion and provide other examples to support it.

Suggested Readings

Freud, S. (1900/1950). *The interpretation of dreams.* New York: Norton.

Freud, S. (1901/1965). *The psychopathology of everyday life.* New York: Norton.

Freud, S. (1923/1962). *The ego and the id.* New York: Norton.

Freud, S. (1930/1961). *Civilization and its discontents.* New York: Norton.

Freud, S. (1966). *The complete introductory lectures on psychoanalysis* (J. Strachey, Trans.). New York: Norton.

Gay, P. (1988). *Freud: A life for our time.* New York: Norton.

Hall, C. S., & Nordly, J. (1973). *A primer of Jungian psychology.* New York: New American Library.

Jacobi, J. (1973). *The psychology of C. G. Jung: An introduction with illustrations.* New Haven, CT: Yale University Press.

Jung, C. G. (1961). *Memories, dreams, reflections* (A. Jaffe, Ed.). New York: Random House.

Jung, C. G. (Ed.). (1964). *Man and his symbols.* New York: Dell.

Masson, J. M. (1984). *The assault on truth: Freud's suppression of the seduction theory.* New York: Farrar, Straus, and Giroux.

◈◈

CHAPTER 6

Psychodynamic Theories II: Adler and the Neoanalysts

CHAPTER OUTLINE

Almost from the moment of its inception Freud's psychoanalytic theory came under attack, not only from those outside the "inner circle," but also from some of Freud's closest colleagues and admirers. Although the loss of Jung, his chosen successor, probably affected Freud most of all, two other prominent members of the Vienna Psychoanalytic Society—Alfred Adler and Otto Rank—had also left the fold by the second decade of the new century. Otto Rank (1884–1939), who achieved widespread recognition for his elaboration of the Freudian conception of the role of the "birth trauma" in anxiety, drew widely from anthropological and historical sources in his writings. Rank, however, was not nearly as influential as Jung and Adler. A principal area of disagreement between Freud and these three men concerned the centrality of the sex instinct in shaping personality and psychoneuroses. Other areas of dispute were Freud's emphasis on the unconscious, his interpretation of the Oedipus complex, and his generally pessimistic, deterministic view of human nature.

Unlike the Ten Commandments, Freud's theory was not written in stone. Substantive changes were made even by the originator himself in the years following the departure of his erstwhile colleagues. Furthermore, other psychoanalysts who had studied under Freud or his students proposed modifications and reconstructions of the theory. These revised theories, however, retained much of the form and substance of classical psychoanalysis. For example, Freud's emphasis on the influence of the first five years of life on adult personality and the significance of dreams were retained in the theoretical writings and therapeutic practices of the revisionists.

Among the group of post-Freudians who became prominent in their own right were Freud's daughter, Anna, Heinz Hartmann, Karen Horney, Harry Stack Sullivan, Erik H. Erikson, and Erich Fromm. Hartmann is sometimes referred to as an *ego psychologist,* because of the greater status that he assigned to the conscious ego in contrast to Freud's emphasis on the unconscious id. Hartmann and other ego analysts expanded the functions of the ego beyond that of a mediator that reduces conflict between the id, the superego, and the external world. The ego was also seen by these analysts as operating in the *conflict-free sphere* of personality, where it promotes activities that assist the individual in adapting to the environment (Hartmann, 1939).

Horney, Sullivan, Erikson, and Fromm also emphasized the importance of consciousness and the ego. All four felt that Freud had overemphasized biological instincts and underestimated the role of social and cultural factors in personality development. Several of them also addressed questions concerning the meaning of life and the role of individual aspirations and goals in reaching one's potential, matters that Freud considered philosophical rather than scientific. In changing the emphasis from "sex" to "social" these *neoanalysts* followed the lead of Alfred Adler. Also like Adler, they took a more positive viewpoint toward human nature than that expressed by the founder of psychoanalysis. Finally, many neoanalysts, such as Erik Erikson, felt that Freud had neglected the effects of postchildhood experiences on personality. Although not denying the importance of the first five years of a person's life, Erikson viewed adolescence and early adulthood as a time for growth and change in personality. He also maintained that psychological growth continues throughout the life span.

Adler and Individual Psychology

Alfred Adler was born in a Viennese suburb in 1870 and died in Aberdeen, Scotland, in 1937. The son of a Jewish grain merchant, Alfred was a sickly child. He almost died of pneumonia when he was five, suffered from rickets, and was nearly killed on two occasions when he was run over by carts. Physical weakness and poor motor skills contributed to his inability to compete successfully in games and athletic contests with his older brother and other playmates. Perhaps his narrow escapes and lack of psychomotor dexterity were instrumental in Adler's decision to become a physician rather than a shoemaker.

Not only was the young Adler inept in sports; initially he was not the best of students. However, he worked hard, even mastering school mathematics after a struggle, was graduated from medical school, and shortly thereafter married a Russian socialist. He practiced ophthalmology for a time, but, as in Jung's case, was attracted to psychoanalysis when he read Freud's *Interpretation of Dreams*. Following Adler's positive review and defense of the book, Freud invited him to join the Wednesday Psychological Circle. In 1910, Adler became the first president of the Vienna Psychoanalytic Society, but he remained in that office for only one year. A disagreement with Freud led to Adler's resignation from the society in 1911. He subsequently founded his own group—the Society for Free Psychoanalytic Research (later called individual psychology) and formulated his own theory and methods of psychological treatment and research.

Adler's differences with Freud should have been obvious to both men as early as 1907, when Adler's essay "Organ Inferiority and Its Physical Compensation" was first published. This paper marked the real beginning of individual psychology, the first serious departure from Freudian psychoanalysis. In the book, Adler presented the thesis that real or imagined organ inferiorities are basic to the feelings of inferiority that characterize all human beings and hence the structure of personality.

Like Carl Jung and others, Adler disagreed with Freud on the importance of the sex instinct in personality and psychoneuroses. Furthermore, in contrast to the iceberg analogy of the Freudian mind, of which the conscious portion forms a much smaller part than the unconscious, Adler's conception of the mind is analogous to a jade tree with its small underground root system (unconscious) and extensive growth above ground (conscious) (see Figure 6–1).

Influenced by his wife and friends, Adler became involved in social causes and the plight of the lower classes of society in particular. He became interested in working with children and their families, and, after a stint as a medical officer in the Austrian army during World War I, he accepted a government commission to set up a series of child guidance clinics in Vienna. Subsequently he achieved international recognition as a child psychologist, an educational psychologist,

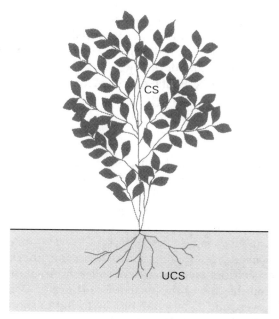

FIGURE 6–1   Adlerian conception of the mind. Unlike the Freudian concept (see Figure 5–2), which views human personality as analogous to an iceberg with most of its mass (the unconscious) below the surface, Adler thought of personality as being more like a jade tree having shallow roots but a luxuriant above-ground growth. (From Hall, C. S., Lindzey, G., Loehlin, J. C., & Manosevitz, M. *Introduction to theories of personality*. Copyright © 1985. Reprinted by permission of John Wiley & Sons, Inc.)

and a pioneer in family therapy. During his middle and later years Adler traveled and lectured widely, in addition to writing and pursuing his therapeutic practice. He settled in America in 1934 and died on a lecture tour in Scotland in 1937. Freud, who had a low tolerance for deviants from traditional psychoanalysis, never forgave Adler for his infidelity. After hearing of Adler's death Freud reportedly remarked that he (Freud) had been responsible for making the little Viennese Jewish boy famous.

Inferiority Complex

To Adler, human infants begin life with a sense of inferiority, a feeling that is never outgrown, no matter how long one's life may be. Adler considered the lifelong struggle to overcome feelings of inferiority, thereby attaining superiority and "perfection," to be the principal motive behind human behavior.

Striving for superiority was viewed as the fundamental fact and force in human nature, but the effort is not always successful. Physical obstacles and personal limitations interfere with one's strivings, and the resulting failures may result in an *inferiority complex*. Such feelings of being greatly inferior to other people and helpless compared with them may completely frustrate an individual's ambitions and lead him or her to retreat into self-absorption and neurosis. In his 1907 paper on organ inferiority, Adler emphasized the role of physical disabilities in creating an inferiority complex, but later he extended the causes of the complex to include limitations in mental abilities and other psychological factors.

Compensation

One method of coping with feelings of inferiority is by compensating. In *compensation,* a person attempts to overcome a real or imagined inferiority in one area by overemphasizing another kind of behavior. Thus the high school boy of average intelligence who is too small or too unskillful to make an athletic team may become a bookworm and overemphasize studying as a means of attaining social acceptability and self-esteem. In a variety of compensation known as *overcompensation,* an attempt is made to overcome inferiority by excessive correction or overperforming in the area of concern. An illustration of overcompensation is seen in the case of the ancient Greek orator Demosthenes. Demosthenes reportedly overcame a speech defect by trying to shout above the noise of sea waves while his mouth was full of pebbles, thus perfecting his elocutionary skills and becoming the greatest orator of his time. Other examples of overcompensation are certain athletic champions or bodybuilders (e.g., Charles Atlas) who were underdeveloped "98-pound weaklings" or sickly children but overcame their physical inferiority by hard work.

Masculine Protest

Another key concept in Adler's earlier writings was that of the *masculine protest*. This phenomenon, which was noted by Freud as well as by Adler, refers to the fact that many women would prefer to be men, while men want to be "real he-men." To Adler, the striving for superiority, and the associated belief that men are superior to women and must constantly prove it, lies at the heart of neurotic problems in both sexes. While Freud viewed the masculine protest as the result of penis envy in women and the castration complex in men, Adler included the concept of masculine protest under the striving for power or superiority. Although Adler perhaps merits the chauvinistic label less than Freud, both men viewed males as superior to females and hence would probably be labeled as male chauvinists by feminists of today.

Child Development

Like Freud, Adler believed that the first five years of life set the stage for later psychological development. If the young child is pampered or neglected (rejected) he will become spoiled on the one hand or cold and unsympathetic on the other. Pampered children, who grow up expecting other people to conform to their desires, tend to be demanding and to have a low tolerance for frustration. They are immature, egocentric, and generally uncooperative. In contrast, rejected children view the world as a threatening, hostile place that must be combated with hostility, distrust, and uncooperativeness. Pampered children are likely to become demanding, infantile neurotics who take without giving, whereas rejected children, who are dominated by the need for revenge, often become delinquents and criminals.

Adler believed that the way in which a child is treated in the family—that is, whether he or she is pampered, neglected, or responded to in some other way—depends to some extent on the child's birth order. Parents tend to pamper both an only child and the youngest child. "Babying, spoiling, and overprotecting" are descriptive of the way in which the youngest child is treated. But the oldest child is likely to be treated more maturely by the parents, and greater maturity and responsibility are expected of him or her. However, all is not well with the oldest child, and he or she, like the only child and the youngest child, has a good chance of becoming neurotic. By being displaced in his parents' affections by younger siblings, the oldest child may come to feel like a deposed monarch and consequently suffer feelings of rejection.

Adler, who himself was a middle child, believed that parental treatment of the middle child tends to be more relaxed. Unlike the oldest child, the middle child has never been the object of exclusive attention by the parents and hence is less likely to be upset or jealous of a younger sibling. Middle children are not always in a happy position, but, according to Adler, as a consequence of their birth order they are generally more cooperative and compromising than first-born and last-born children.

Life-styles and Goals

As children grow and mature, they develop unique *life-styles*, or manners of living consisting of learned approaches to life's demands and techniques of coping with real or imagined inferiorities. A person's life-style is organized and directed by the *creative self*. This self acts and reacts in accordance with the person's *fictional finalisms*, the goals or ends to which the person aspires. The life-style of the person becomes the means by which these fictional finalisms must be attained. The concept of *fictional finalism* was adopted by Adler after reading Hans Vaihinger's (1911) book on *The Philosophy of "As If."* In this book, Vaihinger contended that the actions of people are guided by fictions that they invent to make their lives seem important and directed. For example, a person may act as if he were destined to become a great leader or artist in spite of his lack of success in politics or painting. Such beliefs are not necessarily true, but the person's behavior or life-style is organized and controlled by the idea that the beliefs are more than convenient fictions.

As the concept of fictional finalism makes clear, Adler's theory of development is teleological, in that it focuses on ends, goals, and expectations. Personality is seen as being pulled by the future rather than simply pushed by the past. In this respect as well, Adler anticipated the position of psychological humanists of a later day. Also like the humanists, Adler had an optimistic, purposive view of humanity. People were seen not simply as deterministic dandelions blown this way and that by the winds of heredity and childhood experience, but rather as striving toward goals of their own invention and with the capacity to change their personalities at any time. Because people have control over their futures, they are responsible, at least to some extent, for what happens to them and what they become.

Adler recognized, however, that a person's chosen life-style may be wrong or mistaken for both that person and society. People attempt to safeguard their *mistaken life-styles* by various stratagems (excuses, aggression, distancing, etc.), but these are usually unsuccessful in the long run. In the short run, making excuses (i.e., *rationalization*) may serve to justify the inadequacy of one's behavior, but this *safeguarding strategy* is rarely permanently effective. A second safeguarding strategy, *aggression,* which may involve the deprecation and accusation of others as well as self-accusation, can result in neurosis. A third strategy, *distancing,* which represents an attempt to escape from problems by creating psychological "space" between oneself and them, is also typically ineffective in the long run and characteristic of a neurotic life-style.

By failing to focus on the needs and interests of other people and not merely on one's own needs and preferences, the individual may develop any one of several *mistaken life-styles.* Among these are the *ruling-dominant type,* the *getting-leaning type,* and the *avoiding type.* The ruling-dominant type tries to dominate or control other people, the getting-leaning type exploits others, and the avoiding type avoids problems and potential failure by never trying or taking chances.

To Adler, the most adaptive and productive life-style is the *socially useful type.* Only by developing a genuine *social interest,* a deep concern for the welfare of others, can the individual attain lasting happiness. Only through such a community feeling or sense of being at one with all human beings, can the three major tasks or problems of life—education and work, sex and marriage, family and neighborly love—be accomplished or resolved.[1] Attaining a true social interest facilitates a healthy striving for superiority, but failure to develop a feeling of community results in maladaptive functioning:

> All failures—neurotics, psychotics, criminals, drunkards, problem children, suicides, perverts, and prostitutes—are failures because they are lacking in social interest. They approach the problems of occupation, friendship and sex without the confidence that they can be solved by cooperation. The meaning they give to life is a private meaning. No one else is benefited by the achievement of their aims. . . . Their goal of success is a goal of personal superiority, and their triumphs have meaning only to themselves. (Ansbacher & Ansbacher, 1956, p. 156)

Methods and Evaluation

In his role as a child psychotherapist, Adler placed little emphasis on the classical psychoanalytic techniques of free association and dreams. Rather, in therapy and with parents of problem children, he preferred to explore childhood experiences and feelings by discussion and observation. Reports of first memories, or earliest recollections, were considered especially helpful. Whether or not those memories were true, they revealed the patient's motivations, life-style, and problems. In addition, such matters as sibling rivalry, pampering, rejection, and inferiority feelings were explored in discussions with the patient and others. Adler preferred more direct, commonsense techniques such as reassurance and encouragement to help patients cope with their feelings of inferiority, along with recognition of the importance of focusing on the needs of others rather than solely one's own problems. Through these and other therapeutic techniques, including a mature, reciprocal understanding relationship between the patient and the therapist, Adler tried to foster the self-esteem, courage, responsibility, and social interest of the patient.

The popularity of Adler's psychology has periodically waxed and waned over the years. Today, the membership of the American Society for Individual Psychology, combined with that of Adlerian societies in Canada and Europe, numbers in the thousands. Among the several publications that promote Adlerian psychology is the *Journal of Individual Psychology*.

Critics of Adler's individual psychology have pointed to a lack of operationally defined terms, the somewhat disorganized, unsystematic nature of his theorizing, and consequently the difficulty of testing the theory's propositions and predictions through empirical research. One idea for which research has provided some support is that of the relationship between birth order and personality. Although early investigations failed to confirm much of what Adler postulated concerning the personality characteristics of oldest, youngest, and middle children in families, more recent studies by Stanley Schachter and others have found that, in conjunction with sex and family size, birth order is related to personality (see Vockell, Felker, & Miley, 1973; Ernst & Angst, 1983). For example, in a series of studies concerned with the relationship between anxiety and the need to affiliate, Schachter (1959) showed that, when told that they were going to receive a mild electric shock in a short while, 80 percent of firstborn college students chose to wait together, whereas only 31 percent of later-borns elected to do so. Schachter attributed this difference to a greater need on the part of firstborns to affiliate when anxious, and hence to their greater social orientation.

It has also been found that, compared with later-borns, firstborns are more likely to become alcoholic and to seek psychotherapeutic help (Barry & Blane, 1977), but less likely to enter high-risk occupations such as those of fighter pilot or skydiver (Freedman, 1982). In general, these results are consistent with the conclusions from earlier investigations that firstborns are more anxious and more likely to see social contact as a means of coping with their anxieties (Hoyt & Raven, 1973). These findings are understandable within the framework of Adlerian theory.

The theory and practice of individual psychology are not as clear-cut as classical psychoanalysis, and hence there has been less effort to test the propositions of the theory and or to determine the effectiveness of Adlerian psychotherapy. Despite its shortcomings as a theory, individual psychology has provided an easily understood explanation of human behavior and personality with a great deal of popular appeal. Adler's successors have focused on the fields of clinical and educational psychology and psychiatry, but his influence has been more widespread. For example, in speaking of "the search for glory," Karen Horney (1950) noted that Alfred Adler "was the first psychoanalyst to see it as a comprehensive phenomenon, and to point out its crucial significance in neuroses." Even more comprehensive in its praise was Meerloo's (1970) conclusion:

> We are all plagiarists, though we hate to confess it. Adler's terms and concepts are even used by those who defy him: inferiority complex, compensation, childhood memories, masculine protest, life style. These are only a few. The whole body of social psychiatry would have been impossible without Adler's pioneering zest. (p. 40)

Horney and the Neurotic Personality

Karen Horney (née Danielsen) was born in 1885 in a small town near Hamburg, Germany. Her parents were somewhat of an odd couple: Her father was a rather stern, devoutly religious sea captain, but her mother was a fairly outspoken woman who believed in women's rights and encouraged Karen to assert herself competitively. The only other child in the family was a brother, four years Karen's senior and reportedly the parents' favorite.

After attending the *Gymnasium* for her preparatory work, in 1906 Karen entered the University of Freiburg to study medicine. She was graduated with her medical degree, and soon afterward married Oskar Horney, a friend from her undergraduate days. Karen pursued postgraduate studies with Karl Abraham, a student of Freud, and wrote her first paper on psychoanalysis in 1917. In part because of economic problems, her marriage did not last; she and Oskar were separated in 1924 and divorced in 1939. Karen moved to New York City in 1934, where she taught at the New School for Social Research and became a member of the New York Psychoanalytic Institute. However, criticism by the institute members for her unorthodox views concerning psychoanalysis led to her resignation in 1941. She subsequently formed a rival organization, the Association for the Advancement of Psychoanalysis, and achieved worldwide fame for her writings and lectures on neurosis and feminine psychology. She died of cancer in 1952.

The following were the most influential of Horney's books:

> 1937—*The Neurotic Personality of Our Time*
> 1939—*New Ways in Psychoanalysis*
> 1942—*Self-Analysis*
> 1945—*Our Inner Conflicts*
> 1950—*Neurosis and Human Growth*
> 1923–1937/1967—*Feminine Psychology*

Neurosis and Human Growth was her most scholarly work, but *Self-Analysis,* which was the first self-help book on how to psychoanalyze oneself, was perhaps her most popular.

Basic Anxiety and Neurotic Trends

One of Horney's fundamental concepts is that of *basic anxiety,* a feeling resulting from "being isolated and helpless in a potentially hostile world." To Horney, basic anxiety is not inborn, but is produced by culture and the way in which the child is brought up. Basic anxiety is made more acute by the failure of the parents to provide warmth and affection to the child, leading to resentment and anger on the part of the child. However, the feelings of hostility felt by the mistreated child are repressed when he or she realizes that even more love and security will be lost if those negative feelings are not repressed. Unfortunately, this effort leads to further basic anxiety and hostility, then to an excessive need for affection and a demand for unconditional love, then to feelings on the part of the child of being rejected when its demands are not met. The child's reaction to this perceived rejection is intensified hostility, followed by a need to repress that hostility to avoid losing more love and security, followed by tension and rage, then to basic anxiety and basic hostility, and so on, in a never-ending circle.

The degree of basic anxiety felt by the child is greatly affected by the attitudes of the parents and the treatment accorded the child. Parents may encourage these feelings of anxiety by

> direct or indirect domination, indifference, erratic behavior, lack of respect for the child's individual needs, lack of real guidance, disparaging attitudes, too much admiration or the absence of it, lack of reliable warmth, having to take sides in parental disagreements, too much or too little responsibility, overprotection, isolation from other children, injustice, discrimination, unkept promises, hostile atmosphere, and . . . [a] sense of lurking hypocrisy in the environment. (Horney, 1945, p. 41)

Thus the child is frequently in a state of intrapsychic conflict, a notion which Horney adapted from Freud and viewed as the basis of neurotic behavior.

In an effort to cope with the anxiety stemming from feelings of inadequacy and conflict, the individual begins to reveal certain neurotic needs in his or her behavior. Horney described ten neurotic needs:

1 A need for affection and approval
2 A need for a partner who will control one's life
3 A need to live one's life within narrow limits
4 A need for power
5 A need to exploit others
6 A need for social recognition and prestige
7 A need for personal admiration
8 A need for ambition and personal achievement
9 A need for self-sufficiency and independence
10 A need for perfection and unassailability

These ten needs are, of course, not exclusively neurotic; normal people also experience these needs and attempt to satisfy them. But the neurotic tends to focus on one need exclusively, setting aside or repressing the remaining ones.

In her later writings, Horney combined these ten needs into three neurotic patterns or trends. As with the neurotic needs, a normal person employs these three strategies or orientations in balance, but neurotics emphasize one strategy while repressing the other two.

Moving toward People. The first three neurotic needs listed (1–3) are grouped in the category of "moving toward people." The *compliant type,* who is descriptive of this category, says in effect, "If I give in, I shall not be hurt" (Horney, 1937, p. 97). Such people manifest a strong need for approval and affection from other people, which they get by constantly striving to please and defer to others. Compliant types want to be taken care of, protected, guided, and loved ("clingingly").

Moving against People. The next four neurotic needs listed (4–7) are grouped into the category of "moving against people." The characteristic personality represented by this category is labeled the *hostile type.* The person seems to be saying, "If I have power, no one can hurt me" (Horney, 1937, p. 98). Such an individual has a seemingly insatiable need for power, to exploit other people so he or she can feel superior all the time. To the hostile type, people are meant to be exploited, their weaknesses are to be taken advantage of, and their power is to be seized.

Moving away from People. The last three neurotic needs listed (8–10) fall in the category of "moving away from people." These personalities are referred to as the *detached type,* who says, "If I withdraw, nothing can hurt me" (Horney, 1937, p. 99). They have learned to cope with anxiety by becoming detached, aloof, uninvolved, self-sufficient, and independent of other people. Their desire for privacy is strong, and it is difficult for even the most persistent person to break through that wall.

The *idealized self-images* reflected in these three trends underscore the neurotic's pride and *search for glory.* Unfortunately for the neurotic, the images are impossible to live up to. The compliant, self-effacing type, who moves toward others and is constantly in search of love, has an idealized self-image of being a "generous, good, humble, kind, loving, self-sacrificing, sympathetic, unselfish" individual. The hostile type, who seeks power and control over other people, has an idealized self-image of being "all-powerful and invincible, needing no one's help and being intellectually, physically, and morally superior" to them. The detached type, who seeks to avoid relationships with others, has an idealized self-image of being "independent, free of desires and passions, resourceful, self-contained, self-sufficient, true to oneself, and unique" (Horney, 1942, 1945, 1950).

The neurotic's idealized self-image is governed by a number of unrealistic *shoulds.* The compliant type believes that any love relationship "should" be developed into one of perfect harmony, that one "should" make his (her) partner love him (her), and that one "should" not attempt to get more than one already has. The hostile type believes that he or she "should" accomplish any task, and "should" solve any problem or handle any situation, no matter how difficult or complex it might be. Everything "should" be conquered by sheer will, and one "should" always be right. Finally, the detached type believes that he or she "should" forgo all pleasure, "should" not become emotionally involved with anyone, and "should not" have to adjust to the needs of others. These "shoulds" can become quite tyrannical, dominating one's thoughts and leading one to believe that he or she should be perfectly right, successful, loving, unselfish, and so on all the time.

Clearly, the neurotic's quest for an idealized self-image is almost certain to fail. Such failure, however, is not taken lying down. The neurotic perseveres toward the idealized self-image, making the *neurotic claim* of entitlement to the triumphs and rewards of that image.

Externalization

Any neurotic or normal individual may come to feel that one's influence on his or her own life is limited and that the major influences are outside or external to oneself. This attitude, which Horney called *externalization*, is similar to Julian Rotter's concept of locus of control (see Chapter 8).

With respect to the neurotic trends, the compliant type externalizes anger, hostility, and self-hate, seeing them as coming from outside rather than inside oneself; the hostile type externalizes fear, anxiety, and helplessness; and the detached type externalizes demands for submission and interference with one's life. By externalizing or disowning these impulses and feelings within oneself, the neurotic can better maintain an idealized self-image.

Externalization is only one of several techniques that neurotics use to deal with conflicts that occur when the real self is not consonant with the idealized self-image. Other protective psychological techniques, similar to the Freudian ego defense mechanisms, are blind spots (denial), compartmentalization (applying different rules to different "compartments" in one's life), rationalization, excessive self-control, arbitrary rightness (selecting one answer or position and dogmatically sticking with it), elusiveness (postponing decision making), and cynicism (believing in nothing).

Comparison with Freud

Like other neoanalysts, Horney retained many Freudian concepts, in particular the notions of the unconscious, the role of conflict in neurosis, and the importance of childhood experiences in shaping personality. However, like Adler, Horney disagreed with the Freudian emphasis on sexuality and the Oedipus complex. She also took issue with Freud's psychology of women, and specifically the notion of penis envy.

Reinterpreting the Oedipus complex in terms of anxiety, insecurity, and social factors, Horney (1939) stated:

> The typical conflict leading to anxiety in a child is that between dependency on the parents . . . and hostile impulses against the parents. Hostility may be aroused in a child in many ways: by the parents' lack of respect . . . ; by unreasonable demands and prohibitions; by injustice; by unreliability; by suppression of criticism; by the parents dominating . . . and ascribing these tendencies to love. . . . If a child, in addition to being dependent on . . . parents, is grossly or subtly intimidated by them and hence feels that any expression of hostile impulses against them endangers . . . security, then the existence of such hostile impulses is bound to create anxiety. . . . The resulting picture may look exactly like what Freud describes as the Oedipus complex: passionate clinging to one parent and jealousy toward the other or toward anyone interfering with the claim of exclusive possession. . . . But the dynamic structure of these attachments is entirely different from what Freud conceives as the Oedipus complex. They are an early manifestation of neurotic conflicts rather than a primarily sexual phenomenon. (pp. 81–83)

Horney also criticized Freud's interpretation of feminine psychology, as well as the supposedly weaker moral sense of the fairer sex, in terms of penis envy and the associated Electra complex. She maintained that Freud's image of women had been distorted by the Victorian era in which he lived as a young man and by his exclusive reliance on observations of neurotic women in formulating his feminine psychology. To Horney, both sexes are probably somewhat envious of the other, men being envious of women for their breasts and ability to have children (*womb envy*) (Horney, 1967). However, to Horney, the psychological differences between the sexes are due primarily to social or cultural conditioning and not to invidious comparisons of sex organs. The manner in which females are socialized in a male-dominant society leads to problems of self-confidence and an overdependence on love and compassion rather than aggression and achievement in coping with problems.

Evaluation and Research

Horney's theory of neurosis is parsimonious, in that she employs relatively few concepts. The theory is also limited in its applications and synthesis of research data pertaining to the causes, progress, and treatment of neurotic disorders (Feist, 1990). Horney admittedly did not set out to develop a general theory of personality that could be applied to all people—neurotics and nonneurotics alike. In addition, she stated very few hypotheses in a form that would encourage testing by researchers. Consequently, the theory has stimulated very little research. By creating a kind of amalgam of Freudian and Adlerian ideas in an understandable way, Horney's books have served as effective teaching manuals for psychotherapists who work with neurotic patients.

Beyond her specific theorizing, Horney's writings served to promote greater interest in the role of sociocultural factors in neuroses and inspired feminists and other supporters of women's rights in a later generation. Furthermore, her general positiveness and optimism concerning humanity and its future, and her belief that people possess an inborn drive for self-realization were consistent with the humanistic psychology movement of the 1960s. Her writings were often cited by those humanists who looked for support in the psychoanalytic camp.

Sullivan and Interpersonal Theory

Harry Stack Sullivan (1892–1949), the first American psychiatrist to formulate a theory of personality, was born in Norwich, New York. Sullivan's childhood was not particularly happy; his mother apparently spent a year as a patient in a psychiatric hospital, and Sullivan himself was probably mentally ill for a time. His undergraduate education consisted of less than a year at Cornell University; for both academic and nonacademic reasons, he left Cornell during his second term. In 1915 he gained admission to a small medical school in Chicago, and he received his medical degree in 1917. After graduating from medical school he worked as a psychiatrist in mental hospitals in Baltimore and Washington, D.C., and spent several years in private psychiatric practice in New York.

Sullivan was neither a prolific nor a very skilled writer, but he was a successful therapist, an original thinker, an excellent teacher, and an expert organizer. By the late 1940s he had become quite prominent in American psychiatry and on the international scene as well. His theorizing and practice were greatly influenced by William Alanson White and the Chicago school of sociology. As enunciated by C. H. Cooley, G. H. Mead, and others, the *symbolic interactionism* of the Chicago school conceived of human personality as the result of individual perceptions of how one is seen by others (*reflected appraisals*). Other people were described as "looking glasses" in which we see our attributes and actions approved or disapproved; these reflections prompt us to shape and change what we are and what we think of ourselves.

Sullivan was trained as a psychoanalyst in the 1930s, but his approach was not orthodox Freudian. The one book, *Conceptions of Modern Psychiatry* (1947), that he published during his lifetime and a five-volume posthumously published series containing his lectures describe a conception of personality that is somewhere between classical psychoanalysis and social learning theory. Sullivan's practical experience was principally with schizophrenic patients, with whom he had notable treatment success. It was this work, in addition to his reading and personal associations, that stimulated Sullivan to develop the interpersonal theory of psychiatry. In psychotherapeutic sessions with mental patients he employed the method of *participant observation,* attempting to enter the special world of the patient while maintaining objectivity as a scientific observer.

Personification and the Self

In keeping with an emphasis on interpersonal factors, Sullivan defined personality as "the relatively enduring pattern of recurrent interpersonal situations which characterize a human life" (Sullivan, 1953, p. 11). As this definition implies, Sullivan saw personality as existing only in the presence of real or imagined interpersonal relations. Beginning with infancy, the particular ways of thinking and acting that characterize a person develop from interactions with others.

Sullivan maintained that every situation is an interpersonal one. Even when a person is alone, he or she is responding to past experiences with people and interacting with introjected, internal representations of those people. From these internalized, interpersonal representations the individual develops an image of the *self* and other *personifications*. Satisfying social interactions lead to positive personifications, and unsatisfying social interactions, which are accompanied by anxiety and fear, lead to negative personifications.

As with other personifications (e.g., the "good mother" or "bad mother"), the *self* may be viewed as either positive ("good me") or negative ("bad me"), depending on whether the individual's actions are responded to in a positive or a negative manner by other people. Satisfying experiences, such as being fed and cuddled by mother, enhance the "good me," while disappointing or frustrating experiences enhance the "bad me." In addition to a "good me," about which the person feels good, and a "bad me," about which he or she feels bad, everyone possesses a "not me." The "not me" comprises characteristics and behaviors which the person disowns or from which he or she becomes dissociated. Unlike the conscious "good me" and "bad me," the "not me" is unconscious. Although personifications such as the "good me" or the "bad mother" are imaginary, the child carries on interpersonal exchanges with them as if they were real. In fact, unresolved arguments with the "introjected" persons may continue long after they have disappeared or died.

Dynamisms

Formation of the self and other personifications is driven by *dynamisms*—habitual or characteristic ways of behaving in particular social situations. Dynamisms, the smallest meaningful units of study of an individual, are directed toward attainment of satisfaction and security. Satisfaction results from reduction of a biological drive, and security results from reduction of a social drive. Frustration of either the drive for satisfaction or security increases the individual's anxiety level.

Examples of dynamisms in Sullivan's theory are the self and selective attention. The individual *self* is concerned above all else with controlling anxiety by achieving security. It must constantly monitor and regulate one's interpersonal activities because ineffective interpersonal activities increase anxiety and feelings of insecurity. However, a preoccupation with security can lead to distorted perceptions in the interpersonal arena. Perceptions can be distorted, and anxiety controlled, through various defensive tactics. One such tactic is *selective inattention* or dissociation, that is, simply ignoring or rejecting anxiety-provoking information and experiences. Although selective inattention and other distortions help to control anxiety, they also create misunderstandings. The ultimate result of these misunderstandings is a decline in mental health, which must be restored by improving the person's awareness of his or her interpersonal relations.

Modes of Experiencing

From his observations and interactions with schizophrenics and developing children, Sullivan formulated a distinction between three modes of experiencing—prototaxic, parataxic, and syntaxic. The *prototaxic mode* of experiencing consists of the sensations, images, and feelings that constitute the "stream of consciousness"—experiences that are not tied to logic or linguistic symbolization. This primitive, undifferentiated mode of experiencing, which is characteristic of infants and young children, is private and presymbolic and hence cannot be communicated to other people.

As the young child grows, a *parataxic mode,* a kind of transitional stage of experiencing, develops. In this mode of cognition, a primitive associational sense of causality, aided by the development of language usage, takes place. However, even when cause and effect are not present, they are attributed on the basis of association or contiguity in space and time alone. In the parataxic mode of experiencing, the meanings of many of the individual's utterances are subjective and personalistic, and thereby fail to be communicated accurately.

Parataxic distortions occur when the individual misperceives, mislabels, and misunderstands personifications of the self or others in order to reduce the anxiety produced by certain features of these personifications. Such distortions, which serve to isolate and temporarily protect the self from both its own nature and its relationships with other people, are facilitated by the private, idiosyncratic usage of language in the parataxic mode of experiencing. An extreme example of parataxic distortion is seen in hebephrenic schizophrenia, a thought disorder in which the patient's confused thinking is manifested by the use of non sequiturs, neologisms, word salads, and confabulations. To Sullivan, only by being a participant observer in the world of the schizophrenic can one assist the patient in becoming aware of his or her own self and others and consequently regain mental health.

In normal cognitive development, the child eventually reaches the *syntaxic mode* of experiencing, in which experiences are accurately communicated to others by means of language and as a result can become consensually validated. To attain mental health, a schizophrenic or other emotionally disturbed person must learn the syntaxic mode of experiencing and have his or her experiences validated by interpersonal interactions.

Developmental Epochs

Like Freud, Sullivan emphasized the importance of the first few years of life for personality development. Sullivan believed, however, that social institutions and other influences can have profound effects on personality throughout the life span, particularly during middle childhood and adolescence.

In his life-span schema of personality development, Sullivan delineated seven developmental epochs: infancy, childhood, juvenile, preadolescence, early adolescence, late adolescence, and adulthood. During *infancy,* which lasts from birth until one year of age, the child's empathic perceptions of the moods and feelings of the parents and significant others stimulate the development of the sense of self-esteem. This period ends with the beginnings of articulate speech.

The major task of *childhood* (2–5 years) is the development of language and socialization. The child learns to attain a sense of security by adhering to parental injunctions and by manipulating other people. The *juvenile* period (6–8 years) is marked by socialization beyond the home. A need for playmates is expressed, and the child learns about competition, cooperation, and rejection. During *preadolescence* (9–12 years), the need for companions expands to a need for an intimate relationship with a person of the same sex, a "pal," "buddy," or "best friend." This need represents the transition from an exclusively self-centered orientation to a more other-centered orientation and the beginnings of love.

Early adolescence is marked by an increase in the sex drive and a need for an intimate relationship with a person of the opposite sex. Early adolescence is followed by *late adolescence* (18–early 20s), in which the individual becomes interested in a long-term sexual relationship, an occupation or profession, and financial security. The final developmental stage, in which, at long last, the individual has been changed by means of interpersonal interactions from an animal to a human being, is *adulthood*. During this stage, a career, friendships, and a relatively permanent sexual relationship are achieved.

Evaluation

Similar to many other prominent individuals, much of Sullivan's fame was achieved posthumously. His reputation was nurtured by students, colleagues, and admirers who collected his lectures and other materials into a five-volume series (Sullivan, 1953, 1954, 1956, 1962, 1964). Despite his keen clinical insights and theoretical concepts, little research has been generated by Sullivan's theory. On the other hand, his writings have continued to be useful in training psychiatrists and clinical psychologists, especially those with a more psychoanalytic orientation.

Erikson and Psychosocial Stages

Erik Homberger Erikson was born in Frankfurt, Germany, in 1902, the son of a Danish father and a Jewish mother. The father abandoned the mother even before Erik was born, and three years later she married Theodore Homberger. Young Erik was not told until some years later who his real father was, an event which, according to his own admission, precipitated an identity crisis. The incongruity of his Nordic, "goy" appearance in a Jewish family and among Jewish schoolchildren and playmates also reportedly contributed to Erik's identity problems.

In terms of formal degrees, Erik Erikson received only the equivalent of a high school diploma, but he was well-educated in the book of life. As a young man, he dabbled at being an artist, traveled widely, and became credentialed as a Montessori teacher. He worked for a while as a teacher of young children, in which capacity he met Anna Freud, a prominent child psychiatrist and the daughter of Sigmund Freud. Anna introduced Erik to her father, and, after serving for a time as Freud's chauffeur, in 1933 Erik completed his psychoanalytic training. Shortly thereafter he emigrated to the United States, working and teaching at various universities in New England and California, including Yale, Harvard, and the University of California at Berkeley, and at the prestigious Austin Riggs Center. He conducted a number of field studies of Native American children, and in 1950 wrote his now famous book *Childhood and Society*. In addition to being a practicing child psychoanalyst, a teacher, and a personality theorist, Erikson's books on Martin Luther (*Young Man Luther*, 1958) and Mohandas K. Gandhi (*Gandhi's Truth*, 1969) established his reputation as a psychohistorian.

Ego Psychology

The question of who was the "father of ego psychology," Alfred Adler, Heinz Hartmann, or Erik Erikson, is moot but not critical. A case can be made for Erikson, who, in his analysis of human development, went beyond both classical psychoanalysis and the early revisionists in emphasizing the effects of society and culture on the ego. Although Erikson viewed his work as an extension of rather than a departure from Freudian psychoanalysis, he is actually more in tune with Hartmann and Anna Freud in his emphasis on the ego as opposed to the id. To Erikson, not only does the ego influence the cognitive and social development of the individual, it also affects the sense of self-awareness and identity. He maintained that the ego is so important that psychotherapy should focus on the goal of strengthening the conscious ego rather than attempting to gain insight into the unconscious id and superego.

Psychosocial Stages

Erikson is best known for his analysis of eight stages in psychosocial development and the crises (turning points or conflicts) and goals of each stage. The manner in which the person resolves each crisis affects the direction that personality development takes and how further crises are resolved.

Erikson believed that personality development continues from "womb to tomb," taking place in a series of stages through which the individual may pass successfully or unsuccessfully. Basic to his conception of stages in personality development is a principle borrowed from embryology, that of *epigenesis*. According to this principle, the components comprising an organism develop in sequence, one from the other. As applied to the notion of psychosocial stages, epigenesis means that the ground plan for each stage is present from birth, but that the stages evolve with time and that each stage contains all the others. Thus Erikson's stages are not to be viewed as discrete entities but rather as progressively inclusive with different emphases at different stages.

As listed in Table 6–1, the eight psychosocial stages are infancy (birth–1 year), early childhood (1–3 years), play age (4–5 years), school age (6–11 years), adolescence (12–20 years), young adulthood (20–24 years), middle age (25–64 years), and old age (65–death). During each stage a particular crisis or conflict becomes predominant and must be resolved if psychological development is to proceed normally. Erikson saw each stage as characterized by the emergence of an attribute or virtue that assists the child in coping with problems of development.

The major conflict of *infancy* is basic *trust versus mistrust*—that is, whether, by receiving nourishment, love, and attention, the child comes to view the world as a good place. Of particular importance to the infant is the mothering person, and if she can be trusted when out of sight. Infants who fail to receive an adequate amount of love and care from their mothers and other significant persons develop a basic mistrust of others, an attitude that may persist for life. Associated with the stage of infancy is the virtue of *hope*.

The major crisis of *early childhood* is *autonomy versus shame and doubt*. This is the period during which toilet training takes place, with its attendent feelings of self-control and competence on the one hand or embarrassment and shame on the other. Toddlers who are permitted to explore the environment, express themselves, and try out their growing power are more likely to acquire a sense of self-control or autonomy; otherwise, they fail to achieve a feeling of competence or self-esteem and continue to perceive themselves as incapable and inadequate. The major quality to emerge during the early childhood stage is *will*, the will to do what one is expected to do.

The major crisis of the *play age* (preschool age) is *initiative versus guilt*. The child who fails to develop a sense of initiative at this stage will react to failure with shame, guilt, and resignation. Parents who take time to answer the many questions that preschoolers ask, rather than treating them as a nuisance, will encourage the child's growing sense of initiative. Development of the virtue of *purpose* characterizes this stage.

The *school age* is marked by the crisis of *industry versus inferiority*. The child who enters school with the feeling that he can do anything finds himself faced with tasks and competition which he did not anticipate and which, if not dealt with successfully, can create a lasting sense of inferiority. Success in the classroom and on the playground increases feelings of competence, but failure leads to feelings of inadequacy. Thus the quality of *competence* is the earmark of this stage.

The major crisis of *adolescence* is *identity versus role confusion*. Perhaps the most difficult time of life, the teenage years are marked by a transition from fantasy and play to the task of coming to grips with the questions of who am I, what am I, and what am I going to become? The quest for identity continues, to some extent, throughout life, but that quest is particularly pressing during adolescence. Failure to achieve a sense of identity leads to continuing role confusion and anxiety. The principal virtue that emerges during adolescence is *fidelity,* keeping one's commitments and retaining one's values despite exposure to a wide range of conflicting value systems.

TABLE 6–1 Erikson's Stages of Psychosocial Development

Stage	*Crisis (Conflict)*	*Goal (Resolution)*	*Description*
Infancy	Trust vs. mistrust	Acquire a basic sense of trust	Consistency, continuity, and sameness of experience lead to trust. Inadequate, inconsistent, or negative care may arouse mistrust.
Early childhood	Autonomy vs. doubt	Attain a sense of autonomy	Opportunities to try out skills at own pace and in own way lead to autonomy. Overprotection or lack of support may lead to doubt about ability to control self or environment.
Play age	Initiative vs. guilt	Develop a sense of initiative	Freedom to engage in activities and parents' patient answering of questions lead to initiative. Restrictions of activities and treating questions as a nuisance lead to guilt.
School age	Industry vs. inferiority	Become industrious and competent	Being permitted to make and do things and being praised for accomplishments lead to industry. Limitations on activities and criticism of what is done lead to inferiority.
Adolescence	Identity vs. role confusion	Achieve a personal identity	Recognition of continuity and sameness in one's personality, even when in different situations and when reacted to by different individuals, leads to identity. Inability to establish stability (particularly regarding sex roles and occupational choice) leads to role confusion.
Young adulthood	Intimacy vs. isolation	Become intimate with someone	Fusing of identity with another leads to intimacy. Competitive and combative relations with others may lead to isolation.
Middle age	Generativity vs. self-absorption	Develop an interest in future generations	Establishing and guiding next generation produces sense of generativity. Concern primarily with self leads to self-absorption.
Old age	Integrity vs. despair	Become an integrated and self-accepting person	Acceptance of one's life leads to a sense of integrity. Feeling that it is too late to make up for missed opportunities leads to despair.

After Erikson (1963), as adapted by Biehler, Robert F., *Child Development: An Introduction*, Second Edition. Copyright © 1981 by Houghton Mifflin Company. Used with permission.

Young adulthood is accompanied by the crisis of *intimacy versus isolation,* whether one develops a lasting intimate relationship with another person or continues to jump, in "swinging singles" fashion, from one relationship to another without ever settling down. Remaining isolated from a close relationship during this period can retard emotional development and create permanent unhappiness. Clearly, *love* is the quality that must emerge during this stage if the individual is to grow psychologically.

Erikson's seventh stage, *middle age,* is characterized by the crisis of *generativity versus stagnation.* Now is the time to develop a concern for the next generation and those who will follow it. Failure to acquire an interest in and a sense of responsibility toward future generations leads to *stagnation,* boredom, emotional impoverishment, and a pessimistic feeling that this is where it all ends. To Erikson, middle age is the time when the virtue of *care,* as witnessed by parenting, teaching, supervising, and in other ways assisting the next generation, emerges.

The major crisis of *old age* is *integrity versus despair,* and the principal goal of this stage is to become an integrated and self-accepting person. How the individual handles this crisis depends on personality characteristics that have been developing for years and also on one's physical health, economic situation, and the meaningfulness of the social roles that can be played successfully. Rather than being a consequence of aging per se, a sense of despair in old age more often results from poor health, financial insecurity, social isolation, inactivity, and other debilitating circumstances that so often accompany this stage of life. The virtue that emerges during this last stage of life is *wisdom,* the wisdom to accept the cards that one has been dealt and not to wring one's hands and wrack one's brain with regrets of what might have been. Assuming that the crises of all eight stages have been satisfactorily resolved, later life becomes a time when the individual lives each day with hope, will, purpose, competence, fidelity, love, care, and wisdom.

Although Erikson maintains that each of the eight crises assumes central importance during a particular stage of life, in actuality all eight crises are important throughout an individual's life span. Furthermore, personality is not an "all or none" affair; one pole of a given crisis does not usually overwhelm the other pole. Thus most children develop some degree of mistrust, but they are usually able to maintain a proper balance of trust and mistrust. Likewise, the great majority of older people cannot be characterized as integrated on the one hand or despairing on the other. In fact, a certain amount of despair is realistic, and the usual achievement of old age is not the total victory of integrity over despair but rather a favorable balance between the two.

Evaluation

Like so many theorists in the psychoanalytic camp, Erikson did not set out to construct a theory that could be easily verified by research. Consequently, the validity of his theory of personality development is difficult to test scientifically. A South African study conducted by Ochse and Plug (1986) found some evidence for the validity of Erikson's stages, but in general, research support for the theory has been sparse. Nevertheless, Erikson's ideas have been quite popular among developmental psychologists. The descriptions of the identity versus role confusion crisis of adolescence and the integrity versus despair crisis of old age, in particular, have been widely cited.

In addition to problems with empirical verification, Erikson's theory has been criticized for being too optimistic concerning human nature, too moralistic in tone, and too supportive of the status quo. Other criticisms point to an overemphasis on ego attributes and conscious impulses and the neglect of sexual, aggressive, and unconscious drives. Be that as it may, Erikson's writings have contributed to the shift of emphasis among psychoanalysts away from biological, instinctive urges beyond conscious control and toward the role of sociocultural and developmental factors in personality and mental disorders.

Fromm and Humanistic Psychoanalysis

Erich Fromm (1900–1980), the last psychoanalyst whose theory of personality we shall consider, was, like Erik Erikson, not trained as a physician. Fromm was born in Frankfurt, Germany, and received the Ph.D. in political sociology from the University of Heidelberg in 1922. After immigrating to the United States in 1934, he taught at several institutions in this country and in Latin America. A prolific writer of wide-ranging interests, Fromm acquired an international reputation through his lectures and books, including such volumes as *Escape from Freedom* (1941), *Man for Himself* (1947), *The Forgotten Language* (1951), *The Sane Society* (1955), and *The Art of Loving* (1956).

Fromm, whose writings reflect the influences of both Sigmund Freud and Karl Marx, was as much a philosopher and a political theorist as he was a psychoanalyst. Throughout his life Fromm remained an ardent anti-Nazi and an antiauthoritarian, and his lifelong quest was to understand and explain why people are attracted to totalitarian ideologies and leaders. He proposed the thesis that freedom creates anxiety, an anxiety produced by isolation and loneliness due to separation from nature and other people. Nazism, fascism, communism, and other totalitarian political ideologies provide a way for people to "escape from freedom." The free individual finds the burden of personal responsibility for making choices and taking risks too great, and thereby becomes susceptible to the propaganda of the dictator who promises to relieve him or her of that responsibility.

Basic Needs

To Fromm, since time immemorial human beings have been in a state of conflict between the desire for freedom on the one hand and the desire for security on the other. This conflict is related to five existential human needs: relatedness, transcendence, rootedness, identity, and a frame of reference. These needs are *existential* because they emerged as civilization evolved and people sought meaning in their existence. The *need for relatedness* is a desire to be with, care for, be responsible for, and achieve a union with others. This need may be met by submitting oneself to others, attaining power over them, or expressing love toward them. These three methods of satisfying the need for relatedness may be either productive or unproductive, but love, a "union with somebody or something outside oneself" is potentially the most productive solution.

The *need for transcendence* is a desire to rise above one's biological heritage and become a creative person. Expressions of the need for transcendence, however, may be either positive or negative. The materials and ideas created by a person may either help or harm other people. The *need for rootedness* is concerned with establishing roots or a sense of belongingness in the world. Establishing a physical and psychological home meets the need for rootedness and leads to security and escape from loneliness and anxiety. The *need for identity* prompts the individual to become distinctive and known by identifying with another person or a group of people.

Fromm's fifth basic need, the *need for a frame of reference*, refers to the individual's efforts to find an orientation or "mental road map" to serve as a guide for understanding the world and making one's way in it. Efforts to find such a frame of reference may be successful or go awry, as when an individual follows a destructive creed or philosophy.

In trying to satisfy his or her basic needs and to cope with anxiety and loneliness an individual may unconsciously adopt various mechanisms. Sadistic or masochistic *authoritarianism*, *destructiveness*, and *conformity* are three basic techniques that one can adopt to "escape from freedom" and thereby reduce feelings of alienation, anxiety, and powerlessness.

Character Types

Of all of Fromm's books, the one that deals most closely with the psychology of personality is *Man for Himself*. In this book Fromm describes five personality "characters," four of which he evaluates as undesirable. These character types—receptive, exploitative, hoarding, marketing, and productive—are individual personality patterns that developed as humans evolved and sought to escape from feelings of separateness and loneliness.

People who fit the description of the first character type, the *receptive character type*, take without giving anything in return. Such dependent "wimps" constantly demand support and sustenance from everyone and everything they encounter. They are passive, incorporative recipients of the largesse of the environment who see no connection between their personal actions and the worldly rewards that they deem to be their right.

People of an *exploitative character type* also take what they want from others, but they do it by force or manipulation rather than by simple expectation and demand. These individuals are the "con men" or "ripoff artists" who believe that everyone who has a dollar has at least 90 cents of their money.

People of a *hoarding character type* are selfish and aloof and keep everything that they produce or otherwise acquire for themselves. They are suspicious of the motives of other people and want to be left alone to wallow in their possessions. They view even their mates as possessions, and other people are valued only for what they own.

People of a *marketing character type* see everything in terms of its exchange value. "What can I get or exchange for this or that commodity?" is their guiding interrogative principle. To them, everything is for sale, not only material things, but also beliefs, values, and even self-respect. A marketing character sees himself in the same way: "What are my physical and mental assets, how can I package them most effectively, and what can I get for them?"

In his later writings, Fromm reconceptualized these four character types as being on a productive-nonproductive continuum. Thus each type may vary in the degree to which it is productive or nonproductive in its orientation. In addition, the types are not necessarily distinct. Two or more types may combine to produce a mixed type, such as the receptive-hoarding or the exploitative-marketing type.

According to Fromm, the only healthy character is the fifth one—the *productive type.* These individuals attempt to achieve satisfaction of their needs and to escape from loneliness and anxiety through productive work, reason, and love. Productive work is seen as a means of creative self-expression, and productive love includes care, responsibility, and respect for others.

A supplementary character type described in Fromm's later writings is the *necrophilous type.* As manifested in the worship of power, violence, and weapons of destruction, this type of person is attracted to death, destruction, and decay.

Overview

This brief sketch of Erich Fromm's theory of personality hardly does justice to the volume of his writing on human character and the conflicts, dilemmas, and resolutions of the human condition. Fromm's writings outline a personality and social psychology that tries to connect human character to particular cultural conditions and social structures. The leitmotif or underlying theme of Fromm's theorizing is Rousseau's doctrine that human beings are born good but become corrupted by society. Consequently, individual psychotherapy, which concentrates on the individual, is not enough. It is society that is "sick," a society whose structure must be replaced with one that can satisfy the individual and collective needs of the populace. Fromm referred to such a society as "humanistic communitarian socialism," one "in which man relates to man lovingly, in which he is rooted in bonds of brotherhood and solidarity" (Fromm, 1955, p. 362).

Erich Fromm was something of a maverick in American psychoanalysis, not only because of his nonmedical training, but also because of his versatility and wide-ranging cultural interests. He conducted a number of studies in cultural anthropology, one of the most extensive being an investigation in which *interpretive questionnaires* were administered to 406 peasants in an isolated Mexican village (Fromm & Maccoby, 1970). Consistent with Fromm's expectations, two character types predominated. Lower-class individuals tended to be receptive, and upper-class individuals tended to be hoarding. Within classes, a hoarding orientation was positively associated with economic success. Hoarders tended not to plant sugarcane, but among receptive individuals sugarcane was the favorite crop. These findings supported Fromm's social version of psychoanalytic theory. However, the research is actually an extended case study rather than a carefully controlled research investigation.

In general, Fromm did not achieve renown as a researcher, nor has his theory been subjected to extensive empirical verification by others. Like Horney, Sullivan, and Erikson, Fromm is noted primarily for his writings, his teaching, and, of course, his psychotherapeutic help to troubled people.

Summary

Professional disagreements with Freud's position on the importance of the sex drive, childhood sexuality, the unconscious, and other concepts surfaced even before the turn of the century, but it was during the first decade of the present century that Alfred Adler, Carl Jung, and Otto Rank in particular, all of whom had been members of Freud's inner circle, broke away from their mentor and established theories and psychotherapies of their own. The break with Jung appears to have affected Freud the most. It was Jung whom Freud had groomed as his non-Jewish successor, a selection that presumably would have served as a counterargument to the reputation of psychoanalysis as a Jewish movement.

Disenchantment with classical Freudian psychoanalysis continued among the succeeding generation of psychoanalysts, including such notables as Heinz Hartmann, Karen Horney, Harry Stack Sullivan, Erik Erikson, and Erich Fromm. These dissidents have been referred to as ego analysts and neoanalysts. Although recognizing the importance of the basic unconscious instincts, they saw the ego as having a wider role than simply that of mediating conflicts between the id, the superego, and the external world. An even more extensive role of the ego was in assisting the individual to adapt to the environment.

Adler made a complete break with Freud in reconceptualizing the basic motive of human behavior as the drive for power over the external environment, thereby compensating for deep-seated feelings of inferiority. To Adler, every person develops a life-style based on "fictional finalisms" and consisting of learned coping techniques and safeguarding strategies. That life-style is healthiest when the person has a true social interest. Adler is also noted for his ideas concerning the effects of birth order on personality.

In addition to disagreeing with Freud's emphasis on the unconscious and the id, Karen Horney took issue with his psychology of women, and particularly the concept of penis envy. Horney's theory of personality, which is primarily descriptive of neurotic personalities, emphasizes the effects of parental and societal treatment of the child in producing a vicious circle of anxiety, hostility, fear of rejection, and a neurotic need for love. This vicious circle is associated with ten neurotic needs, which Horney combined into three orientations or trends. Each of these neurotic trends is associated with a particular personality "type": moving toward people (compliant type), moving against people (hostile type), and moving away from people (detached type). The three trends, which reflect the neurotic's need for glory, are governed by a number of unrealistic "shoulds." Techniques such as externalization are employed by the neurotic to deal with conflicts between the real self and the idealized self-image.

Harry Stack Sullivan spent a good part of his professional life attempting to understand and treat schizophrenic patients. His interpersonal theory conceives of personality as shaped by and inseparable from the individual's social interactions. Central to the theory are the concepts of personifications, which are internal representations of the self and other people, and dynamisms, which are characteristic ways of behaving in social situations. Sullivan also emphasized that the developing child has three modes of experiencing—prototaxic, parataxic, and syntaxic, which are associated with the ways in which the child communicates. Although Sullivan wrote only one book, his students and colleagues assured his legacy by compiling his lectures and notes into a multivolume series.

One of the most widely cited of all developmental psychologists is Erik Erikson, whose theory of stages in psychosocial development and whose psychohistorical studies of Martin Luther and Mohandas K. Gandhi were truly ground breaking. The concept of epigenesis, which was borrowed from embryology and refers to the sequential development of organismic components, is basic to Erikson's notion of a series of psychosocial developmental stages. Each psychosocial stage, which comes into focus at a particular chronological age, is considered to be present in rudimentary form at birth and evolves from the preceding stages. At each of the eight stages a particular crisis or conflict must be resolved if the individual is to progress satisfactorily to the next stage. Erikson also pointed out that each stage is associated with a particular quality or virtue, as well as recurring behavior patterns referred to as ritualizations and distortions of ritualizations known as ritualisms.

The last neopsychoanalyst discussed in this chapter is Erik Fromm, whose humanistic orientation may serve as a bridge between this chapter and the next one. Fromm's theory of personality depicts people as torn by the conflict between freedom and security. Human beings desire to be free, but freedom entails separateness from nature and other people and consequently results in loneliness. According to Fromm, the conflict between freedom and security is related to five basic needs—the needs for relatedness, transcendence, rootedness, identity, and a frame of reference.

People attempt to satisfy their basic needs in various ways, for example, by authoritarianism, destructiveness, or conformity. Different character types, including the receptive, exploitative, hoarding, marketing, and productive types, represent patterns of behavior that individuals have developed over millennia to meet their needs and escape from feelings of separateness and aloneness. Only the last of these, the productive type, is seen by Fromm as truly adaptive.

Key Concepts

Character type In Erich Fromm's theory, a relatively permanent pattern of acquired qualities by means of which the individual relates to others and to the world. Examples are the compliant type, the detached type, the hoarding type, the hostile type, the necrophilous type, and the productive type.

Dynamism In H. S. Sullivan's theory, a fairly consistent pattern of behavior that characterizes an individual throughout his or her lifetime. An example is fear of unfamiliar things.

Ego psychology School of neo-Freudians who stress the centrality of the ego, which is viewed as functioning independently from the other components of personality.

Fictional finalism In Alfred Adler's individual psychology, ideal, fictional goals that a person creates from his or her subjective perception of reality and which the person attempts to attain by a particular life-style, thereby becoming a superior individual.

Identity crisis In Erikson's theory of psychosocial developmental stages, the period, especially during adolescence, characterized by a strong concern with acquiring a sense of self. An identity crisis may end in a sense of identity or identity diffusion.

Individual psychology Alfred Adler's theory of personality development, based on a belief in the uniqueness and integrated wholeness of every person and the notion that everyone adjusts to social influences in his or her own individual way.

Inferiority complex Strong, unrealistic feelings of inferiority that interfere with an individual's ability to accomplish anything. Overt inferiority feelings may mask true feelings of superiority (Adler).

Masculine protest Desire for courage, independence, strength, success, and other characteristics that the culture regards as male; may represent an attempt to compensate for feelings of inferiority. Both men and women presumably try to gain power by becoming more "manly" in their behavior (Adler).

Modes of experiencing In H. S. Sullivan's theory, the way in which the individual views and reacts to the world. In the *prototaxic mode,* experiencing is primitive, consisting of sensations, images and feelings in the stream of consciousness and not tied to logic or linguistic symbolization. In the *parataxic mode,* a primitive sense of causality, which is facilitated by linguistic development, is present, but many of the individual's utterances are subjective and personalistic, and *parataxic distortions* occur. In the *syntaxic mode,* experiences are communicated accurately by means of language.

Neurotic needs (neurotic trends) In Horney's theory, ten defensive strategies that, although excessive, allow a person to cope with basic anxiety. The neurotic needs fall into three general categories: moving against people, moving away from people, and moving toward people.

Psychosocial stages Erik Erikson's modification of Freud's theory of psychosexual stages; emphasizes environmental and social problems, as contrasted with biological factors, in the progression of developmental stages from infancy through old age.

Social interest According to Adler, the inborn urge to live peacefully and harmoniously with other people and to work toward the improvement of the environment and society.

Activities and Applications

1. Alfred Adler believed that a child's order of birth in a family affects the personality characteristics of the child. Talk to a dozen friends or acquaintances who were firstborn or last-born children in their families, and ask them to describe how they were treated in their families when they were growing up and how this treatment may have been affected by their birth order and how it affected their personalities. Add your own observations and those of other people to the descriptions of the personalities of these individuals, and see if you can find any differences between the firstborn and last-born children. Do you feel that being born a middle child or an only child affects personality? If so, in what way?

2. Describe your life-style, including not only your typical behavior but also your values, attitudes, and beliefs. What factors influenced your life-style? Do you think that you could change your life-style if, say, you married a person from another culture or accepted a job in which people behave counter to your own beliefs and behaviors?

3. Adler emphasized the importance of early recollections as significant in determining and understanding an individual's life-style. Ask several of your relatives or friends to tell you two or three of their earliest memories. What reasonable interpretations can you make of these memories? Obtain these recollections from individuals who are not very knowledgeable about psychology and presumably less likely than psychology majors to interpret and perhaps censor or embellish their psychologically significant memories. Whether seen from a commonsense viewpoint or a psychodynamic or other theoretical perspective, can such memories be interpreted unambiguously? Do the interpretations make sense, and are they consistent with what you know about the individual from personal observations and other sources?

4. In terms of Horney's three major adjustment techniques, would you say that, in general, you tend to move toward people, away from people, or against people? What experiences or other factors influenced your primary adjustment technique or trend?

5. Using Erikson's terminology, do you think that you have established an *identity*, or are you still in a state of *identity confusion*? How have the following factors been affected by or how are they likely to affect your sense of identity: your college major, your career choice, the person whom you marry, the decision on where you will live (geographical area, section of a city, etc.), how many children you will have, how you spend your leisure time?

6. Can you remember ever idolizing a person—either college, high school, or earlier in life? What made you idolize that person, and what events led you to stop (if you did stop) idolizing the person? Do you think that idolizing someone (hero worship) is healthy? Why or why not?

7. Can you remember experiencing the several crises in growing up to which Erikson refers? What times in your life were particularly enjoyable? Which ones were particularly traumatic? How did you resolve the traumas, or haven't you really done so?

8. Are you fairly satisfied with the kind of person you turned out to be? How would you change your personality if you could?

9. The following scale was devised by Ochse and Plug (1986) to assess the degree to which a person has developed a sense of identity, as defined by Erik Erikson. For each of the 19 items, write 1 if the statement never applies to you, 2 if the statement only occasionally or seldom applies to you, 3 if the statement applies to you fairly often, or 4 if the statement applies to you very often.

_____ **1.** I wonder what sort of person I really am.
_____ **2.** People seem to change their opinion of me.
_____ **3.** I feel certain about what I should do with my life.
_____ **4.** I feel uncertain as to whether something is morally right or wrong.
_____ **5.** Most people seem to agree about what sort of person I am.
_____ **6.** I feel that my way of life suits me.
_____ **7.** My worth is recognized by others.
_____ **8.** I feel freer to be my real self when I am away from those who know me very well.
_____ **9.** I feel that what I am doing in life is not really worthwhile.
_____ **10.** I feel that I fit in well in the community in which I live.
_____ **11.** I feel proud to be the sort of person I am.
_____ **12.** People seem to see me very differently from the way I see myself.
_____ **13.** I feel left out of things.
_____ **14.** People seem to disapprove of me.
_____ **15.** I change my ideas about what I want from life.
_____ **16.** I am unsure as to how people feel about me.
_____ **17.** My feelings about myself change.
_____ **18.** I feel I am putting on an act or doing something for effect.
_____ **19.** I feel proud to be a member of the society in which I live.[2]

Directions for scoring: Subtract each of your numerical answers to items 1, 2, 4, 8, 9, 12, 13, 14, 15, 16, 17, and 18 from 5. Leave the answers to the other items as they are. Then add the resulting scores for all items. The mean score for adults is 57, with a standard deviation of 8. High scores (above 65) indicate a well-developed sense of personal identity, and low scores (below 49) a poorly developed sense of personal identity. Evaluate your score. Compare your score with the scores of your classmates or friends.

Suggested Readings

Ansbacher, H. L., & Ansbacher, R. R. (Eds.). (1956). *The individual psychology of Alfred Adler*. New York: Basic Books.

Ansbacher, H. L., & Ansbacher, R. R. (Eds.). (1979). *Superiority and social interest*. New York: Norton.

Chapman, A. H. (1976). *Harry Stack Sullivan: His life and his work*. New York: Putnam.

Erikson, E. H. (1963). *Childhood and society* (2nd ed.). New York: Norton.

Fromm, E. (1941/1965). *Escape from freedom*. New York: Avon.

Fromm, E. (1956). *The art of loving*. New York: Harper & Brothers.

Horney, K. (1950). *Neurosis and human growth: The struggle toward self-realization*. New York: Norton.

Quinn, S. (1987). *A mind of her own: The life of Karen Horney*. New York: Summit Books.

Roazen, P. (1976). *Erik H. Erikson: The power and limits of a vision*. New York: Free Press.

Westen, D. (1990). Psychoanalytic approaches to personality. In L. A. Pervin (Ed.), *Handbook of personality theory and research* (pp. 21–65). New York: Guilford Press.

Notes

1 A fairly reliable measure of Adler's concept of *social interest* is J. E. Crandall's (1980) Social Interest Scale. The scale consists of 15 pairs of items, each containing one trait closely related to social interest (e.g., helpful, sympathetic, tolerant) and one trait not relevant to social interest (e.g., quick-witted, neat, capable). The respondent is asked to choose the trait in each pair that he or she would rather have. Positive correlations between Social Interest Scale scores and measures of adjustment and well-being have been reported.

2 From Ochse & Plug (1986). Copyright 1986 by the American Psychological Association. Adapted by permission.

CHAPTER 7

Phenomenological Theories

CHAPTER OUTLINE

Classical psychoanalysis has sometimes been characterized as a "hydraulic theory," in the sense that it depicts human thoughts and behaviors as being pushed or pulled by forces or energy systems, which in turn are subject to counter repressive forces. These opposing psychological forces result in dammed-up pressures, which, if not reduced by seepage, result in the formation of unproductive control systems or in explosive releases of psychic energy.

The emphasis on the direction and misdirection of psychic energy in Freud's psychoanalytic theory was an extension of the nineteenth-century mechanistic conception of nature that Helmholtz and other researchers had perfected in the physical sciences. Freud's conception of psychic determinism viewed personality as shaped primarily by forces and events that, for the most part, are not under conscious control and therefore are not the direct results of human volition and rational decision making. This conception was modified by Alfred Adler and the neoanalysts, who accorded more power to the conscious ego and the individual's capacity to shape his or her own destiny. The more optimistic picture of human nature painted by these dissidents from the classical psychoanalytic camp places more emphasis on the planfulness and future orientation of the individual in his or her drive toward self-actualization. The conceptualizations of the neoanalysts recognize that conscious assertiveness and a desire to develop and change are important factors in determining what the individual is capable of becoming and will be.

The four theorists discussed in this chapter—Abraham Maslow, Carl Rogers, Rollo May, and George Kelly—held positions that are consistent with and, to some extent, extensions of concepts proposed by Jung, Adler, Horney, Sullivan, and Fromm. Unlike Freudian analysts, who are seemingly rather pessimistic regarding the human condition, Maslow, Rogers, May, and Kelly express a more optimistic, or humanistic, viewpoint concerning human nature. Rather than being descendants of the nineteenth-century mechanistic tradition, these phenomenologists are more attuned to the doctrine of the eighteenth-century French writer Jean-Jacques Rousseau, who maintained that human beings are born good but are often made bad by social institutions.

In addition to having an optimistic view of humanity, the theorists discussed in this chapter are "phenomenological" in their orientation. *Phenomenology*, a philosophy developed primarily by Edmund Husserl during the early part of the twentieth century, emphasizes the importance of immediate, subjective sense impressions in the individual's conception of reality. From the perspective of phenomenology, reality to the individual is reality as it is experienced. As expressed by Carl Rogers (1961):

> Experience is, for me, the highest authority. . . . Neither the Bible nor the prophets—neither Freud nor research—neither the revelations of God nor man—can take precedence over my own experience. (p. 240)

From the perspective of an external observer, a person's behavior may seem to be inexplicable or at least unusual, but it nevertheless usually makes sense from the frame of reference of the experiencing person. Everyone has a different internal frame of reference, so in order to understand a person one must somehow learn to empathize with that person and see things from his or her point of view. As the term is employed in psychology, phenomenology is the study of the unique, private experiences or meanings that an individual assigns to events. The task of understanding why a person behaves in a certain way requires that we know, not simply what stimuli or events preceded the behavior, but rather the individual's perception of those events—how they are viewed and what they mean against the backdrop of the unique experiences of the individual. The meanings, attitudes, and emotions attached to specific events are crucial in determining and understanding why a person behaves in a certain way when confronted with those events.

As scientists, phenomenological theorists accept the fact that there is a real world beyond the life of any individual. They are not like an egocentric college roommate of mine who planned to destroy the whole world by committing suicide. According to phenomenologists, however, it is not so much the real world that is important to the individual or determines how he thinks and behaves. Rather, it is the world as perceived, the individual's *phenomenal field.* Two subsets of that phenomenal field are of particular importance. One of these is the *self,* that part of the phenomenal field that is related to the individual in a personal way—the "I" or "me" of personality. To William James, perhaps the first psychologist to use the term, the *self* was the "total of all he can call his, not only his body and his psychic powers, but his clothes and his house, his spouse and his children, his ancestors and friends, reputation and worlds, and his land and horse, and yacht and bank account" (James, 1890, p. 291). Although a bit dated and idiosyncratic in its vocabulary, James's definition emphasizes the fact that the self is everything that the individual calls *his.*

A further subset of the phenomenal field, and in fact a subset of the self, is the *self-concept,* the evaluations—good and bad—that the individual places on the personal self. The notion of the self-concept plays an important role in many phenomenological theories of personality, because the self-concept, and in particular discrepancies between the real and ideal self-concepts, is a measure of the satisfaction and happiness of the individual and a window to understanding that person.

Another distinction between psychoanalytic and phenomenological theories is that psychoanalysts emphasize "then and there"—that is, the individual's history or background—as determinants of his or her behavior and personality, whereas phenomenologists are ahistorical in emphasizing "here and now." To the phenomenologist, it is insufficient, and perhaps largely irrelevant, to delve into the personal past in trying to understand an individual. What one must do is focus on the person's current perceptions, attitudes, and thoughts and work toward modifying them if they are sources of discontent.

Phenomenologists believe in the person's creative ability to make choices that will reduce his or her unhappiness and to achieve self-actualization, a state of greater congruence between the real and ideal selves. In this sense, the phenomenologist is a *humanist* who believes in the value and dignity of the individual human being, a being who strives to grow psychologically and to fulfill his or her own unique potentialities. The realization of these potentialities comes about by means of active, self-aware, creative, responsible planning and decision making. Instead of being controlled by basic instincts or regulated by a set of traits, the person is seen as a fundamentally good, self-motivated organism striving to reach a higher plane of functioning. In addition, rather than attempting to analyze personality into a set of constituent parts, phenomenologists view it as an integrated, dynamic organization, a point of view referred to as *holistic*.

Phenomenology, as described here, is closer to the theoretical positions of Abraham Maslow and Carl Rogers than to those of Rollo May and George Kelly. Nevertheless, the existential psychology of May and the personal constructs approach of Kelly are also "phenomenological" in their emphasis on psychological reality as determined by individual perceptions and the ways in which people interpret their experiences and develop their own personalities through conscious control.

Abraham Maslow and Self-actualization

Abraham H. Maslow (1908–1970), the son of an immigrant Russian Jewish father, was born in Brooklyn, New York. The Maslows were the only Jews in the neighborhood where Abe lived as a child, a situation that contributed to the anti-Semitism and sense of isolation that he reportedly felt. Abe's childhood was also an unhappy one in other ways. His physical health was not good, and he was a painfully shy child who often felt alone and rejected. He disliked both of his parents, and, although he later came to terms with his father, he never overcame his intense dislike for his mother. Abe was, however, an exceptionally bright young man with a restless intellect, a quality that brought him to the attention of many teachers and scholars.

Somewhat incongruous for a man who was to become the father of humanistic psychology, Maslow did his doctoral dissertation in animal (monkey) psychology under Harry Harlow at the University of Wisconsin. He left Wisconsin in 1935 to become E. L. Thorndike's research assistant at Columbia University, where he conducted research on human sexuality. A year and a half later he joined the faculty of Brooklyn College, remaining there until he became a professor at Brandeis University in 1951. Somewhat discouraged with the students there, Maslow left Brandeis in 1969 to assume the post of resident fellow at the Laughlin Foundation in California, where he studied and wrote on the political, economic, and ethical implications of humanistic psychology until his death in 1970.

Despite his physical and personal problems, or perhaps in part because of them, Maslow became an influential, eminent psychologist and a founder of *third-force psychology*. He described third-force psychology as a humanistic alternative to the two major "forces" in psychology—psychoanalysis and behaviorism.

Interestingly, Maslow did not perceive himself as either antipsychoanalytic or antibehavioristic, but he felt that these two "schools" of psychology were too limited and too negative concerning their views of humanity. During the late 1930s and 1940s, through the influence of the Gestalt psychologist Max Wertheimer, the anthropologist Ruth Benedict, and several other prominent social scientists (e.g., Alfred Adler, Kurt Goldstein, Karen Horney, Erich Fromm) who were living and working in New York City during those years, Maslow began to develop his own humanistic theory of personality. Two events, the founding of the American Association of Humanistic Psychology (including establishment of the *Journal of Humanistic Psychology*) in 1962 and becoming president of the American Psychological Association in 1969, were perhaps the high points of Maslow's career.

Murray's and Maslow's Needs

The concept of *need* as an inferred internal state which arouses activity and directs behavior toward certain objects or conditions called *goals,* was, of course, not unique to Maslow. For example, Henry Murray had earlier compiled a descriptive list of physiogenic and psychogenic needs as central to his theory of human personality. Like Gordon Allport, Murray believed that the field of personality is best served by intensive study of the single case, and the 20 "needs" that he described are reminiscent of Allport's "traits." A basic principle of Murray's theorizing is that human beings are driven to reduce tensions generated by forces that are internal (*needs*) and external (*press*) to the person. Thus behavior is a function of both needs and press, which are defined as follows:

> A need is a construct . . . which stands for a force (the physico-chemical nature of which is unknown) in the brain region, a force which organizes perception, apperception, intellection, conation, and action in such a way as to transform in a certain direction an existing unsatisfying situation.
>
> The press of an object is what it can *do to the subject* or *for the subject*—the power that it has to affect the well-being of the subject in one way or another. The cathexis of an object . . . is what it can *make the subject do.* (Murray, 1938, p. 121)

Murray labeled the actual, "objective" press from the environment *alpha* press, whereas the "perceived" press was called *beta* press.

Two other concepts, or *hypothetical constructs,* in Murray's theory are *thema* and *vector-value.* A *thema,* of which behavior is a function, results from a combination of a particular need and a particular press. The concept of *vector-value,* or simply *vector,* was added by Murray in 1951 to emphasize the fact that needs, rather than existing alone, operate to serve some value or intent. To a large extent, the notion of *vector,* as a force that serves some value, came to replace that of *need* in Murray's thinking. Examples of such vectors, or behavioral tendencies, are avoidance, expression, reception, and rejection.

Like Murray, Maslow distinguished between two classes of needs, which he called *D* (deficiency) *needs* and *B* (being, or growth-based) *needs.* Strictly speaking,

Maslow's conception of needs is a theory of motivation rather than a theory of personality, but it is more complex than Murray's descriptive list of needs. To Maslow, a person's *basic needs* (or *conative needs*) are hierarchically organized, with psychological needs at the bottom and self-actualization needs at the top of the hierarchy (see Figure 7–1). Examples of *physiological needs* are hunger, thirst, sex, elimination, and sleep; *safety needs,* including order, security, structure, and predictability, are needs to be secure and out of danger; *belongingness and love needs* are needs to be with other people and to be accepted and loved by them; *esteem needs* are needs to achieve, to be strong, competent, and prestigeful; and the *need for self-actualization* is a need to fulfill one's potentialities. This list of needs is a hierarchy because the position of a need in the list is determined by its strength and survival value for most people. Thus the physiological need of hunger is more basic and insistent than the need for self-esteem, and typically the former need must be satisfied before successful efforts are made to satisfy the latter. Likewise, one does not usually concentrate on sex when his or her life is threatened. As a further example, esteem needs are usually more basic than the need for self-actualization: pride may go before a fall, but the need to fulfill one's potentialities usually disappears before the feeling of pride is demolished.

Other features of the hierarchy of needs were described by Maslow: In both evolutionary and individual development, higher needs emerge later than lower

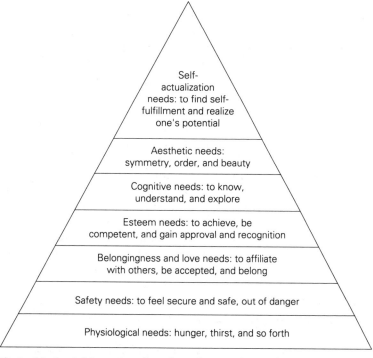

FIGURE 7–1   Maslow's hierarchy of needs. (After Maslow, 1970.)

needs; higher needs are less directly related to survival and hence less urgent than lower needs. The preconditions for satisfying higher needs are greater than those for lower needs, but the satisfaction of higher needs produces greater peace of mind and a richer inner life.

In addition to the basic (*conative*) needs, there are *cognitive needs* (desire to know and understand), *aesthetic needs* (needs for order, symmetry, closure, structure, completion, etc.), and *neurotic needs* (needs that result in stagnation and pathology). Manifestations of neurotic needs are seen in aggression, hostility, hoarding, and similar pathological behaviors that may serve as compensations for the lack of satisfaction of basic needs. Deprivation of the need for self-actualization leads to what Maslow called *metapathology,* in which the individual becomes devoid of values, lacks fulfillment, and loses the meaning of life. Failure to meet one's basic needs may result in stealing, cheating, lying, or even killing. On the other hand, attainment of self-actualization, described as the essence of psychological health, permits the full enjoyment of food, sex, and other sensuous pleasures. This state of self-actualization, however, cannot occur until the basic needs that are lower on the hierarchy have been satisfied. Many of these needs are unconscious—that is, below the individual's momentary level of awareness, where they still affect his or her behavior.

Self-actualization

Most people are not self-actualizers; they become "stuck" at the self-esteem level, in which they are more concerned with ego gratification, pride, and accomplishment than in becoming all that they can be. Fifteen characteristics of self-actualizing people are listed in Table 7–1. As described in this list, self-actualizers are more realistic, more accepting, more spontaneous and natural, "forever young" in their attitudes toward things, less self-centered, more independent, deeply democratic but attached to only a few other people, inner-directed, and highly creative. The growth orientation of such people leads them to focus on what they are, what they are capable of doing, and what they have already accomplished, rather than on what is missing in their lives.

Maslow's procedure in designating historical and contemporary personages whom he considered to be self-actualized was not strictly scientific, but from his study of individuals such as Abraham Lincoln, Thomas Jefferson, Albert Einstein, and Eleanor Roosevelt he concluded that these people possessed a more realistic orientation, were more accepting of themselves and others, were spontaneous in their expressions, had problem-centered rather than self-centered attitudes, and were more independent; they also identified with humanity, had greater emotional depth, democratic values, a philosophical sense of humor, an ability to transcend the environment, and creativity. These are traits which, taken collectively, define them as self-actualized persons.

Particularly characteristic of self-actualized persons is *B cognition* ("being" cognition), a passive mode of perceiving that lets oneself be reached, touched, and affected by events. Whereas *D love* ("deficiency" love) is often replete with

TABLE 7–1 Characteristics of Self-actualizing People

1. They have a more accurate, efficient perception of reality.
2. They are more accepting of themselves, other people, and nature.
3. They show spontaneity, simplicity, and naturalness.
4. They have a continued fresh appreciation of events in their lives.
5. They are more problem-centered and less self-centered.
6. They are able to discriminate more accurately between means and ends, right and wrong.
7. They have a need for privacy and detachment.
8. They are more autonomous, or independent from their environment and culture.
9. They have transcendent, mystical, or "peak" experiences.
10. They have a feeling of oneness or identification with all humanity and a deep desire to help others.
11. They form deep interpersonal attachments with only a few people.
12. They are deeply democratic, free of prejudice, and respecting of all people.
13. They have a well-developed philosophical sense of humor.
14. They are highly creative individuals.
15. They tend to be inner-directed and nonconforming people who resist enculturation.

anxiety, hostility, jealousy, and spitefulness, *B love* is none of these things. Effective B love results in true, penetrating perception of the other person, in a sense, "creating" the person. B love is only one of the *metaneeds* of self-actualized people. Other metaneeds include truth, goodness, beauty, wholeness, aliveness, uniqueness, perfection, justice, order, simplicity, richness, effortlessness, playfulness, self-sufficiency, and completion.

According to Maslow, only about 1 percent of all people attain a state of self-actualization. They may fear and doubt their own abilities and potentialities, thereby developing what he labeled a *Jonah complex*. They may be unwilling to sacrifice their safety or security for personal growth. However, by being open, warm, and friendly and not imposing too many limits, parents can help their children to become more secure and confident and more likely to select experiences that result in personal growth.

When the term *self-actualization* is mentioned, it is natural to think of having reached a state of perfect harmony and contentment and being loved by nearly everyone. Becoming self-actualized, however, is not a uniformly happy state of affairs, often leading to misunderstanding on the part of one's peers and society as a whole. Self-actualizers also possess some negative qualities, including partiality, pride, vanity, silliness, and temper outbursts. Furthermore, the tendency toward self-actualization, although presumably innate, is not achieved by everyone. The drive toward self-actualization is really quite weak and easily frustrated; so relatively few individuals ever reach that apex of Maslow's pyramid.

Despite some problems associated with self-actualization, a person who is not self-actualized is, in a sense, only half a person. Material wants may be satisfied, and one may be loved and respected by the community, yet something is missing and a vague discontent is felt. For those who would take steps toward becoming self-actualized, Maslow (1973) lists eight ways in which one can find the pathway:

1. Experience things fully, vividly, selflessly. Throw yourself into the experiencing of something; concentrate on it fully; let it totally absorb you.

2. Life is an ongoing process of choosing between safety (out of fear and need for defense) and risk (for the sake of progress and growth): make the growth choice "a dozen times a day."

3. Let the self emerge. Try to shut out external clues as to what you should think, feel, say, and so on, and let your experience enable you to say what you truly feel.

4. When in doubt, be honest. If you look into yourself and are honest, you will also take responsibility; taking responsibility is self-actualizing.

5. Listen to your own tastes. Be prepared to be unpopular.

6. Use your intelligence. Work to do well the things you want to do, whether that means finger exercises at a keyboard; memorizing the names of every bone, muscle, hormone, and so on in the human body; or learning how to finish wood so it looks and feels like silk.

7. Make peak experiencing more likely; get rid of illusions and false notions; learn what you are not good at and what your potentialities are not.

8. Find out who you are, what you are, what you like and don't like, what is good and what is bad for you, where you are going, what your mission is. Opening yourself up to yourself in this way means identifying defenses—and then finding the courage to give them up. (pp. 250–252)

Peak Experiences

The term *peak experiencing* in item 7 of the list is a feature of self-actualization referred to frequently by Maslow. *Peak experiences* are feelings of joy or ecstasy at being alive and realizing that one is using one's potentials to the utmost. They include feelings of increased insight and completeness in being at one with the surroundings. Such fleeting moments occur only when feelings are truly spontaneous and one is unconcerned with the constraints of place or time. There are moments when people go, as it were, beyond themselves, beyond immediate space and time and become one with the universe. In his research on peak experiences, Maslow (1968) gave the following instructions to his subjects:

I would like you to think of the most wonderful experience or experiences of your life; happiest moments, ecstatic moments, moments of rapture, perhaps from being in love, or from listening to music or suddenly "being hit" by a book or a painting, or from some great creative moment. First list these. And then try to tell me how you feel in such acute moments, how you feel differently from the way you feel at other times, how you are at the moment a different person in some ways. (p. 81)

It is easy to understand why some of the responses to these instructions are sexual in nature; others concern experiences when viewing a painting, hearing a symphony, or beholding a breathtaking scene. Although such experiences may occur in a passive way, they usually take place when the individual is deeply involved in some sort of activity, at which time the activity seems to "become" the person.

Eupsychia and Transpersonal Psychology

During his later years, Maslow became involved with extending humanistic psychology to the political, economic, and social arenas. In keeping with the zeitgeist of the 1960s, he, like B. F. Skinner with *Walden Two*, conceived of a potential utopian society, Eupsychia as he called it, in which people would be completely cooperative and *synergistic* (working together). The philosophy of the Eupsychians would be Taoistic (based on simplicity, naturalness, and noninterference with the course of natural events), nonintrusive, and basic need gratifying. Maslow advocated applying the same philosophy to industrial management by encouraging managers to become aware of human needs and what it takes to satisfy them. *Eupsychian management* would presumably result in a healthier industry in which working conditions are more conducive to the satisfaction of worker needs than they have been in the past.

Maslow was also a supporter of *ashrams*, or retreats for personal growth. Ashrams, which have existed for hundreds of years in India, are places where people can escape from the stresses of everyday life and, under the guidance of a guru (spiritual teacher or guide), achieve inner peace. The Esalen Institute at Big Sur, California, which was founded by Michael Murphy in 1963, was the first formally established ashram in the United States. Esalen, about which much has been written, was presented as a place where normal people can spend time reflecting on their values and circumstances, searching for themselves, and hopefully becoming healthier and more effectively functioning adults.

Maslow's interest in ashrams signaled his transition into *transpersonal* or *fourth-force psychology*, a psychology that goes beyond the person. Transpersonal psychology emphasizes the study of people having exceptional psychological health, and advocates the use of meditative and yogic techniques and experiences, including altered states of consciousness. Through the understanding and applications of traditional non-Western psychologies, philosophies, and religions, the individual can presumably go beyond his or her own self (ego) and incorporate into consciousness aspects of both the mind and the world that are usually considered foreign to the self. The first issue of the *Journal of Transpersonal Psychology*, dedicated to fourth-force psychology, was published in the year before Maslow's death. This journal is the major publication of the Association for Transpersonal Psychology, which was followed on the world scene by the International Transpersonal Association.

Evaluation and Applications

Although Maslow's theory is replete with suggestions for empirical research, one of the strongest criticisms of the theory is the subjectivity of Maslow's research and that of his colleagues on self-actualization. Efforts have been made to develop objective measures of self-actualization, one of the most popular being the Personal Orientation Inventory (POI) (Shostrom, 1974). This 150-item forced-choice personality inventory is scored first for a Time Ratio, indicating whether the respondent is oriented in the present, past, or future. A second score is a Support Ratio, indicating whether the respondent's reactions are basically toward others or the self. Last, the POI is scored on ten scales designed to measure self-actualizing value, existentiality, feeling reactivity, spontaneity, self-regard, self-acceptance, nature of man, synergy, acceptance of aggression, and capacity for intimate contact. The POI has been used extensively in research, but the reliabilities of its 12 measures are only moderate.

With respect to the hierarchy of needs, it has been noted that many people are able to be productive even when their basic needs are not satisfied, a circumstance which seemingly contradicts Maslow's assertion that basic needs must be satisfied before an individual can fulfill higher needs. Other criticisms of Maslow's theorizing are his use of subjective, and therefore uncontrolled and unreliable, research methods. Finally, as in the case of Alfred Adler, Maslow has been criticized as having an overly optimistic viewpoint concerning human nature.

Despite these criticisms, it must be noted that Maslow's writings have occasioned wide interest and acceptance in developmental psychology and education, as well as in business and religion. Herzberg's (1966) motivator-hygiene theory and Alderfer's (1972) ERG (existence, relatedness, growth) theory, both of which have been applied in numerous organizational settings, are two conceptions of employee motivation based on Maslow's need hierarchy. However, Maslow's writings have not been applied as widely to the psychotherapeutic treatment of personal problems as that of the theorist whom we shall consider next.

Carl Rogers and Self Theory

Carl Ransom Rogers (1902–1987) was born in Oak Park, Illinois, the fourth of six children of a successful civil engineer and his wife. The Rogers family was close-knit, conservative, and quite religious (Protestant). Despite his later rejection of traditional Christianity, throughout his professional career Carl Rogers showed the influence of his Christian upbringing. But Carl was a solitary, painfully shy child, and his home life was not always happy.

As a boy he was deeply interested in science. His first college major at the University of Wisconsin, which he entered in 1919, was in agriculture. In 1922 he was selected to attend the World Student Christian Federation Conference in Peking, China, which led to a six months' trip and an intercultural experience that profoundly affected his thinking. On the way home from China, Rogers came to the conclusion that "Jesus was a man like other men—not divine."

Rogers was graduated from the University of Wisconsin in 1924, and in that same year he married Helen Elliott. Soon afterward he enrolled in Union Theological Seminary, with the intention of becoming a minister. After two years and a few psychology courses he abandoned this plan and decided to study psychology full time at Teachers College, Columbia University. Rogers received the Ph.D. in clinical psychology from Teachers College in 1931, having completed a dissertation on assessing personality adjustment in children.

Rogers' first professional position was that of staff psychologist in a Rochester (New York) child guidance clinic. His first book, *The Clinical Treatment of the Problem Child* (1939), brought him to the attention of the psychology department of Ohio State University, and in 1940 he became a faculty member at that institution. His second book, *Counseling and Psychotherapy: Newer Concepts in Practice* (1942), which introduced the theory and practice of *nondirective psychotherapy*, was written during his tenure at Ohio State. Following a leave of absence from Ohio State in 1944, he became director of counseling services for the United Services Organization in New York City. One year later he accepted a position as professor of psychology and director of the Counseling Center at the University of Chicago. During his 12 years at the University of Chicago he became famous for his client-centered counseling and associated research and completed his most influential book, *Client-Centered Therapy* (1951).

One of the most eventful debates in modern psychology, between the humanist Carl Rogers and the behaviorist B. F. Skinner, occurred during Rogers' last years at Chicago. A principal source of disagreement in these debates, which were not quite as heated as one might have expected, was the prospect of designing a culture according to psychological principles. Skinner proposed that behavioral principles be applied to the design of a society that would be more efficient in satisfying human needs, but Rogers was concerned with the questions of who will be controlled, who will be the controllers, what type of control will be exercised, and what values will be pursued in such controlling.

In 1957, Rogers returned to his alma mater, the University of Wisconsin, with the intention of uniting the professions of psychiatry and psychology. He was unsuccessful in this goal, and for this and other reasons in 1964 he joined the staff of the Western Behavioral Sciences Institute at La Jolla, California. His last professional move was only a short distance to the Center for Studies of the Person, also in La Jolla, which he cofounded and where he tried to apply the person-centered approach that had worked so well in psychological counseling to the wider world of education, industry, and society in general.

Many honors were bestowed upon Carl Rogers during his lifetime, including the presidency of the American Psychological Association in 1946–1947, the first Distinguished Scientific Contribution Award given by that organization (1956), and a Distinguished Professional Contribution Award from the same organization in 1972. This midwestern farm boy, who made the New Testament lesson of love and acceptance a part of psychology and rose to become leader of the humanistic revolution in psychology, died in 1987.

Rogers' Theory of Personality

Rogers' theory of personality, like Freud's psychoanalytic theory, was developed in the context of working with people who had psychological problems. Rogers' clients, who were primarily college students, were, however, less emotionally disturbed than Freud's. Although Maslow dealt with the development, disorders, and other aspects of personality structure and dynamics to some extent, his major focus was on motivation and on the hierarchical nature of motives in particular. While employing some of the same concepts as his fellow humanist, Rogers fashioned a more systematic, detailed theory of personality, a theory that had influences and applications beyond the clinic and into various organizations and institutions of society.

Rogers is often referred to as a *self theorist,* in that he made the *self,* the part of the phenomenal field that becomes differentiated as the "I" or "me," the center of personality. He frequently used *self* and *self-concept* interchangeably, although the latter term usually connotes the individual's perception of the self, and in particular the evaluation of the self. Rogers recognized that *self* is not a unitary concept; every person typically recognizes at least two selves, one being the self as it is (*real self*) and the other the self as the individual would like it to be (*ideal self*). An *incongruency* or disparity between the real and ideal selves is associated with dissatisfaction or lack of mental harmony; only when the real and ideal selves are *congruent* can the individual be self-actualized and at peace with himself.

The concept of *self-actualization* did not, of course, originate with Rogers. Not only Maslow but also certain psychoanalysts and other personality theorists used the term to refer to the striving of the individual to realize his or her potential. To Rogers, the striving for self-actualization is "the inherent tendency of the organism to develop all its capacities in ways which serve to maintain or enhance the person" (Rogers, 1959, p. 1960). People can become *fully functioning* only when they live up to their potential.

A fully functioning person operates according to the *organismic valuing process.* That is, only those experiences that serve to promote growth and self-fulfillment are incorporated into the self; experiences that fail to enhance and actualize the person are ignored or avoided. In other words, organismic valuing is an evaluative process that determines whether a particular behavior contributes to self-actualization. In the process of growing up, however, a person who acts only according to the organismic valuing process usually comes into conflict with the rules and regulations of society. Other people may not always show *unconditional positive regard* for the child; that is, they do not love and value the child regardless of what he or she says or does. They impose *conditions of worth,* or requirements for granting acceptance. Only if the child does the right thing and behaves according to the precepts of society is he or she accepted and approved by others. Thus unconditional positive regard gives way to *conditional positive regard.* From these experiences the child learns that acceptance and love will be forthcoming only if his or her behavior conforms to expected standards imposed by society, and consequently by parents and significant others. For example, John's organismic valuing process may direct him to actualize himself by becoming a teacher, but John's father wants him to become a physician and makes his positive regard for John conditional upon the latter's adherence to the paternal desires. Likewise, Susan may conclude that she can only be herself by dating a certain boy of limited means, but her mother wants her to find a man with money and high social status and will respect Susan only if she does so.

As a consequence of conditions of worth being imposed, a person's efforts to become self-actualized are inhibited and his or her behavior becomes redirected toward satisfying others rather than oneself. Therefore, the child, who eventually becomes an adult, learns to recognize and accept only a part of his or her experiences. The result is an individual who cannot become wholly functioning unless, through psychotherapy or some other self-reorganizing experience, he or she learns to attend once more to the organismic valuing process and its goal of self-actualization.

Rogers included in his theory concepts similar to those of other personality theorists. For example, he recognized a distinction between *experience* and *awareness,* the former encompassing everything that happens to a person and the latter being that part of experience which a person symbolizes. Rogers agreed with Freud that people are not always consciously aware of their experiences, although those experiences can still affect their behavior. A threatening experience may be perceived unconsciously, a process which Rogers referred to as *subception.* Experiences that are incongruent (incompatible) with the self and with internalized conditions of worth are *subceived,* but the threat of their awareness leads to anxiety. In the same way that defense mechanisms operate in psychoanalysis, denial and distortion of experiences may serve to control feelings of anxiety caused by the experience. *Denial* is simply negating an experience by refusing to accept its existence, whereas *distortion* is reducing the threat of an experience by modifying it in some way. The defenses of denial and distortion are, however, not always effective, and when they fail the person becomes aware of and threatened by his or her incongruent experiences. An awareness of these incongruent experiences results in fragmentation of the self-concept, or, in common parlance, a "breakdown."

Rogerian Therapy

To Rogers, the anxiety and depression that characterize many psychological problems are the consequences of a poor self-concept resulting from conditional positive regard, imposed initially by others and subsequently by the individual himself. Owing to a failure to be true to his own natural organismic valuing experiences and his overconcern with the positive regard of other people, the person falsifies these experiences. The result of this failure of openness to experience is a lack of correspondence between external reality and subjective reality. In order to get beyond the impasse of conditional acceptance, achieve reintegration of the self, and put the person back on track toward self-actualization, the psychotherapist must show unconditional positive regard in a free, accepting therapeutic environment. The patient (client) is encouraged to "take charge" of the therapeutic sessions, while the therapist responds to the patient's statements and actions in a nondirective, person-centered, supportive manner. Instead of telling the patient what to do, the therapist acts as a kind of midwife or facilitator of the healing process by employing less directive methods such as simple acceptance, restatement of content, and reflection of feeling, but very little direct interpretation or advice giving.

Q-Sort Technique

When psychotherapy is effective, the patient experiences a reduction in the incongruency between the real and ideal selves, a reduction that can be assessed by means of the Q-sort technique. The *Q-sort technique* requires the client to sort a set of 100 or so statements descriptive of personality into a series of nine categories (piles) varying from "most descriptive" to "least descriptive" of the person. Each card in a Q-sort deck contains a statement such as the following:

Has a wide range of interests.
Is productive; gets things done.
Is self-dramatizing; is histrionic.
Is overreactive to minor frustrations; is irritable.
Seeks reassurance from others.
Appears to have a high degree of intellectual capacity.
Is basically anxious. (Block, 1961, pp. 132–136 passim)

In sorting the statement-containing cards in a Q-sort deck, the respondent is directed to make his or her choices in such a way that a certain number of statements fall in each category and so the resulting frequency distribution of statements across categories has a predetermined shape, usually normal. To approximate a normal distribution for a Q-sort of 100 statements, Block (1961) recommends instructing sorters to place the following numbers of statements into categories 1 through 9: 5, 8, 12, 16, 18, 16, 12, 8, 5. The response to each statement on a Q-sort instrument is assigned an integer ranging from 1 to 9, depending on the category assigned to the statement by the respondent. The results obtained from different sorts or sorters can then be related by computing correlation coefficients between different sorts.

To assess the changes in self-concept resulting from psychotherapy, clients make before-and-after Q-sorts of a series of statements describing their feelings and attitudes. In a series of studies conducted by Rogers and Dymond (1954), each person was directed to make separate Q-sorts according to his or her "real self" and "ideal self." The results showed that, compared with "no-therapy" groups, differences between the "real" and "ideal" self-sorts of clients who had undergone therapy decreased.

Other Applications and Related Research

After leaving Wisconsin in 1964, Rogers devoted much of his efforts to applying his ideas to education, politics, industry, and social problems such as race relations, marital discord, and fostering of creativity among children. Basic to all of these efforts was the humanistic credo that people are basically "good" and that, given freedom and understanding, they will choose a personally and socially productive path to self-actualization. This assumption, which is probably unverifiable, has been a major source of criticism of humanistic psychology. How can one conclude that people are basically good when newspapers are full of stories of vicious, incomprehensible crimes? Rogers was aware of this darker side of human nature, but it was his, some would say, Pollyannish, belief that the goodness in human nature will win out if the individual is given half a chance.

Rogers' ideas have served as a stimulus for a wide range of research studies on the self, including the self-concept, self-awareness, real/ideal-self congruency, self-disclosure, and self-esteem (for reviews see M. H. Davis & Franzoi, 1991; Baumeister, 1991; Markus & Cross, 1990). Descriptions of research and theorizing pertaining to any one of these topics could fill an entire chapter of this textbook, but we shall deal briefly with only two of them—self-disclosure and real/ideal-self congruency.

Self-disclosure. A credo of the humanistic psychologist is that people come to understand themselves by disclosing themselves to others. Self-disclosure, or revealing things about oneself to other people, is important in psychotherapy, in making friends, in achieving a successful career, and in other activities involving social interactions. Self-disclosure should, of course, be exercised with restraint and according to its appropriateness in specific circumstances; it is not simply a matter of "blabbing" everything about oneself to anyone all at once!

Among the findings of research on the effects of self-disclosure are that (1) psychotherapy is most effective when both client and therapist engage in self-disclosure; (2) when socially interacting, people match the extent of their own self-disclosure to that of their co-conversant(s); (3) females tend to disclose more intimate details than males; (4) anxious people engage in less self-disclosure than nonanxious people; (5) well-adjusted people are more flexible in the extent to which they disclose details about themselves, adjusting the amount of self-disclosure to that of their co-conversant(s) and the particular situation; and (6) self-disclosure facilitates mental and physical health (see Derlega & Berg, 1987).

Congruency between Real and Ideal Selves. Although Rogers maintained that the effectiveness of psychotherapy can be gauged by the extent to which the real and ideal selves of the client become more congruent, research on real/ideal-self congruence has revealed seemingly contradictory findings. A number of studies have found, as Rogers maintained, that congruence between real and ideal selves is associated with good adjustment (J. M. Butler, 1968; Gough, Lazzari, & Fioravanti, 1978; Gough, Fioravanti, & Lazzari, 1983). On the other hand, Achenbach and Zigler (1963) obtained a negative relationship between real/ideal-self congruence and social competence scores in psychiatric and nonpsychiatric patients. Furthermore, Katz and Zigler (1967) found that the discrepancy between real-self and ideal-self was greater for older than for younger individuals. Such findings are difficult to explain if one accepts real/ideal-self congruence as a measure of maturity and good adjustment. It might be expected that socially competent and older (and presumably more experienced) individuals would be better adjusted than less socially competent and less experienced individuals. An explanation for the differences between the findings of Zigler and his coworkers and those of other investigators appears to lie in the greater awareness or more complex thought processes of older, brighter, more experienced, and more socially competent individuals. Such people are more likely to see differences between their real and ideal selves—between what they are and what they would like to be—than younger, less experienced, and less socially competent individuals. In fact, complete congruence between real and ideal selves may be interpreted as defensiveness rather than optimal adjustment. Whatever the case may be, the findings of Zigler and his colleagues underscore the fact that mental maturity, experience, and perceptiveness do not ensure good adjustment. Apparently there is some truth in the adages of "the happy idiot," "You don't miss what you don't know about," and "Education and experience can breed dissatisfaction."

Rollo May and Existential Psychology

Existentialism, a philosophy that has its roots in the nineteenth-century writings of Søren Kierkegaard and Friedrich Nietzsche, answers the age-old question of "What or who am I?" with "You are what you do." To Kierkegaard, the meaning of a person's existence is to be found in his or her actions as a participant rather than a spectator in the game of life. People cannot sit idly by on the sidelines and simply watch the passing parade if they wish to find some meaning in life; they must take their chances and get into the game.

The principal maxim of existentialism, *existence is prior to essence,* implies that the theories and methods designed by empirical scientists to assist in understanding the substance, or "objectiveness," of people and other phenonmena are inadequate to the task. It is maintained that science, with all its techniques and laws, will never succeed in telling us who we are and what our lives mean. That meaning must be discovered by *being-in-the-world (Dasein),* by engaging in our own search and finding our own meanings through what we do and how we live.

Social upheavals and human tragedies during the nineteenth and twentieth centuries gave a particular impetus to existential thought. The decline of religious faith and the pursuit of materialism, new styles of working and living that resulted from mechanization and mass production, world wars, genocide, and other sudden changes and catastrophes led to widespread doubt concerning the time-honored belief, as expressed by Robert Browning, that "God's in his heaven—/All's right with the world!" During the 1940s, Jean-Paul Sartre, Victor Frankl, and other victims and resisters of Nazi tyranny reacted to daily reminders of the impermanence of life and found solace in existential philosophy.

Existentialists reject both scientific theories and the notion of causality in explaining human behavior. Unlike behaviorism and other twentieth-century psychologies, existentialism does not clearly distinguish between the person and the environment, the subject and the object. Existentialism does distinguish between *Umwelt* (the physical world), *Mitwelt* (the world of social interactions), and *Eigenwelt* (the intrapersonal world), but the individual is seen as finding meaning only by integrating these three "worlds." Existentialists also emphasize *phenomenology*, the individual perception of reality, as critical to an understanding of behavior. Because perceptions vary from person to person, reality is different for different people and hence subjective. There is an objective reality, but the individual understands and reacts to the world as it is perceived, not as it is in some objective sense. Focusing on an objective world, as science presumably does, provides an incomplete understanding of the individual, what propels him, and what his life means.

An emphasis on individual differences is also seen in existential concepts such as *freedom, choice,* and *authenticity.* Contrary to the viewpoint of scientific determinism that behavior is lawful and hence predictable, existentialists maintain that people are free to choose and to create their own lives, and through their creative efforts to discover their own personal meanings. An urgency to this effort is provided by the awareness of death and the resulting fear of *nothingness.* The term for this sense of urgency is *existential anxiety,* an emotion or motive that may be either normal or neurotic depending on how it is responded to.

The meaning of an individual's life develops from the perception of his or her *destiny,* not only what he or she might become in the future but from that inevitable termination known as *death.* Existentialists maintain, however, that what people fear is not so much death as having lived a meaningless, valueless life. By exercising their freedom, people can lose much of the fear of death and come to view their lives as productive and meaningful. To the existentialist, everyone is basically alone, life lacks any real sustained meaning, and death is absurd—a kind of "cosmic joke" on thinking humanity. Be that as it may, each of us still possesses the freedom to make what he or she will of life. By realizing that one's life may end at any moment, the person is free to make of life what he or she wishes.

Existentialists admit that people are not completely free. Their freedom and the choices they make are limited to some extent by their *thrownness,* including their physical and mental characteristics as well as their environmental circumstances. Nevertheless, people have the capacity and can exert the will to act in such a way as to realize their potentialities—to actualize themselves and strive for an authentic life. But by making certain choices a person must forgo other choices. Choosing one thing, one action, rather than another creates existential *guilt*—a feeling or realization that one has not taken advantage and cannot hope to take advantage of all of life's possibilities.

Although people are free to choose and to attempt to live authentically, they may make unwise choices. The decision to live an authentic life, to take chances on relationships with others, and to accept the challenges that are necessary for personal growth involves risks and therefore requires courage. There are no guarantees with freedom; one acts freely and must assume responsibility for one's choices and their consequences. Regardless of the choices that are made at any moment, existence is always in the process of *becoming*. The goal is to become authentic and completely human; refusal to accept the challenge and pursue this goal results in psychopathology.

Strictly speaking, existentialism is a philosophy rather than a psychology, but several psychologists have adapted existential concepts and ways of thinking to their conceptualizations and practices. Foremost among these psychologists are Ludwig Binswanger, Medard Boss, Victor Frankl, and Rollo May. The writings of all of these men have been instrumental in introducing American psychologists and laymen to existential philosophy and psychology, but May has been the most prolific and popular of these authors.

Biographical Sketch

Rollo May was born in Ada, Ohio, in 1909, but spent most of his childhood in Marine City, Michigan. His childhood, like that of several other theorists whom we have discussed, was not a happy one; his parents quarreled incessantly and eventually separated. Intellectual stimulation in the May family household was almost nonexistent, but Rollo was able to find comfort and curiosity in conversing with the St. Clair River! He developed an interest in art and literature, majored in English at Michigan State University, and was graduated from Oberlin College in 1930. He spent the early 1930s roaming around southern and eastern Europe, where he painted pictures, studied native art, tutored English in Salonika, Greece, and attended Alfred Adler's summer seminars in Vienna.

On returning to the United States, May enrolled in Union Theological Seminary, where he met the eminent theologian Paul Tillich and developed a friendship that lasted for 30 years. Tillich introduced May to existential thought, which the latter continued to study after graduating from Union with a B.D. degree in 1938. After serving for ten years as a student counselor and adviser at Michigan State University, May studied psychoanalysis and joined the faculty of the William Alanson White Institute. He subsequently did doctoral work at Columbia University, where in 1949 he received the first Ph.D. (summa cum laude) in clinical psychology ever offered by that institution.

Another event that contributed to May's interest in existentialism was a bout with tuberculosis during his early 30s. He spent three years at Saranac Sanatorium in Upstate New York, and for a year and a half did not know whether he would live or die. His observations of other patients at Saranac convinced May that a mental attitude of aggressiveness against the disease, rather than giving in to it, was associated with a better chance for recovery. This attitude has come to be characterized by contemporary health psychologists as an aspect of *hardiness* as opposed to *helplessness* (see Chapter 11).

May wrote many influential books having an existential theme, among which are *The Meaning of Anxiety* (1950, 1977) (an expansion of his Ph.D. thesis), *Man's Search for Himself* (1953), *Psychology and the Human Dilemma* (1967), *Love and Will* (1969) (a national best-seller which won the Ralph Waldo Emerson Award for humane scholarship), *Power and Innocence* (1972), and *Freedom and Destiny* (1981).

May's Existential Psychology

Well-versed and trained in both psychoanalysis and existentialism, May did not deny the importance of Freud's contribution to the understanding of human psychology, but he differed with Freud on many key issues. For example, Freud was an atheist, whereas May was an ordained minister who defined an atheist as a person who has failed to find meaning in life. Freud was a scientific determinist, but May believed in free will and personal responsibility.

May (1969) defined *will* as "the capacity to organize oneself so that movement in a certain direction or toward a certain goal may take place" (p. 218). Underlying will and decision is the concept of *intentionality,* the tendency to perceive and assign meaning to objects and events in the world selectively. Through intentionality the individual develops a structure of meaning and then responds to specific experiences in terms of that meaning structure.

Another difference between Freud and May concerns the concept of anxiety. Freud viewed anxiety as caused by unconscious conflict, whereas to May, as to other existentialists, anxiety is a reaction to a conscious threat to one's existence. For May and other existential psychologists, such anxiety is usually normal and becomes neurotic only when it is not dealt with constructively.

May also differed with Freud in regard to the role of the sex instinct. Freud viewed sexual energy (libido) as the driving force of personality, and frustration of its expression was the basis of neurosis. To May, however, sex is merely the biological aspect of love. Depending on the person, either having sex or not having sex may bring about guilt and anxiety, but inhibited sexual impulses are not the inevitable cause of neurosis. Rather than viewing "romantic love" as the sublimation of libidinal desires, May proposed that, in addition to *sex,* there are three other forms of love: eros, philia, and agape. *Eros* is the desire to form a psychological union with or feel as one with a love partner. *Philia* is the feeling of companionship or friendship that a person has with a loved one, even in the absence of sex and eros. Finally, *agape* is unselfishly giving oneself in a love relationship, with no expectation of receiving anything in return.

With respect to the role of the sex drive in determining behavior, May viewed the Oedipal complex not as love for one parent and hatred of the other, but as a struggle between dependence and independence. In addition, he did not subscribe to the Freudian notion of psychosexual stages of development. May's developmental stages (innocence, rebellion, ordinary consciousness of self, creative consciousness of self) are stages in the development of selfhood rather than sexuality.

Unlike Freud, May did not view the goal of psychotherapy to be the alleviation of anxiety and guilt. These symptoms are by-products of deeper problems, those of *powerlessness* and the inability to make effective choices. Consequently, the purpose of psychotherapy becomes one of making people freer, of expanding their consciousness, of making them more aware of the possibilities in their lives, and thereby assisting them in making better choices. Such choices lead to the growth of freedom and responsibility and a greater sense of meaning in one's life.

Also unlike Freud, but like Binswanger and Boss, May professed to have no particular set of psychotherapeutic techniques such as those of classical psychoanalytic therapy. Basically, the existential psychotherapist has only himself to give in attempting to establish an "I-thou" relationship. But, depending on what seems most effective in revealing the patient's existence at a particular time, a variety of psychotherapeutic techniques may be employed.

Criticisms of Existential Psychology

One of the major criticisms of existential psychology, and one that may have led the reader to question why existentialism is even discussed in a book concerned with the scientific study of personality, is the short shrift given to scientific theories and methods. Inherent in this criticism are other reasons why American psychologists have been slow to embrace existentialism. For example, the assumption that people are free to be what they want seems to run counter to everyday experience and clinical findings. To be sure, May rejects Rogers' notion that people are basically good, concluding instead, more in line with popular thought, that they are both good and bad (May's *daimonic*). However, this very notion reveals something of the religious tone of existential psychology, a tone that to scientific psychology smacks too much of unscientific influences and concepts from which psychology has tried to divorce itself. Similarly, existential psychology has been criticized for being more philosophical than psychological. The principal existential concepts are not those of modern psychology, and in any event they are difficult to grasp and essentially impossible to subject to scientific testing. Despite these criticisms, Hall and Lindzey (1985) conclude that

> this new way of studying and comprehending human beings has made a clear contribution to the study of human personality. Whether existential psychology survives, solidifies into a theory, or withers away, it has brought a fresh perspective to old issues and a new excitement to many psychologists concerned with understanding the lives of individual human beings. (p. 260)

George Kelly and Constructive Alternativism

The next and last theorist whom we shall consider in this chapter was a phenomenologist, a humanist, an existentialist, and a cognitivist, although he may very well have denied being any of those things. He was a phenomenologist because he believed in the primacy of conscious experience, a humanist because he stressed the human capacity to improve, an existentialist because he emphasized the present, and a cognitivist because he dealt mainly with cognitive rather than affective or behavioral concepts.

Biographical Sketch

George A. Kelly, a Kansas farm boy, was born April 28, 1905, the only child of a fundamentalist Presbyterian minister. Shortly thereafter the Kelly family moved to Colorado, but returned to Kansas because of the scarcity of work. George attended elementary school in a one-room school house, and at the age of 13 was sent to Wichita, Kansas, for high school. He saw his family very little after then. After graduating from high school he attended Friends University in Wichita, but transferred three years later to Park College. He received the B.A. in physics and mathematics in 1926 and worked as an aeronautical engineer and in various other occupations for a time. Subsequently he enrolled in the University of Kansas, where in 1928 he received the M.A. in educational sociology with a minor in labor relations. His master's thesis dealt with the way workers distribute their leisure-time activities.

After teaching in a labor college, conducting speech classes, and teaching an Americanization class for would-be citizens, Kelly became a member of the faculty of a junior college in Sheldon, Iowa. It was in Sheldon that he met Gladys Thompson, who became his wife. Like many of Kelly's early educational and occupational excursions, his junior-college teaching stint was short-lived. He spent 1929 as an exchange scholar at the University of Edinburgh in Scotland, where he earned a degree in education. On returning to the United States in 1930, he enrolled in the doctoral program in psychology at Iowa State University. He concentrated in physiological psychology and was awarded the Ph.D. in 1931 after writing a dissertation on speech and reading disabilities.

Kelly's first full-time teaching position in psychology was at Fort Hays (Kansas) State College. He gave up the field of physiological psychology for the growing, and economically more promising, field of clinical psychology. In this new position, which he held for 13 years and in which he was self-taught, he honed his clinical skills and laid the foundations for the theory of personality that he developed later at Ohio State University.

During World War II, Kelly joined the U.S. Navy as a psychologist in the Bureau of Medicine and Surgery. After the war he spent a year as an associate professor at the University of Maryland, and in 1946 became professor of psychology and director of the clinical psychology program at Ohio State University. It was at Ohio State that he wrote his 1,200-page *Psychology of Personal Constructs* (G. A. Kelly, 1955), a systematic, detailed, novel conception of human personality.

Kelly was a leader and an organizer who held several important posts in professional organizations and served as an inspiring teacher for many students of psychology. Born on the American prairie, he had a folksy, whimsical, direct manner, somewhat like Will Rogers. Some examples of "Kellyisms" are

If you don't like the way something looks, look at it differently. (1955, p. 11)

If you don't know what's wrong with a client, ask him; he may tell you. (1955, p. 201)

A good deal is said these days about being oneself. . . . It is a little hard for me to understand how one could be anything else. (1964, p. 147)

[Commenting on the S→R paradigm] . . . the most I could make of it was that the "S" was what he had to have in order to account for the "R" and the "R" was put there so the "S" would have something to account for. I never did find out what the arrow stood for—not to this day—and I have pretty well given up trying to figure it out. (1955, p. 47)

[After taking the Rep Test] I wasn't, I said to myself, the overemotional bigoted bastard portrayed there, so I stuck it in a file and did other things. About two weeks later I took it out again and said "yes, I am the overemotional bigoted et cetera portrayed in the grid." (Evans, 1978, p. 7)

Kelly remained at Ohio State until 1965, when he accepted an endowed chair at Brandeis University. He died on March 6, 1967, while working on a revision of his theory of personality.

A Theory of Personal Constructs

The basic unit in Kelly's theory of personality is the *personal construct,* a bipolar dimensional concept employed by the individual to "construe"—that is, classify or interpret—his or her experiences. Illustrative of personal constructs, which vary from person to person and serve to organize and explain one's experiences, are "good-bad," "smart-dumb," and "weak-strong." In the process of developing and interacting with the environment, the person builds up an ordered system of such constructs. An individual's construct system has some features in common with the construct systems of other members of the culture and social group, but it is to a large extent idiosyncratic. This idiosyncratic system of constructs forms the basis of individual personality, a unique pattern of organizing one's experiences and imposing order and predictability upon those experiences.

Just like the white-coated laboratory experimenter, to Kelly the "man-in-the-street" is a scientist who classifies his experiences in terms of a set of constructs, uses those constructs to make predictions about future experiences, and modifies his constructs in the light of experience. This approach to understanding human personality was labeled by Kelly as *constructive alternativism,* referring to the variety of ways in which people are free to select constructs to construe their experiences.

As listed in Table 7–2, Kelly's theory of constructive alternativism has one fundamental postulate and 11 corollaries. The somewhat specialized language of the postulate and corollaries does not make their meaning immediately obvious, but in the interest of precision Kelly avoided popular concepts such as "learning, motivation, and emotion" in formulating his theory. The basic premise of the theory, as stated in the fundamental postulate, is that the psychological processes

TABLE 7–2   Kelly's Fundamental Postulate and Corollaries

Fundamental Postulate
A person's processes are psychologically channelized by the ways in which he anticipates events.

Corollaries
1. *Construction Corollary: A person anticipates events by construing their replications.* This corollary means that personal constructs are formed on the basis of one's recurring experiences.
2. *Individual Corollary: Persons differ from each other in their constructions of events.* This corollary means that each person has a unique way of constructing his or her experiences, and therefore has a unique system of personal constructs.
3. *Organization Corollary: Each person characteristically evolves, for his convenience in anticipating events, a construction system embracing ordinal relationships between corollaries.* This corollary refers to the fact that a person's constructs are hierarchically organized from specific, subordinate constructs to more general, superordinate constructs.
4. *Dichotomy Corollary: A person's construction system is composed of a finite number of dichotomous constructs.* This corollary refers to the bipolarity or dichotomous nature of personality constructs. For example, at one pole of the "smart-dumb" construct dimension are things that are viewed as bright, intelligent, mentally quick, etc.; at the other pole are things that are considered stupid, ignorant, foolish, etc. For Kelly, at least three elements are needed to form a construct; two of these elements must be perceived as similar to each other, and the third as different from the other two. The similar elements are placed at the "similarity pole" of the construct, and the different element at the "contrast pole."
5. *Choice Corollary: A person chooses for himself that alternative in a dichotomized construct through which he anticipates the greater possibility for extension and definition of his system.* This corollary means that people select constructs that serve either to define or extend their existing construct system.
6. *Range Corollary: A construct is convenient for the anticipation of a finite range of events only.* This corollary means that constructs are applicable to a finite range of events. In addition to the "range of convenience," to which a construct is relevant, it has a "focus of convenience," a subset of events within its range of convenience to which it is maximally applicable.
7. *Experience Corollary: A person's construction system varies as he successively construes the replications of events.* This corollary refers to the fact that, as people actively reintegrate and reclassify their experiences, those constructs undergo modification and extension and become more effective in explaining their experiences.
8. *Modulation Corollary: The variation in a person's construction system is limited by the permeability of the constructs within whose ranges of convenience the variants lie.* This corollary means that a construct system containing permeable constructs—that is, constructs that assimilate new experiences more easily—is more adaptable or likely to undergo modification.
9. *Fragmentation Corollary: A person may successively employ a variety of construction subsystems which are inferentially incompatible with each other.* This corollary means that inconsistencies in cognition and behavior may occur as a construct system is tested and confirmed or revised.
10. *Commonality Corollary: To the extent that one person employs a construction of experience which is similar to that employed by another, his psychological processes are similar to those of the other person.* This corollary means that people are similar in personality to the extent that they interpret their experiences in a similar manner; that is, they have similar construct systems.
11. *Sociality Corollary: To the extent that one person construes the construction processes of another, he may play a role in a social process involving the other person.* This corollary means that effective social interaction with another person requires an understanding of how that person construes or interprets his or her experiences.

Source: G. A. Kelly (1955, pp. 103–104).

of an individual, including but not limited to the scientist, are aimed at predicting or anticipating future events. Human beings are seen as basically rational, thinking organisms who are able to plan for and control future events because they can predict them.

Based on the fundamental postulate and the 11 corollaries, Kelly considered a number of other psychological topics, such as roles, emotions, and personality assessment and change. He defined a *role* as acting according to another person's expectations of how one will act. The roles played by a person when interacting with people and groups who are important to that person are referred to as *core roles.* Core roles are central to the identity or self-concept of a person, and the way in which they are performed can have important consequences for the person's life.

People experiment with many roles during their lifetime, but only some of these roles are successful. In *fixed-role therapy,* the client is encouraged by the therapist to assume the role of a fictitious person so the former can try out new ways of construing his or her experiences in a nonthreatening context. The therapist plays a supporting role in this drama, hoping that the client will find the new role effective and, in time, modify his or her existing construct system and adopt the new role as a natural way of behaving.

To Kelly, emotions were signs of a need for a change in one's construct system. A feeling of *threat* occurs when a person becomes aware that one or more of his personal constructs are about to be invalidated and therefore that the construct system must be changed in some way. Associated with threat is *anxiety,* a feeling that an experience lies outside the range of convenience of the individual's system of constructs. *Guilt,* on the other hand, occurs when a person acts in a manner that is inconsistent with a role that he or she has assumed when interacting with a significant person or group. Guilt is a "perception of one's apparent dislodgment from his core role structure" (G. A. Kelly, 1955, p. 502). Threat, anxiety, and guilt may all be associated with abnormal behavior. Such behavior occurs when a person lacks appropriate constructs or when the person's constructs are either too permeable or too impermeable.

Role Construct Repertory Test

According to Kelly's theory of personal constructs, people are scientists, albeit not necessarily good ones. Like scientists, they conceptualize or categorize their experiences in what appears to them to be a logical way. But many people, particularly those who are considered "neurotic," perceive or construe the world incorrectly and develop faulty systems of constructs. Consequently, Kelly believed that to help the neurotic individual the psychotherapist must begin by identifying the system of constructs used by the former in interpreting those people who are important to her or him.

One procedure that Kelly devised for identifying a person's system of constructs is the Role Construct Repertory (Rep) Test. The first step in administering the Rep Test is to have the examinee list the names of the 22 people in his or her life who fill each of the following roles:

1 yourself
2 your mother
3 your father
4 brother nearest to you in age (or person most like a brother)
5 sister nearest to you in age (or person most like a sister)
6 your spouse (or closest friend of opposite sex)
7 friend of opposite sex after person in 6
8 closest friend of same sex as you
9 person once a close friend but no longer
10 religious leader with whom you could discuss feelings about religion
11 your medical doctor
12 neighbor you know best
13 person you know who dislikes you
14 person for whom you feel sorry and would like to help
15 person with whom you feel uncomfortable
16 recent acquaintance you would like to know better
17 most influential teacher when you were in your teens
18 teacher you disagreed with most
19 employer or supervisor under whom you worked while experiencing stress
20 most successful person you know
21 happiest person you know
22 most ethical person you know

After designating the 22 people, the examinee is instructed to compare them in groups of three corresponding to the three circles on each row of Figure 7–2. Thus the first comparison may be among persons 20, 21, and 22, and the second among persons 17, 18, and 19. Then on the appropriate row under the column headed "Construct," a particular examinee may write a word or phrase (e.g., "Motivated") describing how two of the three persons are alike; under "Contrast" the examinee would write a word or phrase (e.g., "Lazy") describing how the third person is different from the other two. Next the examinee draws an X in the circles corresponding to the two people on that row who are alike. For the remaining 19 people on the row, the appropriate box is checked if the "Construct" part applies to them and left blank if it does not apply. This process is continued for the remaining 21 constructs, or as many or few constructs as the examinee wishes to list. Six construct-contrast examples are included in Figure 7–2.

The examinee's performance on the Rep Test is analyzed by noting how many constructs are used and what they are, what aspects of people are emphasized in the constructs (physical, social, etc.), and which people are most like or different from the examinee. Interpreting the results of the Rep Test is a laborious, subjective process, because the test is as much a projective test as a rating scale. In the absence of an objective scoring system it should not be surprising that, although the grid responses appear fairly reliable, the Rep Test

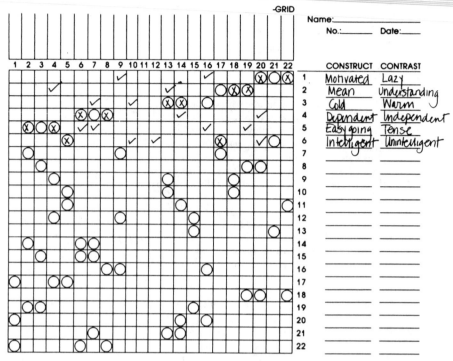

FIGURE 7–2 Typical form used in Role Construct Repertory Test. (Adapted and reproduced with permission from G. A. Kelly, 1955).

has not been widely used for either clinical or research purposes and its validity is largely unknown.

Evaluation of Kelly's Theory

George Kelly's own list of publications concerned with his theory of personality is shorter than that of any other theorist whom we have considered, with the exception of Harry Stack Sullivan. Since the publication of *The Psychology of Personality Constructs* in 1955, and even after Kelly's death in 1967, however, hundreds of papers and a number of books dealing with the theory have been published by other researchers and interpreters of the theory (e.g., Bannister & Fransella, 1971; Bannister, 1984; Maher, 1969; Neimeyer, 1985). Although the theory has not been especially popular in the United States, it has fared better in England, primarily because of the efforts of Bannister. It has also attracted more interest among industrial/organizational psychologists than among clinicians working in mental health settings.

Among the criticisms of personal construct theory are Kelly's rather perfunctory dismissal of learning, motivation, and emotion as unimportant psychological topics, his focus on cognitive or intellectual interpretations of affective processes, and his failure to describe how personal constructs are formed and how personality develops. Furthermore, research findings indicate that, unlike Kelly's assumption that constructs control behavior, in actuality the formulation of constructs often follows behavior rather than vice versa. The narrowness of a personality theory based primarily on midwestern U.S. college students and Kelly's failure to relate the theory to previous research and theorizing in psychology have also been cited as criticisms of the theory. Finally, the validity and utility of the Rep Test as a measure of personal constructs have been questioned.

A number of research studies (e.g., Bieri, 1955; Duck & Craig, 1978; Duck & Spencer, 1972; Neimeyer, 1984) have confirmed certain predictions derived from Kelly's theory, but in general it has not been subjected to rigorous empirical testing. In fairness to Kelly, he considered the theory to be a tentative exposition, and, if he had lived longer, he would undoubtedly have revised it. Despite its shortcomings, the theory remains a significant achievement and an important forerunner of later cognitive theories. It is also a continuing source of fruitful hypotheses for researchers in psychology, communication, and other fields concerned with the acquisition of personal constructs and their effects on personality and behavior.

Summary

Personality theorists of a phenomenological persuasion stress the importance of immediate, personal, subjective experience as the primary determinant of personality. Trait theorists and others who attempt to analyze personality into a set of components are seen as doing an injustice to its integrated, dynamic organization. Phenomenological theorists have, by and large, been quite critical of trait-factor, psychoanalytic, and behavioral theories. In contrast to classical psychoanalytic theory, which sees sexual and aggressive impulses, the unconscious, and psychosexual stages of development as crucial factors in shaping personality, phenomenological psychologists such as Abraham Maslow and Carl Rogers stress perceptions, meanings, feelings, and the self. These psychologists maintain that people respond to the world in terms of their own unique, private perceptions. These perceptions are determined by the individual's experiences and the meanings placed on those experiences in an effort to fully realize one's potentialities. The part of the environment that is perceived and has meaning for the individual is known as the phenomenal field, a portion of which—the self—is related to the individual in a personal way. The evaluations—good and bad—that the individual places on the self become the self-concept.

According to Maslow, Rogers, and other phenomenological theorists, the individual strives to attain a state of self-actualization—a congruence or harmoniousness between his or her real and ideal selves. The basic direction of existence is toward self-actualization and cordial relations with other people, but that natural process can be interfered with in various ways. Rogers points out that most people are not open to or willing to accept the full range of their experiences. In the process of growing up, they learn that they are objects of conditional positive regard: Parents and other significant people in their lives accept their behavior only if it conforms to expected standards, so-called conditions of worth. Consequently, in becoming an adult the child learns to recognize and accept only a part of his or her experiences. The result is an individual who cannot become totally functioning unless he or she receives unconditional positive regard from others.

Although they are not self-theorists in the same sense as Maslow and Rogers, Rollo May and George Kelly also rank among the phenomenologists. Trained in psychoanalysis but imbued with strong artistic and theological interests, May opted for an existential approach in his writings and practice. Taking as a starting point the existentialist credo that "existence is prior to essence," May and other existential psychologists stress the individual's efforts to find meaning in his or her life by being a participant rather than a mere spectator, by attempting to live authentically through exercising one's freedom of choice to create his or her own life. Being free to choose, however, entails responsibility for those choices, whether they are wise ones or not. When people choose poorly, they may need psychotherapy. For May, the goal of psychotherapy is not to alleviate anxiety and guilt, but rather to make a person freer and more aware of the possibilities in life and therefore capable of making better choices.

George Kelly's theory of personal constructs is based on the fundamental postulate that "a person's processes are psychologically channelized by the ways in which he anticipates events." This statement means that a person's psychological processes, like those of the laboratory scientist, are directed toward predicting or anticipating future events. Being able to predict events implies understanding and control over those events.

In elaborating on this postulate and 11 corollaries based on it, Kelly emphasized the personal construct as the basic unit of personality. People tend to anticipate events by construing—that is, interpreting—the replications of those events. The system of personal constructs that is formulated by an individual from his or her observations and successful predictions is, in essence, the person's personality. These dichotomized constructs, which have a range and focus of convenience and a certain degree of permeability, may be similar to or different from those of other people and are subject to change. The success of an individual in construing experiences, as evinced by the validity and consistency of his or her constructs, is an important factor in the person's mental health. The Role Construct Repertory Test (Rep), for elucidating a person's construct system, and fixed-role therapy are two of the techniques that were employed by Kelly in his clinical work.

Key Concepts

Conditions of worth   According to Carl Rogers, the feelings experienced by a person who is evaluated as a totality, and not according to specific actions. The person feels that his or her worth depends on manifesting the right behaviors, attitudes, and values.

Construct   In Kelly's theory of constructive alternativism, a concept used to construe (interpret) events.

Constructive alternativism   Kelly's theory that events can be construed or interpreted in various ways.

Dasein (being-in-the-world)   A existentialist term referring to the sense of self as a free and responsible individual existing in the world of things (*Umwelt*), other people (*Mitwelt*), and one's self (*Einwelt*).

Existentialism   A philosophical school that emphasizes the importance of the individual self as being responsible for its own choices and efforts to find meaning in a purposeless, irrational universe.

Humanistic psychology (phenomenological psychology)   An approach to psychological research and practice that is concerned with subjective experiences and values, focusing on the uniqueness of the person; also referred to as *third-force psychology*.

Ideal self   In Rogers' phenomenological theory, the person whom the individual would like to be (the self he or she would like to possess).

Peak experience   An intense, pleasurable emotional experience leading to personal growth.

Personal construct   In George Kelly's personality theory, the basic unit of personality organization; a conceptual dimension used by the individual to "construe" the environment.

Phenomenal field   That part of the environment that is perceived by and has meaning for the person.

Phenomenology   The study of objects and events as they appear to the experiencing observer; a type of psychotherapy (Rogers, Maslow, etc.) which emphasizes the importance of self-perceptions and impressions of others in determining personality and behavior.

Real self   In Rogers' phenomenological theory, a person's perception of what he or she really is, as contrasted with what he or she would like to be (*ideal self*).

Self   The perceived identity, individuality, or ego; that which consciously knows and experiences.

Self-actualization   Fulfillment of one's potentialities; to attain a state of congruence or harmony between one's real and ideal selves.

Self-concept   Fairly consistent cluster of feelings, ideas, and attitudes toward oneself.

Activities and Applications

1. Do you believe that people are fundamentally good or evil? What are the implications for child rearing, education, government, and other social activities and institutions in the assumption that people are basically good? That they are basically evil? Is there a third alternative concerning human nature, and what are its implications?

2. As we have seen, Freud and many other psychoanalysts placed a great deal of emphasis on irrational, unconscious motivation in determining behavior, whereas phenomenologists and existentialists pay more attention to rational, conscious determinants. How do you personally evaluate the relative importance of conscious and unconscious factors in shaping your own personality? The personalities of other people?

3. Compare and contrast the phenomenological theories discussed in this chapter with the psychodynamic theories discussed in Chapters 5 and 6 with regard to their ability to describe and explain
  a. personality development across the life span.
  b. changes in personality caused by environmental events.
  c. personality disorders.

4. Rate each of the following personality theorists on a scale of 1 to 10 pertaining to their relative optimism or pessimism (a rating of 1 is most pessimistic, and a rating of 10 is most optimistic) concerning the future of humanity:

Alfred Adler
Erik Erikson
Sigmund Freud
Erich Fromm
Karen Horney
Carl Jung
George Kelly
Abraham Maslow
Rollo May
Carl Rogers
Harry Stack Sullivan

What factors or statements by the theorists contributed to your ratings?

5. Consider the personalities of the people whom you know, both relatives and nonrelatives. According to the characteristics of self-actualized people listed in Table 7–1, which individuals whom you know do you believe to be the most self-actualized? Explain.

6. Ask a dozen people or so to respond to the following instructions orally or in writing:

I would like you to think of the most wonderful experience or experiences of your life; happiest moments, ecstatic moments, moments of rapture, perhaps from being in love, or from listening to music or suddenly "being hit" by a book or a painting, or from some great creative moment. First list these. And then try to tell me how you feel in such acute moments, how you feel differently from the way you feel at other times, how you are at the moment a different person in some ways. (Maslow, 1968, p. 71)

What kinds of responses did you obtain? Into what categories can the "peak experiences" be classified? Were there any differences between the reports of males and females? Did the reported experiences provide any information on the personality of the individual?

7. Construct a ten-item self-concept inventory, using a true-false item format. On half the statements the keyed answer should be "true"; on the other half the keyed answer should be "false." Administer your self-concept inventory to several students, and compute their total scores (0–10) as the number of responses they give in the keyed direction. Did you find generally low or generally high scores? How variable were the scores? What evidence can you offer in support of your ten-item inventory as a valid measure of self-concept?

8. Consider the following list of 25 descriptive adjectives. Make a check mark in the second column if the adjective is descriptive of your real self, and make a check mark in the third column if the adjective is descriptive of your ideal self.

Adjective	Descriptive of My Real Self	Descriptive of My Ideal Self
artistic		
athletic		
attractive		
capable		
charming		
courageous		
energetic		
enterprising		
forceful		
friendly		
gentle		
helpful		
intelligent		
kind		
loyal		
organized		
original		
persevering		
popular		
resourceful		
sociable		
studious		
successful		
tactful		
witty		

Now count the number of adjectives for which you placed a check mark in one column but not in the other column. Then subtract this number from 25 and multiply the difference by 4. The resulting percentage figure is a measure of the congruence between your real-self and your ideal-self descriptions. Interpret your score.

9. Take the Role Construct Repertory Test, following the procedure described on pages 190–192. Make a copy of the grid in Figure 7–2, and fill it in with the appropriate circles, constructs, and contrasts pertaining to your own construct system. Interpret your results and compare them with those obtained by administering the test to a friend or acquaintance.

Suggested Readings

Derlega, V. J., & Berg, J. H. (Eds.). (1987). *Self disclosure: Theory, research, and therapy.* New York: Plenum.

Gendlin, E. T. (1988). Carl Rogers (1902–1987). *American Psychologist, 43,* 127–128.

Hoffman, E. (1988). *The right to be human: A biography of Abraham Maslow.* Los Angeles: Tarcher.

Kelly, G. A. (1963). *A theory of personality: The psychology of personal constructs.* New York: Norton.

Kirschenbaum, H. (1979). *On becoming Carl Rogers.* New York: Delacorte Press.

Landfield, A. W., & Epting, F. R. (1987). *Personal construct psychology: Clinical and personality assessment.* New York: Human Sciences Press.

Maslow, A. H. (1987). *Motivation and personality* (3rd ed.). New York: Harper & Row.

May, R. (1969). *Love and will.* New York: Norton.

Rogers, C. R. (1961). *On becoming a person.* Boston: Houghton Mifflin.

Rogers, C. R. (1980). *A way of being.* Boston: Houghton Mifflin.

◈◈

CHAPTER 8

Behavioral and Social Learning Theories

CHAPTER OUTLINE

The early years of the twentieth century were a period of intense activity in American psychology. The influences of introspectionism, evolutionism, and the German tradition of phenomenology all focused on the American scene around 1912. Coupled with the American "practical" philosophy of pragmatism, these ideas gave rise to a number of schools of psychology in the United States, among which were structuralism, functionalism, Gestalt psychology, and behaviorism. These schools consisted of a group of psychologists with a distinct viewpoint concerning the kinds of subject matter or the questions that should be the concern of psychology and the methods that should be used to search for answers to these questions.

The school of *structuralism,* founded in Germany by Wilhelm Wundt and exported to America by E. B. Titchener and others, defined psychology as the study of the normal, adult human mind by means of the method of *introspection* (looking inward to the mind). By having observers introspect into the sensations, images, and feelings they experienced when exposed to a stimulus, the structuralists hoped to devise a kind of "mental chemistry" or structural map of the mind. Representatives of the school of *functionalism* criticized the structuralists for being interested only in answering questions of "what and how" and not the "why" of mental events. Functionalists such as James Angell, Harvey Carr, and Robert Woodworth were greatly influenced by Darwinian evolution, and they extended Darwin's research on the origins of physical differences among species to the functions of mind and behavior. They continued to employ the method of introspection, together with objective observation and experimentation, but their research emphasized the adaptive utility of consciousness and behavior rather than the structure of mind.

The founders of *gestalt psychology*—Max Wertheimer, Kurt Koffka, and Wolfgang Köhler—also objected to the structuralists' emphasis on analyzing the mind into its constituent elements. As seen in their famous dictum "The whole is more than the sum of its parts," the gestaltists noted that what a person perceives is determined not by the parts alone but also by the relationships among the parts. It is generally agreed that gestalt psychology had an invigorating effect on all of psychology, but a greater influence on the direction in which American psychology was to go was exerted by John B. Watson—the founder of *behaviorism.*

Watson and Pavlov

John B. Watson (1878–1958) was repelled by the esoteric philosophizing concerning the structure of consciousness that dominated early scientific psychology and by the unreliability of the method of introspection. He maintained that the proper subject matter of psychology is *behavior,* objectively measured and recorded.

> I believe we can write a psychology . . . and never go back upon our definition; never use the terms consciousness, mental states, mind, content, introspectively verifiable,

imagery, and the like. It can be done in terms of stimulus and response, in terms of habit formation, habit integration, and the like. Furthermore, I believe it is really worth while to make the attempt now. (Watson, 1913, pp. 166–167)

Watson stressed the importance of the environment and learning, as opposed to heredity and instinct, in determining behavior. He believed that, with the exception of a few inherited emotions (fear, rage, and love), behavioral patterns are produced by experience.

As indicated in the following famous quotation, Watson (1924) viewed individual differences and personality as largely determined by learning:

> Give me a dozen healthy infants, well formed, and my own specified world to bring them up in and I'll guarantee to take any one at random and train him to become any type of specialist I might select—doctor, lawyer, merchant, chief, and yes, even beggar-man and thief, regardless of his talents, peculiarities, tendencies, abilities, vocations, and race of his ancestors. There is no such thing as an inheritance of capacity, talent, temperament, mental constitution, and characteristics. (p. 104)

Searching for a technique to demonstrate the importance of learning and the enviroment in fashioning behavior and personality, Watson seized upon the conditioning procedure of the Russian physiologist I. P. Pavlov.

Pavlovian Conditioning

While conducting research on digestion in dogs, Pavlov found that an animal can learn to salivate in response to the ticking of a metronome (or any other stimulus) that regularly precedes the presentation of food. Once such a *conditioned response* to the metronome (the *conditioned stimulus*) was established, the degree of salivation diminished regularly—that is, it became *extinguished*—unless it was periodically reinforced by the presentation of food (the *unconditioned stimulus*). Pavlov and his associates conducted many experiments and discovered a number of principles governing this simple form of learning. Among the phenomena associated with Pavlovian (classical) conditioning are extinction, spontaneous recovery, stimulus generalization, higher-order conditioning, and experimental neurosis. *Extinction* is the gradual diminution of a conditioned response when it is no longer followed by the unconditioned stimulus. However, it is almost impossible to extinguish a conditioned response completely. In fact, after a response has ostensibly been extinguished, it may reappear following a period of rest, a phenomenon known as *spontaneous recovery*. A response that has been conditioned to a particular stimulus may also be elicited by similar stimuli, a phenomenon referred to as *stimulus generalization*. Another phenomenon is *higher-order conditioning*, in which a conditioned stimulus now becomes a reinforcer or unconditioned stimulus and a second stimulus that is associated with it is conditioned to elicit the conditioned response.

Experimental Neurosis

One of Pavlov's most interesting experiments, at least to clinical and personality psychologists, dealt with conditioning a dog to discriminate between a circle and an ellipse. The response was salivation, and the animal, by being reinforced with meat powder when a circle was presented but not reinforced when an ellipse was presented, developed a conditioned discrimination. The dog learned to salivate only when the circle was presented. When the ratio of the axes of the ellipse was changed to 8:9, however, the dog was unable to discriminate between the ellipse and the circle, and its behavior became erratic. It salivated to any stimulus, squealed, barked violently, bit at the apparatus, and could not make even the simpler discriminations that it had made previously. Pavlov called this behavior *experimental neurosis.* He discovered, however, that not all dogs reacted in an excited, aggressive way in this sort of "conflict" situation. Some animals simply went to sleep in the apparatus when they were unable to solve a discrimination problem. Pavlov labeled these two patterns of behavior the *excitatory type* and *inhibitory type,* an understandable distinction to anyone who has observed temperamental differences among dogs.

Watson was especially interested in the conditioned response as a way of studying and explaining how an organism learns, and his experiment on conditioning a young child to fear a white rat is a classic psychological investigation (Watson & Rayner, 1920). From the results of his experiments with children, Watson came to believe that almost all human behavior, either adaptive or maladaptive, is learned and hence can be unlearned. Although Watson was not entirely correct, to many psychologists his ideas came as a fresh wind blowing away the old philosophical, mentalistic cobwebs of consciousness and introspection. Watson left psychology in the 1920s, never to return, but during the 1930s the torch of behaviorism was picked up by a young man at Harvard University.

Skinner and Radical Behaviorism

Perhaps the most famous of all American psychologists, B. F. Skinner, was born in Susquehanna, Pennsylvania, in 1904. As an undergraduate, Skinner attended Hamilton College, where he majored in English with the intent of becoming a creative writer. After a summer in Greenwich Village, however, he concluded that he had nothing to say as a writer, and at that point he decided to enroll as a graduate student in psychology at Harvard University. Skinner received the M.A. in 1930 and the Ph.D. in 1931, then remained at Harvard as a postdoctoral fellow for five years. He began his teaching career at the University of Minnesota in 1936, and in 1945 became chairman of the psychology department at Indiana University. After three years at Indiana he returned to Harvard as professor of psychology, where he remained until his death in 1990.

During his four decades at Harvard, Skinner's name became a household word for "radical behaviorist." His reputation as one of America's foremost psychologists was built on research involving the operant conditioning of organisms ranging from pigeons to people, and on his outspoken views, enunciated in his many books and articles, on social control by means of behavioral principles.

Operant Conditioning

Beginning with his years as a graduate student at Harvard, Skinner's viewpoint on the proper subject matter of psychology and the way to investigate that subject matter did not waver during his lifetime. His penchant for constructing gadgets, combined with persistence, strong self-discipline, and a bit of good luck, resulted in important payoffs for his atheoretical, "empty organism" analysis of behavior. In one sense, Skinner was like Gordon Allport, not that he believed in personality traits, but rather that he believed in focusing on individual data rather than group statistics. However, Skinner was unlike Allport in his belief that an analysis of the interactions between behavior and environment (the *functional analysis of behavior*) in single organisms would yield regularities and principles applicable to all organisms.

Skinner coined the term *operant conditioning* to contrast with *respondent (Pavlovian) conditioning*. He stated that in respondent conditioning, which is the conditioning of responses involving the autonomic nervous system and the law of association, a response is *elicited* by a conditioned stimulus. In operant conditioning, on the other hand, the response involves the skeletal musculature, is *emitted* rather than elicited, and obeys the principle of reinforcement. Skinner maintained that the learning of *operants* (responses that "operate" on the environment) is more typical of everyday learning. Motor and verbal skills are learned by operant conditioning, whereas emotional responses to particular stimuli are learned by respondent conditioning. The term *elicited behavior* is appropriate for respondent conditioning, because in this situation an experimentally manipulated conditioning stimulus comes to elicit a conditioned response. Operant conditioning, on the other hand, deals with *emitted behavior* in which the response is simply "emitted" without any ostensible stimulus being presented.

All of the phenomena demonstrable with respondent conditioning can also be obtained in operant conditioning. For example, once an animal has been conditioned to press the bar in a Skinner box for food reward and suddenly the food no longer appears when the bar is pressed, extinction of the bar-pressing response begins to occur. Illustrative of the extinction of operant behavior in a human being is the cessation of repetitive crying in an infant who is put to bed. When the parents are taught to stop entering the child's bedroom after putting him to bed, the infant's crying is no longer reinforced and gradually becomes extinguished (Williams, 1959).

Also demonstrable in both respondent and operant conditioning are the discrimination and generalization of both stimuli and responses. A *discrimination* between two stimuli may be established in either an animal or a human by rewarding the organism for responding to one stimulus but not the other. A conditioned discrimination, or differentiation, between responses may be established by rewarding one response and not another.

Reinforcement

Basic to Skinner's explanation of learning is the principle that behavior is controlled by its consequences, which may or may not be reinforcing. A *reinforcer* is any stimulus which, when presented after a response is made in a given situation, will affect the probability that the same response will be repeated again in that situation. Predictably, the presentation of a reinforcer is called *reinforcement.* A *positive reinforcer,* when presented, increases the probability of the preceding response, whereas a *negative reinforcer,* when removed, increases the probability of the preceding response. In contrast to negative reinforcement, *punishment* is the application of a stimulus which decreases the probability of an ongoing response. Examples of positive reinforcers used in animal studies are food, water, or other vital substances or conditions of which the animal has been deprived. With human subjects, praise, promotions, and other social rewards are commonly used.

Similar to other psychologists, Skinner advocated the use of positive reinforcement rather than punishment in changing behavior. Laboratory research and personal observations convinced him that strong punishment may temporarily suppress a response but the effects do not last. Illustrative of this point are the results of a study by Estes (1944), who first rewarded rats with food for pressing a bar in a Skinner box and then used the following extinction procedures: Bar-pressing in one group of rats—the nonpunished group—was extinguished by not reinforcing the animals with food. A second group of rats—the punished group—was treated similarly except for the fact that the animals were given an electric shock during the early extinction trials; the shock was administered to the forepaws of the animal through the bar that it was pressing. The results showed that although the rate of bar-pressing was temporarily suppressed in the punished group, the animals eventually made as many bar-pressing responses during extinction as the nonpunished group.

Another distinction pertaining to the concept of reinforcement is that between primary and secondary reinforcers. The reinforcing properties of a *primary reinforcer* are natural, inborn, or unlearned, whereas the reinforcing properties of a *secondary reinforcer* are learned by association with a primary reinforcer. To illustrate, for a hungry rat pressing a bar in a Skinner box to get food, the food is a primary reinforcer and the click of the food-delivery mechanism is a secondary reinforcer. The rat will continue to press the bar for clicks even when food is no longer forthcoming; the click has become a secondary reinforcer.

A distinction should also be made between a secondary reinforcer and a *discriminative stimulus,* which is a stimulus that signals to the respondent that a particular behavior will be followed by reinforcement. Through experience people and animals learn that certain behaviors will be reinforced only when a specific signal or environmental condition is present; that signal or condition is a discriminative stimulus. A rat that has learned to press the bar in a Skinner box only when a light is on, for example, has learned to respond to a discriminative stimulus (the light). In actuality, the same stimulus may serve either as a discriminative stimulus or a secondary reinforcer or both, depending on when it occurs relative to the response. A discriminative stimulus precedes the response, but a secondary reinforcer follows the response. A stimulus occurring concurrently with a response may act either as a discriminative stimulus or a secondary reinforcer.

With respect to the frequency of reinforcement, a distinction should be made between continuous and partial reinforcement. In a *continuous reinforcement schedule,* the animal or person is reinforced every time it makes a designated response; in a *partial reinforcement schedule,* not every correct response is reinforced. Skinner and his coworkers thoroughly investigated the effects of various kinds of partial-reinforcement schedules on behavior (Ferster & Skinner, 1957). Four basic types of reinforcement schedules are fixed-interval, fixed-ratio, variable-interval, and variable-ratio. An organism on a *fixed-interval reinforcement schedule* is reinforced for the first response that it makes when a fixed period of time has elapsed since the last reinforcement. In a *fixed-ratio reinforcement schedule,* reinforcement occurs only on the last of a fixed number of responses; the ratio refers to the number of responses necessary per reinforcement. A fixed-interval schedule is similar to being paid on a fixed weekly or monthly salary, whereas a fixed-ratio schedule is like being paid on a piecework basis. An organism on a *variable-interval reinforcement schedule* is reinforced at irregular intervals, and on a *variable-ratio reinforcement schedule* the number of responses that an organism must make in order to be reinforced changes throughout the course of learning.

Of particular interest is the fact that the rate of responding during acquisition and extinction varies in a predictable manner according to the schedule employed. An organism on a fixed-interval schedule makes few responses until the end of the interval approaches, at which time the rate of responding becomes quite rapid. On the other hand, one of the most impressive effects of the variable-interval schedule is the very high resistance to extinction of learned responses shown by animals trained on this schedule.

Skinner and his associates had notable success in training animals to perform a variety of response patterns ranging from simple bar-pressing to playing Ping-Pong and guiding missiles. The basic principle employed in *shaping* any response is to reward successive approximations to that response. For example, pigeons certainly have no natural inclination to play table tennis, but they can be taught to play a modified version of the game in the following manner: The trainer begins by reinforcing the pigeon for approaching the ball, then reinforces it only if it touches the ball, next only if it rolls the ball with its beak, and finally only if it rolls the ball past another pigeon, similarly trained and waiting on the other side of the table to hit the ball back with its beak.

Although research and applications concerned with reinforcement have focused on animals, the concept has been applied to many different kinds of learning, ranging from simple conditioning of lower animals to complex problem solving and psychotherapy with humans. Extensive research on verbal learning, behavior modification, and programmed instruction, in particular, have increased our understanding of how reinforcement works.

Other Contributions

Behavior therapy did not originate with Skinner, but many of his students have applied the techniques learned under his tutelage to the treatment of drug addiction and alcoholism, autism, speech problems, sexual disorders, phobias, obesity, and delinquency. The use of *token economies* in mental hospitals, training schools, and other institutions, in which token rewards are made contingent on socially approved behavior, originated with Skinner. The basic principle underlying these applications is that behavior can be controlled by manipulating its consequences.

Skinner's restless mind was forever exploring new applications of operant conditioning methodology, even designing and redesigning entire cultures by regulating reinforcement contingencies to encourage certain behaviors and discourage others (*contingency management*). In the books *Walden Two* (1948) and *Beyond Freedom and Dignity* (1971) Skinner argued for the use of behavioral principles to operate and control entire societies. Although based to some extent on laboratory research, the sociopolitical psychology presented in these books is highly speculative and has been widely criticized. Among the major unanswered questions concerning a society organized along Skinnerian lines is "Who will control the controllers?" and "How can such a society keep from becoming fascist?" Humanists in particular have taken issue with Skinner's assumption that people do not possess free will, but rather that their personalities or stylistic behaviors are determined by the reinforcing consequences of their actions.

Drive Theory

Skinner's theoretical position is sometimes characterized as an "empty organism" approach, in that it concentrates on the S and R of the S-O-R (stimulus-organism-response) paradigm. He considered concepts such as ego, self, instincts, drives, and the like as useless internal baggage that add nothing to our understanding of behavior. However, many psychologists who regarded themselves as "behaviorists" did not agree with Skinner's radical behaviorism. Among these psychologists were drive theorists such as Clark Hull, John Dollard, and Neal Miller.

Hull's Hypothetico-Deductive Theory

Drive theory is closely related to the concept of *homeostasis*, the tendency of the body to maintain a relatively constant internal environment. According to drive theory, a drive is aroused by some bodily need, and the drive then activates and directs the organism's behavior toward an incentive that reduces the drive by satisfying the need. Hull (1943, 1951), the most famous drive theorist, developed a learning theory based on the concept of drive as a stimulus resulting from a tissue need. He assumed that the strength of a drive and the resulting behavior that it directs vary with the intensity of a need. Hull also maintained that new responses are learned only if those responses are instrumental in reducing the strength of a drive. According to Hull, the series of events leading to the learning of a new response is as follows: (1) A *drive* is aroused by a need; (2) a stimulus *cue* results in (3) an instrumental *response* that leads to (4) *reward* and consequently (5) *drive reduction*. When the same need is rearoused, the instrumental response will be made more quickly because the organism has learned something about what leads to what.

The organism, of course, typically has a variety of responses in its repertoire (*habit family hierarchy*) that can be made to a specific stimulus situation. In that situation, the dominant response—the response that is highest on the habit family hierarchy—is made first. If that response does not work—that is, if it is not instrumental in reducing the strength of the drive—then the next response in the hierarchy is made, and so on until a drive-reducing response occurs.

According to drive theory, complex psychosocial motives are learned through association with primary motives. Thus it is maintained that a new drive to approach or withdraw from a particular stimulus situation results from the association of that situation with reward or punishment. An experiment by N. E. Miller (1948) illustrates how a new drive is learned. In this experiment, a rat received a painful electric shock in the white compartment but not in the black compartment of a rectangular apparatus painted white on one half of its interior and black on the other half. When the animal was first placed in the compartment, it showed no preference for staying in either the white half or the black half of the apparatus. However, after a mild electric shock was administered to the animal whenever it was in the white half, it began to show a decided preference for remaining in the black half. When the experimenter forced the animal to remain in the white half, it tried frantically to escape, squealing and defecating even when it was not receiving the shock. The behavior of the animal was labeled *fear;* it had learned to "fear" the white but not the black compartment. Unfortunately, fear is just about the only drive that experimenters have succeeded in demonstrating to be a learned drive. An animal or human being can certainly be taught to work for new incentives if these incentives are associated with some stimulus that reduces a primary drive, but the original primary drive, and not some new learned drive, is the animal's motive for working for the new incentive.

Another concept employed by Hull is *habit*. Habits are defined as learned behaviors that are performed when appropriate stimulus conditions for controlling their occurrence are present. Through practice, habits increase in strength and thereby come to be performed more quickly and vigorously. Hull's theory of learning, which was based on drive, habit strength, and associated concepts, is a hypothetico-deductive theory, in the sense that Hull attempted to deduce from

previous findings, hypotheses, and assumptions a series of theoretical propositions about the learning process that could be tested experimentally.

Of great interest to Hull, as well as his students and associates at Yale
University during the 1930s and 1940s, was the possibility of operationally
defining certain psychoanalytic concepts (e.g., frustration, conflict, repression,
the pleasure principle, the unconscious, neurotic behavior, the importance of
early experience) and conducting experiments based upon those concepts.
Among the social scientists at the Yale Institute of Human Relations who pursued
this effort were John Dollard, Neal Miller, Hobart Mowrer, and Robert Sears. A
collaboration between Dollard and Miller during the late 1930s and 1940s
resulted in several important experiments and books, including *Frustration and
Aggression* (1939), *Social Learning and Imitation* (1941), and *Personality and Psychotherapy* (1950).

Frustration and Conflict

One important concept that has been dealt with by psychodynamic theorists as
well as experimental psychologists is *frustration*, defined as an interference with
goal-directed activity. Frustration, however, does not merely block the satisfaction of other motives; it has an energizing and directing function in behavior and
hence qualifies as a motive in its own right.

In the first of the three volumes listed in the previous section, Dollard and
Miller formulated and described their research on the *frustration-aggression hypothesis*. This hypothesis states that *frustration* inevitably causes aggression and that
aggression is invariably the result of frustration; the strength of aggression varies
directly with the degree of frustration. Later research revealed, however, that
although frustration frequently leads to aggression, it does not always do so.
Depending on the individual and the particular circumstances, frustration may
lead to rationalization, regression, withdrawal, or other coping mechanisms. Even
when frustration does lead to aggression, the effect may not be direct. The
aggression resulting from frustration may be *displaced* from the object or person
who is responsible for the frustration to a similar object or person. A timeworn
example of *displaced aggression,* showing how it may produce a chain reaction, is the
case of the man who, after being bawled out by his boss, found fault with his wife,
who then scolded her son, who in turn kicked the family dog.

A person may be frustrated by many things—by an object, a situation, or
another person who gets in the way, by some personal limitation, or by a conflict
between motives. *Conflict,* another concept dealt with by Dollard and Miller, is the
most serious type of frustration. According to psychodynamic theory, an unresolved conflict can lead to mental disorder.

A person is said to have a conflict of motives when two or more motives are
present at the same time but cannot both be satisfied. In human beings, conflicts,
of which there are several types, frequently involve psychosocial motives. One of
the most easily resolved types of conflict is *approach-approach conflict,* in which the
individual is torn between two equally attractive goals. Examples of approach-

approach conflict are the proverbial donkey who starved to death while standing between two stacks of hay and the person who cannot decide which of two films to see. In *avoidance-avoidance conflict,* the individual is "between the devil and the deep blue sea," caught between two equally unattractive goals; withdrawing from one of the negative goals can only be accomplished by approaching the other negative goal. Avoidance-avoidance conflicts endure only when the organism cannot escape from the conflict situation. Examples of this type of conflict are the boy who must climb a tree or be attacked by a dangerous animal and the soldier who must face the enemy or be ridiculed by his comrades.

Probably the most common of all types of conflict is *approach-avoidance conflict,* in which the same goal object has both positive and negative aspects. As shown in Figure 8–1, the strength of the tendency to approach or avoid a goal varies with the distance (physical or psychological) from the goal. When an organism is far from the goal, the tendency to approach is stronger than the tendency to avoid. But, because the avoidance gradient is steeper than the approach gradient, as the organism gets nearer to the goal the tendency to avoid it becomes stronger than the tendency to approach it. The point at which the approach and avoidance gradients cross is called the point of conflict, as manifested by vacillation and other behaviors indicative of uncertainty or conflict. Although Figure 8–1 is based on research with animals, similar results have been obtained with humans. Examples of approach-avoidance conflict on the human level are the student who must study to obtain good grades, the young woman

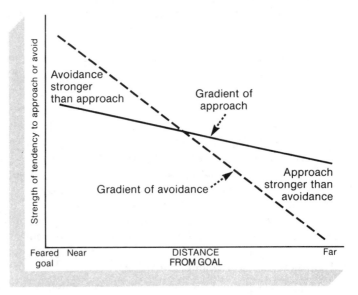

FIGURE 8–1 Graphical representation of an approach-avoidance conflict. (From *Personality and psychotherapy,* by J. Dollard and N. Miller (1950). New York: McGraw-Hill. Reprinted with permission.)

who wants to be independent of her parents but needs the security they afford, and the man who must work at a distasteful job in order to survive.

Dollard and Miller noted that a person in a state of conflict often represses the conflict or tries to forget about it (*suppression*). Repressed but unresolved conflicts, however, may lead to defense mechanisms, and the use of a defense mechanism may have more serious consequences than attempting to deal with the conflict directly. According to Dollard and Miller, most neurotic behavior involves conflict and an associated loss of the ability to discriminate. Neurotics with ineffective defense mechanisms in particular are anxious people who over-generalize their anxieties to a range of situations or circumstances.

Other Psychodynamic Concepts

One of the most important of all psychoanalytic concepts, but an ambiguous one, is anxiety. To Dollard and Miller, anxiety is a drive resulting from frustration and conflict, and consequently any response that leads to decreased anxiety will be learned. One possible response is simply not to think about the anxiety-provoking situation or circumstances; this "not thinking," conditioned-avoidance response is Dollard and Miller's explanation of the Freudian concept of *repression*. In a similar fashion, defense mechanisms may be interpreted as responses that keep anxiety-provoking thoughts from become conscious. Such mechanisms or "symptoms" of neuroses are habits learned in the same way as any other habit and for the same drive-reducing reason.

In *Personality and Psychotherapy*, Dollard and Miller describe in detail the drive reductionist's interpretation of the acquisition of neurotic behavior. Such behavior is learned, and hence it can be unlearned. This unlearning process takes place in psychotherapy in the same way that any conditioned response is un-learned—by extinction. Phobias, compulsions, obsessive thoughts, and other manifestations of neurosis must be permitted to occur in a situation in which they are not reinforced. Like extinction in the animal laboratory, psychotherapy is a gradual process, and to be most therapeutic its effects must generalize from the consulting room to the patient's usual environment. Application of the extinction technique for getting rid of maladaptive behavior was not new with Dollard and Miller. Its effectiveness had been known for at least three decades (e.g., Watson & Rayner, 1920), and it was soon to be supplemented by other behavior modification techniques (Wolpe, 1958).

With respect to psychodynamic theories of the relationships of childhood experiences to adult personality, Dollard and Miller considered four critical developmental tasks: feeding training, cleanliness training, sex training, and training to cope with conflicts between anger and anxiety. They viewed these situations as involving anxiety and other drives and hence leading to the forma-tion of habits that persist and generalize to other situations. If a particular response is ineffective in reducing a certain drive, the individual resorts to a previously learned response (*regression*). If for some reason the individual is unable to learn a new, more adaptive habit, he or she will persist—that is, remain *fixated*—in the old habit.

Evaluation of Drive Theory

Although there are probably still some drive theorists in the ranks of psychologists, enthusiasm for Hullian theory began to abate during the 1950s. The concept of drive or motive, as well as other internal, mediating concepts, became less fashionable and were viewed as unnecessary and perhaps even as interfering with a clearer understanding of personality (Hergenhahn, 1990). With respect to Dollard and Miller's attempted synthesis of psychoanalysis and learning theory, it is recognized as a genuine contribution that paved the way for later efforts to explain personality and personality disorders in behavioristic terminology. The operationally defined and laboratory-based approach to personality and psychotherapy of these two men failed to provide a complete, workable scientific theory of personality. But at least it represents an initial effort to synthesize psychoanalytic theory with learning theory, or to cast the former in terms of the latter and thus make it more susceptible to experimental testing. Dollard and Miller's work also stimulated an extensive amount of research and theorizing on the role of social factors in shaping personality and personality problems, an influence that is seen in the writings of the last three theorists discussed in this chapter.

Rotter's Social Learning Theory

For the better part of the twentieth century, cognitive processes (knowing, understanding, thinking) were treated as separate from personality as an area of study within psychology. The division, however, was never complete, and it was generally recognized that thoughts influence emotions and vice versa. Certain theorists, such as R. B. Cattell, argued for a holistic conception of personality that included both affect (feelings, emotions) and cognition. Also holistic in nature, but emphasizing more cognitive concepts, was George Kelly's "man as scientist" approach to personality. Cognitive concepts have been incorporated into the explanatory systems of the last three theories considered in this chapter. In addition to being cognitive, they can be characterized as social learning theories in that they emphasize the influences of other people in shaping individual personality.

The first social learning theorist, Julian B. Rotter, was born in Brooklyn, New York, on October 22, 1916, the third son of Jewish immigrant parents. Young Julian was a voracious reader and devoured almost all of the books in the local public library. He was graduated from Brooklyn College in 1937. At Iowa, where he studied with the famous field theorist Kurt Lewin, he received a master's degree in 1938 and the Ph.D. in clinical psychology in 1941. He then accepted an appointment at Ohio State University, where he wrote his first and most famous book, *Social Learning and Clinical Psychology* (1954). In addition to having been influenced by Alfred Adler and Kurt Lewin, Rotter benefited from associations with George Kelly and other prominent psychologists during his tenure at Ohio State. He remained at Ohio State until 1963, when he accepted a professorship at the University of Connecticut.

Rotter's attempt to integrate the traditional behavioristic position on the role of reinforcement in learning with the cognitive conceptualizations of Kurt Lewin and other field theorists may be properly labeled the first *social learning theory*. Rotter was, of course, not the first psychologist to note that much human behavior is learned in a social context, but he made a more conscious effort than his predecessors to develop a systematic theory of how this process takes place.

Four basic concepts employed in Rotter's social learning theory are behavior potential, reinforcement value, expectancy, and the psychological situation. *Behavior potential* (BP) is the probability that a given behavior will occur in a particular situation; *reinforcement value* (RV) is the subjective preference for a certain reinforcer; and *expectancy* (E) is the probability that a given behavior will result in reinforcement. Understandably, people are more likely to exert the greatest effort to attain highly valued goals having a high probability of attainment and to exert the least effort to attain goals with low value and a low probability of attainment.

The influence of phenomenology on Rotter's theory is seen in the concept of the *psychological situation,* which is the immediate situation as viewed and interpreted by the behaving person. The nature of the situation is an important feature of the theory, since both expectancy and reinforcement value vary with the particular environmental context in which the person is behaving.

A symbolic statement of Rotter's fundamental theory is his *basic prediction formula,* $BP = f(E, RV)$. In words, the formula states that the potential for the occurrence of a specified behavior BP in a particular situation is a function of (1) the expectancy E that the behavior in question will be followed by reinforcement in that situation and (2) the perceived value of the reinforcement RV in that situation. *Expectancy* refers to the expectation, or anticipation, that a specific reinforcer will follow a particular behavior, and *reinforcement value* is the value or worth of that reinforcer to the individual. As implied in the basic prediction formula, reinforcement is important for performance, but not all reinforcements are equally valued by the individual. Even when the probabilities of occurrence of different reinforcements are equal, certain objects or actions will have greater reinforcement value than others. Responses with higher reinforcement value are more likely to be made. Furthermore, both reinforcement value and expectancy are affected by the psychological relevance or meaning of the situation to the individual, a meaning that must be understood in order to predict the individual's behavior in the situation.

Locus of Control

The cognitive concept of *expectancy* in the basic prediction formula represents a departure from traditional behaviorism and requires some elaboration. Expectancies may be specific to a given situation or more general to a variety of situations. Two *generalized expectancies* that Rotter has assessed and investigated are internal/external locus of control and interpersonal trust. *Locus of control* refers to the typical direction from which people perceive themselves as being controlled—*internal* (from within oneself) or *external* (by other people or outside events). The I-E Scale, which was designed to measure locus of control, consists of 23 forced-choice item pairs and six filler items. In the following list, one member (the A statement) of each item pair is associated with the belief that a person can control his or her own life (*internal locus of control*), and the other (the B statement) with the belief that a person's life is controlled by fate or luck (*external locus of control*). Examinees indicate which member of each pair best applies, and their responses are scored on a scale of 0 to 23 (higher scores indicate higher external locus of control).

1A Many of the unhappy things in people's lives are partly due to bad luck.
1B People's misfortunes result from the mistakes they make.
2A No matter how hard you try, some people just don't like you.
2B People who can't get others to like them don't understand how to get along with others.
3A In the case of the well-prepared student, there is rarely if ever such a thing as an unfair test.
3B Many times exam questions tend to be so unrelated to course work that studying is really useless.
4A Becoming a success is a matter of hard work; luck has little or nothing to do with it.
4B Getting a good job depends mainly on being in the right place at the right time.
5A The average citizen can have an influence in government decisions.
5B This world is run by the few people in power, and there is not much the little guy can do about it.[1]

Research by Rotter and others (e.g., Seeman & Evans, 1962; V. C. Crandall, 1973; Phares, 1976; Eskew & Riche, 1982) has shown that internal locus of control increases with age and is fostered by warm, responsive, supportive parents who encourage independence. Table 8–1 is a summary of findings obtained from research comparing the characteristics and behavior of individuals scoring in the internal-locus-of-control and external-locus-of-control ranges of the I-E Scale.

More recent research has questioned the underlying assumption of the I-E Scale that locus of control is a general trait that is manifested in a wide range of situations. Several investigations (Levenson, 1981; Paulhus, 1983) have maintained that the same person may be "internal" about some things and "external" about others. For example, you may feel that whether or not you get good grades depends mostly on your effort and ability, but whether or not you get a good job after graduation depends more on the economic situation and other factors beyond your control. In addition, you may qualify as an "external" at certain times and an "internal" at other times. When you are young, strong, and energetic, you may feel capable of overcoming all odds and view the future with confidence, but as you age and all your dreams have not come true you may become more "external" in outlook. Realizing the existence of situational and

TABLE 8–1   Comparisons between Internals and Externals on the I-E Scale

Compared with externals, internals:
Are more likely to attribute failure to lack of ability.
Are more likely to be successful with weight-reduction programs.
Are more likely to take actions that will keep them healthy.
Are more likely to use seat belts.
Are more perceptive and ready to learn about surroundings.
Ask more questions and process information more efficiently.
Have greater mastery tendencies.
Have better problem-solving abilities.
Have higher achievement.
Are more inquisitive.
Cope with sickness more effectively.
Are better versed about critical political events.
Give in to authority less readily.
Judge others more severely.
Are more likely to advocate harsh punishment for violating rules.
Make more independent judgments.
Try harder to control the behavior of other people.
Tend to assume more responsibility.
Are more likely to know about conditions that lead to good physical and emotional health.
Are more likely to take steps to improve their health.
Suffer less from hypertension.
Are less likely to have heart attacks.
Cope with illness more adequately.
Derive more benefit from social support.
Compared with internals, externals:
Are more likely to attribute failure to task difficulty or bad luck.
Are more likely to attempt suicide.
Are more likely to conform.
Are more likely to suffer from psychological disorders.
Tend to be more anxious and depressed.
Tend to be more vulnerable to stress.
Are more likely to develop defensive strategies that invite failure in coping.
Are more likely to use defensive strategies to explain their failures.
Are more likely to be females.

temporal variations in locus of control, several psychologists have constructed inventories to measure locus of control in more specific contexts. Among these are classroom situations (Crandall, Katkovsky, & Crandall, 1965), health-related situations (Wallston & Wallston, 1981), and marital situations (P. C. Miller, Lefcourt, & Ware, 1983).

Interpersonal Trust

Another personality assessment instrument constructed by Rotter to measure a generalized expectancy is the Interpersonal Trust Scale. This instrument was designed to measure *interpersonal trust,* an expectancy on the part of an individual or group "that the word, promise, verbal or written statement of another individual or group can be relied upon" (Rotter, 1967 p. 651). The degree of interpersonal trust depends not only on the likelihood that the statements one is asked to believe are true, but also on the reputation of the source. It has also been found that people who score high in interpersonal trust tend to be higher in socioeconomic status, to have had strong parental support as children, to be happier and less conflicted, to have more friends, to be less likely to lie, and, although not gullible, to be more willing to give people a second chance (Rotter, 1980).

A General Prediction Formula

The basic prediction formula, $BP = f(E, RV)$, was designed to apply in specific situations, and because of that limitation Rotter proposed another formula to predict functionally related behaviors in general situations. This general prediction formula, $NP = f(FM, NV)$, states that need potential NP is a function of freedom of movement and need value NV. Like other psychologists, Rotter distinguished between unlearned, biologically based needs and psychological needs. Six categories of psychological needs, which are internal cognitive states that result from experience rather than biological factors, are described in Table 8–2.

The concept of *need potential* refers to the possible occurrence of a set of functionally related behaviors directed toward the satisfaction of the same goal or a similar set of goals. Similar to the concept of reinforcement value in the basic prediction formula is the concept of *need value*—the extent to which a person prefers one set of reinforcements to another. Differences in need value are associated with different personalities. The third variable in the general prediction formula, *freedom of movement*, is similar to the expectancy variable in the basic prediction form. Freedom of movement refers to a person's perception of the

---

TABLE 8–2   Rotter's Needs

1. *Recognition-status:* The need to excel, to be considered competent, good or better than others in school occupation, profession, athletics, social position, physical appeal, or play; that is, the need to obtain high position in a socially valued competitive scale.
2. *Dominance:* The need to control the actions of other people, including family and friends; to be in a position of power, to have others follow one's own ideas and desires.
3. *Independence:* The need to make one's own decisions, to rely on oneself, to develop the skill necessary to obtain satisfaction and reach goals without the help of others.
4. *Protection-dependency:* The need to have another person or persons prevent frustration, provide protection and security, and help obtain other desired goals.
5. *Love and affection:* The need for acceptance and liking by other people, to have their warm regard, interest, concern, and devotion.
6. *Physical comfort:* The need for physical satisfactions that have become associated with security and a state of well-being, the avoidance of pain, and the desire for bodily pleasures.

Source: From *Clinical Psychology* (2nd ed., p. 60) by J. B. Rotter, © 1971. Reprinted by permission of Prentice Hall, Inc., Englewood Cliffs, NJ.

number of available avenues through which a particular need can be satisfied, that is, how many routes to reinforcement exist. Freedom of movement varies with the individual, and hence it is an aspect of personality. A problem arises when need value coupled with low freedom of movement leads to a frustrated, ineffective individual who may resort to excessive fantasizing or other neurotic behavior. All three of the components in the general prediction formula are subsumed under the concept of *need*, which, as implied in the general prediction formula, refers to a set of behaviors that are related in the sense that they result in the same or similar reinforcements.

Evaluation

Rotter's social learning theory represents a kind of amalgam of behavioral, gestalt, cognitive, and teleological concepts. It is teleological in the sense that it emphasizes the importance of goals and goal-directed behavior. For example, Rotter defines *maladaptive behavior* as actions that fail to move a person closer to a desired goal. To change a person's maladaptive behavior, Rotter would change his or her goals and eliminate low expectancies.

Rotter's social learning theory deserves some praise because it was one of the first serious efforts to combine behavioral with cognitive concepts, but it obviously has limitations. For example, it lacks the range of versatility of psychoanalysis in dealing with the structure, dynamics, and development of personality. It also fails to provide a systematic approach to changing behavior, maladaptive and otherwise. On the other hand, Rotter's efforts have stimulated a great deal of research, particularly on expectancy versus reinforcement value and locus of control. In fact, Rotter's 1966 monograph describing the I-E Scale has been one of the most widely quoted papers in psychology.

Also of importance to psychodiagnosticians is the popular Rotter Incomplete Sentences Blank (ISB) (Rotter & Rafferty, 1950). Responses to the 30 sentence fragments on the ISB are scored as "conflict or unhealthy, neutral, or positive or healthy." Perhaps Rotter's most important contribution, however, is that he provided a stimulus and a first approximation to a social learning theory of personality that would be followed up by Albert Bandura, Walter Mischel, and other cognitive behaviorists.

Bandura's Cognitive Social Learning Theory

An important assumption of both Hullian and Skinnerian behaviorism is that learning cannot occur in the absence of an unreinforced response. However, even during the early 1930s this assumption was called into question by E. C. Tolman (1932), who maintained that rats and other animals can learn mazes without being reinforced. When placed in a maze without food in the goal box, the animal wanders about, making a series of right and left turns and, according to Tolman, constructs a mental picture, or *cognitive map,* of the maze. During these nonreinforced trials *latent learning* of the maze, as represented by the cognitive map, occurs, but learning is not apparent until the animal is reinforced with food in the goal box. On the basis of his experiments on latent learning in rats, Tolman made a distinction between learning and performance. He concluded that reinforcement is not necessary for learning to occur, although it is necessary for performance. The theorist whom we shall discuss next, Albert Bandura, extended Tolman's distinction between learning (acquisition) and performance to the human level. Bandura also profited from Dollard and Miller's (1950) research on imitation and the psychoanalytic concept of identification, both of which stress the importance of observation.

Albert Bandura was born in Mundare, a small town in Alberta, Canada, on December 4, 1925. He completed his undergraduate work at the University of British Columbia and his graduate work in psychology at the University of Iowa. After receiving the Ph.D. in 1951, followed by a clinical internship at the Wichita, Kansas, Guidance Center, he accepted a position at Stanford University. Bandura's first and second books, *Adolescent Aggression* (1959) and *Social Learning and Personality Development* (1963), were coauthored with his first doctoral student, Richard Walters. He subsequently published several other books, the two most recent being *Social Learning Theory* (1977) and *Social Foundations of Thought and Action* (1986).

Modeling and the Bobo Doll

Bandura's most famous series of research investigations involved the use of a large inflated Bobo doll (see Figure 8–2). In an early study (Bandura, Ross, & Ross, 1963), a group of preschool children (the experimental group) observed a film of an adult playing with a Bobo doll, hitting and kicking it while shouting "Sock him in the nose!" "Throw him in the air!" and similar outbursts. A second group of children (the control group) did not see the film. Later, when both groups were permitted to play with the doll, the play of the experimental group was twice as aggressive as that of the control group. In other words, the experimental group modeled the behavior of the aggressive adult.

To answer the question of whether the results of the model's behavior would make a difference in whether that behavior was imitated, Bandura (1965) used three groups of children. The first group ("Model rewarded") saw the model being rewarded for being aggressive; the second group ("Model punished") observed the model being punished for being aggressive; the third group ("No consequences") observed no consequences of the model's behavior. The results showed that, when given the opportunity to play with the doll, the "Model rewarded" group was most aggressive, the "Model punished" group was least aggressive, and the "No consequences" group fell between the first and second groups in aggressiveness. However, when offered an incentive if they would replicate the model's behavior, the children in all three groups did so (see Figure 8–3). These results were interpreted as indicating that all of the children had

FIGURE 8–2   Children reproducing the aggressive behavior of a female model observed in a film. (From Bandura, Ross, & Ross, 1963.)

learned the aggressive behavior toward the doll by observing the model, but it was more likely to be expressed when the model was seen being reinforced or the child observer was led to expect reinforcement for engaging in the same behavior as the model. To Bandura and Walters this result meant that learning can occur simply from observing, but whether or not learning is translated into performance depends on the *behavior-outcome expectancies* of the observer.

From his research on modeling, Bandura (1969, p. 108) concluded that "virtually all learning phenomena resulting from direct experiences can occur on a vicarious basis through observation of other persons' behavior and its consequences to them." These learning phenomena include not only verbal and motor skills but a wide variety of complex, socially oriented behaviors ranging from altruism to self-control. Aggression, fears, sex-typed behaviors, and many other emotional and stylistic reactions are learned by observing and modeling. When emotional reactions are learned from observing other people, the process is referred to as *vicarious conditioning*.

Violence and the Media

With respect to research on modeling aggressive behavior, the results of numerous laboratory and field studies suggest that viewing aggression and violence in the media increases the likelihood of aggressive behavior on the part of the viewer (e.g., Friedrich-Cofer & Huston, 1986; Geen & Thomas, 1986; Huesmann

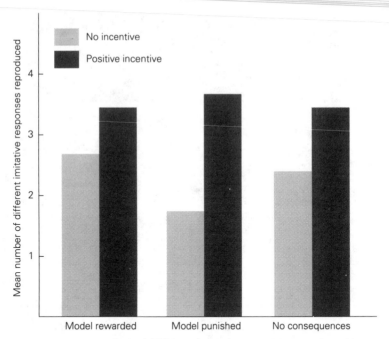

FIGURE 8–3 Mean number of different imitative responses produced by children as a function of response consequences to the model and positive incentives. (From Bandura, 1965. Copyright 1965 by the American Psychological Association. Reprinted by permission.)

& Malamuth, 1986; Eron, 1987). Children and adults view murders in the home, in the street, and in war zones almost daily on television. As a result, they may become conditioned to guns as symbols of violence and become aroused by the sight of them. They learn how to kill by mail, by bombs, by military-style assault weapons, and by means of other instruments provided by modern technology. Of course, caution should be exercised in generalizing the results of any study linking violence in real life to vicariously experienced violence (Freedman, 1984, 1986). Children who watch violent television may be more violent to begin with than those who prefer less violent programs, perhaps as much because of hereditary factors as experiential ones.

Cognitive Processes in Modeling

Behavior-outcome expectancies are, of course, cognitive processes, so Bandura's theory of learning by modeling is both social and cognitive. But not all individuals model the same behaviors, whether or not those behaviors are reinforced in the observer or the model. According to Bandura, four factors determine whether modeling occurs and is translated into behavior: attentional processes, retention processes, motor reproduction processes, and motivational processes (see Figure

8–4). *Attentional processes* include characteristics of the modeling stimuli and the observer that influence the degree to which the observer pays attention to the model. In addition to the factors listed in the first box of Figure 8–4, Bandura (1977) found that low self-esteem, incompetence, high dependency, and high motivation are characteristics of observers that influence modeling.

Given that the model's behavior has been attended to, the observer must remember it (retention processes), be capable of enacting it (motor reproduction processes), and expect that the behavior will be rewarded (motivational pro-

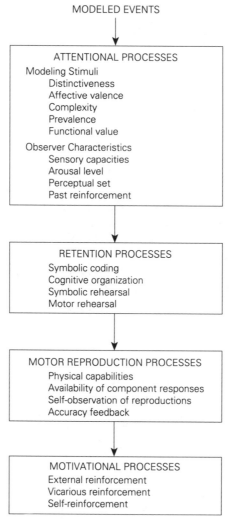

MODELED EVENTS

ATTENTIONAL PROCESSES
Modeling Stimuli
　　Distinctiveness
　　Affective valence
　　Complexity
　　Prevalence
　　Functional value

Observer Characteristics
　　Sensory capacities
　　Arousal level
　　Perceptual set
　　Past reinforcement

RETENTION PROCESSES
Symbolic coding
Cognitive organization
Symbolic rehearsal
Motor rehearsal

MOTOR REPRODUCTION PROCESSES
　　Physical capabilities
　　Availability of component responses
　　Self-observation of reproductions
　　Accuracy feedback

MOTIVATIONAL PROCESSES
　　External reinforcement
　　Vicarious reinforcement
　　Self-reinforcement

FIGURE 8–4　Factors determining modeling and whether it is translated into behavior. (From Albert Bandura, *Social Learning Theory*, © 1977, p. 23. Adapted by permission of Prentice Hall, Englewood Cliffs, NJ.)

cesses). *Retention processes* consist of the ways in which experiences are stored in memory, and *motor reproduction processes* are concerned with the physical capabilities of the observer and other processes that are responsible for translating learning into performance. Finally, *motivational processes* are various sources of external, vicarious, self-reinforcement. *External reinforcement* occurs when the observer is rewarded by another person or circumstance, *vicarious reinforcement* is when the model is reinforced, and *self-reinforcement* is when the observer provides his or her own reinforcement. Both external and vicarious reinforcement provide information to the observer that contributes to behavior-outcome expectancies. Bandura believes that motivation is stronger than the other three processes in determining whether or not a response is made. People who believe that their actions will lead to either short- or long-term rewards are more likely to imitate the behavior of another person.

Reciprocal Determinism

Bandura emphasizes the fact the people are not passive, push-button automata who act only when acted upon; they influence and are influenced by the social environment. Central to Bandura's social learning theory is the concept of *reciprocal determinism,* a three-part paradigm based on the mutual interactions of the person, the environment, and behavior. To Bandura and Mischel, the person (including cognitive variables and other personal factors) interacts with both environmental (situational) factors and behavior, which also interact with and mutually influence each other. For example, a student who dislikes people (personal factor) may be induced to give a talk on neighborly love (behavior) for which he receives strong approval from the listeners (situational factor). As a result, his attitude toward others becomes more positive. He may then decide to present talks on similar subjects in the future, further increasing his feeling of community.

Self-efficacy

An especially important personal factor in Bandura's learning theory is *self-efficacy,* a person's expectation that he or she is capable of learning or performing the particular behaviors that will result in desirable outcomes in a particular situation. Self-efficacy is different from behavior-outcome expectancies in that the latter are concerned with the expected outcomes of particular actions in given situations and the former with one's ability to carry out those actions. Whether or not an individual decides to strive toward a particular goal depends greatly on his or her perceived self-efficacy to do what is required to attain the goal.

Among the sources or variables that influence self-efficacy are performance accomplishments, vicarious experience, verbal persuasion, and emotional arousal. *Performance accomplishments,* which are probably the most important factor in determining self-efficacy, consist of the successes and failures experienced by the individual in the past. Depending on how a person views his or her own capabilities with respect to those of other people, *vicarious experience,* which consists of observing the successes and failures of other people in similar situations, can also contribute to self-efficacy. *Verbal persuasion*—that is, being told by other people whether or not one is capable of accomplishing a particular task—is probably the weakest of all variables influencing self-efficacy. *Emotional arousal,* the quality and intensity of emotion experienced by an individual in the situation, is also related to self-efficacy. With respect to the quality of emotion, being overjoyed obviously has a different effect on self-efficacy than being anxious, particularly if the level of anxiety is high.

A persistent feeling of low self-efficacy is indicative of the need for psychotherapy to change the person's self-perceptions. Depending on whether or not one believes that the self-efficacies of most other people are also low, the result may be either feelings of apathy or depression. One's self-efficacy may be unrealistically high in some situations and unrealistically low in others. In general, however, high self-efficacy is associated with high performance. When high self-efficacy is not accompanied by a high level of performance, the individual may feel resentment toward what he or she perceives to be an unresponsive social environment.

Self-efficacy is an aspect of the individual's *self system,* which, for Bandura, is a cognitive structure that provides a frame of reference for perceiving, evaluating, and regulating one's behavior. Part of the self system consists of *performance standards* which the individual acquires by experience and according to which his or her performance is evaluated. Of particular importance in determining one's performance standards are parents, siblings, peers, and other individuals who play significant roles in the person's life. Whatever one's performance standards may be, they are obviously important in making plans, setting goals, and self-regulating behavior. Realistically, it is best to set short-range (proximal) goals, the attainment of which will enhance self-efficacy and lead to increased interest in the particular skill involved.

As implied in the preceding paragraphs, Bandura stresses the idea that learning and behavior are mediated by perceptions and cognitions. People form internal, symbolic representations of the environment, and these representations mediate changes in their behavior. By manipulating these internal symbols, the individual learns to visualize the consequences of certain actions and hence to regulate his or her behavior. A similar cognitive approach has been proposed by Walter Mischel, one of Bandura's associates. This approach may be viewed as an extension of the latter's cognitive social learning theory.

Mischel's Person/Situation Theory

Walter Mischel was born in Vienna, Austria, but the family emigrated to the United States during the 1930s and resettled in New York City. After graduating from the City College of New York, he accepted employment as a social worker. Subsequently he attended Ohio State University, where in 1956 he received the

Ph.D. in clinical psychology. Mischel began his academic career at the University of Colorado, spent four years at Harvard University and more than 20 years at Stanford University, and then returned to New York City as a professor of psychology at Columbia University.

Mischel is perhaps best known for his attack on trait theories of personality (Mischel, 1968) and the resulting controversy concerning the consistency of behavior and the relative importance of the person and the situation in determining behavior (see Chapter 4). Although he was very critical of personality theories that placed more emphasis on *person variables* than on *situation variables,* he has recently expressed an interactionist viewpoint in which the importance of both sets of variables in determining behavior is recognized (Mischel, 1986).

Rather than attempting to define personality in terms of a collection of traits, Mischel is more interested in how and why people employ trait constructs and what purposes are served by these constructs. And rather than simply predicting behavior, he is interested in analyzing it to better understand basic psychological processes and to clarify the structure and functioning of human personality (Mischel, 1984, 1986). Mischel is a cognitive theorist, but one with a strong behavioristic orientation. Like other behaviorists, he emphasizes the importance of the environment in determining what people do. He acknowledges the roles of both person variables and situation variables, but rather than emphasizing generalized predictions about people, he limits himself to predicting and understanding the behavior of the *person in the situation.*

Mischel's *person* variables are not adjectival traits such as "friendliness," "conscientiousness," "aggressiveness," or "cooperativeness," but rather cognitive or information-processing concepts such as "construction competencies," "encoding strategies," "expectancies," "goals and values," and "self-regulatory systems and plans." The influences of Kelly, Rotter, and Bandura are all evident in the descriptions of these five sets of person variables, which are linked to basic psychological processes that control a person's behavior in particular situations.

The first person variable, *construction competencies,* is concerned with an individual's cognitive and behavioral competencies—that is, his or her intellectual, social, and physical abilities to generate diverse behaviors under appropriate conditions. In other words, what does a person know, and what skills does he or she possess?

The second variable, *encoding strategies,* is concerned with how people perceive, group, and construe events or entities (including themselves) and categorize situations. For example, a situation that is frightening to one person may be exciting or even boring to someone else.

Mischel's third person variable, *expectancies,* is also a key concept in Rotter's theory. The concept refers to an individual's specific expectations of what will occur under specified conditions. For example, "What will happen if I take this job rather than another one?" Included among the expectancies are self-efficacy expectations ("How will I do?"), one of the major variables in Bandura's theory.

Mischel's fourth person variable is *goals and subjective values.* People who possess similar expectations but different goals or subjective values may behave differently because the same outcomes are not equally important to different people.

The fifth person variable described by Mischel consists of *self-regulatory (self-control) systems and plans.* These systems and plans are different rules or standards that people adopt to regulate their behavior (Mischel, 1984). Mischel considers most behavior to be self-regulated by intrinsic reinforcement rather than by extrinsic reinforcers applied from a source external to the individual.

Mischel (1984, 1986) argues that person variables such as self-efficacy expectations—how effective the individual expects to be in coping with a particular situation—are good predictors of such outcomes as the success of psychotherapy, reactions to stress, and performance attainment (see Bandura, 1982). The research conduct by Mischel and his colleagues on how people can learn self-control by focusing their attention on other stimuli is particularly noteworthy (e.g., Mischel & Moore, 1973; Mischel & Baker, 1975).

Evaluating Theories of Personality

In closing this section of theories of personality, it should be pointed out that all of the theories have some interesting features but none has escaped criticism. Perhaps because it was one of the first and most ambitious of all conceptions of human personality, the greatest amount of criticism has been directed toward psychoanalytic theory. In fact, phenomenological and behavioral theories of personality arose in part as a result of the perceived shortcomings of psychoanalysis. Although no other theory of personality possesses the scope of classical psychoanalysis, Freud was clearly in error on many counts. He overemphasized the importance of the sex drive or pleasure principle as a motivating force in human behavior. He overgeneralized the role of the Oedipus complex and reified concepts such as the unconscious, the ego, the superego, and the id. In addition, classical psychoanalytic theory has been criticized for being pessimistic, deterministic, and fatalistic in its outlook regarding human nature.

In contrast to psychoanalysis, phenomenological theories—Rogers' self theory in particular—are more optimistic and more comfortable with the concept of free will and the responsibility of the individual for his own destiny. Although traditional behaviorism is certainly deterministic, it cannot be said to be pessimistic about human fate. Finally, the social learning theories of Rotter, Bandura, and Mischel are fairly optimistic and nonfatalistic in their viewpoints.

By modifying radical behaviorism to include nonobservable variables such as expectations and self-efficacy, social learning theorists have made their theorizing more palatable to phenomenologists and other nonbehaviorists. Unfortunately, these invisible variables have often proved difficult to tie down and deal with in an operational way. In addition, social learning theories have been faulted for slighting heredity and maturation as shapers of personality and for not paying enough attention to personality development.

At the end of this section on personality theories, we are faced with the question of whether and in what ways these theories can assist our efforts to understand the origins and consequences of individual differences. Do the theories help us to predict and understand human behavior? Do they help us to deal with our own problems and those of other people? Such questions cannot be easily answered, for different theories arose from different motives and were meant to serve different purposes. For example, trait-factor theory has guided the development of a number of personality assessment instruments, and psychoanalysis has influenced the construction of other devices. Unlike trait-factor theory, psychoanalytic and phenomenological theories have been concerned more with psychotherapy and other interventions. Behaviorism and social learning theory have also shown less concern with instrument development and more concern with the modification of behavior. Furthermore, if origin is a key to applicability, it may be worthwhile to recall that both psychoanalysis and self theory arose in clinical contexts, whereas behaviorism and social learning theory originated in the psychological laboratory.

Perhaps the best approach to deciding what choices to make among the various theories is to keep one's options open and adopt an eclectic attitude.[2] This means that we must be familiar with all of the theories and "be on our toes" for situations in which one theory or theoretical construct rather than another seems to be most relevant or applicable. It is not necessary to accept every assumption or principle of a given theory. However, we should be aware of those assumptions and principles so we can confirm or disconfirm, select or reject them for our own purposes. In the end, the theories, and hence our acceptance of them, will stand or fall on the basis of empirical evidence. In the remainder of this book we shall be concerned more with evidence and methods than with theories, but within the context of our discussion of particular research findings and techniques it should become clear what the influences and applications of particular theories of personality have been and continue to be.

Summary

The study of *learning,* defined as any change in behavior resulting from experience, is not the exclusive province of the psychologist, but it is one in which psychologists have taken a great deal of interest since the turn of the century. Patterns of individual differences in behavior are, of course, not produced by means of learning alone. As we shall see in the next chapter, biological factors and their interaction with the environment are also important considerations in accounting for human personality and its idiosyncrasies.

Research on the procedures and processes by which people and animals learn received a strong impetus from Watson's behaviorist manifesto. Many prominent psychologists—for example, Guthrie, Tolman, Hull, Skinner, and

Dollard and Miller during the 1930s through the 1950s, and other more clinically oriented psychologists such as Rotter, Bandura, and Mischel since the 1950s— have contributed to our understanding of learning.

Hull's drive-reduction theory viewed learned performance as a joint function of previous learning (habit strength) and motivation (drive). Hull emphasized the importance of drives (primary and secondary) and the necessity of drive-reduction for learning to take place. Extension of Hull's ideas to clinical contexts, and the reinterpretation of psychoanalytic concepts in Hullian terms, was made by a number of his students and colleagues, John Dollard and Neal Miller in particular. Dollard and Miller's analysis of conflict, the role of anxiety as a drive in learning, and formulation of the frustration-aggression hypothesis were three of their most significant contributions.

Radical, empty-organism behaviorists such as B. F. Skinner gave short shrift to internal, mediating concepts of the sort described by Dollard and Miller. From Skinner's perspective, there is a tendency to reify concepts such as drive, anxiety, aggression, and the like. Skinner believed that these concepts are useless unless they can be operationally defined in terms of observable behavior and specific environmental variables. A fundamental principle of Skinner's radical behaviorism is that behavior is controlled by its consequences. If those consequences are reinforcing, the behavior of interest will tend to be repeated; if not, it won't. Unlike respondent behavior, which is elicited by an external stimulus, operant behavior is simply emitted. Of course, operants may be brought under stimulus control by using discriminative stimuli. Generalizing from rats and pigeons to humans, Skinner has advocated the application of operant conditioning methodology to the modification of behavior in a wide variety of situations, including teaching (teaching machines and programmed instruction), psychotherapy (behavior modification), institutions (control by token economies), and even the design of entire societies.

Rotter, Bandura, and Mischel, the three principal social learning theorists considered in this chapter, accept the study of behavior as the proper pursuit of psychologists and recognize the importance of reinforcement in learning and performance. However, they have gone beyond empty-organism behaviorism in their view of the human being as a thinking, planning person who has needs, expectancies, and feelings of self-efficacy and employs observational abilities, strategies, values, and plans to regulate his or her own behavior. Furthermore, unlike the credo of earlier behaviorists who maintained that reinforcement is essential for learning to occur, Bandura in particular has concluded that most learning occurs by simple observation of a model. Reinforcement is necessary for the performance of a specific action or skill, but not for its acquisition. All three of these men have described applications of their ideas to the treatment of behavioral disorders and have conducted research on the effectiveness of particular assessment and therapeutic techniques.

Owing to the influence of theorists such as Rotter, Bandura, and Mischel, the radical behaviorism of the 1950s has definitely changed in the direction of an inclusion of cognitive processes. Following Jean Piaget and other developmental psychologists as well as research in neurophysiology, concepts such as plans, schema, scripts, encoding, and other information-processing ideas have been introduced to help explain the seeming vagaries of human personality.

Key Concepts

Approach-avoidance conflict   Mental stage in which a person is both attracted to and repelled by the same object, person, or situation and has difficulty deciding whether to approach or avoid (withdraw from) it.

Conflict   A mental state in which opposing or mutually exclusive impulses, desires, or tendencies are present at the same time. See *approach-avoidance conflict.*

Drive theory   Theory of learning, such as C. L. Hull's hypothetico-deductive theory of rote learning, which maintains that drive reduction is essential for learning to occur.

Expectancy   Julian Rotter's term for the subjective probability that a given behavior will be instrumental in obtaining a certain reinforcer.

Frustration-aggression hypothesis   Hypothesis that frustration (interference with goal-directed activity) results in aggressive behavior.

Interpersonal trust   Generalized expectancy (Rotter) to believe other people.

Locus of control   J. B. Rotter's term for a cognitive-perceptual style characterized by the typical direction ("internal" or self versus "external" or other) from which individuals perceive themselves to be controlled.

Modeling   Learning social and cognitive behaviors by observing and imitating other people.

Operant conditioning   Learning that occurs when positive or negative consequences follow behavior.

Reinforcement   Application or removal of a stimulus that affects the probability of a response.

Respondent conditioning   Classical conditioning, in which the response is elicited by a known stimulus rather than emitted.

Self-efficacy   A person's belief that he or she can successfully accomplish a given action.

Unconscious   In psychoanalytic theory, that part of the personality that is below the level of conscious awareness and is brought into consciousness only in disguised form.

Activities and Applications

1. Make a copy of the following Behavioral Checklist for Performance Anxiety and use it to record your observations of a person over eight time periods of ten minutes each. Put a check mark after the behavior in the appropriate time-period column if the behavior occurs during that time. Make multiple check marks if the same behavior is observed more than once during the time period. How consistent was each of the behaviors across the eight time periods, and how many times did each behavior occur? Would you characterize the person whom you observed as an "anxious person"? Do you believe that all of the 20 behaviors listed in this checklist are indicative of "anxiety"? Why or why not?

Checklist for Performance Anxiety

	Time Period							
Behavior Observed	1	2	3	4	5	6	7	8
1. Paces								
2. Sways								
3. Shuffles feet								
4. Knees tremble								
5. Extraneous arm and hand movement (swings, scratches, toys, etc.)								
6. Arms rigid								
7. Hands restrained (in pockets, behind back, clasped)								
8. Hand tremors								
9. No eye contact								
10. Face muscles tense (drawn, tics, grimaces)								
11. Face "deadpan"								
12. Face pale								
13. Face flushed (blushes)								
14. Moistens lips								
15. Swallows								
16. Clears throat								
17. Breathes heavily								
18. Perspires (face, hands, armpits)								
19. Voice quivers								
20. Speech blocks or stammers								

Reprinted from *Insight vs. Desensitization in Psychotherapy* by Gordon L. Paul, with the permission of the publishers, Stanford University Press. © 1966 by the Board of Trustees of the Leland Stanford Junior University.

2. Select a particular habit of yours, such as smoking, chewing gum, eating some favorite food, or looking at television. Keep a diary for one week, recording when and where you were when you had the urge to express the habit and for how long you engaged in it. At the end of the week, compare your entries on day 7 with those on day 1. Was there any change in the frequency of time in which you engaged in the habit? If so, how can the change be explained?

3. Considering your own behavior, do you find that you explicitly or implicitly take into account the probability of success and the amount of reward before beginning a less than pleasant task? How does the expectation or probability and the value of the outcome affect the amount of energy which you put into a task?

4. Engage in conversations with several people, and reinforce a particular part of their speech by nodding your head or looking more interested when they use that part of speech. Examples of enunciations which you might select to reinforce are plural nouns, "you know," "like," "uh," or even particular topics such as members of the opposite sex or professors. Make a count of any changes (increase or decrease) in the target speech behavior that you choose to reinforce.

5. Describe a case of conditioned fear or anger toward some innocuous object in yourself or a friend. Did you or the friend get over the fear or anger? How?

6. Describe one good behavior and one bad behavior that you acquired by modeling the behavior of someone else. Who was the model for your behavior? Did you consciously decide to imitate the behavior, or did it just occur without thinking?

7. Consider the traits versus situations controversy ignited by Walter Mischel and discussed at some length in Chapter 4. Take a position in defense of the assertion that behavior is determined largely by traits that manifest themselves across various situations. Now take the opposite position that behavior is determined primarily by the specific situation in which it occurs. With which position do you feel most comfortable, and why?

8. The sixth Suggested Reading contains Rotter's I-E Scale. Make a copy of the I-E Scale, then complete and score it. Are the results consistent with your own subjective evaluation of your standing on the internal-external locus of control dimension? Why or why not?

9. Consider Albert Bandura's concept of self-efficacy. Construct a ten-item true-false inventory of self-efficacy, including five items that would tend to be answered "true" and five items that would tend to be answered "false" by a person high in self-efficacy. An example of an item of the first type is "I feel confident that I can accomplish the goals that I have set for myself." An example of an item of the second type is "I frequently have doubts about my capabilities." Administer your completed ten-item scale to a dozen students. The scores will range from 0 to 10. Compute the correlation between scores on your SE Inventory and grade-point averages of the students. Did you find the expected positive correlation? Why or why not?

Suggested Readings

Bandura, A. (1986). *Social foundations of thought and action: A social cognitive theory.* Englewood Cliffs, NJ: Prentice Hall.

Bandura, A. (1988). Social cognitive theory. In A. Vasta (Ed.), *Annals of child development* (Vol. 6). Greenwich, CT: JAI Press.

Dollard, J., & Miller, N. E. (1950). *Personality and psychotherapy.* New York: McGraw-Hill.

Huesmann, R. L., & Malamuth, N. M. (Eds.). (1986). Special issue: Media violence and antisocial behavior. *Journal of Social Issues, 42*(3).

Mischel, W. (1986). *Introduction to personality.* New York: Holt, Rinehart & Winston.

Rotter, J. B. (1966). Generalized expectancies for internal versus external control of reinforcement. *Psychological Monographs, 80*(1, Whole No. 609).

Rotter, J. B. (1982a). Introduction. In J. B. Rotter, *The development and applications of social learning theory: Selected papers* (pp. 1–12). New York: Praeger.

Rotter, J. B. (1982b). Social learning theory. In N. T. Feather (Ed.), *Expectations and action: Expectancy-value models in psychology* (pp. 241–260). Hillsdale, NJ: Erlbaum.

Skinner, B. F. (1953). *Science and human behavior.* New York: Macmillan.

Notes

1 From Rotter (1966). Copyright 1966 by the American Psychological Association. Reprinted by permission.
2 McAdams (1990) takes a somewhat different point of view in urging his readers to "make a choice" among the various personality theorists. Although it is certainly worthwhile to consider theories in depth, one should not be too hasty in embracing a particular theory before investigating all of them. Furthermore, enthusiasm for a specific theory is stimulating but may not be warranted on the basis of what the theory is able to explain. All theories of personality have defects, but the defects are usually in different places. At this stage of theoretical development in personality study, this author stands by his recommendation to be eclectic. The student should try to be selective and choose whatever seems to fit best as an explanation of the psychological phenomenon in which he or she is interested and not go overboard for a single theory.

CHAPTER 9

Biological Foundations of Personality

CHAPTER OUTLINE

Unlike Aristotle, who believed that the heart is the site of mental activity, modern psychologists recognize the brain as the center of cognitive, as well as affective and psychomotor, processes. As the seat of consciousness and the controller of behavior, the brain governs and regulates not only the nervous system, but also the muscles, glands, and other body systems that contribute to what people are and do.

It is possible to discuss human personality by restricting oneself to behavioral data, focusing on observable peripheral actions without taking into consideration the biological "black box" that is responsible for those actions. Following John B. Watson and B. F. Skinner, a science of personality can be constructed without considering what is known by geneticists, neurophysiologists, biochemists, and other biological and physical scientists. However, the study of personality divorced from biology and chemistry is too limited for most psychologists. Failure to take into account relevant biological and biochemical knowledge leads to a situation like the one experienced by the blind men of Indostan, who were aware of only a portion of what constitutes an elephant. For certain purposes a portion of the truth concerning human uniqueness may be sufficient, but a better understanding of individual differences comes from a knowledge of their biological and chemical substrates.

As we shall see in this chapter, contemporary knowledge of the biology of personality is incomplete but nonetheless interesting. That knowledge has been obtained from a variety of sources: experimental and population genetics; studies of diseases, accidents, and other fortuitous events in humans and animals; laboratory experiments with animals; and noninvasive correlational and experimental investigations of humans. Advances in biotechnology during the past century have brought us a long way from the beginnings of neurophysiology in the 1800s. The techniques and machinery for exploring the central and peripheral nervous systems, as well as the muscular, circulatory, endocrine, and immune systems, that are now available are truly amazing when compared with the cruder biomedical research procedures of yesteryear. Despite the sophistication of contemporary biological research methods, investigators of the biology of human behavior typically encounter a second door behind the first, a third door behind the second, and so on—a complex, multifaceted domain in which one question leads to another and ultimate truth is a will-o'-the-wisp that seems forever out of reach. Nevertheless, the elusiveness of total understanding should be viewed as a challenge rather than a frustration. Scientific discoveries are never final, but what researchers learn is frequently sufficient to encourage and tantalize them into continuing their explorations.

Research Methods in Population Genetics

For thousands of years the results of breeding farm and hunting animals for specific temperamental and behavioral traits has revealed that certain characteristics of ability and temperament are inborn. Controlled breeding experiments with laboratory animals have also demonstrated the inheritance of measures of emotionality, maze-learning ability, and other psychological characteristics. For example, interbreeding successive generations of white rats that manifested greater emotionality when placed in an open area (as indicated by defecating, squealing, urinating, and the like) resulted in offspring that were more emotional than the offspring of less emotional rats (Hall, 1938). Although the differences in temperament among humans have also been recognized as to some extent inborn, there has been a greater reluctance to attribute behavioral and mental characteristics to heredity than to environment. Human personality was, and still is, perceived as being formed more by upbringing and individual experience than by biological inheritance.

Family Trees

As most children are taught in elementary or junior high school, the formal science of genetics was begun by an Austrian monk, Gregor Mendel, during the nineteenth century. Charles Darwin's theory of evolution, which also gained prominence during that time, underscored the importance of inheritance in determining the physical characteristics of animals and, by extension, their behaviors. Early investigations in human genetics were conducted by a cousin of Darwin, Sir Francis Galton, whose book *Hereditary Genius* (1865) inaugurated the systematic study of human pedigrees or family trees. Galton concentrated on the inheritance of exceptional mental ability, as manifested by the attainment of eminence in fields such as art, law, letters, religion, and science, but subsequent investigators dealt with the inheritance of character and personality as well as mental abilities (e.g., Dugdale, 1877; Goddard, 1912).

Unfortunately, studies of family trees suggest but do not firmly establish the role of heredity in determining a characteristic of interest. One such study traced the descendants of a revolutionary war soldier who produced two family trees, one by a feebleminded tavern girl and another by a Quaker lady whom he married (see Figure 9–1). Henry Goddard (1912) traced the two lines of the soldier Martin Kallikak (a fictitious name) over six generations. Among the 480 descendants of Kallikak's liaison with the tavern girl were 37 prostitutes, 24 alcoholics, and 3 criminals. On the other hand, the line stemming from Kallikak and his wife consisted principally of professional people (doctors, lawyers, judges) and other upstanding citizens. Although it would appear obvious that the differences between the two Kallikak lines may have been due as much to environment as to heredity, Goddard concluded that heredity alone was responsible for the high incidence of feeblemindedness and social degeneracy in the illegitimate side of the Kallikak lineage. This conclusion gained popular and even political support during the early twentieth century.

Twin Studies

Because the selective breeding of human beings is unethical, we must seek another method of obtaining information concerning the effects of environment

MARTIN KALLIKAK

He dallied with a feeble-minded tavern girl

He married a worthy Quakeress

She bore a son known as "Old Horror" who had ten children

She bore seven upright worthy children

From "Old Horror's" ten children came hundreds of the lowest types of human beings

From these seven worthy children came hundreds of the highest types of human beings

FIGURE 9–1 The two branches of the Kallikak family. The Kallikaks (fictitious name) were the focus of a sociological study by Henry Goddard (1912). One branch consisted of feebleminded descendants, most of whom were social degenerates; the other, of individuals of normal intelligence who were mostly successful.

on abilities and personality. The available method that is least ambiguous is to conduct an experiment with several sets of monozygotic (identical) twins, who have identical heredities. Some twin pairs would be separated at birth by assigning them to different experimentally contrived environments, whereas other twin pairs would be kept together in the same environment. If greater differences in trait scores are obtained between twin pairs reared in different environments than between twin pairs reared in the same environment, the results may be interpreted as support for the hypothesis that environment influences the characteristics of interest. Because society will not permit even well-intentioned scientists to move children around like chess pieces, nonexperimental methods of assessing the relative effects of heredity and environment must be employed. Nature's own experiments, which permit comparisons of genetically related individuals reared together or apart and comparisons of adopted children with natural children in the same families, must be relied upon.

Much of the available information pertaining to the role of heredity in determining abilities and personality comes from studies of individuals having different genetic relationships, monozygotic and dizygotic twins in particular. A shortcoming of all such studies, however, is that differences in the environment in which individuals are reared are not controlled or even measured carefully. Recognizing the problem of control, a variety of complex statistical procedures have been applied to the analysis of data obtained from such studies. The simplest and most common statistical approach is to compute a concordance rate or a correlation coefficient.

Concordance Rate

The *concordance rate* is the percentage of individuals, usually genetically related to a specified person having a particular characteristic or condition (a *proband* or *index case*), who also possess that characteristic or condition. The genetic basis of a psychological characteristic or disorder is determined by comparing the concordance rate between probands and their relatives with the base rate for the condition in the general population. For example, Allen (1976) estimated that the concordance rate for monozygotic twins suffering from depression is 40 percent. This means that if one monozygotic twin has a depressive disorder, the chances are 40 out of 100 that the other twin will also suffer from depression. Concordance rates have been determined for many other mental disorders, such as schizophrenia and bipolar disorder, as well as personal-social problems such as adult criminal behavior, alcoholism, and childhood behavior problems. The results of studies by Eysenck (1964), for example, show that the concordance rates for identical twins are significantly higher than those for fraternal twins on a variety of problem or socially deviant behaviors. As illustrated in Figure 9–2, included among these are adult crime, childhood behavior problems, alcoholism, and homosexuality.

A somewhat more accurate measure of the influence of heredity on a dichotomous trait is the *probandwise concordance rate,* a measure of the extent to which pairs of relatives share the same trait. This statistic can be compared with the incidence or risk of the condition in the general population—the percentage of people who develop the condition over their lifetime. The probandwise concordance rate is computed by dividing the number of individuals in the sample who are concordant pairs for the trait by the total number of individuals in the sample who have the trait. Suppose that we have a sample of 50 identical twin pairs. Let us say that in 30 pairs both twins have a particular trait, but in the remaining 20 pairs only one twin in each pair has the trait. Of the 100 people in the sample, then, a total of 2(30) + 20 = 80 have the trait. Of these 80 people, however, only 2(30) = 60 have identical siblings with the trait. Dividing 60 by 80 gives the probandwise concordance rate (.75) for this sample.

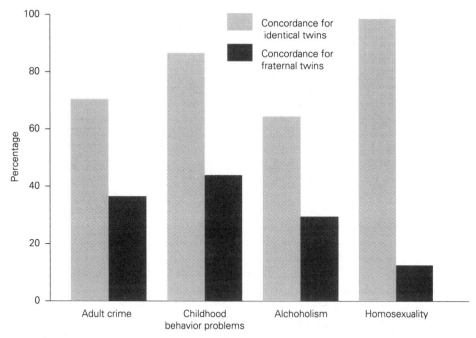

FIGURE 9–2 Concordance rates for four types of deviant social behavior. (After Eysenck, 1964.)

Correlation and Heritability Coefficients

When the characteristic of interest is continuous rather than dichotomous, the Pearson product-moment correlation is the most commonly applied statistic in heritability studies. Correlating the trait scores of genetically related persons reared together and apart is one of several genetic research methods devised by Francis Galton. The resulting correlation coefficients provide estimates of the relative influences of heredity and environment on that particular trait. For example, a correlation of .69 between the IQs of monozygotic (identical) twins reared apart, compared with a correlation of .88 between the IQs of identical twins reared together, indicates that both heredity and environment affect intelligence but that heredity exerts the stronger influence.

If the correlation between the ability or personality test scores of monozygotic twins (r_{mz}) and the correlation between the scores of dizygotic twins (r_{dz}) are known, a *heritability coefficient* (h^2) can be computed. The heritability coefficient, which ranges from 0 to 1, is the proportion of trait variance in the designated population that can be attributed to heredity. The heritability coefficient for a particular trait is computed as $h^2 = 2(r_{mz} - r_{dz})$. For example, if $r_{mz} = .85$ and $r_{dz} = .58$, the heritability coefficient is $2(.85 - .58) = .54$. This means that approximately 54 percent of the variance of this trait in the population can be attributed to heredity.

Subtracting the heritability coefficient from one yields an estimate of the proportion of variance in the trait that can be attributed to a combination of environmental differences and errors of measurement (.46 in this example). A portion of the environmental variance is due to experiences that the related persons have in common (*shared* or *common environmental variance*), and a portion is due to experiences that the related persons do not have in common (*unshared* or *specific environmental variance*).

Other statistical procedures for determining the relative effects of heredity and environment on a psychological characteristic include structural equation modeling and multiple abstract variance analysis. These procedures are described briefly in the following paragraphs.

Structural Equation Modeling. The first of these procedures, *structural equation modeling*, consists of determining the best-fitting equation to estimate the correlations among the trait scores of people having different genetic relationships. The procedure yields estimates of the genetic and environmental parameters that provide the best account of the variance attributable to each familial correlation. Interactive computer programs using maximum-likelihood or least-squares criteria are applied to determine the parameter estimates that do the best job of generating the familial correlations. A good structural equation model can reproduce the empirically determined familial correlations within a small range of error. Structural equation modeling can be used to assess the effects of certain practices, such as the selective placement of children in adoptive families that match the intellectual ability of the children's biological parents (Derlega, Winstead, & Jones, 1991).

Multiple Abstract Variance Analysis. A second approach, *multiple abstract variance analysis (MAVA)*, involves administering several measures of personality to individuals with varying genetic relationships who are reared together in the same family or apart in different families. The scores on these measures are statistically analyzed to determine the degree to which each measure is related to the amount of genetic overlap between different individuals (Cattell, 1965, 1982). The MAVA procedure yields four variance estimates: between-family environmental variance, within-family environmental variance, between-family hereditary variance, and within-family hereditary variance. Statistical equations are applied to determine the effects of heredity and environment on the characteristic.

Application of the MAVA technique in one study revealed that an estimated 40 to 45 percent of the variance in scores on a test of neuroticism could be accounted for by heredity. However, considerably smaller percentages of the variance in scores on measures of emotional sensitivity and carefreeness (versus cautiousness) were accounted for by heredity. Application of the MAVA technique to a wide range of personality variables led the researchers to conclude that approximately one-third of the overall variance in scores on measures of personality is due to heredity and two-thirds to environment (Hundleby, Pawlik, & Cattell, 1965).

Interpreting the Results of Heritability Studies

It should be emphasized that heritability and environmental coefficients or variances reveal nothing about the relative importance of heredity or environment as determinants of the personality characteristics of a specific individual. These coefficients, as well as the results of population genetics studies in general, apply only to the population of which the particular sample selected for study is representative. Because no two samples are exactly alike, different results can be expected with different samples. Depending on the way in which the particular characteristic is measured as well as the manner in which samples were selected, the range of heritability statistics may be narrow or wide.

Another important point is that even the most ardent proponent of the genetic basis of human behavior on the one hand or the most dedicated environmentalist on the other realizes that *both* heredity and environment are important in shaping personality. The two sources of influence—heredity and environment—usually covary and interact in a complex manner to determine a particular characteristic or trait. Consequently, a simple additive model that depicts the variance due to heredity and the variance due to environment as summing in a straightforward manner provides only an approximation, and often a very rough approximation, to the way in which these two sources of variation actually combine.

As shown by the correlations in Table 9–1, a large number of biological and psychological variables have been examined for their genetic bases. The high correlations for anthropometric variables such as fingerprint ridge count and the small differences between the correlations for monozygotic twins reared together and apart point to strong genetic influences on these variables. As might be expected, the smallest correlations are for psychological interests and social attitudes, but moderate to high correlations have been found for certain measures of personality and mental ability.

Heritability of Mental Abilities

A holistic definition of personality as "the pattern of collective character, behavioral, temperamental, emotional and mental traits of an individual" (*American Heritage Dictionary, 1982*) can be used to justify the inclusion of research findings on the genetic basis of intelligence in a chapter on the biology of personality. Scientific research concerned with the hereditary basis of intelligence, the most extensively investigated of all psychological characteristics, began with Francis Galton. However, belief in the genetic determination of mental abilities goes back to antiquity. In the famous "myth of metals" found in *The Republic*, Plato recognizes not only the inheritance of ability but also the diversity of that inheritance:

> You, citizens, are all brothers, but the God who created you has put different metals into your composition—gold into those who are fit to be rulers, silver into those who

TABLE 9–1   Correlations between Monozygotic Twins Reared Apart and Together for Nine Classes of Variables

Variable	Reared Together	Reared Apart
Anthropometric variables		
Fingerprint ridge count	.96	.97
Height	.93	.86
Weight	.83	.73
Electroencephalographic variables		
Amount of 8–12 Hz (alpha) activity	.81	.80
Midfrequency of alpha activity	.82	.80
Psychophysiologic variables		
Systolic blood pressure	.70	.64
Heart rate	.54	.49
Electrodermal response amplitude:		
Males	.78	.82
Females	.54	.30
Trials to habituation EDR	.42	.43
Information processing ability factors		
Speed of response	.73	.56
Acquisition speed	NA	.20
Speed of spatial processing	NA	.36
Mental ability–general factor		
WAIS IQ–Full Scale	.88	.69
WAIS IQ–Verbal	.88	.64
WAIS IQ–Performance	.79	.71
Raven, Mill–Hill composite	.76	.78
Special mental abilities		
Mean of 15 Hawaii-battery scales	NA	.45
Mean of 13 Comprehensive Ability Battery scales	NA	.48
Personality variables		
Mean of 11 Multidimensional Personality Questionnaire (MPQ) scales	.49	.50
Mean of 18 California Psychological Inventory (CPI) scales	.49	.48
Psychological interests		
Mean of 23 Strong Campbell Interest Inventory scales (SCII)	.48	.39
Mean of 34 Jackson Vocational Interest Survey scales (JVIS)	NA	.43
Mean of 17 Minnesota Occupational Interest scales	.49	.40
Social attitudes		
Mean of two religiosity scales	.51	.49
Mean of 14 nonreligious social attitude items	.28	.34
MPQ traditionalism scale	.50	.53

Source: Adapted from "Sources of Human Psychological Differences: The Minnesota Study of Twins Reared Apart" by T. J. Bouchard, Jr., D. T. Lykken, M. McGue, N. L. Segal, and A. Tellengen, 1990, *Science, 250*, p. 226.

are to act as their executives, and in those whose task it will be to cultivate the soil or manufacture goods he has mixed iron or brass. Most children resemble their parents. Yet occasionally a golden parent may beget a silver child or a silver parent a child of gold; indeed, any kind of parent may at times give birth to any kind of child.

During our own century, one of the staunchest believers in the inheritance of intelligence was H. H. Goddard. In one of his more controversial assertions, Goddard (1920) proposed that human society be reconstructed according to the intellectual abilities of its members:

> If mental level plays anything like the role it seems to, and if in each human being it is the fixed quantity that many believe it is, then it is no useless speculation that tries to see what would happen if society were organized so as to recognize and make use of the doctrine of mental levels. . . . Testing intelligence is no longer an experiment or of doubted value. It is fast becoming an exact science. Greater efficiency, we are always working for. Can these new facts be used to increase our efficiency? No question! We only await the Human Engineer who will undertake the work. (pp. v–vii)

The great majority of contemporary psychologists undoubtedly believe that general intelligence, or at least a predisposition to develop intellectually, is to some extent inherited. This belief is based in large measure on the results of studies in which correlations between the IQs of monozygotic twins reared together are compared with the IQs of monozygotic twins reared apart. An examination of the correlations between the IQs of individuals having different degrees of genetic relationship is also instructive.

Despite the difficulties of locating pairs of monozygotic twins who have been reared apart, several noteworthy investigations of this kind have been conducted (see Plomin & Foch, 1980; Bouchard & McGue, 1981; and Bouchard, Lykken, McGue, Segal, & Tellengen, 1990 for summaries). As shown in Table 9–2, the correlation between the IQs of identical twins reared together is higher than that of identical twins reared apart, although both correlations are significant. Table 9–2 also shows that the closer the genetic relationship between individuals, the higher the correlations between their intelligence test scores. Furthermore, correlations such as those reported in this table lead to the conclusion that the effects of environment on intelligence are not nearly as great as those of heredity. Additional support for this conclusion is provided by Bouchard et al. (1990). As shown in Table 9–1, the correlations between the WAIS Total IQs of monozygotic twins reared together and monozygotic twins reared apart averaged .88 and .69, respectively.

Another approach to evaluating the differential effects of heredity and environment on mental abilities is represented by adoption research such as the Minnesota Adoption Studies (Scarr & Weinberg, 1983) and the Texas Adoption Project (Horn, 1983). These investigations compared the IQs of large samples of adopted children with those of their nonadopted siblings and those of their adoptive and biological parents. Horn's (1983) findings are typical in that the IQs of the 3–10-year-old adopted children whom he studied were much closer to the

TABLE 9–2   **Median Correlations between IQs of Persons Having Different Degrees of Kinship**

Comparison	*Median Correlation*
Monozygotic twins reared together	.85
Monozygotic twins reared apart	.67
Dizygotic twins reared together	.58
Siblings reared together	.45
Siblings reared apart	.24
Half siblings	.35
Parent and offspring (together)	.385
Parent and offspring (apart)	.22
Cousins	.145
Nonbiological siblings reared together	.29
Adoptive parent and offspring	.18

Source: Adapted from "Familial Studies of Intelligence: A Review" by T. J. Bouchard and M. McGue, 1981, *Science, 212*, p. 1056. Copyright 1981 by AAAS.

IQs of their biological mothers, from whom they had been separated almost since birth, than to the IQs of their adoptive parents. The IQs of the adolescents in Scarr and Weinberg's (1983) study were also more highly correlated with the IQs of their biological mothers than with the IQs of their adoptive mothers.

The fact that genetic influences often become more important with age was underscored by the results of the Louisville Twin Study (R. S. Wilson, 1983). In this investigation of 500 pairs of twins, the IQs of monozygotic twins became increasingly similar with age, but the IQs of dizygotic twins became less similar from infancy to adolescence. The results of the Minnesota Adoption Studies (Scarr & Weinberg, 1983) and the Louisville Twin Study agree in finding that the home environment has some impact on IQ, particularly during early childhood, but the effects of home environment are substantially less than those of heredity. The findings of all three of these studies support the notion that people are born with an intellectual potential, but the manner and extent to which that potential is expressed depends on the specific experiences of the person.

Heritability of Personality

A wealth of correlational data points to significant relationships between genetic factors and personality (Loehlin & Nichols, 1976; Rushton, Fulker, Neale, Nias, & Eysenck, 1986; Floderus-Myrhed, Pederson, & Rasmuson, 1980; Plomin, 1986; Rose, Koskenvuo, Kaprio, Sarna, & Langinvainio, 1988), but the exact nature and amount of the influence has not been determined. Comparisons between trait correlations for monozygotic twins reared together (MZT) with trait correlations for dizygotic twins reared together (DZT) seldom provide a true picture of hereditary influence. Monozygotic twins are usually treated more alike than dizygotic twins, so the MZT:DZT ratio or MZT − DZT difference is probably inflated by environmental factors. Correlations between monozygotic twins reared apart (MZA) and dizygotic twins reared apart (DZA) are believed to provide a better indication of the effects of heredity (Plomin, Chipuer, & Loehlin, 1990), but even in these cases environmental influences are not completely eliminated.

After considering the results of numerous studies of individuals, reared together and reared apart and having different genetic makeups, a ballpark estimate of around 50 percent may be suggested as the percentage of the variance in personality that can be attributed to heredity. This figure is, of course, merely an average estimate, and it varies with the particular trait as well as the size and composition of the sample of individuals.

Interaction between Heredity and Environment

The effects of genetics on personality may also interact in a complex manner with environment, chronological age, and sex. Studies have shown that, depending on the specific traits, differences between MZ and DZ correlations may not show up until maturity (Dworkin, Burke, Maher, & Gottesman, 1976) and may be significantly different for males and females (Rose et al., 1988).

Concerning the effects of environment on personality, it is becoming increasingly clear that they are mediated by genetic factors. The fact that meager differences between MZT and MZA correlations are found on many personality variables (see Table 9–1) points to a relatively small environmental variance.

Although developmental psychologists and laymen alike have tended to believe that environmental manipulation can have a pronounced effect on almost any personality trait, David Rowe concluded, "Every parent of one child is an environmentalist, and every parent of more than one becomes a geneticist" ("How genes shape personality," 1987, p. 59). Observing the dramatic differences in personality between two nonidentical siblings reared in what is ostensibly the same environment may remind one of the old saying that you can't make a silk purse out of a sow's ear.

Parents, of course, are not the only source of potential influence on a child's personality, particularly as the child matures and other factors such as peer acceptance may become even more important than parental approval. To a large extent, depending on their genetic makeup, children create or shape their own environments. The fact that members of the same family frequently have quite different personalities indicates that, whatever the effects of environment may be, they are neither as direct nor as decisive as many child-rearing experts have assumed. The sex, physique, temperament, and abilities of a child—all of which bear the stamp of genetic causation—affect how other people react to the child, the activities the child engages in, and whether or not these efforts are successful. The opportunities and rewards provided for different behaviors vary with the sociocultural environment in which a person functions, but there is typically a wide range of acceptable and applauded behavior in any society. Within that range, the biological constitution of the person plays a critical role in forming his or her own life space and life-style.

In every culture, and particularly when extensive freedom of choice is permitted, children tend to elicit and select experiences that are congruent with their own genetic endowment. Children with particular hereditarily based talents and temperaments pursue activities that allow expression of and reward for those characteristics. They make different choices regarding what to pay attention to and what to ignore than children with other genes. For example, temperamentally active or emotional babies elicit different responses from caretakers than calm, docile babies. Well-behaved and attractive youngsters are likely to stimulate greater parental affection and interest than difficult, unattractive youngsters. On the other hand, parental characteristics also interact with the child's disposition. For example, highly emotional parents are likely to create unstable environments that have a more negative effect on children with certain genetically determined dispositions. The child's reactions then further exacerbate the parent's problem, and so on in reciprocal, transactive fashion.

Studies of Temperament Traits

According to the sociobiologist E. O. Wilson (1978, p. 47), "Genes . . . probably influence the ranges of the form and intensity of emotional responses, the thresholds of arousal, the readiness to learn certain stimuli as opposed to others, and the pattern of sensitivity to additional environmental factors that point cultural evolution in one direction as opposed to another." These are characteristics of temperament, which even such staunch environmentalists as the philosopher John ("tabula rasa") Locke recognized as inherited.

The results of a number of longitudinal studies of young children bear on the question of the inheritance of temperament. For example, in a developmental study by Thomas, Chess, and Birch (1968), 231 children were followed from infancy through adolescence to determine which features of basic behavioral style, or temperament, remained constant from birth to the teenage years. The study revealed a substantial degree of consistency in various measures of temperament, including activity level, regularity of biological functioning, readiness to accept new people and situations, adaptability to changes in routine, sensitivity to sensory stimuli, mood, intensity of responding, distractibility, and persistence. The children varied greatly from one another on these measures, and many children changed their behavior in response to parental handling. However, there was a strong tendency for the children to persist in their initial style well into adolescence.

Other developmental studies of temperament have been conducted by Buss and Plomin (1975, 1984, 1986). Using a variety of measures of frequency, duration, and amplitude (intensity) of behavioral and physiological responses, these investigators conceptualized temperament in terms of four general dispositions; emotionality (E), activity (A), sociability (S), and impulsivity (I). In their later research, the last variable (impulsivity) was dropped. Behavioral ratings were used to assess these dispositions in children, whereas the EAS Temperament Scale (see Figure 9–3) was administered to adults.

The three EAS dimensions are defined as follows. The first dimension,

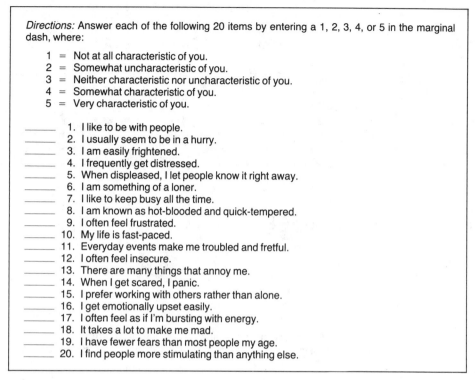

Directions: Answer each of the following 20 items by entering a 1, 2, 3, 4, or 5 in the marginal dash, where:

1 = Not at all characteristic of you.
2 = Somewhat uncharacteristic of you.
3 = Neither characteristic nor uncharacteristic of you.
4 = Somewhat characteristic of you.
5 = Very characteristic of you.

_____ 1. I like to be with people.
_____ 2. I usually seem to be in a hurry.
_____ 3. I am easily frightened.
_____ 4. I frequently get distressed.
_____ 5. When displeased, I let people know it right away.
_____ 6. I am something of a loner.
_____ 7. I like to keep busy all the time.
_____ 8. I am known as hot-blooded and quick-tempered.
_____ 9. I often feel frustrated.
_____ 10. My life is fast-paced.
_____ 11. Everyday events make me troubled and fretful.
_____ 12. I often feel insecure.
_____ 13. There are many things that annoy me.
_____ 14. When I get scared, I panic.
_____ 15. I prefer working with others rather than alone.
_____ 16. I get emotionally upset easily.
_____ 17. I often feel as if I'm bursting with energy.
_____ 18. It takes a lot to make me mad.
_____ 19. I have fewer fears than most people my age.
_____ 20. I find people more stimulating than anything else.

FIGURE 9–3   EAS Temperament Scale for Adults. (From Buss & Plomin, 1984. Reprinted by permission.)

emotionality (E), refers to the intensity of a person's emotional reactions. Emotionality is divided into distress, fearfulness, and anger. A highly emotional child is easily and frequently aroused (distressed, frightened, or angered). The second dimension, *activity* (A), refers to the general level of energy output. A highly active child cannot sit still for long and prefers games or other pursuits requiring a great deal of movement. The third dimension, *sociability* (S), refers to the tendency to interact and affiliate with other people. A highly sociable child likes to play with other people and seeks them out frequently.

The results of several correlational studies of twins support the hypothesis of genetic determinants of temperamental dispositions of emotionality (Thomas & Chess, 1977; Worobey, 1986), activity (Torgerson, 1985; Riese, 1988), and sociability (Floderus-Myrhed et al., 1980; Royce & Powell, 1983). The findings depicted in Figure 9–4 are typical of the MZ and DZ correlations.

Shyness. Related to Buss and Plomin's dimensions of emotionality and sociability are the results of studies of shyness (Kagan & Moss, 1962; Kagan, Reznick, & Snidman, 1988). Shy or inhibited children, who tend to be passive and cautious in new situations or around strangers, are contrasted with uninhibited children,

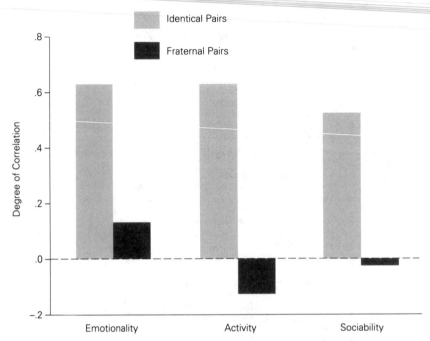

FIGURE 9–4   Average correlations of parental ratings of identical and fraternal twins on emotionality, activity level, and sociability. (Adapted from Buss & Plomin, 1984.)

who express themselves freely, energetically, and spontaneously. Kagan and his coworkers found that the tendency to be shy, as measured by behavior as well as physiological indices (heart rate, pupillary dilation, etc.) is quite consistent from age 21 months through age 51/2 years and presumably on into adulthood (Kagan et al. 1988; Reznick, Kagan, Snidman, Gersten, Baak, & Rosenberg, 1988). In addition to being shy, these children were more likely to be irritable and to experience sleep disturbances and constipation during the first few months of life. The inherited factor in this case may simply be a predisposition to develop a more easily aroused sympathetic nervous system.

Introversion and Extroversion. Essentially the same as Buss and Plomin's sociability (S) disposition is the dimension of introversion and extroversion. Regarding the genetic basis of introversion versus extroversion, the findings of Floderus-Myrhed et al. (1980) in Sweden and Rose et al. (1988) in Finland provide the most convincing evidence. Correlations between the introversion/extroversion scores of large samples of Swedes and Finns were .54 and .48 for monozygotic females, .47 and .46 for monozygotic males, .21 and .14 for dizygotic females, and .20 and .15 for dizygotic females, respectively.

Altruism and Aggressiveness. Also of interest are the findings of Rushton et al. (1986) with respect to the variables of altruism and aggressiveness. *Altruism* was defined as unselfish concern or devotion to the welfare of other people. In this large-sample study of twins, the correlations between self-reported altruism scores were .53 for monozygotic twins and .25 for dizygotic twins. The correlations between aggressiveness scores were .40 for monozygotic twins and .04 for dizygotic twins.

The fact that the heritability coefficient for several of the temperament variables discussed previously is higher than the correlation between scores for monozygotic twins should, however, serve as a caution against accepting them at face value. In theory, the monozygotic correlation is the maximum possible value of the heritability coefficient h^2. As indicated previously, these inflated estimates of h^2 are probably due, at least in part, to the fact that the environments of monozygotic twins reared together are more alike than those of dizygotic twins reared together.

Heritability of Mental and Behavioral Disorders

Sociobiologists, who combine findings from anthropology, biology, economics, law, psychology, and sociology, consider most personality traits—both normal and abnormal—from a heredity-environment systems perspective. This approach is a recognition of the fact that psychological traits are shaped by a multiplicity of interacting biological and psychosocial events (E. O. Wilson, 1975). Among the behavioral and mental disorders that have been studied from such a perspective are alcoholism, juvenile delinquency, criminality, abnormal fears, neuroticism, depression, obesity, bipolar disorder, and schizophrenia. The concordance rate for alcoholism is more than twice as high for monozygotic as dizygotic twins (Eysenck, 1964; Schuckit & Rayses, 1979; Cloninger, Reich, Sigvardsson, von Knorring, & Bohman, 1986). The results of breeding experiments with rats and certain other animal species also indicate that a preference for alcohol is inherited (Rodgers, 1966).

Criminality

Concordance rates for childhood behavior problems, juvenile delinquency, and adult criminality are substantially higher for monozygotic than for dizygotic twins (Eysenck, 1964; Cadoret, Cain, & Crowe, 1983). Evidence of this kind is partially responsible for the continuing influence of the nineteenth-century notion of the "bad seed" on theories concerning the causes of criminal behavior (Yochelson & Samenow, 1976; J. Q. Wilson & Herrnstein, 1985). Although not denying the importance of environment, supporters of a genetic basis for criminality maintain that a predisposition toward such behavior, as manifested in temperamental characteristics such as impulsiveness or low frustration tolerance, is inherited. Some years ago, the XYY, or so-called "supermale," chromosomal pattern received a great deal of attention as a possible biological determinant of

TABLE 9–3   Percentages of Sons Convicted When Biological and Adoptive Parents Convicted or Not Convicted

	Biological Parents	
Adoptive Parents	*Convicted*	*Not Convicted*
Convicted	24.5%	14.7%
Not Convicted	20.0%	15.5%

Source: From "Genetic Influences in Criminal Convictions: Evidence from an Adoption Cohort" by S. A. Mednick, W. F. Gabrielli, and B. Hutchings, 1984, *Science, 224,* 891–894.

aggressiveness and impulsive murder, but the research findings were largely unsupportive.

Although few people today subscribe to Cesare Lombroso's theory that criminals are evolutionary throwbacks to an apelike ancestor (Lombroso, 1911), the notion that a person can inherit a predisposition to criminal behavior has been supported by the results of several twin and adoption studies. For example, in a study of 15,000 adopted Danish children, a closer relationship between criminality in adopted sons and their biological parents was found than between criminality in adopted sons and their adoptive parents (see Table 9–3) (Mednick, Gabrielli, & Hutchings 1984). The results of this study and others are summaried by J. Q. Wilson and Herrnstein (1985). In their book *Crime and Human Nature*, which has been criticized as a modern version of Lombroso's throwback thesis (Leo, 1985), Wilson and Herrnstein (1985) characterize lawbreakers as tending to be young, male, mesomorphic individuals of low normal to borderline intelligence, who are likely to be emotionally unstable, impulsive, suspicious, hostile, egocentric, unhappy, worried, and dissatisfied.

Neuroses and Psychoses

Evidence has been obtained for the influence of heredity on a variety of psychoneurotic conditions, including abnormal fears such as agoraphobia (Rose & Ditto, 1983; Ohman, 1986; Breier, Charney, & Heninger, 1984) and anxiety and obsessive disorders (Gottesman, 1962; Inouye, 1965; Gregory & Rosen, 1965; Weissman, Leckman, Merikangas, Gammon, & Prusoff, 1984). Emotional problems, as manifested in symptoms such as bed-wetting, car sickness, nail biting, and sleepwalking, are also believed to have a genetic component (Bakwin, 1971a,b,c,d).

The two mental disorders that have received the most research attention with respect to the role of heredity are schizophrenia and manic-depressive psychosis (bipolar disorder). There is considerable evidence for a genetic influence on both of these disorders, but the nature of that influence remains unclear. According to the *diathesis stress model*, what is inherited is a predisposition to the disorder, but whether or not one actually acquires the disorder depends on the stressfulness of the environment.

Systematic studies of the concordance rate for schizophrenia place it at 44–50 percent for monozygotic twins (Kallman & Jarvik, 1959; Gottesman & Shields, 1973, 1982), 9–12 percent for dizygotic twins, and approximately 10 percent for biological parents and children (Heston, 1966). Whether the hereditary factor in schizophrenia is transmitted by a major gene or by a combination of minor genes and whether the transmission pattern varies with the type of schizophrenia have been matters of speculation. Two possible locations for a schizophrenic gene— one on chromosome 5 and the other on the X chromosome—have been posited (Bassett, McGillivray, Jones, & Pantzar, 1988) but not confirmed.

Affective disorders such as depression and bipolar illness have also been the subjects of intense genetic research. Concordance rates for bipolar disorder, in which the patient fluctuates periodically between extreme elation and deep depression, are typically higher than those for schizophrenia (Allen, 1976; Egeland, Gerhard, Pauls, Sussex, Kidd, et al., 1987) and higher than those for simple depression (*unipolar disorder*) (Mendlewicz, 1985). Particularly strong support for the genetic basis of bipolar disorder was obtained in an investigation of 32 cases of the disorder, every one of which went back several generations, among several thousand Amish in Lancaster County, Pennsylvania (Egeland et al., 1987).

One, and possibly two, genes for depression have been identified by laboratory research methods (Holden, 1987), and sites on the short arm of chromosome 11 and on the X chromosome have been found to be associated with bipolar disorder. In particular, Egeland et al. (1987) found that the presence of bipolar disorder is related to certain proteins controlled by genes located on the short arm of chromosome 11. The findings of Egeland et al. (1987), however, have not been confirmed by other researchers (Byerly et al., 1989; Kelsoe et al., 1989).

Physiological Correlates and Substrates of Personality

Physiological measures such as blood pressure and volume, heart rate, respiration rate, muscle tension, temperature, the galvanic skin response (GSR) and intrinsic (EEG) and evoked (EP) electrical activity of the brain have been used in research and applied contexts (e.g., lie detection) for many years. Such measures, which are regulated by the autonomic system, the reticular formation, and other parts of the nervous system, are frequently monitored as indicators of emotional arousal or level of activation. Many of these so-called bioelectric indicators have a hereditary component, as documented by twin research (e.g., Jost & Sontag, 1944; Lehtovaara, Saarinen, & Jarvinen, 1965; Bouchard et al., 1990).

Researchers have attempted to find evidence of distinctive physiological or biochemical patterns associated with different emotions and personality characteristics, but success has proved elusive. The theory of Hippocrates and Galen, discussed in Chapter 1, was the first scientific effort to relate body chemistry to personality. However, surely no one today would argue that irritability, depression, aggressiveness, and laziness are caused by excesses of yellow bile, black bile, blood, and phlegm!

Significant relationships between physiological measures and personality have been found in some studies—for example, lower heart rate in depressed persons (Henriques & Davidson, 1989), higher heart rates with faster acquisition of conditioned fears (Hodes, Cook, & Lang, 1985), and slower speed of habituation of the galvanic skin response in anxious and neurotic individuals (Coles, Gale, & Kline, 1971; see O'Gorman, 1983, for review). In a longitudinal study of shyness, Kagan, et al. (1988) found that, in comparison with more outgoing children, shy children have faster heart rates, more widely dilated pupils, and increased tension in their voice box muscles when confronted with a new situation or person. Another finding of this study was a significant correlation between shyness and monoamine oxidase (MAO), a chemical compound that regulates certain neurotransmitters in the brain.

Brain Damage and Functioning

Relationships of personality to brain activity (e.g., alpha rhythm), cerebral blood flow, and brain damage have also been documented. An oft-quoted illustration of the effects of severe brain damage on personality and behavior is the case of Phineas Gage, a nineteenth-century railroad foreman who survived an accident in which an iron bar he was using to tamp dynamite was driven through his left frontal lobe. As described by an observer, the changes in Gage, who had reportedly been a conscientious man of average intelligence prior to the accident, were quite dramatic:

> The equilibrium or balance between his intellectual faculties and animal propensities seems to have been destroyed. He is fitful, irreverent, indulging at times in the grossest profanity, manifesting little deference for his fellows, impatient of restraint or advice when it conflicts with his desires, yet capricious and vacillating, devising many plans of operation, which [are] no sooner arranged than they are abandoned in turn for others appearing more feasible. A child in his intellectual capacity and manifestations, he has the animal passions of a strong man. (Blumer & Benson, 1975, p.153)

The results of several studies (Gainotti, 1972; R. G. Robinson, Kubos, Starr, Rao, & Price, 1984; Sackeim, Weinman, Gur, Greenberg, Hungerbuhler, & Geschwind, 1982) point to a relationship between depression and damage to the left anterior region of the brain. Other research indicates that more negative emotions are accompanied by selective activation of the right-anterior region of the brain, while more positive emotions are associated with activity in the left anterior region (Ahern & Schwartz, 1985; Davidson, 1991).

Neural Bases of Introversion and Extroversion

Taking a cue from Pavlov's differentiation between friendly, outgoing dogs that were conditioned less readily and more easily conditioned, timid, fearful dogs, Eysenck (1967) speculated that a similar differentiation exists on the human level. According to Eysenck, the reason why extroverts condition less readily than introverts is that cortical excitation levels are lower and sensory thresholds are higher in the former than the latter. Having a lower cortical excitation level than introverts, extroverts are more apt to seek external stimulation to elevate that level. Empirical support for Eysenck's hypothesis has been reported by several researchers (Eysenck, 1967; Geen, 1984; J. H. Howard, Cunningham, & Rechnitzer, 1987; Nichols & Newman, 1986; Pearce-McCall & Newman, 1986; Davis & Cowles, 1988).

Eysenck includes autonomic nervous system reactivity in his physiological differentiation between neuroticism and normality (see Table 9–4). In general, neurotics are presumed to have more arousable autonomic nervous systems than normals, but level of cortical excitation in normals and neurotics is different for introverts and extroverts. Neurotic introverts (anxiety, phobic, and obsessive-compulsive neurotics), who suffer from what Eysenck labels *disorders of the first kind,* have higher cortical excitation levels than normal introverts. On the other hand, in neurotic extroverts, who suffer from *disorders of the second kind*, cortical excitation levels are higher than in normal extroverts but lower than in normal introverts. According to Eysenck, this pattern of neural activity results in insufficient fear to inhibit the expression of impulses in neurotic extroverts—psychopathic or antisocial personalities who have frequent difficulties with the law.

Related to Eysenck's introversion/extroversion dimension is Petrie's (1978) concept of augmentation/reduction. According to Petrie, some people tend to augment or enhance their sensory experiences, whereas others reduce or moderate those experiences. On Petrie's block test, *augmenters* perceive the blocks to be

TABLE 9–4 Physiological Differentiation between Introversion/Extroversion and Normality/Neuroticism

	Activation of Cerebral Cortex	*Activation of Autonomic Nervous System*
Introvert		
Normal	High	Low
Neurotic	High	High
Extrovert		
Normal	Low	Low
Neurotic	Low	High

Source: Adapted from *The Biological Basis of Personality* by H. J. Eysenck, 1967, Springfield, IL: Thomas.

wider and *reducers* perceive them to be narrower than they actually are. Like Eysenck's introverts, Petrie's augmenters are easily overstimulated individuals who are less tolerant of pain stimulation but more tolerant of sensory deprivation or monotony than reducers. In contrast, reducers, like extroverts, can stand pain better than augmenters or introverts, but are less tolerant of sensory deprivation.

The degree of augmentation versus reduction can also be assessed without verbal report by measuring the electrical potentials evoked in the cerebral cortex when the individual is exposed to an external stimulus such as a light flash or tone. Compared with reducers, augmenters show larger increases in evoked cortical potentials as the intensity of the stimulus is increased. (Buchsbaum & Silverman, 1968).

Introversion and extroversion are also related to Zuckerman's (1983) concept of *sensation seeking*. The "Sensation Seeking Scale" (see Figure 9–5) was

---

Directions: For each item, select the response (a or b) that best describes your true feeling. If you do not like either response, mark the one you dislike the least. Do not leave any items blank.

1. a. I have no patience with dull or boring persons.
   b. I find something interesting in almost every person I talk to.
2. a. A good painting should shock or jolt the senses.
   b. A good painting should provide a feeling of peace and security.
3. a. People who ride motorcycles must have some kind of unconscious need to hurt themselves.
   b. I would like to drive or ride a motorcycle.
4. a. I would prefer living in an ideal society in which everyone is safe, secure, and happy.
   b. I would have preferred living in the unsettled days of history.
5. a. I sometimes like to do things that are a little frightening.
   b. A sensible person avoids dangerous activities.
6. a. I would not like to be hypnotized.
   b. I would like to be hypnotized.
7. a. The most important goal of life is to live to the fullest and experience as much as possible.
   b. The most important goal of life is to find peace and happiness.
8. a. I would like to try parachute jumping.
   b. I would never want to try jumping from a plane, with or without a parachute.
9. a. I enter cold water gradually, giving myself time to get used to it.
   b. I like to dive or jump right into the ocean or a cold pool.
10. a. When I go on a vacation, I prefer the comfort of a good room and bed.
    b. When I go on a vacation, I prefer the change of camping out.
11. a. I prefer people who are emotionally expressive even if they are a bit unstable.
    b. I prefer people who are calm and even-tempered.
12. a. I would prefer a job in one location.
    b. I would like a job that requires traveling.
13. a. I can't wait to get indoors on a cold day.
    b. I am invigorated by a brisk, cold day.
14. a. I get bored seeing the same faces.
    b. I like the comfortable familiarity of everyday friends.

FIGURE 9–5   Sensation Seeking Scale. (Test items courtesy Marvin Zuckerman.)

designed to measure a person's thrill-seeking behavior—the desire for new experiences or willingness to take risks. High scorers ("sensation seekers") tend to seek out new, varied, and exciting experiences. The relationship of sensation seeking to introversion versus extroversion is seen in the finding that extroverts tend to score higher on this scale than introverts (Zuckerman, 1983). High scorers also tend to have lower blood levels of the monoamine oxidase (MAO) enzyme than low scorers. The concentration of two neurotransmitters thought to be important in emotion and motivation are regulated by MAO. Because the level of MAO in the blood is affected by heredity (as well as other factors), these findings suggest that risk taking may be due in part to biochemical inheritance.

Sex Differences

In addition to being a biological variable, sex may be conceptualized as a psychological characteristic. Masculinity/femininity, sex role, and gender identity are a few of the terms that have been used to designate the cluster of personality and behavioral traits that are related to biological gender. The higher aggressiveness and spatial abilities of boys are the most authenticated psychological differences between the sexes (Maccoby & Jacklin, 1974).

The influence of androgens, estrogens, and other sex hormones on the behavior of animals and humans is well-documented (Money, 1980; Bell, Weinberg, & Hammersmith, 1981; Ehrhardt et al., 1985). Eysenck (1967) argued that evidence for the role of male sex hormones as a biological factor in personality is found in the fact that men, who have a higher concentration of androgens than women, also score higher on the psychoticism (P) personality dimension. High P types are found more often in jails, reform schools, and other institutions.

Too little or too much male hormone during critical stages of fetal development can have a dramatic effect on sexual differentiation (Money & Alexander, 1969; Money & Ehrhardt, 1972; Money, 1974, 1980). Experiments in animal husbandry have shown that the development of the sex organs and sexual behavior can be affected by injecting the fetus with sex hormones during a critical period in its development. In humans, sexual preferences have also been linked to concentrations of sex hormones in the prenatal environment. Exposure to high concentrations of androgens prior to birth, for example, can influence a person's later potential for physical aggressiveness (Remisch, 1981).

Later sex role behavior can also be affected prior to conception. Nondisjunction in the 23rd pair of chromosomes during meiotic division can result in an XO, XXY, or XXX individual. Individuals with the XO condition (Turner's syndrome) tend to be emotionally immature, less socially adept, less self-confident, and markedly low in self-esteem. Individuals with an XXY condition (Klinefelter's syndrome) or an XXX condition tend to be passive and shy. However, whether the behavior of Turner's and Klinefelter's children is due primarily to biological factors or to the child's perception of herself or himself as (sexually) different is debatable.

Depression

Depression and mood disorders have been found to be associated with a number of environmental variables, including sunlight (winter depression or seasonal affective disorder), negative and positive ions in the air (Baron, Russell, & Arms, 1985; Charrey & Hawkinshead, 1981), and ozone level (Rotton & Frey, 1985). On the biochemical level, depression has been related to insufficient activity of monoamine neurons, leading to a deficit of norepinephrine and serotonin. It has been hypothesized that chronic depression is the result of abnormally low levels and mania the result of abnormally high levels of noradrenergic activity (Bunney & Davis, 1965; Schildkraut, 1965). Whatever its causes may be, the biological basis of certain kinds of depression is revealed by means of a *dexamethasone suppression test (DST)*. This test is based on the fact that dexamethasone suppresses the production of cortisol, a hormone found in the cerebral cortex. The DST suppression effect lasts for a shorter time period in some depressed people, those presumed to have a biological predisposition for depression (Carroll, 1982). However, the results of the test are not always valid, so they should be interpreted cautiously (Carroll, 1985).

Schizophrenia

More money and effort have been expended in trying to find a biological basis and a medical cure for schizophrenia than for any other mental disorder. Numerous interesting findings—for example, that the ventricles of the brain are abnormally large in schizophrenics (Andreasen, 1982)—have been reported, but medical and psychological researchers are probably still a long way from discovering the causes and cures for this disorder. It has been suggested that schizophrenia is caused by a gradual neurological degenerative process, but if so we do not understand at present how to arrest or reverse the process.

The neurotransmitter that has been studied most intensively with respect to schizophrenia is dopamine. The hypothesis that has guided this research is that schizophrenia is caused by overactivity of dopamine-producing neurons in various areas and pathways of the brain (neocortex, limbic system, tegmentum, etc.). The action of dopamine, a catecholamine that is a precursor of norepinephrine, at synaptic receptor sites is blocked by antipsychotic medication. If an excess of dopamine were the direct biochemical cause of schizophrenia, the effects of antipsychotic drugs on the symptoms of this disorder should be immediate. Unfortunately, these effects are more prolonged, indicating that the dopamine hypothesis is untenable or at least requires extensive modification. Any revision of the dopaminergic hypothesis must also take into account the fact that only a portion of schizophrenics—those displaying so-called positive signs (thought disorder, hallucinations, delusions)—respond favorably to antipsychotic medication. Chronic patients who display the so-called negative signs of schizophrenia (flat affect, poverty of speech, loss of drive) respond less favorably to the medication (Crow, 1982).

Organic Personality Syndrome

Traditionally, schizophrenia has been classified as a *functional mental disorder*, which means that it was assumed to be caused by improper functioning of the brain rather than by some demonstrable structural anomaly. On the other hand, disorders of personality and behavior in which structural change in the brain could be observed were referred to as *organic mental disorders*. These disorders could be caused by hereditary factors, external trauma (accidents), disease, or aging, and the mental or behavioral symptoms might vary greatly from patient to patient—even among patients manifesting the same structural aberration.

In a sense, any damage to the nervous system is a source of stress, and the particular symptomatology depends to some extent on the patient's premorbid personality—the kind of person the patient was before the trauma or disease occurred. However, when the damage is severe patients generally suffer some loss of impulse control and motivation; they show rapidly fluctuating and shallow emotions or mood, decreased concern about the consequences of their actions, and an inability to direct their activities toward appropriate goals. They may become either apathetic or lustful and, as a consequence of poor control, engage in antisocial behavior which they would not have dared or even dreamed of before the disorder occurred. For example, a gentle old man may make sexual advances toward a child, or a previously cautious businessman may engage in wild financial schemes. This cluster of symptoms is referred to as an *organic personality syndrome*, and it is more typical of patients who have sustained injury to the frontal lobes of the cerebral cortex (Crockett, Clark, & Klonoff, 1987; Sherwin & Geschwind, 1978).

Summary

Debate over the relative importance of heredity and environment in shaping human personality has continued throughout the twentieth century, sometimes favoring one side and sometimes the other. From the 1930s through the 1950s, Watson's behaviorist manifesto, with its legacy perpetuated by Hull and Skinner, was the stimulus for an era of environmentalism. Lip service was paid to heredity, but child rearing practices and individual learning history were considered more critical in determining what a person became and did.

Since the discovery during the 1950s of the structure of the DNA molecule, the hereditarian's star has burned more brightly. Not only have sophisticated genetic research methods and models led to the discovery of the hereditary bases of a host of physical disorders, but temperament, intelligence, and other psychological characteristics and disorders have also been shown to have genetic underpinnings. However, the answer to the question of exactly how heredity combines with environment to fashion complex behavioral and mental traits remains as elusive as ever.

The bulk of research on the role of heredity in determining personality is correlational in nature, involving studies of monozygotic and dizygotic twins and people having other genetic relationships, reared together or reared apart. In the case of a dichotomous condition or disorder, concordance rates and proband-wise concordance rates are computed on a sample of people having a specified genetic relationship and then compared with the incidence (or risk) of the condition in the general population. When measures of the characteristic are continuous or scaled, statistics such as the correlation coefficient or heritability coefficient are computed to assess the importance of heredity. More complex statistical procedures, such as structural equation modeling and multiple abstract variance analysis, are also used to estimate the proportion of trait variance attributable to heredity, environment, and various interactive or covarying combinations of these two sources of influence. The accuracy of any of these statistics depends on the validity of the assessment instrument, whether the sample is representative of the target population, and the logic of the statistical model that is employed. Other cautions to be exercised in interpreting the results of such studies are that (1) the results apply only to populations and not individuals and (2) correlation does not imply causation.

The findings of twin studies in particular point to a substantial hereditary component in measures of general mental ability (intelligence) and certain temperament traits. Three temperament variables that appear to be greatly influenced by heredity are emotionality, activity level, and sociability. Related to these three variables are measures of introversion/extroversion, augmentation/reduction, and sensation seeking. Among other "normal" characteristics of personality that have been found to have a genetic component are shyness, altruism, and aggressiveness. Alcoholism, juvenile delinquency, criminality, phobias, psychoneurosis, chronic depression, bipolar disorder, and schizophrenia are examples of abnormal characteristics or disorders that have been examined from a sociobiological systems perspective and found to have a genetic basis.

Significant relationships between physiological measures and behavioral or personality variables have been found, but many of these findings can be attributed to increased physiological arousal in stressful or strange situations. Studies of brain-damaged individuals have also revealed personality changes when certain brain areas are injured or destroyed.

Some evidence has been obtained for differential levels of cortical arousal in introverts and extroverts as well as differential arousal of the autonomic nervous system in neurotics and normals. Another brain research finding is that more positive emotions appear to be associated with activation of the left anterior region of the brain and more negative emotions with activation of the right anterior region.

The results of experimental studies on animals and correlational studies of humans indicate that too much or too little male hormone during critical stages of fetal development can have dramatic effects on sexual differentiation and later sexual and sex-role behavior. Structural abnormalities produced by nondisjunction can also affect gender identification and other personality characteristics.

Extensive research has been conducted on the biological basis of depression, bipolar disorder, and schizophrenia. Neurochemical investigations have revealed links between high dopamine levels and schizophrenia as well as relationships between abnormally low levels of noradrenalin and serotonin with depression. However, the biochemical bases of these disorders are complex, and definitive answers must await future research.

Key Concepts

Bipolar disorder   Condition in which an individual's mood fluctuates between euphoric mania and depression.

Concordance rate   Degree to which other people have the same characteristic as a specified individual (the *proband* or *index case*). The extent to which the characteristic is genetically based is determined by comparing the concordance rates for the proband's relatives and those of the general population.

Diathesis stress model   Theory of psychopathology that each person is more or less vulnerable to stress, depending on his or her inherited predisposition. Whether or not psychopathology develops when the individual is exposed to stress depends on the inherited predisposition and the individual's ability to cope with stressors.

Fraternal (dizygotic) twins   Twins resulting from coincident pregnancies in the same person. Originating from two separately fertilized eggs, fraternal twins are genetically no more alike than nontwin siblings.

Genotype   The underlying genetic structure of a characteristic, which may or may not be manifested in the individual's appearance or behavior (see *phenotype*).

Heritability coefficient   The ratio of the test score variance attributable to heredity to the variance attributable to both heredity and environment in combination; an index of the extent to which a characteristic is genetically based.

Identical (monozygotic) twins   Twins produced by a single fertilized egg. Because they are genetically identical, they are often used to investigate the differential effects of heredity and environment on personality and behavior.

Neurotransmitter   One of many chemicals secreted at the ends of axons that affect the transmission of nervous impulses across synapses.

Phenotype   The manner in which a genetically determined characteristic is actually manifested in the individual's appearance or behavior.

Schizophrenic disorders   Psychoses characterized by withdrawal from reality and disturbances of thinking, emotion, and behavior; a breakdown of integrated personality functioning.

Sensation seeking   Thrill-seeking behavior, the desire for new experiences or a willingness to take risks. Can be assessed by Zuckerman's Sensation Seeking Scale.

Temperament   General mood, activity level, and reactivity to stimulation, presumably based on genetic factors and present from birth.

Activities and Applications

1. Three personality characteristics for which research indicates a strong hereditary component are emotionality, activity, and sociability (Buss & Plomin, 1984). Take the EAS Temperament Scale for Adults in Figure 9–3, score it, and evaluate your scores on the three variables with respect to the means for adults given in the table.

Directions for Scoring: Begin by subtracting your numerical answers to items 6, 16, and 19 from the value 6. Then score each of the five scales (Distress, Fearfulness, Anger, Activity, Sociability) separately. The score on scale D (Distress) is the sum of scores on items 4, 9, 11, and 16. The score on scale F (Fearfulness) is the sum of scores on items 3, 12, 14, and 19. The score on scale An (Anger) is the sum of scores on items 5, 8, 13, and 18. The score on scale Ac (Activity) is the sum of the scores on items 2, 7, 10, and 17. The score on scale S (Sociability) is the sum of the scores on items 1, 6, 15, and 20. Compare your scores with the following mean score norms based on adult averages:

	Mean Score	
Scale	*Women*	*Men*
Emotionality (E)		
Distress (D)	10.08	9.72
Fearfulness (F)	10.60	8.95
Anger (An)	10.28	10.80
Activity (Ac)	13.40	12.80
Sociability (S)	15.24	14.60

Reprinted by permission from Buss and Plomin (1984).

2. One personality variable that is thought to have a biochemical basis is thrill-seeking behavior. Take the measure of this variable (Sensation Seeking Scale) in Figure 9–5, score it, and compare your score with the norms given below.

Directions for Scoring: Count one point for each item that you marked as follows: 1-a, 2-a, 3-b, 4-b, 5-a, 6-b, 7-a, 8-a, 9-b, 10-b, 11-a, 12-b, 13-b, 14-a. Find the total of your points and compare this "sensation seeking score" with the following norms:

  0–3: Very low   4–5: Low   6–9: Average   10–11: High   12–14: Very High

3. The average correlations for three temperament traits measured in monozygotic and dizygotic twins are as follows (Buss & Plomin, 1984):

	Monozygotic Twins	*Dizygotic Twins*
Emotionality	.63	.12
Activity	.62	−.13
Sociability	.53	−.03

A frequently used formula for computing the heritability coefficient is $h^2 = 2(r_{mz} - r_{dz})$, where r_{mz} is the correlation between the scores of monozygotic (identical) twins and r_{dz} the correlation between the scores of dizygotic (fraternal) twins. Using the correlations in the table, compute and interpret the heritability coefficients for the three personality variables. The proportion of total trait variance that is due to shared and unshared environmental factors is known as the environmentality coefficient. That coefficient can best be computed as the difference between the correlations for identical twins reared together and apart. However, approximations to the total, shared, and unshared environmentality coefficients can be determined as follows: Compute $e_{su} = 1 - h^2$, an estimate of the total trait variance due to both shared and unshared factors; $e_s = 2r_{dz} - r_{mz}$, an estimate of the proportion of total trait variance due to shared (common) environmental factors; and $e_u = 1 - r_{mz}$, an estimate of the proportion of total trait variance due to unshared (specific) environmental factors. These formulas assume that the error of measurement is zero, a tenuous assumption at best. Interpret the results of your computations.

4. Write five statements indicative of introversion (e.g., "I like to be by myself a lot") and five statements indicative of extroversion (e.g., I like to spend a lot of time with other people"). Using appropriate directions, administer your ten statements as a true-false inventory (call it your I/E Inventory) to ten people. Score the results on a scale of 0 to 10. A score of 0 can be obtained by answering "true" to all of the introversion statements and "false" to all of the extroversion statements. A score of 10 can be obtained by answering all the introversion items "false" and all the extroversion items "true." In your opinion, do the I/E scores of your examinees correspond to their observable behaviors? Why or why not?

5. Recall some of the relatives or friends whom you knew when they were young children and whom you still know. Do you feel that the levels of emotionality, activity, and sociability of these people have remained fairly constant over the years? If so, would you consider this observation to be evidence for the genetic basis of these variables? Why or why not? Now look at your own personality. In what ways has it remained constant over the years? In what ways has it changed?

6. Differences in the level of activity of the two halves of the human brain are related to behavior and mental abilities, and probably to personality as well. In right-handed people, the left brain is typically the dominant half of the brain, but, depending on the task, either the left or right side may be most active. A simple test of *hemisphericity,* which refers to individual differences in the level of activation of the two cerebral hemispheres, is to observe the direction of a person's eye movements when he or she presented with a task or problem. In a right-handed person, eye movements to the left indicate relatively greater activity in the right hemisphere, and eye movements to the right indicate relatively greater activity in the left hemisphere (Gur & Reivich, 1980). The pattern of hemispheric activation is more complex in left-handed people and cannot be determined without additional testing. Read each of the following statements to a friend or fellow student who is right-handed, and observe the direction of his or her eye movements after each problem is presented:

a. Tell me how you feel when you are anxious.

b. Visualize and describe the most upsetting photograph you have ever seen.

c. Imagine that you are relaxing on the beach, looking westward over the Pacific Ocean on a clear, sunny day. Your friend is resting peacefully with his back toward your right side and looking straight ahead. In what direction is he looking?

d. Make up a sentence using the words "shock" and "anger."

e. Try to visualize your mother's face, and tell me what feeling or emotion you experience.

f. Tell me how you feel when you are frustrated.

g. Picture and describe the most joyous scene you have recently been in.

h. Imagine that you are a veterinarian and must make a long and deep incision upon a dog. You must cut a straight line from the dog's left eye to his right shoulder. Visualize making the incision and tell me what parts of the dog's face you would cut through.

i. Make up a sentence using the words "rhapsody" and "pleasure."

j. Visualize and describe the most beautiful photograph you have recently seen.

If the eyes of the examinee to whom you gave this test moved to the right on seven or more of the items, he or she showed activation in the left hemisphere; if the eyes moved to the left on seven or more items, the examinee showed right activation. The test has been adapted from a study by Schwartz, Davidson, and Maer (1975) and is not a conclusive measure of hemisphericity. However, research has suggested that people who consistently move their eyes to the left are affected more by negative emotional content, but individuals who consistently move their eyes to the right are affected more by positive emotional content. Was this true of your examinee, considering that items a, b, d, f, and h contain negative emotional content whereas items c, e, g, i, and j contain positive emotional content?

Suggested Readings

Bouchard, T. J., Jr., Lykken, D. T., McGue, M., Segal, N. L., & Tellengen, A. (1990). Sources of human psychological differences: The Minnesota study of twins reared apart. *Science, 250*, 223–228.

Buss, D. M. (Ed.). (1990). Biological foundations of personality: Evolution, behavior genetics, and psychophysiology. *Journal of Personality, 58*(1).

Cattell, R. B. (1982). *The inheritance of personality and ability.* New York: Academic Press.

Eysenck, H. J. (1990). Biological dimensions of personality. In L. A. Pervin (Ed.), *Handbook of personality theory and research* (pp. 244–276). New York: Guilford Press.

Kagan, J., Reznick, J. S., & Snidman, N. (1988). Biological bases of childhood shyness. *Science, 240*, 167–171.

Kolata, G. (1986). Manic depression: Is it inherited? *Science, 232*, 575–576.

Loehlin, J. C., Willerman, L., & Horn, J. M. (1987). Personality resemblance in adoptive families: a ten-year follow-up. *Journal of Personality and Social Psychology, 53*, 961–969.

Plomin, R., Chipuer, H. M., & Loehlin, J. C. (1990). Behavior genetics and personality. In L. A. Pervin (Ed.), *Handbook of personality theory and research* (pp. 225–243). New York: Guilford Press.

Plomin, R., DeFries, J. C., & McClearn, G. E. (1990). *Behavior genetics: A primer* (2nd ed.). New York: W. H. Freeman.

Plomin, R., & Rende, K. (1991). Human behavioral genetics. *Annual Review of Psychology, 42*, 161–190.

Rowe, D. (1989). Personality theory and behavior genetics: Contributions and issues. In

D. M. Buss & N. Cantor (Eds.), *Personality psychology: Recent trends and emerging directions* (pp. 294–307). New York: Springer-Verlag.

Strelau, J., Farley, F., & Gale, A. (Eds.). (1985). *The biological bases of personality and behavior* (Vol. 1). New York: Hemisphere.

Tellengen, A., Lykken, D. T., Bouchard, T. J., Jr., Wilcox, K. J., Segal, N. L., & Rick, S. (1988). Personality similarity in twins reared apart and together. *Journal of Personality and Social Psychology, 54,* 1031–1039.

Note

1 People also differ in their circadian rhythms, or "internal clocks." Some individuals are said to be "morning persons" or "larks," whereas others are more active in the evening ("night owls"). To what extent these differences are inborn or acquired is not clear, but they certainly affect the choices of occupations and life-styles. Needless to say, early retirees and early risers are not necessarily healthier, wealthier, or wiser than their later-night, sleep-in counterparts. One's best work may be done either after the witching hour, when most people have gone to bed, or in the wee morning hours before they get up. Circadian rhythms are not related to so-called biorhythms, which are based on false, commercially promoted ideas founded on the notion that every person goes through three cycles—a 23-day physical cycle, a 28-day emotional cycle, and a 33-day intellectual cycle. A lining up of the person's cycles on critical days is said to increase the risk of an accident or the likelihood of a personal problem on those days. The empirical evidence is strongly against biorhythm theory, so one should not try to blame one's disasters or failures on biorhythms (Louis, 1978; Lester, 1990; Wolcott et al., 1977).

CHAPTER 10

Social Foundations of Personality

CHAPTER OUTLINE

Disagreement over the relative contributions of heredity and environment in determining personality is at least hundreds and perhaps thousands of years old. Even in ancient Greece there were those who took a nativistic point of view that in large measure people are born with different abilities and temperaments, in contrast to those who advocated an empiricistic viewpoint that experience or environment plays the larger role in making us what we are.

In our own time, some psychologists have favored Jean-Jacques Rousseau's nativistic belief that people are born free and "good," and others have sided with John Locke's environmental determinism—the notion of the neonate's mind as being a blank slate on which nurture etches a personality. The pioneer American psychologist William James revealed himself as a supporter of Locke's empiricism when he described the world of the newborn as a "blooming, buzzing confusion," with no nativistically determined organization or preformed patterns to guide the process of experiencing. However, twentieth-century research in psychology has demonstrated that newborn babies are capable of performing all sorts of behavior. As described in Chapter 9, genetic inheritance is important in determining what we are, what we are capable of doing, and even what we are likely to become. But as we shall see in this chapter, biology is not destiny. Environment—in early, middle, and late life—is at least as important as heredity in forming one's "personhood." From the very beginnings of our lives, heredity and environment are *joint* contributors to our personalities. These two influences never act independently, but are confounded and interactive in their effects from birth onward. For example, genetic inheritance influences the kind of environment a person is likely to experience. Sad but true, not only are all men not created equal, but even in America they are not born with equal opportunities. Rousseau's assertion that "man is born free but is everywhere in chains" is not a fair statement of the lot of contemporary man, but there is no question that we are constrained by both our genetic endowment and the environments in which we live.

The Individual and the Environment

The influence of environment on personality is due not so much to experiences that are shared with other family members as to the *unshared experiences* resulting from individual differences in variables such as physical appearance, gender, ordinal position (birth order), chronological age, and age spacing of children within families. Any of these variables can affect the way in which children are treated by their parents, siblings, and other relatives. For example, the experiences of little girls are different from those of little boys, and the experiences of older children are different from those of their younger siblings. Furthermore, experiences outside the family, such as having nonoverlapping friends, different teachers, and idiosyncratic experiences, contribute to personality differences among siblings. The opportunities for different experiences vary with the status and roles assigned to the individual within the family and the wider society.

Accidents, illnesses, and prenatal exposure to harmful substances also vary from child to child and can have pronounced effects on personality.

The influence of unshared experiences is seen in comparisons of monozygotic (identical) and dizygotic (fraternal) twins. From the very outset, monozygotic twins are treated more alike and hence have fewer unshared experiences than dizygotic twins. Differences in the experiences of dizygotic twins, as well as ordinary siblings, increase with age, resulting in greater divergences in personality. Similarities between the personalities of monozgotic twins, however, do not diminish appreciably across time or rearing environments (Scarr, 1988; Scarr & McCartney, 1983). This continuing likeness could be due either to genetically based similarities or to a greater frequency of shared experiences in these identical twins.

Ordinal Position in the Family

Birth order is a variable that Alfred Adler maintained was significantly related to personality (see Chapter 6). In particular, Adler focused on personality differences among the oldest, the youngest, and the middle child in a family. Although Adler's characterizations have not been entirely supported by research, empirical evidence for differences between the psychological characteristics of firstborn and later-born children goes back to the time of Francis Galton (late nineteenth century). Summarizing research on the topic through the early 1960s, Altus (1966) concluded that firstborns constitute a greater portion of the intellectually superior population than of the population as a whole. With respect to their cognitive abilities, firstborns talk earlier and more clearly, learn to read earlier, are better at problem-solving and perceptual tasks, score higher on intelligence tests, and are higher achievers in school than later borns. Temperamentally, firstborns tend to be more cautious, more conscientious, more serious, more responsible, and more dependent on adults. Later-born children, on the other hand, tend to be more physically aggressive and athletic, more socially outgoing, more relaxed and unrestrained, and more imaginative than firstborns.

One explanation for these differences is that parents usually treat firstborn children, particularly boys, differently from subsequently born children. Perhaps because of greater expectations and less experience with children, both parents tend to be more attentive and stimulating, as well as stricter and more concerned, with firstborn children and more relaxed and permissive with later-borns (Kilbride, Johnson, & Streissguth, 1977). Parents spend more time with firstborn children, talking to them and engaging in direct achievement training (Thoman, Leiderman, & Olson, 1972). Parents tend to offer more encouragement and help on developmental tasks such as walking, talking, and reading at the appropriate age to firstborn children (Rothbart, 1971). Of course, when there is only one child in the family, a child who, at least for a time, does not share the parents' attention with other children, parents have more time to spend encouraging and in other ways being helpful to the child. Not surprisingly, only children, who are perpetual firstborns, possess many of the same characteristics as firstborn children in multichild families.

Gender and Gender Identity

In contrast to *norms,* which are standards applicable to all individuals in a group, *roles* are particular patterns of behavior that given individuals are expected to display in specific social situations. Like norms, roles are learned ways of behaving. An important way in which children learn particular roles is by observing other people and being rewarded or punished for copying their behavior. Thus little girls typically receive approval from adults, and other children, when they act like little ladies; little boys are similarly reinforced for acting "manly." The roles acquired by an individual are largely determined by the culture in which he or she grows up. As whimsically and somewhat grotesquely expressed by Roger Brown (1965, p. 141) a generation ago and still somewhat in evidence:

> In the United States, a *real* boy climbs trees, disdains girls, dirties his knees, plays with soldiers, and takes blue for his favorite color. A real girl dresses dolls, jumps rope, plays hopscotch, and takes pink for her favorite color. When they go to school, real girls like English and music and "auditorium"; real boys prefer manual training, gym, and arithmetic. In college the boys smoke pipes, drink beer, and major in engineering or physics; the girls chew Juicy Fruit gum, drink cherry Cokes, and major in fine arts. The real boy matures into a "man's man" who plays poker, goes hunting, drinks brandy, and dies in the war; the real girl becomes a "feminine" woman who loves children, embroiders handkerchiefs, drinks weak tea, and "succumbs" to consumption.

Traditionally, little American girls are dressed differently, treated differently, and expected to behave differently from little American boys. Newborn girls are described as "pretty and delicate"; newborn boys are "strong and manly." Compared with little boys, little girls are encouraged to show consideration for other people and not be aggressive. They are expected to be more agreeable and person oriented, and little boys more aggressive and task oriented.

It is a commonly observed fact that children tend to pattern their behavior after that of their parents, and especially the like-sex parent. In a traditional American family, a little girl identifies with and models her behavior after her mother, and a little boy tries to be like his father. As stated by Freud, by means of this process of *identification* the child takes on the characteristics of the like-sex parent, including his or her sex roles and gender identity.

Although very young children do not consistently differentiate between boys and girls, they can easily and accurately identify another child's sex by the age of three (Thompson, 1975). And by the age of 5–7 years both sexes know what sex they are and what it means to be a boy or girl (Guardo & Bohan, 1971; Kohlberg, 1966). By the time they enter elementary school, most children have a fairly good idea of what is considered sex-appropriate behavior and what might happen to children who fail to adhere to their assigned sex roles (Stoddart & Turiel, 1985) (see Table 10–1).

The greater value placed on babies of one sex over the other and the roles that each sex is expected to play vary with the particular culture. In a comparison study of sex and temperament in three primitive societies, Margaret Mead demonstrated the importance of the environment and social customs in prescribing sex roles. These three New Guinea societies—the Arapesh, the Mundugumor, and the Tchambuli—although geographically close, were far apart in the roles assigned to males and females. Among the Arapesh, who lived in the mountains, both men and women were characterized as passive, gentle, loving, and submissive—traits that are usually construed as "feminine" in Western societies. In contrast, Mundugumor men and women, who lived by a river and had been cannibalistic at one time, were both highly individualistic and aggressive, or "masculine." Among the lake-dwelling Tchambuli, the sex roles of men and women were opposite to those considered normal in most Western societies:

TABLE 10–1   Periods in the Development of Gender Identity

Developmental Period	Events and Outcomes
Prenatal	The fetus develops the morphological characteristics of a male or a female, which others will react to once the child is born.
Birth to 3 years	Parents and other companions label the child as a boy or a girl, frequently remind the child of his or her gender, and begin to encourage gender-consistent behavior while discouraging cross-sex activities. As a result of these social experiences and the development of very basic classification skills, the young child acquires some sex-typed behavioral preferences and the knowledge that he or she is a a boy or a girl (basic gender identity).
3–6 years	Once children acquire a basic gender identity, they begin to seek information about sex differences, form gender schemata, and become intrinsically motivated to perform those acts that are viewed as "appropriate" for their own sex. When acquiring gender schemata, children attend to both male and female models. And once their "own sex" schemata are well established, these youngsters are apt to imitate behaviors considered appropriate for their sex, regardless of the gender of the model who displays them.
Ages 6 to 7 and beyond	Children finally acquire a sense of gender consistency—a firm, future-oriented image of themselves as boys who must necessarily become men or girls who will obviously become women. At this point they begin to rely less exclusively on gender schemata and more on the behavior of same-sex models to acquire those mannerisms and attributes that are consistent with their firm categorization of self as a male or female.

Source: From *Social and Personality Development* (2nd ed., p. 384) by D. R. Shaffer, 1988, Pacific Grove, CA: Brooks/Cole. Reprinted with permission.

Tchambuli women did all the work while the men spent their time in artistic, ceremonial, and other "feminine" pursuits.

Biological differences between the sexes, including the greater physical strength and gross motor activity of boys, the superior fine motor activity of girls, and the greater vulnerability of males to disease and death, are well-known and little cause for debate. Not so with sex differences in cognitive and affective variables, which have been a continuing sources of dispute with respect to their existence and origin. Summarizing the results of empirical findings on sex differences in American society, Maccoby and Jacklin (1974) concluded that girls are superior to boys in verbal ability, whereas boys have better visual-spatial and mathematical ability and are also more aggressive than girls. Although there is no question that particular ways of expressing aggression are learned, the fact that boys are more physically aggressive than girls as early as ages 2–3 years suggests a genetic basis or biochemical substrate for aggressiveness (Fagot, Leinbach, & Hagan, 1986). On the other hand, more subtle forms of aggression, such as snubbing or ignoring one's peers and gossiping, appear to be more common among girls than boys (Feshbach, 1969; Lagerspetz, Bjorkquist, & Peltorer, 1988).

Additional research findings indicate that girls are more people oriented and compliant with adults (Block, 1973, 1976). They display greater empathy and sensitivity to others (Eisenberg & Lennon, 1983), greater dependency and fearfulness, less self-confidence, and perhaps greater irritability and demandingness than boys. Boys, on the other hand, are said to be more active, exploratory, and impulsive than girls (Feshbach & Weiner, 1991).

Beginning with the "women's liberation movement" of the 1960s, the dichotomy *masculine versus feminine* has been viewed by certain writers as an artificial dichotomy that interferes with an appreciation of individual worth and with equitable relations between the sexes. The traditional way of labeling behavior as "masculine" or "feminine" has been deemed misleading, and certain psychologists have advocated rearing children without the sex-role stereotypes that are a consequence of such labels (Pogrebin, 1980). Rather, it is recommended that children be taught the value of both traditional feminine and traditional masculine activities and become more *androgynous* by engaging in both sets of sex-typed activities. In recent years the traditional conceptions of the American male as a self-confident, self-sufficient, powerful, tough individual with high expectations and the American female as a dependent, tender, weak person who is uncertain of her abilities have been changing. Cross-sex exchanges and the sharing of responsibilities have become more commonplace, and the emphasis on "masculinity" versus "femininity" as a personality dichotomy has diminished (Morawski, 1987).

Differences between the preferences and activities of males and females have been considered so obvious that in the past it was a routine procedure to standardize psychological tests and inventories separately by sex. Although this procedure may have been and may still be justified under certain circumstances, unisex test scoring and norms have become more common. The idea that psychological tests may contribute to sex discrimination is seen in the allegation that interest inventories administered for purposes of vocational counseling in schools contributed to sex discrimination by directing young women into traditional women's occupations such as teaching, nursing, and clerical work (Diamond, 1979).

Concern over sex discrimination and an interest in the nature and origin of sex differences in psychological characteristics also prompted the development of a number of measures of sex role. Two prominent examples are the Bem Sex-Role Inventory (from Consulting Psychologists Press, 1978–81) and the Personal Attributes Questionnaire (Spence & Helmreich, 1978). Both of these inventories are oriented toward a dualistic rather than a bipolar conception of masculinity and femininity, in that the two constructs are viewed as different dimensions rather than simply opposite ends of the same masculinity-femininity continuum.

A more recent conception of the development of sex-role behavior is "gender schema theory," in which gender is viewed as a category used by individuals to cognitively organize information about themselves. By attending to the verbal and nonverbal behaviors of other people, the growing child learns gender-linked associations, or *gender schemata*. A gender schema serves as a guide that motivates and regulates behavior according to cultural definitions of maleness and femaleness. In S. L. Bem's (1984) words:

> Males and females behave differently from one another on the average because, as individuals, they have each come to perceive, evaluate, and regulate their own behavior and the behavior of others in accordance with cultural definitions of gender appropriateness. (p. 188)

Three Interactions

Not only do different children respond differently to the same environment; they also prompt different reactions in other people and eventually try to structure the environment to suit themselves. One way of characterizing the dynamic interactions between individuals and their environments is in terms of reactive, evocative, or proactive types (Scarr, 1988; Scarr & McCartney, 1983). All three types of person-environment interactions are important in shaping personality.

Reactive interaction occurs when a child experiences, interprets, and reacts to the environment in ways that are different from those of other people. For example, a more aggressive child will respond differently to physical punishment or other forms of parental discipline than a less aggressive child.

A child's particular physical, mental, emotional, and behavioral characteristics also affect how other people respond to that child. This stimulus-response sequence, which initiates reciprocal reactions on the part of the child, describes an *evocative interaction*. For example, a cute, friendly child may be easier to love and forgive than a homely child who has frequent temper tantrums.

As children grow older, they move beyond the immediate family and begin to select and construct their own environments. In this way, rather than being mere passive recipients of external stimulation, they become active agents in shaping their own personalities. For example, an extroversive child will seek out playmates and engage in competitive play, thereby reinforcing his or her gregariousness. On the other hand, an introversive child may prefer to watch television, look at a book, or engage in some other solitary activity, thereby strengthening his or her introversive inclinations. This behavioral process, which is referred to as *proactive interaction*, is responsible, at least in part, for the decreasing relationship between genetic and environmental factors as children mature.

Cultural Differences

The finding that within-family differences in personality are equal to or greater than between-family differences may be attributable to the similarity of experiences of children in American culture, regardless of their family background. Presumably, significant between-family differences in personality could be demonstrated if a sufficiently wide range of families in different societies or cultures were studied. Comparisons between Western and non-Western cultures, in particular, might be expected to reveal important effects of between-family cultural differences on personality.

Culture consists of the behavior patterns, mores, attitudes, motivations, and organizations that are handed down from generation to generation and become characteristic ways of thinking and acting in a large group of people. In other words, culture is the part of an individual's environment that has been made by other people. The characteristics and effects of particular cultures are studied by cultural anthropologists who, along with other techniques, employ the *cross-cultural method* of comparing the behavior of people in different societies. Information for making cross-cultural comparisons may be obtained by objective observation (participant and otherwise), interviewing, and administering various tests or tasks to the members of specific cultural groups.

Cultural anthropologists have tended to emphasize the role of environmental factors, particularly cultural conditioning, in the development of temperamental differences among people (M. Mead, 1935). To both the sociologist and the cultural anthropologist, individual and cultural differences in personality and behavior are viewed as due largely to differences in socialization. Extensive studies by cultural anthropologists such as Bronislaw Malinowski, Ruth Benedict, and Margaret Mead have revealed a number of significant relationships between culture and personality. Particularly noteworthy are the analyses of cross-cultural data on child development obtained by Yale University researchers. Unfortunately, many of these studies have been faulted for certain methodological problems. They have also been criticized for being based on psychoanalytic theory and for fostering stereotypes of certain ethnic and national groups. However, the results of the studies did call into question a number of psychoanalytic principles and provided evidence for the role of socialization, as contrasted with biology, in determining culture-specific behavior patterns.

Despite advances in theory and research methodology, interest in investigations of personality and culture has waned during the past several decades. Be that as it may, the results of many of the studies, both older and more recent, are pertinent to an understanding of the role and process of socialization and culture in personality development. Particularly noteworthy among more recent cross-cultural projects for their documentation of relationships between child-rearing practices and personality are the Six Cultures Project, the Harvard values project at Rimrock, the Cornell-Aro project, the Culture and Ecology in East Africa project, and the Fromm-Maccoby study of social character in a Mexican town. Details of these and other researches may be found in Barnouw (1985).

The emphasis on independence, self-assertiveness, and achievement motivation in American culture tends to produce children who have those characteristics. In contrast, certain non-Western cultures stress social interdependence and encourage children to cooperate rather than compete (Edwards & Whiting, 1980; Whiting & Edwards, 1988). The uses of reward and punishment in child rearing also vary from culture to culture. Certain cultures, for example, punish "bad" behavior but do not reward "good" behavior. Some cultures reinforce shyness and formality in new situations, whereas others emphasize boldness and risk taking.

Depending on the nature of its economy and what is deemed necessary for survival of a particular society, different cultures place a premium on the development of different personal characteristics. Children in agricultural societies, in which group cooperativeness is essential for planting, tending, harvesting, and storing crops, emphasize responsibility, reliability, and obedience. On the other hand, hunting societies, in which individual ability, initiative, and bravery are more important, stress the importance of achievement, self-reliance, and independence (Barry, Child, & Bacon, 1959). Of course, particular societies are not always successful in fostering culturally desirable characteristics in all their members. As any teacher knows, lessons seem to "take" better with some children, depending on the abilities and temperament of each child as well as the alternative models to which he or she is exposed.

Personality Development in Childhood

Of all factors affecting a child's personality, perhaps the one that has evoked the greatest research interest is the degree of stimulation and attention received during the first year or so after birth. The reason for this interest is that the first few years of life have a great formative influence on the personality of the child. The kinds of experiences that one has during those early years are important determiners of the abilities, degree of security and trust, and overall attitude toward life of the person.

The law of primacy in personality development, which originated with the Jesuits and was adopted by Freud, maintains that forces acting early in life have a greater influence in shaping personality than those acting later. The Jesuits asked only that the child be given to them for the first seven years of life, and he would presumably thereafter remain a good Jesuit. Freud also conceived of the script of personality as being essentially written during the formative preschool years, a script which, with few changes, is followed for life.

Certainly William James's conception of the newborn as "an alimentary canal with a loud noise at one end and no sense of responsibility at the other" is quickly changed when the infant begins to smile at familiar faces and shows other signs of being a "real person." The development of this person depends critically, but not exclusively, on social experiences during the early years of life. Becoming attached to other people, learning to differentiate between "self" and "nonself," acquiring a gender identity and a sense of morality, learning to control one's feelings and behavior, and, in sum, shaping an effective personality, are important development tasks during childhood.

Human development, however, does not stop abruptly with the end of childhood; development is a continuing, hopefully progressive, process from the cradle to the grave. Shakespeare's play *As You Like It* describes, albeit rather unflatteringly, seven stages of human development:

> All the world's a stage,
> And all the men and women merely players,
> They have their exits and their entrances,
> And one man in his time plays many parts,
> His acts being seven ages. At first the infant,
> Mewling and puking in the nurse's arms.
> Then the whining schoolboy with his satchel
> And shining morning face, creeping like snail
> Unwillingly to school. And then the lover,
> Sighing like furnace, with a woeful ballad
> Made to his mistress' eyebrow. Then, a soldier,
> Full of strange oaths, and bearded like the pard,
> Jealous in honour, sudden, and quick in quarrel,
> Seeking the bubble reputation
> Even in the cannon's mouth. And then the justice,
> In fair round belly with good capon lined,
> With eyes severe and beard of formal cut,
> Full of wise saws and modern instances;
> And so he plays his part. The sixth age shifts
> Into the lean and slippered pantaloon,
> With spectacles on nose and pouch on side,
> His youthful hose, well saved, a world too wide
> For his shrunk shank, and his big, manly voice,
> Turning again toward childish treble, pipes
> And whistles in his sound. Last scene of all,
> That ends this strange, eventful history,
> Is second childishness and mere oblivion,
> Sans teeth, sans eyes, and sans taste, sans everything.[1]

Modern "stage theorists," such as Robert Havighurst (1953), have based their conceptualizations, an illustration of which is given in Table 10–2, on more

TABLE 10–2 Some Developmental Tasks

Period	Age Range in Years	Developmental Tasks
Infancy	1–1½	Creeping, interpreting sensations, adapting to feeding schedule, weaning, learning to manipulate objects
Early childhood	2–4	Walking, talking, accepting social regulations, identifying with parent, developing social skills
Early school years	5–9	Adjusting to organization, controlling emotions, accepting rules and rights of others, personal grooming, developing play and tool skills, learning schoolwork, acquiring physical skills
Middle childhood	10–11	Participating in group activities, conducting long-range projects, working by self, earning money, developing interests
Early adolescence	12–16	Dating, planning for future, needing less direction, being accepted by opposite sex, accepting own physical and mental abilities, acquiring a vocational direction
Later adolescence	17–20	Preparing for work, courting, sticking to schedules and completing tasks, deciding by self and taking responsibility, selecting vocational goal and working toward it
Early adulthood	21–35	Mating, establishing home, starting in occupation, rearing children, accepting civic responsibilities
Middle age	35–60	Helping younger people, developing leisure-time activities, fulfilling civic and social responsibilities, adjusting to physiological changes with age
Later maturity	60+	Adjusting to decreasing strength, retiring, adjusting to death of spouse and affiliating with one's age group

After Havighurst (1953).

empirical research than Shakespeare. Note that the majority of the developmental tasks listed in Table 10–2 involve other people, a fact that underscores the importance of social factors in personality development.

Of particular relevance to personality development are Erik Erikson's eight stages (crises and goals) discussed in Chapter 6 (see Table 6–1). To Erikson, the major goal of infancy (0–1 year) is to acquire a basic sense of trust; the major goal of early childhood (1–4 years) is to attain a sense of autonomy; the major goal of the play age (4–6 years) is to develop a sense of initiative; and the major goal of the school age (6–12 years) is to become industrious and competent.

Stimulation in Infancy

Many observers have noted profound effects on the behavior and well-being of an infant separated from its mother for a prolonged period of time. Margaret Ribble (1944) coined the term *marasmus* for the physical and psychological "wasting away" that she observed in infants deprived of their mothers. Some years later, Rene Spitz (1953) provided detailed descriptions of the physical and behavioral characteristics of institutionalized children who had received only about a 15th as much "maternal" attention as most children. The institutional children showed retarded physical development, increased susceptibility to disease, and behaviors such as weepiness, sadness, rocking, genital play, absence of expression, and immobility—a group of symptoms constituting the disorder of *hospitalism* or *anaclitic depression*. Spitz argued that an emotional closeness or "affective interchange" between mother and infant is critical to the physical and behaviorial well-being of the infant. Depriving an infant of this relationship is said to handicap his or her personality development in every sphere.

Pinneau (1955) criticized early research on maternal deprivation and the work of Spitz in particular. Pinneau's major criticisms of Spitz's research are that (1) the exact amount and the kind of contacts that the infants had with personnel in the institutions were not indicated; (2) descriptions of the health of the children and the care given to them are inconsistent; and (3) the heredity and socioeconmic background of the children were not controlled. Despite these criticisms, it is probably fair to conclude that some factor related to maternal deprivation in infancy can affect the development of the child but that the nature of that factor is unclear.

More satisfactory from a methodological viewpoint was an investigation conducted by Goldfarb (1955). Fifteen 12- to 14-year-old children who had been placed in foster homes when they were approximately three years old, after having spent all but the first few months of life in an institution, were compared with controls who had spent no time in an institution. The foster homes of the institutional and control children were similar in socioeconomic status. During their three-year stay in the institution, the former group of infants were kept in isolated cubicles for the first nine months (from age 3 months to 1 year); during this time they had only brief contacts with adults. During their last two years in the institution, however, the children were only slightly deprived of stimulation. Because the physical conditions of the institution and the foster homes were equivalent, the only essential difference between the treatment of the institutional children and that of the control children was in the amount of attention received during infancy. But when tested during adolescence, the personalities of the children who had previously been in the institution were quite different from those of the controls. When compared with the controls, the institutional children (1) were less socially mature; (2) had poorer speech development; (3) made lower scores on tests of intelligence, reading, arithmetic, and conceptualizing ability; and (4) showed less ability to keep rules and less guilt on breaking them.

Another study of children reared in institutions was conducted by Dennis and Najarian (1957). The subjects were children in institutions in Lebanon, where "mothering" was at a minimum and the infants were swaddled during the first few months of life. Tests given to these children at a later age showed them to be from three to 12 months retarded in intelligence, a finding interpreted as a result of the fact that the infants had little experience with materials like those on the test. However, no emotional effects of the sort reported by Spitz and no permanent effects of environmental restriction were noted.

Taken as a whole, these studies indicate that lack of sensory stimulation or attention during infancy results in retarded intellectual development. Furthermore, tactile stimulation of premature infants has been shown to have a significant effect on their weight gain (White & La Barba, 1976). The findings on the effects of restriction on emotional development, however, are less clear. Experimental research with animals has demonstrated that environmental restriction of young animals can retard their emotional development (e.g., Melzack, 1954). In addition, Harlow's (1958) research on mothering in monkeys demonstrates that tactile contact is a significant variable in emotional development.

All well and good, but many psychologists feel that the reported consequences of maternal deprivation in humans are due to sensory deprivation and not to the severing of some intangible bond between mother and child. They maintain that the infant needs attention from the mother and suffers in its absence because she provides the infant with varied stimulation. Other researchers have emphasized the importance of learning in determining these effects. Johnson and Medinnus (1965), for example, maintained that taking a child away from its mother during the last six months of the first year of life has the most harmful effects on the infant; they suggest that the cause is an emotional bond established between mother and child through learning during the first six months of life and that separation after the bond is established has harmful emotional effects on the child.

Research on Attachment

Building on the work of Ribble, Spitz, and others, more recent—and more carefully controlled—research has focused on the concept of *attachment*. Becoming socially and emotionally attached to a mothering person is considered to be critical for socialization and the development of a sense of dependency and trust. Attachment, indicated by proximity to the mother or other care giver, and the related phenomenon of *separation anxiety* typically emerge during the last six months of the first year. Behaviors such as babbling, smiling, looking at the caretaker, and following or clinging to him are all indicative of attachment. These behaviors become more pronounced at about the same time as babies show evidence of understanding the concept of object permanence; they look for objects that they have seen but are now out of sight.

As shown in observations of humans and animals, physical contact, including holding, cuddling, grooming, and the like, is crucial to the development of a sense of attachment and the security that it provides. The well-known experiments conducted by Harry Harlow with wire and cloth mothers demonstrate the role of contact comfort and socialization in providing security to and fostering normal social and sexual development in infant monkeys. Because monkeys are so humanlike in their structure and behavior, the results of these experiments have important implications for understanding the effects of "mothering" and its deprivation on human development (Harlow, 1958; Harlow & Zimmerman, 1959; Harlow & Suomi, 1971). After years of research, Harlow concluded that cloth mothers are better than wire mothers, but real monkey mothers are best of all. Without the opportunity to interact with a real monkey mother, or at least peer monkeys, during the first six months of life, the young monkey's later social development is retarded.

The development of attachment on the human level normally begins with a preference for people over other objects, progresses to a preference for familiar people over unfamiliar ones, and culminates in a preference for certain people, usually the mother or primary caretaker. This three-stage sequence in the development of attachment has been found in both Western and non-Western societies (Schaffer & Emerson, 1964; Ainsworth, 1963; Kermoian & Leiderman, 1986; Takahaski, 1986). Because of its cross-cultural generality, Bowlby (1973) inferred that attachment has a genetic basis.

Strange-Situation Procedure. An experimental procedure—the *strange situation procedure*—has been employed by Ainsworth and her coworkers to study attachment and stranger anxiety (Ainsworth, Blehar, Waters, & Wall, 1978; Sroufe, 1985). A typical experiment begins with the mother and baby entering an unfamiliar room. The mother sits down, and the baby is free to explore. Next, an unfamiliar adult enters the room. The mother leaves the baby alone with the stranger. After a time the mother comes back into the room, and the stranger leaves. A few more minutes pass, the stranger returns, and the mother leaves. Finally, the mother returns, and the stranger leaves for good.

When Ainsworth and her colleagues placed one-year-old infants in this situation, they observed three patterns of attachment behavior. The most common category, to which 66 percent of the babies were designated as belonging, was *securely attached*. These babies readily endured separation from their mothers and explored their surroundings. When separated from their mothers they sought comfort in some way and then returned to their exploration. Twenty percent of the infants were designated as belonging to the second, or *avoidant*, category. Although these infants rarely cried when separated from the mother, unlike the securely attached infants they avoided her when she returned. Also unlike the the securely attached infants, who were usually cooperative and free of anger in the situation, the avoidant infants did not reach out in time of need, disliked being held and disliked being put down even more, and tended to be very angry. The 12 percent of the infants in the third, or *ambivalent*, category became anxious even before their mothers left the room. Although they became extremely upset when she left, on her return they behaved ambivalently by simultaneously seeking and resisting contact by kicking and squirming.

Maternal Behavior and Child Personality. Ainsworth and her colleagues found differences in the behaviors of mothers of securely attached, avoidant, and ambivalent babies. Mothers of securely attached babies tended to be more responsive to the needs of their infants, providing more social stimulation and expressing greater parental affection than mothers of other infants. However, the relationship between the care giver's (mother's) behavior and the security manifested by the infant is not a one-way street. The mother's responsiveness can be affected by the infant's behavior as well as the reverse (Clarke-Stewart, 1973). For example, with reference to the nine aspects of temperament found in the New York Longitudinal Study, three categories of children have been identified: easy child, difficult child, and slow-to-warm-up child (Thomas, Chess, & Birch, 1968). It is easy to see how these differences between children, which show up soon after birth and remain relatively stable throughout childhood, could affect the mother's or other caretaker's treatment of the child. Another study pointing to the existence of temperament differences at birth, which can undoubtedly affect the responsiveness of the mother or other care giver, was conducted by Sostek and Wyatt (1981). These researchers found that neonates having low levels of monoamine oxidase (MAO) are more active, more excitable, and crankier than those having higher levels of this enzyme.

Whatever the cause of their insecurity may be, less securely attached one-year-olds are more easily frustrated, more dependent on adults, and more socially withdrawn (Matas, Arend, & Sroufe, 1978; Sroufe, Fox, & Pancake, 1983; Waters, Wippman, & Sroufe, 1979). They also experience more difficulty in problem solving at ages 2–3 (Sroufe, 1978). It has been observed that an inability to form secure attachments during the early years contributes to later failure to form close relationships with siblings, friends, and marital partners (Bowlby, 1973; Rutter, 1979; Ainsworth, 1989). Ainsworth (1982) pointed out, however, that childhood experiences can overcome a failure to form close attachments during infancy. Children are not irreparably damaged for life simply because they experience poor social relationships or emotional trauma in early life. Subsequent experiences can compensate for these deficits and produce a happy, well-adjusted child despite a poor start.

Cross-national comparisons have revealed somewhat different patterns of infant attachment in different groups. For example, in a study conducted by Van Ijzendoorn and Kroonenberg (1988) the majority of the infants who were examined in the sampled countries were described as *secure*. However, a higher proportion of infants in West European nations displayed an *insecure* rather than an *avoidant* pattern, whereas the reverse was true for Japanese and Israeli children. Infants in the United States fell somewhere in between: More were classified as *insecure* than *avoidant*, but the difference was proportionally smaller than that for the West European countries.

Day Care. Approximately 50 percent of American mothers who have young children work outside the home, and while their mothers are at work many of these children remain in day-care centers. Questions concerning not only the quality of care offered by these centers but also the effects of day care on attachment between mother and child and the feelings of security and trust engendered in the child have been the subjects of considerable discussion and research. Despite some evidence to the contrary, most researchers have found no reduction in quality of the mother-child relationship due to day care. This conclusion is particularly true when working mothers set aside uninterrupted time for their children, paying exclusive attention to them during this special time (Hoffman, 1984). Furthermore, the multiple attachments that a child develops toward the day-care staff and mother seem to have generally positive effects on the child's social development (Moore, 1975). Day-care centers are obviously not equally effective in maximizing healthy child development, and working parents would be wise to compare the features of particular centers with those recommended by specialists in child development (e.g., Kagan, Kearsley, & Zelazo, 1977).

Self and Self-concept Development

"Know thyself" advised the oracle at Delphi, but what is it that the oracle wished us to know? Multiple definitions and differentiations have been suggested, including "self as object" and "self as agent" and between "material, spiritual, and social selves." A common definition of *self* is "the perceived, consciously known and experienced identity, individuality, or ego of the person."

As discussed in Chapter 7, phenomenologists consider the self to be that part of the phenomenal field (or "awareness") perceived by a person as his or her own personality. The existence of this "self," or conscious awareness of individuality, is one of the many things that differentiate humans from other animals. As far as we know, other animals do not plan their activities for the following day or week, contemplate the meaning of their existence (but perhaps their navels!), or understand that their days are numbered. One needs a self, an awareness of the difference between "me" and "thou" and between "me" and "it," in order to engage in such contemplations. Small wonder that the analysis of human consciousness, which includes an awareness of individuality or uniqueness, was viewed by many late-nineteenth-century psychologists as the primary task of psychology, a task which, incidentally, they failed to complete.

Although a newborn baby is an individual, it cannot truly be said to possess a self. Infants do not distinguish between *self* and *nonself* until 4–6 months of age, at which time they begin to learn through personal experience the limits of their own bodies and their influences on other human and nonhuman parts of the environment. One proof of the existence of a "self," the ability to recognize a mirror image or a picture of oneself, is not in evidence until the infant is approximately 18 months old (Amsterdam, 1972; Lewis & Brooks, 1975). Whereas 9- and 12-month-old infants do not respond to rouge on their noses (as viewed in a mirror), infants in the latter half of the second year do react to it (Lewis & Brooks-Gunn, 1979). Incidentally, using the rouge test as a criterion, adult chimpanzees, who also respond to reflections of themselves with red noses, must have selves!

Separation of the infant from its mother is an important factor in the process of *individuation* or self-development. The child learns through pain, deprivation, and frustration that it is no longer symbiotically attached to its mother, that everyone does not always conform to its desires and sometimes it must conform to the needs of others. It also learns that it is a boy or a girl and a member of a particular family. Imitation of and identification with one's parents and other family members is crucial to the development of an identity or self in the young child. But when the child begins to leave the home, he or she discovers other models—friends, teachers, coaches, and even nonpresent models such as film stars and professional athletes.

Self-concept and Self-esteem

Through trial and error, the two-year-old learns what he or she can and cannot do and thus sows the seeds of a self-concept. As the child grows and develops a differentiated self, a conception of that self is also acquired. The *self-concept*, which consists of how one views himself or herself, depends on the person's physical characteristics, abilities, and temperament, as compared with those of other individuals. People may come to evaluate themselves highly (high self-esteem) or lowly (low self-esteem). That self-concept includes not only the image the person has of his or her own body, but also the person's attitudes, aspirations, and social roles.

Whereas self-concept refers to the ideas or beliefs that an individual has about himself or herself, *self-esteem* consists of how the self is evaluated by the individual. Children who have high self-esteem want to succeed and hate to fail. When they do fail they may try to avoid the failure situation, but if it proves impossible to do so, they will try even harder and more persistently on the next occasion. In contrast, children with low self-esteem are less persistent and tend to settle for moderate success. They are also less likely than those with high self-esteem to be persuaded to try harder, and they are more critical of other people (Shrauger & Sorman, 1977; McFarlin, Baumeister, & Blascovich, 1984; Crocker & Schwartz, 1985).

With the development of perception and cognitive skills, children become aware of similarities and differences between their own desires and those of other people, and they learn to behave in more realistic, socially appropriate ways. Children also learn to respond in terms of how they see themselves, a view determined in large measure by the reactions of people who are significant to them. C. H. Cooley (1922) referred to these self-development processes as the "looking glass concept of the self," that is, the individual's perceptions of how other people perceive and react to his or her person and behavior. Through such social interactions children come to modify their behavior and conceptions of themselves.

Self-monitoring and Attributions

As the child's world expands and he or she becomes more aware of the characteristics of other people and has experiences with success and failure, the child's feelings of self-esteem, self-confidence, self-efficacy, and self-awareness all undergo modification. Some people (*high self-monitors*) are more sensitive to socially appropriate behaviors and act accordingly; other people (*low self-monitors*) are less sensitive to external cues and act more in response to their own internal attitudes and feelings.

In general people tend to attribute their successes to their personal efforts and ability (*internal attributions*) and their failures to the difficulty of the task or bad luck (*external attributions*) (Weary, 1978). The reverse may be true with regard to our attributions of the causes of successes and failures experienced by other people. In any event, the tendency to attribute success and failure to forces within or outside oneself varies with the individual and therefore qualifies as a personality variable.

The acquisition of language is particularly important in the development of a self. Acquiring a language enables the child to communicate with other people, learning and confirming or disconfirming assumptions about oneself and other aspects of the world. Language facilitates learning about things that one has not directly experienced and aids in acquiring motives and goals of a more intangible nature. However, nonverbal behaviors, such as eye contact, gestures, postures, and manner of speaking, as well as dress and other behaviors that signify who one is, are also important in creating the self.

Stages of Moral Development

Learning the rules of right conduct and adhering to them is an important developmental task that faces all children in a given culture. To Sigmund Freud (1930), acquisition of a sense of right and wrong, or morality, occurs with the development of the superego, that portion of the personality which consists in large measure of the internalization of parental prohibitions and sanctions. Conflict between the superego and the id was said to result in *moral anxiety*, an apprehensiveness that the id will cause immoral behavior or temptations that will result in the expression of guilt by the superego or shame at having violated, or having been tempted to violate, the moral code. Freud felt that the superego, which consists of the conscience and the ego ideal, is essentially in place by the end of the preschool period. Through the process of socialization and identification with parents and other significant adults, the child's conscience—the bases of moral choices—had become instilled by that time. According to Freud, resolution of the Oedipus complex through fear of castration and resulting identification with the father creates a deeper reservoir of fear and guilt in the male child, and hence a stronger conscience, than in the female.

Whereas Freud and other psychoanalysts stressed the development of moral feelings or emotions, Jean Piaget and Lawrence Kohlberg took a cognitive approach in theorizing about morality. Piaget saw the maturation of moral judgment as occurring in a series of stages that roughly parallel the preoperational, concrete operational, and formal operational periods of cognitive development. The first stage in the development of moral judgment is that of *moral realism*. During this stage, which lasts until age seven or eight, the child believes in rigid rules and unquestioned reliance on authority. Adherence to a belief in moral realism gives way to a second, or *morality of cooperation*, stage lasting until approximately age 11. At this stage, the child comes to believe in equal treatment or reciprocity ("taking turns") as a basis for determining what is fair. The highest, or *moral relativism*, stage of moral judgment comes into play around age 11 or 12. Now the child realizes that the particular situation or circumstances leading to a given action, including the intentions of the perpetrator, affect whether that action should be judged as good or bad.

In a related stage theory of moral development, Lawrence Kohlberg (1969, 1976) maintained that the development of personal moral judgment progresses through three ascending levels, consisting of two stages each. At the lowest level (Level I, or *preconventional morality*), moral judgments are based on obedience to authority figures (stage 1) or on a kind of naive pleasure-pain philosophy (stage 2). At an intermediate level (Level II, or *conventional morality*), moral judgments are based either on social approval ("good boy/good girl" morality) (stage 3) or on a law and order orientation (stage 4). In the first stage of the highest level (Level III, or *postconventional morality*), moral judgments are based on the acceptance of a contract or democratically determined agreement ("the good of all") (stage 5) or on one's own internal, self-accepted set of moral principles and a conscience that directs judgment and behavior (stage 6).

To assess the stage of moral judgment attained by a particular child, Kohlberg developed the Moral Judgment Scale. Administration of this scale consists of presenting to the examinee each of nine hypothetical moral dilemmas and eliciting a judgment and reasons for the judgment pertaining to the dilemma. One such dilemma, that of Heinz and the druggist, is as follows:

> In Europe, a woman was near death from a special kind of cancer. There was one drug that the doctors thought might save her. It was a form of radium that a druggest in the same town had recently discovered. The drug was expensive to make, but the druggist was charging ten times what the drug cost him to make. He paid $200 for the radium and charged $2000 for a small dose of the drug. The sick woman's husband, Heinz, went to everyone he knew to borrow the money, but he could only get together about $1000, which was half of what it cost. He told the druggist that his wife was dying, and asked him to sell it cheaper or let him pay later. But the druggist said, "No, I discovered the drug and I'm going to make money from it." So Heinz got desperate and broke into the man's store to steal the drug for his wife. (Kohlberg & Elfenbein, 1975)

Scoring responses to the dilemmas posed by the Moral Judgment Scale is an elaborate process of making subjective evaluations of the responses in terms of the six stages. Unfortunately, the scoring is not very reliable.

Kohlberg's theory of a universally fixed sequence of six stages of moral development has not received extensive research support, although at least one longitudinal study of Turkish children and adolescents found a stage sequence of moral judgments similar to the one postulated by Kohlberg (Nisan & Kohlberg, 1982). In addition, it should be emphasized that moral judgment, which is highly dependent on the level of cognitive development, is not the same as moral behavior or moral feelings. Many children and adults can logically determine and easily verbalize the difference between right and wrong, and yet, often with no expressed feelings of guilt or remorse, violate those very principles in their behavior.

Kohlberg's theory of moral development was based on an all-male sample, and as such it may reflect only a male orientation toward morality. Gilligan (1982) has taken exception to the generalization of the theory to women, alleging that the theory neglects morality based on responsibility and caring. She contends that men and women follow different patterns in their moral development. This contention, however, has not been strongly supported by research (Walker, 1984).

Unlike theories that presuppose a general trait of morality, social learning theorists view moral behavior as highly situation-specific: Whether a person lies, cheats, steals, or in other ways behaves immorally is said to depend on the situation or circumstances. A classic demonstration of the situational specificity of morality was the Character Education Inquiry of Hartshorne and May (1928). In this series of investigations, children were surreptitiously provided with an opportunity to demonstrate their honesty, altruism, and other character traits. For example, to test for honesty the investigators placed the children in a situation where they could steal some coins and in another situation where they could copy test answers, seemingly without being detected. Not all children were equally honest or dishonest in all situations. Older children, less intelligent children, children of lower socioeconomic status, and more emotionally unstable children tended to be less honest in all of the contrived situations. But the most widely cited finding of these investigations was that honesty and other character traits varied as much with the situation as with the individual. In other words, a child's honesty, altruism, and other moral behaviors were highly dependent on the situation in which he or she was observed. Although subsequent reanalyses of the Hartshorne and May data (Burton, 1963; Epstein, 1979) yielded greater behavioral consistency than originally reported, a great deal of situational specificity in behavior remained. Thus the findings of the Hartshorne and May studies appear to be explicable more in terms of social learning theory, which emphasizes the role of situations in determining behavior, than by a trait theory of moral behavior.

Other Prosocial and Antisocial Behaviors

Similar evidence of situational specificity has been found in research on other kinds of prosocial behavior. An example is *bystander intervention,* that is, whether or not a person chooses to come to the aid of someone who is being attacked or has had an accident. In their studies of bystander intervention, Latane and Darley (1970) found that whether or not an observer decides to assist a victim depends greatly on the actions of other spectators at the scene. When many people are present, responsibility may become so diffuse that a given individual is less likely to intervene. Unless a particular person is focused on by the victim or other bystanders to render assistance, that person may assume it is not his or her responsibility to help. Darley and Latane also found that the personality and

---

Attitude toward People

Directions: Indicate the extent of your agreement or disagreement with each of the following statements by writing in the blank next to the statement number:

SA if you "strongly agree" with the statement.
A   if you "agree" with the statement.
U   if you are "undecided."
D   if you "disagree" with the statement.
SD if you "strongly disagree" with the statement.

_____ 1. I want to live a life that is filled with caring for and service to others.
_____ 2. Admittedly I'm a rather self-centered person, but after all that's only normal.
_____ 3. I have great respect for Mother Teresa, the nun who devoted her life to serving the "poorest of the poor."
_____ 4. In this life one had better look after oneself first and worry about helping other people second.
_____ 5. Most people don't really appreciate it when someone tries to help them, so why bother?
_____ 6. There is nothing finer and nobler than a person who goes out of the way to assist another human being.
_____ 7. People should be more concerned with the feelings and welfare of others than with how everything affects them personally.
_____ 8. Enlightened self-interest is a very realistic and appropriate philosophy of life in most situations and circumstances.
_____ 9. I'm willing to dedicate my life to helping people who are less fortunate than I.
_____ 10. Like most people, I'm primarily concerned with my own life and how events and circumstances affect me personally.
_____ 11. I would be willing to sacrifice my life to save the life of a friend or relative whom I loved or respected greatly.
_____ 12. Intelligent people stick to their own affairs and let other people take care of themselves.
_____ 13. It is usually not wise to get involved or interfere when a stranger is in trouble or suffering in some way.
_____ 14. I am quite willing to donate money and time to charitable causes that provide assistance to needy people.
_____ 15. I'm not willing to donate a kidney or any other duplicate but important body organ to save someone else while I'm still alive.

FIGURE 10–1   Scale to measure altruism.

demographic characteristics of bystanders were not very predictive of whether they tried to render assistance to a victim.

Altruism, an unselfish concern for or devotion to the welfare of others (see Figure 10–1), is related to bystander intervention. Thus one might expect more altruistic individuals to come to the aid of a suffering fellow human (Oliner & Oliner, 1988). Teaching children, by modeling and otherwise, to be altruistic should also reduce aggressiveness and bystander apathy in them. Furthermore, altruism is an aspect of generosity and cooperativeness, a willingness to contribute and work with other people to achieve a common goal.

The fact that prosocial behavior such as bystander intervention, altruism, generosity, and cooperativeness can be taught by example and differential rewards in families and schools has been documented by a number of studies (e.g., Knight & Kagan, 1977; Midlarsky & Bryan, 1972; Rushton, 1976). Oliner and Oliner (1988) found, for example, that rescuers of other people in crisis situations were three times as likely as idle bystanders to report that their parents had taught them to care for others.

In general, altruistic, generous, and cooperative parents, teachers, and peers tend to ensure that children will develop similar prosocial behaviors. All of these behaviors depend to some extent on *empathy,* the ability to experience vicariously the feelings, thoughts, and attitudes of another person. Empathy seems to vary with the degree of similarity (in age, sex, ethnicity, etc.) between two people, as well as one's ability to observe carefully and listen attentively to another person.

Authoritarian Personality. Contrasted with Good Samaritan prosocial behaviors is social prejudice or ethnocentrism. An ethnocentric person believes that the behavior of people in his or her cultural group is superior in all respects to that of members of other groups. Frequently associated with ethnocentrism is a complex of personality traits including rigidity, conventionality, cynicism, extreme moralizing, superstitiousness, political conservatism, a craving for power, a tendency to hold stereotypes, and scapegoating—traits that in combination constitute an *authoritarian personality.* Rokeach (1960), who subsequently referred to the authoritarian personality as "the authority-dependent personality," saw it as consisting of seven characteristics: rigidity, compulsiveness, conformity, dogmatism, concreteness, literalness, and pedantry.

From their studies of authoritarian personalities, Adorno and his colleagues (Adorno et al., 1950) concluded that as children such people were subjected to strict parental control. Although the overcontrolled child may have felt resentment toward his or her parents, expressing it would have resulted in severe punishment. Consequently, the child suppressed the resentment but continued to feel angry. As adults, authoritarian personalities keep their unresolved hostility toward their parents unconscious by being overobedient to authority and displacing the hostility onto minority groups and other "safe" objects. They express their hostility quite generally—toward Jews, blacks, and almost any foreigner or minority group member—tending to be prejudiced toward all groups that are in any way different from their own.

The percentage of prejudiced people who actually fit the description of an authoritarian personality is probably not very high. Also, authoritarianism is only one of many variables that correlate with prejudice. The fact that a person may be highly prejudiced without being highly authoritarian was demonstrated by the results of Pettigrew's (1958) study of white South Africans. These individuals were more racially prejudiced than white Americans, but the degree of authoritarianism was approximately the same in both countries.

Additional support for the proposition that attitudes toward other groups of people are frequently an expression of a general personality trait was obtained in a study by Anisfield, Munoz, and Lambert (1963). The attitudes of Jewish high school students toward both Gentiles and Jews were measured and correlated with several other variables. It was found that self-accepting students were also more positive in their attitudes toward their parents, Jews, and Gentiles. But students who were high in hostility held less favorable attitudes toward their parents and toward both Jews and Gentiles.

Parental Treatment and Child Personality

The immediate family is a miniature society in which the child has his or her first contacts with other people. These early social experiences condition the child to expect certain things and to behave in certain ways when he or she goes out into the larger society. A feeling of security or insecurity acquired in the family situation tends to generalize to other social situations. Thus a child who is loved and understood at home will feel more secure outside the home than one who is rejected at home.

Training and Discipline. According to classical psychoanalytic theory as well as other theories of human development, specific child-training practices such as early versus late weaning or toilet training have a profound effect on the individual's personality. In general, however, research has failed to support the contention that specific experiences are such important determinants of personality (e.g., Sewell & Mussen, 1952). What appears to be more important than a specific training practice is the attitude of the family, and especially the primary care giver, toward the child. A relaxed, affectionate, and accepting attitude on the part of the mother is far more effective in producing a mentally healthy child than is a specific practice such as self-demand feeding, gradual weaning, or permissive toilet training. One variable that seems to have a pronounced effect on child behavior, however, is the way in which the child is disciplined for misbehavior. The results of a classic survey conducted to determine the relationships between techniques used to discipline a child and variables such as feeding problems, conscience development, and dependency in children are instructive. Some of the findings of this investigation (Sears, Maccoby, & Levin, 1957) are as follows:

1 The percentage with feeding problems was greater (a) for children whose parents used physical punishment fairly often than for children whose parents used it infrequently or never, and (b) for children whose mothers were less affectionate or even cold than for children whose mothers were warm and affectionate toward their children.
2 The percentage rating high on conscience development was greater for children whose mothers were relatively warm and used withdrawal of love fairly often than for children whose mothers were either relatively cold or used no withdrawal of love.
3 The percentage manifesting considerable dependency at kindergarten age was greatest (a) for children whose parents used withdrawal of love fairly often as opposed to occasionally or seldom, (b) for children whose parents used severe or moderate punishment for offenses, and (c) for children whose parents used some rejection as opposed to no rejection of the child.

Types of Parents. It has frequently been observed that parents tend to treat their children in much the same way as they were treated as children. In this way, certain personality characteristics or ways of behaving are perpetuated for generations within families without direct hereditary transmission. Assuming that this view is correct, it is understandable why considerable interest has been shown by child development researchers in the effects of parental behaviors on the personalities of their children. One influential typology of parental behaviors is that proposed by Baumrind (1971, 1972), who identified three types of parents—authoritarian, permissive, and authoritative, each of which is presumably associated with specific behaviors on the part of children. *Authoritarian parents* are generally restrictive, rule-emphasizing individuals who expect unquestioning obedience from the child and punish behavior that deviates from their code. *Permissive parents,* on the other hand, make few demands on their children and permit them to play a role in establishing their own standards of conduct. The typical behavior of children whose parents are either authoritarian or permissive is similar in certain respects, in that the sons manifest greater hostility than normal, whereas the daughters are socially retiring individuals who give up easily.

According to Baumrind (1972), the most effective type of all are *authoritative parents.* These parents set behavioral limits and standards, enforcing them with a combination of power and reasoning. Their children are encouraged to conform to these limits but are also permitted to contribute their reasoning about them. The results, according to Baumrind, are sons and daughters who are able to conform to group norms without sacrificing their own individuality.

A modification of Baumrind's typology, combined with a two-dimensional model proposed earlier by E. S. Schaefer (1959) and Becker (1964), has been advocated by Maccoby and Martin (1983). As shown in Table 10–3, the two dimensions of parental behavior in Becker and Schaefer's model are permissiveness/restrictiveness and warmth/acceptingness. Maccoby and Martin renamed these dimensions *demandingness* and *responsiveness* to the child, respectively. The Maccoby and Martin model includes four types of parents—authoritative, authoritarian, indulgent, and neglecting (see Table 10–4).

Authoritative parents in the Maccoby/Martin model are described as accept-

TABLE 10–3 Becker and Schaefer's Model of Two Dimensions of Parenting and Their Relationships to Child Personality

Permissiveness/Restrictiveness Parenting Dimension	*Child Personality Characteristics on Warmth/Acceptingness Parenting Dimension*	
	Warm, Accepting	*Hostile, Rejecting*
Permissive, reasonably controlling	Socially outgoing, independent, creative, low in hostility	Aggressive, noncompliant, delinquent
Restrictive, overcontrolling	Submissive, nonaggressive, dependent	Quarrelsome, shy, psychological problems

Source: Adapted from Becker (1964) and E. S. Schaefer (1959).

TABLE 10–4   Maccoby and Martin's Two-Dimensional Model of Parenting

Demandingness Parenting Dimension	Responsiveness Parenting Dimension	
	Accepting, Responsive, Child-Centered	*Rejecting, Unresponsive, Parent-Centered*
Demanding, controlling	Authoritative-reciprocal, high in bidirectional communication	Authoritarian, power-assertive
Undemanding, low in control attempts	Indulgent	Neglecting, ignoring, indifferent, uninvolved

Source: Adapted from Maccoby and Martin (1983), p. 39.

ing, responsive, child-centered, and yet controlling. They expect their children to behave according to their ages and abilities, and they solicit the children's opinions and feelings in family decision making. These warm, nurturing parents are not averse to imposing punitive and restrictive measures, but they provide reasons and explanations when they do so. Presumably as a result of this kind of treatment, the children tend to become independent, self-assertive, friendly, and cooperative.

In contrast to authoritative parents, *authoritarian parents* assert their power without warmth, nurturance, or two-way communication between parent and child. Valuing obedience, respect for authority, work, tradition, and the preservation of order, authoritarian parents attempt to control and evaluate the child's behavior according to a set of absolute standards. The children of authoritarian parents tend to be moderately competent and responsible, but socially withdrawn and lacking in spontaneity. The daughters tend to be dependent and low in achievement motivation, whereas the sons are higher in aggressiveness but lower in self-esteem than other boys their age (Coopersmith, 1967).

"Accepting, responsive, child-centered people who make few demands on their children" is a description of *indulgent parents* in Maccoby and Martin's model. Although the children of such parents have more positive moods and greater vitality than the children of authoritarian parents, they tend to lack maturity, impulse control, and a sense of social responsibility. Like the children of authoritarian parents, the children of indulgent parents have little self-reliance and experience difficulties handling aggression.

Neglecting parents, who ignore their children and are indifferent to and uninvolved with them, constitute the fourth category of the Maccoby and Martin model. These parents are not necessarily child abusers, but they are parent centered rather than child centered in their behavior. Much of the time they are unaware of where their children are or what they are doing; they take little interest in the activities or opinions of their children, and they have few conversations with them. A number of studies (e.g., Egeland & Sroufe, 1981a, 1981b; Pulkkinen, 1982) have revealed some of the negative effects on children of chronic parental neglect. Impulsiveness, moodiness, inability to concentrate, low frustration tolerance, difficulty controlling aggression, truancy, and lack of emotional attachment to other people are common in such children.

Despite the face validity of models linking parental behavior to the personality characteristics and behavior of children, it must be emphasized that these are correlational rather than experimental studies. They tell us nothing about the direction and magnitude of causation. A reasonable supposition is that parental and child behavior form a reciprocal, interactive relationship, in which the child's actions affect the attitudes and responses of the parents and vice versa. In addition, although the correlations between parent and child behaviors are often statistically significant, in most cases they are small to moderate in size. As indicated in Chapter 9, differences between families in the ways that children are treated probably have less effect on their personalities than genetic factors.

Social and Personality Development after Childhood

As children grow older, the number and variety of their social experiences increase. From an early social environment consisting of only the primary family group, a child's world expands to encompass neighborhood playmates and school acquaintances. Inevitably, not all of these social experiences are friendly. Sibling rivalry, in which brothers and sisters become jealous and hostile toward each other, frequently competing for parental attention or possessions, is quite common. It is interesting to observe, however, that the number of friendly contacts among children is positively correlated with the number of unfriendly contacts. As the interactions among children increase, they show greater sympathy and cooperation as well as more aggressive and quarrelsome behavior.

Social development after age three is also characterized by an increasing attachment to a few friends. This becomes particularly evident during the "gang stage" from seven to 12 years of age. Belonging to a "gang" or small "crowd" provides the prepubertal child with experience in learning to cooperate with others. But the prepubertal gang is not as important to the child or as stable as the cliques or peer groups of adolescence. Getting along with other people is of utmost importance to a typical adolescent, and the peer group provides security and support in the struggle to be independent from one's parents and make one's own way in the world.

Adolescent Development

Adolescence need not be a period of storm and stress, as G. Stanley Hall (1916) characterized it, but it is a time of change, unrest, and searching. The biological changes of adolescence are accompanied by cognitive and emotional changes, and these lead to new challenges and questions. The impact of external events on adolescents is particularly important, because the way in which they are treated changes as they mature. Consequently, the adolescent's self-concept must be continually adjusted even if it was accurate and healthy before. According to Erik Erikson (1968), the major crisis of adolescence is *identity versus role confusion,* and the goal is to achieve a personal identity, particularly in regard to sex roles and occupational choice. The search for a personal identity does not cease with adolescence, but it is especially acute at this time and typically leads to extensive exploration and uncertainty.

The rate of physical maturation can affect an adolescent's feelings of self-adequacy or self-confidence, feelings that often persist into adulthood. Both early-maturing boys and early-maturing girls tend to have more friends and to assume leadership roles, particularly in sports and other physical activities. Late maturation can create personal and social difficulties for both boys and girls, but it is more of a problem for the former. Late-maturing girls tend to be less relaxed and less self-confident in social situations, but not to the degree experienced by late-maturing boys (Mussen & Jones, 1957; Livson & Peskin, 1980). Though late-maturing boys may attempt to compensate for their physical inadequacies by clowning and other attention-seeking behaviors, they are frequently censured or rejected by their age mates.

A typical adolescent possesses essentially the same personality as in childhood, but hormonal changes, coupled with new experiences and modifications in the environment, lead to an intensification of old traits and the appearance of new ones. To older adults, adolescents may appear to be impulsive, impatient, inconsiderate, and even bizarre in their behavior. But this strangeness has a purpose, and the individual is still recognizably the same personality as before.

Adult Development

In the stage theories of Erikson and others, adolescence ends at young adulthood. At this time the individual typically becomes intimate with someone else and fuses his or her identity with that of the other person. Young adulthood, in turn, gives way to middle age, a period of maximum generativity for most people. Then in time the middle-aged person hopefully becomes the integrated and self-accepting person of later life. An alternative to Erikson's stage theory of personality development is transition theories. These theories assume that psychological needs are not satisfied once and for all but must be continually renegotiated. According to Nancy Schlossberg (quoted by Tavris, 1987), such needs include control over one's life, enthusiasm for activities and commitments to other people and values, and the feeling that one matters to others. Transition theorists emphasize the individuality of development. As expressed by Orville Brim, "Unlike child development, which is powerfully governed by maturation and biological changes, adult development is affected by psychology and experience" (Tavris, 1987). Brim and Wheeler (1966) see personality change in terms of the changing demands and expectations of society as the individual passes through the age-graded social structure. Age-related changes in socially expected behaviors lead the aging individual to acquire new attitudes, roles, and beliefs (Reedy, 1983).

   A kind of combination stage and transition theory was proposed by Daniel Levinson (1978), who based many of his concepts on in-depth interviews of 40 men (10 each in four occupational groups). According to Levinson, the goal of adult development is to build a life structure, consisting of an external, sociocultural side as well as an internal, personal side. Shaping one's life structure takes place in a series of stable stages of 6–8 years in length, alternating with transition periods of 4–5 years. As described in Table 10–5, there are five transition periods: early adult transition, age 30 transition, midlife transition, age 50 transition, and late adult transition. During each of these transition periods the individual reexamines his life and prepares for the next stage.

   Perhaps Levinson's most famous concept is that of the *midlife crisis*. Taking place either during the midlife transition or the age 50 transition, the midlife crisis is precipitated by a personal review and reevaluation of one's past. According to Roger Gould (1980), midlife is the time to shed one's irrational notions about life, including the illusions that (1) I will be safe forever, (2) death cannot happen to me or my loved ones, (3) it is impossible to live without a partner in the world, (4) no change of life exists beyond the family, and (5) I am no innocent being.

   Also of particular significance in Levinson's theory is the Late Adult Transition, the time between ages 60 and 65 when the person realizes that he can no longer occupy center stage. The heavy responsibilities of middle adulthood must be reduced as the aging individual learns to function in a changed relationship between himself and society. In the end, what matters most is "one's view from the

---

TABLE 10–5   Levinson's Stages and Transitions in Adult Development

1. *Early adult transition* (17–22)
   Goal is to terminate adolescent life structure and form a basis for living in the adult world.
2. *Entering the adult world* (22–28)
   Form and test out preliminary life structures and provide a link between self and adult society.
3. *Age 30 transition* (30–33)
   Revise life structure of previous period and form a basis for more satisfactory life structure to be created in the settling down stage.
4. *Settling down stage* (33–40)
   Establish one's niche in society ("early settling down"), work at advancement, and strive for further success ("become one's own man").
5. *Midlife transition* (40–45)
   Evaluate success in attaining goals of settling down stage, take steps toward initiating midlife, and deal with relationships between oneself and external world (*individuation*).
6. *Entering middle adulthood* (45–50)
7. *Age 50 transition* (50–55)
8. *Building a second middle adult structure* (55–60)
   Analogous to settling down stage of young adulthood.
9. *Late adult transition* (60–65)
   Changing mental and physical capacities intensify one's own aging and sense of mortality.

Source: Adapted from Levinson (1978).

bridge"—the final sense of what life is all about and what it means. Such a perception typically takes place as a result of what Robert Butler (1971) termed a *life review*, a process of looking back over one's life and sorting the good from the bad.

Levinson's theory of developmental stages and transitions, although based on research with adult males, undoubtedly has implications for women as well. However, the ways in which men typically "find themselves" are different in many respects from the ways in which women develop personal identities. Men are more likely to strive for individual achievement by breaking away from their families and pursuing their individual interests. Women, on the other hand, are more likely to attain their identities through the responsibilities and attachments that characterize their relationships with other people (Gilligan, 1982; Baruch, Barnett, & Rivers, 1983; Notman, 1980). For example, the self-descriptions of the men interviewed by Gilligan (1982) were in terms of individual achievements, whereas the women tended to describe themselves in terms of successful relationships. To the women, the establishment of intimacy and the fusion of one's identity with those of others, rather than the attainment of academic or professional distinction, were more indicative of a successful life.

Continuity and Change in Personality

Both stage and transition theorists emphasize the changes in personality and ways of adjusting to the environment over time. However, the results of a number of investigations have revealed that, although personality can change across the life span, there is a great deal of continuity or consistency in certain characteristics. From the results of a study of changes in personality over a seven-year period in eight different age cohorts, Schaie and Parham (1976, p. 157) concluded that the "stability of personality traits is the rule rather than the exception." Intelligence in particular, and temperamental traits such as aggression, extroversion, emotionality, and impulse control are fairly constant, but interests, attitudes, and opinions show less consistency over a 5- to 10-year period (Conley, 1984). The relationship between early infant disturbances and subsequent psychopathology is also quite low (Sameroff & Chandler, 1975). Impulsive children tend to become more restless and impatient than other adults, but not so impulsive as they were as children (Stewart & Olds, 1973).

Factors other than motivation or aging can, of course, lead to changes in personality. Serendipitous events such as physical or psychological trauma, education, or altered circumstances, as well as self-initiated events such as drug or alcohol abuse, psychotherapy, and religious experiences, may precipitate personality changes (Campbell, 1984).

Longitudinal Studies of Personality

The continuity of personality from adolescence to adulthood has been documented by two extensive longitudinal studies—the Berkeley Guidance Study and the Oakland Growth Study. The first study, conducted by the Institute of Human Development at the University of California at Berkeley, followed a large sample of children from birth through adulthood. A special psychometric technique involving the use of Q-sorts was used to correlate personality ratings of the subjects when they were in junior high school (age 13), in senior high school (age 16), and in adulthood (age 30 or 37). The findings revealed considerable consistency in personality ratings from junior to senior high school, and less, but still substantial, consistency from senior high school to adulthood. Similar findings were obtained in the Oakland study, which followed 212 children from the fifth grade through adolescence and interviewed them again at ages 37, 47, and 57.

Of particular interest in these two longitudinal studies was information on differences between the characteristics of individuals who showed substantial change ("changers") in personality compared with those who showed little change ("nonchangers"). As shown in Table 10–6, the nonchangers were described as better adjusted in adolescence than the changers. Descriptions of the male and female changers were similar, but it was found that female changers were more likely than male changers to grow out of their problems.

In a follow-up analysis of data from the archives of the Institute of Human Development (IHD), Caspi and Herbener (1989) asked the question whether spouses who were more alike in personality would produce greater personality continuity in each other. Dividing 126 couples into three groups (least similar

TABLE 10–6 Characteristics of Adolescent Changers and Nonchangers in Personality in IHD Study

	Nonchangers	*Changers*
Males	Ambitious	Hostile toward adults
	Dependable	Other directed
	Insightful	Psychologically brittle
	Productive	Self-defeating
	Satisfied with self	Self-pitying
	Value intellectual matters	Uncomfortable with uncertainty
	Verbally fluent	
Females	Ambitious	Deceitful
	Arouse liking and nurturance in others	Distrustful
	Conservative	Hostile
	Consistent	Psychologically brittle
	Dependable	Rebellious
	Intellectual	Self-defensive
	Productive	Self-dramatizing
	Self-satisfied	Self-indulgent
	Straightforward	Undercontrolled
	Submissive	
	Sympathetic	
	Warm	

Source: Block (1971). Used by permission.

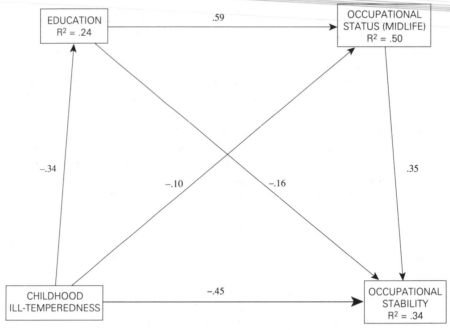

FIGURE 10–2   Midlife occupational status and stability in adult men as a function of childhood ill-temperedness. (From Caspi, Elder, & Bem, 1987. Copyright 1987 by the American Psychological Association. Reprinted by permission.)

spouses, moderately similar spouses, most similar spouses) according to their similarity on Q-sort personality ratings, greater continuity of personality was found for the moderately similar than for the least similar spouses and greater continuity for the most similar spouses than for the moderately similar spouses.

In another study employing the IHD archival data, Caspi, Elder, and Bem (1987a) asked the question whether ill-tempered boys become ill-tempered men. The findings led to an affirmative answer to the question, in that temper-tantrum scores in late childhood were significantly correlated with peer descriptions of the individuals 20 years later as being undercontrolled, irritable, and moody. A further analysis of the data, using a statistical procedure known as *path analysis,* was conducted to try to determine whether or not ill-temperedness in childhood contributes to occupational disadvantage in adulthood. The four measures that were intercorrelated in this study were ill-temperedness in childhood, educational level, occupational status, and occupational stability. The numbers in Figure 10–2, which are measures of relationship between the two variables connected by the associated line, show that the relationship between education and occupational stability is quite low (−.16) and nonsignificant but that there is a direct moderate relationship between childhood ill-temperedness and occupational stability (−.45).

Personality Changes in Middle Age and Late Life

According to continuity theorists, personality may change with aging, but the modifications are quantitative rather than qualitative. The pattern of one's personality traits, established early in life, becomes more pronounced in response to the stresses of later life (Neugarten, 1971, 1973). But styles of coping, achieving life satisfaction, and goal-directed behavior remain consistent after midlife (Neugarten & Associates, 1964; Botwinick, 1978; Ward, 1979). Evidence for the continuity of personality is impressive, although certain traits change with age to some degree. Evidence for an age-related increase in "rigidity" is inconsistent, but the finding of increased attention to the self, or introversion ("interiority") with aging is well-documented (Botwinick, 1978; Neugarten, 1977). People who were more extroverted in their youth are still likely to be fairly outgoing, even though they tend to become more introverted and introspective during middle and late life (Neugarten, 1977).

With respect to sex differences, the role relationships between the sexes may reverse in later life. Women tend to become more aggressive or assertive and men more submissive and nurturant. Aging tends to make men more mellow and less ambitious, more nurturing and more interested in intimate relationships, whereas women become more assertive, self-confident, achievement-oriented, and controlling (Gutmann, 1972; McGee & Wells, 1982; Neugarten, 1968). Interestingly enough, the typical result of these age changes in men and women is a reduction in emotional tension, easier communication, and greater sharing of feelings between the sexes.

Rather than developing suddenly as a result of hormonal changes in middle age, the relatively greater aggressiveness shown by older women may result from the release of aggressive urges that have been there all along (Gutmann, 1964, 1967). During the years when she is rearing her children, a typical married woman suppresses her aggressive impulses, as is required by the nurturant, mothering role she plays at that time. When her children have grown up and moved away, she may feel free to release those impulses and express long-dormant aspects of her personality.

Choices and Script Theory

A certain amount of the observed continuity in personality is attributable to the fact that people are attracted to environments that "fit" their personalities and hence do not require much change on their part (Ahammer, 1973). For example, slow-paced, gentle people tend to prefer living in small towns, and shy people do not speak in public. In this way, individual decisions about preferred living environments and life-styles result in greater stability of personality—a stability that is created more by the individual than by the environment (Lerner & Busch-Rossnagel, 1981).

According to one cognitive theory of personality, *script theory,* individuals attempt to maintain a sense of continuity or order (the "script") in the critical events, or *scenes*, of their lives:

> Personality development is best understood as the formation, growth or decline of (a) scenes that represent important features of an individual's life and (b) scripts that enable the person to anticipate, respond to, control, or create events in a meaningful fashion. An essential premise of script theory is that personality development is not plotted as a one-way progression from earlier to later constructions of experience. Instead, there is two-way traffic through time. Constructions of the past may be radically changed in the light of later experience; anticipations of the future may color the present and revise the past; old experiences may return to alter the present. (Carlson, 1981, p. 503)

As recognized by both continuity theory and script theory, there is no final stage of personality development. Although different lives follow different courses, with a large majority of individuals manifesting a great deal of stability and others changing substantially even in later life, all retain the potential for modification and adaptation. Human personality is not completely static; it is changed to some extent by the very process of aging and the success of one's attempts to cope with the challenges and problems presented at different stages of life.

Summary

Environment is at least as important as heredity in shaping personality, but the influences of unshared experiences appear to be greater than those of shared experiences. Birth order has some relationship to personality, in that firstborn and only children tend to be more achievement-oriented and more serious, whereas later-borns are more outgoing and sociable. Parents usually spend more time with firstborns and in other ways treat them differently from later-born children.

In most families, girls are treated quite differently from boys, and different behaviors are expected of them. Girls are expected to be less aggressive and more socially considerate than boys and to identify with their mothers rather than their fathers. In such traditional families, girls tend to be more empathic and sensitive to other people, but more dependent and less self-confident than boys. Boys, on the other hand, are more active, exploring, and impulsive than girls. On the other hand, in families that are more androgynous in their orientation and practice equality between the sexes, boys and girls assume many of the traditional tasks of the opposite sex.

Reactive, evocative, and proactive interactions, in which the individual reacts to the environment, prompts reactions from other people, and structures the environment, respectively, are all important in shaping personality. Although the preschool years are considered critical to personality development, personality continues developing throughout childhood and even thereafter.

The pioneering studies of Ribble and Spitz on marasmus or hospitalism paved the way for Harlow's research on mothering in monkeys and Ainsworth's research on the attachment of human infants to their mothers. The strange-situation procedure, in which the infant's reactions are noted when its mother leaves the room and a stranger enters, was designed to study attachment and the effects of separation on infants. Three types of attachment—securely attached, avoidant, and ambivalent—have been noted in this situation and related to maternal behavior. Attachment between infant and mother is, however, a two-way street: The appearance and behavior of the baby affect the mother's reactions, and the mother's behavior in turn affects the baby. Attachment or bonding between mother and child is universal, but it varies to some extent with the culture.

Infants begin to distinguish between "self" and "nonself" at about 4–6 months of age. However, they do not pass the "rouge test" of reacting to rouge on their noses as seen in a mirror until 18+ months. Separation from the mother, which serves as a stimulus for individuation, is important for self-development. The development of a differentiated self leads to a self-concept—an appraisal or evaluation of one's self.

Whereas the Freudian theory of personality describes the development of the superego according to the moral principle, and resulting feelings of "guilt" when the superego comes into conflict with the id, the stage theories of Piaget and Kohlberg are concerned with moral judgment rather than moral feelings or moral behavior. Kohlberg's theory has inspired a great deal of research on morality, but support for the idea of six fixed stages through which individuals pass in the development of a mature sense of morality is meager. In addition, as demonstrated by Hartshorne and May's classic studies of character, honesty and other moral behaviors are not very generalizable across different situations.

Although research on prosocial behavior, such as bystander intervention and altruism, has emphasized the influence of the specific social situation in determining such behaviors, evidence of a general trait cluster—an *authoritarian personality*—related to ethnocentrism has been obtained.

Baumrind identified three types of parents—authoritarian, permissive, and authoritative—each of which is associated with a specific set of behaviors on the part of children. A related model of parental behavior, that of Maccoby and Martin, includes four types of parents—authoritative, authoritarian, indulgent, and neglecting.

The search for a personal identity does not cease with adolescence, but it is especially acute at this time and typically leads to extensive exploration and uncertainty. Late-maturing boys and girls usually experience more problems with respect to feelings of self-adequacy, self-confidence, and social acceptance.

Levinson views the goal of adult development as building an external and internal life structure through a series of four stages and five transition periods. During each transition period the individual reexamines his or her life and prepares for the next stage. The concept of *midlife crisis,* when people must shed their irrational notions about life and dispense with their illusions, is Levinson's most popular concept. Whereas men are more likely to strive for and measure success in terms of individual achievements, women tend to view success more in terms of personal relationships.

Although personality continues to grow and change over a lifetime, it actually manifests a great deal of continuity from early to late life. Particularly stable are general intelligence and characteristics of temperament such as aggression, extroversion, emotionality, and impulse control. The findings of longitudinal studies conducted at Berkeley and Oakland, California, underscore the continuity of personality from junior high school through adulthood. The Berkeley studies also found many of the characteristics of people whose personalities changed the most—so-called changers—to be different from those of nonchangers. With respect to personality changes in middle and late life, the changes tend to be quantitative rather than qualitative; each sex also takes on some of the characteristics of the other.

Key Concepts

Altruism   Unselfish concern or devotion to the welfare of other people at the cost of some sacrifice to oneself.

Attachment   Development by a young child or animal of a close, lasting relationship with another person; bonding.

Attribution   Process of interpreting the cause of a person's successes and failures as one's personal efforts and ability (*internal attributions*) or as the difficulty of the task or bad luck (*external attributions*).

Authoritarian personality   A tendency to view the world in terms of a strict social hierarchy in which a person higher on the hierarchy demands cooperation and deference from those below him or her.

Authoritative parents   Parents who set behavioral limits and standards, enforcing them with a combination of power and reasoning.

Bystander intervention   Whether or not a person chooses to come to the aid of someone who is being attacked or has had an accident.

Gender identity   Inner sense of being male or female, resulting from child-rearing practices combined with genetic and hormonal factors. In contrast to gender identity, *gender role* consists of the patterns of appearance and behavior associated by a society or culture with being male or female. Gender roles are learned from gender-linked associations, or *gender schemata*.

Identification   Taking on the personal characteristics of another person, as when a developing child identifies with a significant "other" person. Also, in psychoanalytic theory, an ego defense mechanism for coping with anxiety.

Midlife crisis   Crisis precipitated during midlife by a personal review and reevaluation of one's past.

Script   General plans developed by the individual to enable him or her to anticipate, respond to, control, or create events in a meaningful fashion. *Script theory* holds that people attempt to maintain a sense of continuity or order in the critical events, or *scenes,* of their lives.

Self   The perceived, consciously known and experienced identity, individuality or ego of the person. The *self-concept* consists of how a person views himself (herself), and *self-esteem* consists of how the self is evaluated by the individual.

Self-monitoring   The extent to which people are sensitive to, or monitor, their own behavior according to environmental cues. High self-monitors are more sensitive to what is situationally appropriate and act accordingly. Low self-monitors are less sensitive to external cues and act more in response to their own internal attitudes and feelings.

Strange-situation procedure   An experimental procedure involving a stranger entering a room with a mother and young child, and then the mother leaving. Three patterns of child behavior have been observed in this situation: securely attached, avoidant, and ambivalent.

Activities and Applications

1. Granting that all personality characteristics are influenced by both heredity and environment, make a list of those characteristics or traits that you consider to be influenced more by heredity and a second list of those characteristics that you consider to be influenced more by environment. Compare your two lists with those of your classmates.

2. Write a brief autobiography, describing yourself to a pen pal of the same sex whom you have never met. Now rewrite your autobiography for a letter to a pen pal of the opposite sex. What are the similarities and differences between the two autobiographies? How do you explain them?

3. An important feature of the process of becoming intimate with someone is self-disclosure—revealing personal or private information about your thoughts, experiences, and behavior. However, the timing of self-disclosure is critical for establishing a lasting relationship. Explain what is meant by this statement, and provide examples from your own background.

4. The dictionary defines *altruism* as "unselfish concern for or devotion to the welfare of others." Administer the questionnaire in Figure 10–1 to ten men and ten women students. Score it according to the following directions: Score items 1, 3, 6, 7, 9, 11, and 14 as SA = 4, A = 3, U = 2, D = 1, SD = 0; score items 2, 4, 5, 8, 10, 12, and 13 as SA = 0, A = 1, U = 2, D = 3, SD = 4. Then add the scoring weights. Possible scores range from 0 to 60. Finally, conduct a statistical test of the significance of the difference between the mean scores of the two sexes. Did you expect the women to score higher than the men? Why? Did they do so?

5. Describe one or more persons who have influenced your moral and ethical development. What did that or those persons say and do that had such a strong effect on your morals and character?

6. Read a description of any three of the following countries in the *Encyclopedia Americana,* the *Encyclopaedia Britannica,* and other sources: Iran, Ireland, Israel, Japan,

People's Republic of China, Russia. Pay particular attention to information concerning the ways in which the people live and make their living, their religious and other beliefs and attitudes, and how they bring up their children. Then compare and contrast the child-rearing practices of the three countries and their resulting effects on child and adult personality. If you are a non-American student, you may wish to compare the relationship between child-rearing practices in your own country and those in the United States. Do you find more similarities than differences between the personalities, attitudes, and ambitions of children and adults in different countries? Why or why not?

7. Administer the following "Rights of the Sexes" inventory to ten men and ten women students. Score it according to the directions given below the inventory, and conduct a statistical test of the significance of the difference between the mean scores of the two sexes. Did you expect the women to score higher than the men? Why? Did they do so?

Rights of the Sexes

Directions: Indicate the extent of your agreement or disagreement with each of the following statements by writing in the blank next to the statement number:

    SA if you "strongly agree" with the statement.
    A if you "agree" with the statement.
    U if you are "undecided" whether you agree or disagree with the statement.
    D if you "disagree" with the statement.
    SD if you "strongly disagree" with the statement.

_____ 1. A woman's husband should be more important to her than a career.
_____ 2. A wife's opinion should have no less weight than that of her husband in deciding what purchases to make for the home.
_____ 3. Women deserve to have just as much freedom of action as men.
_____ 4. A woman should concentrate more on becoming a good wife and mother than on pursuing a career outside the home.
_____ 5. A married woman should have the right to either withhold or initiate sexual intimacy with her husband.
_____ 6. Women are just as intelligent and capable as men.
_____ 7. Women should subordinate their careers to home duties to a greater extent than men.
_____ 8. A wife should bear more responsibility than a husband for grocery shopping, meal preparation, and house cleaning.
_____ 9. The husband and wife have equal rights and responsibilities with respect to legal matters concerning their marriage.
_____ 10. Women can perform almost any occupation as well as men and should be permitted to do so when qualified by training and experience.

Directions for Scoring: Score items 1, 4, 7, and 8 as SA = 0, A = 1, U = 2, D = 3, SD = 4. Score items 2, 3, 5, 6, 9, and 10 as SA = 4, A = 3, U = 2, D = 1, SD = 0.

---

8. Despite the legal and social emphases on equal rights for the sexes, the results of recent surveys show that schoolteachers and counselors continue to have different expectations for boys and girls and to treat them differently. For example, many girls are discouraged from applying for programs or preparing for professions for which advanced math is a requirement. The stated reasons are that girls are not good in mathematics and that they are only inviting frustration and failure by entering such fields. Is the differential treatment of males and females good or bad, and what are some possible reasons for and results of it?

Suggested Readings

Ainsworth, M.D.S. (1991). An ethological approach to personality development. *American Psychologist, 46,* 333–341.

Ashmore, R. D. (1990). Sex, gender, and the individual. In L. A. Pervin (Ed.), *Handbook of personality theory and research* (pp. 486–526). New York: Guilford Press.

Barnouw, V. (1985). *Culture and personality* (4th ed.). Belmont, CA: Wadsworth.

Caspi, A. (1989). On the continuities and consequences of personality: A life-course perspective. In D.M. Buss & N. Cantor (Eds.), *Personality psychology: Recent trends and emerging directions* (pp. 85–98). New York: Springer-Verlag.

Caspi, A., & Bem, D. J. (1990). Personality continuity and change across the life course. In L. A. Pervin (Ed.), *Handbook of personality theory and research* (pp. 549–575). New York: Guilford Press.

Collins, W. A., & Gunnmar, M. R. (1990). Social and personality development. *Annual Review of Psychology, 41,* 387–416.

Costa, P. T., Jr., & McCrae, R. R. (1985). Personality as a lifelong determinant of well-being. In C. Malatesta & C. Izard (Eds.), *Affective processes in adult development and aging.* New York: Sage.

Deaux, K. (1984). From individual differences to social categories: Analysis of a decade's research on gender. *American Psychologist, 39,* 105–116.

Emler, N. (1991). Moral character. In V. J. Derlega, B. A. Winstead, & W. H. Jones (Eds.), *Personality: Contemporary theory and research* (pp. 381–406). Chicago: Nelson-Hall.

Kogan, N. (1990). Personality and aging. In J. E. Birren & K. W. Schaie (Eds.), *Handbook of the psychology of aging* (3rd ed., pp. 330–346). New York: Academic Press.

Magnusson, D. (1990). Personality development from an interactional perspective. In L. A. Pervin (Ed.), *Handbook of personality theory and research* (pp. 193–222). New York: Guilford Press.

Plomin, R. (1989). Environment and genes: Determinants of behavior. *American Psychologist, 44,* 105–111.

West, S. G., & Graziano, W. G. (Eds.). (1989). Long-term stability and change in personality. *Journal of Personality, 57* (2).

Note

1 William Shakespeare, *As You Like It,* Act 2, Scene 7. Quoted from S. Wills and G. Taylor (Gen. Eds.), *The Complete Oxford Shakespeare,* Vol. 2: *Comedies,* 1987, Oxford University Press.

CHAPTER 11

Health, Personality, and Behavior

CHAPTER OUTLINE

Psychosomatic Medicine and Health Psychology
    Personality Factors and Specific Illness
    Psychodiagnosis and Health Psychology
    Retrospective and Prospective Studies
The Emergency Pattern and Stress
    Stress and the General Adaptation Syndrome
    Stress-Related Disorders
    Personality Adjustment and Health
    Life Changes and Health
The Personality/Health Connection Revisited
    Type A Behavior and Personality
    Cancer
    Anorexia and Bulimia
Coping with Stress-Related Illness
    Coping Mechanisms
    Personality Variables Related to Control
    Social Factors in Physical Illness
    Techniques for Treating Stress
Summary
Key Concepts
Activities and Applications
Suggested Readings

It has been known at least since Aristotle's time that psychological factors may play a role in the genesis and progression of physical disorders. In addition to more magical explanations and "cures" for illness, prayers, incantations, and other noninvasive rituals, along with bleeding, purgatives, herbs, surgery, and other physical techniques, were employed by people in former times to treat the sick. The curative powers of many of these treatments can probably be attributed to what is now known as the *placebo effect,* the beneficial effect of an inert substance or neutral condition on a disorder. In fact, it has been said that the survival of medicine from ancient times to the nineteenth century is attributable in large measure to the power of "faith" in healing (Shapiro & Morris, 1978).

Psychosomatic Medicine and Health Psychology

During the 1930s and 1940s, the specialty of *psychosomatic medicine,* which is concerned with a host of aches and pains that are caused or made worse by emotions and psychological stress, was founded. Among the "psychosomatic" disorders are fairly minor conditions such as chronic backache, constipation, fatigue, headaches, and skin rashes, as well as more serious illnesses such as asthma, eczema, high blood pressure, and ulcers.

Certain late-nineteenth- and early twentieth-century physicians went overboard in proposing psychological explanations for physical disorders. Despite excesses in both the psychogenic ("psychologically caused") and physiogenic ("biologically caused") camps, the medical community as a whole came to accept the notion that a patient's anxieties, attitudes, and conflicts are important contributors to health and illness. Charcot, Freud, and certain other psychiatrists had demonstrated that in cases of hysteria or conversion neuroses a bodily organ is not actually diseased or damaged, but the patient acts as if it were. Freud maintained that the anxiety resulting from psychological conflicts is converted into physical symptoms; these symptoms provide clues to the nature of the conflict. In the case of psychosomatic disorders, however, detectable damage or malfunctioning of tissues, organs, or systems are precipitated or aggravated by the patient's thoughts and emotions. Bacteria, viruses, and other pathogens are recognized as necessary causes of disease, but psychological factors presumably contribute to the disorder by lowering the patient's resistance to pathogenic agents.

Personality Factors and Specific Illness

Inspired to some extent by the findings of researchers such as Wolf and Wolff (1942), Ax (1953), and Funkenstein, King, and Drolette (1957) on the relationships between emotional and physiological responses, for years medical and psychophysiological researchers tried to identify connections between specific emotions and specific diseases. The possibility of such connections was bolstered by research suggesting that emotional and cognitive variables are important in determining patterns of body responses to threat (Mason, 1975).

A half century ago psychodynamically oriented researchers such as Franz Alexander (1939, 1950) and Flanders Dunbar (1943) speculated that every psychosomatic illness is associated with a particular personality pattern or conflict that predisposes the patient to the disorder. The affected "target organ" or system of the disorder was presumed to have a symbolic connection to an intrapsychic conflict. Alexander was perhaps the first to link psychological conflict to disease, and both he and Dunbar focused on personality profiles associated with particular illnesses. Dunbar's thesis is reflected in his statement that it is "more important to know what kind of patient has the disease than what kind of disease the patient has" (Dunbar, 1943, p. 23). Alexander and French (1948) maintained that many physical illnesses, including bronchial asthma, diabetes, essential hypertension, and peptic ulcers, are related to special oral, anal, maternal, and other conflicts. Whenever a particular conflict is triggered by an environmental event, the emotional reaction of the individual presumably gives rise to symptoms of the associated physical disorder. Chronic repressed hostility, for example, is reportedly a precipitating factor in rheumatoid arthritis. Arthritics have also been described as being perfectionistic, excessively interested in athletics, competitive, and passive (Moos, 1964).

The presumed relationships between psychological states and other psychosomatic illnesses include the following:

Acne with guilt over exhibitionism
Bronchial asthma with fear of separation from the mother
Colitis with an inability to fulfill obligations
Diabetes with chronic anxiety and depression stemming from frustrated dependency needs
Hyperthyroidism with psychic trauma such as the loss of one's mother during childhood
Migraine headaches with perfectionism, rigidity, resentment, unconscious hostility, and preoccupation with success
Tension headaches with dependency, depression, worry, and sexual conflicts (Blanchard, Andrasik, & Arena, 1984)
Gastric ulcers with passivity and dependency (always ready to be fed)
Hypertension with hostility and competitiveness (always ready to fight)

With respect to hypertension, Alexander (1950) attributed the chronic high blood pressure that is fairly common in black Americans to the frustration and hostility engendered by their inferior position in U.S. society. Other psychodynamic theorists, such as Menninger (1935) and Dunbar (1954), viewed diabetic patients as anxious, depressed individuals who have dependence-independence conflicts and poor sexual adjustment.

Similar to the notion of the cold, distant "schizophrenogenic mother," Block, Harvey, Jennings, and Simpson (1966) hypothesized that the frequency and severity of attacks in an asthmatic child are increased by having an "asthmatogenic mother." Asthmatogenic mothers were described as overprotective, rigid individuals who blur the boundaries between the role of parent and child. Because of the presumed influence of the mother on the child's illness, it has been maintained that it is better to treat asthmatic children outside the home rather than within the home environment (see Peshkin, 1960).

During the past two decades or so researchers have concluded that the relationships between personality characteristics and specific illnesses proposed by Alexander, Dunbar, and others for the most part simply do not exist (H. Weiner, 1977). Even when such relationships are confirmed, in many instances the direction of causation is reversed: Rather than the illness being caused by the psychological state, the illness itself is responsible for the emotional or personality problems experienced by the individual. In the case of diabetes, for example, psychological problems are more likely to be the result than the cause of the illness (Ezrin, 1977).

Recent research findings have indicated that, rather than being chronically anxious and depressed, most diabetic children, adolescents, and adults are actually well-adjusted individuals (Dunn & Turtle, 1981). Likewise, there is little or no support for specific psychopathological characteristics in asthmatic patients or their parents (Creer & Kotses, 1983). And in the case of rheumatoid arthritis, whatever psychological disturbances the patient may manifest are more likely to be reactions to physical suffering rather than predisposing or precipitating causes of the disorder (Spergel, Ehrlich, & Glass, 1978). In certain instances, however, it still appears reasonable to conclude that psychological problems are directly related to specific illnesses such as headaches (Blanchard, Andrasik, & Arena, 1984). The psychosomatic hypothesis that hostility (anger) is a contributory factor in hypertension and heart disease has also received some empirical support (e.g., Barefoot, Dahlstrom, & Williams, 1983).

Psychodiagnosis and Health Psychology

The *Diagnostic and Statistical Manual of Mental Disorders* (American Psychiatric Association, 1968, 1980, 1987) is the official guide for psychodiagnosis followed by most psychiatrists and psychologists in the United States. In the second (1980) edition of this manual, the diagnosis "psychosomatic disorders" of the first edition was changed to *psychophysiologic disorders*. An even more drastic change occurred with the publication of the revision of the third (1987) edition of the manual (DSM-III-R) (American Psychiatric Association, 1987). In the multiaxial diagnostic system of DSM-III-R, Axis I includes the diagnostic category "Psychological Factors Affecting Physical Condition," but the actual physical disorder is classified on Axis III. This biaxial classification is employed when psychological factors have either definitely or probably played a significant role in initiating or aggravating a physical disorder.

The change from DSM-II to DSM-III-R in the manner of classifying physical disorders to which psychological factors contribute came about because psychiatrists and psychologists recognized that psychological factors can affect almost any physical problem. The list of professional journals in Table 11–1 is an

TABLE 11–1   Periodicals Dealing Most Closely with Topics in Health Psychology

Behavior Research and Therapy
Behavior Therapy
Behavioral Medicine Update
Biofeedback and Self-regulation
Brain, Behavior, and Immunity
Clinical Biofeedback and Health
Health Psychologist Newsletter
Health Psychology
Journal of Behavioral Medicine
Journal of Health and Human Behavior
Journal of Health and Social Behavior
Journal of Human Stress
Journal of Psychosomatic Research
Psychological Medicine
Psychology and Health
Psychophysiology
Psychosomatic Medicine
Psychosomatics
Social Science and Medicine
Stress Medicine

indication of the extensiveness of published research and applications on the psychology of health and disease. Another sign of the growing recognition of the importance of psychological factors in both illness and wellness was the founding of the field of *health psychology*. As defined by Matarazzo (1980, p. 815), health psychology is concerned with the "educational, scientific, and professional contributions of the discipline of psychology to the promotion and maintenance of health, the prevention and treatment of illness, and the identification of etiological and diagnostic correlates of health, illness, and related dysfunction." A significant event in the growth of health psychology as a profession was the establishment in 1978 of Division 38, the Division of Health Psychology, of the American Psychological Association. Health psychology is a broad discipline that includes such specializations as neuropsychology, pediatric psychology, geropsychology, and health enhancement (I. B. Weiner, 1983).

Health psychologists are interested in the role played by attitudes, emotions, stress, and personality, not only in traditional psychosomatic disorders such as duodenal ulcers and migraine headaches but also in life-threatening illnesses such as cardiovascular disorders and cancer (Holroyd, 1979). Clinical psychologists, in particular, may be called upon to identify psychological factors related to various physical disorders, to help diagnose specific illnesses, and to assist in planning intervention or treatment. In particular, the field of *behavioral medicine*, which is a subspecialty of health psychology, has made significant contributions to the treatment and management of patients by means of behavior modification procedures.

Retrospective and Prospective Studies

Research psychologists and psychiatrists with an interest in physical health have conducted a variety of research investigations concerned with psychological variables impacting on health and disease. The majority of these investigations have been either retrospective or prospective studies of the relationships of specific disorders to selected characteristics of personality and behavior. In a *retrospective study* the investigator looks back at the history of a group of people having a certain disease or characteristic and attempts to identify variables that mark those individuals as different from people who do not have the illness or condition. In a *prospective study* the researcher follows the forward development of a group of people to determine what variables distinguish between those who develop a particular illness or characteristic and those who do not. Both of these longitudinal approaches, which are borrowed from research in epidemiology, are basically correlational in nature. Consequently, causal conclusions are not justified from the results of either approach. The results of prospective studies, however, are usually viewed as more trustworthy and meaningful than those obtained from retrospective investigations, particularly when the prospective study is experimental rather than merely descriptive in nature.

The Emergency Pattern and Stress

Human beings are equipped by nature to respond to emergencies, whether real or imagined. The sympathetic division of the autonomic nervous system, which is regulated by the hypothalamus, controls a complex of bodily changes constituting what Walter Cannon (1929) called the *emergency pattern*. The following components of the emergency pattern result from increased activity of the sympathetic system. Circulatory system changes include: an increase in blood pressure and more rapid pumping of the blood due to an accelerated and stronger heartbeat; the release of red blood cells needed to carry extra oxygen from the spleen; an increase in the amount of coagulant in the blood, and therefore more rapid clotting; a change in the acid-alkaline balance of the blood; an increase in the amount of epinephrine secreted by the adrenal medulla into the blood; and redistribution of the blood supply from the viscera and skin to the muscles and brain. Other changes include stimulation of the liver, causing it to release stored sugar that provides greater energy for the muscles; an increase in the ratio of inhaled oxygen volume to exhaled carbon dioxide volume; inhibition of gastrointestinal movements; pilomotor response (goose pimples); inhibition of salivary secretion; increased perspiration; enlargement of the pupils of the eyes; increased muscle tension; and tremor. These responses, which are initiated by action of the sympathetic system, are prolonged by the circulating epinephrine in the blood.

The emergency "fight-or-flight" reaction pattern has the function of permitting short-term expenditure of the maximum amount of energy needed in states of emergency. It is useful in certain situations, but, as we shall see, it can also result in difficulties and disease in civilized human beings. This reaction pattern is associated with a wide range of emotions, including excitement, distress, rage, and fear, which can be destructive if not properly directed. Cannon (1929) noted that many of the gastrointenstinal, cardiovascular, and other psychogenic diseases of civilization are more common in industrialized than in nonindustrialized societies such as the aborigines of Western Australia (Kidson & Jones, 1968). Unfortunately, as preindustrial societies become more westernized, the incidence of stress-related illness increases.

Stress and the General Adaptation Syndrome

The concept of *stress,* which has played a central role in health psychology, was defined by Hans Selye (1982) as "the nonspecific (that is, common) result of any demand on the body, be the effect mental or somatic" (p. 7). *Stressors,* or stimuli that produce stress and hence lead to the mobilization of bodily resources and the expenditure of a greater amount of energy than usual, range from physical conditions such as bodily injury, lack of sleep, and inadequate or improper nourishment through various psychological states (frustration, conflict, etc.). Relatively minor stressors include everyday *hassles* such as getting to school or work on time and getting caught in traffic (see Table 11–2). These hassles, or "background stressors" as they have been called, are annoying or irritating but are usually dealt with fairly easily. On the other hand, more "personal stressors," including major life events such as the death of a relative or close friend, being diagnosed has having a serious illness, losing a job, or experiencing a personal failure, produce more intense and persisting reactions. Finally, natural disasters (plane crashes, tornadoes, etc.) and other cataclysmic events can produce stress in a number of people at the same time. Interestingly enough, many of the physical symptoms of stress (see Table 11–3) are predicted better by daily hassles than by major life events (R. S. Lazarus, 1984). Facilitating these predictions are Lazarus and Folkman's Hassles and Uplifts Scale, a 305-item inventory published by Consulting Psychologists Press.

Unlike Franz Alexander and Flanders Dunbar, who postulated that different physiological reactions are associated with different personality characteristics or psychological conflicts, Hans Selye (1976, 1982) hypothesized that a similar somatic reaction pattern is triggered by different physical or psychological stimuli. According to Selye, who introduced the concept of stress into medicine, the human body reacts to any stressor with the same basic three-stage pattern of changes. Selye labeled this response pattern the *general adaptation syndrome (GAS).*

The first stage of the general adaptation syndrome—the *alarm reaction*—occurs when the affected person becomes aware of the presence of a stressor.

TABLE 11–2　Worries (in Rank Order) of 335 College Students

1. Grades (marks)
2. Tests or examinations
3. Finances (money and bills)
4. Course paper assignments
5. Too much homework
6. Uncertainty about my future
7. Job prospects after graduation
8. My parents or other family members
9. Lack of exercise
10. Relationships with my boyfriend or girlfriend
11. Dieting
12. Friendships (other than romantic)
13. Living conditions (room, roommate, etc.)
14. Participation in an athletic team
15. My health
16. Overeating
17. Deciding on a major
18. Marital plans
19. Transportation
20. Meetings
21. Fear of AIDS
22. Boredom
23. Poor class schedule
24. Problems with my present job
25. My neighbors

This stage consists of mobilization of the body's resources through increased activity of the autonomic nervous system and associated changes of the sort described under the *emergency pattern*. Other physiological changes occurring during this first stage include an enlargement of the cortex of the adrenal glands and increased secretion of corticosteroid hormones. On the other hand, the thymus gland and lymph nodes, which are parts of the immune system, decrease in size. These structures are responsible for the antibody-producing B cells, which serve as an immediate defense against invading microorganisms, and the multifunction T cells. By acting as predisposing or precipitating factors in the alarm reaction, psychological stress can affect the functioning of the immune system.

During the second stage of the GAS—the *stage of resistance*—the adrenal cortex shrinks and the lymph nodes become normal in size again. However, the level of physiological arousal and sensitivity to stressors remains high. If the resistance is inadequate and the original stressor is not reduced, or if the individual is exposed to a new stressor, the body's resources can become depleted, and the last stage of the GAS—the *stage of exhaustion*—may be entered. During this stage the capacity to withstand stressors declines, and the individual will become permanently incapacitated if stress continues.

TABLE 11–3   Stress Reactions (in Rank Order) of 335 College Students

 1. Anxiety
 2. Feelings of frustration
 3. Anger
 4. Irritability
 5. Extreme fatigue
 6. Depression
 7. Tension headaches
 8. Crying
 9. Biting one's fingernails or lips
10. Neckaches
11. Acne flare-ups
12. Upset stomach
13. Insomnia (trouble sleeping)
14. Backache
15. Loss of appetite
16. Muscle tension or spasms
17. Oversleeping
18. Indigestion
19. Colds or other respiratory problems
20. Shouting or screaming
21. Menstrual irregularities
22. Panic attacks
23. Increased blood pressure
24. Lightheadedness
25. Migraine headaches
26. Irregular heartbeat
27. Heavy perspiration
28. Dizziness
29. Shortness of breath
30. Diarrhea
31. Vomiting
32. Uncontrollable trembling
33. Tightness in throat or chest
34. Itching skin
35. Dermatitis (skin inflammation)
36. Constipation
37. Blurred vision
38. Allergy flare-ups
39. Skin rashes (other than acne)
40. Hyperventilation (excessively rapid and deep breathing)
41. Dandruff flare-ups

Stress-Related Disorders

Prolonged stress can result in a variety of psychophysiological changes, including persistent anxiety, depression, irritability, fatigue, loss of appetite, headache, and backache. Almost any organ or system of the body may show structural and functional changes when stress continues indefinitely. One plausible hypothesis is that the "target" or affected structure in stress is the weakest organ or system, perhaps the stomach (gastrointestinal disorders), perhaps the musculoskeletal system (backache, muscle tension and chronic fatigue), perhaps the respiratory system (bronchial asthma), perhaps the skin (neurodermatitis, etc.).

Peptic ulcers and other gastrointestinal reactions are the most publicized stress-related disorders, but the course and severity of migraine headaches, skin conditions, chronic backache, and bronchial asthma are also affected by persistent emotional stress. In fact, it is generally acknowledged by medical scientists that all physical illnesses and their prognoses may be influenced by the patient's emotional state. Furthermore, feelings of anxiety, nightmares, and "flashbacks" associated with stressful experiences may occur for months or even years after the event. These and others symptoms (insomnia, problems with social relationships, substance abuse) of *posttraumatic stress disorder* have been experienced by a substantial number of Vietnam War veterans (Roberts, 1988).

Burnout. One stress-related condition that has received a great deal of attention in the workplace is job *burnout.* Precipitated by the stress of overwork, the burnout syndrome is characterized by emotional exhaustion, lessened productivity, and feelings of depersonalization. The emotional exhaustion experienced by burned-out employees is associated with headaches, backaches, and other physical problems, in addition to social withdrawal. A useful instrument for identifying burnout victims and counseling them is the Maslach Burnout Inventory, a 22-item inventory designed by C. Maslach and S. E. Jackson and available from Consulting Psychologists Press.

Burnout occurs more often in compulsive, insecure, workaholic individuals whose jobs have ceased to provide them with feelings of self-fulfillment. Such individuals tend to lack self-esteem off the job and attempt to find it by becoming workaholics. These efforts often lead to recognition and rewards at the workplace, but the effects of overwork finally catch up with them. Studies have found that burnout is more common among women managers than men managers ("Stress, Burnout," 1988), among divorced than married employees, and among employees who lack opportunities for job promotion (Gaines & Jermier, 1983).

Retirement. Another potentially stressful job-related experience is retirement. A 65-year-old whose job has provided a sense of importance and meaning may view retirement as an insulting indication that society considers him or her to be old and useless, ready to be put "on the shelf" or "out to pasture." The activity orientation and work ethic of Western culture do little to prepare retirees for the potential trauma of leaving the job. When a person is almost religiously devoted to work, the experience of suddenly becoming unemployed and presumably unproductive can be very damaging to his or her self-esteem. In such instances, retirement is often accompanied by feelings of diminished usefulness, insignificance, loss of independence, and sometimes a sense of despair that life is essentially over. The loss of meaning and significance that can occur in one's life after retirement may, like any prolonged stress, accelerate the age-related pro-cess of physical decline.

> In retirement, otherwise perfectly healthy men and women may develop headaches, depression, gastrointestinal symptoms, and oversleeping. . . . Irritability, loss of interest, lack of energy, increased alcoholic intake, and reduced efficiency are all familiar and common reactions. (Butler & Lewis, 1982, pp. 128, 130)

Bereavement. Experiencing the death of a spouse is, like retirement, more com-mon in later life and typically more stressful. Among the physical and psychologi-cal symptoms experienced by recently widowed persons are depression, sleep disturbances, lack of appetite or weight loss, chronic fatigue, loss of interest in things, and difficulty concentrating. Reactions to the death of a spouse may be so intense that severe physical illness, a serious accident, or even death may occur. For example, in a study of 4,500 British widowers aged 55 and over, it was found that 213 died during the first six months of their bereavement. The rate of death, most instances of which apparently resulted from heart failure, was 40 percent higher than expected in this age group (Parkes, Benjamin, & Fitzgerald, 1969).

Of course, not all people who are subjected to seemingly stressful conditions develop stress-related disorders. For example, only a small number of combat air crews serving during World War II developed psychosomatic or psychophys-iological illnesses (Grinker & Spiegel, 1945). In order to be stressful, not only must a situation be perceived as threatening, but the individual must also lack adequate physical and mental resources to cope with it (Folkman, Dunkel-Schetter, DeLongis, & Gruen, 1986). In general, threats that are immediate, expected to continue for a long time, and expected to have an effect on a number of the individual's goals are more likely to be stressful (Paterson & Neufeld, 1987).

Personality Adjustment and Health

Although the evidence linking specific personality traits to specific illness is tenuous, personality adjustment, which may either contribute to or be affected by stress, appears to be a factor in some physical illnesses. This conclusion was the result of a prospective study of 204 men who were students at Harvard Univer-sity in the 1940s and who were followed up over a period of 30 years (Vaillant, 1979). Men who had been diagnosed as "poorly adjusted" as students proved much more likely to become seriously ill and die in their middle years than those who had been diagnosed as "well adjusted." In contrast to the well-adjusted men, the poorly adjusted men had a greater incidence of cancer, coronary disorders, high blood pressure, emphysema, back disorders, and suicide. From these re-sults, Vaillant concluded that personality adjustment, or mental health status, has a definite effect on a person's physical health in midlife. Good adjustment and positive mental health appear to retard the physical decline that begins in the middle years of life, whereas poor adjustment hastens it.

Life Changes and Health

It does not require a traumatic experience to produce an adjustment problem. The process of change itself, whether unpleasant or pleasant, can create a disruption in daily living that is stressful. Holmes and Rahe (1967) maintained that the stress of change, which requires behavioral and physiological readjustment, increases one's susceptibility to disease. The degree of increased susceptibility to disease varies with the extent of readjustment necessitated by the change.

Holmes and Rahe constructed a "Social Readjustment Scale" on which events requiring changes in the pattern of daily living are scaled from 0 to 100, depending on the degree of readjustment ("points") required (see Figure 11–1). The greater the degree of readjustment required in a given year, the greater the individual's chances of developing a stress-related illness. Unfortunately, it is not clear from the Holmes and Rahe (1967) data and subsequent research investigations whether life change is a cause or a consequence of illness. Preexisting illness may lead to higher scores on the Social Readjustment Scale and thereby account, at least in part, for the correlation between life change and illness.

Although research findings have not uniformly supported the theory that life change contributes to physical illness, the evidence for a relationship between *negative* life events and illness is persuasive. Schwartz and Griffin (1986), for example, found that among people who have experienced many life changes, negative ones in particular, there is a significantly higher incidence of cardiovascular disease, depression, diabetes, leukemia, schizophrenia, and difficulties with pregnancy.

The Personality/Health Connection Revisited

Since the 1950s *stress* has been recognized as the most important concept in relating psychological factors to physical illness. Attempts to establish relationships between specific personality characteristics and syndromes of specific illnesses have not been abandoned, but psychological stress has been viewed as a more useful concept in that its influence on a host of illnesses can be traced.

Meta-analysis of the findings of a wide range of research studies linking personality to illness has suggested that a generally negative affective style, including anxiety, depression, repression, and to some extent, hostility, is associated with the development of a large number of illnesses. Included among these are asthma, coronary heart disease, recurrent headaches, ulcers, and arthritis (Friedman & Booth-Kewley, 1987). It has been speculated that there is such a thing as a general *disease-prone personality*, characterized by a pervasive negative emotional state that has a profound effect on health-related behavior.

Directions: Circle the number on the left corresponding to each event which you have experienced during the past year.

1. Beginning or ceasing formal schooling (26)
2. Being fired at work (47)
3. Change in residence (20)
4. Changing to a different line of work (36)
5. Changing to a new school (20)
6. Christmas (12)
7. Death of a close friend (37)
8. Death of a close family member (63)
9. Death of a spouse (100)
10. Detention in jail or other institution (63)
11. Divorce (73)
12. Foreclosure on a mortgage or loan (30)
13. Gaining a new family member (e.g., through birth, adoption, oldster moving in, etc.) (39)
14. Major business readjustment (e.g., merger, reorganization, bankruptcy, etc.) (39)
15. Major change in church activities (e.g., a lot more or a lot less than usual) (19)
16. Major change in eating habits (a lot more or a lot less food intake, or very different meal hours or surroundings) (15)
17. Major change in financial state (e.g., a lot worse off or a lot better off than usual) (38)
18. Major change in health or behavior of a family member (44)
19. Major change in living conditions (e.g., building a new home, remodeling, deterioration of home or neighborhood) (25)
20. Major change in responsibilities at work (e.g., promotion, demotion, lateral transfer) (29)
21. Major change in sleeping habits (a lot more or a lot less sleep or change in part of day when asleep) (16)
22. Major change in social activities (e.g., clubs, dancing, movies, visiting, etc.) (18)
23. Major change in number of family get-togethers (e.g., a lot more or a lot less than usual) (15)
24. Major change in the number of arguments with spouse (e.g., either a lot more or a lot less than usual regarding child rearing, personal habits, etc.) (35)
25. Major change in usual type and/or amount of recreation (19)
26. Major change in working hours or conditions (20)
27. Major personal injury or illness (53)
28. Marital reconciliation with mate (45)
29. Marital separation from mate (65)
30. Marriage (50)
31. Minor violations of the law (e.g., traffic tickets, jaywalking, disturbing the peace, etc.) (11)
32. Outstanding personal achievement (28)
33. Pregnancy (40)
34. Retirement from work (45)
35. Revision of personal habits (dress, manners, associations, etc.) (24)
36. Sexual difficulties (39)
37. Son or daughter leaving home (e.g., marriage, attending college, etc.) (29)
38. Taking out a mortgage or loan for a lesser purchase (e.g., for a car, TV, freezer, etc.) (17)
39. Taking out a mortgage or loan for a major purchase (e.g., for a home, business, etc.) (31)
40. Trouble with boss (23)
41. Trouble with in-laws (29)
42. Vacation (13)
43. Wife beginning or ceasing work outside the home (26)

FIGURE 11–1   Social Readjustment Rating Scale. The scale is scored by summing the numbers in parentheses after the statements whose numbers have been circled by the respondent. (Reprinted with permission from *Journal of Psychosomatic Research,* 1967, Vol. 11, by T. H. Holmes & R. H. Rahe, Pergamon Press Ltd. Oxford, England.)

Type A Behavior and Personality

The belief that particular personality traits are related to specific physical disorders was given a boost by the studies of the Western Collaborative Group on the relationships between Type A behavior and heart disease (Rosenman, Brand, Jenkins, Friedman, Straus, & Wurm, 1975). The findings of other research investigations, such as those based on the hypothesis that cancer is related to depression, have also contributed to the renewed interest in personality and health. However, research on Type A behavior and personality has been particularly influential in stimulating a reexamination of the connection between personality and physical health.

Type A individuals are described as driven, aggressive, ambitious, extremely competitive, preoccupied with achievement, challenged, self-centered (selfish), impatient, restless in their movements, staccato-like in their speech, and dominated by feelings of being under pressure (Rosenman et al., 1975; Matthews, 1982; Yarnold, Grimm, & Mueser, 1986).

> Type A's may be found attempting to view television, read a newspaper or trade journal, and eat lunch or dinner all at the same time. "When the commercials come on, I turn down the volume and read my newspaper," is a statement we hear repeatedly. It is not unusual for a Type A to view two football games on two different television sets as he irons a shirt or treads an exercise bicycle. (Friedman & Ulmer, 1984)

In contrast to the Type A behavioral pattern, Type B individuals are described as more relaxed, easygoing, and patient, and they speak and act more slowly and evenly. Compared with Type B's, Type A individuals reportedly have a significantly higher incidence of heart attacks, even when differences in age, serum cholesterol level, smoking frequency, and blood pressure are statistically controlled. The American Heart Association recognizes the Type A pattern as a significant risk factor in coronary and blood vessel diseases, although not to the same extent as smoking, high blood pressure, or high blood cholesterol.

The original, and perhaps most valid, method of assessing Type A behavior is to conduct a specially designed Structured Interview (SI) that evaluates the interviewee's behavior (movements, etc.) as well as his or her answers to specific questions. A more efficient, but different, procedure is to administer the Jenkins Activity Survey (JAS), a 52-item, self-report inventory designed for adults aged 25–65 (from The Psychological Corporation). The JAS divides each of the A and B types into two subtypes (A1 and A2, B3 and B4), depending on the degree to which Type A or Type B characteristics are manifested. People in the A1 subtype show most Type A behaviors to an intense degree, whereas these behaviors are entirely absent in B4 people. The behaviors of A2 and B3 people are intermediate between the A1 and B4 extremes. The JAS is scored on Type A, as well as three factorially independent scales: Speed and Impatience, Job Involvement, and Hard Driving and Competitive. Illustrative of items on each of these three scales are the following:

1 When you listen to someone talking, and this person takes too long to come to the point, do you feel like hurrying him along?

2 How often do you bring your work home with you at night or study materials related to your job?

3 Nowadays, do you consider yourself to be
   a. Definitely hard-driving and competitive?
   b. Probably hard-driving and competitive?
   c. Probably more relaxed and easygoing?
   d. Definitely more relaxed and easygoing?

Unfortunately, the JAS and the Structured Interview do not measure exactly the same variables, a fact which has contributed to some of the inconsistencies in the research literature on Type A behavior.

Despite a great deal of work on Type A behavior, the role of psychological factors in heart disease remains unclear. According to certain researchers (e.g., Ragland & Brand, 1988), it is not necessarily a high achievement drive per se but rather frustration resulting from a discrepancy between ambition and achievement that promotes cardiovascular illness. Research findings also point to hostility, characterized by a lack of trust in other people or fear that other people are out to get one, as an important contributing factor in the blockage of coronary arteries.

The results of a long-term follow-up study of patients who took part in a 1960s study that helped to advance Type A theory call into question the original findings. This follow-up study found that people with Type A personalities are no more likely to die suddenly of a heart attack than Type B's (Ragland & Brand, 1988). Of 257 men who suffered heart attacks between the time they took part in the original (1960s) study and 1983, twenty-six died within 24 hours after suffering an attack. But there was no significant difference between the average death rates of those identified as Type A's and the Type B's. Furthermore, among the 231 men who survived at least 24 hours after an attack, the death rate for the Type A's was only 58 percent that of the Type B's. Such findings might lead to the conclusion that, rather than increasing the risk of death after a heart attack, a Type A personality may actually serve to decrease that risk or to protect the victim against death. However, research on the relationship between Type A personality and heart disorders continues.

Whatever the role of psychological factors in coronary heart disease may prove to be, the use of intervention techniques such as messages and stories on television and in other media, posters, community demonstrations, and other approaches urging people to quit smoking, to monitor their diet for fat intake, to have their blood pressure checked regularly and to have hypertension treated, can play an important role in the prevention and treatment of heart disease (e.g., Puska, 1984).

Cancer

Observational and correlational data suggest that psychological variables such as an attitude of passivity and hopelessness in the face of stress, can affect the growth, if not the genesis, of cancer cells (Schmale, 1972; Derogatis, Abeloff, & Melisaratos, 1979). A tendency to keep resentment and anger within oneself rather than expressing it and a "marked inability to forgive" have been said to be typical of cancer patients (Greer & Morris, 1975; Renneker, 1981). Cancer patients reportedly have difficulty forming long-term relationships with other people (e.g., Thomas, Duszynski, & Schaffer, 1979); they also tend to engage in an above-average amount of self-pity and to have poor self-images (Scarf, 1980). These studies, unfortunately, do not make clear whether the psychological variables are contributory or consequential factors in cancer, or whether they merely promote behaviors, such as smoking, poor diet, and noncompliance with medical orders, which are known risk factors for the disease.

It has also been argued that personality variables are more important in the progress than in the precipitation of cancer. For example, the results of one investigation showed that cancer progressed more rapidly in overly polite, passive individuals than in aggressive patients (Derogatis et al., 1979). Another study found that people who were able to maintain a "fighting spirit"—a belief that they were going to lick the disease no matter what the odds—were more likely to recover than pessimists who resigned themselves to being "goners" (Pettingale, Morris, Greer, & Haybittle, 1985).

Convinced of the importance of psychological factors in the prognosis of cancer, Carl and Stephanie Simonton (Simonton, Matthews-Simonton, & Creighton, 1978) supplemented physical treatment methods (surgery, radiation, chemotherapy) with psychological techniques. Their purpose was to get patients to think positively and confidently about their ability to control their illness and to stimulate their immune system by proper thoughts. Relaxation to control anxiety, combined with visual imagery, in which patients imagine that their white blood cells are attacking and destroying cancer cells, are among the techniques employed. Significant results have been reported using these methods, but most physicians remain skeptical. In general, oncologists (physicians specializing in the treatment of cancer) seem to feel that psychological treatment in conjunction with physicochemical treatment is worth trying, but they warn against the danger and cruelty of unduly raising the hopes of cancer patients.

Anorexia and Bulimia

A number of other illnesses, including anorexia/bulimia, recurrent headaches, essential hypertension, peptic ulcer, alcoholism, and AIDS, have also been studied for their possible connections with personality and other psychological variables. With the possible exception of anorexia, the results to date have not been encouraging. Just as there does not seem to be an "accident-prone personality" or an "alcoholic personality," there appears to be no such thing as a "headache personality," an "ulcer personality," or an "AIDS personality."

The psychogenic basis of *anorexia nervosa*, a severe loss of weight accompanied by an intense fear of putting on weight and a belief that one is too fat, has been studied extensively over the past few years. This disorder, which occurs almost exclusively in females, typically begins when the individual is undergoing a life change that requires unfamiliar skills and consequently precipitates feelings of inadequacy. Through their comments and other behavior, anorexics manifest feelings of body dissatisfaction, ineffectiveness, perfectionism, interpersonal distrust, and fears of maturing. They typically describe their mothers as dominant, ambivalent, intrusive, and overbearing, and their fathers as "emotional absentees." The psychodynamics of anorexia are unclear, but treatment that focuses only on losing weight and neglects family relationships and other problems experienced by the patient is clearly inadequate and likely to lead to recidivism. Family therapy, in which as many members as possible of the immediate family, and not just the anorexic member, are treated as a group, has shown promising results (Minuchin, 1974). Behavior modification approaches are useful in getting the anorexic to eat properly and to change certain aspects of her interpersonal behavior.

Bulimics, who experience recurrent episodes of uncontrollable binge eating, are more aware than anorexics of the abnormality of their behavior and therefore are potentially more receptive to treatment. Bulimics have pronounced fears that they will be unable to stop eating. They are preoccupied with weight gain, and engage in periodic attempts to lose weight by fasting, overusing laxatives and diuretics, and self-induced vomiting (purging). Binging and purging often develop into a cycle that is difficult to break.

Anorexia and bulimia have sometimes been referred to by the combined term *bulimarexia* to emphasize their common psychological features: obsession with food and body proportions, low self-esteem, social withdrawal, and preoccupation with pleasing other people. Cultural factors, such as the preoccupation with thinness in Western society, combined with psychological problems related to food ingestion and body appearance, are the focus of research on causes and treatments of these eating disorders. Rather than having a single cause, it is likely that anorexia and bulimia, like asthma, hypertension, ulcers, and headaches, have multiple causes and dynamics.

Coping with Stress-Related Illness

A story is told of a fraternity that decided to initiate a new pledge in what they considered a particularly imaginative way. They bound his arms and legs, blindfolded him, and tied him to a railroad track. Unbeknown to the poor pledge, they tied him to a track that was never used, but which was adjacent to one that was used. Along came a train. Although the young man was in no physical danger, he had every reason to believe he was, and he died. (Kalat, 1984, pp. 23–25)

Death resulting from extreme stress and fear, as in the above account, is referred to as *sympathetic death*. Belief in voodoo curses that are placed on people can literally scare them to death. Breaking taboos may also contribute to the deaths of violators who are convinced that they will be killed for their transgressions, as seems to have occurred in the following story:

In New Zealand, a Maori woman ate some fruit which she subsequently learned had come from a tabooed place. She explained that the sanctity of her chief had been profaned thereby and that his spirit would kill her. She apparently died within twenty-four hours. (Barker, 1968, p. 19)

Such deaths are referred to as "sympathetic" because they are associated with overactivity of the sympathetic nervous system, as indicated by increased heart rate and elevated blood pressure.

In contrast to sympathetic death is the plight of certain nursing-home patients and other ill or otherwise desperate people who "give up" and give in to *parasympathetic death.* In these cases, the parasympathetic nervous system becomes excessively active, resulting in an extreme relaxation, a slowing down of heart action, and a fatal lowering of blood pressure (Seligman, 1992).

Parasympathetic death is believed to be the result in many instances of feeling helpless and hopeless. Death attributable to loss of hope and simply giving up has been observed in convicts, prisoners of war, and other institutionalized persons (see Report 11–1). These individuals apparently felt that their efforts to resist or otherwise deal with external events were no longer effective. They resigned themselves to being unable to cope with whatever physical and psychological stress they were experiencing and simply gave up and died, the only choice that seemed to be left open to them.

Coping Mechanisms

Most sick people have a long way to go and many resources to expend before they feel helpless and hopeless enough to give up and die. When faced with a stressful situation, the normal reaction is to call on a hierarchy of previously effective coping strategies that help one endure and combat the situation. Among the many coping mechanisms reported by college students are those listed in Table 11–4. These responses were given in a survey of the same 335 students on whom the responses in Tables 11–2 and 11–3 were compiled. The denial or distraction mechanisms seen in many of these responses might strike the observer as ineffective and unproductive in the long run, but denial is not necessarily an unreasonable way of dealing with stress under certain circumstances. Denial may buy time for the person, helping him or her to get through the early period of stress when little can be done, and thus it may leave room for hope.

The effectiveness of denial or avoidance is seen in the results of a study by Cohen and Lazarus (1973) of the postsurgical recovery of a sample of hospital patients. One group of patients, who were classified as *avoiders,* denied the emotional or threatening aspects of the surgery and did not want to think about their illness or listen to anything concerning it. But another group of patients, who were classified as *vigilants,* were sensitive to the emotional and threatening aspects of the surgery and attempted to control every aspect of the situation. In comparison with the vigilants, the avoiders recovered more quickly from surgery: They required less pain medication, showed less distress, and had fewer headaches, fevers, and infections. In this investigation, the techniques of avoid-

Case Example of the Effects of Helplessness and Hopelessness

When, in early 1973, medical army officer Major F. Harold Kushner returned from five and a half years as a prisoner of war in South Vietnam, he told me a stark and chilling tale. His story represents one of the few cases on record in which a trained medical observer witnessed from start to finish what I can only call death from helplessness.

Major Kushner was shot down in a helicopter in Vietnam in November 1967. He was captured, seriously wounded, by the Viet Cong. He spent the next three years in a hell called First Camp. Through the camp passed 27 Americans: 5 were released by the Viet Cong, 10 died in the camp, and 12 survived to be released from Hanoi in 1973. The camp's conditions beggar description. At any time there were about eleven men who lived in a bamboo hut, sleeping on one crowded bamboo bed about sixteen feet across. The basic diet was three small cups of red, rotten vermin-infested rice a day. Within the first year the average prisoner lost 40 to 50 percent of his body weight, and acquired running sores and atrophied muscles. There were two prominent killers: malnutrition and helplessness. When Kushner was first captured, he was asked to make antiwar statements. He said that he would rather die, and his captor responded with words Kushner remembered every day of his captivity: "Dying is easy; it's living that's hard." The will to live and the catastrophic consequences of the loss of hope are the theme of Kushner's story. . . .

When Major Kushner arrived at First Camp in January 1968, Robert had already been captive for two years. He was a rugged and intelligent corporal from a crack marine unit, austere, stoic, and oblivious to pain and suffering. He was 24 years old and had been trained as a parachutist and a scuba diver. Like the rest of the men, he was down to a weight of ninety pounds and was forced to make long, shoeless treks daily with ninety pounds of manioc root on his back. He never griped. "Grit your teeth and tighten your belt," he used to repeat. Despite malnutrition and a terrible skin disease, he remained in very good physical and mental health. The cause of his relatively fine shape was clear to Kushner. Robert was convinced that he would soon be released. The Viet Cong had made it a practice to release, as examples, a few men who had cooperated with them and adopted the correct attitudes. Robert had done so, and the camp commander had indicated that he was next in line for release, to come in six months.

As expected, six months later, the event occurred that had preceded these token releases in the past. A very high-ranking Viet Cong cadre appeared to give the prisoners a political course; it was understood that the outstanding pupil would be released. Robert was chosen as leader of the thought-reform group. He made the statements required and was told to expect release within the month.

The month came and went, and he began to sense a change in the guards' attitude toward him. Finally it dawned on him that he had been deceived—that he had already served his captors' purpose, and he wasn't going to be released. He stopped working and showed signs of severe depression: he refused food and lay on his bed in a fetal position, sucking his thumb. His fellow prisoners tried to bring him around. They hugged him, babied him, and, when this didn't work, tried to bring him out of his stupor with their fists.

He defecated and urinated in the bed. After a few weeks, it was apparent to Kushner that Robert was moribund: although otherwise his gross physical shape was still better than most of the others, he was dusky and cyanotic. In the early hours of a November morning he lay dying in Kushner's arms. For the first time in days his eyes focused and he spoke: "Doc, Post Office Box 161, Texarkana, Texas. Mom, Dad, I love you very much. Barbara, I forgive you." Within seconds he was dead.

Robert's was typical of a number of such deaths that Major Kushner saw. What killed him? Kushner could not perform an autopsy, since the Viet Cong allowed him no surgical tools. To Kushner's eyes the immediate cause was "gross electrolyte imbalance." But given Robert's relatively good physical state, psychological precursors rather than psychological state seem a more specifiable cause of death. Hope of release sustained Robert. When he gave up hope, when he believed that all his efforts had failed and would continue to fail, he died.

Source: From Helplessness: On Development, Depression, and Death, by M.E.P. Seligman. Copyright © 1975 and 1992 by Martin E. P. Seligman. Reprinted by permission of W. H. Freeman and Company.

TABLE 11–4   Stress-Coping Techniques (in Rank Order) of 335 College Students

1. Analyze the situation
2. Talk with someone about it
3. Make a list of what I have to do
4. Go to sleep
5. Listen to music
6. Rest
7. Get away from the source of stress
8. Reevaluate and reorganize things
9. Exercise more
10. Buy something to cheer myself up
11. Pray or read the Bible
12. Try to remain calm
13. Do something constructive about the stress
14. Withdraw into myself
15. Go to a movie
16. Drink coffee or soda, or eat something good
17. Go to a party
18. Drink beer or another alcoholic beverage
19. Cook, construct, or design something
20. Write in my journal or diary
21. Take deep breaths
22. Put it out of my mind
23. Bury myself in work
24. Talk myself out of it
25. Smoke cigarettes
26. Hit something or somebody
27. Read a good book or something inspiring
28. Take tranquilizers or other drugs

ance and vigilance were treated as a dichotomy. These approaches to coping with stress are, however, not all-or-none matters. Rather, they exist on a continuum. A similar distinction—that between repression and sensitization—was made by Byrne (1964). Information-avoidance behaviors are nearer to the repression end and information-seeking behaviors nearer to the sensitization end of the *repression-sensitization* continuum. Whatever one may call the technique—denial, avoidance, or repression—it is not invariably effective in coping with stress. There are occasions on which it is better to "take the bull by the horns" and face reality directly, rather than trying to deny, avoid, or repress it.

Other coping strategies, including rest and relaxation, attempting to control the stressful situation by direct action, and calling on other people for emotional support and advice, are seen in the responses listed in Table 11–4. Inherent in many of the more active attempts to combat stress is the concept of *control*, exerting efforts to master or manage the situation and change it to one's own advantage.

Personality Variables Related to Control

Whether or not one believes that a situation can be controlled depends on both the situation itself and the personality of the individual. Among the various personality variables that have been studied for their relationships to individual effectiveness in controlling stress are optimism-pessimism, internal-external locus of control, self-concept, self-efficacy, and explanatory style (causal attributions). In general, more optimistic people with more positive self-concepts and a greater sense of self-efficacy (a "can-do" attitude) are more effective in mastering stress. Such people also tend to have a more internal locus of control and to make internal causal attributions: They believe that the responsibility for their experiences and the outcomes of their behavior depend to a large extent upon their own efforts. The personal resources that an individual possesses for coping with stress can also be assessed by psychometric instruments such as the "Ways of Coping Questionnaire" and the "Coping Resources Inventory," both of which were designed by A. L. Hammer and M. S. Marting and are available from Consulting Psychologists Press.

Explanations of coping ability based on concepts such as self-concept, self-efficacy, optimism-pessimism, locus of control, and explanatory style are, however, not necessarily causal. When research finds that people who are able to exert more control over events are the ones who believe that they can do so, it is not clear whether the success in coping is a consequence of the personality variable or vice versa. In all likelihood the direction of causation is reciprocal and interactive rather than one-way: Believing in one's ability to cope enhances the ability to do so, and effectively coping increases one's self-confidence in the ability to do so.

Hardiness. One of the most general, and most extensively researched, of all personality variables related to success in coping with stress is *hardiness*, defined as the ability to withstand stress and remain healthy in the face of it. As described by Kobasa (1979), hardiness consists of three characteristics: commitment, control, and challenge. *Commitment* consists of a clear sense of purpose, involvement with other people, and an ability to recognize one's goals, priorities, and values. *Control* refers to the ability to select a course of action, to incorporate external events into a dynamic life plan, and to be motivated to achieve. *Challenge* is a feeling that change is positive and that one has an opportunity to integrate his or her life goals into new situations. The relationships of these components to illness have been studied by Kobasa and others (e.g., Kobasa, 1979; Kobasa, Maddi, & Kahn, 1982; Peterson & Stunkard, 1986). Kobasa and her coworkers found that people who report having a low incidence of physical illness scored higher on all three components of hardiness than people who report a high incidence of illness. Hardy individuals were also found to be more likely to maintain good health practices when under stress (Wiebe & McCallum, 1986) and to come from a home environment that encourages self-mastery and includes encouragement (Kobasa et al., 1982). Results of other investigations seemed to support the conclusions that hardiness develops rather early in life, is related to physical endowment as well as developmental experiences, and helps protect people from physical illness.

Not all research findings are consistent with Kobasa's thesis that hardiness acts as a buffer against physical illness. In addition, the three components of commitment, control, and challenge that were identified by Kobasa are not independent of each other or other psychological variables (e.g., neuroticism) (Schmied & Lawler, 1986; Allred & Smith, 1989; Contrada, 1989).

Identity Disruption. Another personality variable that has been proposed to account for the effects of psychological stress on illness is *identity disruption* (J. D. Brown & McGill, 1989). Identity disruption, which is an erosion of a person's identity or sense of self, occurs when the person is exposed to events that are inconsistent with that identity. According to Brown and McGill, identity disruption is a source of stress that can increase one's vulnerability to pathogenic agents. Such disruption may occur in the face of any change—positive or negative—of one's life circumstances, because change produces a new perception of the self and forces a readjustment of the self-concept. In studies of high school and college students, these researchers found that, in contrast to students who possessed high self-esteem, students with low self-esteem experienced more illness symptoms following positive life events.

Research on the validity of the concepts of hardiness and identity disruption as explanatory variables in health and disease is continuing. A problem with research that attempts to link psychological concepts such as these to physical illness is that the findings are, for the most part, based on individual reports or responses to questionnaires rather than direct observations of illness. Again, then, we are faced not only with the question of the reliability of these reports but also with whether specific personality factors promote physical health or physical health affects scores on self-report measures of the personality factors. Whether they are causes, effects, or a bit of both, variables such as optimism-pessimism, self-efficacy, self-concept, locus of control, explanatory style, hardiness, and identity disruption can help to predict, if not necessarily explain, individual health status.

Social Factors in Physical Illness

Fairly widely accepted is the proposition that social support from caring, interested people can reduce the level of stress that must be endured by a physically ill person (Schaefer, Coyne, & Lazarus, 1981; Dunkel-Schetter, Folkman, & Lazarus, 1987). Self-disclosure of one's personal experiences and fears also appears to reduce the incidence of health problems (Pennebaker & O'Heeron, 1984). Compared with those who keep things to themselves, people who talk about their problems with others tend to be physically healthier (Larson, 1988). Social interaction not only provides emotional support in times of stress but also supplies information about the nature of the stressor and what can be expected. Accurate expectations about a stressor prior to being exposed to it reduce its threat by enabling a person to prepare and buffer himself or herself against it (E. J. Langer & Saegert, 1977; Baum, Fisher, & Solomon, 1981; Minkler, 1989).

Much of the social support given to adults appears to be obtained in the context of marriage. However, not all people find that a spouse and the marital situation are as supportive as they might seem to be. Although unmarried men usually have fewer social ties and a lower social status than married men, the roles of married women appear to be more confining and frustrating than those of married men (Gove, 1973; Kobrin & Hendershot, 1977). Widows, divorcees, and single women have as many interpersonal ties as married women, and unattached single women may possess even higher social status than married women. Consequently, from a psychological viewpoint women are seen as benefiting less from marriage and suffering less from being single than men. Close social ties and higher social status, which are more likely to be found in marriages than outside it, favor greater longevity, but this statement is truer for men than for women. Unmarried men typically have fewer social ties and lower social status than married men, but unmarried women usually retain their interpersonal ties and may have even greater social status than they would as male-dominated members of families (Aiken, 1991a).

Whether or not a person is married, the results of certain studies suggest that loneliness may have as great an impact on the death rate as drinking alcohol, overeating or not eating the right foods, smoking, and lack of exercise. The results of studies conducted in Alameda County, California, indicate that social isolation is at least as strongly associated with mortality as cigarette smoking and lack of exercise (Berkman & Syme, 1979). Supporting evidence for the importance of social interaction in promoting longevity was obtained in a study conducted in Tecumseh, Michigan (House, Robbins, & Metzner, 1982). The findings showed that married men who were involved in active rather than passive leisure activities and women who attended church frequently but watched television infrequently had lower mortality rates than their less socially involved peers.

Techniques for Treating Stress

Many medical tests and treatment procedures involve invasive procedures such as *angioplasty,* in which a catheter is passed into an obstructed artery and the tip inflated to flatten out deposits of plaque and thereby restore some circulation in the artery. Providing patients with accurate information about this and other stressful medical procedures that they must undergo can reduce the anxiety associated with the procedure. Information and social support are two common methods for reducing stress and buffering oneself against it. Other stress-reduction techniques include progressive muscle relaxation, biofeedback, stress-inoculation training, desensitization, counterconditioning, modeling, assertiveness training, cognitive restructuring, and related procedures of the sort used in treating anxiety-based disorders (see Chapter 13). The twin goals in all of these procedures are to reduce the emotional response to stress and provide the patient with cognitive techniques for coping with stress. Many of these techniques are not new, but have probably been used for centuries by both physicians and laypersons. One or more of these procedures, together with medical treatment of the physical condition by means of drugs, surgery, exercise, and other physical therapies, are recommended in the treatment of a variety of illnesses in which psychological factors act as predisposing or precipitating factors or have an effect on the course and prognosis of the illness.

In Jacobson's technique of *progressive relaxation* (or *relaxation training*), muscle tension and associated muscular pain are reduced and anxiety is allayed by attending to the differences in sensation when alternately tensing and relaxing various muscles. Relaxation training is often used in conjunction with *biofeedback.* This term refers to any technique whereby a person learns to control some physiological change in his or her body. A special apparatus is used to measure the physiological variable (blood pressure, pulse rate, respiration rate, heart rate, muscle tension, brain waves, galvanic skin response, etc.) and "feed back" information on its status to the patient. Abnormal readings on the selected variable are presumably associated with stress and can be brought under control with practice. By trying to relax and by other techniques that he or she may not even be aware of, the patient attempts to bring the monitored measurement under control.

The most common type of biofeedback involves the measurement of muscle tension by means of an *electromyograph,* in which electrodes are placed over selected groups of muscles, typically in the forehead, neck, or back. Electromyographic feedback has been used in treating muscle spasms, headaches, and low back pain in particular. Two other types of biofeedback that have had some success in the treatment of psychological stress and physical pain are temperature feedback (with a *thermistor*) and brain wave feedback (with an *electroencephalograph*). The effects of biofeedback can often be attributed to the fact that the procedure teaches the patient how to relax. In fact, it has been found in practice that relaxation training alone is often just as effective in reducing stress as relaxation plus biofeedback (Andrasik, Blanchard, & Edlund, 1985).

Summary

Research on the relationships of psychological factors to physical illness originated in psychosomatic medicine. Early research in this area was greatly influenced by the psychoanalytic hypothesis that the affected organ is symbolically related to a mental conflict. Another proposed explanation that received attention was the "weakest organ" hypothesis that the weakest body organ is affected by conflict, stress, and strong emotions.

Despite a few positive results, efforts to find specific physical reaction patterns associated with specific emotions have been largely unsuccessful. Likewise, early attempts to find connections between personality characteristics and physical illness met with little success. Although some psychiatrists and psychologists claim otherwise, the notions of a bronchial asthma personality, an essential hypertension personality, a peptic ulcers personality, a diabetes personality, a rheumatoid arthritis personality, and the like are generally viewed as unsubstantiated by research. Even when a significant relationship between a personality variable and a specific illness is found, it is unclear which causes which or whether they cause each other.

The advent of the field of health psychology has led to more carefully conducted research on the relationships between physical illness and psychological variables. Much of this research, which has been both retrospective and prospective, is based on Selye's concepts of stress and the general adaptation syndrome. The GAS, a generalized response of the body to any physical or psychological stressor, consists of three stages: alarm reaction, stage of resistance, and stage of exhaustion. Almost any organ or organ system (gastrointestinal, musculoskeletal, respiratory, etc.) may show structural and functional changes when stress continues indefinitely. Among the many disorders that have been found to be associated with prolonged stress are peptic ulcers, migraine headaches, chronic backache, bronchial asthma, and syndromes such as posttraumatic stress disorder and burnout. Retirement, bereavement, natural disasters, and other losses or traumatic events may also precipitate a variety of stress symptoms. These stressful experiences can result in physical decline and even premature death. The extent to which these events, or any changes in one's life, are perceived as stressful varies with the physical and mental resources of the individual.

The findings of a wide range of research studies linking personality to illness have suggested that a generally negative affective style, including anxiety, depression, repression, and to some extent, hostility, is associated with the development of a large number of physical illnesses. A pervasive negative emotional state, which is felt to have a profound effect on health, is said to characterize the disease-prone personality.

Although the findings are somewhat mixed, there is support for a particular behavioral or personality pattern associated with a greater incidence of coronary heart disease. This Type A pattern is characterized as driven, aggressive, ambitious, extremely competitive, preoccupied with achievement, challenged, self-centered, impatient, restless in movements, staccato-like in speech, and dominated by feelings of being under pressure. The contrasting pattern is shown by Type B people, who are described as more relaxed, easygoing, patient individuals who speak and act more slowly and evenly than Type A's. The Type A personality pattern is assessed by means of a Structured Interview or the Jenkins Activity Survey, but the two measures yield somewhat different results. Recent research on Type A behavior suggests that cardiovascular illness is promoted by hostility or frustration resulting from a discrepancy between ambition and achievement, rather than by a high achievement drive alone.

Observational and correlational data suggest that psychological variables such as an attitude of passivity and hopelessness in the face of stress, can affect the growth, if not the genesis, of cancer cells. A tendency to "bottle up" one's anger, a "marked inability to forgive," and difficulty in forming long-term relationships are also said to be typical of cancer patients. Like many other studies in health psychology, however, these results are based on correlational data and hence do not permit separation of cause and effect.

The role of psychological factors in eating disorders such as anorexia nervosa and bulimia has received a great deal of research attention, but the findings are seldom clear-cut. In general, anorexics are perfectionistic, interpersonally distrustful girls who are dissatisfied with their bodies and have fears of maturing. They describe their mothers as dominant and overbearing and their fathers as "emotional absentees." The prognosis in anorexia is not as good as that for bulimia, but treatment focuses on getting the anorexic to start eating and to work on her interpersonal problems. Family therapy and behavior-modification approaches have been more effective than other psychotherapeutic interventions in treating anorexics.

When faced with a stressful situation, a normal response is to employ one or more coping strategies. These include denial, avoidance, rest and relaxation, direct action, and enlisting the support of other people. Denial or avoidance is often more effective in coping with stress, especially during its initial stages, than being overly concerned and completely informed about the nature of the stress situation. Optimistic individuals who have a high self-concept or high self-efficacy and an internal locus of control and who make internal causal attributions tend to have greater control over stress and to cope with it more effectively. In contrast, pessimistic individuals who have a low self-concept or low self-efficacy and an external locus of control and who make external causal attributions cope with stress less effectively. Hardiness, which consists of commitment, control, and challenge, has also been found to be associated with better physical health and the ability to cope with stress.

One important factor in dealing with stress is social support, either within or outside of the institution of marriage. Social isolation leads to loneliness, which may have as great an impact on death rate as drinking, overeating, smoking, and lack of exercise. Self-disclosure not only serves to reduce the tension associated with stress but leaves one more open to information on methods for dealing with it. Information about medical procedures such as angioplasty can reduce the stress associated with such procedures. Particularly useful in treating the anxiety and tension associated with stressful situations is progressive muscle relaxation, either with or without biofeedback.

Key Concepts

Behavioral medicine   Broad multidisciplinary field of scientific investigation, education, and practice concerned with the relationships of behavior to health, illness, and psychological dysfunctions.

Biofeedback   The process of learning to control autonomic body functions by means of visual or auditory cues.

General adaptation syndrome (GAS)   Selye's three-stage bodily stress response (alarm reaction, stage of resistance, stage of exhaustion) resulting from exposure to a stressor.

Hardiness   A personality characteristic (including commitment, challenge, and control) associated with a lower rate of stress-related illness.

Health psychology   A branch of psychology concerned with research and applications directed toward the promotion of health and the prevention of illness.

Learned helplessness   Acquired perception on the part of the individual of his or her lack of influence or control over external events; can lead to apathy and depression.

Posttraumatic stress disorder   A persisting anxiety reaction precipitated by a severely stressful experience, such as military combat; characterized by a reexperiencing of the stressful event and avoidance of stimuli associated with it. Other symptoms include feelings of estrangement, recurring dreams and nightmares, and a tendency to be easily startled.

Progressive muscle relaxation   Alternately tensing and relaxing each one of the 16 muscle groups of the body while attending to the feelings of tension and relaxation. Progressive relaxation is a common therapeutic procedure for coping with stress and a part of systematic desensitization in the treatment of phobias.

Prospective study   Research investigation which follows up, over time, people having different characteristics or life-styles to determine which ones develop a particular condition or disorder.

Psychosomatic disorders   Physical illnesses based on psychological stress, such as duodenal ulcers and tension headaches.

Repression-sensitization   Donald Byrne's conceptualization of a personality continuum representing an individual's typical response to threat; information-avoidance behaviors are at one end of the continuum and information-seeking behaviors at the other end.

Retrospective study   A researcher looks back at the history of a group of people with a certain disease or characteristic and attempts to identify variables that mark these people as different from those who do not have the condition.

Stress   Defined either as a stimulus or a response to a stressor; associated with psychological and/or physiological tension or imbalance in an organism.

Type A personality   Personality pattern characterized by a combination of behaviors, including aggressivity, competitiveness, hostility, quick actions, and constant striving; associated with a high incidence of coronary heart disease.

Type B personality   Personality pattern characterized by a relaxed, easygoing, patient, noncompetitive life-style; associated with a low incidence of coronary heart disease.

Activities and Applications

1. Make a list of the common problems or worries that you have experienced in college, and compare your list with that of a friend and with the list in Table 11–2. What are the similarities and differences between your list and the list in Table 11–2? Between your list and your friend's list? Do the differences between your responses and those of your friend and those in Table 11–2 tell you anything about your personality? About your friend's personality?

2. Administer the following questionnaire to a sample of students in your classes, tabulate and analyze the results, and draw whatever conclusions you feel are warranted. In particular, compare the responses to Part IV with those to Parts I–III. Are there any differences between males and females? Between freshmen, sophomores, juniors, and seniors?

Questionnaire

Directions: This questionnaire is anonymous, and your answers will be kept confidential. The results will be used to help us understand students and their problems. Please answer all parts of the questionnaire as accurately as possible.

What is your sex? (Check correct category)
_____ Female
_____ Male

What is your classification? (Check correct category)
_____ Freshman
_____ Sophomore
_____ Junior
_____ Senior

Part I. Check each of the following that is a cause of worry or stress for you at this time in your life:

_____   1. Boredom
_____   2. Course paper assignments
_____   3. Deciding on a major
_____   4. Dieting
_____   5. Fear of AIDS
_____   6. Finances (money and bills)
_____   7. Friendships (other than romantic)
_____   8. Grades (marks)
_____   9. Job prospects after graduation
_____ 10. Lack of exercise

_____ 11. Living conditions (room, roommate, etc.)
_____ 12. Marital plans
_____ 13. Meetings
_____ 14. My health
_____ 15. My neighbors
_____ 16. My parents or other family members
_____ 17. Overeating
_____ 18. Participation in an athletic team or other organization
_____ 19. Poor class schedule
_____ 20. Problems with my present job
_____ 21. Relationship with my boyfriend or girlfriend
_____ 22. Tests or examinations
_____ 23. Too much homework
_____ 24. Transportation
_____ 25. Uncertainty about my future
_____ 26. Other worries (describe)

Part II. Check each of the following that you have experienced during times of stress:

_____ 1. Acne flare-ups
_____ 2. Allergy flare-ups
_____ 3. Anger
_____ 4. Anxiety
_____ 5. Backache
_____ 6. Biting fingernails or lips
_____ 7. Blurred vision
_____ 8. Colds or other respiratory problems
_____ 9. Constipation
_____ 10. Crying
_____ 11. Dandruff flare-ups
_____ 12. Depression
_____ 13. Dermatitis (skin inflammation)
_____ 14. Diarrhea
_____ 15. Dizziness
_____ 16. Fatigue (extreme)
_____ 17. Feelings of frustration
_____ 18. Heavy perspiration
_____ 19. Hyperventilation (excessively rapid and deep breathing)
_____ 20. Increased blood pressure
_____ 21. Indigestion
_____ 22. Insomnia (trouble sleeping)
_____ 23. Irregular heartbeat
_____ 24. Irritability
_____ 25. Itching skin
_____ 26. Lightheadedness
_____ 27. Loss of appetite
_____ 28. Menstrual irregularities
_____ 29. Migraine headaches
_____ 30. Muscle tension or spasms
_____ 31. Neckaches
_____ 32. Oversleeping
_____ 33. Panic attacks
_____ 34. Shouting or screaming
_____ 35. Shortness of breath
_____ 36. Skin rashes (other than acne)
_____ 37. Tension headaches
_____ 38. Tightness in throat or chest
_____ 39. Uncontrollable trembling
_____ 40. Upset stomach

_____ 41. Vomiting
_____ 42. Other (specify)

Part III. Check each of the following techniques that you typically use to cope with stress:

_____ 1. Analyze the situation
_____ 2. Bury myself in work
_____ 3. Buy something to cheer me up
_____ 4. Cook, construct, or design something
_____ 5. Do something constructive about the stress
_____ 6. Drink beer or another alcoholic beverage
_____ 7. Drink coffee or soda or eat something good
_____ 8. Exercise more
_____ 9. Get away from the source of stress
_____ 10. Go to a movie
_____ 11. Go to a party
_____ 12. Go to sleep
_____ 13. Hit something or somebody
_____ 14. Listen to music
_____ 15. Make a list of what I have to do
_____ 16. Pray or read the Bible
_____ 17. Put it out of my mind
_____ 18. Read a good book or something inspiring
_____ 19. Reevaluate and reorganize things
_____ 20. Rest
_____ 21. Smoke cigarettes
_____ 22. Take deep breaths
_____ 23. Take tranquilizers or other drugs
_____ 24. Talk with someone about it
_____ 25. Talk myself out of it
_____ 26. Try to remain calm
_____ 27. Withdraw into myself
_____ 28. Write in my journal or diary
_____ 29. Other (describe)

Part IV. Rate yourself on each of the following personality scales by checking the appropriate line segment:

affectionate	___ ___ ___ ___ ___ ___ ___	reserved
careful	___ ___ ___ ___ ___ ___ ___	careless
fun-loving	___ ___ ___ ___ ___ ___ ___	sober
helpful	___ ___ ___ ___ ___ ___ ___	uncooperative
imaginative	___ ___ ___ ___ ___ ___ ___	down-to-earth
independent	___ ___ ___ ___ ___ ___ ___	conforming
insecure	___ ___ ___ ___ ___ ___ ___	secure
prefer variety	___ ___ ___ ___ ___ ___ ___	prefer routine
self-disciplined	___ ___ ___ ___ ___ ___ ___	weak-willed
self-pitying	___ ___ ___ ___ ___ ___ ___	self-satisfied
sociable	___ ___ ___ ___ ___ ___ ___	retiring
softhearted	___ ___ ___ ___ ___ ___ ___	ruthless
trusting	___ ___ ___ ___ ___ ___ ___	suspicious
well-organized	___ ___ ___ ___ ___ ___ ___	disorganized
worrying	___ ___ ___ ___ ___ ___ ___	calm

3. Research has shown that learned helplessness, optimism versus pessimism, self-efficacy, locus of control, hardiness, attributional style, and self-concept are all related to the acquisition and persistence of certain physical illnesses. However, for the most part the data on which such conclusions are based are correlational in nature and hence do not permit conclusions concerning the direction of causation. How can you be certain that feelings of helplessness, for example, are a consequence rather than a contributor to poor health? What research procedures and findings would convince you that psychological factors contribute to physical illness rather than vice versa?

4. With respect to measures of optimism-pessimism, learned helplessness, self-efficacy, locus of control, attributional style, self-concept, and hardiness, assuming that all six of these variables are causally related to physical health, what might be the common factor or factors underlying these relationships?

5. One problem with the research literature on Type A behavior is that different assessment methods—for example, interview and questionnaire—do not yield the same results. Although questionnaires such as the Jenkins Activity Survey are more efficient than interviews, Rosenman (1986) and others have rejected such self-report measures because Type A personalities presumably have little insight into their own behavior. One way of testing this hypothesis is to compare self-ratings of behavior with ratings of behavior made by unbiased observers. With this in mind, select a few students who seem to fit the description of the Type A personality given in the chapter, and administer the following checklist to each of them. Then have someone who knows the person well fill out the same checklist to describe that person. Compare the self-ratings with the other-ratings using a convenient statistical procedure.

Checklist

Directions: Check each of the following terms or phrases which is descriptive of you:

_____   1. Achievement-oriented
_____   2. Aggressive
_____   3. Ambitious
_____   4. Competitive
_____   5. Constant worker
_____   6. Dislikes wasting time
_____   7. Easily angered
_____   8. Easily aroused to action
_____   9. Easily frustrated
_____ 10. Efficient
_____ 11. Emotionally explosive
_____ 12. Fast worker
_____ 13. Hard worker
_____ 14. Highly motivated
_____ 15. Impatient
_____ 16. Likes challenges
_____ 17. Likes to lead
_____ 18. Likes responsibility
_____ 19. Restless
_____ 20. Tries hard to succeed

---

6. Take and score the Social Readjustment Rating Scale in Figure 11–1. Compare your score with the scores of several other people to whom you administer the scale.

7. Differentiate between retrospective and prospective research investigations, including the purposes, design, advantages, and disadvantages of each.

8. Do you believe that changes in one's life circumstances, whether positive or negative, act as stressors that contribute to physical illness? Think back over your own life. Are you aware of any relationship between rather abrupt changes in your life, such as those listed in Figure 11–1, and your own physical health?

Suggested Readings

Blany, P. H. (1985). Psychological considerations in cancer. In N. Schneiderman & J. T. Tapp (Eds.), *Behavioral medicine: The biopsychosocial approach* (pp. 533–563). Hillsdale, NJ: Erlbaum.

Cohen, S., Tyrrell, D.A.J., & Smith, A. P. (1991). Psychological stress and susceptibility to the common cold. *New England Journal of Medicine, 325*(9), 606–612.

Contrada, R. J., Leventhal, H., & O'Leary, A. (1990). Personality and health. In L. A. Pervin (Ed.), *Handbook of personality: Theory and research* (pp. 638–669). New York: Guilford Press.

Cowen, E. L. (1991). In pursuit of wellness. *American Psychologist, 46,* 404–408.

Dembroski, T. M., MacDougall, M. J., Herd, J. A., & Shields, J. (1983). Perspectives on coronary-prone behavior. In D. S. Krantz, A. Baum, & J. E. Singer (Eds.), *Handbook of psychology* (pp. 57–83). Hillsdale, NJ: Erlbaum.

Friedman, H. S., & Booth-Kewley, S. (1987). The "disease-prone personality." *American Psychologist, 42,* 539–555.

Kobasa, S. (1990). The stress resistant personality. In R. Ornstein & C. Swencionis (Eds.), *The healing brain: A scientific reader.* New York: Guilford Press.

Prokop, C. K., Bradley, L. A., Burisch, T. G., Anderson, K. O., & Fox, J. E. (1991). *Health psychology: Clinical methods and research.* New York: Macmillan.

Roth, S., & Cohen, L. J. (1986). Approach, avoidance, and coping with stress. *American Psychologist, 41,* 813–819.

Suls, J., & Rittenhouse, J. D. (Eds.). (1987). Personality and physical health (Special issue). *Journal of Personality, 55*(2).

Taylor, S. E. (1990). Health psychology: The science and the field. *American Psychologist, 45,* 40–50.

CHAPTER 12

Mental Disorders

CHAPTER OUTLINE

In every society and time there have been individuals who were looked upon as peculiar, difficult to live with, and different from others in their behavior. Contrary to what may have been believed in previous centuries, these people were not witches or possessed by demons. They were, for a combination of biological and psychological reasons, mentally disordered and hence in need of therapeutic help.

In general, modern psychological and psychiatric principles are inconsistent with an oversimplified conception of good versus evil, right versus wrong, or normal versus insane. However, the laws of most countries continue to employ the concept of *insanity* in determining punishment for a crime. The standard of legal insanity applied most frequently by the judicial system in the United States is the American Law Institute (ALI) rule, introduced in 1962 and later (1972) adopted by the D.C. Court of Appeals:

> (1) A person is not responsible for criminal conduct if at the time of such conduct as a result of mental disease or defect he lacks substantial capacity either to appreciate the criminality (wrongfulness) of his conduct or to conform his conduct to the requirement of the law; (2) As used in the Article, the terms "mental disease or defect" do not include an abnormality manifested only by repeated criminal or otherwise anti-social conduct [United States v. Brawner, 471 F 2d 969 (D.C. Dir. 1972]).

The ALI rule incorporates two standards of insanity: an inability to appreciate wrongfulness of an act (cognitive standard); and an inability to conform conduct to requirements of law (volitional standard). The second of these two standards was removed by the Congressional Insanity Reform Act of 1984, and now only the cognitive standard is applied in determining whether the defendant was insane at the time of the crime (see Rogers, 1987).

Definition, Demographics, and Diagnosis of Abnormal Behavior

To a great extent, normality and abnormality of behavior are statistical concepts that vary in meaning with the particular society and time. Sociocultural factors, such as the attitudes and tolerance of other people, are important in determining what is normal or acceptable behavior. These factors are emphasized when an abnormal person is defined as one who has poor interpersonal relations, displays socially inappropriate behavior, and has no acceptable goals. According to this definition, people who repeatedly violate social norms are abnormal. But whether abnormal behavior is punished; ignored; treated with drugs, shock, surgery, or psychotherapy; or even lauded, depends on society's interpretation of the value of the behavior and the extent to which other people are willing to tolerate it.

Most psychologists are not satisfied with a purely cultural or statistical definition of abnormality. In determining whether or not a mental disorder is present, they look further into the personal experiences of the person, studying the satisfactions attained, the tension, anxiety, depression, and sense of isolation that are felt, and the effort expended by the person in attempting to cope. Disruptive thought processes, perceptions, and attitudes, which are not always apparent in behavior, are also important. Society may be willing to tolerate strange behavior or even be unaware of the problems experienced by a person, who may continue to function fairly effectively over a lifetime while enduring invisible anxieties and insecurities.

> Whenever Richard Cory went down town,
> We people on the pavement looked at him:
> He was a gentleman from sole to crown,
> Clean favored, and imperially slim.
>
> And he was always quietly arrayed,
> And he was always human when he talked;
> But still he fluttered pulses when he said,
> "Good-morning," and he glittered when he walked.
>
> And he was rich—yes, richer than a king—
> And admirably schooled in every grace:
> In fine, we thought that he was every thing
> To make us wish that we were in his place.
>
> So on we worked, and waited for the light,
> And went without the meat, and cursed the bread;
> And Richard Cory, one calm summer night,
> Went home and put a bullet through his head.[1]
>
> —*E. A. Robinson*

Demographics of Mental Disorders

It is sometimes maintained that the stress of modern living is responsible for the high incidence of mental disorders in the twentieth century. Because diagnostic criteria and other factors affecting mental hospital admission rates vary with time and place, the question of whether people are more likely to become mentally disordered in contemporary society than they were in former times is difficult to answer. It can be argued that it is just as easy to become anxious and depressed in a horse cart as in an automobile or an airplane, and the available data indicate that the twentieth century has not produced a greater proportion of mental disorders (Goldhamer & Marshall, 1953). It is true that the *number* of first admissions to mental hospitals has increased during the twentieth century, but the admission *rate* has not changed, and the average length of residence in mental hospitals has declined. During the past few decades there has been a drop in first admissions to mental hospitals for all patients—young and old. Unfortunately, this drop has not been due to a decrease in the number of mentally disturbed people but rather to the fact that other facilities and institutions—nursing homes in particular—are housing larger numbers of patients.

Although the rate of serious psychotic disorders in American men under 40 and women under 50 did not change appreciably from 1885 to 1950 (Goldhamer

& Marshall, 1953), during the twentieth century there has been an increase in mental disorders associated with old age. The increase is interpreted as due largely to the fact that people are living longer and consequently are more likely to develop age-related or organic brain disorders and attendant mental symptoms.

Psychodiagnosis

The trend today is to avoid assigning nonuseful, potentially stigmatizing diagnostic labels to mental disorders whenever possible and to attempt to identify the causes of disordered behavior. However, for purposes of record keeping, treatment, and research, diagnosing mental disorders is an important part of the work of many clinical psychologists and psychiatrists.

Psychodiagnosis is the process of examining a person from a psychological viewpoint to determine the nature and extent of a mental or behavioral disorder. In the traditional *medical model,* the diagnostician observes, interviews, and tests the patient to determine the presence or absence of certain psychological (and physical) symptoms. He or she then compares the patient's symptoms with standard descriptions of abnormal behavior to determine in which category or categories the patient best fits. The end result of the process is a psychiatric classification or succinct description of the patient. In addition to diagnosing the disorder, a *prognosis,* or prediction of its likely outcome, is made.

The most popular system of psychodiagnosis, although by no means the only one, is that described in the *Diagnostic and Statistical Manual of Mental Disorders.* In the first two editions of this manual, which were published in 1952 and 1968, the categories of mental disorders used by Sigmund Freud, Emil Kraepelin, and other famous psychiatrists were combined. The third edition of the manual (DSM-III), which grouped 200 specific disorders and conditions into 17 major categories, represented a major departure from its predecessors (see Table 12–1). A revision of DSM-III known as DSM-III-R, published in 1987, incorporated further changes in diagnostic criteria (American Psychiatric Association, 1987). The DSM-III-R system is multiaxial, in that a patient may be classified on five separate axes, or dimensions. Explicit criteria and decision-branching sequences for reaching a diagnosis are provided, with the various disorders being grouped according to very specific behavioral symptoms without specifying their origins or methods of treatment.

In the multiaxial evaluation of the DSM-III-R system, each case is assessed on five axes referring to different kinds of information about the patient. Axis I consists of the clinical syndromes and V codes ("conditions not attributable to a mental disorder that are a focus of attention or treatment"), and Axis II of developmental disorders and personality disorders. In addition to labeling and numbering each disorder with a five-digit code on Axis I and Axis II, the severity of the disorder may be specified as mild, moderate, severe, or in partial or complete remission. Axis III provides a classification of accompanying physical disorders and conditions, Axis IV a classification of the severity of psychosocial

TABLE 12–1   Major Categories of the *Diagnostic and Statistical Manual of Mental Disorders* (Third Edition–Revised)

Disorders usually first evident in infancy, childhood, or adolescence
Organic mental syndromes and disorders
Psychoactive substance use disorders
Schizophrenia
Delusional disorder
Psychotic disorders not elsewhere classified
Mood disorders
Anxiety disorders
Somatoform disorders
Dissociative disorders
Sexual disorders
Sleep disorders
Factitious disorders
Impulse control disorders not elsewhere classified
Adjustment disorder
Psychological factors affecting physical condition
Personality disorders

Source: American Psychiatric Association (1987).

stressors, and Axis V a global assessment of functioning (GAF) on a numerical scale. DSM-III-R permits multiple diagnoses of a patient's condition on Axes I and II. As indicated by the following example, such diagnoses may be quite complex:

Axis I	296.23	Major depression, single episode, severe without psychotic features
	303.90	Alcohol dependence
Axis II	301.60	Dependent personality disorder (provisional, rule out borderline personality disorder)
Axis III		Alcoholic cirrhosis of liver
Axis IV		Psychosocial stressors: anticipated retirement and change in residence, with loss of contact with friends
Axis V		Current GAF: 44

Although it would appear that, by providing more precise psychodiagnostic criteria, DSM-III-R would possess greater reliability than previous systems, questions concerning its validity have been raised. Some authorities have argued that the criteria are too rigid to apply to all patients, whereas others question the appropriateness and possible dangers of any kind of psychiatric labeling (Vaillant, 1984). One criticism of DSM-III-R is that diagnostic labels such as schizophrenia and depression are not always assigned consistently. In addition to varying with the theoretical orientation and personal biases of the psychodiagnostician, and the socioeconomic status and ethnicity of the patient, diagnoses differ from institution to institution, community to community, and country to country (Cooper, Kendall, Gurland, Sharp, Copeland, & Simon, 1972).

Variations in diagnoses of the same disorder are also a product of the preoccupations and concerns of the diagnostician. In general, clinical psychologists and psychiatrists have tended to be more concerned with detecting signs of abnormality than with denoting indicators of health and coping abilities. Depending on the perceived repercussions or payoffs for making a patient appear more or less disordered, the diagnostician may either exaggerate or minimize the severity of symptoms. For example, if a government agency or private insurance company pays for treatment or awards other compensation to patients who are diagnosed as psychotic or brain-damaged but does not pay for other diagnosed conditions, the result may be a greater number of diagnoses of psychosis and brain damage. In some states, however, where a patient diagnosed as "psychotic" loses many of his or her legal rights, diagnosticians may be reluctant to assign this label.

Advocates of psychodiagnostic classification point out that, by reducing the amount of long-winded explanation, diagnostic terms can improve communication among mental health professionals. Furthermore, classifying mental disorders can assist in making diagnostic predictions and in conducting research on abnormal behavior (Meehl, 1962; Spitzer, 1976). In any event, great care must be exercised in selecting the appropriate terms or categories to be included in the report of a psychological examination. Labels such as psychotic, neurotic, psychopathic, and the like too often act as self-fulfilling prophecies in which the patient becomes—at least in the eyes of others—what he or she is labeled as being (Rosenhan, 1973).

Frustration, Conflict, and Defense Mechanisms[2]

Three concepts that have traditionally been associated with mental disorders are psychological stress, frustration, and conflict. Many types of psychological reactions to stress, some adaptive and others maladaptive, occur in people of all ages. Precisely how an individual reacts to stress and frustration depends upon many factors, including heredity and earlier experiences. Of course, parents cannot and should not overprotect their children from all stressful situations; overprotection may result in even greater inability to tolerate frustration and cope with such situations. Frustration tolerance and coping ability must, like most other things in a child's life, be learned. Thus the child who is successful in solving difficult, frustrating problems will learn to tolerate frustration better than one who fails or is never given a chance to try.

In his or her efforts to cope with stress and frustration, however, the individual often reaches an impasse—a state of conflict—in things that are important. When a person is *ego-involved* in a task or situation—that is, personally involved to such an extent that failure results in a loss of self-esteem—he or she becomes tense, and frequently anxious or hostile.

Emotional reactions to a frustrating or conflict situation form a vicious circle from which one may find it difficult to get free. One's initial reaction will probably be anger and aggression, but because parents and society in general have punished the person for displaying these reactions, he or she may respond to such negative feelings with anxiety or fear. Anxiety and fear, of course, prompt the person to withdraw from the frustrating situation, but withdrawal itself may produce further anxiety over failing to attain the desired goal. This anxiety is also frustrating, and back we go through the vicious circle once again.

Another emotion that frequently accompanies anxiety is guilt. Guilt, which is felt when the individual either has done or imagines that he or she has done something wrong, is a frequent accompaniment of a conflict between what a person wants to do and what he knows he should not do. Depression is another emotional reaction to frustration, either directly or by way of anxiety and guilt.

Although anger, anxiety, guilt, and depression may all result from frustration and conflict, most people do not remain in these emotional states for very long. If a person is chronically upset by such feelings, he or she becomes unable to function effectively. What is required, then, is some means of protecting oneself from these feelings. This is the function served by what psychodynamic theories refer to as *defense mechanisms* and other psychologists as *coping mechanisms*. Examples of such defense or coping mechanisms are rationalization, denial, fantasy, displaced aggression, projection, compensation, sublimation, and reaction formation. All of these mechanisms may be adaptive in the short run but maladaptive when used to excess.

Rationalization consists of giving false but socially acceptable reasons for failing to deal with a situation, whereas *denial* is simply denying the seriousness of a problem or that it even exists. Related to denial is the act of withdrawing from potentially threatening situations, because of the feeling that being close to others is risky and that the best way to cope is self-isolation or retreat into fantasy. In *fantasy*, the individual vicariously satisfies his or her desires, fulfills wishes, and creates a private, less frustrating world. Although fantasy is very common in normal people, and may help to cushion the shock of disappointment and even assist in planning for the future, excessive use of fantasy is counterproductive and symptomatic of severe mental disorder.

Another reaction to stress, *displaced aggression*, is becoming angry at someone or something other than the direct cause of frustration. In this case the victim has nothing to do with the frustrating circumstances but is merely a convenient scapegoat. Somewhat related to displaced aggression is *projection*, a defense mechanism in which the individual perceives other people as possessing the impulses and desires that are felt by the projecting person. A person who unrealistically views others as being against him or "having it in for him" is projecting. This common mechanism is self-reinforcing, because people who believe that others are against them typically react aggressively toward those people and, as a consequence, provoke counterhostility.

Another common defense mechanism is *compensation*, in which a person attempts to overcome a real or imagined inferiority in one area by overemphasizing another kind of behavior. For example, a high school boy of average intelligence who is too small or too unskillful to make an athletic team may become a "greasy grind" and overemphasize book learning as a means of obtaining self-esteem and social acceptability.

In *sublimation,* basic drives such as those of sex and aggression are channeled into socially approved activities. Although there is some question whether instances of clear-cut sublimation actually occur, some frequently cited examples are writing romantic poetry to sublimate the sex drive, taking care of other people's children as a sublimation of the urge to have children of one's own, or becoming active in certain sports or occupations (butcher, surgeon) as a way of sublimating one's aggressive impulses. Also fairly uncommon is *reaction formation,* a mechanism in which the individual behaves in a manner directly opposite to an unconscious wish or impulse, for instance, being kind instead of cruel.

Another reaction to frustration and conflict is to become helpless or overly dependent on other people. Individuals with strong dependency needs may also exaggerate and exploit a physical illness and associated depression. In this way they gain attention, sympathy, and an excuse for not attempting to fight their own battles against stress-provoking circumstances.

These defense mechanisms are usually maladaptive, because they are not permanent solutions to problems and usually create further difficulties for the person. Used to excess, many defense mechanisms can lead to more serious mental disturbances—for example, paranoia is a result of excessive anger or schizophrenia as a result of withdrawal.

Neuroses and Psychoses

It has been estimated that anywhere from 8 to 25 percent of all American adults are neurotic, probably about 30 million people in all. (National Institute of Mental Health, 1985). *Neuroses*[3] which are based on faulty learning of certain habits and attitudes, interfere with effective junctioning but do not usually require hospitalization. Even though they are not dangerous or out of touch with reality, neurotics may be bothersome to other people. Some neuroses are short-lived and others of long duration, but predisposing factors exist in every case.

A widely accepted explanation of neurotic symptoms is that they serve to reduce anxiety. The history of a neurotic individual usually involves a limited ability to tolerate frustration and the failure of defense mechanisms. These factors, coupled with a traumatic experience or other precipitating stress, result in a high level of uncontrolled anxiety. At this point the person may "stumble onto" or devise a neurotic symptom that is instrumental in reducing anxiety. Because tension-reducing behaviors are learned, the neurotic behavior comes to be employed repeatedly in stressful situations.

Although the symptoms vary with the particular neurosis, certain characteristics are common to neurotics. Horney (1937) listed these characteristics as rigid personality, feelings of inferiority and self-doubt, general unhappiness and dissatisfaction, inflexibility in confronting problems, and a difference between

actual and potential achievement. Horney and other psychoanalysts also emphasized that the basic cause of neuroses is anxiety produced by conflict—conflict
between an individual's personal desires and impulses and his or her perception
of the demands of society.

Classification of Neuroses

The classical neuroses are grouped into three categories—anxiety disorders, somatoform disorders, and dissociative disorders—by DSM-III-R (American Psychiatric
Association, 1987). Under anxiety disorders are grouped phobias (agoraphobia,
social phobia, simple phobia, etc.), obsessive-compulsive neuroses, posttraumatic
stress disorder, and generalized anxiety disorder. Conversion (hysterical) neurosis,
hypochondriasis, and somatization disorder are grouped under somatoform disorders. Dissociative disorders include multiple personality, psychogenic fugue, psychogenic amnesia, and depersonalization disorder.

Phobias. A *phobia* is an overwhelming fear of something, such as enclosed places,
high places, open places, animals, death, darkness, crowds, or even the number
13. According to psychoanalytic theory, in phobias anxiety becomes displaced
onto some object or situation. In this way the phobic symptom serves to hide, or
substitute for, the real source of anxiety. A classical case of phobia was that of the
five-year-old boy Hans's fear of horses, which Sigmund Freud analyzed as being
a displacement of the original, basic fear that the child had of his father (Freud,
1925). According to behavior theory, phobias result from the more straightforward processes of conditioning and stimulus generalization. This is illustrated in
The Locomotive God (Leonard, 1927), a book that relates how a lifelong fear of
locomotives was produced when a passing train scalded a child with hot steam.

Obsessive-Compulsive Neurosis. An *obsession* is an unwanted idea that continually
intrudes into consciousness, whereas a *compulsion* is a strong, repetitive urge to
perform an irrational act of some kind. Examples of compulsions are repeated,
unnecessary handwashing or bathing, continually looking under one's bed,
checking the locks on one's doors and windows, and ritualistic touching, count-
ing, and avoiding particular things. The person feels tense and is driven to
perform the compulsive act, and the tension is reduced by the performance of
the act.

Obsessive-compulsive neuroses may involve either obsessive thoughts, compulsive acts, or a combination of the two. The French psychiatrist Pierre Janet,
who classified both phobias and obsessive-compulsive neuroses as "psychasthe-
nias," maintained that obsessive-compulsive neuroses are more common in intelligent people. In contrast, he considered conversion or hysterical neurosis to be a
"malady of the intellectually inferior" person. Consistent with Janet's hypothesis
is the fact that during World War I the incidence of hysteria was proportionally
greater among enlisted men, whereas obsessive-compulsive symptoms occurred
more frequently among officers.

Generalized Anxiety Disorder. The classical interpretation of an *anxiety neurosis* is that it is the basic form of neurosis—in other words, a neurosis before a specific defense mechanism has developed. Generalized anxiety disorder is characterized by an anxious expectation or diffuse fear that something dreadful is going to happen. The individual is tense, perspires freely, experiences heart palpitations, is nauseated, and feels hopeless. In addition, he or she is frequently hypersensitive, is unable to sleep or eat, and may have nightmares. These symptoms are commonly observed in *posttraumatic stress disorder* precipitated by physical or psychological trauma as in battle, during an earthquake, or in any other extremely stressful situation.

Conversion or Hysterical Neurosis. This disorder is characterized by sensory symptoms such as blindness, deafness, and other anesthesias, or by motor symptoms such as paralysis of a body organ, tics, tremors, and convulsions. There is no demonstrable organic basic for the particular physical symptom, and it usually disappears under hypnosis or drug therapy. The incidence of conversion neurosis is apparently lower than it once was, and a number of people who were initially diagnosed as hysterical neurotics were found on reevaluation to be suffering from an anxiety reaction, depression, schizophrenia, or even organic brain disorder. It is noteworthy that conversion neurosis was the first neurotic disorder to be treated by Sigmund Freud, in the case of Anna O.

The psychoanalytic interpretation of conversion neurosis is that the symptom serves to control anxiety: The anxiety is "converted" into a physical symptom. Thus a soldier who is afraid of being killed may develop a paralysis of the legs, or the arms of a man who secretly desires to harm someone may become paralyzed. In this way, the symptom is said to reduce the disturbing feelings and impulses. In addition, secondary gains frequently result from conversion symptoms. For example, other people may express sympathy for a person with a "bad back" or some other "physical" ailment, and the person may also receive financial compensation from the government or an insurance company. It should be emphasized, however, that the conversion neurotic is not considered to be a malingerer. The patient truly believes that there is an organic basis for the symptoms, and like a person with a hypochondriacal neurosis, may visit several physicians in search of a cure. Fortunately, the prognosis in conversion hysteria is usually good.

Hypochondriasis. A hypochondriac is a person who worries continuously and needlessly about his or her health and imagines all sorts of unreal illnesses. Physicians are often plagued by these people, who complain of numerous aches and pains in the absence of any true organic pathology and usually take various kinds of pills and tonics. As in the case of other neurotic disorders, the symptoms of hypochondriasis are considered to be learned ways of controlling anxiety. Of interest is the fact that hypochondriasis tends to run in families. There is probably no hereditary basis for the disorder, but the children of hypochondriacal parents learn by imitation and reward to become excessively concerned about their own health and to focus on physical illness as a socially manipulative means of controlling anxiety.

Dissociative Disorders. A group of neurotic conditions that are frequently confused with psychoses are the dissociative disorders. In these conditions, particular aspects of personality become separated from the personality as a whole. The psychoanalytic interpretation of dissociative disorders is that the personality is no longer an integrated whole, because certain significant aspects are "dissociated" from the remainder. The most prominent defense mechanism in dissociative disorders is repression, but the repressed thoughts, memories, or other aspects of personality do not simply cease to exist. They are expressed in various ways—in feelings of depersonalization, amnesia, and fugue states, and very rarely as a multiple personality.

The memory loss that occurs in *psychogenic amnesia* is usually a forgetting of convenience, in that the patient gains satisfaction and relief from trying to forget. But he or she is not purposefully trying to forget, and expresses a strong interest in recovering the lost memories. Related to psychogenic amnesia is *psychogenic fugue,* which is amnesia accompanied by actual physical flight. For example, during wartime a soldier may be found wandering far from the scene of battle, professing no memory of his identity or experiences. Individuals in such fugue states may engage in behavior, perhaps even criminal in nature, that they fail to recall on "coming to themselves."

Probably no mental disorder has so captured the public imagination as *multiple personality*. In this neurosis, the same individual has two or more fairly distinct, separate personalities. A classic example of multiple personality is the case of Sally Beauchamp (Prince, 1905; also see Rosenzweig, 1988). This young woman, who was a student at Radcliffe College, manifested three distinct personalities during the six years in which she was studied by Morton Prince. A more recent and famous case is that of Eve White, a serious-minded, conscientious young woman who occasionally became Eve Black, an extroversive, vibrant flirt (Thigpen & Cleckley, 1957). A typical finding in cases of multiple personality is demonstrated by the fact that Eve Black was aware of Eve White, but the latter did not know of the former's existence. Thigpen and Cleckley concluded that the "split" that produced the two personalities was caused by a difference in identification. Eve White reportedly identified with her mother, and Eve Black with her father. During the process of treatment, a more mature personality known as Jane emerged. However, as related in Eve's own story (Lancaster & Poling, 1958), Jane eventually broke down. A fourth personality then reportedly developed to finally resolve the conflict between Eve White and Eve Black (also see Schreiber, 1973).

For the most part, neurotic behavior in adulthood is merely a continuation and intensification of personality characteristics that have been present since childhood. The particular neurotic symptoms depend, however, on the existing personality structure as well as the social reinforcements that the individual receives for the symptoms. For example, the greater frequency of hypochondriasis among women is probably a reflection of the fact that the dependent, sick role is a more socially acceptable pattern of behavior in women than in men.

Psychotic Disorders

People who suffer from milder mental disorders such as neuroses can benefit from treatment and sometimes require hospitalization. Such patients, however, rarely show the severe distortion of reality, bizarre behavior, and extensive personality disorganization seen in institutionalized patients. The label *psychosis* implies the presence of a disorder in which the ability to recognize reality is severely affected. The distortion of reality is manifested by deficits in perception, language, and memory, as well as changes in mood. Approximately 50 percent of patients diagnosed as psychotic have a detectable brain disorder, and there appears to be a biochemical basis for many of the remaining 50 percent.

Schizophrenia. The three major types of psychoses for which there is no known organic basis are schizophrenia, delusional disorder, and mood disorders. Schizophrenics, who comprise the largest category, have severe disturbances in thinking and sometimes perception. They withdraw from contact with reality and lose empathy with other people. Disturbances in concept formation and regressive, bizarre behavior are characteristic of schizophrenics; hallucinations (false perceptions) and delusions (false beliefs) may also be present.

Some schizophrenics spend a large portion of their lives, continuously or intermittently, in mental hospitals, growing old in institutions. Generally speaking, these long-term patients are meek and mild individuals who have adapted to institutional life and would probably be unable to cope with the decisions and stresses outside an institution. If they are not being treated for the disorder, a nursing home or some other less expensive facility is preferable to life in a mental hospital. Because of the law that people who are not actively being treated and are not considered to be dangerous to themselves or others cannot be retained indefinitely in a mental institution, many schizophrenics end up on city streets. There they somehow manage to survive, but receive little assistance from the community and are perceived as an eyesore and an annoyance.

Delusional (Paranoid) Disorder. The delusional or paranoid category of psychosis includes a broad range of mental disorders of varying severity characterized by suspiciousness, projection, excessive feelings of self-importance, and frequently complex delusions of grandeur, persecution, and ideas of reference. The frequency of delusional disorder tends to increase with age, being second only to depression in mental disturbances among the elderly (Pfeiffer, 1977). On rare occasions, two or more people share the same delusional system, as in *folie à deux* ("madness of two") or *folie à trois* ("madness of three").

Mood Disorders. Also fairly common are disorders involving disturbances in mood—either extreme elation (mania), profound depression, or periodic fluctuation between the two. In addition to extremes of mood, there is a loss of contact with reality. The major types of mood disorders are *bipolar disorder* and *depressive (unipolar) disorder*. The symptom picture in bipolar disorder consists of severe mood swings from depression to elation, remission, and then recurrence. With aging, the manic and depressive phases of the cycle become more regular and hence predictable. During the manic state the patient is overtalkative, elated, or irritable, and shows increased motor activity and bizarre ideation. During the depressive phase of the cycle the patient is deeply depressed in mood and activity; expressions of guilt and self-deprecation, bodily complaints, and motor inhibition (stuporousness) or agitation are also seen in some instances.

The symptoms of depression include feelings of intense sadness, hopelessness, pessimism, low self-regard, a loss of interest in people and things, problems in eating and sleeping, physical aches and pains, fatigue, and difficulty remembering. Attempted suicide is an ever-present danger in severe depression, and an estimated 30,000 Americans choose this way out every year (U.S. Dept. of Health & Human Services, 1992). The suicide rate for women remains fairly constant throughout the adult years, but it increases dramatically in elderly men.

Disorders of Childhood

Whatever mistakes Sigmund Freud may have made in theorizing about personality, he was right in at least one assertion: The child is father to the man. Many behavioral disturbances of childhood are precursors of mild to severe mental disorders in adulthood. Furthermore, a number of childhood disorders, which are problematic enough in their own right, either remain unchanged or become less severe as development proceeds. In DSM-III-R, some of the disorders that are usually first evident in infancy, childhood, or adolescence have been placed on Axis I and others on Axis II. Table 12–2 lists the major categories of the developmental disorders, which are coded on Axis II. The remaining eight categories of childhood disorders are coded on Axis I. These 12 diagnostic categories represent a substantial increase over the two childhood emotional disorders—childhood schizophrenia and adjustment reaction of childhood—included in the first edition of DSM (American Psychiatric Association, 1952). Rather than describing each of the several disorders in each category, we shall limit the discussion to three of the most common, and the most troublesome. One of these—autistic disorder—is coded on Axis II under pervasive developmental disorders, and the other two—attention-deficit hyperactivity disorder and conduct disorder—on Axis I under disruptive behavior disorders.

Autistic Disorder

Autism is a rare disorder occurring in approximately 1 out of 10,000 children (Lovaas, 1987) and usually identifiable during the first 30 months of life. The child shows almost no signs of attachment to other people, failing to smile, laugh,

TABLE 12–2   Developmental Disorders

(These disorders usually appear and are first evident in infancy, childhood, or adolescence.)

Autistic disorder: Characterized by qualitative impairment in the development of reciprocal social interaction and in the development of verbal and nonverbal communication skills.

Attention-deficit hyperactivity disorder: Characterized by developmentally inappropriate degrees of inattention, impulsiveness, and hyperactivity.

Conduct disorder: Persistent pattern of conduct in which the basic rights of others and major age-appropriate societal norms or rules are violated.

Avoidant disorder of childhood or adolescence: Excessive shrinking from contact with unfamiliar people, for a period of six months or longer, sufficiently severe to interfere with social functioning in peer relationships.

Gender identity disorder: Persistent and intense distress about being a male or female, and a stated desire to be a member of the opposite sex or insistence that one is a member of that sex.

Identity disorder: Severe subjective distress regarding inability to integrate aspects of the self into a relatively coherent and acceptable sense of self.

Reactive attachment disorder of infancy or early childhood: Markedly disturbed social relatedness in most contexts that begins before the age of five and is not due to mental retardation or autism.

Source: Adapted from descriptions in *Diagnostic and Statistical Manual of Mental Disorders* (3rd ed., rev.) by the American Psychiatric Association (1987).

or make eye contact, and frantically resisting being held or cuddled. He or she manifests few socialization skills and little desire to play with other children, fails to develop self-help skills, and frequently has aggressive outbursts or tantrums. Although the child's behavior suggests a sensory or perceptual defect, as indicated by inattentiveness and a seeming inability to appreciate fully the impact of physical pain, the sense organs are not defective. Autistic children frequently show a pronounced aversion to auditory stimuli, sometimes screaming or crying even at the sound of the human voice.

Characteristic of autism is an "interest in sameness": The child becomes quite upset when things are moved around or the environment changed in any way. Autistic children may spend hours in self-stimulatory activities: rocking, head banging, flapping their arms, playing with the same object over and over in a stereotyped, ritualistic manner, lining objects up in a row, or staring persistently at a spinning top or fan. Language development is seriously deficient, and many autistic children never learn to speak at all. Their vocalizations may consist merely of the echolalic (parrotlike) repetition of certain sounds or words, and no attempt is made to establish conversational contact with parents or other persons.

The cause of autism is not known; the older theory that it is due to parents who are "emotional refrigerators" has been discounted. There is no known genetic basis for the disorder, but abnormally high levels of the brain's natural opiates (endorphins) may contribute to the lack of interest in human contact and comfort shown by autistic children (Herman et al., 1986). Administration of a long-lasting opiate antagonist such as naltrexone (brand name Trexan) has yielded some positive results, as in reducing the injuries which these children inflict on themselves (Sahley & Panksepp, 1987). In addition, it has been suggested that a problem of cell communication in the language areas of the brains of autistic children is a contributing factor (Minshew, Payton, & Sclabassi, 1986). In some cases, psychological treatment (e.g., behavior modification) results in improvements in language and social interaction. However, less than one-fourth of the autistic children who are treated are able to make even marginal adjustments (Carson, Butcher, & Coleman, 1988).

Attention-Deficit Hyperactivity Disorder

Attention-deficit hyperactivity disorder, which is the most common reason for referring children to mental health and pediatric facilities, affects an estimated 3–5 percent of elementary school children (A. O. Ross & Pelham, 1981). The *hyperactive* or *hyperkinetic* child, who is 6–9 times more likely to be a boy than a girl, consistently exhibits a high level of activity in situations where it is clearly inappropriate. The excessive movement is particularly likely in classrooms and other situations that require attentiveness and stillness. Hyperactive children are inattentive and impulsive, have low frustration tolerance and difficulty concentrating, and are usually unable to inhibit the excessive activity even when commanded to do so. They continually annoy and exhaust other people, and consequently have problems getting along with both children and adults. Not surprisingly, the delinquency rate and the incidence of other maladaptive behaviors are higher in individuals who have been hyperactive during childhood (Hechtman, Weiss, & Perlman, 1984).

The exact causes of hyperactivity in children are unclear, but problems in the home, including parental personality disorders (Morrison, 1980), are associated with the disorder (D. Ross & S. Ross, 1976; Morrison, 1980). Contrary to their effects on adults, cerebral stimulants such as amphetamines have a calming effect on hyperactive children. In addition, training the child to think before acting, encouraging him or her to signal for a "time out" period when needed to regain self-control, and other behavioral and cognitive techniques are helpful. Even without treatment, hyperactivity tends to diminish by the time the child reaches the middle teens.

Conduct Disorders

Conduct disorders, defined as a persistent pattern of conduct in which the basic rights of other people and age-appropriate social norms or rules are violated, are associated with both hyperactivity and delinquency. In addition, conduct disorders are precursors of antisocial personality, which is discussed in a later section of the chapter. An estimated 9 percent of boys and 2 percent of girls have conduct disorders (American Psychiatric Association, 1978), manifested by physical and verbal aggressiveness, disobedience, cruelty, meanness, theft, and, in girls, precocious sexual behavior. Other symptomatic behaviors include lying, stealing, and temper tantrums. As a child grows older and becomes stronger and more experienced, purse snatching, armed robbery, rape, and other assaults may occur. Use of tobacco, alcohol, and other drugs are associated factors.

The characteristic family background of children who fit this predelinquent syndrome is a rejecting, unstable, frustrating place for the child, a place where discipline is harsh and inconsistent and parental separation or divorce is common. The child "acts out" his or her feelings of rejection and frustration by socially disruptive or delinquent behavior or by becoming a runaway. Because of the central role played by the home environment in conduct disorders, effective treatment necessitates finding some means of modifying that environment or removing the child from it.

Personality Disorders

Unlike posttraumatic stress disorder, in which some identifiable stimulus or situation produces anxiety, depression, and other symptoms of stress, *personality disorders*[4] are not caused by specific, identifiable physical or psychological stressors. Rather, the pattern of behavior in such individuals is deep-seated, having developed over a lifetime. The individual does not feel anxious or disturbed, even though the personality appears warped to such an extent that he or she is unable to become a fully functioning member of society. Perception, thinking, and social interactions may all be maladaptive as a result of certain inflexible characteristics or traits that are exhibited in a wide range of situations.

Personality disorders are pervasive, persistent, and highly resistant to change. However, the associated behavior causes difficulties for other people rather than anxiety and depression in the disordered person. The disorders are also associated with other problems, such as drug and alcohol addiction, family problems and divorce, and criminality. Hospitalization or institutionalization may be required in certain cases, but not to the extent found in psychotic disorders. Occasionally, however, a personality disorder may be a forerunner of a more serious psychotic illness. Certain personality disorders are also related to disorders of childhood or adolescence: Antisocial personality disorder is related to conduct disorder; avoidant personality disorder, to avoidance disorder of childhood or adolescence; and borderline personality disorder, to identity disorder.

DSM-III-R lists 11 personality disorders—three in Cluster A, four in Cluster B, and four in Cluster C. As shown in Table 12–3, paranoid personality disorder, schizoid personality disorder, and schizotypal personality disorder are grouped in Cluster A, the major symptoms of which are odd or eccentric behavior. Antisocial personality disorder, borderline personality disorder, histrionic personality disorder, and narcissistic personality disorder, all of which involve dramatic, emotional, or erratic behavior, are in Cluster B. Avoidant personality disorder, dependent personality disorder, obsessive-compulsive per-

TABLE 12–3   Personality Disorders

(Specific patterns of behavior described for each disorder are pervasive, are shown in a variety of contexts, and begin in early adulthood.)

Cluster A: Odd or eccentric behavior.
1. *Paranoid personality disorder:* Unwarranted tendency to interpret actions of other people as deliberately demeaning or threatening.
2. *Schizoid personality disorder:* Indifference to social relationships and a restricted range of emotional experience and expression.
3. *Schizotypal personality disorder:* Peculiarities of ideation, appearance, and behavior, and deficits in interpersonal relatedness, but not severe enough to warrant diagnosis of schizophrenia.

Cluster B: Dramatic, emotional, or erratic behavior.
4. *Antisocial personality disorders:* Irresponsible and antisocial behavior; patient must be at least 18 years of age and have a history of conduct disorder before age of 15.
5. *Borderline personality disorder:* Instability of self-image, interpersonal relationships, and mood.
6. *Histrionic personality disorder:* Excessive emotionality and attention-seeking behavior.
7. *Narcissistic personality disorder:* Grandiosity (in fantasy or behavior), hypersensitivity to the evaluation of others, and lack of empathy.

Cluster C: Frequent anxiety and fearfulness.
8. *Avoidant personality disorder:* Social discomfort, fear of negative evaluation, and timidity.
9. *Dependent personality disorder:* Dependent and submissive behavior.
10. *Obsessive-compulsive personality disorder:* Perfectionism and inflexibility.
11. *Passive-aggressive personality disorder:* Passive resistance to demands for adequate social and occupational performance.

Source: Adapted from descriptions in *Diagnostic and Statistical Manual of Mental Disorders* (3rd ed., rev.) by the American Psychiatric Association (1987).

sonality disorder, and passive-aggressive personality disorder are grouped in Cluster C, which is characterized by frequent anxiety and fearfulness.

Paranoid, Schizoid, and Schizotypal Personalities

The first of the disorders in Cluster A, *paranoid personality disorder,* involves suspiciousness, hypersensitivity, mistrustfulness, secretiveness, deviousness, and feelings of persecution. The individual blames other people for his or her problems, is rigid and argumentative, may feel others are plotting against him or her, and in general "makes mountains out of molehills." Charles Clay in the following description is an example of a paranoid personality:

> Charles Clay, aged 45, owned what had been a successful 24-hour-a-day grocery store. . . . Until 5 years ago he had been a cheerful, friendly merchant. Then his wife died, and his personality seemed to undergo a change. Increasingly, he worried that people were trying to shoplift his merchandise. . . . As time went on, he began to confront customers with his suspicions and even to demand that some of them submit to a search.
>
> Mr. Clay's business began to decline. When this happened, he got very angry and even more suspicious. The culminating event was an attempt he made to search a

woman who entered the store, walked around for a few minutes, and then bought a newspaper. When he tried to search her (at the same time yelling, "Don't tell me you were just looking around!"), she ran from the store and summoned the police. The police investigation led Mr. Clay to seek advice from his lawyer, who had been a friend since high school. Although Mr. Clay insisted that "there is nothing the matter with me," his anger and suspiciousness bothered the lawyer. With deft touches of tact and persuasion, the lawyer got Mr. Clay to agree to visit a psychiatrist. Unfortunately, the visit did not work out well. Mr. Clay was reluctant to talk about his concerns and was angered by what he thought of as the psychiatrist's inquisitiveness. . . . Several months later Mr. Clay was arrested and convicted of physically attacking another customer.[5]

The second disorder in Cluster A, *schizoid personality disorder,* consists of aloof, detached, humorless individuals who are unable to establish or are uninterested in establishing social relationships and prefer solitary interests and occupations. They are cold, seclusive loners who may become schizophrenic but usually do not.

The third disorder in Cluster A, *schizotypal personality disorder,* is similar in many respects to schizoid personality. Because of its similarity to full-blown schizophrenia, schizotypal personality disorder has been referred to as ambulatory, borderline, or latent schizophrenia. Schizotypal personalities show pronounced eccentricities of behavior, perception, and thinking, along with a colorless emotionality and an egocentric estrangement from other people. They are sometimes drifters, sometimes cultists, and sometimes seeming innovators who never succeed. They seldom marry or establish a home of their own, but live meaningless, idle, ineffectual lives.

Antisocial Personalities

Formerly known as psychopathic or sociopathic personalities, people with *antisocial personality disorder* are irresponsible, unpredictable, unreliable, aggressive individuals who lie, steal, abuse drugs, and commit vandalism and violence—all with no apparent sense of guilt. It has been said that there is honor among thieves except when the thieves are psychopaths, such as the professor making the following confession:

> I had always wanted lots of things; as a child I can remember wanting a bullet that a friend of mine had brought in to show the class. I took it and put it into my school bag and when my friend noticed it was missing, I was the one who stayed after school with him and searched the room, and I was the one who sat with him and bitched about the other kids and how one of them took his bullet. I even went home with him to help him break the news to his uncle, who had brought it home from the war for him.
>
> But that was petty compared with the stuff I did later. I wanted a Ph.D. very badly, but I didn't want to work very hard—just enough to get by. I never did the experiments I reported; hell, I was smart enough to make up the results. I knew enough about statistics to make anything look plausible. I got my master's degree without even spending one hour in a laboratory. I mean, the professors believed

anything. I'd stay out all night drinking and being with my friends, and the next day I'd get in just before them and tell 'em I'd been in the lab all night. They'd actually feel sorry for me. I did my doctoral research the same way, except it got published and there was some excitement about my findings. The research helped me get my first college teaching job. Then my goal was tenure.

The rules at my university were about the same as at any other. You had to publish and you had to be an effective teacher. "Gathering" data and publishing it was never any problem for me, so that was fine. But teaching was evaluated on the basis of forms completed by students at the end of each semester. I'm a fair-to-good teacher, but I had to be sure that my record showed me as excellent. The task was simple. Each semester, I collected the evaluation forms, took out all the fair-to-bad ones and replaced them with doctored ones. It would take me a whole evening, but I'd sit down with a bunch of different colored pens and pencils and would fill in as many as 300 of the forms. Needless to say, I was awarded tenure. (Duke & Nowicki, 1979, pp. 309–310)

Antisocial personalities tend to be superficially charming, to have good verbal skills (be "good talkers"), and to be average or above average in intelligence. When coupled with an adventurous, thrill-seeking attitude, these traits make them successful manipulators, con men, or swindlers. Certain kinds of swindles practiced by antisocial personalities are so common that they have been christened with special names. Two of these bunco schemes are the "pigeon drop" and the "bank examiner swindle":

The Pigeon Drop. The victim is approached by one of the swindlers and engaged in a conversation on any sympathetic subject. Let's say the victim is an older man. When the swindler has gained his confidence, she mentions a large sum of money found by a second swindler who, at the moment, "happens" to pass by. The victim is led to believe that whoever lost the money probably came by it unlawfully. The swindlers discuss with the victim what to do with the money. One of the swindlers says that she works in the vicinity, and decides to contact her "employer" for advice. She returns in a few minutes and states that her boss has counted the money and verified the amount, and that he agrees that as the money undoubtedly was stolen or belonged to a gambler (or some such variation on a theme), they should keep and divide the money three ways but that each should show evidence of financial responsibility and good faith before collecting a share. The victim is then induced to draw his "good faith" money from his bank. After he has done this, either alone or in the company of one of the swindlers, the money is taken by the swindler to her "employer." Upon the swindler's return, the victim is given the name and address of the employer and told he is waiting with his share of the money. The victim leaves and, of course, cannot find the employer or sometimes even the address. When he returns to where he left the swindlers they, of course, are gone.

The Bank Examiner Swindle. A phony bank or savings and loan "investigator" calls you or comes to your home. He is very serious, and may have brought along deposit slips from your bank and other official-looking papers. He tells you that the bank is checking up on a dishonest employee and explains how you can help. He says he wants to make a test to see what the suspected employee does when a customer draws money out of his account. He suggests that you go to your bank, draw out a specified amount of money, then let him use it for the test. Either he or a "bonded messenger" or some other official will pick up the money at some nearby point. You withdraw the money. Advised of the need for "absolute secrecy" and that the money must be cash "in order to check serial numbers," you ignore the bank teller's concern that you are drawing out such a large sum of cash. You give the money to the "examiner," who hands you a receipt, thanks you for your "cooperation," and may tell you how he plans to use it to trap the suspected employee. Once he is gone, you'll never see him again, or your money. The bank, of course, has never heard of him. (from Aiken, 1989, p. 273)

During the nineteenth century antisocial personalities were labeled "morally insane," because they were viewed as socially troublesome individuals but not legally insane. The crime sprees and ultimately self-defeating life-styles of Billy the Kid, Bonnie and Clyde, and other antisocial personalities have been depicted in many novels and films. Two recent examples are Truman Capote's *In Cold Blood* and Norman Mailer's *The Executioner's Song*.

The typical behavioral pattern in antisocial personality usually begins before age 15, may be punctuated by a series of stints behind bars, and usually becomes more moderate in middle age ("burned out psychopath"). However, not all antisocial personalities come to the attention of the law; they may actually be quite successful as "soldiers of fortune" or other adventuresome types who get away with "living on the edge." Although the causal picture in antisocial personality disorder is not clear, the fact that many of these individuals show poor emotional conditioning and abnormal brain-wave patterns points to a physiological basis for the disorder (Hare, 1970, 1978). Other possible contributing factors include broken homes, parental rejection, a conflict-filled childhood, and a background of poverty.

Other Personality Disorders in Cluster B

Borderline Personality Disorder. Having features of both personality disorders and more serious psychotic illness are *borderline personalities*. These individuals are profoundly unstable in both mood and interpersonal relationships and have a basically negative outlook. They are impulsive, unpredictable (especially where gambling, sex, and drugs are concerned), and unclear regarding their self-identity. Multiple emotions—rage, love, and guilt—may be expressed simultaneously toward the same individuals. There are occasions on which they appear to be out of contact with reality, having extreme emotional outbursts and engaging in self-mutilation.

Histrionic Personality Disorder. The pervasive pattern of behavior in *histrionic personality* is described as overly dramatic, self-centered, and attention-seeking. Like many actors, they are vain individuals with affected speech and manner who hunger for the approval of others. In their immature, shallow, unstable enthusiasm, histrionic personalities never seem to get enough excitement or social acceptance. To these egocentric, dependent individuals the show must go on forever, because the only thing worth living for is the stimulation of public approbation and applause.

Narcissistic Personality Disorder. In myth, the youthful Narcissus fell in love with his own image reflected in a pool, wasted away from unsatisfied desire, and was subsequently transformed into a flower. The primary symptoms of narcissistic personality disorder are similar to those of histrionic personality. They are an excessive need for attention and admiration and an exaggerated sense of self-importance and personal accomplishment. These individuals frequently make grandiose plans and set impossible goals, most of which cannot be realized. Like antisocial personalities, they are interpersonally exploitative and have a defective conscience. They see things only through their own eyes and from their own viewpoint, and they lack any real empathy for other people. Consequently, it is not surprising that their interpersonal relations are frequently strained or disturbed.

Personality Disorders in Cluster C

The four personality disorders in Cluster C are characterized by a pervasive pattern of social discomfort, fear of negative evaluation, and timidity in various contexts (American Psychiatric Association, 1987). Individuals classified in the first category of the cluster, *avoidant personality disorder,* are overly sensitive to potential rejection, derogation, or humiliation. They are reluctant to enter into an interpersonal relationship unless unconditional acceptance is guaranteed, and they refuse to play games unless assured of success. They are fearful of criticism and embarrassment, and tend to see ridicule when it is unintended.

Persons in the second category of Cluster C—*dependent personality disorder*—are noted for assuming a passive-submissive orientation. Lacking confidence in their ability to function independently, they let other people assume responsibility and make the major decisions affecting their lives. In short, they are helpless, clinging, ingenuous individuals who dislike being alone or in other circumstances in which they must take control of their own lives.

Persons in the third category of Cluster C, *obsessive-compulsive personality disorder,* are described as perfectionistic, excessively conforming, obstinate, overconscientious, overdutiful, and rigid. They are efficient, orderly individuals who are preoccupied with trivial details, concerned with rules, and have a high capacity for work. They always want things their own way, and are impatient and intolerant with sloppiness, laziness, or inefficiency. Like the other personalities in Cluster C, they have difficulty getting along with people.

Individuals in the fourth category of Cluster C, *passive-aggressive personality disorder,* attempt to cope with what they perceive as unreasonable demands and expectations on the part of other people by passively resisting those demands with procrastination, criticalness, stubbornness, intentional inefficiency, and "forgetfulness." They are sulky, grumbling, unaccommodating, faultfinders who react with hostile negativism rather than overt aggression when frustrated.

Other Personality Disorders

In addition to the 11 disorders already described, two other personality disorders—self-defeating personality disorder and sadistic personality disorder—have been proposed. These diagnoses, which are described in Appendix A or DSM-III-R, are, however, quite controversial. They have been criticized in particular by women's rights organizations, which view them as misleading categories that provide a psychiatric rationalization for the abuse of women by men.

Self-defeating personalities avoid pleasurable experiences and show an inclination toward becoming involved in relationships in which they suffer. Although they possess the ability to succeed, these persons fail to attain their own personal objectives or goals. On the other hand, individuals who are diagnosed as having *sadistic personality disorder* show a pervasive pattern of cruelty, aggression, and demeaning behavior toward others. They are typically fascinated with violence, including its techniques and weapons.

With respect to the causes of personality disorders in general, it has been suggested that constitutional or hereditary variables may act as predisposing factors in the development of specific conditions. It should also be noted that the personality disorders are typically secondary diagnoses, and that a given patient may be assigned to more than one diagnostic (personality disorder) category. Furthermore, the utility of the 11–13 personality disorders described in DSM-III-R has been questioned, and these categories will undoubtedly be extensively revised in the forthcoming DSM-IV.

Summary

To a great extent, normality and abnormality are statistical concepts that depend on the frequency of certain kinds of behavior in a society as well as the extent to which members of that society are willing to tolerate certain behaviors, thoughts, and feelings. In addition, distinction is made between *mental disorder,* which is a psychiatric concept, and *insanity,* which is a legal concept. Statistics on admissions to U.S. mental hospitals over the past century indicate that the number has increased as the population has grown, but the relative percentages of various kinds of disorders have not changed appreciably in young and middle-aged Americans.

Admission and retention of patients by mental hospitals depend on the specific symptoms and diagnoses. Psychodiagnosis consists of an analysis of psychological and physical symptoms to classify and label an individual as belonging to a particular psychiatric category. The most widely used classification system for mental disorders in the United States is described in the *Diagnostic and Statistical Manual of Mental Disorders, Third Edition–Revised (DSM-III-R).* DSM-III-R is recognized as an improvement over its predecessors, but the shortcomings and dangers of any sort of psychopathological labeling and the subjectivity of the diagnostic process are sources of continuing controversy.

Anxiety and depression are characteristic symptoms of mental disturbances, but pervasive hostility, hallucinations, delusions, and other indicators of disordered thinking and behavior may occur. Anxiety is caused by a threat to a person's self-esteem, which may result from unresolved frustration and conflict. According to psychodynamic theories of personality, defense mechanisms serve to protect and defend the individual from anxiety. These mechanisms include rationalization, denial, fantasy, displaced aggression, projection, compensation, sublimation, and reaction formation. When used in moderation, many of these mechanisms enable the individual to cope with the stresses of living. When used to excess, however, they become symptomatic of major mental disorder.

Neuroses are moderate to severe mental disorders in which the individual does not lose contact with reality but in which the efficiency of personal functioning is demonstrably impaired as a result of anxiety and other symptoms stemming from unresolved problems. Neuroses are the results of learning faulty habits and attitudes, and are characterized by rigidity of personality, feelings of inferiority and self-doubt, general unhappiness, and dissatisfaction. The major categories of neuroses described in DSM-III-R are anxiety disorders (phobias, obsessive-compulsive neuroses, posttraumatic stress disorder, and generalized anxiety disorder), somatoform disorders (conversion or hysterical neurosis, hypochondriasis, and somatization disorder), and dissociative disorders (psychogenic amnesia, psychogenic fugue, depersonalization disorder, and multiple personality).

The most severe mental disorders are the psychoses, which involve distortions of reality, mental deterioration, and disturbed emotions. Approximately 50 percent of the cases diagnosed as psychotic disorders are classified in DSM-III-R under organic mental disorders. The majority of the remainder, for which there is no known organic basis, are grouped under the categories of schizophrenia, delusional (paranoid) disorder, and mood disorder (bipolar disorder, depressive disorder).

Several other categories of mental disorders—for example, sexual disorders, sleep disorders, factitious disorders, adjustment disorder, and certain "disorders usually first evident in infancy, childhood, or adolescence"—are classified on Axis I of DSM-III-R. The last of these categories contains a number of disorders that occur in childhood, including disruptive behavior disorders such as hyperactivity and conduct disorder. Several chronic developmental disorders, such as pervasive developmental disorder (e.g., autism), are classified on Axis II of DSM-III-R.

Also classified on Axis II are personality disorders, which are pervasive, persistent, maladaptive patterns of behavior that are highly resistant to change. These disorders are grouped into three clusters. The disorders in Cluster A, which include paranoid, schizoid, and schizotypal personality disorders, are characterized by odd or eccentric behavior. The disorders in Cluster B are characterized by dramatic, emotional, or erratic behavior; they include antisocial, borderline, histrionic, and narcissistic personality disorders. In Cluster C, which includes disorders marked by frequent anxiety and fearfulness, are grouped avoidant, dependent, obsessive-compulsive, and passive-aggressive personality disorders. Two additional, but controversial, personality disorders are described in an appendix of DSM-III-R: self-defeating personality disorder and sadistic personality disorder.

Key Concepts

Antisocial personality   Formerly called *psychopathic personality,* a disorder of personality characterized by inadequate development of moral and ethical restraints. Such a person is extremely self-centered, acts in a hostile, hurtful way without feeling guilty, has difficulty forming close relationships, behaves in a manipulative, dishonest fashion, and is seemingly unable to profit from punitive experiences.

Anxiety disorder   Chronic feelings of apprehension or uneasiness. This diagnostic label includes generalized anxiety disorder, panic disorder, obsessive-compulsive disorder, posttraumatic stress disorder, and phobic disorder.

Bipolar disorder   An affective disorder in which an individual's mood fluctuates between euphoric mania and depression. During the mania phase the patient is excessively agitated and excitable; this mood alternates with depression.

Delusion   A false belief that is resistant to reason or reality, e.g., a delusion of persecution or grandeur.

Depression   Mood disorder characterized by dejection, loss of interest in things, negative thoughts (including suicidal thoughts), and various physical symptoms (e.g., loss of appetite, insomnia, fatigue).

Dissociation   Separation of a cluster of mental processes from the main body of consciousness, as in amnesia, fugue, somnambulism, hysteria, and multiple personality.

Insanity   Legal term for mental disorder in which a person cannot tell the difference between right and wrong (McNaghten Rule) or cannot control his actions and manage his life. Insanity is not equivalent to *incompetency,* a legal decision that a person is suffering from a mental disorder that causes a defect of judgment such that the person is unable to manage his or her own property, enter into contracts, and take care of other affairs.

Multiple personality   Dissociative disorder in which two or more personalities exist within the same individual.

Narcissistic personality   A person having an exaggerated sense of self-importance, often combined with self-doubt.

Neurosis (psychoneurosis)   Nonpsychotic mental disorder characterized by anxiety, obsessions, compulsions, phobias, or bodily complaints or dysfunctions having no demonstrable physical cause.

Obsessive-compulsive disorder   A neurotic disorder of which obsessions (recurring thoughts or ideas) and compulsions (uncontrollable acts) are symptomatic.

Paranoid personality   Personality disorder characterized by projection, suspiciousness, extreme jealousy or envy, and stubbornness. Paranoid personality is not the same as *paranoid schizophrenia,* which is a psychotic disorder characterized by paranoid delusions (of grandeur, persecution, etc.), illogical thinking, and unpredictable behavior.

Passive-aggressive personality   Personality disorder in which aggressive feelings are characteristically expressed in a passive manner (by pouting, stubbornness, refusal to cooperate, etc.).

Phobic disorder   A mental disorder in which the individual is unreasonably afraid of some situation or object that typically poses no actual threat, as in *agoraphobia* or *claustrophobia*.

Psychosis   Severe mental disorder characterized by faulty perception of reality, deficits of language and memory, disturbances in the emotional sphere, and other bizarre symptoms.

Schizophrenic disorders   Psychoses characterized by withdrawal from reality and disturbances of thinking, emotion, and behavior; a breakdown of integrated personality functioning.

Schizotypal personality   Personality pattern similar to but less intense than schizophrenia. Characterized by shyness, eccentricity, oversensitivity, and seclusiveness.

Activities and Applications

1. What are the advantages and disadvantages of viewing abnormal behaviors as diseases, as in the medical model of mental illness? Do you believe that Thomas Szasz (1966, 1987) is correct in asserting that mental illness is a myth perpetuated by the diagnostic system and the procedures followed by psychiatrists and psychologists? Why or why not?

2. Many famous artists or writers, such as Vincent van Gogh, Lord Byron, Edvard Munch, and Anne Sexton suffered from personality problems of one kind or another. Certain film stars (e.g., Marilyn Monroe, Freddie Prinze), rock stars (e.g., Janis Joplin), and famous athletes have also had serious psychological problems. Can you think of other examples? What problems did they have and how did they deal with them?

3. Some "normal" college students, and even certain professional psychologists, seem to admire many of the characteristics possessed by antisocial personalities. Why should they admire such traits? What could possibly be desirable or attractive about an antisocial personality?

4. How would you classify serial murderers—as antisocial personalities, paranoid personalities, sex deviates, or in some other diagnostic category? On the basis of what criteria would you make your diagnosis?

5. What do you consider the relative roles of heredity and environment in determining each of the mental disorders described in this chapter? Support your conclusions by citing specific research studies if possible. Also, if and when it becomes possible to identify individuals who have an inherited predisposition to schizophrenia, bipolar disorder, or other mental disorders, should these individuals be told? Should they receive genetic counseling?

6. Construct a checklist of symptoms for each of the conditions described in the section of personality disorders in this chapter. Consult DSM-III-R or a textbook on abnormal psychology (e.g., Carson, Butcher, & Coleman, 1992; Willerman & Cohen, 1990) for more complete descriptions.

   7. What are the pros and cons of psychodiagnosis, that is, classifying and assigning a label or labels to people having specific psychological problems? Consider DSM-III-R as an illustration, as well as criticisms of it (see Vaillant, 1984; Millon & Klerman, 1986).

   8. Make arrangements with one of your psychology professors (or some other influential person!) to visit a mental hospital in your vicinity. Write a paper on your experiences and impressions during the visit.

Suggested Readings

Cleckley, H. (1976). *The mask of sanity* (5th ed., reprint). Augusta, GA: E. S. Cleckley.

Costa, P. T., Jr., & McCrae, R. R. (1985). In C. Malatesta & C. Izard (Eds.), *Affective processes in adult development and aging.* New York: Sage.

Henker, B., & Whalen, C. R. (1989). Hyperactivity and attention deficits. *American Psychologist, 44,* 216–223.

Millon, T. (1990). The disorders of personality. In L. A. Pervin (Ed.), *Handbook of personality theory and research* (pp. 339–370). New York: Guilford Press.

Oldham, J. (Ed.). (1991). *Personality disorders: New perspectives diagnostic validity.* Washington, DC: American Psychiatric Association.

Rosenzweig, S. (1988). The identity and idiodynamics of the multiple personality "Sally Beauchamp." *American Psychologist, 43,* 45–48.

Schreiber, F. R. (1973). *Sybil.* Chicago: Regency.

Szasz, T. S. (1987). *Insanity: The idea and its consequences.* New York: Wiley.

Turkat, I. D. (1990). *The personality disorders: A psychological approach to clinical management.* New York: Pergamon Press.

Notes

1 "Richard Cory" is reproduced with the permission of Charles Scribner's Sons from *The Children of the Night* (1897, p. 35) by Edwin Arlington Robinson.

2 Much of this material has been introduced in the previous chapters of psychodynamic and social learning theories. It is elaborated on and extended here to emphasize its importance as a foundation for understanding abnormal behavior and mental disorders.

3 The term "neurosis" is not a category in the current official diagnostic system of the American Psychiatric Association (DSM-III-R), but it continues to be part of the nomenclature of psychopathology.

4 It may appear that a disproportionate amount of attention has been given in this text to personality disorders. The author's justification is that this is a book on *personality*, and hence it should provide a fairly thorough treatment of the behavioral symptoms and classification of "abnormal" personalities as well as a description and explanation of "normal" personality.

5 Irwin G. Sarason and Barbara R. Sarason, *Abnormal Psychology: The Problem of Maladaptive Behavior* (4th ed.), © 1984. Reprinted by permission of Prentice Hall, Englewood Cliffs, NJ.

CHAPTER 13

Psychological Treatment and Behavioral Change

CHAPTER OUTLINE

Psychotherapy, the "talking cure" as it is sometimes called, has been practiced since the first primitive man or woman confided a personal problem to a friend or relative. Psychotherapy of a sort has also been practiced since time immemorial by priests with their parishioners, by lawyers with their clients, by teachers with the students, and in all walks of life by counselors with their counselees. Not until the late nineteenth century, however, was psychotherapy recognized by physicians as a useful method for treating mental disorders.

Counseling versus Psychotherapy

The distinction between *counseling* and *psychotherapy* is not clear-cut, and the terms are often used interchangeably. Both involve discussing one's problems with a professionally trained person, but in counseling these discussions are usually of shorter duration. Counseling techniques also tend to be more superficial than psychotherapy, and the goals more limited. The discussions that take place in counseling and psychotherapy are encouraged by the development of a positive interpersonal relationship between the counselor (therapist) and counselee (client, patient). These discussions hopefully provide a psychological climate in which the counselee, client, or patient can examine his or her psychological problems and explore possible solutions to them. Psychotherapy is best viewed as a kind of emotional reeducation of the client. Although the specific activities of the therapist that stimulate the client's emotional growth and reeducation vary with the persons and the situation, all varieties of psychotherapy are similar in certain respects.

Common to all systems of psychotherapy is *catharsis,* the release of emotion and tension by reliving unpleasant past experiences. By "talking through" his or her problems, the patient or client reexperiences much of the emotion associated with the original situation. But the difference between the original and the therapeutic situations is that in the latter the accepting and noncritical attitude of the therapist enables the client to tolerate the unpleasant memory and "drain off" some of the emotion associated with it. Another important characteristic of psychotherapy is the degree of rapport that exists between client and therapist. *Rapport* is a special kind of relationship, not quite the same as friendship or love, but rather a trusting, confident, helping relationship that enables the client to move toward emotional maturity.

It is true that catharsis and rapport are important fundamentals in a psychotherapeutic relationship, but they are not sufficient to produce the emotional growth and other personal changes that are the goals of successful psychotherapy. Additional therapeutic techniques, depending on the age of the client, the severity of his or her psychological problem, and the time and resources he or she is willing to invest, are employed. In a number of cases, simply modifying some aspect of the client's environment or providing emotional support may be all that can or should be done. For example, changing the environment is often indicated for children with behavioral disorders, whereas supporting and strengthening defense mechanisms is often advisable in treating older adults.

Serious mental health problems, such as severe anxiety and depressive reactions, may require in-depth personal counseling or psychotherapy. On the other hand, patients with debilitating physical problems, which are aggravated by emotional reactions, may require only supportive measures. Included in supportive counseling are techniques such as sensitive listening and reassurance, in addition to efforts to motivate the person, elevate his or her spirits, and reinforce the will to recover, "regroup," and go on. These approaches are especially necessary when the person receives little or no emotional support from family and friends.

Counseling and psychotherapy are also needed by people residing in hospitals, nursing homes, and penal institutions, as well as in educational and employment situations. Personal counseling and other psychological interventions can assist in the redevelopment of feelings of worth and independence to sustain patients in an institution and help them cope with life outside. Another type of counseling, avocational counseling, can be combined with retraining to assist persons in handling feelings of resentment and apathy accompanying unemployment and retirement.

Psychotherapists and counselors may be psychiatrists, psychologists, clergymen (pastoral counselors), social workers, and certain other "helpers." In some states and countries, however, almost anyone can call himself a psychotherapist or counselor and "treat" people for a fee. Because of the danger of psychological quackery, people who need psychological treatment should be aware of the credentials of the person to whom they are referred. A list of competent professional psychotherapists can usually be obtained from a family physician, clergyman, or public mental health agency. In addition, mental health organizations in most cities publish directories of professionals who are qualified to offer psychological assistance.

Psychodynamic Therapies

From the classical psychoanalytic viewpoint, the basic goal of psychotherapy is to bring into conscious awareness repressed impulses and conflicts that are causing anxiety. One of the goals of psychotherapy as practiced by psychoanalysts and other psychodynamic therapists is for the client to achieve insight, or in-depth understanding, into the causes of the disorder. The major techniques of psychoanalytic therapy, as developed by Sigmund Freud and his followers, are free association, the analysis of transference, the analysis of resistance, and dream analysis. These techniques were referred to in Chapters 5 and 6, but we shall discuss them in more detail here.

Methods of Psychoanalytic Therapy

Free Association. The most basic technique used by psychoanalytic therapists is *free association,* in which the patient (or analysand) is encouraged to express, without hesitation or equivocation, whatever thoughts are feelings come into his or her mind. In his early work, Freud used hypnosis to get at the unconscious motives and urges of a patient, but this technique was soon abandoned in favor of the method of free association. The assumption behind the use of free association is that by saying whatever comes to mind, the patient will eventually say something that has significance for the problem or disorder that confronts him or her—material which had previously been unconscious. Most of the time in psychoanalysis is spent in free association, that is, getting significant repressed material into consciousness where it can be understood and dealt with.

Analysis of Transference. To Freud, the patient's attitudes toward the analyst were an important part of treatment. Freud observed that patients often behave toward therapists as they behaved in the past toward significant persons in their lives. During the early stages of therapy this *transference* is usually positive; that is, the patient has a positive emotional reaction to the analyst. As therapy proceeds, however, the transference may become negative, in which case the patient develops unfriendly feelings toward the analyst. A *countertransference,* in which the analyst has strong feelings toward the patient, may also occur during the course of therapy and interfere with its progress. One purpose of a training analysis, in which the would-be psychoanalyst is psychoanalyzed, is to make the fledgling analyst more aware of potential sources of countertransference and force him or her to deal with these problems before attempting to psychoanalyze patients.

Interpretation of the transference relationship by the analyst enables patients to gain insight into their behavior and feelings toward people who are, or were, important influences in creating the particular problem that caused the patient to seek psychoanalytic treatment. Analysis of transference is viewed as the key to discovering patients' childhood relationships with their parents and the sources of the problems being experienced by the adult patients.

Analysis of Resistance. As therapy progresses, the patient will often use various techniques to keep the therapist from discovering unconscious material. These techniques are known as *resistances,* examples of which are refusing to talk about certain subjects, being late for a therapy appointment, and even bringing presents to the therapists. As described by Meissner (1980), resistance is shown when

> the patient pauses abruptly, corrects himself, makes a slip of the tongue, stammers, remains silent, fidgets with some part of his clothing, asks irrelevant questions, intellectualizes, arrives late for appointments, finds excuses for not keeping them, offers critical evaluations of the rationale underlying the treatment method, simply cannot think of anything to say, or censors thoughts that do occur to him and decides that they are banal, uninteresting, or irrelevant and not worth mentioning. (p. 722)

Again, as in the case of transference, analyzing these resistances helps both the therapist and the patient understand more about the problem.

Dream Analysis. Freud held that dreams are "the royal road to the unconscious" because they express, in disguised form, the basic fears, desires, and conflicts felt by a person. By interpreting the manifest content—the content of the dream as it appears to the dreamer—the analyst and patient are able to understand the latent content, that is, what the dream actually means. Having their dreams interpreted for them, or interpreting the dreams themselves, is another method by which patients gain insights into their conflicts, personality dynamics, and behavior. Understanding the meaning of dreams is facilitated by having the patient free-associate to the manifest content and indicate what it suggests or might connote.

Progress in psychoanalytic therapy occurs as the patient begins to examine and reexamine his or her conflicts, and as a result comes to understand them. This process consists of reexperiencing and working through painful emotions, particularly those experienced initially in childhood. With the support of the analyst, the patient learns to confront or face the anxiety and other negative emotions associated with conflicts and problems. Eventually the patient comes to discover and comprehend the underlying causes of his or her behavior and learns how to deal with them more effectively and realistically. An example of a fairly brief and successful psychoanalytic treatment is give in Report 13–1.

Other Psychodynamic Therapies

Many variations of classical psychoanalysis have been developed, among which are Jungian psychotherapy, Adlerian therapy, Sullivan's interpersonal therapy, and Berne's transactional analysis. Jungian therapy is somewhat difficult to define because Jung did not delineate a clear-cut set of procedures of the sort followed by Freud. In Jungian therapy the therapist is more active and self-disclosing than in Freudian psychoanalysis. Jungian analysts engage in a dialogue, or dialectical procedure, with the patient. Confession, which is somewhat like Freud's free association, occurs during the early stages of Jungian therapy. The patient's dreams are also interpreted, but no distinction is made between the manifest and latent content, and the analyst concentrates on a series of dreams rather than a single dream. The aim of the Jungian psychotherapist is to help the patient achieve self-understanding, an achievement that is facilitated by an active imagination.

Like Jungian therapy, Adlerian therapy is somewhat eclectic. The particular procedures that are followed are adapted to the patient's personality and problems. Adlerian therapy begins with efforts on the part of the therapist to establish contact with the patient and to win his or her confidence. Next, the therapist analyzes the patient's style of life and tries to point out the errors in that way of living. The patient is encouraged to act as if the old limiting fictions of his or her life-style are false and to have the courage to change them. In a very real sense the Adlerian therapist is a teacher who tries to reeducate the patient in the art of living constructively. The patient learns to deal with feelings of resentment

REPORT 13–1

Example of a Psychodynamically Oriented Treatment Case

A college-educated woman in her late 20s complained of extreme passivity, interpersonal alienation, and obsessive thoughts of wanting to harm her young children. Therapy made slow progress and the cause of these feelings remained mysterious until her mother happened to give away a childhood violin. She then became very angry, revealing that the violin had been a gift from the father just before he died. Following this, she now remembered with photographic precision and intense emotion her father's lingering illness and death, facts she had previously insisted could not be recalled.

Between that therapy session and the next, she vented considerable anger at her husband and reported the absence of hostile feelings toward her children. She then came to see her therapist in a more realistic light, now citing numerous therapeutic errors he had made. This was important because she seemed to have idolized her therapist earlier, an indication of her transference misperceptions.

Discussing her father's death revealed deep feelings of loss and resentment about his illness and its disruption of her life. When he died, she felt that her hostile fantasies were responsible, with the consequence that all her expressions of anger brought on feelings of guilt and a sense of imminent danger. By examining the original feelings from a more mature perspective, she was able to become appropriately assertive in current interpersonal relationships without apprehension.

Source: From Willerman, L., and Cohen, D.B. (1990). *Psycopathology* (pp. 607–608). New York: McGraw-Hill. Reprinted with permission.

and rejection and replace them with a positive attitude and an interest in other people (social interest). In successful Adlerian therapy the patient learns that a genuine feeling of superiority can be attained only by subordinating his or her personal interests to the welfare of others.

As noted previously, modifications in the theory and practice of psychoanalysis by Freud's colleagues and followers took place even during his lifetime. Neoanalysts such as Horney, Fromm, and Sullivan followed Adler to some extent in their emphasis on social factors in personality development and change. In addition, many of these post-Freudians advocated reducing the dominating position of the analyst and focusing instead on the establishment of a cooperative relationship between patient and therapist. More recent variants of psychoanalytic therapy include setting upper limits to the number of sessions (usually 25), psychoanalytic group therapy, and the use of medication in conjunction with psychotherapy (Luborsky, 1988).

Transactional Analysis

Particularly influential among the various psychoanalytically oriented therapies is *transactional analysis*. As described by Eric Berne (1964), transactional analysis conceives of human personality as being composed of three ego states—adult, parent, and child. These three states are similar to the ego, superego, and id of classical psychoanalysis, but unlike the psychoanalytic emphasis on the unconscious, transactional analysis focuses on conscious, observable behavior. Similar to the Freudian notion of psychic conflict, the interactions, or *transactions,* among these three ego states lead to maladaptive personality development or emotional problems.

The following goals of transactional analysis, which takes place in a group setting, were described by Berne (1966):

1 To help the client decontaminate any damaged ego state.
2 To develop in the client the capacity to use all ego states where appropriate.
3 To assist the client in developing the full use of his or her adult state.
4 To help the client rid himself or herself of an inappropriately chosen life position and life script, replacing them with an "I'm OK" position and a new, productive life script.

To accomplish these goals, the counselor tries to understand the intent of the client's communications and to help the client become aware of the structures of his or her ego states ("structural analysis"), the transactions in which the client usually engages ("transactional analysis"), the payoffs that a client receives for playing certain games ("games analysis"), and the fact that the client's whole life script has been a mistake ("script analysis"). As described in *Games People Play* (Berne, 1964), in their social interactions people often play destructive games marked by subterfuge and deceit. Examples of these games, which are usually deadly serious and highly destructive, are "Why Don't You—Yes But" (WDYYB), "Wooden Leg," and "Now I've Got You, You Son of a Bitch" (NIGYYSOB).

Phenomenological Therapies

Among the many ways in which the practice of psychotherapy varies with the practitioner is the degree of direction provided by the therapist. A generally "directive" type of psychotherapy is one in which the therapist asks direct questions, provides information and advice, and offers interpretations of the patient's symptoms and problems. In contrast, generally, "nondirective" techniques such as those emphasized by *client-centered therapy* involve a minimum of questioning, advising, and interpreting.

According to Carl Rogers, Abraham Maslow, and other phenomenological or humanistic theories, people have an inherent capacity to grow and change in the direction of self-actualization, that is, toward becoming more fully functioning persons. Phenomenological therapists emphasize the importance of the client's experiences, and they view psychotherapy as a process of examining and either confirming or disconfirming the validity of interpretations of those experiences. The development of experiential understanding and self-awareness leads to self-acceptance, self-reliance, and greater interpersonal effectiveness. By accepting the principle that people are basically good and worthy of respect, the phenomenological therapist is able to help the client identify his or her creative potential—the power to be—and to realize that potential through changes in attitudes, perceptions, and behavior.

Rogers' Client-Centered Therapy

Carl Rogers (1951, 1966) and certain other psychologists who were greatly influenced by phenomenological and existential philosophers emphasized an ahistorical, "here-and-now" (as opposed to "there-and-then") approach to counseling. Counselors subscribing to this point of view engage in a minimum of questioning, advising and interpreting. Rogers' client-centered counseling, for example, is based on the premise that people are free to control their own behavior and hence should assume responsibility for solving their own problems. The counselor acts as a facilitator, simply accepting what the client says, reflecting and clarifying the feeling tone in the client's statements, or restating the implicit and explicit cognitive (i.e., intellectual) content of the client's statements. By providing an open, accepting, empathic, nonjudgmental atmosphere ("unconditional positive regard") in which clients can examine their own experiences freely and be themselves, the counselor encourages clients to use their own resources to solve personal problems and change their attitudes and behavior. It is made clear that, although the therapist will encourage and guide the therapeutic process to some extent, the major responsibility for solving the client's personal problems rest squarely on the shoulders of the client.

Rogers emphasized that people have the ability to grow and fulfill their potentialities—that is, to "become" themselves in the right kind of social atmosphere. In successful counseling, clients initially express rather low, predominantly negative self-evaluations. But these evaluations become more positive as the counseling process proceeds and the client begins to feel more hopeful. In general, the frequency of reiterating problems or symptoms by the client decreases, and the frequency of insightful or understanding statements by the client increases, over successive therapy sessions (Seeman, 1949). As with any type of therapy, there is no guarantee of success with client-centered counseling, especially when the counselee is highly dependent or has a severe emotional disorder. The client-centered approach tends to be more effective with mildly maladjusted but fairly self-sufficient people. An excerpt from a client-centered therapy session is given in Report 13–2.

Other Phenomenological Therapies

Two other pioneers in the humanistic movement—Abraham Maslow and Rollo May—devised their own systems of psychotherapy. Maslow's (1970) approach

REPORT 13–2

Excerpt from Client-Centered Therapy with a Depressed Young Woman

Client: . . . I cannot be the kind of person I want to be. I guess maybe I haven't the guts or the strength to kill myself and if someone else would relieve me of the responsibility or I would be in an accident, I, I . . . just don't want to live.

Therapist: At the present time things look so black that you can't see much point in living. (Note the use of empathic reflection and the absence of any criticism.)

Client: Yes. I wish I'd never started this therapy. I was happy when I was living in my dream world. Then I could be the kind of person I wanted to be. But now there is such a wide, wide gap between my ideal and what I am. . . . (Notice how the client responds to reflection by giving more information.)

Therapist: It's really a tough struggle digging into this like you are and at times the shelter of your dream world looks more attractive and comfortable. (Reflection)

Client: My dream world or suicide. . . . So I don't see why I should waste your time— coming in twice a week—I'm not worth it—What do you think?

Therapist: It's up to you. . . . It isn't wasting my time. I'd be glad to see you whenever you come but it's how you feel about it. . . . (Note the congruence in stating an honest desire to see the client and the unconditional positive regard in trusting her capacity and responsibility for choice.)

Client: You're not going to suggest that I come in oftener? You're not alarmed and think I ought to come in every day until I get out of this?

Therapist: I believe you are able to make your own decision. I'll see you whenever you want to come. (Positive regard)

Client: (Note of awe in her voice) I don't believe you are alarmed about—I see—I may be afraid of myself but you aren't afraid for me. (She experiences the therapist's confidence in her.)

Therapist: You say you may be afraid of yourself and are wondering why I don't seem to be afraid for you? (Reflection)

Client: You have more confidence in me than I have. I'll see you next week . . . maybe.

Source: From Rogers, Carl R. *Client-Centered Therapy* (p. 49). Copyright © 1951 by Houghton Mifflin Company. Used with permission.

stemmed from his conception of a hierarchy of needs, and, like Rogers, he emphasized that people have a natural tendency to grow and become self-actualized. Effective psychotherapy in the Maslovian framework capitalizes on that tendency.

Rollo May's therapeutic system also follows Rogers to a large extent. May saw the purpose of therapy as one of expanding the consciousness of the client so he or she could be free to make wiser choices. It is fine when psychotherapy results in a diminution of maladaptive behavior or symptoms, but from May's perspective the main purpose of therapy is not symptom eradication but rather helping people to experience their existence. The interaction between therapist and client is an "I-thou" encounter that carries risks of anxiety, guilt, and despair. However, the therapist must be willing to risk the potentially negative outcomes of that encounter if therapy is to be effective.

Gestalt therapy, as pioneered by Fritz Perls (1967, 1970), is also a phenomenological approach that emphasizes the here-and-now rather than the there-and-then of experience. The gestalt therapist employs a variety of techniques to integrate the feelings, thoughts, and behavior of the client into a harmonious whole, or *gestalt.* Participants in gestalt therapy sessions, which are conducted in a group setting, examine their previous (especially childhood) experiences carefully and often try to act out or role-play those earlier experiences that are related to their current problems and conflicts. Participants are encouraged to try to understand the emotions that are affecting them and to assume personal responsibility for their behavior.

A number of variations and extensions on Rogers' client-centered psychotherapy have also been devised. A noteworthy example is Carkhuff's (1969) model, which is based on three counseling goals: self-exploration, self-understanding, and action. The counselor uses six conditions—empathy, respect, concreteness, genuineness, confrontation, and immediacy—to assist the client in attaining these goals. The first four conditions are most important during the initial or facilitation stage of counseling. This stage has as its primary objective the establishment of a working relationship such that the client will feel free to begin self-exploration, which will hopefully lead to self-understanding. During the second, or action, stage of counseling, the last two conditions—confronting the client with discrepancies and getting the client to focus on the immediate situation in counseling—are most important.

Behavioral and Cognitive Therapies

For many years almost all psychotherapists subscribed to the following beliefs of psychoanalytic depth therapists:

1 Simply removing symptoms rather than treating root causes does not produce permanent cures.
2 Causes, and hence "cures," can only be found by studying the patient's life history in detail.
3 A transference relationship between patient and therapist must develop if therapy is to be successful.
4 The patient can be cured only by gaining insight into his or her problems and personality.

Although these beliefs are not held as tenaciously by phenomenological counselors, the latter still subscribe to the notion that clients must achieve some degree of self-understanding, or "in-sight," in order to solve their emotional problems. Since the 1950s, however, an increasing number of psychotherapists and counselors, particularly clinical psychologists who have been trained in learning theory, have questioned whether these beliefs are correct. Even some psychoanalysts have expressed doubts concerning the necessity of treating root causes, studying the patient's life history, developing a strong transference relationship, and attaining insight (see Ellis, 1962).

Behavioral Therapy

Behavior theorists maintain that because many adjustment problems are the consequences of faulty learning, it should be possible to arrange conditions so that inappropriate behavior is unlearned. Behavioral approaches to psychological treatment, referred to as *behavior therapy* or *behavior modification*, are based on principles of learning and motivation (e.g., operant and respondent conditioning, stimulus discrimination, response differentiation, generalization, extinction, etc.) formulated from the results of laboratory experiments on animals and humans. The procedures of behavior modification based on these principles are designed to change maladaptive behaviors to more personally and socially accepted behaviors.

Behavior therapists attempt to develop intervention or modification programs for maladaptive behaviors by identifying the antecedents and consequences of the behavior. A basic tenet of behavior modification is that behavior is controlled by its consequences. Therefore, to design a program for correcting problem behavior one must identify the reinforcing consequences that sustain the behavior, in addition to the conditions that trigger it. The process of behavior modification is preceded by a functional analysis of the problem behavior, consisting of a sequence of (1) the *antecedent conditions*, (2) the *problem behavior*, and (3) the *consequences* of the behavior. The therapy itself consists of modifying the problem behavior by controlling for the antecedent conditions and changing the consequences of the behavior. The antecedents and consequences of the target behavior may be either overt, objectively observable conditions or covert mental events reported by the person whose behavior is to be modified.

Research and practice have shown that maladaptive behaviors, which may consist of excesses, deficits, or other inadequacies of action, can be modified through specialized techniques such as differential reinforcement, systematic desensitization, counterconditioning, and extinction. To assess the effectiveness of these techniques in modifying the target behavior, a *baseline* (operant) level of the frequency or intensity of the behavior is first determined. The baseline response level may then be compared with the frequency or intensity of the behavior after the particular behavior modification procedure has been applied to determine whether the frequency of the maladaptive or inappropriate behavior has declined and the frequency of more socially appropriate behavior has increased.

Among the maladaptive behaviors that have received special attention by behavior modifiers are specific fears (or phobias), smoking, overeating, alcoholism, drug addiction, underassertiveness, bed-wetting, chronic tension and pain, and sexual inadequacies of various kinds. Whatever the *target behaviors* or responses may be, they should be defined precisely and occur with sufficient frequency to be recordable and modifiable.

Contingency Management. A behavior modification approach that has been fairly successful with patients or inmates in institutions is *contingency management.* This approach makes positive reinforcement (pleasures or privileges of various kinds) contingent on socially approved behavior (keeping neat and clean, eating properly, interacting with other patients, etc.). As with all behavior modification procedures, the ultimate goal of contingency management is for patients to learn to monitor and control their own behavior.

Systematic Desensitization. A number of behavioral techniques have been devised for dealing with anxiety, which is considered to be at the core of many emotional disorders. In the technique of *systematic desensitization* the patient is exposed to an anxiety-arousing, or phobic, situation under contrived, "safe" conditions. Other, more normal responses can be conditioned to the situation by controlling anxiety responses. For example, the therapist may encourage and teach the patient to become progressively more relaxed, after which increasingly more fearful stimuli are presented. The therapist begins with stimuli that normally produce a weak fear response and then presents more frightening stimuli while the patient is relaxed. An illustration of a desensitization hierarchy of increasingly anxiety-provoking stimuli used with a patient who had a fear of flying is given in Table 13–1. The desensitization procedure began with item 1 in the hierarchy and worked up gradually to item 15 while the patient concentrated on relaxing. Besides relaxation, assertive behavior, sexual behavior, and eating responses have also been used to control anxiety.

Self-monitoring. An effective behavior technique for modifying compulsive behaviors such as smoking is self-observation or *self-monitoring.* Patients are instructed to carry materials such as a notepad, a diary, a wrist counter, and a timer with them at all times to keep a record of occurrences of the target behavior and the time, place, and circumstances in which it occurred. The recorded information is then reported and discussed with the therapist at the next therapy session. For example, an overweight student might keep a detailed record of everything she eats, including the time of day and the circumstances under which it was eaten, as well as the caloric value of the food. Interestingly enough, the very process of self-monitoring—observing and tabulating occurrences of specific behaviors in which one engages—can affect the occurrences of these behaviors, often in a therapeutic way (Ciminero, Nelson, & Lipinski, 1977). Thus a heavy smoker may find himself smoking less when he has to keep track of how often and how long he smokes.

TABLE 13–1   The First 15 Scenes of a Desensitization Hierarchy for a Person Who Was Afraid of Flying

1. You are reading the paper and notice an ad for an airline.
2. You are watching a television program that shows a group of people boarding a plane.
3. Your boss tells you that you need to make a business trip by air.
4. It is two weeks before your trip, and you ask your secretary to make airline reservations.
5. You are in your bedroom, packing a suitcase for your trip.
6. You are in the shower on the morning of your trip.
7. You are in a taxi on the way to the airport.
8. You are checking in for your flight and the agent says, "Would you like a window or aisle seat?"
9. You are in the waiting lounge and hear an announcement that your flight is now ready for boarding.
10. You are in line, just about to board the airplane.
11. You are in your seat and hear the plane's engines start.
12. The plane begins to move as you hear the flight attendant say, "Be sure your seatbelts are securely fastened."
13. You look at the runway as the plane waits to take off.
14. You look out the window as the plane begins to roll down the runway.
15. You look out the window as the plane leaves the ground.

Source: From Bernstein, Douglas A., Edward J. Roy, Thomas K. Srull, and Christopher D. Wickens. *Psychology*, Second Edition (p. 640). Copyright © 1991 by Houghton Mifflin Company. Used with permission.

Modeling. As discussed in Chapter 8, *modeling* the behavior of another person has been shown to be an effective approach to overcoming phobias and certain compulsive behaviors. In this form of behavioral therapy, the patient watches another person interacting with the feared object or performing the feared act without showing any fear. The model may be on film, or it may be a real live model. In addition, the patient may be encouraged to rehearse the feared behavior in a role-playing situation before actually engaging in it. Figure 13–1 shows the results of a comparison among four approaches to treating snake phobia (fear of snakes). Note that although systematic desensitization and symbolic modeling (watching filmed models) were more effective than no treatment (control) in reducing the fear of snakes, the number of approach responses to snakes was greatest in the case of live modeling with actual participation by the person with the snake phobia.

Cognitive Therapy

Although target behaviors have typically been rather narrowly defined by behavior therapists, cognitive behavior therapists have also tackled more general problems such as a negative self-concept or an identity crisis. Furthermore, the target behaviors consist not only of nonverbal movements but also of verbal reports of thoughts and feelings.

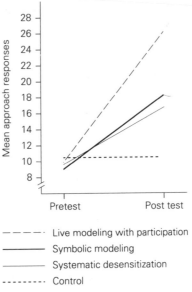

FIGURE 13–1 Results of a study of comparative effects of systematic desensitization, participant modeling, and symbolic modeling and control (no treatment) on the fear of snakes. (From Bandura, Blanchard, & Ritter, 1969. Copyright 1969 by the American Psychological Association. Reprinted by permission.)

Cognitive therapists emphasize the role of maladaptive thought patterns (specific attitudes, beliefs, expectations, etc.) in determining adjustment problems. Using self-monitoring, thought stopping, and other procedures, patients are taught how to identify and gain control over their automatic, idiosyncratic mental reactions to disturbing stimuli. Cognitively oriented therapy has been particularly useful in the treatment of depression (Beck, 1967). Depressed patients tend to be very negative and self-critical in evaluating events; so cognitive therapy focuses on changing their thoughts in a more realistic, less self-destructive direction. For example, the patient is encouraged to keep a diary of pleasant and unpleasant daily experiences and automatic negative thoughts. The patient meets with the therapist for an hour each week to discuss and analyze the material recorded in the diary. In this way patients gradually become aware of how they are making themselves miserable, and they learn to cope with their negative thoughts and behaviors.

Three cognitive therapy techniques that are particularly useful in helping people cope with anxiety and stress are assertiveness training, cognitive restructuring, and stress inoculation. The goal of *assertiveness training* is to reduce the anxiety and tension experienced by people when they must reject a demand made by someone else or must compete with another person. Through the use of role playing and related procedures, assertiveness training teaches people to make legitimate requests of others and to reject their unreasonable demands.

Cognitive Restructuring. The cognitive-restructuring technique is based on the assumptions that specific thoughts or self-verbalizations give rise to anxiety and that the patient must modify such negative self-verbalizations and replace them with positive self-statements (Meichenbaum, 1974). Similar in effectiveness to systematic desensitization in its ability to reduce anxiety, cognitive restructuring employs procedures such as *thought stopping:*

> The client is asked to concentrate on the anxiety-inducing thoughts, and, after a short period of time, the therapist suddenly and emphatically says "stop" (any loud noise . . . may also suffice). After this procedure has been repeated several times (and the client reports that his thoughts were indeed interrupted or blocked), the locus of control is shifted from the therapist to the client. Specifically, the client is taught to emit a subvocal "stop" whenever he begins to engage in a self-defeating rumination. (Rimm & Masters, 1979, p. 430)

Stress Inoculation. Another coping strategy pioneered by Meichenbaum (Meichenbaum & Cameron, 1983) is *stress inoculation.* Similar to inoculation against a physical disease, the purpose of stress inoculation is to teach people how to manage stressful situations by exposing them to small amounts of stress and equipping them with suggestions for making adaptive rather than maladaptive responses to stress. The focus of stress inoculation is on specific cognitions (automatic thoughts, dysfunctional expectancies, irrational beliefs) that contribute to maladaptive behavior. The entire process consists of three stages: conceptualization, skills acquisition rehearsal, and follow-through. In the *conceptualization* stage, information is obtained by interviewing, observation, and other data-collection procedures to identify the determinants of the person's problem and his or her ability to cope with it. During the second stage, the *skills acquisition rehearsal* stage, the person learns and practices new ways of coping with stress. During the final stage, *application and follow-through,* skill rehearsal continues by means of imagery, role playing, and performing in real or simulated stress situations.

Rational-Emotive and Reality Therapy

Rational-Emotive Therapy. Although Albert Ellis was trained as a psychoanalyst, his *rational emotive therapy* (*RET*) is actually more akin to cognitive behavioral therapy. The goal of RET is to restructure the patient's belief system (*B*) so that he or she comes to realize that it is *B* rather than an antecedent event (*A*) that leads to an unfortunate consequence (*C*). RET takes a cue from the ancient Stoic philosophers Epictetus and Marcus Aurelius, who concluded, "It is not this thing which disturbs you, but your own judgment about it" (Marcus Aurelius, 1945, p. 87); and so, "Take away the opinion and there is taken away the complaint" (p. 35). Some of the most common faulty thought patterns or beliefs that cause trouble for people are listed in Table 13–2, and an excerpt from an RET session is given in Report 13–3.

TABLE 13–2   Some Common Irrational Beliefs

Obvious Irrational Beliefs

"Because I strongly desire to perform important tasks competently and successfully, I *absolutely must* perform them well at all times."

"Because I strongly desire to be approved by people I find significant, I *absolutely must* always have their approval."

"Because I strongly desire people to treat me considerately and fairly, they *absolutely must* at all times and under all conditions do so."

"Because I strongly desire to have a safe, comfortable, and satisfying life, the conditions under which I live *absolutely must* at all times be easy, convenient, and gratifying."

Subtle and Tricky Irrational Beliefs

"Because I strongly desire to perform important tasks competently and successfully, and because I want to succeed at them only *some* of the time, I *absolutely must* perform these tasks well."

"Because I strongly desire to be approved by people I find significant, and because I only want a *little* approval from them, I *absolutely must* have it."

"Because I strongly desire people to treat me considerately and fairly, and because I am almost always considerate and fair to others, they *absolutely must* treat me well."

"Because I strongly desire to have a safe, comfortable, and satisfying life, and because I am a nice person who tries to help others lead this kind of life, the conditions under which I live *absolutely must* be easy, convenient, and gratifying."

Source: From "The Impossibility of Achieving Consistently Good Mental Health" by A. E. Ellis, 1987, *American Psychologist, 52,* 364–375. Copyright 1987 by the American Psychological Association. Reprinted by permission.

Reality Therapy. Like behavior therapy, *reality therapy* did not stem from a complex theory of personality development and adjustment. Rather, this approach is based on a set of practical techniques devised by William Glasser (1965) from his personal experiences with emotionally disturbed adolescents. Glasser conceptualizes human personality in terms of how well people meet their needs, especially the needs to be loved and to feel worthwhile. The goal of reality therapy is to teach the client to meet his or her own needs by using the three R's of "right, responsibility, and reality" as a guide. "Right" is an accepted standard or norm of behavior; "responsibility" means satisfying one's own needs without interfering with those of others; "reality" means understanding that there is a real world in which one's needs have to be satisfied.

A reality therapist uses the following techniques to teach the client to govern his or her life according to the three R's (Hansen, Stevic, & Warner, 1977):

1 Communicating to the client that he or she cares.
2 Getting the client to focus on present behavior rather than feelings.
3 Helping the client to evaluate his or her own irresponsible behavior.
4 Getting the client to make a commitment to a specific plan to change his or her irresponsible behavior.
5 Refusing to accept excuses for failure to stick to a plan but not punishing the client for failing.

REPORT 13–3

Excerpt from a Rational-Emotive Therapy Session

Client: Well, this is all a part of something that's bothered me for a long time. I'm always afraid of making a mistake.

Ellis: Why? What's the horror?

Client: I don't know.

Ellis: You're saying that you're a bitch, you're a louse when you make a mistake.

Client: But this is the way I've always been. Every time I make a mistake, I die a thousand deaths over it.

Ellis: You blame yourself. But why? What's the horror? Is it going to make you better next time? Is it going to make you make fewer mistakes?

Client: No.

Ellis: Then why blame yourself? Why are you a louse for making a mistake? Who said so?

Client: I guess it's one of those feelings I have.

Ellis: One of those *beliefs*. The belief is: "I am a louse!" And then you get the feeling; "Oh, how awful! How shameful!" But the feeling follows the belief. And again, you're saying, "I should be different; I *shouldn't* make mistakes!" Instead of: "Oh, look: I made a mistake. It's undesirable to make mistakes. Now, how am I going to stop making one next time?". . .

Client: It might all go back to, as you said, the need for approval. If I don't make mistakes, then people will look up to me. If I do it all perfectly—

Ellis: Yes, that's part of it. That is the erroneous belief: that if you never make mistakes everybody will love you and that it is necessary that they do. . . . But is it true? Suppose you never did make mistakes—*would* people love you? They'd sometimes hate your guts, wouldn't they?

Source: Reprinted by permission from Ellis (1971).

Special Psychotherapeutic Methods

There are literally dozens of psychotherapies, but those based on psychodynamic, phenomenological, and behavioral theories are the most popular. In addition, a number of special psychotherapeutic techniques are of interest. Four such techniques are role therapy, play therapy, psychodrama, and group therapy.

Role Therapy

In *role therapy*, characterization that clients have written describing their views of themselves are studied by one or more therapists. The therapist(s) then write a second characterization, describing what the client should strive to become. The client is encouraged to try out this new role, the theory being that as he or she experiments with the new role, it will gradually be found to be more and more satisfying, and, in a sense, the client will become the person he or she is pretending to be.

A type of psychotherapeutic role playing in which patients act out situations relevant to their conflicts and problems was devised by J. L. Moreno (1946). In this procedure, known as *psychodrama,* a stage, an audience, and supporting characters are used to help the patient reexperience, or even experience for the first time, a situation, fantasy, or role related to his or her problem. During the action, the therapist analyzes and interprets the situation to the patient.

Play Therapy

Play therapy is a psychotherapeutic technique used with children in which a play situation is the basis of therapy. Depending on the age and sex of the child, various kinds of play materials, including dolls, small houses, construction materials, and the like may be used. Most play therapy involves a degree of emotional release, in that the child is given an opportunity to vent his or her feelings— usually hostile or aggressive ones. These feelings are the result of acting out, in the play situation, real-life problem situations that the child has experienced with the parents or other significant persons in his or her life. Also of importance in some types of play therapy is the relationship between the therapist and the child. Under certain circumstances the therapist may consider it advisable to interpret to the child, or try to put into words, how the child feels and the reasons why the child behaves in a certain way. Like role playing and group therapy, play therapy may be adapted to almost any theory of personality and psychotherapy— psychoanalytic, phenomenological, or behavioral—but most often it is an eclectic procedure that does not adhere rigidly to a specific theory.

Group Therapy

All psychotherapy is concerned with interpersonal relationships, but the interpersonal aspect is emphasized in group therapy. People who are experiencing feelings of alienation, loneliness, loss of self-esteem, and even despair can be helped greatly by group-oriented techniques.

Group therapy is psychotherapy conducted simultaneously with a small group of people (typically 6–12) coordinated by a therapist or group leader. Not only does the method save time over that required for individual therapy, but the group also provides an opportunity for the patient to communicate with someone other than the therapist. In this way, patients are exposed to the kind of interpersonal stresses that have contributed to their problems and with which they must learn to cope. Patients in group therapy also gain social support, the realization that their troubles are not unique, and the advice and counsel of other people who have experienced similar problems.

Like play therapy, group therapy may follow a particular theory of personality change, but it is usually eclectic. Group therapy may also incorporate a number of other psychotherapeutic procedures, such as role playing, scribotherapy, and self-image therapy. Role playing in a group setting consists of having particular members of the group act out situations related to their conflicts and problems while other members of the group play the roles of supporting characters. In this way a particular group member reexperiences a situation pertaining to his or her most significant problem. In the technique of *scribotherapy,* group members record their feelings about certain topics and then, after group discussion and individual interviews, develop them into a news format. Another "literary" technique that has been applied in group-therapy contexts is *self-image therapy:* A book selected by the group is read and discussed as a means of developing group cohesiveness and a sense of security among group members.

Support groups of various kinds have been formed in communities throughout the nation. Among these groups are *compeers,* which are support groups of mental patients; other examples are grief groups, groups of reformed alcoholics and substance abusers, and parent effectiveness groups. Some of these groups are crisis oriented, but most have regular meetings that focus on long-term counseling and rehabilitation. A list of some of the self-help groups in one city, San Diego, California, is given in Table 13–3.

Family therapy is a special type of age-integrated group therapy in which two or more members of a family interact with each other and the therapist(s). The goal of marital and family therapy is to make people more sensitive to each other's feelings and needs and to find ways to handle their interpersonal conflicts. Because family relationships are a common source of difficulty for children and adults, it is often important to include the family in therapy sessions. Marital problems, behavioral problems in children, bereavement, and many other stressful circumstances involving several individuals in the same family are often treated by means of family therapy. In a very real sense, the family is a dynamic "system" in which the problems being experienced by one member can affect the sense of well-being and behaviors of the other family members. An example is a *schismatic family,* in which the parents contemptuously compete with one another and use the children as pawns in their arguments and manipulations. Among other results of effective family therapy is the adoption by participants of more constructive intrafamilial roles (Minuchin, 1974).

Milieu Therapy and Prevention

The counseling and psychotherapeutic techniques discussed thus far are remedial, but preventive counseling is potentially even more contributory to good adjustment and mental health. Environmental arrangements or changes of the sort that play a role in prevention can also be used in remediation. Mental health professionals realize that a patient's physical and social surroundings are important in the course and treatment of psychological problems and disorders, a realization that is basic to the concepts of a *therapeutic community* and *milieu therapy.*

TABLE 13–3   Some Self-help Groups

AIDS Counseling Program
AIRS (teenage chemical dependency)
Adult Children of Alcoholics
Adults Molested as Children
Affective Disorders Group (mood disorders)
Al-Anon (families of alcoholics)
Ala-Teen (teenage alcohol abuse)
Alcoholics Anonymous
Alzheimer's Disease Family Support Group
Arthritis Support Group
Battered Women's Support Group
Bi-Polar Support Group (manic-depression)
CREATE (college students recovering from mental illness)
Emotional Health Anonymous
Epilepsy Support Group
Gay Men's Coming Out Group
Grandmother's Support Group (mothers of teenage mothers)
Lesbian Support Group
Loss Support (grief recovery)
Make Today Count (breast cancer support)
Narcotics Anonymous
PMS Association (Pre-Menstrual Syndrome)
Parent Aid (parents at risk for child abuse)
Parents United (sexual abuse)
Parkinson's Disease Support Group
Pre Ala-Teen (child alcohol dependency)
Project Return (recovering mental patients)
Recovery, Inc.
Phobia Foundation
Single Parent Support Group
Sudden Infant Death Syndrome
Survivors of Suicide
Teen Mothers Support Group
Victims of Homicide (family and loved ones)
Voices (schizophrenic support group)

Source: San Diego Mental Health Association.

For example, it has been found that the introduction of simple changes—a record player, a decorated bulletin board, games, dressing patients in white shirts and ties, serving beer and crackers every day at two o'clock—can markedly alter the behavior of patients on a senile ward (Volpe & Kastenbaum, 1967). Such changes have been found to result in decreased incontinence, a lessened need for restraint and medication, and marked improvement in the social functioning of patients. These improvements may be interpreted as stemming from better patient attitudes, accompanied by an increase in the expectations of the institutional staff and the patients of what the latter are able to do.

Of course, this cuts both ways: Maladaptive behavior can be exacerbated in patients who are treated by the institutional staff as "sick inmates" who are incapable of making decisions or doing anything constructive for themselves. At least to an extent, mental patients—and people in general—become what they are viewed or labeled as being, and they do what other people expect them to do.

Comparing and Evaluating Psychotherapies

Although the informal practice of psychotherapy is very old, it is still fairly young as a formal treatment method to be evaluated by scientific means. An indication of the somewhat inexact state of the art and science of psychotherapy in 1959 is given in Harper's (1959) book describing 36 systems of psychotherapy, none of which was generally agreed to be the "best" method. Any attempt to evaluate the effects of psychotherapy must specify rather precisely the goals and procedures employed.

In 1952, Hans Eysenck wrote a paper summarizing a group of investigations concerned with the effects of psychotherapy. He concluded that mental patients who had received little or no psychotherapy recovered at least as often as those who had received extensive psychotherapy. In fact, Eysenck reported that only 64 percent of patients who had undergone intensive, prolonged psychotherapy showed improvement, compared with 72 percent of patients who had received treatment from a general practitioner or simple custodial care. Some years later, Eysenck (1960) published a second paper that left the conclusions of the first report essentially unchanged. However, both the 1952 and the 1961 reports were severely criticized on methodological grounds. For example, the "symptom remission" criterion of improvement used by Eysenck is unacceptable to many therapists, especially those who are psychodynamically oriented. It is possible, for example, for a particular treatment to have an effect on specific target symptoms but to have no impact on the basic disorder. Therapists of different persuasions differ not only in the kinds of problems that they treat but also on the indicators of therapeutic effectiveness to which they attend. Whereas behavioral therapists focus on specific maladaptive behaviors, psychoanalysts and other dynamic therapists are more concerned with helping patients deal with inner conflicts. In any case, it was concluded that Eysenck's findings were by no means the final word on the issue of the effectiveness of psychotherapy (Smith & Glass, 1977; Landman & Dawes, 1982).

Evaluating the effectiveness of psychotherapy is, of course, a complex affair. For example, what should be the criterion of improvement through psychotherapy—a person's statement that he or she feels better or is happier than before? Most clinicians realize that subjective reports of this kind are not usually very reliable or valid. In fact, patients will often tell the therapist that they have been helped simply through a sense of human decency or reciprocity, or perhaps they actually believe that they have improved because a prestigious, understanding person has spent so much time and effort trying to help them.

Evaluating Client-Centered Therapy

One of the most carefully controlled studies of psychotherapy was conducted by Rogers and Dymond (1954) to evaluate the effects of client-centered therapy. This investigation is particularly noteworthy because extreme care was taken to employ adequate control groups. Before and after client-centered therapy, the clients made judgments (Q-sorts) of how they actually perceived themselves as being ("real self") and also how they would ideally like to be ("ideal self"). The results showed that whereas there was typically a marked discrepancy between an individual's "real self" ratings and his or her "ideal self" ratings at the beginning of therapy, the discrepancy became smaller as therapy progressed. As noted in Chapter 7, however, the real-self/ideal-self discrepancy may not be a true indicator of personality adjustment or therapeutic effectiveness.

Does the Type of Psychotherapy Make a Difference?

More recent studies have shown that patients apparently improve under all kinds of psychotherapy and that the extent of improvement is directly related to the number of therapy sessions (see Figure 13–2). For example, Smith, Glass, and Miller (1980) concluded that, despite the variation among success rates of differ-

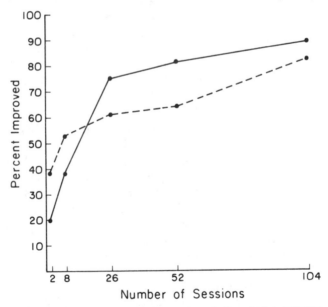

Note. Objective ratings at termination are shown by the solid line; subjective ratings during therapy are shown by the broken line.

FIGURE 13–2   Improvement with psychotherapy. (Reprinted with permission from Howard, Kopta, Krause, & Orlinsky, 1986. Copyright 1986 by the American Psychological Association. Reprinted by permission.)

ent forms of psychotherapy, the success rates are not greatly different from therapy to therapy (also see Shapiro & Shapiro, 1982; Berman, Miller, & Massman, 1985). Behavioral and cognitive approaches may boast a slightly higher overall success rate, but this superiority may be due to the kinds of cases treated. Treatment success is greater for behavioral cognitive therapy in the case of simple phobias and other specific symptom disorders, but identity crises and deep-seated conflicts tend to be more effectively treated by psychodynamic techniques. If the goal is to eliminate specific behaviors, then behavioral or cognitive therapy usually works best; if the goal is self-understanding, then phenomenological or psychoanalytic therapy works best. In fact, one study found that a sizable percentage of behavioral therapists who themselves needed treatment chose to seek help from psychodynamic therapists (Lazarus, 1971)!

Not only are different therapeutic approaches more appropriate for different disorders, but different therapists also work better with certain patients and certain kinds of problems than with other patients or problems. This lesson, unfortunately, is sometimes learned too late, and it may happen that psychotherapy actually ends up hurting people rather than helping them. Harm may be done, for example, when a therapist decides to use an insight approach with an older adult, attempting to strip away the patient's defense mechanisms and refashion his or her personality. Perhaps all that is needed in such cases is a sympathetic ear and the ability to reinforce those heretofore serviceable defenses:

> A farmer's wife came and told a tragic story where nothing could be done, but her compassion and strength made it possible to continue. As usual with these cases, I asked if she would care to come again; she look a little surprised, and said, "There is no need. I've told you everything." She had only wanted to confide in someone she respected, in case there was more she could do, and not to be so alone in her hard life. . . . One visit was enough for her. (Scott-Maxwell, 1968)

In this case, one visit apparently was all that was needed. In other cases, however, the patient may fail to return for a second session because he or she felt that the psychotherapeutic experience was ineffective or useless.

Common Factors in Different Psychotherapies

Although different therapies appear to be more effective than others in treating certain kinds of mental disorders, as predicted by Freud many years ago none of the therapies is demonstrably effective in treating psychotic disorders such as schizophrenia or bipolar illness. In addition, all successful psychotherapies share certain common elements, and it may be those common elements rather than the therapy-specific techniques that account for much of the success of different therapies. Among the characteristics that are common to almost all successful psychotherapies are the following (Garfield, 1980; Orlinsky & Howard, 1987):

1 A warm and trusting interpersonal relationship between therapist and client.
2 Reassurance and support provided by the therapist (and group members in the case of group therapy).

3 Desensitizing or extinguishing the patient's maladaptive thoughts and emotional reactions.

4 Reinforcing the patient for adaptive responses.

5 Understanding or insight of oneself gained by the patient.

[The most effective therapists recognize the importance of these factors and make use of them in therapy.]

Summary

Psychotherapy consists of using psychological methods to treat adjustment problems and mental disorders. In psychoanalytic psychotherapy, the patient free-associates and reports his or her feelings, impressions, and dreams to the therapist. The therapist listens and occasionally remarks on the patient's statements, offering interpretations and analyses of the patient's condition. The therapist's analysis is based on the association, dreams, and resistances of the patients, as well as the nature of the transference relationship. In this way, patients gain insight into their disordered behavior and hopefully show improvement.

In client-centered therapy, it is assumed that clients have the capacity to grow emotionally and will assume primary responsibility for solving their own problems. Client-centered therapists (or counselors) are limited to the relatively nondirective techniques of simple acceptance, restating the content of the client's statements, and reflecting the emotional feelings in what their clients say.

Behavior therapy is based on the assumption that because emotional disorders are learned, they can be unlearned. Unlearning may be accomplished either by gradually desensitizing the individual to objects, persons, or situations that make him or her anxious or arranging for the stimuli that trigger anxiety to be presented when the individual is making responses that are incompatible with anxiety. Other behavior modification techniques include modeling, reinforcement, extinction, implosion (flooding), and aversion therapy. Cognitive therapy is an extension of behavior therapy that concentrates on making patients aware of their self-destructive thoughts and finding ways of dealing with such thoughts. Three cognitive techniques are assertiveness training, cognitive restructuring, and stress inoculation.

Among the many special psychotherapeutic methods are role therapy, psychodrama, play therapy, group therapy, family therapy, and milieu therapy. Role therapy and psychodrama are especially useful in helping to reduce the level of anxiety associated with traumatic experiences. Play therapy is a means of permitting children to act out their feelings and gain understanding in a play situation. Group therapy is an efficient method of therapy, particularly when difficulties with social interactions form a significant part of the client's problem. Marital therapy and family therapy are types of group therapy in which the marital or family unit is treated as a dynamic unit or system.

Despite some initial evaluations by Hans Eysenck that cast doubt on the effectiveness of psychotherapy, more recent research findings indicate that almost all types of psychotherapy are better than no psychological treatment at all. Psychotherapy is ineffective or destructive in a minority of cases. Behavior and cognitive therapies appear to be somewhat more successful than psychodynamic and phenomenologically oriented therapies in treating specific symptoms such as phobias or compulsions, but less successful in treating more pervasive disorders such as identity crises or generalized anxiety reactions. The effectiveness of psychotherapy increases, at least up to a point, as the number of therapy sessions increases. For certain disorders, psychotherapy may be even more helpful when used in conjunction with medication, environmental manipulation, or other specialized procedures. However, on the whole psychotherapy does not appear to be productive in the treatment of psychotic illness such as schizophrenia or bipolar disorder.

Key Concepts

Behavior modification   Psychotherapeutic procedures, based on learning theory and research, designed to change inappropriate behavior to more personally and socially acceptable behavior. Examples of such procedures are reinforcement, systematic desensitization, counterconditioning, aversion, extinction, implosion (flooding), and modeling.

Catharsis   Release of anxiety or tension through indirect verbal expression or fantasy.

Client-centered therapy   A type of psychotherapy, pioneered by Carl Rogers, in which the client decides what to talk about and when, without direction, judgment, or interpretation on the part of the therapist. Unconditional positive regard, empathy, and congruence characterize the therapist's attitude in this type of therapy.

Cognitive behavioral therapy   Psychotherapeutic process in which a person's faulty cognitions or beliefs are changed to more realistic ones.

Contingency management   Control of institutionalized persons by differentially reinforcing them for socially approved and socially disapproved behavior; makes certain kinds of pleasures or privileges contingent upon keeping neat and clean, eating properly, interacting with other patients, or engaging in other socially acceptable behaviors. Also known as *token economy* when the reinforcers are tokens that can be exchanged for something desired by the individual.

Counterconditioning (reciprocal inhibition)   Extinction of an undesirable response to a stimulus through introduction of a more desirable, often incompatible, response; involves presentation of the conditioned stimuli for an anxiety response while the individual is making responses that are incompatible with anxiety.

Delusion   A false belief that is resistant to reason or reality, e.g., a delusion of persecution or grandeur.

Family therapy   Treatment of psychological problems in a family setting; based on the doctrine that many, if not most, psychological problems originate in the interpersonal family situation and hence can be treated more effectively in that context.

Group therapy   Type of psychotherapy in which several individuals share their feelings, experiences, and expectations with each other under the direction or guidance of a therapist or group leader.

Psychodrama   A psychotherapeutic method, pioneered by J. L. Moreno, in which the problems and experiences of a person are acted out in a stage setting by the person and other "actors."

Rational-emotive therapy (RET)   A form of cognitive restructuring devised by Albert Ellis; directive approach designed to change a person's beliefs about himself (herself) by pointing out and getting him (her) to accept that things are not what they seem but are affected by one's beliefs.

Systematic desensitization   Behavioral therapy technique in which a hierarchy of anxiety-provoking situations is imagined or directly experienced while the individual is in a deeply relaxed state. In this manner, the situations gradually come to be experienced without anxiety.

Transactional analysis   A group-therapeutic approach, pioneered by Eric Berne, in which the therapist observes the behavior of the group members and clarifies the destructive aspects of their life scripts and life positions and the associated games that they play in social interactions.

Activities and Applications

1. Describe the various approaches to psychotherapy discussed in this chapter and the kinds of adjustment problems or disorders for which each is considered most appropriate.

2. Select one form of psychotherapy and write a comprehensive paper on it, including criticisms and an overall evaluation.

3. Look under "psychiatrists," "psychologists," "psychotherapists," and "counselors" in a city telephone directory. How many listings did you find under each title? Did the listings indicate the specializations, that is, the kinds of problems in which the person specializes? What conclusions can you draw from this exercise concerning the availability of psychological treatment in your city?

4. What are the similarities and differences between the various psychotherapies? In particular, what features do different approaches to psychotherapy have in common? That is, what appear to be the "basics" of all psychotherapeutic approaches?

5. Select a target behavior, such as a mannerism of speech or movement in a person with whom you are talking, and reinforce it with a smile or nod every time that it is emitted during a ten-minute conversation. Were you successful in increasing the frequency of the target behavior by using positive reinforcement? Why or why not?

6. A great deal has been written about psychotherapists taking sexual liberties with their patients (clients). Describe what you know about this matter from reading or other sources of information. Why should engaging in a sexual or romantic relationship with a patient (client) be considered unethical by the American Psychological Association and other mental health organizations?

7. In keeping with the recent emphasis on the legal rights of individuals, some attorneys and psychiatrists have argued that mental patients have a right to refuse treatment, to retain their personal property when placed in an institution, to be legally represented by counsel who is not a member of the institutional staff, and to request an alternative to confinement in a mental hospital. What are the pros and cons of allowing these "rights" or privileges to mental patients?

8. What are the major differences between Freud's approach to psychotherapy and the approaches of other psychoanalysts? Are the differences greater than the similarities or vice versa?

9. Administer the following questionnaire concerning psychotherapy anonymously to 10 psychology majors (five men and five women) and 10 nonpsychology majors (five men and five women). Compare the responses to each of the items of the 10 men with the responses of the 10 women and the responses of the 10 psychology majors with those of the 10 nonpsychology majors. What conclusions can you draw from these comparisons?

Opinions of Psychotherapy

Directions: Write the letter(s) corresponding to your opinion concerning the truth of each statement in the blank next to the statement. Use the following letters:
SD = Strongly Disagree, D = Disagree, U = Undecided, A = Agree, SA = Strongly Agree.

_____ 1. Good psychotherapists are born, not made by a lot of fancy education and training.
_____ 2. Effective psychotherapy is more of an art than a science.
_____ 3. Psychotherapy is useful in treating both major and minor mental health problems, ranging from mild stress reactions all the way to psychoses.
_____ 4. Prolonged psychotherapy is usually unnecessary; one or two sessions are typically enough for most problems.
_____ 5. All that one needs to be an effective psychotherapist is the ability to listen carefully and nonjudgmentally.
_____ 6. In many cases psychotherapy actually does more harm than good.
_____ 7. Most people are better off after having received psychotherapeutic help.
_____ 8. When psychotherapy does work, it is usually because of the placebo effect: The patient thinks he or she must be getting better because a prestigious person is trying to help.
_____ 9. One reason why psychotherapy works is because the patient is paying so much money for it.
_____10. In psychotherapy, as in many other things in life, "it takes one to know one." That is, a person who has had mental problems and has worked through them is in a better position to help other people with their personal problems.
_____11. A person needs little or no training to be an effective psychotherapist; it's mostly a matter of interpersonal warmth, understanding, common sense, and a genuine interest in helping people.
_____12. Most people could benefit from psychotherapy at some time during their lives.

Suggested Readings

Corsini, R., & Wedding, D. (Eds.). (1989). *Current psychotherapies.* Itasca, IL: F. E. Peacock.
Hunt, M. (1987, August 30). Navigating the therapy maze. *New York Times Magazine,* pp. 28–30, 37–49.
Kanfer, F. H., & Goldstein, A. P. (Eds.). (1986). *Helping people change* (3rd ed.). New York: Pergamon Press.
London, P. (1986). *The modes and morals of psychotherapy.* New York: Harper & Row.

Marmar, C. R. (1990). Psychotherapy process research: Progress, dilemmas, and future directions. *Journal of Consulting and Clinical Psychology, 58,* 265–272.

Messer, S. B., & Warren, S. (1990). Personality change and psychotherapy. *Handbook of personality theory and research* (pp. 371–398). New York: Guilford Press.

O'Leary, K. D., & Wilson, G. T. (1987). *Behavior therapy: Applications and outcomes* (2nd ed.). Englewood Cliffs, NJ: Prentice Hall.

VandenBos, G. A. (1986). Psychotherapy research (Special issue). *American Psychologist, 41*(2).

Yalom, I. D. (1980). *Love's executioner and other tales of psychotherapy.* New York: Basic Books.

CHAPTER 14

Applications, Issues, and Outlook

CHAPTER OUTLINE

Methods, theories, and research concerning human personality have been discussed in the preceding 13 chapters of this book. Any one of these chapters could be expanded into a book, and entire books focusing on the material in a given chapter have already been written. It is hoped, however, that the overview presented in the previous chapters has provided the reader with some understanding of the varied backgrounds and interests of personality theorists and researchers, as well as the ways in which they have gone about trying to answer the question of why people behave as they do. Now, by way of summing up and completing this survey of the psychology of personality, it is appropriate to look at some additional practical applications of research findings and theories, as well as some of the criticisms and issues that continue to be of concern. Finally, though it may seem presumptuous and loaded with the possibility of making mistakes, we shall take a stab at answering the question of where we go from here.

Personality Theories and Research in Applied Contexts

For centuries, applications of scientific discoveries to practical problems lagged behind basic science. The progress of science during the Renaissance and the Enlightenment periods from the 1300s through the 1970s was truly remarkable, but still limited. Even Isaac Newton, one of the foremost scientists of all time, confessed:

> I do not know what I may appear to the world; but to myself I seem to have been only like a boy playing on the seashore, and diverting myself in now and then finding a smoother pebble or a prettier shell than ordinary, whilst the great ocean of truth lay all undiscovered before me.

With the advent of the industrial revolution, the demand for new technology exceeded the available scientific knowledge. At that time, new applications became stalled until the relevant basic research had been conducted. Today we are faced with a somewhat similar problem in psychology. Although there are many who would claim otherwise, our knowledge concerning the functioning of the human brain and the dynamics of behavior and personality is relatively meager. Consequently, much of applied psychology is "off the top of one's head" or "by the seat of one's pants," so to speak. Clinical, industrial-organizational, educational, and other applied psychologists are, for the most part, practical individuals who depend little on the library of facts that have accumulated over the past hundred years or so of scientific psychology. These practitioners try to deduce workable conclusions and prescriptions from their own personal experiences "in the field." Sometimes these judgments or conclusions are valid, but just as often they are wrong. Preconceived notions, failure to consider the base rate of particular events, the hindsight bias, and overconfidence in intuitive understanding can cloud one's perceptions, predictions, and conclusions. An example of a *preconceived notion* is the illusory correlation problem of focusing on the number of times that a symptom and a disorder have occurred together and overlooking the number of times they have not occurred together. Another factor that can detract from clinical judgment is a low *base rate,* that is, a low frequency of occurrence of a characteristic or condition. Variables having low base rates are harder to predict than those with high base rates. The third factor described by Arkes (1985), the *hindsight bias,* concerns the belief that, after an event has occurred, one could have predicted it beforehand. For example, people who commit violent acts are viewed, with 20-20 hindsight, as always having been "a little bit strange and uncontrollable." The fourth facto⁻ that impairs clinical judgments is the tendency of people who are the poorest forecasters to be the most confident in their judgments. Such *overconfidence* in one's judgments leads the clinician to reject assistance, correction, or remediation from others, thereby solidifying his or her false overconfidence in judging people and predicting behavioral events. Despite the scarcity of tried-and-true principles and procedures for understanding, predicting, and controlling human behavior, there is a danger that the field of psychology will become flooded with poorly trained clinicians and other applied specialists who harbor a downright dislike for science and research. This possibility creates an uncertain future for the science and practice of psychology, or at least a future that is radically different from the one envisioned by the founding fathers in the late nineteenth and early twentieth centuries.

To be fair, practitioners may reply that they would be happy to embrace the theories, methods, and findings of research psychologists if it could be shown that they are applicable to the world of the clinic, the hospital, and the job, and not just to the restricted environment of the laboratory, the library, and the classroom. To quote Pervin (1985):

> I continue to be impressed with and distressed by the gap between what I read in the literature and what I see in my office. In particular, I am struck with the power of conflicting motivations in my patients and the absence of concern with such phenomena in the literature, with the diversity of personally significant emotions reported by patients and the more restricted concerns of psychologists with anxiety and depression, with the importance of implicit causal (if-then) beliefs held by people and the narrow perspective of much of attribution theory. On the whole, I continue to feel that I am more in touch with and learn more about people in my office than I do in reading the personality literature. (p. 105)

After all is said and done, have there really been any demonstrable contributions of personality research and theorizing to the solution of practical problems? Although perhaps not as many as one might wish, there have been and continue to be numerous contributions. Several of these contributions—to human development, health psychology, and psychotherapy in particular—are discussed in Chapters 11–13. Some of the other contributions that have been made in fields such as business, education, law, and even politics and athletics are considered in the following sections.

Business and Industrial Settings

Among the applications of personality theory, research, and assessment in business and industrial contexts are those concerned with (1) selecting, placing, and promoting employees; (2) determining the causes of accidents; (3) understanding and predicting consumer behavior; and (4) determining the presence and causes of stress-related disorders. In this section we shall be concerned with the first three of these areas; the fourth was discussed to some extent in Chapter 11.

Employment, Placement, and Promotion. Personality assessment instruments such as rating scales, checklists, inventories, projective techniques, interview forms, and biographical data banks have been used extensively in employment situations to screen, place, and promote individuals having particular personality characteristics (e.g., honesty, a sense of responsibility, organizational ability, conscientiousness, consideration). Whether a person adapts and succeeds or maladapts and fails on a job depends, as in other walks of life, not only on the ability to do the job but also on the motivations, interests, and temperament characteristics of the employee.

One popular approach to selecting higher-level executive personnel is the *assessment center,* in which six to 12 executive candidates are observed and studied intensively. In addition to objective observations, interviews, management games, and group problem-solving exercises, a number of personality tests are used to assess the candidates over a period of several days. In a *leaderless group discussion* (LGD) exercise, participants are assigned a topic concerning a specific administrative, political, or social problem and asked to discuss it for a period of 30 minutes to an hour. The performances of individual members of the group are rated by both external observers and other members of the group. Reliable ratings are usually made in terms of the dimensions of ascendance, task facilitation, and sociability. The principal criteria on which the overall performance of candidates is evaluated in the assessment center are their degree of active participation, their organizational skills, and their decision-making ability.

Personality tests have also been used as selection devices in the public sector, particularly for positions in government and military service. For example, situational tests were administered during World War II by the Office of Strategic Services to select espionage agents, and the MMPI was used during the 1960s to select candidates for the Peace Corps. In addition, the polygraph and other "lie detector tests" have been used by the U.S. government to screen applicants for positions in which security is considered particularly important. However, the inaccuracy of polygraph tests prompted the U.S. Congress in 1988 to ban their use for most purposes in government and in the private workplace. Certain tests of honesty and integrity remain in use in employment situations, and apparently a number of these measures possess acceptable reliabilities and validities for screening purposes (DeAngelis, 1991).

The MMPI and certain other personality inventories have occasionally been the objects of civil suits, in which it has been alleged that the administration of such instruments for purposes of employee selection is discriminatory or an invasion of the applicant's right to privacy. Questions concerning sexual preferences and religious beliefs, in particular, have been the targets of legal action. The Uniform Guidelines on Employee Selection (Equal Employment Opportunity Commission, 1978), which serve as a reference in such cases, do not expressly forbid the use of personality inventories and tests in employee selection. Nor do these guidelines require that each personality test item be valididated against a criterion of job performance. What must be demonstrated in using such assessment devices for employment purposes is that scores on the test or inventory are job related ("The Future of Personality Tests," 1992). Unfortunately, this point is sometimes difficult to prove in practice.

Accident Proneness. Another problem that plagues certain business and industrial organizations is a high frequency of accidents on the job. Since World War II the notion that there is an *accident proneness* syndrome, characterized by a worker having a significantly above-average number of accidents, has been the topic of considerable research. Some early research seemed to find that accident proneness was associated with certain personality characteristics.

It is certainly true that temporary emotional problems, resulting from the stress of an unhappy home life, may increase distractibility and hence contribute to accidents. Understandably, frustrated, worried, and angry workers may have more accidents than happy and contented workers. For example, Shaw and Sichel (1971) reported that accident repeaters are less emotionally stable, more hostile toward authority, and higher in anxiety than nonrepeaters. Accident repeaters also experience more problems getting along with others and have less stable work histories than nonrepeaters. In addition, it has been found that air traffic controllers who display Type A behavior (see Chapter 11) are more likely than those showing a Type B behavior pattern to incur injuries on the job (Niemcryk, Jenkins, Rose, & Hurst, 1987). Other studies have found an association between high accident rate and personality characteristics such as excessive ambition and revengeful attitudes (McGuire, 1976). Despite these findings, the concept of accident proneness is believed to be in large matter a statistical artifact rather than a genuine phenomenon (Schultz & Schultz, 1990).

Consumer Behavior. Among other things, consumer psychology is concerned with identifying attitudes, interests, opinions, values, personality traits, and life-styles that are associated with preferences for and purchases of certain products and services. A particular focus is on *psychographics,* which attempts through research to describe the characteristic patterns of temperament, cognition, and behavior that differentiate between diverse human components of the marketplace. The results of psychographic research may contribute to segmenting a particular market according to consumer personality and behavioral characteristics and then designing advertising, packaging, and promotional efforts to appeal to that market.

To give just one illustration, Sadalla and Burroughs (1981) classified foods as vegetarian, gourmet, health, fast, and synthetic (processed bacon or cheese snacks, instant eggs or drinks, etc.). Groups of individuals who preferred foods in each of these five categories then rated themselves and were rated by other people on a variety of behaviors and preferences. The raters concurred in describing consumers who preferred vegetarian foods as "noncompetitive, sexual, and liking carafe and folk dancing." Those preferring gourmet foods were described as "using drugs, living alone, liberal, and liking glamour sports and gambling." Those who preferred fast foods were described as "religious, logical, conservative people who wear polyester clothing, have no favorite hobbies, and show a particular liking for fast-food hamburgers."

Two of the most common approaches in psychographic studies are AIO inventories and VALS (values and life-styles). An *AIO inventory* consists of statements of the activities, interests, and opinions of specified groups. Illustrative of this approach are the following items on an AIO inventory administered to a sample of 18–24-year-old men who both drank and drove (Lastovicka, Murray, Joachimsthaler, Bhalla, and Scheurich, 1987):

> It seems like no matter what my friends and I do on a weekend, we almost always end up at a bar getting smashed.
> A party wouldn't be a party without some liquor.
> I've been drunk at least five times this month.
> Being drunk is fun.
> The chances of an accident or losing a driver's license from drinking and driving are low.
> Drinking helps me to have fun and do better with girls.
> A few drinks will have no noticeable effect on my coordination and self-control.

The *VALS* approach is based on a typology consisting of three broad categories of consumers: (1) need driven, (2) outer directed, and (3) inner directed (Mitchell, 1983). As illustrated in Figure 14–1, need-driven individuals, who are classified as sustainers or survivors, are at the lower end of the double hierarchy. The left (outer-directed) side of the hierarchy ranges from belongers at the bottom to emulators and achievers at the top. The right (inner-directed) side of the hierarchy ranges from the I-am-me's to the experientials and the societally conscious. The left and right sides of the double hierarchy meet at the top in the integrated person category. The nine types represented in the VALS hierarchy are described as follows:

I   *Need-drivens* spend according to need rather than preference.
   A. *Survivors* struggle for survival and are distrustful, social misfits who are ruled by appetites.
   B. *Sustainers* are concerned with safety and want law and order; they are insecure, compulsive, dependent, following individuals with a strong need for security.
II   *Outer-directeds* are extensive purchasers who buy from a sensitivity to what other people think of them and their purchases.
   A. *Belongers* are conforming, conventional, unexperimental, traditional, and formal.

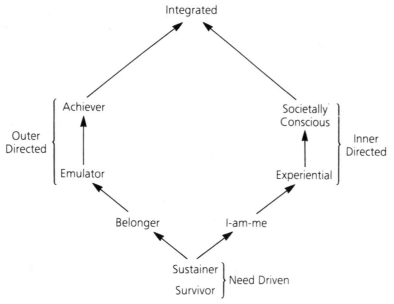

FIGURE 14–1 The VALS double hierarchy. (Reprinted with the permission of Macmillan Publishing Company from *The Nine American Lifestyles* by Arnold Mitchell. Copyright © 1983 by Arnold Mitchell.)

    B. *Emulators* are ambitious, status conscious show-offs who are upwardly mobile, macho, and competitive.

    C. *Achievers* are achievement-motivated, materialistic, efficient people who possess leadership ability and desire comfort.

III *Inner-directeds* are governed more by individual needs than by externally oriented values.

    A. *I-am-me's* are fiercely individualistic, dramatic, impulsive, and volatile.

    B. *Experientials* are driven toward direct experience; they are active, participative, person-centered, and artistic.

    C. *Societally conscious* are socially responsible people who live simply on a small scale and emphasize inner growth in a simple fashion.

IV *Integrateds* are psychologically mature and have a sense of what is fitting; they are tolerant, self-actualizing, and possess a world perspective.

Though used widely in marketing, VALS is limited by the fact that consumers do not usually fit into a single category; also, the data and keys on which the scoring is based are confidential and proprietary.

Academic Settings

Psychological tests were first used in schools for the purpose of determining whether children had sufficient intellectual ability to profit from regular classroom instruction. By the 1930s standardized tests of intelligence, achievement, and special aptitudes were widely administered in academic settings for screening, placement, and counseling purposes. One of the first personality tests to be used with schoolchildren was the Bernreuter Personality Inventory, published in 1931, which was scored for neurotic tendency, self-sufficiency, introversion-extroversion, dominance-submission, sociability, and confidence. The Bernreuter was administered to a generation of American public school pupils for the purpose of identifying those with personality problems.

Since the heyday of the Bernreuter, many personality assessment devices have been administered in school settings. Included among these are the California Test of Personality, the Mooney Problem Checklist, and the California Psychological Inventory. Certain inventories, such as the Jesness Inventory of Adolescent Personality for juvenile offenders, have been directed toward special groups, including emotionally disturbed, learning disabled, and physically impaired children.

The ideas of Freud, Adler, Rogers, Glasser, and other personality theorists have also been applied in school settings, not only as guides in the development of personality assessment instruments but in the training of school psychologists, pupil personnel workers, and teachers. Therapists in child guidance clinics, which maintain close ties with the schools, are usually trained extensively in one or more therapeutic techniques based on a particular theory of personality. With respect to teacher training, the author and many of his colleagues have had some success in applying the reality therapy concepts of William Glasser (1965, 1969) with teachers who were experiencing problems in maintaining classroom control or discipline. Teachers of young children have benefited especially from Adler's concept of the inferiority complex, the striving for superiority, and the relationship of ordinal position to child behavior. In addition, the writings of Rogers and Maslow on self-actualization have influenced many teachers who wished to bring out the creative spark in their pupils and provide an atmosphere in which children would have a better chance of fulfilling their potentialities.

Legal and Political Settings

Psychologists who work in legal settings are called upon to perform a variety of tasks, many of a diagnostic nature. In a court case, a psychologist may be asked by either the prosecution or the defense to examine the plaintiff for signs of mental disorder, dangerous or violent behavior, incompetency to stand trial or handle his (her) own affairs, inability to serve as a suitable parent (in a child custody hearing), or many other purposes. The legal case may involve anything from a simple divorce proceeding to first-degree homicide.

Not only the defendant but also other persons (witnesses, etc.) associated with a legal dispute may require examination by a psychologist. The psychologist may be asked for an opinion concerning an unknown or unapprehended criminal, whether a child will be better off if placed with one of the parents or with some other person, and even how potential jurors are likely to vote.[1]

Ability measures such as the Wechsler Intelligence Scales are often administered in court cases, but the Minnesota Multiphasic Personality Inventory

(MMPI) and the Rorschach Inkblot Test are the most commonly administered personality assessment instruments in such contexts. Other psychological measures include the Georgia Competency Test (Wildman et al., 1980), the Rogers Criminal Responsibility Scales (Psychological Assessment Resources), the Clarke Sex History Questionnaire for Males (Langevin, 1983), and the Georgetown Screening Interview for Competency to Stand Trial (Bukatman, Foy, & De Grazia, 1971). Unfortunately, none of these instruments is perfectly valid, and there is a need for psychodiagnostic measures that provide more accurate answers to legal questions than the instruments that are currently available.

Criminal Personality. As noted in Chapter 9, research on criminal characteristics goes back at least as far as the early twentieth century (Lombroso, 1911). The notion that certain childhood experiences and personality traits are more common in criminals has also been a popular theme among criminologists and psychologists. For example, Sigmund Freud interpreted much criminal behavior as a compulsive need for punishment resulting from guilt feelings associated with the Oedipus complex. Other psychoanalysts have maintained that criminality is characteristic of immature personalities who lack adequate control over id impulses, or that it is due to a failure to internalize the reality principle and hence control the drive toward immediate gratification (Nietzel, 1979).

Hans Eysenck (1964), who is primarily a dispositional theorist, took an interactionist position in his assertion that criminal behavior is due to an interaction of environmental and hereditary factors. Yochelson and Samenow (1976) and J. Q. Wilson and Herrnstein (1985) would appear to agree with Eysenck's position. Yochelson and Samenow (1976; Samenow, 1984) maintained that criminals possess a different way of perceiving and thinking about the world, a way that cannot be explained simply as the result of learning or differential associations with other lawbreakers. Although evidence in support of these theories of criminal behavior is fragile, some data point to an unusual and characteristic pattern of brain organization in antisocial personalities (Jutai, Hare, & Connolly, 1987; also see Goleman, 1987a, 1987b).

While not discounting the role of learning in criminal behavior, dispositional theorists place less emphasis on interpersonal interactions, modeling, and reinforcement in a variety of situations than do sociopsychological theorists. To the latter, criminal behavior is acquired through social interactions or interchanges. Criminal behavior is seen as a consequence of differential positive reinforcement for antisocial behavior (Bandura, 1977; Conger, 1980). Punishment or restriction, or a lack of same, is also believed to be an important variable in criminality. Thus people are said to learn to behave in an antisocial manner because they are not adequately controlled by external social pressures (Reckless, 1961, 1967).

Personalities of Police Officers. Although not as extensively studied as the personalities of lawbreakers, the personality characteristics of law enforcers and lawmakers have also been investigated. In contrast to the popular conception of police officers as highly authoritarian, rigid, and almost pathologically paranoid, as a group they appear to be relatively normal and far from homogeneous with respect to personality. Lefkowitz (1975) cites evidence for two clusters of personality traits shared by police officers. The first cluster consists of the traits of isolation and secrecy, defensiveness and suspiciousness, cynicism, and probably insecurity. The second cluster comprises authoritarianism, status concerns, and violence. The labels "authoritarian" and "violent," as applied to police officers, may be somewhat justified, but not to a pathological degree. Police officers tend to respect authority, particularly as represented by government and laws, and they see themselves as representatives of the legal establishment and enforcers of society's laws. Thus showing disrespect for a police officer is likely to be interpreted by the officer as disrespect for the higher legal authority of which he or she is a visible manifestation.

Allegations that the police discriminate against people of lower socioeconomic status and in favor of middle-class suspects and others who possess political power may also be justified. This tendency is frequently reinforced by the petty lower-class criminals with whom street officers typically come into contact. These experiences with the so-called dregs of humanity may serve to bolster any incipient and perhaps realistic paranoia felt by an officer.

Most police officers come from working-class homes, a background that is reflected in their high need for security. Police officers typically score in the average to high-average range on intelligence tests, and when examined by clinical (impressionistic) techniques, they show up as physically aggressive, rather impulsive risk takers who are preoccupied with self-image (Lefkowitz, 1975). Still, as a group police officers have a strong sense of comaraderie and a pronounced secondary interest in being of service to society.

Political Leaders. Above the legions of lawbreakers and law enforcers are the political leaders who encourage, make, modify, interpret, and defend the law. Psychobiographical studies of many famous people, including political leaders such as Adolf Hitler (Binion, 1976; Langer, 1972), Mohandas Gandhi (Erikson, 1969), and a number of American presidents (Freud & Bullitt, 1967; Brodie, 1983; Kearns, 1976; Glad, 1980), have been conducted for both theoretical and practical reasons. The practical reasons have centered on providing opposition leaders (or others who are forced to contend with certain political figures) with insights into the personality and behavior of those leaders and some means of predicting what they might do under certain circumstances. One of the first such psychobiographies was written by Sigmund Freud and William C. Bullitt to provide psychological data concerning President Woodrow Wilson, which presumably could then be used as political ammunition against him (Freud & Bullitt, 1967). Similar motives reportedly led to Langer's (1972) analysis of Hitler, and perhaps analyses of other political personalities as well.

Although most psychobiographies have been written by historians or psychoanalysts, psychologists with a dispositional perspective have also conducted studies of the characteristics of political leaders. Among the most famous of these are studies of the *authoritarian personality* (see Chapter 10) conducted with a paper-and-pencil inventory known as the F ("fascism") Scale (Adorno et al., 1950). Simonton (1990) views the psychological construct of authoritarianism as being similar to Rokeach's (1960) concepts of *dogmatism* and the variable of *integrative complexity* (Schroder, Driver, & Streufert, 1967). Higher scorers on the F Scale and the Dogmatism Scale tend to think in rigid, simplistic terms, whereas persons who are high on integrative complexity deal with information in a much more sophisticated way.

Political psychologists have also analyzed the roles of concepts such as the power motive, the achievement motive, and the affiliation motive in shaping the actions of political leaders. Measures of dominance, extroversion, flexibility, intelligence, morality, idealism, and Machiavellianism have also been found to be related to political behavior (see Simonton, 1990). Other variables that have been examined by researchers in their efforts to account for the behavior of political leaders are birth order and situational influences, and in particular the interaction between individual characteristics and situational variables. How valid the resulting conclusions are and whether they should be used for practical purposes, however, remain open questions.

Sports and Personality

Applications of psychology to professional sports began with an emphasis on techniques for enhancing the performance of athletes (see Butt, 1987). Clinical psychologists, working with athletic coaches, have served as both advisers and psychotherapists to professional athletes striving to attain a winning edge in high-level competition. A variety of individual and group techniques have been applied by sports psychologists, and a separate division, the Division of Exercise and Sport Psychology, was established within the American Psychological Association.

Currently the psychology of sport is a broad field of research, theory, and application that deals not only with maximizing the performance of elite athletes, but also with a variety of other topics pertaining to the physical activities of all age groups and all levels of athletic competence (see Butt, 1987; LeUnes & Nation, 1989). For example, sports psychologists have conducted numerous studies concerned with the selection of potentially winning athletes. Among the personality assessment instruments administered in such studies are the Athletic Motivation Inventory, the Minnesota Multiphasic Personality Inventory, the Sixteen Personality Factor Questionnaire, the Eysenck Personality Inventory, and the Edwards Personality Inventory. Although none of these instruments has proven to be an especially valid predictor of athletic performance, somewhat more encouraging results have been obtained with the Profile of Mood States (POMS). Morgan (1980) compared the POMS scores of Olympic rowers, wrestlers, and distance runners with the scores of unsuccessful candidates in these sports. In all three sports, successful candidates scored lower than unsuccessful candidates on the tension (TEN), depression (DEP), anger (ANG), fatigue (FAT), and confu-

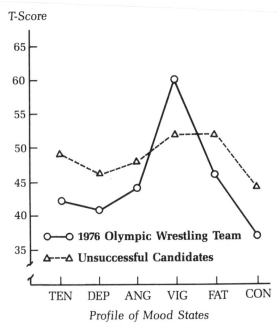

T-Score

FIGURE 14–2   Morgan's iceberg profile (Reprinted with permission from "Test of Champions: The Iceberg Profile" by W. P. Morgan, 1980, *Psychology Today*, 14[2], 92–102, 108.)

sion (CON) scales, but higher on the vigor (VIG) scale of the POMS. This so-called iceberg profile (see Figure 14–2) has also been reported by other investigators (e.g., Joesting, 1981; Ungeleiter & Golding, 1989).

Another kind of investigation of the relationships of personality variables to athletic performance and exercise has examined the effects of exercise on mood and other affective variables. The overall results of these studies indicate that physical exercise has a significant effect on anxiety, depression, self-esteem, and other indices of mental well-being. Not only does exercise reduce anxiety (Morgan, 1973) and depression (Greist, 1984), but it also promotes self-esteem (Sonstroem, 1984) and acts as a buffer against stress (Roth & Holmes, 1985).

Issues in the Study of Personality

Since the time of Freud, personality theory and research findings have been continuously debated. The Freudian emphases on childhood sexuality, the Oedipus complex, stages in psychosexual development, and the influence of unconscious motivation on behavior have been the topics of both controversy and fascination by psychologists and nonpsychologists alike. Despite many shortcomings in his theory of personality development, Freud unquestionably was right in asserting that, to a large extent, the child is father to the man. It is now generally accepted that childhood experiences can have an enduring effect on personality development, and on adult personality in particular. However, most contemporary theorists recognize that Freud overemphasized the formative influence of infantile sexuality on adult personality.

The Status of Personality Theories

Not only does the zeitgeist, or spirit and culture of the times, in which a personality theorist lives affect the nature of the theory, but the particular experiences and personality of the theorist also play a significant role in shaping the theory. It is a truism that no one can completely divorce himself from his time or self in fashioning whatever picture he develops of the world.

The fact that the personality of the theorist and the sociocultural context in which he lives are intertwined with his theorizing does not necessarily mean that the theory is wrong. It does suggest, however, that the theory is limited in what it can explain. Such limitations and idiosyncrasies are seen, for example, in comparing the theories of Sigmund Freud and Carl Rogers. Freud was a Jewish physician who spent his formative years in Vienna, Austria, where he experienced anti-Semitism and the social values of the Victorian era. The 100 or so patients whom Freud treated during his professional career were, for the most part, well-to-do, middle-class neurotics. Rogers, on the other hand, who was the son of a deeply religious Protestant father, grew up in a midwestern American rural community and spent most of his professional life teaching and counseling American university students. Although Freud and Rogers were both highly intelligent and well-educated, it takes no great stretch of the imagination to realize that the differences in backgrounds of these men influenced their philosophies of life and presumably their conceptions of personality in particular and humanity in general.

In addition to the notion that the cultural environment of a theorist is affected by his or her experiences and hence plays a significant role in shaping the theorist's picture of human personality, another statement concerning personality theorists also seems certain to be true: In one way or another, all personality theorists since Freud have been influenced by his ideas. This statement does not mean that all subsequent theorists agreed completely or even substantially with Freud's teachings, but he did influence them in either a positive or a negative way. For Harry S. Sullivan and Erik Erikson the influence was mainly positive; for Gordon Allport and Carl Rogers, it was presumably more negative.

In some ways, the status of personality theories appears more uncertain as the twentieth century draws to a close than it was a few decades ago. The situation is perhaps characteristic of psychology as a whole. Many years ago when the author was a graduate student it seemed as if psychology, which we were told was handicapped by getting a late start, would attain the exactness and status of the physical, or at least the biological, sciences within the foreseeable future. Today that hope has dimmed considerably.

Although the influence of psychoanalytic theory can still be felt, no single theory of personality has attained a dominant position. Diversity and disagreement over concepts, methodology, and applications are the rule rather than the exception. The roles of biological versus social factors, conscious versus unconscious determinants, determinism versus free will, and behavior versus cognitions and feelings are illustrative of the many bipolar issues that divide personality theorists (Feist, 1990). Beginning with Dollard and Miller's (1950) laudable efforts to combine psychoanalysis and Hullian behaviorism, attempts have been made to create a synthesis or rapprochement between various theories. None of these efforts, however, has been particularly successful.

Today most practicing psychologists are reluctant to subscribe to any single theoretical position, preferring to assume an eclectic stance in which whatever seems appropriate is adopted from different theories to serve as a guide in psychotherapy and other psychological intervention procedures. Perhaps a more general theory of personality, one that is applicable to a wider range of problems and situations, is just beyond the horizon. The likelihood that some genius will come along and achieve such a monumental goal, however, is not particularly high. Still, one can argue that progress can come out of conflict and chaos, and that understanding usually advances by small steps rather than by earth-shattering insights.

Continuing Controversies

Many of the older disputes in personality theory and research have abated with time. For example, the idiographic versus nomothetic controversy and the clinical versus statistical prediction debates are little discussed today.

Idiographic versus Nomothetic and Clinical versus Statistical. As described in Chapter 4, the distinction between the idiographic and nomethetic approaches to conceptualizing personality was first made by Gordon Allport (1937, 1961). In the *idiographic approach,* each person is viewed as a lawful, integrated system to be studied in his or her own right. In contrast, the *nomothetic approach* consists of searching for laws of personality that apply to all people. It is true that clinical psychologists are, on the whole, more inclined toward an idiographic approach and experimental psychologists toward a nomothetic approach, but the clash between these two ways of viewing human personality is not as heated as it once was. Likewise, the *clinical approach,* in which diagnostic judgments are made intuitively or impressionistically and conclusions are drawn from subjective experiences combined with a theory of personality, does not seem to contrast as vividly as it once did with the *statistical approach* to data collection, analysis, and prediction. Although clinical psychologists have, by and large, retained their intuitive bent, they are not now as reluctant as previously to combine subjective judgment with statistically evaluated data and actuarial predictions based on objective rules. Recognition of the efficiency of such statistical or actuarial methods has led to the current emphasis on using computers to administer, score, and interpret personality assessment instruments of various types.

Heredity versus Environment. Two issues that are still widely debated, if perhaps not as vociferously as they were at one time, are the relative importance of heredity versus environment and traits versus situations in shaping personality and behavior. With respect to the former issue, American pychologists have traditionally been primarily environmentalistic or nurture centered in their explanations of the origins of behavior. This environmentalist bias is to some extent a reflection of the prominence of learning as a topic of research by American psychologists during the twentieth century.[2] Research by behaviorists and social learning theorists such as John Dollard and Neal Miller, Julian Rotter, and Albert Bandura has demonstrated that the emphasis on the role of learning in personality development has not been misdirected. The effects of environment and learning appear to be particularly important during the formative years of human development, when the child is still growing and exploring.

Even the most radical behaviorists recognize, however, that personality characteristics result from the joint action of environment and heredity. Evidence for a genetic basis for personality characteristics and certain mental disorders, a topic considered in some detail in Chapter 9, is truly impressive and expanding. The ways in which heredity and environment interact to shape human personality are complex and still not clearly understood, but one thing is clear: Personality is the result of reciprocal interactions, exchanges, or transactions between people and their physical and social environments. Children who possess different genetically based physiques and temperaments react differently to the same environment and are in turn acted upon by that environment. The response of the physical and social environment to a child's genetically based characteristics and behavior further mold those characteristics. The resulting changes in personal characteristics or behaviors, in turn, produce further reactions from the environment, and so forth, in a back-and-forth interactive manner.

Traits versus Situations. The issue of traits versus situations was discussed in some detail in Chapter 4, but it may be instructive to review the topic here. Dispositional theorists have traditionally assumed that behavior is influenced to a great extent by an aggregate of traits that are consistently manifested in a variety of situations. Although it has long been recognized that environmental situations affect behavior, the emphasis of dispositional theorists in particular has been on personality traits or types. After reviewing a mass of research reports, Walter Mischel (1968) concluded that, although cognitive abilities are fairly consistent across different situations, personal-social behavior is highly dependent on the situation in which it occurs. Mischel maintained that measures of personality traits and inferences made from scores on such measures show little transsituational generality. To Mischel, "Traditional trait-state conceptualizations of personality, while often paying lip-service to man's complexity and the uniqueness of each person, in fact lead to a grossly oversimplified view that misses both the richness and the uniqueness of individual lives" (1968, p. 301).

Mischel's criticism of dispositional theories of personality did not go unanswered. During the past two decades a great deal of research has led to a more balanced perspective regarding the interactive roles of traits and situations in determining behavior (e.g., Bem & Allen, 1974; Block, 1977; Bem & Funder, 1978). Analyses of situations into categories such as "strong" versus "weak" have underscored the fact that the influences of personal characteristics vary appreciably with the situation. Under certain circumstances personal characteristics exert a powerful influence in determining how a person behaves; in other contexts, situational influences are more pronounced. Certain behaviors are responses to specific stimuli and hence likely to be consistent across situations in which those stimuli are present. Other behaviors do not require specific eliciting stimuli and hence are likely to occur in a broader range of situations and to be influenced more by personality traits.

It is now recognized that some behaviors, as well as some people, show high consistency in some situations but are quite variable in others (Chaplin & Goldberg, 1984; Zuckerman, Koestner, DeBoy, Garcia, et al., 1988). Certain situations may elicit the expression of personality characteristics that are not manifested in other situations, but the extent to which this generalization is true varies with the person. Some people are more rigid or less flexible in their behaviors, acting in much the same manner regardless of changed external circumstances. Other people are virtually chameleon-like in the way their behavior varies from place to place and time to time. In this regard, Snyder (1974, 1979) constructed the Self-Monitoring Scale to measure the extent to which people are very attentive to situational cues (*high self-monitors*) as opposed to relying on internal cues (*low self-monitors*); the latter are more consistent in their behavior in different situations.

The low to moderate reliabilities of both trait and situation measures obviously detract from the careful assessment of the roles of these variables and of the ways in which they interact in influencing behavior. One suggestion, although not a complete solution, is to increase the reliability of trait measures by aggregating (combining) them across different times and different situations (Epstein, 1979). In addition, conceptual models of how personality dispositions and situational features interact are sorely needed (McReynolds, 1979). If the resulting measures are sufficiently precise, analysis-of-variance statistical procedures can be used to separate the main effects of traits and situations from the effects of their interaction. Another proposal is the *template-matching technique* (Bem & Funder, 1978), according to which the degree of similarity between a given person's behavior in a specified situation is compared with a template of how a person ideally behaves in that situation. This is an interesting suggestion, but it is far from a complete situation-trait transactive theory of the sort that is needed.

In summary, both personal and situational determinants are now recognized as important and essential factors in individual behavior. Today, the controversy over the supremacy of traits versus situations in shaping behavior has definitely subsided (Buss, 1989; Kenrick & Funder, 1988). We now see dispositional and behavioral/social learning theorists concurring on the significance of both traits and situations in guiding behavior. The task that faces personality theorists and researchers, as in the case of heredity versus environment, is to determine precisely how the multiplicity of personal and situational influences combine and interact to prompt a person to behave in one way rather than another.

Computers, Cognitions, and Personality

Perhaps the single most important event that has influenced personality research and assessment during the past two or three decades has been the technological advance represented by the digital computer. The increased speed, versatility, and accessibility of computers has led to ever more complex techniques and models in almost every area of psychological investigation and evaluation. Computers can be programmed not only to analyze and interpret data, but also to conduct interviews and experiments, perform psychological counseling, and simulate real-life behavior patterns. It is therefore no wonder that several recent conceptualizations or theoretical systems concerning personality and behavior have incorporated concepts and processes basic to the design and operation of computers.

Information-Processing and Cognitive Theories

Computers are essentially information-processing machines, a description that in some measure can also be applied to the functioning of the human brain. Like a computer, the brain encodes, stores, organizes, and retrieves information. Although the processes of the brain are analogous to those of a computer, the brain is not merely a "simply divine automatic computer," referred to by the acronym SDAC. Perception, problem solving, and responding have their counterparts in the input, central-processing-unit, and output functions of a computer, but research on artificial intelligence has revealed that it is not an easy task to replace the complex functions of a thinking human being with those of a machine. Consequently, it will undoubtedly be quite some time, if ever, before an understanding of the inner workings of a computer is able to provide an in-depth understanding of human behavior and personality. In fact, some authorities question the assumption that the brain can ever understand itself well enough to design a machine that can do everything that is done by the brain itself. An effective computer model of human thinking must take into account the fact that human beings are not passive responders to stimuli, but that they actively select and analyze available information in terms of its compatibility with their own purposes, plans, and goals.

Consistent with an emphasis on computer models of human behavior and thinking are cognitive theories of personality. A number of cognitive theories, those of George Kelly, Julian Rotter, Albert Bandura, and Walter Mischel, are discussed in Chapters 7 and 8. More recent cognitive theories, however, employ the language and concepts of information theory and computer science. These theories, of which there are several, view the human being as an information-processing system that represents reality in symbolic form, makes plans, devises schemata, formulates and follows scripts, and in general operates according to modifiable programs to satisfy its needs and cope with its problems.

According to Jean Piaget, a *schema* is a cognitive structure that guides the processing of information. It is a mental process by which a person comes to organize and understand his or her experiences. For example, when a child tries to use one hand to grasp a glass container after having just grasped a rattle with that hand, he or she is attempting to assimilate the glass into a preexisting schema for grasping. If unsuccessful in grasping the glass with one hand, the child will be forced to accommodate the grasping schema to the reality of the situation. That is, the child will have to modify his or her approach by using two hands. As the child matures, the grasping schema and other mental structures and the associated patterns of behavior become elaborated and refined in response to experience. Thus a schema of an intelligent adult might be a philosophy of pacifism, which may have to be accommodated to external reality when the person is physically attacked. Elementary schemata are also organized into higher-order, integrated schemata.

In contrast to schemata, *scripts* consist of patterns of expectations and behaviors considered appropriate to a particular situation and according to which a person regulates his or her life. As described by Schank and Abelson (1977), people develop scripts as elaborate, stereotyped frameworks for understanding or construing sequential events such as going to a movie, eating at a restaurant, performing the tasks constituting an occupation, and other patterns of behavior that flow and change with time.

Through the analysis of schemata, scripts, and other cognitive variables, psychological researchers are attempting to answer the question of how people process and apply information from their physical, social, and personal environments to accomplish the work and attain the goals of their lives. According to this approach, the ways in which a person's ideas and beliefs about his or her experiences are organized and utilized comprise the personality of that individual. Those experiences are organized into conceptual categories of various levels of abstraction, categories that simplify and construe experience into a more or less efficient way of dealing with the environment. As noted by George Kelly (1955) (see Chapter 7), the categories according to which a person construes (constructs) his or her experiences with the world become the personality of that person. These categories, of course, do not always represent the most useful or realistic ways of construing one's experience. Such shortcomings are seen in the maladaptive ways employed by mentally disordered individuals to process the information that is available to them. The aim of therapy with such individuals is to find ways of dealing with or changing these unrealistic, maladaptive cognitions to more realistic, socially acceptable and personally gratifying cognitions (e.g., Beck, Rush, Shaw, & Emery, 1979; Meichenbaum, 1985).

Other Research Areas Related to Personality

In addition to keeping up with research and developments in computer science, future personologists will need to be attentive to advances in neurophysiology, biochemistry, and genetics. Even now, there appears to be a greater readiness than heretofore to incorporate physiological and genetic concepts and data into explanations of personality differences and changes. Psychoanalytic constructs such as the unconscious mind are also being resurrected by information theorists, who find evidence for different levels of awareness and the unconscious processing of information (e.g., Cheesman & Merikle, 1986). Noteworthy progress has also been made in understanding the physiological and genetic bases of a variety of disorders (e.g., Alzheimer's disease, autism, depression, schizophrenia) and emotions that are of interest to personality psychologists.

Would-be personality researchers and theorists must also keep in touch with developmental psychology, cross-cultural research, and psychometrics. As we have seen in Chapter 10, a great deal of research is currently under way on developmental processes, and there is every reason to expect that it will continue. Furthermore, rather than being limited to twentieth-century Western culture, the field of personality psychology must incorporate the findings and analyses of sociologists, cultural anthropologists, and historians on how behavior varies with the sociocultural setting and the times in which children develop.

With respect to psychometrics, recent work in structural equation modeling, path analysis, causal modeling, factor analysis, and related techniques designed to make psychological data more interpretable (e.g., Bentler & Newcomb, 1986) should be followed carefully and applied judiciously to questions concerning the development of personality characteristics and their influences on behavior. Applications of these statistical procedures enable researchers to go beyond simple correlation coefficients and investigate the complex interrelationships and causal connections among more fundamental underlying variables.

It should be clear from the preceding paragraphs that future researchers and theorists in personality psychology will need to consider multiple sources of information and adopt multiple approaches to obtaining further information. Progress in the field of personology will undoubtedly continue to be slow, punctuated as it has been in the recent past by minitheories concerning specific concepts or processes such as aggression, causal attributions, sex roles, competitiveness, and altruism. Research on the concept of *self*, which is viewed as a kind of unitary causal agent in personality, will probably continue and may give rise to theories more closely connected with research findings. Other concepts that many psychologists of yesteryear considered too "mentalistic" to be the proper topics of research in their discipline are now receiving reconsideration. Research on cognitive teleological concepts such as intentions, plans, purposes, and goals indicates movement from a "push" to a "pull" theory of motivation during the late twentieth century.

Ultimately, the construction of a more general theory of personality will require the efforts of a team of researchers equipped with a variety of knowledge and skills. Such a theory should be parsimonious and clear in its concepts, firmly based on a multitude of factors obtained from empirical research, and comprised of propositions that are testable and lead to verifiable predictions. It should be congruent with the findings in all areas of psychology and other sciences, and it should lead to the generation of valid assessment instruments and effective intervention procedures.

Postscript

So where have we arrived in our quest to understand the mystery of the human personality? Hopefully we have made some progress, but admittedly we are not very far along the road to enlightenment. At least one thing seems clear at this juncture: On one level people are fairly easy to understand. As William James asserted more than 100 years ago, human behavior is to a large extent habitual and motivated to acquire those things that ensure survival and satisfaction of a person's needs. B. F. Skinner was also right in his assertion that behavior is controlled by the reinforcement contingencies that follow it. And Albert Bandura is right: When in Rome all kinds of people act as the Romans do, because imitating or modeling the behavior of others saves a lot of time and also satisfies one's social motives to be accepted and respected by others.

Be that as it may, understanding why people behave and think in certain ways becomes more difficult as we probe more deeply in our quest for enlightenment. Some individuals, among whom Sigmund Freud and Carl Rogers should be counted, appear to be equipped with a kind of sixth sense or ability to understand the inner experiences and suffering of other people. Individuals who possess this empathic sensitivity have learned to observe carefully, to "listen with the third ear" (as in the following quotation), and to refrain from making hasty judgments and glib overgeneralizations. But even these seemingly insightful psychologists cannot know the entirety of another human being.

> After a few sentences about the eventful day, the patient fell into a long silence. She assured me that nothing was in her thoughts. Silence from me. After many minutes she complained about a toothache. She told me that she had been to the dentist yesterday. He had given her an injection and then had pulled a wisdom tooth. The spot was hurting again. New and longer silence. She pointed to my bookcase in the corner and said, "There's a book standing on its head."
>
> Without the slightest hesitation and in a reproachful voice I said, "But why did you not tell me that you had an abortion?" I had said it without an inkling of what I would say and why I would say it. It felt as if, not I, but something in me had said that. The patient jumped up and looked at me as if I were a ghost. Nobody knew or could know that her love, the physician, had performed an abortion on her. The

operation, especially dangerous because of the advanced state of her pregnancy was, of course, kept very secret because abortion in the case of gentiles was punishable by death in Germany. To protect the man she still loved, she had decided to tell me all except this secret.[3]

I once interviewed a young man who had the delusion that the words written on billboards and certain other signs were symbolic messages directed to him personally. For some time he expressed this belief to other people, but eventually he was committed to a mental hospital. When he was finally released, I asked him if he still felt that the signs were personal messages meant for him alone. After a while he looked at me and said, "Can you keep a secret?" When I assured him that our conversation was confidential, he replied, "Yes, I still feel the same way, but I know that if I admit it to other people they will lock me up again. So I have learned to keep quiet about my feelings." In a sense, this man was still mentally ill, but he had learned to play the role of a sane person. Such is the subtlety and complexity of human personality, a realization with which we began and will end this book.

Summary

The systematic, scientific study of personality began during the late nineteenth and early twentieth centuries with investigations of abnormal behavior and individual differences in mental abilities. The oldest conceptions of human personality, which were proposed by novelists, playwrights, and other storytellers and sages long before psychology became a science and a profession, depicted it in terms of types, traits, and other dispositional constructs. Lists of instincts, motives, phobias, and other compilations were devised in the hope of providing exhaustive descriptions and explanations of individual differences in stylistic patterns of thinking and acting.

Although they were the oldest and most commonly applied in everyday speech, dispositional theories had less influence than psychoanalytic depth psychology on later theories and research pertaining to personality. Freud's 1909 visit stimulated professional interest in psychoanalysis in the United States and had profound effects on the diagnosis and treatment of mental disorders. The influence of psychoanalysis reached a peak during the 1930s and 1940s, after which behavioristic and phenomenological-humanistic theories and methods gained in popularity. Today, a kind of amalgam of behavioristic and cognitive constructs has become prominent in clinical and personality psychology. What other aspiring theories are waiting in the wings remains to be seen, but information-processing models of problem solving and thinking will certainly play a role.

Psychologists, no less than other human beings, have disagreements, politely referred to as "issues" rather than "arguments." Among the topics of controversy are the polarities of heredity versus environment, traits versus situations, idiographic versus nomothetic approaches, and clinical versus statistical methods. Debate over which end of each polarity is nearer to the truth has diminished in recent years, as a kind of working eclecticism that recognizes the virtue of multiple viewpoints and the importance of interactionism has emerged. Psychologists of all persuasions now recognize that both heredity *and* environment, as well as traits *and* situations, are important in personality development and functioning. Likewise, the idiographic versus nomothetic and the clinical versus statistical approaches to data collection, diagnosis, and prediction have achieved something of a marriage.

In addition to their traditional applications in counseling and psychotherapy, as well as other health-related contexts, research findings and theories concerning personality have been applied to a variety of problems in education, business and industry, and law enforcement and politics. The effectiveness of these applications is hampered to some extent by problems with the validities of our assessment instruments as well as untested procedures and inadequately trained practitioners. It seems certain, however, that the demand for applications of personality theories, diagnostic and research methods, and assessment instruments will continue. For this and other reasons, it is essential for students of personality psychology to receive a thorough grounding in scientific and statistical methods and more than a passing acquaintance with computer science, genetics, physiological and development psychology, sociology, and cultural anthropology.

Key Concepts

Accident proneness   The largely discounted theory that a particular personality type is associated with a greater tendency to have accidents.

AIO inventory   An inventory consisting of statements designed to analyze differences in the activities, interests, and opinions of specified groups (market segments) for product-marketing purposes.

Assessment center   Technique, used primarily in the selection of executive personnel, for evaluating the personality characteristics and behavior of a small group of individuals by having them perform a variety of tasks during a period of a few days.

Clinical (impressionistic) approach   Approach to behavioral prediction and diagnosis in which psychologists assign their own judgmental weights to the predictor variables and then combine them in a subjective manner to make behavioral forecasts or diagnoses.

Dogmatism   Personality trait characterized by repeated, unfounded assertions of one's opinions as being the truth; may be assessed by Rokeach's Dogmatism Scale.

Information processing   Perceptual-cognitive process by which information is taken in, stored, and used.

Leaderless group discussion (LGD)   A session in which approximately six individuals (for example, candidates for an executive position) are observed while discussing an assigned problem to determine their effectiveness in working with a group and reaching a solution.

Psychographics Consumer research directed toward describing the psychological profiles, or characteristic patterns of behavior and thinking, that differentiate one consumer group from another.

Schema A cognitive structure that abstractly represents events, objects, or relationships in the external world.

Script General plans developed by the individual to enable him or her to anticipate, respond to, control, or create events in a meaningful fashion.

Self The perceived identity, individuality, or ego; that which consciously knows and experiences.

Statistical (actuarial) approach Approach to data collection and behavior prediction consisting of the application of a statistical formula, a set of rules, or an actuarial table to assessment data.

Activities and Applications

1. Which theories of personality discussed in Chapters 4–8 of this book do you think are helpful in understanding and predicting consumer behavior? Be as specific and detailed as you can, considering dispositional (trait-factor), psychodynamic (psychoanalytic), phenomenological (self, humanistic, and existential), and behavioral/social learning theories.

2. Write a short paper on the relationships of personality to criminal behavior, including excerpts from newspaper and magazines stories as well as books and journal articles. The following references should help get you started:
Goleman, D. (1987, April 7). The bully: New research depicts a paranoid, lifelong loser. *New York Times*, 19, 23.
Samenow, S. E. (1984). *Inside the criminal mind*. New York: Times Books.
Yochelson, S., & Samenow, S. E. (1976). *The criminal personality Vol. I: A profile for change*. New York: Jason Aronson.
Wilson, J. Q., & Herrnstein, R. (1985). *Crime and human nature*. New York: Simon & Schuster.

3. It has been claimed that famous novelists and biographers often display a keener understanding of human personality and behavior than professional psychologists, psychiatrists, and other behavioral scientists. Defend the validity or invalidity of this proposition. Make certain that your arguments are logical and based as much as possible on direct evidence.

4. The question of whether success in sports is due primarily to the efforts of individual athletes or to cooperative team efforts has been debated at some length. It is likely that the answer to this question varies with whether one is talking about an individual sport or a team sport. The following questionnaire was designed to assess opinions on whether success in sports is due to individual or team efforts. Administer it to a sample of athletes in several team sports (basketball, volleyball, football, etc.) and to another group of athletes in several individual sports (tennis, golf, swimming, etc.). We will overlook the fact that some individual sports are also team sports. Score the questionnaires and calculate the mean scores of the sample of team sport athletes and the individual sport athletes. Is there a significant difference between the means? Is it in the predicted direction, that is, higher for the athletes in individual sports?

Questionnaire

Directions: For each of the following statements, write the appropriate letters in the marginal dash to indicate your degree of agreement or disagreement with the statement: SA = Strongly Agree, A = Agree, U = Undecided, D = Disagree, SD = Strongly Disagree.

_____ 1. Success in sports is attained more by individual effort than by cooperative group effort.

_____ 2. People who try to separate themselves from the needs of others usually end up getting hurt in one way or another.

_____ 3. The most successful people are those who are able to break free from group conformity and rely on themselves.

_____ 4. As with success in any endeavor, winning a game depends on the cooperation of all players rather than just the efforts of one or two.

_____ 5. You can depend on other people only so far, and then it is up to you to accomplish what you want to do.

_____ 6. In general, it is better to do what other people expect of you even if it conflicts with what you yourself would rather do.

_____ 7. Children should be taught to do their best even if it is not always the best thing for their friends or teammates.

_____ 8. I have learned in life that it is better not to be self-centered, but rather to try to cooperate with others.

_____ 9. It is a sign of weakness to be too dependent on other people.

_____ 10. The most important thing that a coach can say about a person is that he is a "real team player."

_____ 11. I attribute much of my success to the fact that I paid more attention to my own beliefs and feelings than to the demands and expectations of other people.

_____ 12. The world would be a much better place if people were less self-centered and more socially oriented.

_____ 13. I listen to what other people have to say, but in the end I usually do it my own way.

_____ 14. Relying exclusively on one's own abilities is bad for the group and, in the end, bad for oneself.

_____ 15. To accomplish your goals you have to separate yourself from other people and depend more on your own physical and mental resources.

_____ 16. I attribute much of my success to the fact that I tried to do what my family, my friends, and my teammates expected of me.

_____ 17. In the end a person has to rely on his or her own abilities and beliefs rather than those of other people.

_____ 18. Before I make an important decision I usually try to consider what other people might think about what I decide to do.

_____ 19. In the main, successful people do things their own way without paying much attention to what others think of them.

_____ 20. Individual success is usually the result of cooperative efforts.

Scoring: Responses to the odd-numbered items are scored as SA = 4, A = 3, U = 2, D = 1, and SD = 0; responses to the even-numbered items are scored as SA = 0, A = 1, U = 2, D = 3, and SD = 4. The highest possible score is 80. The higher the score, the more individualistic or self-centered the respondent.

5. Summarize research findings on the following:
   a. Idiographic and nomothetic approaches to personality study.
   b. Heredity and environment as determiners of personality.
   c. Traits and situations as determiners of personality.
   d. Clinical and statistical methods of personality assessment.

6. What changes do you predict will occur in personality theory, research, and assessment during the next 20 years or so? What new kinds of methods or procedures for studying personality will be forthcoming, and what new applications will be found for theories and research results concerned with personality? See Pervin (1990) in the Suggested Readings.

7. Give examples of contexts in which the situation would be expected to exert a more powerful influence on the individual's behavior, and other contexts in which personality traits would be expected to have a greater effort on how a person behaves.

Suggested Readings

Buss, A. H. (1989). Personality as traits. *American Psychologist, 44,* 1378–1388.
Buss, A. H., & Cantor, N. (Eds.). (1989). *Personality psychology: Recent trends and emerging directions.* New York: Springer-Verlag.
Kenrick, D. T., & Funder, D. C. (1988). Profiting from controversy: Lessons from the person-situation debate. *American Psychologist, 43,* 23–34.
LeUnes, A. D., & Nation, J. R. (1989). Personality variables and sport. In A. D. LeUnes & J. R. Nation, *Sport psychology: An introduction* (pp. 231–271). Chicago: Nelson Hall.
McAdams, D. P., & Ochberg, R. L. (Eds.). (1988). Psychobiography and life narratives. *Journal of Personality, 56* (1).
Mischel, W. (1984). On the predictability of behavior and the structure of personality. In R. A. Zucker, J. C. Aronoff, & A. I. Rabin (Eds.), *Personality and the prediction of behavior.* New York: Academic Press.
Pervin, L. A. (1985). Personality: Curent controversies, issues, and directions. *Annual Review of Psychology, 36,* 83–114.
Pervin, L. A. (1990). Personality theory and research: Prospects for the future. In L. A. Pervin (Ed.), *Handbook of personality theory and research* (pp. 723–727). New York: Guilford Press.
Rowe, D. C. (1987). Resolving the person-situation debate. *American Psychologist, 42,* 218–227.
Simonton, D. K. (1990). Personality and politics. In L. A. Pervin (Ed.), *Handbook of personality theory and research* (pp. 670–692). New York: Guilford Press.
West, S. G. (1986). Methodological developments in personality research: An introduction. *Journal of Personality, 54,* 1–17.

Notes

1 Another judicial situation in which experts in personality analysis have been or might be called upon to assist is the process of jury selection in criminal or civil trials. Many attorneys consider the *voir dire,* or questioning of the jury to decide whether to accept or dismiss a potential juror, to be one of the most important phases of a trial. Although both the defense and prosecution attorneys in a legal dispute presumably desire to see

justice done, to the prosecution *justice* usually means a guilty verdict, and to the defense it means a not guilty verdict. The makeup of the juror, as much as the actual evidence presented in the trial, affects which of these verdicts is handed down. Generally speaking, prosecutors in criminal trials are inclined to select jurors who, from their dress, manner, hobbies, or occupation, appear to be conservative in their political and legal views. Defense attorneys, on the other hand, are more likely to select jurors who appear liberal in their thoughts and behavior. Nordic-appearing types with crew cuts tend to be favored by prosecutors and long-haired Latins by defenders. Sometimes whether a potential juror is prosecution oriented or defense oriented can be determined from his or her occupation. Bankers and engineers, for example, are said to be prosecution oriented, whereas teachers and social workers tend to be defense oriented. Even the most conservative-appearing professional, however, may harbor liberal sentiments. And who would have guessed that the most prosecution-oriented of all occupational groups are secretaries (Bugliosi, 1991)?

2 Of course, the emphasis on the study of learning can be viewed as a reflection of the individualism, egalitarianism, and democratic philosophy that have permeated much of American social and political life from the very beginnings of the United States.

3 From *Listening with the Third Ear* (pp. 263–264) by T. Reik, 1948, New York: Grove Press. Reprinted with permission.

APPENDIX A

Glossary

Accident proneness   The now largely discounted theory of a particular personality type that is associated with a greater tendency to have accidents.

Acquiescence response set (style)   Tendency of a person to answer affirmatively ("yes" or "true") on personality test items and in other alternative response situations.

Acquired motive (drive)   A learned motive, such as the motive or drive to acquire money, a secondary reinforcer.

Actuarial approach   Combining quantified clinical information according to empirically established rules, and then making behavioral predictions or diagnoses on the basis of the results.

Adjustment   Ability to cope in social situations and achieve satisfaction of one's needs.

Adjustment disorder   Difficulty in adjusting to stress and in meeting one's psychological needs.

Affective assessment   The measurement of noncognitive (nonintellective) variables or characteristics. Affective variables include temperament, emotion, interests, attitudes, personal style, and other behaviors, traits, or processes typical of an individual.

Affective disorders   Mental disorders characterized by extreme disturbance of mood and emotion.

Agoraphobia   An abnormal fear of being alone or in open, public places, where escape might be difficult in case of a panic attack.

Alarm reaction   The first stage of Selye's *general adaptation syndrome*, in which the body is mobilized for fight or flight by increased activity of the sympathetic nervous system and the resulting muscular and glandular changes.

Alienation   State of withdrawal or isolation from other people through indifference or disaffection.

Altruism   Unselfish concern or devotion to the welfare of other people at the cost of some sacrifice to oneself.

Anal stage   According to Freud, the period of life (second year) during which the major focus of tension and excitation is the anal region of the body; interest and conflict center on the retention and expulsion of feces. Negativism, manifested by defiance of parental orders and frequently associated with toilet training, is most acute during the anal stage.

Analysis of resistance   Assessment/therapeutic procedure in psychoanalysis which involves analyzing the behavioral signs of resistance to therapeutic progress, (e.g., appearing late for appointments, refusing to talk about certain matters, bringing presents to the analyst).

Analysis of transference   Assessment/therapeutic process in psychoanalysis which involves analyzing the relationship (positive or negative) between the analyst and the patient. Transference occurs when the patient behaves toward the analyst as the patient has acted toward some significant other person in his or her life (e.g., acting as if the analyst were a father or mother figure).

Analytical psychology   C. G. Jung's mystical theory of personality, including the belief that the desire to be creative resulted in the libido.

Androgyny   Personality characteristic composed of both masculine and feminine characteristics.

Anima/animus   In C. G. Jung's theory of personality, the archetype consisting of the feminine principle (*anima*), especially in the male, and the masculine principle (*animus*), especially in the female.

Anorexia nervosa   An eating disorder characterized by a pathological fear of being fat, and consequent excessive dieting and emaciation; occurs primarily in adolescent girls.

Antisocial personality   Formerly called *psychopathic personality*, a disorder of personality characterized by inadequate development of moral and ethical restraints. Such a person acts in a hostile, hurtful way without feeling guilty, has difficulty forming close relationships, and behaves in a manipulative, dishonest fashion.

Anxiety   Vague feeling of uneasiness or apprehension, not necessarily directed toward a specific object or situation.

Anxiety disorders   Chronic feelings of apprehension or uneasiness. This diagnostic label includes generalized anxiety disorder, panic disorder, obsessive-compulsive disorder, posttraumatic stress disorder, and phobic disorder.

Approach-avoidance conflict   Mental stage in which a person is both attracted to and repelled by the same object, person, or situation and has difficulty deciding whether to approach or avoid (withdraw from) it.

Archetype   In C. G. Jung's theory of personality, a collectively inherited, conscious idea, thought pattern, or image that is present in everyone.

Assertiveness training (conditioning)   Techniques of teaching anxious or socially unproductive or inhibited people how to become more comfortable and effective in interacting with others.

Assessment   Appraising the presence or magnitude of one or more personal characteristics. Assessing human behavior and mental processes includes such procedures as observations, interviews, rating scales, checklists, inventories, projectives, and tests.

Astrology   Pseudoscience of interpreting an individual's personality and future circumstances from his or her birth date and the relative positions of the moon and planets.

Attachment   Development by a young child or animal of a close, lasting relationship with another person; bonding.

Attitude   Tendency to react positively or negatively to some object, person, or situation.

Attitude scale   A paper-and-pencil instrument consisting of a series of statements concerning an institution, situation, person, event, etc. The examinee responds to each statement by endorsing it or by indicating his degree or agreement or disagreement with it.

Attribution   Process of interpreting the cause of a person's behavior as forces within (internal atrribution) or outside (external attribution) the person.

Aunt Fanny error   Accepting as accurate a trivial, highly generalized personality description that could pertain to almost anyone, even one's "Aunt Fanny."

Authoritarian personality   A tendency to view the world in terms of a strict social hierarchy in which a person higher on the hierarchy demands cooperation and deference from those below him or her.

Autism   Developmental disorder characterized by impaired communication, emotional detachment, and excessive rigidity.

Aversion therapy (conditioning)   Helping a person to break an undesirable habit by associating it with unpleasant experiences or consequences.

Barnum effect   Belief in a personality description phrased in generalities, truisms, and other statements that sound specific to a given person but are actually applicable to almost anyone. Same as *Aunt Fanny error*.

Base rate   Proportion of a specified population of people who possess a characteristic that is of interest. The base rate should be taken into account when evaluating the effectiveness of a psychometric instrument in identifying and diagnosing people who have that characteristic.

Behavior analysis   Procedures that focus on objectively describing a particular behavior and identifying the antecedents and consequences of that behavior. Behavior analysis may be conducted for research purposes or to obtain information in planning a behavior modification program.

Behavior modification   Psychotherapeutic procedures, based on learning theory and research, designed to change inappropriate behavior to more personally and socially acceptable behavior. Examples of such procedures are reinforcement, systematic desensitization, counterconditioning, aversion, extinction, implosion (flooding), and modeling.

Behavioral assessment   The use of direct measures of behavior to describe personality.

Behavioral medicine   Broad multidisciplinary field of scientific investigation, education, and practice concerned with the relationships of behavior to health, illness, and physiological dysfunctions.

Biofeedback   The process of learning to control autonomic body functions by means of visual or auditory cues.

Biographical inventory   Questionnaire composed of items designed to collect information on an individual's background, interests, and other personal data.

Biorhythms   Theory that one's mental or physical effectiveness on a given day is affected by the physical, mental, and emotional "cycles" fixed in the individual since birth.

Bipolar disorder   Condition in which an individual's mood fluctuates between euphoric mania and depression.

Bulimia Disorder in which a person eats massive amounts of food and then eliminates the food by self-induced vomiting or strong laxatives.

Cardinal trait According to G. W. Allport, a disposition or theme so dominant in a person's life that it is expressed in almost all of his or her behavior (e.g., power striving, self-love).

Case study Detailed study of an individual, designed to provide a comprehensive, in-depth understanding of personality. Information for a case study is obtained from biographical, interview, observational, and test data.

Castration anxiety The fear experienced by a boy during the phallic stage of psychosexual development that his genital organs will be cut off.

Catastrophizing A common cognitive stress response in which the individual dwells on and overemphasizes the consequences of negative events.

Catatonic schizophrenia A type of schizophrenic disorder characterized by a movement condition in which the patient may show total immobility or stupor (including maintaining uncomfortable positions for long periods of time), alternating with wild excitement.

Catharsis Release of anxiety or tension through indirect verbal expression or fantasy.

Cathexis Investment of emotional significance in an activity, object, or idea.

Central trait According to G. W. Allport, tendency to behave in a particular way in various situations, but less general or pervasive than a *cardinal trait*. Examples of central traits are sociability and affectionateness.

Cerebrotonia In Sheldon's temperament typology, the tendency to be introversive and prefer mental to physical or social activities; most closely related to ectomorphic body build.

Checklist List of words, phrases, or statements descriptive of personal characteristics; respondents endorse (check) those items characteristic of themselves (self-ratings) or other people (other-ratings).

Claustrophobia Abnormal fear of narrow or enclosed places.

Client-centered therapy A type of psychotherapy, pioneered by Carl Rogers, in which the client decides what to talk about and when, without direction, judgment, or interpretation on the part of the therapist. Unconditional positive regard, empathy, and congruence characterize the therapist's attitude in this type of therapy.

Clinical (impressionistic) approach Approach to behavioral prediction and diagnosis in which psychologists assign their own judgmental weights to the predictor variables and then combine them in a subjective manner to make behavioral forecasts or diagnoses.

Clinical psychologist A psychologist trained to diagnose and treat emotional and behavioral disorders.

Cognitive-behavioral therapy Psychotherapeutic process in which a person's faulty cognitions or beliefs are changed to more realistic ones.

Cognitive complexity The degree of elaborateness of a system of personal constructs, usually indicated by the number of personal constructs in the system.

Cognitive restructuring Psychotherapeutic procedures designed to change the way in which people process information and think about themselves and the world.

Cognitive style Strategies or approaches to perceiving, remembering, and thinking that a person comes to prefer in attempting to understand and cope with the world (e.g., field independence-dependence, reflectivity-impulsivity, and internal-external locus of control).

Cohort A group of people of the same age, class membership, or culture (e.g., all people born in 1900).

Cohort differences Physical and psychological differences between individuals born in different time periods and hence belonging to different generations.

Collective unconscious According to Jung's analytical theory of personality, that part of the unconscious mind that contains material common to all people in a given culture. See *personal unconscious.*

Communality Proportion of variance in a measured variable accounted for by variance that the variable has in common with other variables.

Compensation A defense mechanism in which a person attempts to overcome a real or imagined inferiority in one area by overemphasizing another kind of behavior.

Competency Legal determination that a person's judgment is sound and that he or she is able to manage his or her own property, enter into contracts, and so on.

Complex A system of interrelated, emotionally charged ideas, feelings, memories, and impulses, usually repressed and resulting in abnormal behavior.

Compulsive personality A person who feels compelled to behave in a rigid, repetitive manner, e.g., a compulsion to be clean.

Concordance rate Degree to which other people have the same characteristic as a specified individual (the proband or index case). The extent to which the characteristic is genetically based is determined by comparing the concordance rates for the proband's relatives with those of the general population.

Concurrent validity The extent to which the scores obtained by a group of individuals on a particular psychometric instrument are related to their simultaneously determined scores on another measure (criterion) of the same characteristic that the instrument is supposed to measure.

Conditioned (secondary) reinforcer An environmental object or event that becomes reinforcing in its own right by being associated with a primary reinforcer such as food or sex.

Conditions of worth According to Carl Rogers, the feelings experienced by a person who is evaluated as a totality, and not according to specific actions. The person feels that his or her worth depends on manifesting the right behaviors, attitudes, and values.

Conflict A mental state in which opposing or mutually exclusive impulses, desires, or tendencies are present at the same time. See *approach-avoidance conflict.*

Congruence In client-centered therapy, consistency between the therapist's feelings and actions toward the client. The empathy and unconditional positive regard expressed by the therapist are genuine, not pretended.

Construct In Kelly's theory of constructive alternativism, a concept used to construe (interpret) events.

Construct validity   The extent to which scores on a psychometric instrument designed to measure a certain characteristic are related to measures of behavior in situations in which the characteristic is supposed to be an important determinant of behavior.

Constructive alternativism   Kelly's theory that events can be construed or interpreted in various ways.

Content analysis   Method of studying and analyzing written (or oral) communications in a systematic, objective, and quantitative manner to assess certain psychological variables.

Content validity   A test or other psychometric instrument is said to have *content validity* if a group of experts on the material with which the instrument is concerned agree that it measures what it was intended to measure.

Contingency management   Control of institutionalized persons by differentially reinforcing them for socially approved and socially disapproved behavior; makes certain kinds of pleasures or privileges contingent upon keeping neat and clean, eating properly, interacting with other patients, or engaging in other socially acceptable behaviors. Also known as *token economy* when the reinforcers are tokens that can be exchanged for something desired by the individual.

Continuity theory   Persistence of personality characteristics and typical behaviors throughout the individual's lifetime.

Contrast error   In interviewing or rating, the tendency to evaluate a person more positively if an immediately preceding individual was assigned a highly negative evaluation, or to evaluate a person more negatively if an immediately preceding individual was given a highly positive evaluation.

Convergent validity   Situation in which an assessment instrument has high correlations with other measures of (or methods of measuring) the same construct. (see *discriminant validity*)

Conversion disorder   A dissociative or somatoform disorder in which the individual appears to be, but actually is not, blind, deaf, paralyzed, or insensitive to pain in various parts of the body, or even pregnant (pseudocyesis).

Coping   Controlling, reducing, or learning to tolerate stress-provoking events.

Correlation   The degree of relationship between two variables, signified by an index number (a correlation coefficient) ranging from -1.00 (a perfect negative relationship) to $+1.00$ (a perfect positive relationship).

Counseling   A general term for providing advice and guidance to individuals who need assistance with vocational, academic, or personal problems.

Counterconditioning (reciprocal inhibition)   Extinction of an undesirable response to a stimulus through introduction of a more desirable, often incompatible, response; involves presentation of the conditioned stimuli for an anxiety response while the individual is making responses that are incompatible with anxiety.

Cross-sectional study   Comparisons of the physical and psychological characteristics of people of different chronological ages.

Cross-sequential study   Developmental research study in which two or more successive cohorts are studied longitudinally. For example, the change from 1970 to 1980 in the personality characteristics of individuals born in 1910, 1930, and 1950 is compared.

Daimonic   In May's theory of personality, any natural function that comes to dominate a person's behavior.

Dasein (being-in-the-world)   A existentialist term referring to the sense of self as a free and responsible individual existing in the world of things (Umwelt), other people (Mitwelt), and one's self (Einwelt).

Defense mechanisms   In psychodynamic theory, psychological techniques that defend the ego against anxiety, guilt, and a loss of self-esteem resulting from awareness of certain impulses or realities.

Delusion   A false belief that is resistant to reason or reality, e.g., a delusion of persecution or grandeur.

Dementia   Impairment of intellectual functioning and disintegration of personality brought on by damage to the brain, as in aging.

Demonological model   Explanation of abnormal behavior as due to the devil or other supernatural forces.

Denial   Psychological defense mechanism in which anxiety is alleviated by denying thoughts, feelings, or events that are intolerable to the ego.

Depersonalization   Condition in which the reality of oneself or the environment is no longer perceived.

Depressant   Any drug that slows down nervous system activity. Examples of depressants are alcohol, barbiturates, and opiates.

Depression   Mood disorder characterized by dejection, loss of interest in things, negative thoughts (including suicidal thoughts), and various physical symptoms (e.g., loss of appetite, insomnia, fatigue).

Determinism   The doctrine that all events, including human thoughts and actions (psychic determinism), have natural, explicable causes.

Diagnostic interview   An interview designed to obtain information on a person's thoughts, feelings, perceptions, and behavior; used in making a diagnostic decision about the person.

Diathesis stress model   Theory of psychopathology that each person is more or less vulnerable to stress, depending on his or her inherited predisposition. Whether or not psychopathology develops when the individual is exposed to stress depends on the inherited predisposition and the individual's ability to cope with stressors.

Discriminant validity   Situation in which a psychometric instrument has low correlations with other measures of (or methods of measuring) different psychological constructs.

Displaced aggression   Directing one's anger or frustration toward a person or thing other than that which caused it.

Displacement   Directing an unwanted thought or feeling from its original source to another object, person, or situation.

Dispositional approach   Includes any one of many different theories of personality based on the assumption of stable, enduring internal dispositions to feel, think, or act in certain ways. Different dispositions are considered to be characteristic of different individuals and to be expressed across a variety of situations.

Dissociation Separation of a cluster of mental processes from the main body of consciousness, as in amnesia, fugue, hysteria, and multiple personality.

Dissociative disorder Mental disorder characterized by a sudden, temporary change in personality, as in multiple personality.

Dogmatism Personality trait characterized by chronic unfounded assertions of one's opinions as being the truth; may be assessed by Rokeach's Dogmatism Scale.

Dream analysis In psychoanalysis, analyzing the manifest content of a dream to reveal the underlying latent content, including the patient's unconscious wishes and conflicts.

Dreamwork Various techniques, including condensation, displacement, distortion, and symbolism, used in a dream to disguise its real meaning (latent content).

Ectomorph In Sheldon's somatotype system, a person having a tall, thin body build; related to the cerebrotonic (thinking, introversive) temperament type.

Ego Loosely speaking, the "I" or "self" of personality. In psychoanalytic theory, the executive, reality-oriented aspect of personality, which acts as a mediator between id and superego.

Ego ideal That part of the superego which consists of a composite of those persons with whom an individual identifies most closely.

Ego psychology School of neo-Freudians who stress the centrality of the ego, which is viewed as functioning independently from the other components of personality.

Electra complex Unconscious sexual desires of a daughter for her father.

Electroconvulsive therapy (ECT) The application of electric current to the brain to induce a seizure or convulsion; used especially in the treatment of depression.

Electromyograph (EMG) Electronic apparatus designed to measure muscular activity or tension.

Empathy Vicarious experiencing of the thoughts, emotions, attitudes, etc., of another person, thus increasing the likelihood of being able to respond to the person's needs.

Endomorph In Sheldon's somatotype system, a person having a rotund body shape (fat); related to the viscerotonic (relaxed, sociable) temperament.

Endorphins Endogenous morphines. A group of peptides occurring in the brain that resemble opiates in their effects, that is, elevating the pain threshold.

Exhaustion stage The third stage of Selye's general adaptation syndrome, in which failure to adapt to or cope with a stressor leads to serious physical and/or psychological problems.

Existentialism A philosophical school that emphasizes the importance of the individual self as being responsible for its own choices and that stresses efforts to find meaning in a purposeless, irrational universe.

Expectancy Julian Rotter's term for the subjective probability that a given behavior will be instrumental in obtaining a certain reinforcer.

Extrovert Jung's term for individuals who are oriented, in their thoughts or social orientation, toward the external environment and other people rather than toward their own thoughts and feelings.

Factor A dimension, trait, or characteristic of personality revealed by factor-analyzing the matrix of correlations computed from the scores of a large number of people on several different tests or items.

Factor analysis A mathematical procedure for analyzing a matrix of correlations among measurements to determine what factors (constructs) are sufficient to explain the correlations.

Factor loadings In factor analysis, the resulting correlations (weights) between tests (or other variables) and the extracted factors.

Family therapy Treatment of psychological problems in a family setting; based on the doctrine that many, if not most, psychological problems originate in the interpersonal family situation and hence can be treated more effectively in that context.

Field dependence A perceptual style in which the perceiver depends primarily on cues from the surrounding visual environment, rather than kinesthetic (gravitational) cues, to determine the upright position on Witkin's rod-and-frame test.

Field independence A perceptual style in which the perceiver depends primarily on kinesthetic (gravitational) cues rather than visual cues from the surrounding environment to determine the upright position on Witkin's rod-and-frame test.

Fixation Partial arrest of personality development at an early age, a result of severe frustration or overgratification; any stereotyped form of behavior resulting from frustration and resistance to change.

Fraternal (dizygotic) twins Twins resulting from coincident pregnancies in the same person. Originating from two separately fertilized eggs, fraternal twins are genetically no more alike than nontwin siblings.

Free association In psychoanalytic therapy, the uncensored, uninhibited expression of ideas or feelings by the patient.

Free-floating anxiety Generalized anxiety disorder involving relatively mild but persisting, unfocused anxiety.

Freudian slip Mistake or substitution of words in speaking or writing contrary to the person's conscious intent and presumably reflective of unconscious thoughts and feelings.

Frustration Interference with goal-directed activity; also the feeling resulting from such interference.

Frustration-aggression hypothesis Tenet that interference with goal-directed activity results in an increment in aggressive impulses.

Functional analysis of behavior Analysis of the interactions between environmental events and behavior.

Functional autonomy of motives Gordon Allport's term for the persistence of a behavior pattern long after the original impetus for the behavior has disappeared.

Functional psychosis An older term for a psychotic disorder having no clearly defined structural (organic) basis.

Fundamental attribution error Tendency to attribute one's own behavior to situational influences but to attribute the behavior of other people to dispositional causes.

Gender identity Inner sense of being male or female, resulting from child-rearing practices combined with genetic and hormonal factors.

Gender role Patterns of appearance and behavior associated by a society or culture with being male or female.

General adaptation syndrome (GAS) Selye's three-stage bodily stress response (alarm reaction, stage of resistance, stage of exhaustion) resulting from exposure to a stressor.

Genital stage The last of Freud's five stages of psychosexual development, beginning at puberty. Interest in the opposite sex becomes predominant during this stage, culminating eventually in heterosexual union.

Genotype The underlying genetic structure of a characteristic, which may or may not be manifested in the individual's appearance or behavior (see *phenotype*).

Graphology The analysis of handwriting to ascertain the character or personality of the writer.

Group therapy Type of psychotherapy in which several individuals share their feelings, experiences, and expectations with each other under the direction or guidance of a therapist or other group leader.

Hallucination Perception of an object or situation in the absence of an external stimulus.

Hallucinogens Drugs or chemicals that produce hallucinations.

Halo effect Rating a person high on one characteristic merely because he or she rates high on other characteristics.

Hardiness A personality characteristic (including commitment, challenge, and control) associated with a lower rate of stress-related illness.

Health psychology A branch of psychology concerned with research and applications directed toward the promotion of health and the prevention of illness.

Heritability coefficient The ratio of the test score variance attributable to heredity to the variance attributable to both heredity and environment in combination; an index of the extent to which a characteristic is genetically based.

Histrionic personality Type of personality characterized by deliberately affected, overly dramatic, self-consciously emotional speech and actions.

Humanistic psychology (phenomenological psychology) An approach to psychological research and practice that is concerned with subjective experiences and values, focusing on the uniqueness of the person; also referred to as third-force psychology.

Humanistic therapy Type of psychotherapy which assumes that the client (patient) is responsible for solving his or her own problems and can exercise control over his or her own behavior and hence make constructive choices.

Id In the psychoanalytic three-part theory of personality, the reservoir of instinctive impulses and strivings. The id, or "animal nature" of humans, is concerned only with immediate gratification of the pleasure and destructive impulses.

Ideal self In Rogers' phenomenological theory, the person whom the individual would like to be (the self he or she would like to possess).

Identical twins (monozygotic twins) Twins produced by a single fertilized egg. Because they are genetically identical, identical twins are often used to investigate the differential effects of heredity and environment on personality and behavior.

Identification Taking on the personal characteristics of another person, as when a developing child identifies with a significant "other" person. Also, in psychoanalytic theory, an ego defense mechanism for coping with anxiety.

Identity Term used to describe the individual's gradually emerging, and continually changing, sense of self.

Identity crisis In Erikson's theory of psychosocial developmental stages, the period, especially during adolescence, characterized by a strong concern with acquiring a sense of self. An identity crisis may end in either a sense of identity or identity diffusion.

Idiographic approach Approach to personality assessment and research in which the individual is viewed as a lawful, integrated system in his or her own right (see *nomothetic approach*).

Immune system First line of defense of the body against invading pathogens. Consists of T cells, which attack cells infected by viruses; B cells, which form antibodies; and natural killer cells, which kill tumor cells and cells infected by viruses.

Incompetency Legal decision that a person is suffering from a mental disorder, that causes a defect of judgment such that the person is unable to manage his or her own property, enter into contracts, and take care of other affairs.

Independent variable The variable whose effects (on the dependent variable) are attempting to be determined in an experiment.

Individual psychology Alfred Adler's theory of personality development, based on a belief in the uniqueness of every person and the notion that everyone adjusts to social influences in his or her own individual way.

Individual test A test administered to one examinee at a time.

Inferiority complex Feelings of being greatly inferior to other people and helpless compared with them.

Information processing Perceptual-cognitive process by which information is taken in, stored, and used.

Insanity An imprecise legal term for severe mental disorders involving lack of responsibility for one's actions. According to the M'Nagten Rule, an insane person is one who cannot distinguish right from wrong. However, other precedents, such as the Durham decision, are generally referred to in determining the presence of insanity.

Intellectualization Defense mechanism in which the individual attempts to become isolated from emotional experiences by dealing with them in an abstract, intellectual manner.

Intelligence Many definitions of intelligence have been proposed, such as "the ability to judge well, understand well, and reason well" (Binet), "the capacity for abstract thinking" (Terman), and "the aggregate or global capacity of an individual" (Wechsler).

Intelligence test A psychological test designed to measure an individual's aptitude for scholastic work or other kinds of activities involving verbal ability and problem solving. In general, what is measured by intelligence tests is the ability to succeed in school-type tasks.

Interest inventory   A test or checklist, such as the Strong Interest Inventory and the Kuder General Interest Survey, designed to assess an individual's preferences for certain activities and topics.

Interpersonal trust   Generalized expectancy (Rotter) to believe other people.

Interview   Systematic procedure for obtaining information by asking questions and, in general, verbally interacting with a person.

Introversion-extroversion   Dimension of personality, first formulated by Carl Jung, characterized by the degree to which an individual is oriented inwardly toward the self (introversion) or outwardly toward the external world (extroversion).

Introvert   Jung's term for an individual who is oriented toward the self, primarily concerned with one's own thoughts and feelings rather than with the external environment or other people; one whose preference is for solitary activities.

Inventory   A set of questions or statements to which the individual responds (for example, by indicating agreement or disagreement), designed to provide a measure of personality, interest, attitude, or behavior.

Latency period   Psychosexual developmental stage, during middle childhood, following resolution of the Oedipus complex and in which sexual desires are relatively mild.

Latent content   The underlying or real meaning of a dream, which is distorted by the dreamwork to form the *manifest content*.

Learned helplessness   Acquired perception on the part of the individual of his or her lack of influence or control over external events; can lead to apathy and depression.

Libido   Psychic energy of the sexual drive.

Life space   Kurt Lewin's term for that part of the environment in which the individual lives and works, and hence by which he or she is influenced.

Life-style   Composite of habits, attitudes, preferences, socioeconomic status, etc., constituting an individual's manner of living.

Locus of control   J. B. Rotter's term for a cognitive-perceptual style characterized by the typical direction ("internal" or self versus "external" or other) from which individuals perceive themselves to be controlled.

Machiavellianism   Personality trait in which the individual is concerned with manipulating other people or using them for his or her own purposes.

Man-to-man scale   Procedure in which ratings on a specific trait (e.g., leadership) are made by comparing each person to be rated with several other people whose standings on the trait have already been determined.

Mandala   In Jungian psychology, a symbol (a circle) representing an effort on the part of the person to reunify the self.

Manic-depressive psychosis (bipolar disorder)   An affective disorder characterized by severe mood swings and excitability.

Manic disorder   Excessive agitation and excitability, which may or may not alternate with depression (see *manic-depressive psychosis*).

Manifest content   A dream as it appears to the dreamer, in disguised, symbolic form. See *latent content*.

Masculine protest   Term used by Alfred Adler to refer to an attempt to compensate for feelings of inferiority.

Meditation   An altered state of consciousness characterized by a greatly relaxed state and feelings of being apart from the external world; achieved by procedures such as regulated breathing, restricted attention to a particular object or thought, and assumption of a yogalike posture.

Mesomorph   W. H. Sheldon's term for a person having an athletic physique; correlated with a somatotonic temperament (active, aggressive, energetic).

Modeling   Learning social and cognitive behaviors by observing and imitating other people.

Moral anxiety   Feelings of guilt or shame resulting from a conflict between the id and superego (see *neurotic anxiety*).

Multiple abstract variance analysis (MAVA)   Statistical procedure, devised by R. B. Cattell, for estimating the relative effects of heredity and environment in determining a particular personality characteristic.

Multiple personality   Dissociative disorder in which two or more personalities exist within the same individual.

Multitrait-multimethod matrix   Matrix of correlation coefficients resulting from correlating measures of the same trait by the same method, different traits by the same method, the same trait by different methods, and different traits by different methods. The relative magnitudes of the four types of correlations are compared in evaluating the construct validity of a test.

Narcissistic personality   A person having an exaggerated sense of self-importance, often combined with self-doubt.

Need   Biological or psychological lack or deficit within a person.

Need achievement   Motive to excel or attain success in some field or endeavor; a trait measured and studied extensively by D. McClelland.

Neurosis (psychoneurosis)   Nonpsychotic mental disorder characterized by anxiety, obsessions, compulsions, phobias, or bodily complaints or dysfunctions having no demonstrable physical basis.

Neurotic anxiety   Anxiety caused when irrational id impulses threaten to become uncontrollable by the ego.

Neuroticism-stability   In Hans Eysenck's conceptualization of personality, the dimension ranging from extreme moodiness to even-temperedness.

Neurotransmitter   One of many chemicals secreted at the ends of axons that affect the transmission of nervous impulses across synapses.

Nomothetic approach   A search for general laws of behavior and personality that apply to all individuals (see *idiographic approach*).

Nonverbal behavior   Any behavior in which the respondent does not make word sounds or signs. Nonverbal behavior serving a communicative function includes movements of large (macrokinesics) and small (microkinesics) body parts, interpersonal distance or territoriality (proxemics), tone and rate of voice sounds (paralinguistics), and communications imparted by culturally prescribed matters relating to time, dress, memberships, and the like (culturics).

Norms   Average scores on a test or other measuring instrument of people falling in a given demographic category (age, sex, race, geographical region, etc.) on a psychological test or other assessment device; norms are expressed as percentile ranks, standard scores, or other transformed scores of a group of examinees on whom a test has been standardized.

Numerology   The study of numbers, such as the digits representing the year of a person's birth, to analyze their presumed effects on the person's life and future.

Objective test   A test scored by comparing the examinee's responses to a list of correct answers (a "key") prepared beforehand, in contrast to a subjectively scored test. Examples of objective test items are multiple-choice and true-false.

Oblique rotation   In a factor analysis, a rotation in which the factor axes are allowed to form acute or obtuse angles with each other; consequently, the factors are correlated (see *orthogonal rotation*).

Observation method   Observing behavior in a controlled or uncontrolled situation and making a formal or informal record of the observations.

Observational learning   Learning by observing the behavior of other people.

Obsession   A recurring thought or idea.

Obsessive-compulsive disorder   A neurotic disorder of which obsessions and compulsions are symptomatic.

Oedipus complex   A composite of sexual feelings toward the mother and dislike of the father in a 3- to 6-year-old boy; viewed by Freud as a universal phenomenon. The comparable situation in a girl, disliking the mother and loving the father, is referred to as the *Electra complex*.

Operant conditioning   Learning that occurs when positive or negative consequences follow behavior.

Oral stage   The first of Freud's psychosexual developmental stages, occurring from birth to 1½ years. During the oral stage, pleasure is derived primarily from stimulation of the mouth and lips, as in sucking, biting, and swallowing.

Orthogonal rotation   In a factor analysis, a rotation that maintains the independence of factors; that is, the angles between factors are kept at 90 degrees and hence the factors are uncorrelated (see *oblique rotation*).

Panic disorder   The manifestation of anxiety through panic attacks.

Parallel forms   Two tests that are equivalent in the sense that they contain the same kinds of items of equal difficulty and are highly correlated. Examinees' scores on one form of the test are very close to their scores on the other form.

Parallel-forms reliability   An index of reliability determined by correlating the scores of individuals on parallel forms of a test.

Paranoid personality   Personality disorder characterized by projection, suspiciousness, extreme jealousy or envy, and stubbornness.

Paranoid schizophrenia   Psychotic disorder characterized by paranoid delusions (of grandeur, persecution, etc.), ideas of reference, illogical thinking, and unpredictable behavior.

Parasympathetic death   Death due to overactivity of the parasympathetic nervous system, resulting in an extreme reduction in heart action and a fatal lowering of blood pressure; may occur when a sick or despairing person feels so helpless or desperate that he or she simply "gives up" and quits trying to fight or live.

Participant observation   A research technique, used mainly by cultural anthropologists, in which the observer attempts to minimize the intrusiveness of his or her presence and observational activities by becoming part of the group that is being observed, e.g., by dressing and behaving like the other group members.

Passive-aggressive personality   Personality disorder in which aggressive feelings are characteristically expressed in a passive manner (by pouting, stubbornness, refusal to cooperate, etc.).

Peak experience   An intense, pleasurable emotional experience leading to personal growth.

Penis envy   In Freud's psychology of women, the desire of a female to have a penis and be like a male.

Percentile norms   A list of raw scores and the corresponding percentages of the test standardization group whose scores fall below the given percentile.

Perceptual defense   Unconscious mechanism that keeps a person from perceiving threatening stimuli.

Persona   In Carl Jung's analytical theory, the external or public personality that an individual presents to others to satisfy environmental demands, and not the real, inner personality.

Personal construct   In George Kelly's personality theory, the basic unit of personality organization; a conceptual dimension used by the individual to "construe" the environment.

Personal unconscious   In Carl Jung's theory of personality, that part of the unconscious mind that is unique to the individual. The individual is not immediately aware of his (her) personal unconscious, but can easily become so.

Personality   Sum total of all the qualities, traits, and behaviors that characterize a person's individuality and by which, together with his or her physical attributes, the person is recognized as unique.

Personality assessment   The description and analysis of personality by means of various techniques, including personality inventories, observations, interviews, checklists, rating scales, and projective techniques.

Personality disorder   Maladaptive behavioral syndrome originating in childhood but not characterized by psychoneurotic or psychotic symptoms.

Personality inventory   A self-report inventory or questionnaire consisting of statements concerned with personal characteristics and behaviors. On a true-false inventory, the respondent indicates whether or not each test item or statement is self-descriptive; on a multiple-choice or forced-choice inventory, the respondent selects the statements that are self-descriptive.

Personality profile Graph of scores on a battery or set of scales of a personality inventory or rating scale. The elevation and scatter of the profile assists in the assessment of personality and mental disorders.

Personality psychology The study of consistencies and changes in behavior and the psychological characteristics that differentiate one person from another.

Personality test Any one of several methods of analyzing personality, such as checklists, personality inventories, and projective techniques.

Personology The scientific study of personality.

Phallic stage The third of Freud's stages of psychosexual development. During this stage (3–6 years), the genital area is of greatest interest, indicated by rubbing, touching, and exhibiting one's genital organs. It is during the phallic stage that the Oedipus complex develops.

Phenomenal field That part of the environment that is perceived by and has meaning for the person.

Phenomenology The study of objects and events as they appear to the experiencing observer; a type of psychotherapy (Rogers, Maslow, etc.) that emphasizes the importance of self-perceptions and impressions of others in determining personality and behavior.

Phenotype The manner in which a genetically determined characteristic is actually manifested in the individual's appearance or behavior.

Phobia An irrational, persisting fear of something, as in *agoraphobia* or *claustrophobia*.

Phobic disorder Neurotic condition in which the individual is unreasonably afraid of some situation or object that typically poses no actual threat.

Phrenology Discredited theory and practice of Gall and Spurzheim relating affective and cognitive characteristics to the configuration (bumps) of the skull.

Physiognomy A pseudoscience which maintains that the personal characteristics of an individual are revealed by the form or features of the body, and especially the face.

Pleasure principle The principle on which the id operates, i.e., expression of sexual and aggressive impulses.

Polygraph So-called lie detector machine, which measures heart rate, blood pressure, respiration rate, and the galvanic skin response. Changes in these responses from baseline levels are considered to be indicative of lying.

Posttraumatic stress disorder A persisting anxiety reaction precipitated by a severely stressful experience, such as military combat; characterized by a reexperiencing of the stressful event and avoidance of stimuli associated with it. Other symptoms include feelings of estrangement, recurring dreams and nightmares, and a tendency to be easily startled.

Predictive validity Extent to which scores on a test are predictive of performance on some criterion measure assessed at a later time; usually expressed as a correlation between the test (predictor variable) and the criterion variable.

Press Henry Murray's term for environmental circumstances that affect behavior.

Primary process Process by which a mental image of a need-satisfying object is produced by the id to reduce psychic tension.

Primary reinforcer   A reinforcer whose reinforcing properties are not acquired through a process of learning.

Progressive muscle relaxation   Alternately tensing and relaxing each one of the 16 muscle groups of the body while attending to the feelings of tension and relaxation. Progressive relaxation is a common therapeutic procedure for coping with stress and a part of systematic desensitization in the treatment of phobias.

Projection   Defense mechanism in which an individual attributes his or her own unacceptable desires and impulses to other people.

Projective technique   A relatively unstructured personality test in which the examinee responds to materials such as inkblots, ambiguous pictures, incomplete sentences, and other materials by telling what he or she perceives, making up stories, or constructing and arranging sentences and objects. Theoretically, because the material is fairly unstructured, whatever structure the examinee imposes on it represents a projection of his or her own personality characteristics (needs, conflicts, sources of anxiety, etc.).

Proprium   The "self" in Gordon Allport's trait theory of personality.

Prospective study   Research investigation which follows up, over time, people having different characteristics or life-styles to determine which ones develop a particular condition or disorder.

Psychoanalysis   As developed by Sigmund Freud, psychoanalysis is (1) a theory of personality concerned with the interaction between the conscious and unconscious, (2) a psychotherapeutic method for dealing with personality problems, and (3) a research method for studying personality.

Psychodiagnosis   Examination and evaluation of personality in terms of behavioral, cognitive, and affective characteristics and the interactions among them.

Psychodrama   A psychotherapeutic method, pioneered by J. L. Moreno, in which the problems and experiences of a person are acted out in a stage setting by the person and other "actors."

Psychodynamic theory   Theory emphasizing the interaction of conscious and unconscious mental processes in determining thoughts, feelings, and behavior.

Psychogenic needs   According to Henry Murray, a psychological, as contrasted with a physiological, predisposition to behave in a certain way. Examples of psychogenic needs are the needs for achievement, affiliation, and power.

Psychographics   Study of the relationships of consumer behavior to personality characteristics and life-styles.

Psychohistory   Biography, such as Erikson's *Young Man Luther* (1958) or *Gandhi's Truth* (1969), written from a psychoanalytic point of view.

Psychopathic personality   Personality pattern characterized by antisocial behavior, lack of ability to establish meaningful relationships, extreme self-centeredness, and a seeming inability to profit from punitive experiences.

Psychosexual disorder   Psychologically based dysfunction in the ability to give or receive sexual gratification.

Psychosexual stages   Sequence of stages in sexual development (oral, anal, phallic, latency, genital) characterized by a focus on different erogenous zones.

Psychosis   Severe mental disorder characterized by faulty perception of reality, deficits of language and memory, disturbances in the emotional sphere, and other bizarre symptoms.

Psychosocial stages   Erik Erikson's modification of Freud's theory of psychosexual stages; emphasizes environmental and social problems, as contrasted with biological factors, in the progression of developmental stages from infancy through old age.

Psychosomatic disorders   Physical illnesses based on psychological stress, such as duodenal ulcers and tension headaches.

Psychotherapy   Psychological methods of treating mental disorders, involving communications between patient and therapist and the use of other special techniques.

Psychotic disorders (psychoses)   Extreme personality disorders characterized by loss of contact with reality, bizarre behavior, and distortions of personality; usually require hospitalization.

Q data   R. B. Cattell's term for personality data obtained from questionnaires.

Q-technique   A set of procedures, used to conduct research on the individual, that center on sorting decks of cards called Q-sorts and correlating the responses of different individuals to the Q-sorts.

Rapport   A warm, friendly relationship between the examiner and the examinee, which is important to establish at the beginning of an assessment session so the examinee will be motivated and respond conscientiously on a test of personality or ability.

Rational-emotive therapy (RET)   A form of *cognitive restructuring* devised by Albert Ellis.

Rationalization   Maintaining self-esteem by giving plausible but false reasons for one's behavior. Examples of rationalization are the "sour grapes" and "sweet lemon" philosophies.

Reaction formation   A defense mechanism in which a person's behavior is the opposite of his or her unconscious desires.

Reactive psychosis   Severe mental disorder which develops suddenly and is precipitated by identifiable stressors; marked by confusion and intense emotional turmoil.

Real self   In Rogers' phenomenological theory, a person's perception of what he or she really is, as contrasted with what he or she would like to be (ideal self).

Reality principle   The psychoanalytic principle on which the ego operates; gratification of instinctual drives is accommodated to the realities of the external world (see *pleasure principle*).

Reciprocal interaction   Joint effects of the person and the environment on each other; the person changes the environment, and the environment changes the person.

Regression   A defense mechanism in which conflict or frustration results in the repetition of behavior more characteristic of an earlier stage of development (e.g., thumb sucking or temper tantrums in an older child or adult).

Reinforcement   Application or removal of a stimulus that affects the probability of a response.

Reliability   The extent to which a psychological assessment instrument measures anything consistently. A reliable instrument is relatively free from errors of measurement, so the scores obtained by examinees are close in numerical value to their true scores.

Reliability coefficient   A numerical index, between .00 and 1.00, of the reliability of an assessment instrument. Methods of determining reliability include test-retest, parallel-forms, and internal consistency.

Repression   According to psychoanalytic theory, an automatic process by which anxiety-producing conflicts or experiences are relegated to the unconscious, below the level of conscious awareness.

Repression-sensitization   Donald Byrne's conceptualization of a personality continuum representing an individual's typical response to threat; information-avoidance behaviors are at one end of the continuum and information-seeking behaviors at the other end.

Resistance stage   The second stage of Hans Selye's general adaptation syndrome; the signs of the alarm reaction diminish, while activity of the adrenal cortex and other indicators of settling in by the body for a long-term siege become prominent.

Respondent conditioning   Classical conditioning, in which response is elicited by a known stimulus rather than being emitted.

Response sets (styles)   Tendencies for individuals to respond in relatively fixed or stereotyped ways in situations where there are two or more response choices, such as on personality inventories. Tendencies to guess, to answer true (acquiescence), and to give socially desirable answers are examples of response sets that have been investigated.

Retrospective study   Comparisons of the incidence of a disorder or other condition in two or more groups of people having different backgrounds, behaviors, or other characteristics.

Role   The rights, obligations, and behaviors expected of an individual having a certain social or occupational status.

Schema   A cognitive structure that abstractly represents events, objects, or relationships in the external world.

Schizoid personality   Personality disorder characterized by shyness, eccentricity, oversensitivity, and seclusiveness.

Schizophrenic disorders   Psychoses characterized by withdrawal from reality and disturbances of thinking, emotion, and behavior; a breakdown of integrated personality functioning.

Schizotypal personality   Personality pattern similar to but less intense than schizophrenia.

Scribotherapy   Form of psychotherapy in which patients write out their feelings concerning certain topics.

Script   General plans developed by the individual to enable him or her to anticipate, respond to, control, or create events in a meaningful fashion.

Secondary process   Ego process of reducing intrapsychic tension by thinking, problem solving, and compromising with external reality (see *primary process*).

Secondary trait   Less important personality traits, such as preferences or interests, that affect behavior less than *central* or *cardinal traits*.

Self   The perceived identity, individuality, or ego; that which consciously knows and experiences.

Self-actualization   Fulfillment of one's potentialities; to attain a state of congruence or harmony between one's real and ideal selves.

Self-concept   Fairly consistent cluster of feelings, ideas, and attitudes toward oneself.

Self-disclosure   Revealing intimate, private information about oneself to another person.

Self-efficacy   A person's belief that he or she can successfully accomplish a given action.

Self-fulfilling prophecy   An expectation that leads one to behave in such a manner that the expectation becomes reality.

Self-monitoring   The extent to which people are sensitive to, or monitor, their own behavior according to environmental cues. High self-monitors are more sensitive to what is situationally appropriate and act accordingly. Low self-monitors are less sensitive to external cues and act more in response to their own internal attitudes and feelings.

Semantic differential   A rating scale, introduced by C. Osgood, for evaluating the connotative meanings that selected concepts have for a person. Each concept is rated on a seven-point, bipolar, adjectival scale.

Sensory deprivation   Restriction of sensory input or information.

Sentence completion test   A personality (projective) test consisting of a series of incomplete sentences that the examinee is instructed to complete as quickly as possible.

Sex roles   An aggregate of traits and behaviors that males and females in a given culture are expected to display.

Sex typing   Process of acquiring attitudes and behaviors considered by society as appropriate for a person of a given sex.

Shadow   In Jungian theory, the archetype representing the evil side of human nature.

Situation(al) test   A performance test in which the examinee is placed in a realistic but contrived situation and directed to accomplish a specified goal. Situation tests are sometimes employed to assess personality characteristics such as honesty and frustration tolerance.

Social desirability response set   Response set or style affecting scores on personality inventories. It refers to the tendency on the part of an examinee to respond to the assessment materials in a more socially desirable direction rather than responding in a manner that is truly characteristic or descriptive of his or her personality.

Social learning theory   Conceptualizations of learning that occur by imitation or interactions with other people.

Sociopathic personality   See *psychopathic personality.*

Somatotonia   Athletic, aggressive temperament type in W. H. Sheldon's three-component system of personality; most closely correlated with a mesomorphic (muscular) body build.

Somatotype   Classification of body build (physique) in W. H. Sheldon's three-component system (*endomorph, mesomorph, ectomorph*).

Source traits   R. B. Cattell's term for organizing structures or dimensio: : of personality that underlie and determine surface traits.

Standard scores   A group of scores, such as z scores, *T* scores, or stanine scores, having a desired mean and standard deviation. Standard scores are computed by transforming raw scores to z scores, multiplying the z scores by the desired standard deviation, and then adding the desired mean to the product.

Standardization   Administering a carefully constructed test to a large, representative sample of people under standard conditions for the purpose of determining norms.

State anxiety   A temporary state of anxiety, precipitated by a specific situation.

Statistical (actuarial) approach   Approach to data collection and behavior prediction consisting of the application of a statistical formula, a set of rules, or an actuarial table to assessment data.

Stimulus generalization   Making a similar response to a stimulus that is similar to the stimulus to which a response was originally conditioned.

Stress   Defined either as a stimulus or a response to a stressor; associated with psychological or physiological tension or imbalance in an organism.

Stress interview   Interviewing procedure in which the interviewer applies psychologically stressful techniques (critical and hostile questioning, frequent interruptions, prolonged silences, etc.) to break down the interviewee's defenses or determine how the interviewee reacts under pressure.

Structured interview   Interviewing procedure in which the interviewee is asked a series of preplanned questions.

Sublimation   A defense mechanism in which unacceptable unconscious impulses are expressed in indirect, socially acceptable ways.

Subliminal perception   Perception of a stimulus without conscious awareness.

Superego   In psychoanalytic theory, the part of the personality that acts according to the moral, idealistic principle, incorporating parental (societal) prohibitions, and sanctions.

Surface traits   Publicly manifested characteristics of personality; observable expressions of source traits.

Sympathetic death   Death resulting from extreme stress and fear, as in voodoo; extreme shock leads to excessive activity of the sympathetic nervous system and consequently to dramatic increases in heart rate and blood pressure.

Systematic desensitization   Behavioral therapy technique in which a hierarchy of anxiety-provoking situations is imagined or directly experienced while the individual is in a deeply relaxed state. In this manner, the situations gradually come to be experienced without anxiety.

Target behaviors   Specific, objectively defined behaviors observed and measured in behavioral assessments. Of particular interest are the effects on these behaviors of antecedent and consequent events in the environment.

Temperament   General mood, activity level, and reactivity to stimulation, presumably based on genetic factors and present from birth.

Template-matching technique   Bem and Fudner's conceptualization of a situation template as a pattern of behavior characterizing the way that a person (person I) is ideally expected to behave in that situation. The extent to which another person (person J) behaves similarly in the same situation depends on the match between the personality characteristics of person I and J.

Test anxiety   A feeling of fear or uneasiness that one will not do well on a test. Although severe test anxiety can interfere with effective test performance, a moderate degree of test anxiety is normal and does not greatly disrupt test performance.

Theory   A set of assumptions or propositions set forth to explain available information and to predict new facts concerning some phenomenon. Theories are typically conjectural rather than being established fact, and they are usually fairly broad in scope.

Time-lag design   Developmental research procedure for examining several cohorts, each in a different time period.

Token economy   Systematically controlled environment in which patients or inmates earn tokens, which can be exchanged for primary reinforcers and privileges for performing specified behaviors.

Trait   A cognitive, affective, or psychomotor characteristic possessed in different amounts by different people.

Trait anxiety   Generalized level of anxiety expressed in a variety of situations.

Trait theory   Personality theory that conceptualizes human personality as consisting of a combination of traits.

Transactional analysis   A group-therapeutic approach, pioneered by Eric Berne, in which the therapist observes the behavior of the group in social interaction and clarifies the destructive aspects of group members' life scripts and life positions and the associated games that members play in social interactions.

Transference   Psychotherapeutic phenomenon in which the patient transfers to the therapist unconscious feelings held toward another person.

Type   A larger dimension of personality than *trait*; a combination of traits characterizing a particular kind of personality, e.g., Type A or Type B.

Type A personality   Personality pattern characterized by a combination of behaviors, including aggressivity, competitiveness, hostility, quick actions, and constant striving; associated with a high incidence of coronary heart disease.

Type B personality   Personality pattern characterized by a relaxed, easygoing, patient, noncompetitive life-style; associated with a low incidence of coronary heart disease.

Unconditional positive regard   In client-centered therapy, an accepting, sincere attitude on the part of the therapist, regardless of the feelings or actions revealed by the client.

Unconscious   In psychoanalytic theory, the part of the personality that is below the level of conscious awareness and is brought into consciousness only in disguised form.

Unconscious motive   A motive or drive of which the individual is not consciously aware and which can be brought to consciousness only in disguised form.

Unobtrusive observations   Observations made without the awareness of the person whose behavior is being observed.

Unstructured interview   Interview procedure in which the questions asked are not preplanned but vary with the progress or flow of the interview.

Validity   The extent to which an assessment instrument measures what it is designed to measure. Validity can be assessed in several ways: by an analysis of the instrument's content (*content validity*), by relating scores on the test to a criterion (*predictive* and *concurrent validity*), and by a more thorough study of the extent to which the test is a measure of a certain psychological construct (*construct validity*).

Viscerotonia   Jolly, sociable temperament type in W. H. Sheldon's three-component description of personality; most closely correlated with the endomorphic (rotund) body build.

Will to power   The principal motive in Alfred Adler's theory of personality—to achieve power and hence control over feelings of inferiority.

Wish fulfillment   Satisfaction of an id impulse by imagining the desired object.

Word association test   A list of words that is read aloud to an examinee who has been instructed to respond to each one with the first word that comes to mind. Introduced as a clinical tool by Carl Jung, a word association test is often used in the analysis of personality.

APPENDIX B

A Brief Introduction to Factor Analysis

We shall begin our introduction to factor analysis with Table B–1, a matrix of correlations among the scores of 588 females on the 15 need scales of the Adjective Check List (scales 5–19 in Table 3–3). If the matrix is divided into two triangular portions by drawing a line from the upper left to the lower right corner, it can be seen that it is a symmetric matrix in which the first row contains the same values as the first column, the second row the same elements as the second column, etc. Also notice that the numbers on the principal diagonal (upper left to lower right) are all 1.00, the presumed correlation of each item with itself.

Computing the correlation coefficients in this matrix is the first step in a *factor analysis,* a mathematical procedure for reducing the number of variables (items or tests) to a smaller number of dimensions, or *factors,* by taking into account the overlap (correlations) among the various measures. The goal of factor analysis, as applied in psychological research and instrument development, is to find a few salient factors that account for the major part of the variance in a group of scores on different tests or other psychometric measures. Thus the factors extracted by a factor analysis should account for a large percentage of the overlap among the variances of the measures represented in the correlation matrix.

In this example there are 15 variables, or scales; so the goal of the factor analysis is to find the matrix of *factor loadings,* or correlations between the factors and scales, that most effectively accounts for the correlations among the scales. There are many approaches to factor analysis, but all involve two stages: (1) factoring the correlation matrix to yield an original, or unrotated, factor matrix, and then (2) *rotating* the factor matrix to provide the simplest possible configu-

TABLE B–1 Intercorrelation Matrix for 15 Need Scales from Adjective Checklist

Scale	Ach	Dom	End	Ord	Int	Nur	Aff	Het	Exh	Aut	Agg	Cha	Suc	Aba	Def
Ach	1.00	.73	.72	.55	.39	.19	.39	.25	.18	.15	.13	.09	-.51	-.49	-.17
Dom	.73	1.00	.38	.19	.20	.08	.33	.39	.61	.49	.48	.31	-.59	-.79	-.52
End	.72	.38	1.00	.85	.48	.39	.40	.08	-.17	-.22	-.24	-.34	-.36	-.21	.20
Ord	.55	.19	.85	1.00	.41	.16	.26	-.10	-.31	-.28	-.28	-.53	-.26	-.10	.29
Int	.39	.20	.48	.41	1.00	.64	.63	.27	-.20	-.30	-.45	-.01	-.37	-.09	-.30
Nur	.19	.08	.39	.16	.64	1.00	.74	.46	-.11	-.52	-.51	.03	-.13	.09	.48
Aff	.39	.33	.40	.26	.63	.74	1.00	.52	.08	-.26	-.37	.12	-.35	-.19	.27
Het	.25	.39	.08	-.10	.27	.46	.52	1.00	.40	.07	.10	.42	-.22	-.26	-.11
Exh	.18	.61	-.17	-.31	-.20	-.11	.08	.40	1.00	.57	.68	.49	-.12	-.54	-.63
Aut	.15	.49	-.22	-.28	-.30	-.52	-.26	.07	.57	1.00	.69	.32	-.31	-.61	-.86
Agg	.13	.48	-.24	-.28	-.45	-.51	-.37	.10	.68	.69	1.00	.34	.01	-.47	-.76
Cha	.09	.31	-.34	-.53	-.01	.03	.12	.42	.49	.32	.34	1.00	-.11	-.25	-.46
Suc	-.51	-.59	-.36	-.26	-.37	-.13	-.35	-.22	-.12	-.31	.01	-.11	1.00	.66	.26
Aba	-.49	-.79	-.21	-.10	-.09	.09	-.19	-.26	-.54	-.61	-.47	-.25	.66	1.00	.63
Def	-.17	-.52	.20	.29	-.30	.48	.27	-.11	-.63	-.86	-.76	-.46	.26	.63	1.00

ration of factor loadings. The purpose of the factoring process is to determine the number of factors required to account for the relationships among the various tests and provide initial estimates of the numerical loadings of each test on each factor. The purpose of factor rotation is to make the factors more interpretable by producing a rotated factor matrix in which only a few tests have high loadings and the majority of tests have low loadings on any given factor. One of the most common factoring procedures is the *principal axis* method, and a popular rotation procedure is *varimax rotation*. These are the procedures that we shall use in this example.

The correlation matrix in Table B–1 was factored by the principal axis procedure by using subprogram FACTOR of the computer package of statistical programs known as SPSS/PC+ (Norusis, 1990). The resulting unrotated factor matrix is shown in Table B–2. Observe that the computer program yielded a three-factor solution, the three factors designated as A, B, and C. The decimal numbers listed under each factor column are the correlations, or *loadings*, of the 15 scales on that factor. Thus the first scale, Achievement, has a loading of .335 on Factor A, .758 on Factor B, and −.288 on Factor C. The sum of the squared loadings for each item is the item's *communality*, or proportion of the variance of that item which is accounted for by the three common factors. For example, the communality of the Achievement scale is $(.335)^2 + (.758)^2 + (−.288)^2 = .770$. This means that 77.0 percent of the variance of the scores on this scale is accounted for by these three factors.

It is also of interest to determine the proportion of total test variance (or item variance in this case) specific to a given test. To compute this *specificity* of a test (or scale), we use the equation

TABLE B–2 Unrotated Factor Matrix of Need Scales on Adjective Checklist

Scale	Factor Loadings			Communality
	Factor A	Factor B	Factor C	
Achievement	.335	.758	−.288	.770
Dominance	.741	.572	−.078	.882
Endurance	−.137	.791	−.455	.851
Order	−.276	.640	−.610	.858
Intraception	−.243	.757	.186	.667
Nurturance	−.364	.641	.545	.840
Affiliation	−.094	.776	.442	.806
Heterosexuality	.300	.434	.625	.669
Exhibition	.801	.005	.267	.713
Autonomy	.858	−.184	−.171	.799
Aggression	.818	−.294	−.124	.771
Change	.545	−.043	.608	.669
Succorance	−.390	−.608	.148	.544
Abasement	−.775	−.399	.157	.784
Deference	−.900	.178	.107	.853

Specificity = Reliability − Communality

As discussed in Chapter 2, *reliability* refers to the consistency of measurement, that is, the extent to which the scores on a test or other psychometric instrument are free from errors of measurement. A *reliability coefficient* is an index number ranging from .00 (complete unreliability) to 1.00 (perfect reliability). Like communality and reliability, specificity ranges from .00 to 1.00; the larger a test's specificity, the more specific whatever that test measures is to that test itself. The larger a test's communality, the more common whatever that test measures is to the other tests in the group of tests being factor analyzed.

The rotated factor matrix is shown in Table B–3. The communality of each item is the same as in the unrotated factor matrix, but the rotated factors are easier to interpret than those in Table B–2. Varimax rotation is an *orthogonal rotation* procedure, in that the factor axes remain at right angles to each other. In contrast, the factor axes in *oblique rotation* make acute or obtuse angles with each other. Orthogonal factors are usually easier to interpret than oblique factors, because the factors are uncorrelated, or independent. Table B–3 was obtained by the varimax rotation procedure, and hence the three factors are orthogonal, or independent of one another.

In interpreting the rotated factor matrix, we pay particular attention to the items that have high loadings (plus or minus .50 or greater) on a given factor. It can be seen in Table B–3 that seven of the 15 need scales—Dominance, Exhibition, Autonomy, Aggression, Change, Abasement, and Deference—have high loadings on Factor A′; the first five of these scales have high positive loadings on Factor A′, and the last two scales have high negative loadings on this factor. An

TABLE B–3 Rotated Factor Matrix of Need Scales on Adjective Checklist

Scale	Factor Loadings		
	Factor A′	*Factor B′*	*Factor C′*
Achievement	.333	.769	.260
Dominance	.743	.496	.291
Endurance	−.143	.897	.164
Order	−.287	.880	−.048
Intraception	−.232	.457	.635
Nurturance	−.346	.136	.838
Affiliation	−.078	.308	.839
Heterosexuality	.318	−.066	.750
Exhibition	.807	−.159	.188
Autonomy	.852	−.022	−.270
Aggression	.813	−.136	−.304
Change	.560	−.419	.425
Succorance	−.390	−.565	−.269
Abasement	−.774	−.415	−.119
Deference	−.896	.058	.217

inspection of the adjectives defining these seven scales suggests that an appropriate name for Factor A′ is "Self-Confidence" or "Ego Strength." Four scales have high loadings on Factor B′: Achievement, Endurance, Order, and Succorance. The first three of these scales have positive loadings, and the last has a negative loading on Factor B′. Inspection of the adjectives on these four scales suggests that an appropriate label for Factor B′ is "Goal Orientation." Last, four scales have high loadings, all of which are positive, on Factor C′: Intraception, Nurturance, Affiliation, and Heterosexuality. An inspection of the adjectives on these four scales suggests that an appropriate name for Factor C′ is "Social Interactiveness" or "Friendliness."

Obviously there is much more to factor analysis than has been sketched here; entire books have been written on the subject (e.g., Harman, 1976). As these books reveal, factor analysis is a complex topic that involves higher-order mathematics such as matrix algebra and the analytic geometry of space. The topic is also a controversial one. Not only is there disagreement concerning the most appropriate procedures of factoring and rotation, but the interpretation of factors and their psychological bases have been the source of dispute for many years. At the very least, however, factor analysis provides the psychometrician with a tool for understanding the relationships among psychological variables and events. It has proven to be particularly useful in the design of psychological assessment instruments, in research concerned with the validity of those instruments, and in theorizing about the structure of personality.

References

Achenbach, T., & Zigler, E. (1963). Social competence and self-image disparity in psychiatric and nonpsychiatric patients. *Journal of Abnormal and Social Psychology, 67,* 197–205.

Adorno, T. W., Frenkel-Brunswik, E., Levinson, D., & Sanford, N. (1950). *The authoritarian personality.* New York: Harper.

Agras, W. S., Sylvester, D., & Oliveau, D. (1969). The epidemiology of common fears and phobias. *Comprehensive Psychiatry, 10,* 151–156.

Ahammer, L. M. (1973). Social-learning theory as a framework for the study of adult personality development. In P. B. Baltes & K. W. Schaie (Eds.), *Life-span developmental psychology: Personality and socialization* (pp. 256–294). New York: Academic Press.

Ahern, G. L., & Schwartz, G. E. (1985). Differential lateralization for positive and negative emotion in the human brain: EEG spectral analysis. *Neuropsychologists, 23,* 745–756.

Aiken, L. R. (1987). *Assessment of intellectual functioning.* Boston: Allyn & Bacon.

Aiken, L. R. (1989). *Later life* (3rd ed.). Hillsdale, NJ: Lawrence Erlbaum.

Aiken, L. R. (1991a). *Dying, death, and bereavement* (2nd ed.). Boston: Allyn & Bacon.

Aiken, L. R. (1991b). *Psychological testing and assessment* (7th ed.). Needham Heights, MA: Allyn & Bacon.

Aiken, L. R., & Zweigenhaft, R. (1978). Signature size, sex and status: A cross-cultural replication. *Journal of Social Psychology, 106,* 273–274.

Ainsworth, M. D. (1963). The development of infant-mother interactions among the Ganda. In D. M. Foss (Ed.), *Determinants of infant behavior* (Vol. 2). New York: Wiley.

Ainsworth, M.D.S. (1982). Attachment: Retrospect and prospect. In C. M. Parkes & J. Stevenson-Hinde (Eds.), *The place of attachment human behavior.* New York: Basic Books.

Ainsworth, M.D.S. (1989). Attachments beyond infancy. *American Psychologist, 44,* 709–717.

Ainsworth, M. D., Blehar, M. C., Waters, E., & Wall, S. (1978). *Patterns of attachment.* Hillsdale, NJ: Lawrence Erlbaum.

Alderfer, C. P. (1972). *Existence, relatedness, and growth: Human needs in organizational settings.* New York: Free Press.

Alexander, F. (1939). Emotional factors in essential hypertension. *Psychosomatic Medicine, 1,* 139–152.

Alexander, F. (1950). *Psychosomatic medicine: Its principles and applications.* New York: Norton.

Alexander, F., & French, T. M. (1948). *Studies in psychosomatic medicine.* New York: Ronald Press.

Allen, M. G. (1976). Twin studies of affective illness. *Archives of General Psychiatry, 33*, 1476–1478.

Allport, G. W. (1937). *Personality: A psychological interpretation*. New York: Holt.

Allport, G. W. (1961). *Pattern and growth in personality*. New York: Holt, Rinehart & Winston.

Allport, G. W. (Ed.). (1965). *Letters from Jenny*. New York: Harcourt, Brace & World.

Allport G. W., & Odbert, H. S. (1936). Trait-names, a psycholexical study. *Psychological Monographs, 47* (Whole No. 211).

Allred, K. D., & Smith, T.W. (1989). The hardy personality: Cognitive and physiological responses to evaluative threat. *Journal of Personality and Social Psychology, 56*, 257–266.

Altus, W. D. (1966). Birth order and its sequelae. *Science, 151*, 44–49.

American Educational Research Association, American Psychological Association, & National Council on Measurement in Education. (1985). *Standards for educational and psychological testing*. Washington, DC: American Psychological Association.

American Law Institute. (1956). *Model penal code*. Tentative Draft Number 4.

American Psychiatric Association. (1952). *Diagnostic and statistical manual of mental disorders*. Washington, DC: Author.

American Psychiatric Association. (1968). *Diagnostic and statistical manual of mental disorders* (2nd ed.). Washington, DC: Author.

American Psychiatric Association. (1980). *Diagnostic and statistical manual of mental disorders* (3rd ed.). Washington, DC: Author.

American Psychiatric Association. (1987). *Diagnostic and statistical manual of mental disorders* (3rd ed., rev). Washington, DC: Author.

American Psychological Association. (1992, May). APA continues to reform its Ethics Code. *APA Monitor, 123* (5), 38–42.

Amsterdam, B. (1972). Mirror self-image reactions before age two. *Developmental Psychobiology, 5*, 297–305.

Andrasik, E., Blanchard, E. B., & Edlund, S. R. (1985). Physiological responding during biofeedback. In S. R. Burchfield (Ed.), *Stress: Psychological and physiological interactions*. Washington, DC: Hemisphere.

Andreasen, N. C. (1982). Negative symptoms in schizophrenia: Definition and reliability. *Archives of General Psychiatry, 39*, 784–788.

Anisfield, M. S., Munoz, S. R., & Lambert, W. E. (1963). The structure and dynamics of the ethnic attitudes of Jewish adolescents. *Journal of Abnormal and Social Psychology, 66*, 31–36.

Ansbacher, H. L., & Ansbacher, R. R. (Eds.). (1956). *The individual psychology of Alfred Adler*. New York: Basic Books.

Arkes, H. R. (1985). Clinical judgment. In R. J. Corsini (Ed.), *Encyclopedia of psychology* (Vol. 1, pp. 223–224). New York: Wiley.

Atkinson, R. L., Atkinson, R. C., Smith, E. E., & Bem, D. J. (1990). *Introduction to psychology* (10th ed.). San Diego, CA: Harcourt Brace Jovanovich.

Atkinson, J. W., & Litwin, G. H. (1960). Achievement motive and test anxiety conceived as motive to approach success and motive to avoid failure. *Journal of Abnormal and Social Psychology, 60*, 52–63.

Ax, A. F. (1953). The physiological differentiation between fear and anger in humans. *Psychosomatic Medicine, 15*, 433–442.

Bakan, P. (1957). Extraversion-introversion and improvement in an auditory vigilance task. *Medical Research Council*, A.P.U. 311/57.

Bakwin, H. (1971a). Car-sickness in twins. *Developmental Medicine and Child Neurology, 13*, 310–312.

Bakwin, H. (1971b). Constipation in twins. *Journal of Diseases of Children, 121*, 179–181.

Bakwin, H. (1971c). Nail-biting in twins. *Developmental Medicine and Child Neurology, 13*, 304–307.

Bakwin, H. (1971d). Enuresis in twins. *American Journal of Diseases of Children, 121,* 222–225.

Bandura, A. (1965). Influence of models' reinforcement contingencies on the acquisition of imitative responses. *Journal of Personality and Social Psychology, 1,* 589–595.

Bandura, A. (1969). *Principles of behavior modification.* New York: Holt, Rinehart & Winston.

Bandura, A. (1977). *Social learning theory.* Englewood Cliffs, NJ: Prentice Hall.

Bandura, A. (1982). Self-efficacy mechanism in human agency. *American Psychologist, 37,* 122–147.

Bandura, A. (1986). *Social foundations of thought and action: A social cognitive theory.* Englewood Cliffs, NJ: Prentice Hall.

Bandura, A., Blanchard, E. B., & Ritter, B. (1969). The relative efficacy of desensitization and modeling approaches for inducing behavioral, affective, and attitudinal changes. *Journal of Personality and Social Psychology, 13,* 173–199.

Bandura, A., Ross, D., & Ross, S. A. (1963). Imitation of film-mediated aggressive models. *Journal of Abnormal and Social Psychology, 66,* 3–11.

Bandura, A., & Walters, R. H. (1959). *Adolescent aggression.* New York: Ronald.

Bandura, A., & Walters, R. H. (1963). *Social learning and personality development.* New York: Holt.

Bannister, D. (Ed.). (1984). *Further perspectives in personal construct theory.* New York: Academic Press.

Bannister, D., & Fransella, F. (1971). *Inquiring man: The theory of personal constructs.* New York: Penguin.

Barefoot, J. C., Dahlstrom, W. C., & Williams, R. B. (1983). Hostility, CHD incidence, and total mortality: A 25-year follow-up study of 255 physicians. *Psychosomatic Medicine, 45,* 59–63.

Barker, J. (1968). *Scared to death.* London: Frederick Muller.

Barnouw, V. (1985). *Culture and personality* (4th ed.). Belmont, CA: Wadsworth.

Baron, R. A., Russell, G. W., & Arms, R. L. (1985). Negative ions and behavior: Impact on mood, memory, and aggression among Type A and Type B persons. *Journal of Personality and Social Psychology, 48,* 746–754.

Barry, H., & Blane, H. T. (1977). Birth order of alcoholics. *Journal of Individual Psychology, 33,* 62–69.

Barry, H., Child, I., & Bacon, M. (1959). Relation of child training to subsistence economy. *American Anthropologist, 61,* 51–63.

Baruch, G., Barnett, R., & Rivers, C. (1983). *Lifeprints.* New York: McGraw-Hill.

Bassett, A. S., McGillvray, B. C., Jones, B. D., & Pantzar, J. T. (1988, April 9). Partial trisomy chromosome 5 cosegregating with schizophrenia. *Lancet,* 799–801.

Baum, A., Fisher, J. D., & Solomon, S. (1981). Type of information, familiarity, and the reduction of crowding stress. *Journal of Personality and Social Psychology, 40*(1), 11–23.

Baumeister, R. F. (1991). Self-concept and identity. In V. J. Derlega, B. A. Winstead, & W. H. Jones (Eds.), *Personality: Contemporary theory and research* (pp. 349–380). Chicago: Nelson-Hall.

Baumrind, D. (1971). Current patterns of parental authority. *Developmental Psychology Monographs, 1,* 1–103.

Baumrind, D. (1972). Socialization and instrumental competence in young children. In W. W. Harrup (Ed.), *The young child: Reviews of research* (Vol. 2). Washington, DC: National Association for the Education of Young Children.

Beck, A. T. (1967). *Depression: Clinical, experimental, and theoretical aspects.* New York: Harper & Row.

Beck, A. T., Rush, A. J., Shaw, B. F., & Emery, G. (1979). *Cognitive therapy of depression.* New York: Guilford.

Becker, W. C. (1964). Consequences of different kinds of parental discipline. In M. L.

Hoffman & L. W. Hoffman (Eds.), *Review of child development research* (Vol. 1). New York: Russell Sage.

Bell, A. P., Weinberg, M. S., & Hammersmith, S. K. (1981). *Sexual preference: Its development in men and women.* Bloomington: Indiana University Press.

Bellak, L. (1986). *The T.A.T., C.A.T., and S.A.T. in clinical use* (4th ed.). New York: Grune & Stratton.

Bem, D. J., & Allen, A. (1974). On predicting some of the people some of the time: The search for cross-situational consistencies in behavior. *Psychological Review, 81,* 506–520.

Bem, D. J., & Funder, D. C. (1978). Predicting some of the people more of the time: Assessing the personality of situations. *Psychological Review, 85,* 485–501.

Bem, S. L. (1984). Androgyny and gender schema theory: A conceptual and empirical integration. *Nebraska Symposium on Motivation, 32,* 179–226.

Ben-Shakhar, G., Bar-Hillel, M., Bilu, Y., Ben-Abba, E., & Flug, A. (1986). Can graphology predict occupational success? Two empirical studies and some methodological ruminations. *Journal of Applied Psychology, 71,* 645–653.

Bentler, P. M., & Newcomb, M. D. (1986). Personality, sexual behavior, and drug use revealed through latent variable methods. *Clinical Psychology Review, 6*(5), 363–386.

Berkman, L., & Syme, S. L. (1979). Social networks, host resistance, and mortality: A nine-year follow-up study of Alameda County residents. *American Journal of Epidemiology, 109,* 186–204.

Berman, J. S., Miller, R. C., & Massman, P. J. (1985). Cognitive therapy versus systematic desensitization: Is one treatment superior? *Psychological Bulletin, 97,* 451–461.

Berne, E. (1964). *Games people play.* New York: Grove Press.

Berne, E. (1966). *Principles of group treatment.* New York: Oxford University Press.

Bieri, J. (1955). Cognitive complexity-simplicity and predictive behavior. *Journal of Abnormal and Social Psychology, 1,* 61–66.

Binion, R. (1976). *Hitler among the Germans.* New York: Elsevier.

Blanchard, E. B., Andrasik, F., & Arena, J. G. (1984). Personality and chronic headache. In B. A. Maher & W. B. Maher (Eds.), *Progress in experimental personality research: Vol. 13. Normal personality processes* (pp. 303–364). New York: Academic Press.

Block, J. (1961). *The Q-sort method in personality assessment and psychiatric research.* Springfield, IL: Thomas.

Block, J. (1971). *Lives through time.* Berkeley, CA: Bancroft.

Block, J. (1977). Advancing the psychology of personality: Paradigmatic shift in improving the quality of research. In D. Magnusson & N. S. Endler (Eds.), *Personality at the crossroads: Current issues in interactional psychology.* Hillsdale, NJ: Erlbaum.

Block, J., Harvey, E., Jennings, P. H., & Simpson, E. (1966). Clinicians' conceptions of the asthmatogenic mother. *Archives of General Psychiatry, 15,* 610.

Block, J. H. (1973). Conceptions of sex role: Some cross-cultural and longitudinal perspectives. *American Psychologist, 28,* 512–529.

Block, J. H. (1976). Issues, problems and pitfalls in assessing sex differences. *Merrill-Palmer Quarterly, 22,* 283–308.

Blumer, D., & Benson, D. F. (1975). Personality changes with frontal and temporal lobe lesions. In D. F. Benson & D. Blumer (Eds.), *Psychiatric aspects of neurological disease* (pp. 151–170). New York: Grune & Stratton.

Botwinick, J. (1978). *Aging and behavior: A comprehensive integration of research findings* (2nd ed.). New York: Springer-Verlag.

Bouchard, T. J., Jr., Lykken, D. T., McGue, M., Segal, N. L., & Tellengen, A. (1990). Sources of human psychological differences: The Minnesota study of twins reared apart. *Science, 250,* 223–228.

Bouchard, T. J., Jr., & McGue, M. (1981). Familial studies of intelligence: A review. *Science, 212,* 1055–1059.

Bowlby, J. (1973). *Attachment and loss: Vol. 2. Separation: Anxiety and anger.* New York: Basic Books.

Bradley, R. H., & Caldwell, B. M. (1977). Home observation for the measurement of the environment: A validation study of screening efficiency. *American Journal of Mental Deficiency, 81,* 417–420.

Breier, A., Charney, D. S., & Heninger, G. R. (1984). Major depression in patients with agoraphobia and panic disorder. *Archives of General Psychiatry, 41,* 1129–1135.

Brim, O. G., Jr., & Wheeler, S. (1966). *Socialization after childhood.* New York: Wiley.

Brodie, F. M. (1983). *Richard Nixon: The shaping of his character.* Cambridge, MA: Harvard University Press.

Brown, J. D., & McGill, K. L. (1989). The cost of good fortune: When positive life events produce negative health consequences. *Journal of Personality and Social Psychology, 57,* 1103–1110.

Brown, R. (1965). *Social psychology.* New York: Free Press.

Buchsbaum, M. S., & Silverman, J. (1968). Stimulus intensity control and the cortical evoked response. *Psychosomatic Medicine, 30,* 12–22.

Bugliosi, V. (1991). *And the sea will tell.* New York: Ivy Books.

Bukatman, B. A., Foy, J. L., & De Grazia, E. (1971). What is competency to stand trial? *American Journal of Psychiatry, 127,* 1225–1229.

Bunney, W. E., & Davis, J. M. (1965). Norepinephrine in depressive reactions: A review. *Archives of General Psychiatry, 13,* 483–494.

Burton, R. V. (1963). Generality of honesty reconsidered. *Psychological Review, 70,* 481–499.

Buss, A. H. (1989). Personality as traits. *American Psychologist, 44,* 1378–1388.

Buss, A. H., & Plomin, R. (1975). *A temperament theory of personality development.* New York: Wiley.

Buss, A. H., & Plomin, R. (1984). *Temperament: Early developing personality traits.* Hillsdale, NJ: Erlbaum.

Buss, A. H., & Plomin, R. (1986). The EAS approach to temperament. In R. Plomin & J. Dunn (Eds.), *The study of temperament: Changes, continuities and challenges* (pp. 67–79). Hillsdale, NJ: Erlbaum.

Butler, J. M. (1968). Self-ideal congruence in psychotherapy. *Psychotherapy: Research and Practice, 5,* 13–17.

Butler, R. N. (1971). Age: The life review. *Psychology Today, 5*(7), 49–55 ff.

Butler, R. N., & Lewis, M. I. (1982). *Aging and mental health* (3rd ed.). St Louis: Mosby.

Butt, D. S. (1987). *Psychology of sport* (2nd ed.). New York: Van Nostrand Reinhold.

Byerly, W., Mellon, C., O'Connell, P., Lalouel, J.-M., Nakamura, Y., Leppert, M., & White, R. (1989). Mapping genes for manic-depression and schizophrenia with DNA markers. *Trends in Neurosciences, 12,* 46–48.

Byrne, D. (1961). The Repression-Sensitization Scale: Rationale, reliability, and validity. *Journal of Personality, 29,* 334–349.

Byrne, D. (1964). Repression-sensitization as a dimension of personality. In B. A. Maher (Ed.), *Progress in experimental personality research* (Vol. 1). New York: Academic Press.

Cadoret, R. J., Cain, C. A., & Crowe, R. R. (1983). Evidence for gene-environment interaction in the development of adolescent antisocial behavior. *Behavioral Genetics, 13,* 301–310.

Campbell, J. B. (1984). Personality changes. In R. J. Corsini (Ed.), *Encyclopedia of psychology* (Vol. 3, pp. 14–15). New York: Wiley.

Cannon, W. B. (1929). *Bodily changes in pain, hunger, fear, and rage* (2nd ed.). New York: Appleton.

Carkhuff, R. R. (1969). *Helping and human relations* (Vols. 1 & 2). New York: Holt, Rinehart & Winston.

Carlson, R. (1981). Studies in script theory: I. Adult analogs of a childhood nuclear scene. *Journal of Personality and Social Psychology, 40,* 501–510.

Carroll, B. J. (1982). The dexamethasone suppression test for melancholia. *British Journal of Psychiatry, 140*, 292–304.

Carroll, B. J. (1985). Dexamethasone suppression test: A review of contemporary confusion. *Journal of Clinical Psychiatry, 46*, 13–24.

Carson, R. C., Butcher, J. N., & Coleman, J. C. (1992). *Abnormal psychology and modern life* (9th ed.). Glenview, IL: Scott Foresman.

Caspi, A., Elder, G. H., Jr., & Bem, D. J. (1987a). Moving against the world: Life course patterns of explosive children. *Developmental Psychology, 23*, 308-313.

Caspi, A. Elder, G. H., Jr., & Bem, D. J. (1987b). *Moving toward the world: Life-course patterns of dependent children.* Unpublished manuscript, Harvard University.

Caspi, A., & Herbener, E. S. (1989). *Continuity and change: Assortative marriage and the consistency of personality in adulthood.* Unpublished manuscript, Harvard University.

Cattell, R. B. (1950). *Personality: A systematic, theoretical, and factual study.* New York: McGraw-Hill.

Cattell, R. B. (1965). *The scientific analysis of personality.* New York: Penguin.

Cattell, R. B. (1982). *The inheritance of personality and ability.* New York: Academic Press.

Chaplin, W. F., & Goldberg, L. R. (1984). A failure to replicate the Bem and Allen study of individual differences in cross-situational consistency. *Journal of Personality and Social Psychology, 47*, 1074–1090.

Charrey, J. M., & Hawkinshead, F.B.W. (1981). Effects of atmospheric electricity on some substrates of disordered social behavior. *Journal of Personality and Social Psychology, 41*, 185–197.

Cheek, J. (1982). Aggregation, moderator variables, and the validity of personality tests: A peer-rating study. *Journal of Personality and Social Psychology, 43*, 1254–1269.

Cheesman, J., & Merikle, P. M. (1986). Distinguishing conscious from unconscious perception. *Canadian Journal of Psychology, 40*, 343–367.

Ciminero, A. R., Nelson, R. O., & Lipinski, D. P. (1977). Self-monitoring procedures. In A. R. Ciminero, K. S. Calhoun, & H. E. Adams (Eds.), *Handbook of behavioral assessment.* New York: Wiley.

Claridge, G. (1960). The excitation-inhibition balance in neurotics. In H. J. Eysenck (Ed.), *Experiments in personality.* London: Routledge & Kegan Paul.

Clarke-Stewart, K. A. (1973). Interactions between mothers and their young children: Characteristics and consequences. *Monographs of the Society for Research in Child Development, 38*(6 & 7, Serial No. 153).

Cloninger, C. R., Reich, T., Sigvardsson, S., von Knorring, A. L., & Bohman, M. (1986). The effects of changes in alcohol use between generations on the inheritance of alcohol abuse. In *Alcholism: A medical disorder.* Proceedings of the 76th Annual Meeting of the American Psychopathological Association.

Cohen, F., & Lazarus, R. (1973). Active coping processes, coping dispositions, and recovery from surgery. *Psychosomatic Medicine, 35*, 375–389.

Coles, M.G.H., Gale, A., & Kline P. (1971). Personality and habituation of the orienting reaction: Tonic and response measures of electrodermal activity. *Psychophysiology, 8*, 54–63.

Conger, R. (1980). Juvenile delinquency: Behavior restraint or behavior facilitation? In T. Hirschi & M. Gottfredson (Eds.), *Understanding crime: Current theory and research* (pp. 131–142). Newbury Park, CA: Sage.

Conley, J. J. (1984). The hierarchy of consistency: A review and model of longitudinal findings on adult individual differences in intelligence, personality, and self-opinion. *Personality and Individual Differences, 5*, 11–25.

Conley, J. J. (1985). Longitudinal stability of personality traits: A multitrait-multimethod-multioccasion analysis. *Journal of Personality and Social Psychology, 49*, 1266–1282.

Conoley, J. C., & Kramer, J. J. (Eds.). (1989). *The tenth mental measurements yearbook.* Lincoln: Buros Institute of Mental Measurements, University of Nebraska–Lincoln.

Contrada, R. J. (1989). Type A behavior, personality hardiness, and cardiovascular response to stress. *Journal of Personality and Social Psychology, 57,* 895–903.

Cooley, C. H. (1922). *Human nature and the social order.* New York: Scribners.

Cooper, J. E., Kendall, R. E., Gurland, B. J., Sharp, L., Copeland, J.R.M., & Simon, R. (1972). *Psychiatric diagnosis in New York and London: A comparative study of mental hospital admissions.* New York: Oxford University Press.

Coopersmith, H. S. (1967). *The antecedents of self-esteem.* San Francisco: Freeman.

Costa, P. T., Jr., & McCrae, R. R. (1986). Personality stability and its implications for clinical psychology. *Clinical Psychology Review, 6,* 407–423.

Crandall, J. E. (1980). Adler's concept of social interest: Theory, measurement, and implications for adjustment. *Journal of Personality and Social Psychology, 39,* 481–495.

Crandall, V. C. (1973). Achievement. In H. Stevenson (Ed.), *Child psychology.* Chicago, IL: University of Chicago Press.

Crandall, V. C., Katkovsky, W., & Crandall, V. J. (1965). Children's beliefs in their own control of reinforcements in intellectual-academic situations. *Child Development, 36,* 91–109.

Creer, T. L., & Kotses, H. (1983). Asthma: Psychological aspects and management. In E. Middleton, Jr., C. Reed, & E. Ellis (Eds.), *Allergy: Principles and practice* (2nd ed.). St. Louis: Mosby.

Crocker, J., & Schwartz, I. (1985). Prejudice and ingroup favoritism in a minimal inter-group situation: Effects of self-esteem. *Personality and Social Psychology Bulletin, 11,* 379–386.

Crockett, D., Clark, C., & Klonoff, H. (1987). Introduction—an overview of neuropsychology. In S. B. Filskov & T. J. Boll (Eds.), *Handbook of clinical neuropsychology.* New York: Wiley.

Crow, T. J. (1982). Two syndromes in schizophrenia? *Trends in Neurosciences, 5,* 351–354.

Davidson, R. J. (1991). Biological approaches to the study of personality. In V. J. Derlega, B. A. Winstead, & W. H. Jones (Eds.), *Personality: Contemporary theory and research* (pp. 87–112). Chicago: Nelson-Hall.

Davis, C., & Cowles, M. (1988). A laboratory study of temperament and arousal: A test of Gale's hypothesis. *Journal of Research in Personality, 22,* 101–116.

Davis, M. H., & Franzoi, S. L. (1991). Self-awareness and self-consciousness. In V. J. Derlega, B. A. Winstead, & W. H. Jones (Eds.), *Personality: Contemporary theory and research* (pp. 313–347). Chicago: Nelson-Hall.

DeAngelis, T. (1991). Honesty tests weigh in with improved ratings. *APA Monitor, 22*(6), 6.

Dennis, W., & Najarian, P. (1957). Infant development under environmental handicap. *Psychological Monographs, 71,* No. 7.

Derlega, V. J., & Berg, J. H. (Eds.) (1987). *Self-disclosure: Theory, research and therapy.* New York: Plenum.

Derlega, V. J., Winstead, B. A., & Jones, W. H. (1991). *Personality: Contemporary theory and research.* Chicago: Nelson-Hall.

Derogatis, L., Abeloff, M., & Melisaratos, N. (1979). Psychological coping mechanisms and survival time in metastatic breast cancer. *Journal of the American Medical Association, 112,* 45–56.

Diamond, E. E. (1979). Sex equality and measurement practices. *New Directions for Testing and Measurement, 3,* 31–78.

Disbrow, M. A., Doerr, H. O., & Caulfield, C. (1977, March). *Measures to predict child abuse.* Final report of Grant MC-R530351, Maternal and Child Health. Washington, DC: National Institute of Mental Health.

Dollard, J., Doob, L. W., Miller, N. E., Mowrer, O. H., & Sears, R. R. (1939). *Frustration and aggression.* New Haven, CT: Yale University Press.

Dollard, J., & Miller, N. (1941). *Social learning and imitation.* New Haven, CT: Yale University Press.

Dollard, J., & Miller, N. E. (1950). *Personality and psychotherapy: An analysis in terms of learning, thinking, and culture.* New York: McGraw-Hill.

Duck, S. W., & Craig, G. (1978). Personality similarity and the development of friendship: A longitudinal study. *British Journal of Social and Clinical Psychology, 17,* 237–242.

Duck, S. W., & Spencer, C. (1972). Personal constructs, and friendship formation. *Journal of Personality and Social Psychology, 23,* 40–45.

Dugdale, R. L. (1877). *The Jukes: A study in crime, pauperism, disease and heredity.* New York: Putnam.

Duke, M. P., & Nowicki, S., Jr. (1979). *Abnormal psychology: Perspectives on being different.* Monterey, CA: Brooks/Cole.

Dunbar, F. (1943). *Psychosomatic diagnosis.* New York: Harper & Row.

Dunbar, H. F. (1954). *Emotions and bodily changes.* New York: Columbia University Press.

Dunkel-Schetter, C., Folkman, S., & Lazarus, R. S. (1987). Correlates of social support receipt. *Journal of Personality and Social Psychology, 53*(1), 71–80.

Dunn, S. M., & Turtle, J. R. (1981). The myth of the diabetic personality. *Diabetes Care, 4,* 640–646.

Dworkin, R. H., Burke, B. W., Maher, B. A., & Gottesman, I. I. (1976). A longitudinal study of the genetics of personality. *Journal of Personality and Social Psychology, 34,* 510–518.

Edmonds, J. M. (Ed. and Trans.). (1929). *The characters of Theophrastus.* Cambridge, MA: Harvard University Press.

Edwards, C. P., & Whiting, B. B. (1980). Differential socialization of girls and boys in light of cross-cultural research. In C. Super & S. Harkness (Eds.), *Anthropological perspectives on child development.* San Francisco: Jossey-Bass.

Egeland, J. A., Gerhard, D. S., Pauls, D. L., Sussex, J. N., Kidd, K. K., et al. (1987). Bipolar affective disorders linked to DNA markers on chromosome 11. *Nature, 325,* 783–787.

Egeland, B., & Sroufe, L. A. (1981a). Attachment and early maltreatment. *Child Development, 52,* 44–52.

Egeland, B., & Sroufe, L. A. (1981b). Developmental sequelae of maltreatment in infancy. *New Directions for Child Development, 11,* 77–92.

Ehrhardt, A. A., Meyer-Bahlburg, H.F.L., Rosen, L. R., Feldman, J. F., Veridiano, N. P., Zimmerman, I., & McEwen, B. S. (1985). Sexual orientation after prenatal exposure to exogenous estrogen. *Archives of Sexual Behavior, 14,* 75–77.

Eisenberg, N., & Lennon, R. (1983). Sex differences in empathy and related capacities. *Psychological Bulletin, 94,* 100–131.

Ekman, P., & Friesen, W. V. (1984). *Unmasking the face* (Reprint ed.). Palo Alto, CA: Consulting Psychologists Press.

Ellis, A. E. (1962). *Reason and emotion in psychotherapy.* New York: Lyle Stuart.

Ellis, A. E. (1971). *Growth through reason: Verbatim cases in rational-emotive therapy.* North Hollywood, CA: Wilshire.

Epstein, S. (1979). The stability of behavior: I. On predicting most of the people much of the time. *Journal of Personality and Social Psychology, 37,* 1097–1126.

Equal Employment Opportunity Commission, Civil Service Commission, Department of Labor, & Department of Justice. (1978). Adoption by four agencies of guidelines on employee selection procedures. *Federal Register, 43*(166), 38315–38290.

Erikson, E. H. (1958). *Young man Luther: A study in psychoanalysis and history.* New York: Norton.

Erikson, E. H. (1963). *Childhood and society* (2nd ed.). New York: Norton.

Erikson, E. H. (1968). *Identity: Youth and crisis.* New York: Norton.

Erikson, E. H. (1969). *Gandhi's truth: On the origins of militant nonviolence.* New York: Norton.

Ernst, C., & Angst, J. (1983). *Birth order: Its influence on personality.* Berlin: Springer-Verlag.

Eron, I. D. (1987). The development of aggressive behavior from the perspective of a developing behaviorism. *American Psychologist, 42,* 435–442.

Eskew, R. T., & Riche, C. V. (1982). Pacing and locus of control in quality control inspection. *Human Factors, 24,* 411–415.

Estes, W. K. (1944). An experimental study of punishment. *Psychological Monographs, 57* (Whole No. 263).

Ethical principles of psychologists (Amended June 2, 1990). *American Psychologist, 45,* 390–395.

Evans, R. I. (1978, July). Donald Bannister: On clinical psychology in Britain. *APA Monitor* (Vol. 9, No. 7), pp. 6–7.

Exner, J. E. (1978). *The Rorschach: A comprehensive system: Vol. II. Current research and advanced interpretation.* New York: Wiley.

Exner, J. E. (1986). *The Rorschach: A comprehensive system* (Vol. 1, 2nd ed.). New York: Wiley.

Eysenck, H. J. (1952). The effects of psychotherapy: An evaluation. *Journal of Consulting Psychology, 16,* 319–324.

Eysenck, H. J. (1960). The effects of psychotherapy. In H. J. Eysenck (Ed.), *Handbook of abnormal psychology: An experimental approach.* London: Pittman Medical Publishing.

Eysenck, H. J. (1961). *Handbook of abnormal psychology: An experimental approach.* New York: Basic Books.

Eysenck, H. J. (1964). *Crime and personality.* Boston: Houghton Mifflin.

Eysenck, H. J. (1967). *The biological basis of personality.* Springfield, IL: Charles C Thomas.

Eysenck, H. J. (1982). *Personality, genetics, and behavior.* New York: Praeger.

Eysenck, H. J., & Eysenck, S.B.G. (1968). *Manual for the Eysenck Personality Inventory.* San Diego, CA: Educational and Industrial Testing Service.

Eysenck, H. J., & Eysenck, S.B.G. (1975). *Manual of the Eysenck Personality Questionnaire.* San Diego: Educational and Industrial Testing Service.

Ezrin, C. (1977). Psychiatric aspects of endocrine and metabolic disorders. In E. D. Wittkower & H. Warnes (Eds.), *Psychosomatic medicine: Its clinical applications* (pp. 280–295). New York: Harper & Row.

Fadiman, C. (Ed.). (1945). *The short stories of Henry James.* New York: Random House.

Fagot, B. I., Leinbach, M. D., & Hagan, R. (1986). Gender labeling and the adoption of sex-typed behaviors. *Developmental Psychology, 22,* 440–443.

Farley, F., & Farley, S. V. (1967). Extroversion and stimulus-seeking motivation. *Journal of Consulting Psychology, 31,* 215–216.

Feist, J. (1990). *Theories of personality* (2nd ed.). New York: Holt Rinehart Winston.

Ferster, C. B., & Skinner, B. F. (1957). *Schedules of reinforcement.* New York: Appleton.

Feshbach, N. D. (1969). Sex differences in children's modes of aggressive responses toward outsiders. *Merrill-Palmer Quarterly, 15,* 249–258.

Feshbach, S., & Weiner, B. (1991). *Personality* (3rd ed.). Lexington, MA: D. C. Heath.

Fisher, S., & Greenberg, R. P. (1977). *The scientific credibility of Freud's theories and therapy.* New York: Basic Books.

Floderus-Myrhed, B., Pedersen, N., & Rasmuson, I. (1980). Assessment of heritability for personality based on a short form of the Eysenck Personality Inventory: A study of 12,898 twin pairs. *Behavior Genetics, 10,* 153–162.

Folkman, S., Dunkel-Schetter, C., DeLongis, A., & Gruen, R. (1986). The dynamics of a stressful encounter: Cognitive appraisal, coping, and encounter outcomes. *Journal of Personality and Social Psychology, 50,* 992–1003.

Forer, B. R. (1949). The fallacy of personal validation: A classroom demonstration of gullibility. *Journal of Abnormal and Social Psychology, 44,* 118–123.

Fowler, O. L. (1890). *Practical phrenology* (rev. ed.). New York: Fowler & Wells Co.

Freedman, J. L. (1982). *Introductory psychology* (2nd ed.). Reading, MA: Addison-Wesley.

Freedman, J. L. (1984). Effect of television violence on aggressiveness. *Psychological Bulletin, 96,* 227–246.

Freedman, J. L. (1986). Television violence and aggression: A rejoinder. *Psychological Bulletin, 100,* 372–378.

Freud, S. (1900). *The interpretation of dreams. Collected works* (Vol. 4). London: Hogarth.

Freud, S. (1901) *The psychopathology of everyday life. Collected works* (Vol. 4). London: Hogarth.

Freud, S. (1905a, reprinted 1969). Fragment of an analysis of a case of hysteria. In *Collected papers* (Vol. 3). New York: Basic Books.

Freud, S. (1905 b/1960). *Jokes and their relation to the unconscious.* London: Hogarth Press.

Freud, S. (1925). Analysis of a phobia in a 5-year-old child. In *Collected papers.* (Vol. 3, pp. 149–289). New York: International Psychoanalytic Press. (Analyse der Phobie eines 5 jarhigen Knaben. In *Jahrbuch für psychoanalytische und psychopathologische forschungen.* Leipzig und Wien: F. Deuticke, 1909.)

Freud, S. (1926). *The problem of anxiety.* New York: W. W. Norton, 1935.

Freud, S. (1930). *Civilization and its discontents.* London: Hogarth.

Freud, S. (1933). *New introductory lectures on psychoanalysis.* New York: Norton, 1961.

Freud S., & Bullitt, W. C. (1967). *Thomas Woodrow Wilson.* Boston: Houghton Mifflin.

Friedman, H. S., & Booth-Kewley, S. (1987). Personality, Type A behavior, and coronary heart disease: The role of emotional expression. *Journal of Personality and Social Psychology, 53,* 783–792.

Friedman, M., & Ulmer, D. (1984). *Treating Type A behavior and your heart.* New York: Knopf.

Friedrich-Cofer, L., & Huston, A. C. (1986). Television violence and aggression: The debate continues. *Psychological Bulletin, 100,* 364–371.

Fromm, E. (1941). *Escape from freedom.* New York: Holt, Rinehart & Winston.

Fromm, E. (1947). *Man for himself: An inquiry into the psychology of ethics.* New York: Holt, Rinehart & Winston.

Fromm, E. (1951). *The forgotten language: An introduction to the understainding of dreams, fairy tales and myths.* New York: Rinehart.

Fromm, E. (1955). *The sane society.* New York: Holt, Rinehart & Winston.

Fromm, E. (1956). *The art of loving.* New York: Harper & Brothers.

Fromm, E., & Maccoby, M. (1970). *Social character in a Mexican village.* Englewood Cliffs, NJ: Prentice Hall.

Funkenstein, D. H., King, S. H., & Drolette, M. E. (1957). *Mastery of stress.* Cambridge, MA: Harvard University Press.

The future of personality tests in employment settings. (1992, January/February). *Psychological Science Agenda* (pp. 2–3). Washington, DC: American Psychological Association.

Gaines, J., & Jermier, J. M. (1983). Emotional exhaustion in a high stress organization. *Academy of Management Journal, 26,* 567–586.

Gainotti, G. (1972). Emotional behavior and hemispheric side of lesion. *Cortex, 8,* 41–55.

Galton, F. (1865). *Hereditary genius: An inquiry into its laws and consequences.* London: Macmillan (Cleveland: World Publishing, 1962).

Galton, L. (1979, June 3). Best friend, best therapy? *Parade,* p. 20.

Garfield, S. L. (1980). *Psychotherapy: An eclectic approach.* New York: Wiley-Interscience.

Geen, R. A., & Thomas, S. L. (1986). The immediated effects of media violence on behavior. *Journal of Social Issues, 42*(3), 7–28.

Geen, R. G. (1984). Preferred stimulation levels in introverts and extraverts: Effects on arousal and performance. *Journal of Personality and Social Psychology, 46,* 1303–1312.

Gilligan, C. (1982). *In a different voice: Psychological theory and women's development.* Cambridge, MA: Harvard University Press.

Glad, B. (1980). *Jimmy Carter: In search of the great White House.* New York: Norton.

Glasser, W. (1965). *Reality therapy: A new approach in psychiatry.* New York: Harper & Row.

Glasser, W. (1969). *Schools without failure.* New York: Harper & Row.

Goddard, H. H. (1912). *The Kallikak family: A study in the heredity of feeble-mindedness.* New York: Macmillan.

Goddard, H. H. (1920). *Human efficiency and levels of intelligence.* Princeton, NJ: Princeton University Press.

Goldberg, L. R. (1980, April). *Some ruminations about the structure of individual differences: Developing a common lexicon for the major characteristics of human personality.* Paper presented at the annual meeting of the Western Psychological Association, Honolulu, HI.

Goldfarb, W. (1955). Emotional and intellectual consequences of psychological deprivation in infancy. In E. Hoch & J. Zubin (Eds.), *Psychopathology in childhood* (pp. 105–119). New York: Grune.

Goldhamer, H., & Marshall, A. W. (1953). *Psychosis and civilization.* Glencoe, IL: Free Press.

Goldstein, K. (1939). *The organism.* New York: American Book Company.

Goleman, D. (1987a, April 7). The bully: New research depicts a paranoid, lifelong loser. *New York Times,* 19, 23.

Goleman, D. (1987b, July 7). Brain defect tied to utter amorality of the psychopath. *New York Times,* 13, 16.

Gottesman, I. I. (1962). Differential inheritance of the psychoneuroses. *Eugenics Quarterly, 9,* 223–227.

Gottesman, I. I., & Shields, J. (1973). *Schizophrenia and genetics: A twin study vantage point.* New York: Academic Press.

Gottesman, I. I., & Shields, J. (1982). *Schizophrenia: The epigenetic puzzle.* New York: Cambridge University Press.

Gough, H. G., Fiorvanti, M., & Lazzari, R. (1983). Some implications of self versus ideal-self congruence on the Revised Adjective Check List. *Journal of Personality and Social Psychology, 44,* 1214–1220.

Gough, H. G., Lazzari, R., & Fiorvanti, M. (1978). Self versus ideal self: A comparison of five Adjective Check list indices. *Journal of Consulting and Clinical Psychology, 46,* 1085–1091.

Gould, R. L. (1980). Transformation during early and middle adult years. In N. J. Smelser & E. H. Erikson (Eds.), *Themes of work and love in adulthood.* Cambridge, MA: Harvard University Press.

Gove, W. (1973). Sex, marital status, and mortality. *American Journal of Sociology, 79*(1), 45–67.

Greer, S., & Morris, T. (1975). Psychological attributes of women who develop breast cancer. *Psychosomatic Research, 19,* 147–153.

Gregory, I., & Rosen, E. (1965). *Abnormal psychology.* Philadelphia: W. B. Saunders.

Greist, J. H. (1984). Exercise in the treatment of depression. *Coping with mental stress: The potential and limits of exercise intervention.* Washington, DC: National Institute of Mental Health.

Grinker, R. R., & Spiegel, J. P. (1945). *Men under stress.* Philadelphia: Blackiston.

Guardo, C. J., & Bohan, J. B. (1971). Development of a sense of self-identity in children. *Child Development, 42,* 1909–1921.

Gur, R. C., & Reivich, M. (1980). Cognitive task effects on hemispheric blood flow in humans: Evidence for individual differences in hemispheric activation. *Brain and Language, 9,* 78–92.

Gutmann, D. L. (1964). An exploration of ego configurations in middle and later life. In B. L. Neugarten (Ed.), *Personality in middle and late life: Empirical studies* (pp. 114–148). New York: Atherton Press.

Gutmann, D. L. (1967). Aging among the Highland Maya: A comparative study. *Journal of Personality and Social Psychology, 7,* 28–35.

Gutmann, D. L. (1972). Ego psychological and developmental approaches to the retirement crisis in men. In F. M. Carp (Ed.), *Retirement* (pp. 267–305). New York: Behavioral Publications.

Hall, C. S. (1938). The inheritance of emotionality. *Sigma Xi Quarterly, 26,* 17–27.

Hall, C. S., & Lindzey, G. (1957). *Theories of personality*. New York: Wiley.

Hall, C. S., Lindzey, G., Loehlin, J. C., & Manosevitz, M. (1985). *Introduction to theories of personality*. New York: Wiley.

Hall, G. S. (1916). *Adolescence*. New York: Appleton.

Hansen, J. C., Stevic, R. R., & Warner, R. W. (1977). *Counseling theory and process* (2nd ed.). Boston: Allyn & Bacon.

Hare, R. D. (1970). *Psychopathy: Theory and research*. New York: Wiley.

Hare, R. D. (1978). Psychopathy and physiological activity during anticipation of an aversive stimulus in a distraction paradigm. *Psychophysiology, 15,* 165–172.

Harkins, S., & Green, R. G. (1975). Discriminability and criterion differences between extraverts and introverts during vigilance. *Journal of Research in Personality, 9,* 335–340.

Harlow, H. F. (1958). The nature of love. *American Psychologist, 13,* 673–685.

Harlow, H. F., & Suomi, S. J. (1971). Social recovery by isolation-reared monkeys. *Proceedings of the National Academy of Sciences, 68,* 1534–1558.

Harlow, H. F., & Zimmerman, R. R. (1959). Affectional responses in the infant monkey. *Science, 130,* 421–432.

Harman, H. H. (1976). *Modern factor analysis* (3rd ed.). Chicago: University of Chicago Press.

Harper, R. A. (1959). *Psychoanalysis and psychotherapy: 36 systems*. Englewood Cliffs, NJ: Prentice Hall.

Hartmann, H. (1939). *Ego psychology and the problem of adaptation* (D. Rapaport, Trans.). New York: International Universities Press.

Hartshorne, H., & May, M. A. (1928). *Studies in the nature of character: Vol. 1. Studies in deceit.* New York: Macmillan.

Hathaway, S. R., & McKinley, J. C. (1943). *The Minnesota Mutliphasic Personality Inventory* (rev. ed.) Minneapolis, MN: University of Minnesota Press.

Havighurst, R. J. (1953). *Human development and education*. New York: Longmans.

Hechtman, L., Weiss, G., & Perlman, T. (1984). Hyperactives as young adults: Past and current substance abuse and antisocial behavior. *American Journal of Orthopsychiatry, 54,* 415–425.

Henriques, J. B., & Davidson, R. J. (1989). Affective disorders. In G. Turpin (Ed.), *Handbook of clinical psychophysiology* (pp. 357–392). London: Wiley.

Hergenhahn, B. R. (1990). *Theories of pesonality* (3rd ed.). Englewood Cliffs, NJ: Prentice Hall.

Herman B. H., Hammock, M. K., Arthur-Smith, A., Egan, J., Chatoor, I., Zelnik, N., Carradine, M., Applegate, K., Boecks, R., & Sharp, S. D. (1986, November). Role of opioid peptides in autism: Effects of acute administration of naltrexone. *Society for Neuroscience Abstracts, 12.*

Herzberg, F. (1966). *Work and the nature of man*. Cleveland: World.

Heston, L. L. (1966). Psychiatric disorders in foster home reared children of schizophrenic mothers. *British Journal of Psychiatry, 112,* 819–825.

Hodes, R. L., Cook, E. W., & Lang, P. (1985). Individual differences in autonomic response: Conditioned association or conditioned fear? *Psychophysiology, 22,* 545–560.

Hoffman, L. W. (1984). Maternal employment and the young child. In M. Perlmutter (Ed.), *Parent-child interaction and parent-child relations in child development. Minnesota Symposia on Child Psychology, Vol. 17.* Hillsdale, NJ: Erlbaum.

Holden, C. (1975). Lie detectors: PSE gains audience despite critics' doubt. *Science, 190,* 359–362.

Holmes, T. H., & Rahe, R. H. (1967). The Social Readjustment Rating Scale. *Journal of Psychosomatic Research, 11,* 213–218.

Holroyd, K. A. (1979). Stress, coping, and the treatment of a stress-related illness. In J. R.

McNamara (Ed.), *Behavioral approaches to medicine: Applications and analysis.* New York: Plenum.

Horn, J. (1983). The Texas Adoption Project: Adopted children and their intellectual resemblance to biological and adoptive parents. *Child Development, 54,* 268–275.

Horney, K. (1937). *The neurotic personality of our time.* New York: Norton.

Horney, K. (1939). *New ways in psychoanalysis.* New York: Norton.

Horney, K. (1942). *Self-analysis.* New York: Norton.

Horney, K. (1945). *Our inner conflicts: A constructive theory of neurosis.* New York: Norton.

Horney, K. (1950). *Neurosis and human growth: The struggle toward self-realization.* New York: Norton.

Horney, K. (1967). *Feminine psychology.* New York: Norton.

House, J. S., Robbins, C., & Metzner, H. L. (1982). The association of social relationships and activities with mortality. *American Journal of Epidemiology, 116,* 123–140.

How genes shape personality. (1987, April 13). *U.S. News & World Report,* pp. 58–59, 61.

Howard, J. H., Cunningham, D. A., & Rechnitzer, P. A. (1987). Personality and fitness decline in middle-aged men. *International Journal of Sport Psychology, 18,* 100–111.

Howard, K. I., Kopta, S. M., Krause, M. S., & Orlinsky, D. E. (1986). The dose-effect relationship in psychotherapy. *American Psychologist, 41,* 159–164.

Hoyt, M. F., & Raven, B. H. (1973). Birth order and the 1971 Los Angeles earthquake. *Journal of Personality and Social Psychology, 28,* 123–128.

Huesmann, L. R., & Malamuth, N. M. (1986). Media violence and antisocial behavior. *Journal of Social Issues, 42*(3), 1–6.

Hull, C. L. (1943). *Principles of behavior.* New York: Appleton.

Hull, C. L. (1951). *Essentials of behavior.* New Haven, CT: Yale University Press.

Hundleby, J. D., Pawlik, K., & Cattell, R. B. (1965). *Personality factors in objective test devices: A critical integration of a quarter of a century's research.* San Diego: Knapp.

Hunt, J. McV. (1979). Psychological development: Early experience. *Annual Review of Psychology, 30,* 103–144.

Hunt, J. McV. (1986). Personality. *Collier's Encyclopedia* (Vol. 18, pp. 594–594C). New York: Macmillan.

Inouye, E. (1965). Similar and dissimilar manifestations of obsessive-compulsive neuroses in monozygotic twins. *American Journal of Psychology, 121,* 1171–1175.

James, W. (1890). *The principles of psychology* (2 vols.). New York: Holt.

Jenkins, C. D., Zyzanski, S. J., & Rosenman, R. H. (1979). *Jenkins Activity Survey: Manual.* New York: Psychological Corporation.

Joesting, J. (1981). Comparison of personalities of athletes who sail to those who run. *Perceptual and Motor Skills, 52,* 514.

Johnson, R. C., & Medinnus, G. R. (1965). *Child psychology.* New York: Wiley.

Jones, E. (1990). Freud, Sigmund. *Encyclopedia Americana* (Vol. 12, pp. 83–87). Danbury, CT: Grolier.

Jones, E. E., & Nisbett, R. E. (1972). The actor and the observer: Divergent perceptions of the cause of behavior. In E. E. Jones, D. E. Karouse, H. H. Kelley, R. E. Nisbett, S. Valins, & B. Weiner (Eds.), *Attribution: Perceiving the causes of behavior.* Morristown, NJ: Learning Press.

Jost, H., & Sontag, L. (1944). The genetic factor in autonomic nervous system function. *Psychosomatic Medicine, 6,* 308–310.

Jung, C. G. (1928). *Contributions to analytical psychology.* New York: Harcourt, Brace.

Jung, C. G. (1931/1954). The aims of psychotherapy. In *The collected works of C. G. Jung* (Vol. 16). New York: Pantheon Books.

Jutai, J. W., Hare, R. D., & Connolly, J. F. (1987). Psychopathy and event-related brain potentials (ERPs) associated with attention to speech stimuli. *Personality and Individual Differences, 8,* 175–184.

Kagan, J., Kearsley, R. B., & Zelazo, P. R. (1977). The effects of infant day care on psychological development. *Educational Quarterly, 1,* 109–142.

Kagan, J., & Kogan, N. (1970). Individual variation in cognitive processes. In P. Mussen (Ed.), *Carmichael's manual of child psychology* (3rd ed., Vol. 1). New York: Wiley.

Kagan, J., & Moss, H. A. (1962). *Birth to maturity.* New York: Wiley.

Kagan, J., Reznick, J. S., & Snidman, N. (1988). Biological bases of childhood shyness. *Science, 240,* 167–171.

Kagan, J., Rosman, B. L., Day, D., Albert, J., & Phillips, W. (1964). Information processing in the child: Significance of analytic and reflective attitudes. *Psychological Monographs, 78* (Whole No. 578).

Kalat, J. W. (1984). *Biological psychology* (2nd ed.). Belmont, CA: Wadsworth.

Kallman, F. J., & Jarvik, L. (1959). Individual differences in constitution and genetic background. In J. E. Birren (Ed.), *Handbook of aging and the individual.* Chicago: University of Chicago Press.

Kantorwitz, D. A. (1978). Personality and conditioning of tumescence and detumescence. *Behavioral Research Therapy, 16,* 117–128.

Katz, P. A., & Zigler, E. (1967). Self-image disparity: A development approach. *Journal of Personality and Social Psychology, 5,* 186–195.

Kearns, D. (1976). *Lyndon Johnson and the American dream.* New York: Wilson.

Kelly, E. L. (1987). Graphology. In R. J. Corsini (Ed.), *Concise encyclopedia of psychology* (p. 469). New York: Wiley.

Kelly, G. A. (1955). *The psychology of personal constructs* (2 vols.). New York: Norton.

Kelly, G. A. (1964). The language of hypotheses: Man's psychological instrument. *Journal of Individual Psychology, 20,* 137–152.

Kelsoe, J. R., Ginns, E. I., Egeland, J. A., Gerhard, D. S., Goldstein, A. M., Bale, S. J., Pauls, D. L., Long, R. T., Kidd, K. K., Conte, G., Housman, D. E., & Paul, S. M. (1989). Reevaluation of the linkage relationship between chromosome lip loci and the gene for bipolar affective disorder in the Old Order Amish. *Nature, 342,* 238–243.

Kenrick, D. T., & Funder, D. C. (1988). Profiting from controversy: Lessons from the person-situation debate. *American Psychologist, 43,* 23–34.

Kermoian, R., & Leiderman, P. H. (1986). Infant attachment to mother and child caretaker in an East African community. (Special Issue: Cross-cultural human development.) *International Journal of Behavioral Development, 9,* 455–469.

Keyser, D. J., & Sweetland, R. C. (Eds.). (1984–1988). *Test critiques,* Vols. 1–7. Kansas City, MO: Test Corporation of America.

Kidson, M., & Jones, I. (1968). Psychiatric disorders among aborigines of the Australian Western Desert. *Archives of General Psychiatry, 19,* 413–422.

Kilbride, H. W., Johnson, D. L., & Streissguth, A. P. (1977). Social class, birth order, and newborn experience. *Child Development, 48,* 1686–1688.

Kline, P. (1972). *Fact and fantasy in Freudian theory.* London: Methuen.

Knight, G. P., & Kagan, S. (1977). Development of prosocial and competitive behaviors in Anglo-American and Mexican-American children. *Child Development, 48,* 1385–1394.

Kobasa, S. C. (1979). Stressful life events, personality, and health: An inquiry into hardiness. *Journal of Personality and Social Psychology, 37,* 1–11.

Kobasa, S. C., Maddi, S., & Kahn, S. (1982). Hardiness and health: A prospective study. *Journal of Personality and Social Psychology, 42,* 168–177.

Kobrin, F., & Hendershot, G. (1977). Do family ties reduce mortality? Evidence from the United States, 1966–68. *Journal of Marriage and the Family, 39,* 737–745.

Kohlberg, L. (1966). A cognitive-development analysis of children's sex-role concepts and attitudes. In E. Maccoby (Ed.), *The development of sex differences.* Stanford, CA: Stanford University Press.

Kohlberg, L. (1969). *Stages in the development of moral thought and action.* New York: Holt.

Kohlberg, L. (1976). Stages and moralization: The cognitive-developmental approach. In T. Liskona (Ed.), *Moral development and behavior: Theory, research and social issues.* New York: Holt, Rinehart & Winston.

Kohlberg, L., & Elfenbein, D. (1975). The development of moral judgments concerning capital punishment. *American Journal of Orthopsychiatry, 45,* 614–639.

Kubis, J. F. (1962). Cited in B. M. Smith, The polygraph. In R. C. Atkinson (Ed.), *Contemporary psychology.* San Francisco: Freeman.

Lagerspetz, K. M., Bjorkqvist, K., & Peltorer, T. (1988). Is indirect aggression typical of females? Gender differences in aggressiveness in 11 to 12 year old children. *Aggressive Behavior, 14,* 403–414.

Lancaster, E., & Poling, J. (1958). *The final face of Eve.* New York: McGraw-Hill.

Landman, J. T., & Dawes, R. M. (1982). Psychotherapy outcomes. *American Psychologist, 37,* 504–516.

Langer, E. J., & Saegert, S. (1977). Crowding and cognitive control. *Journal of Personality and Social Psychology, 35,* 175–182.

Langer, W. C. (1972). *The mind of Adolf Hitler.* New York: Basic Books.

Langevin, R. (1983). *Sexual strands: Understanding and treating sexual anomalies in men.* Hillsdale, NJ: Erlbaum.

Larson, D. G. (1988). *Self-concealment: Conceptualization, measurement, and health implications.* Unpublished manuscript.

Lastovicka, J. L., Murray, J. P., Joachimsthaler, E. A., Bhalla, G., & Scheurich, J. (1987). A lifestyle typology to model young male drinking and driving. *Journal of Consumer Research, 14,* 257–263.

Latane, B., & Darley, J. (1970). Social determinants of bystander intervention in emergencies. In J. Macaulay & L. Berkowitz (Eds.), *Altriusm and helping behavior.* New York: Academic Press.

Lazarus, A. A. (1971). Where do behavior therapists take their troubles? *Psychological Reports, 28,* 349–350.

Lazarus, R. S. (1984). Puzzles in the study of daily hassles. *Journal of Behavioral Medicine, 7,* 375–389.

Lefkowitz, J. (1975). Psychological attributes of policemen: A review of research and opinion. *Journal of Social Issues, 31*(1), 3–26.

Lehtovaara, A., Saarinen, P., & Jarvinen, I. (1965). *Psychological attudies of twins: I. GSR reactions.* Psychological Institute, University of Helsinki.

Leo, J. (1985, October 21). Are criminals born, not made? *Time,* p. 94.

Leonard, W. E. (1927). *The locomotive God.* New York: Appleton.

Lerner, R. M., & Busch-Rossnagel, N. (Eds.). (1981). *Individuals as producers of their own development.* New York: Academic Press.

Lester, D. (1990). Biorhythms and the timing of death. *The Skeptical Inquirer, 14*(4), 410–411.

LeUnes, A. D., & Nation, J. R. (1989). *Sport psychology: An introduction.* Chicago: Nelson-Hall.

Levenson, H. (1981). Differentiating among internality, powerful others, and chance. In H. M. Lefcourt (Ed.), *Research with the locus of control construct* (Vol. 1, pp. 15–63). New York: Academic Press.

Levinson, D. J. (1978). *The seasons of a man's life.* New York: Knopf.

Lewin, K. (1935). *A dynamic theory of personality.* New York: McGraw-Hill.

Lewis, M., & Brooks, J. (1975). Infants' social perception: A constructionist view. In L. Cohen & S. Salopatele (Eds.), *Infant perception: From sensation to cognition. Perception of space, speech and sound* (Vol. 2). New York: Academic Press.

Lewis, M., & Brooks-Gunn, J. (1979). *Social cognition and the acquisition of the self.* New York: Plenum.

Livson, N., & Peskin, H. (1980). Perspectives on adolescence from longitudinal research. In J. Adelson (Ed.), *Handbook of adolescent psychology* (pp. 47–98). New York: Wiley.

Loehlin, J. C., & Nichols, R. C. (1976). *Heredity, environment and personality: A study of 850 sets of twins.* Austin: University of Texas Press.

Lombroso, C. (1911). *Criminal man.* New York: Putnam.

Louis, A. M. (1978, April). Should you buy biorhythms? *Psychology Today,* 93–96.

Lovaas, O. I. (1987). Behavioral treatment and normal educational and intellectual functioning in young autistic children. *Journal of Consulting and Clinical Psychology, 55,* 3–9.

Luborsky, L. (1970). New directions in research on neurotic and psychosomatic symptoms. *American Scientist, 58,* 661–668.

Luborsky, L. (1988). *Who will benefit from psychotherapy?* New York: Basic Books.

Lynn, R., & Eysenck, H. J. (1961). Tolerance for pain, extraversion and neuroticism. *Perceptual and Motor Skills, 12,* 161–162.

Maccoby, E., & Jacklin, C. (1974). *The psychology of sex differences.* Stanford, CA: Stanford University Press.

Maccoby, E. E., & Martin, J. A. (1983). Socialization in the context of the family: Parent-child interaction. In P. H. Mussen (Ed.), *Handbook of child psychology: Vol. 4, Socialization, personality, and social development.* New York: Wiley.

Macoby, E. E., & Maccoby, N. (1954). The interview: A tool of social science. In G. Lindzey (Ed.), *Handbook of social psychology* (pp. 449–487). Cambridge, MA: Addison-Wesley.

Maddi, S. R. (1972). *Personality theories: A comparative analysis* (2nd ed.). Homewood, IL: Dorsey.

Maddi, S. R. (1980). *Personality theories: A comparative analysis* (4th ed.). Homewood, IL: Dorsey.

Maher, B. (Ed.). (1969). *Clinical psychology and personality: The selected papers of George Kelly.* New York: Wiley.

Malinowski, B. (1927/1955). *Sex and repression in savage society.* London: Routledge & Kegan Paul.

Marcus Aurelius. (1945). The meditations of Marcus Aurelius. In *Marcus Aurelius and his times.* New York. Black.

Markus, H., & Cross, S. (1990). The interpersonal self. In L. A. Pervin (Ed.), *Handbook of personality theory and research* (pp. 576–608). New York: Guilford Press.

Masling, J. (Ed.). (1983). *Empirical studies of psychoanalytical theories* (Vol. 1). Hillsdale, NJ: Erlbaum.

Maslow, A. H. (1968). *Toward a psychology of being* (2nd ed.). New York: Van Nostrand.

Maslow, A. H. (1970). *Motivation and personality* (2nd ed.). New York: Harper & Row.

Maslow, A. H. (1973). Self-actualizing and beyond. In G. Lindzey, C. S. Hall, & M. Manosevitz (Eds.), *Theories of personality: Primary sources and research* (2nd ed.). New York: Wiley.

Mason, J. W. (1975). A historical view of the stress field. *Journal of Human Stress, 1,* 6–12, 22–37.

Masson, J. M. (1984). *The assault on truth: Freud's suppression of the seduction theory.* New York: Farrar, Straus, & Giroux.

Matarazzo, J. D. (1980). Behavioral health and behavioral medicine: Frontiers for a new health psychology. *American Psychologist, 35,* 807–817.

Matas, L., Arend, R. A., & Sroufe, L. A. (1978). Continuity of adaptation in the second year: The relationship between quality of attachment and later competence. *Child Development, 49,* 483–494.

Matthews, R. A. (1982). Psychological perspectives on the Type A behavior pattern. *Psychological Bulletin, 91,* 293–323.

May, R. (1950, 1977). *The meaning of anxiety.* New York: Ronald Press.

May, R. (1953). *Man's search for himself.* New York: Norton.

May, R. (1967). *Psychology and the human dilemma.* New York: Van Nostrand.

May R. (1969). *Love and will.* New York: Norton.

May, R. (1972). *Power and innocence: A search for the sources of violence.* New York: Norton.

May, R. (1981). *Freedom and destiny.* New York: Norton.

McAdams, D. P. (1990). *The person: An introduction to personality psychology.* San Diego: Harcourt Brace Jovanovich.

McClelland, D. C. (1961). *The achieving society.* Princeton, NJ: Van Nostrand.

McClelland, D. C. (1975). *Power: The inner experience.* New York: Wiley.

McClelland, D. C., Atkinson, J. W., Clark, R. A., & Lowell, E. L. (1953). *The achievement motive.* New York: Appleton.

McCrae, R. R., & Costa, P. T. (1987). Validation of the five-factor model of personality across instruments and observers. *Journal of Personality and Social Psychology, 52,* 81–90.

McFarlin, D. B., Baumeister, R. F., & Blascovich, J. (1984). On knowing when to quit: Task failure, self-esteem, advice, and nonproductive persistence. *Journal of Personality, 52,* 138–155.

McGee, J., & Wells, K. (1982). Gender typing and androgyny in later life. *Human Development, 25,* 116–139.

McGinnies, E. (1949). Emotionality and perceptual defense. *Psychological Review, 56,* 244–251.

McGuire, F. L. (1976). Personality factors in highway accidents. *Human Factors, 18,* 433–442.

McReynolds, P. (1979). The case for interactional assessment. *Behavioral Assessment, 1,* 237–247.

Mead, M. (1935). *Sex and temperament in three primitive societies.* New York: Morrow.

Mednick, S. A., Gabrielli, W. F., & Hutchings, B. (1984). Genetic influences in criminal convictions: Evidence from an adoption cohort. *Science, 224,* 891–894.

Meehl, P. E. (1962). Schizotaxia, schizotypy, schizophrenia. *American Psychologist, 17,* 827–838.

Meerloo, J. (1970). Pervasiveness of terms and concepts. (Tribute to Alfred Adler on his 100th birthday). *Journal of Individual Psychology, 26,* 14.

Meichenbaum, D. (1974). *Cognitive behavior modification.* Boston: General Learning Press.

Meichenbaum, D. (1985). *Stress inoculation training.* New York: Pergamon.

Meichenbaum, D., & Cameron, R. (1983). Stress inoculation training: Toward a general paradigm for training coping skills. In D. Meichenbaum & M. E. Jaremko (Eds.), *Stress reduction and prevention.* New York: Plenum Press.

Meissner, W. W. (1980). Theories of personality and psychopathology: Classical psychoanalysis. In H. I. Kaplan, A. M. Freedman, & B. J. Sadock (Eds.), *Comprehensive textbook of psychiatry* (3rd ed., Vol. 1). Baltimore: Williams & Wilkins.

Melzack, R. (1954). The genesis of emotional behavior: An experimental study of the dog. *Journal of Comparative and Physiological Psychology, 47,* 166–168.

Mendlewicz, J. (1985). Genetic research in depressive disorders. In E. E. Beckham & W. R. Leber (Eds.), *Handbook of depression: Treatment, assessment and research.* Homewood, IL: Dorsey Press.

Menninger, W. C. (1935). Psychological factors in the etiology of diabetes. *Journal of Nervous and Mental Diseases, 81,* 1–13.

Midlarsky, E., & Bryan, J. H. (1972). Affect expressions and children's imitative altruism. *Journal of Experimental Research in Personality, 6,* 195–203.

Miller, N. E. (1948). Theory and experiment relating psychoanalytic displacement to stimulus-response generalization. *Journal of Abnormal and Social Psychology, 43,* 155–178.

Miller, P. C., Lefcourt, H. M., & Ware, E. E. (1983). The construction and development of the Miller Marital Locus of Control Scale. *Canadian Journal of Behaviorial Science, 15,* 266–279.

Millon, T., & Klerman, G. L. (1986). *Contemporary directions in psychopathology: Toward the DSM-IV*. New York: Guilford Press.

Minkler, M. (1989). Health education, health promotion and the open society: An historical perspective. *Health Education Quarterly, 16*(1), 17–30.

Minshew, N. J., Payton, J. B., & Sclabassi, R. J. (1986). Cortical neurophysiologic abnormalities in autism. *Neurology, 36* (Suppl. 1), 194.

Minuchin, S. (1974). *Families and family therapy*. Cambridge, MA: Harvard University Press.

Mischel, W. (1968). *Personality and assessment*. New York: Wiley.

Mischel, W. (1984). On the predictability of behavior and the structure of personality. In R. A. Zucker, J. C. Aronoff, & A. I. Rabin (Eds.), *Personality and the prediction of behavior*. New York: Academic.

Mischel, W. (1986). *Introduction to personality* (4th ed.). New York: Holt, Rinehart & Winston.

Mischel, W., & Baker, N. (1975). Cognitive transformations of reward objects through instructions. *Journal of Personality and Social Psychology, 31*, 254–261.

Mischel, W., & Moore, B. (1973). Effects of attention to symbolically-presented rewards on self-control. *Journal of Personality and Social Psychology, 28*, 172–179.

Mitchell, A. (1983). *The nine American lifestyles*. New York: Macmillan.

Money, J. (1974). Prenatal hormones and postnatal socialization in gender identity differentiation. In J. K. Cole & R. Dienstbier (Eds.), *Nebraska symposium on motivation, 1973* (pp. 221–295). Lincoln, NE: University of Nebraska Press.

Money, J. (1980). *Love and love sickness: The science of sex, gender difference, and pair-bonding*. Baltimore: Johns Hopkins University Press.

Money, J., & Alexander, D. (1969). Psychosexual development and absence of homosexuality in males with precocious puberty. *Journal of Nervous and Mental Diseases, 148*(2), 111–123.

Money, J., & Ehrhardt, A. E. (1972). *Man & woman, boy & girl*. Baltimore: Johns Hopkins University Press.

Monson, T. C., Hesley, J. W., & Chernick, L. (1982). Specifying when personality traits can and cannot predict behavior: An alternative to abandoning the attempt to predict single-act criteria. *Journal of Personality and Social Psychology, 43*, 385–399.

Moore, T. (1975). Training for what? Alterantive emphasis? *AEP—Association of Educational Psychologists Journal, 3*, 21–24.

Moos, R. H. (1964). Personality factors associated with rheumatoid arthritis: A review. *Journal of Chronic Diseases, 17*, 18–29.

Morawski, J. G. (1987). The troubled quest for masculinity, femininity, and androgyny. In P. Shaveer & C. Hendrick (Eds.), *Sex and gender* (pp. 44–69). Beverly, Hills, CA: Sage.

Moreno, J. L. (1946). *Psychodrama*. New York: Beacon House.

Morgan, W. P. (1973). Influence of acute physical activity on state anxiety. In *Proceedings of the College Physical Education Association*. Pittsburgh.

Morgan, W. P. (1980). Test of champions. *Psychology Today, 14*, 92–108.

Morrison, J. (1980). Adult psychiatric disorders in parents of hyperactive children. *American Journal of Psychiatry, 137*(7), 825–827.

Murray, H. A. (and collaborators). (1938). *Explorations in personality*. New York: Oxford University Press.

Mussen, P. H., & Jones, M. C. (1957). Self-conceptions, motivations, and interpersonal attitudes of late- and early-maturing boys. *Child Development, 28*, 243–256.

National Institute of Mental Health (1985). *Mental Health, United States, 1985*. Washington, DC: U.S. Governmenting Printing Office.

Neimeyer, R. A. (1984). Toward a personal construct conceptualization of depression and suicide. In F. R. Epting & R. A. Neimeyer (Eds.), *Personal meanings of death:*

Applications of personal construct theory to clinical practice (pp. 127–173). New York: Hemisphere/McGraw-Hill.

Neimeyer, R. A. (1985). *The development of personal construct psychology.* Lincoln: University of Nebraska Press.

Neugarten, B. L. (1968). Adult personality: Toward a psychology of the life cycle. In B. L. Neugarten (Ed.), *Middle age and aging: A reader in social psychology* (pp. 137–147). Chicago: University of Chicago Press.

Neugarten, B. L. (1971). Grow old along with me! The best is yet to be. *Psychology Today, 5*(7), 45–48 ff.

Neugarten, B. L. (1973). Personality changes in late life: A developmental perspective. In C. Eisdorfer & M. P. Lawton (Eds.), *The psychology of adult development and aging* (pp. 311–338). Washington, DC: American Psychological Association.

Neugarten, B. L. (1977). Personality and aging. In J. E. Birren & K. W. Schaie (Eds.), *Handbook of the psychology of aging* (pp. 626–649). New York: Van Nostrand Reinhold.

Neugarten, B. L., & Associates. (1964). *Personality in middle and late life.* New York: Atherton.

Nichols, S. L., & Newman, J. P. (1986). Effects of punishment on response latency in extroverts. *Journal of Personality and Social Psychology, 50,* 624–630.

Niemcryk, S. J., Jenkins, C. D., Rose, R. M., & Hurst, M. W. (1987). The prospective impact of psychosocial variables on rates of illness and injury in professional employees. *Journal of Occupational Medicine, 29*(8), 645–652.

Nietzel, M. T. (1979). *Crime and its modifications: A social learning perspective.* New York: Pergamon Press.

Nisan, M., & Kohlberg, L. (1982). Universality and variation in moral judgment: A longitudinal and cross-sectional study in Turkey. *Child Development, 53,* 865–876.

Norusis, M. (1990). *SPSS/PC + statistics 4.0.* Chicago: SPSS, Inc.

Notman, M. T. (1980). Adult life cycles: Changing roles and changing hormones. In J. E. Parsons (Ed.), *The psychology of sex differences and sex roles.* New York: McGraw-Hill.

Nunnally, J. (1978). *Psychometric theory.* New York: McGraw-Hill.

Ochse, R., & Plug, C. (1986). Cross-cultural investigation of the validity of Erikson's theory of personality development. *Journal of Personality and Social Psychology, 50,* 1240–1252.

O'Gorman, J. G. (1983). Habituation and personality. In A. Gale & J. A. Edwards (Eds.), *Physiological correlates of human behavior: Vol. 3. Individual differences and psychopathology* (pp. 45–61). London: Academic Press.

Ohman, A. (1986). Face the beast and fear the face: Animal and social fears as prototypes for evolutionary analyses of emotion. *Psychophysiology, 23,* 123–145.

Oliner, S. P., & Oliner, P. M. (1988). *The altruistic personality: Rescuers of Jews in Nazi Europe.* New York: The Free Press.

Orlinsky, D. E., & Howard, K. I. (1987). A generic model of psychotherapy. *Journal of Integrative and Eclectic Psychotherapy, 6,* 282–293.

Orne, M. T. (1962). On the social psychology of the psychological experiment: With particular reference to demand characteristics and their implications. *American Psychologist, 17,* 776–783.

Osgood, C. E., Suci, G. J., & Tannenbaum, P. H. (1957). *The measurement of meaning.* Urbana: University of Illinois Press.

Pagano, R. R. (1990). *Understanding statistics in the behavioral sciences* (3rd ed.). St. Paul, MN: West.

Parkes, C. M., Benjamin, B., & Fitzgerald, R. G. (1969). Broken heart: A statistical study of increased mortality among widowers. *British Medical Journal, 1,* 740–743.

Paterson, R. J., & Neufeld, R.W.J. (1987). Clear danger: Situational determinants of the appraisal of threat. *Psychological Bulletin, 101,* 404–416.

Paulhus, D. L. (1983). Sphere-specific measures of perceived control. *Journal of Personality and Social Psychology, 44,* 1253–1265.

Peabody, D. (1987). Selecting representative trait adjectives. *Journal of Personality and Social Psychology, 52,* 59–71.

Pearce-McCall, D., & Newman, J. P. (1986). Expectations of success following noncontingent punishment in introverts and extroverts. *Journal of Personality and Social Psychology, 50,* 439–446.

Pennebaker, J. W., & O'Heeron, R. C. (1984). Confiding in others and illness rates among spouses of suicide and accidental-death victims. *Journal of Abnormal Psychology, 93,* 473–476.

Perls, F. S. (1967). Group vs. individual therapy. *ETC: A review of general semantics, 34,* 306–312.

Perls, F. S. (1970). *Gestalt therapy now: Therapy, techniques, applications.* Palo Alto, CA: Science and Behavior Books.

Pervin, L. A. (1985). Personality: Current controversies, issues and directions. *Annual Review of Psychology, 36,* 83–114.

Peshkin, M. M. (1960). Management of the institutionalized child with intractable asthma. *Annals of Allergy, 18,* 75–79.

Peterson, C., & Stunkard, A. J. (1986). *Personal control and health promotion.* Unpublished manuscript, Virginia Polytechnic Institute and State University.

Petrie, A. (1967). *Individuality in pain and suffering.* Chicago: University of Chicago Press.

Petrie, A. (1978). *Individuality in pain and suffering* (2nd ed.). Chicago: University of Chicago Press.

Pettigrew, T. F. (1958). Personality and socio-cultural factors in intergroup attitudes: A cross-national comparison. *Journal of Conflict Resolution, 2,* 29–42.

Pettingale, K. W., Morris, T., Greer, S., & Haybittle, J. L. (1985). Mental attitudes to cancer: An additional prognostic factor. *Lancet, 1,* 750.

Petzelt, J. T., & Craddick, R. (1978). Present meaning of assessment in psychology. *Professional Psychology: Research and Practice, 9,* 587–591.

Pfeiffer, E. (1977). Psychopathology and social pathology. In J. E. Birren & K. W. Schaie (Eds.), *Handbook of the psychology of aging* (pp. 650–671). New York: Van Nostrand Reinhold.

Phares, E. J. (1976). *Locus of control in personality.* Morristown, NJ: General Learning Press.

Pinneau, S. R. (1955). The infantile disorders of hospitalism and anaclitic depression. *Psychological Bulletin, 52,* 429–452.

Plomin, R. (1986). Behavioral genetic methods. *Journal of Personality, 54,* 226–261.

Plomin, R., Chipuer, H. M., & Loehlin, J. C. (1990). Behavior genetics and personality. In L. A. Pervin (Ed.), *Handbook of personality theory and research* (pp. 225–243). New York: Guilford.

Plomin, R., & DeFries, J. C. (1985). *Origins of individual differences in infancy: The Colorado Adoption Project.* New York: Academic Press.

Plomin, R., & Foch, T. T. (1980). A twin study of objectively assessed personality in childhood. *Journal of Personality and Social Psychology, 39,* 680–688.

Pogrebin, L. C. (1980). *Growing up free.* New York: McGraw-Hill.

Prince, M. (1905). *The dissociation of a personality.* New York: Longmans.

Pulkkinen, L. (1982). Self-control and continuity from childhood to adolescence. In P. B. Baltes & O. G. Brim, Jr. (Eds.), *Lifespan development and behavior* (Vol. 4). New York: Academic Press.

Puska, P. (1984). Community based prevention of cardiovascular disease: The North Karelia Project. In J. D. Matarazzo, S. M. Weiss, et al. (Eds.), *Behavioral health.* New York: Wiley.

Ragland, D. B., & Brand, R. J. (1988, January 14). Type A behavior and mortality from coronary heart disease. *New England Journal of Medicine, 318,* 65–69.

Ramirez, M., III, & Casteneda, A. (1974). *Cultural democracy, biocognitive development, and education.* New York Academic Press.

Reckless, W. C. (1961). *The crime problem.* New York: Appleton-Century-Crofts.

Reckless, W. C. (1967). *The crime problem* (4th ed.). New York: Meredith.

Reedy, M. N. (1983). Personality and aging. In D. S. Woodruff & J. E. Birren (Eds.), *Aging: Scientific perspectives and social issues* (2nd ed., pp. 112–136). Monterey, CA: Brooks/Cole.

Remisch, J. M. (1981). Prenatal exposure to synthetic progestins increases potential for aggression in humans. *Science, 211,* 1171–1173.

Renneker, R. (1981). Cancer and psychotherapy. In J. Goldberg (Ed.), *Psychotherapeutic treatment of cancer patients.* New York: Free Press.

Reznick, J. S., Kagan, J., Snidman, N., Gersten, M., Baak, K., & Rosenberg, A. (1986). Inhibited and uninhibited children: A follow-up study. *Child Development, 57,* 660–680.

Ribble, M. A. (1944). Infantile experience in relation to personality development. In J. M. Hunt (Ed.), *Personality and the behavior disorders.* New York: Ronald.

Riese, M. (1988). Temperament in full-term and preterm infants: Stability over ages 6–24 months. *Journal of Developmental and Behavioral Pediatrics, 9,* 6–11.

Rimm, D. C., & Masters, J. C. (1979). *Behavioral therapy: Techniques and empirical findings* (2nd ed.). New York: Academic Press.

Roberts, L. (1988, July 8). Vietnam's psychological toll. *Science, 241,* 159–161.

Robinson, R. G., Kubos, K. L., Starr, B., Rao, K., & Price, T. R. (1984). Mood disorders in stroke patients: Importance of location of lesion. *Brain, 07,* 81–93.

Rodgers, D. A. (1966). Factors underlying differences in alcohol preference among inbred strains of mice. *Psychosomatic Medicine, 28,* 498–513.

Rogers, C. R. (1939). *The clinical treatment of the problem child.* Boston: Houghton Mifflin.

Rogers, C. R. (1942). *Counseling and psychotherapy: Newer concepts in practice.* Boston: Houghton Mifflin.

Rogers, C. R. (1951). *Client-centered therapy: Its current practice, implications, and theory.* Boston: Houghton Mifflin.

Rogers, C. R. (1959). A theory of therapy, personality, and interpersonal relationships, as developed in the client-centered framework. In S. Koch (Ed.), *Psychology: A study of a science* (Vol. 3). New York: McGraw-Hill.

Rogers, C. R. (1961). *On becoming a person: A therapist's view of psychotherapy.* Boston: Houghton Mifflin.

Rogers, C. R. (1966). Client-centered therapy. In S. Arieti (Ed.), *American handbook of psychiatry.* New York: Basic Books.

Rogers, C. R., & Dymond, R. F. (Eds.). (1954). *Psychotherapy and personality change.* Chicago: University of Chicago Press.

Rogers, R. (1987). APA's position on the insanity defense: Empiricism versus emotionalism. *American Psychologist, 42,* 840–848.

Rokeach, M. (1960). *The open and closed mind.* New York: Basic Books.

Rorschach, H. (1921). *Psychodiagnostik.* Berne: Birchen.

Rose, R. J., & Ditto, W. B. (1983). A developmental genetic analysis of common fears from early adolescence to early adulthood. *Child Development, 54,* 361–368.

Rose, R. J., Koskenvuo, M., Kaprio, J., Sarna, S., & Langinvainio, H. (1988). Shared genes, shared experiences, and similarity of personality: Data from 14,288 adult Finnish co-twins. *Journal of Personality and Social Psychology, 54,* 161–171.

Rosenhan, D. L. (1973). On being sane in insane places. *Science, 179,* 250–258.

Rosenman, R. H. (1986). Current and past history of Type A behavior pattern. In T. H. Schmidt, T. M. Dembroski, & G. Blumchen (Eds.), *Biological and psychological factors in cardiovascular disease* (pp. 15–40). New York: Springer-Verlag.

Rosenman, R. H., Brand, R. J., Jenkins, C. D., Friedman, M., Straus, R., & Wurm, M.

(1975). Coronary heart disease in the Western Colloborative Group Study: Final follow-up of 8½ years. *Journal of the American Medical Association, 233,* 872–877.

Rosenthal R., Hall, J. A., DiMatteo, M. R., Rogers, P. L., & Archer, D. (1979). *Sensitivity to nonverbal communication: The PONS tests.* Baltimore: Johns Hopkins University Press.

Rosenzweig, S. (1988). The identity and idiodynamics of the multiple personality "Sally Beauchamp." *American Psychologist, 43,* 45–48.

Ross, A. O., & Pelham, W. E. (1981). Child psychopathology. *Annual Review of Psychology, 32,* 243–278.

Ross, D., & Ross, S. (1976). *Hyperactivity: Research, theory, action.* New York: Wiley.

Roth, D. L., & Holmes, D. S. (1985). Influence of physical fitness in deterring the impact of stressful events on physical and psychologic health. *Psychosomatic Medicine, 47,* 164–173.

Rothbart, M. K. (1971). Birth order and mother-child interaction in an achievement-oriented situation. *Journal of Personality and Social Psychology, 17,* 113–120.

Rothenberg, M. G. (1990). Graphology. *Encyclopedia Americana* (Vol. 13, pp. 190–191). Danbury, CT: Grolier, Inc.

Rotter, J. B. (1954). *Social learning and clinical psychology.* Englewood Cliffs, NJ: Prentice Hall.

Rotter, J. B. (1966). Generalized expectancies for internal versus external control of reinforcement. *Psychological Monographs, 81* (1, Whole No. 609).

Rotter, J. B. (1967). A new scale for the measurement of interpersonal trust. *Journal of Personality, 35,* 651–655.

Rotter, J. B. (1980). Interpersonal trust, trustworthiness, and gullibility. American Psychlogist, 35, 1–7.

Rotter, J. B., & Rafferty, J. E. (1950). *The Rotter Incomplete Sentences Blank manual: College form.* New York: Psychological Corporation.

Rotton, J., & Frey, J. (1985). Air pollution, weather, and violent crimes: Concomitant, time-series analysis of archival data. *Journal of Personality and Social Psychology, 49,* 1207–1220.

Rowe, D. C. (1987). Resolving the person-situation debate: Invitation to an interdisciplinary dialogue. *American Psychologist, 42,* 218–227.

Royce, J. R., & Powell, A. (1983). *Theory of personality and individual differences: Factors, systems, and processes.* Englewood Cliffs, NJ: Prentice Hall.

Rushton, J. P. (1976). Socialization and the altruistic behavior of children. *Psychological Bulletin, 83,* 898–913.

Rushton, J. P., Brainerd, C. J., & Pressley, M. (1983). Behavioral development and construct validity: The principle of aggregation. *Psychological Bulletin, 94,* 18–38.

Rushton, J. P., Fulker, D. W., Neale, M. C., Nias, D.K.B., & Eysenck, H. J. (1986). Altruism and aggression: The heritability of individual differences. *Journal of Personality and Social Psychology, 50,* 1192–1198.

Rutter, M. (1979). Maternal deprivation, 1972–1978: New findings, new concepts, new approaches. *Child Development, 50,* 283–305.

Sackeim, H. A., Weinman, A. L., Gur, R. C., Greenberg, M. Hungerbuhler, J. P., & Geschwind, N. (1982). Pathological laughter and crying: Functional brain asymmetry in the expression of positive and negative emotions. *Archives of Neurology, 39,* 210–218.

Sadalla, E., & Burroughs, J. (1981). Profiles in eating: Sexy vegetarians and other diet-based social stereotypes. *Psychology Today, 15,* 51–57.

Sahley, T. L., & Panksepp, J. (1987). Brain opioids and autism: An updated analysis of possible linkages. *Journal of Autism and Developmental Disorders, 17,* 201–216.

St. George–Hyslop, P. H., et al. (1987). Absence of duplication of chromosome 21 genes in familial and sporadic Alzheimer's disease. *Science, 238,* 664–666.

Samenow, S. E. (1984). *Inside the criminal mind.* New York: Times Books.

Sameroff, A. J., & Chandler, M. J. (1975). Reproductive right and the continuum of caretaking casualty. In F. D. Horowitz (Ed.), *Review of child development research* (Vol. 4). Chicago: University of Chicago Press.

Sarason, I. G., & Sarason, B. G. (1984). *Abnormal psychology.* Englewood Cliffs, NJ: Prentice Hall.

Scarf, M. (1980). Images that heal: A doubtful idea whose time has come. *Psychology Today, 14*(4), 32–46.

Scarr, S. (1988). New genotypes and environments combine: Development and individual differences. In N. Bolger, A. Caspi, G. Downey, & M. Moorehouse (Eds.), *Persons in context: Developmental processes.* New York: Cambridge University Press.

Scarr, S., & McCartney, K. (1983). How people make their own environments: A theory of genotype-environment effects. *Child Development, 54,* 424–435.

Scarr, S., & Weinberg, R. A. (1983). The Minnesota adoption studies: Genetic differences and malleability. *Child Development, 54,* 260–267.

Schachter, S. (1959). *The psychology of affiliation: Experimental studies of the sources of gregariousness.* Stanford, CA: Stanford University Press.

Schaefer, C., Coyne, J. C., & Lazarus, R. S. (1981). The health-related functions of social support. *Journal of Behavioral Medicine, 4,* 381–406.

Schaefer, E. S. (1959). A circumplex model for maternal behavior. *Journal of Abnormal and Social Psychology, 59,* 226–235.

Schaffer, H. R., & Emerson, P. E. (1964). The development of social attachments in infancy. *Monographs of the Society for Research in Child Development, 29* (3, Serial No. 94).

Schaie, K. W., & Parham, I. A. (1976). Stability of adult personality traits: Fact or fable? *Journal of Personality and Social Psychology, 34,* 146–158.

Schank, R., & Abelson, R. (1977). *Scripts, plans, goals, and understanding.* Hillsdale, NJ: Erlbaum.

Schildkraut, J. J. (1965). The catecholamine hypothesis of affective disorders: A review of supporting evidence. *American Journal of Psychiatry, 122,* 509–522.

Schmale, A. H., Jr. (1972). Giving up as a final common pathway to changes in health. *Advances in Psychosomatic Medicine, 8,* 20–40.

Schmied, L. A., & Lawler, K. A. (1986). Hardiness, Type A behavior, and the stress-illness relation in working women. *Journal of Personality and Social Psychology, 51,* 1218–1223.

Schreiber, F. R. (1973). *Sybil.* Chicago: Regency.

Schroder, H. M., Driver, M. J., & Streufert, S. (1967). *Human information processing.* New York: Holt, Rinehart, & Winston.

Schuckit, M. A., & Rayses, V. (1979). Ethanol ingestion: Differences in blood acetaldehyde concetrations in relatives of alcoholics and controls. *Science, 203,* 54–55.

Schultz, D. P., & Schultz, S. E. (1990). *Psychology and industry today* (5th ed.). New York: Macmillan.

Schwartz, G. E., Davidson, R. J., & Maer, F. (1975). Right hemisphere lateralization for emotion in the human brain: Interactions with cognition. *Science, 190,* 286–288.

Schwartz, S., & Griffin, T. (1986). *Medical thinking: The psychology of medical judgment and decision making.* New York: Springer-Verlag.

Scott-Maxwell, F. (1968). *The measure of my days.* New York: Knopf.

Sears, R. R. (1943). *Survey of objective studies of psychoanalytic concepts.* New York: Social Science Research Council.

Sears, R. R., Maccoby, E. E., & Levin, H. (1957). *Patterns of child rearing.* New York: Harper.

Seeman, J. (1949). A study of the process of nondirective therapy. *Journal of Consulting Psychology, 13,* 157–168.

Seeman, M., & Evans, J. W. (1962). Alienation and learning in a hospital setting. *American Sociological Review, 27,* 772–782.

Seligman, M.E.P. (1975). *Helplessness.* San Francisco: Freeman.

Seligman, M.E.P. (1992). *Helplessness.* (2nd ed.). San Francisco: Freeman.

Selye, H. (1976). *The stress of life* (rev. ed.). New York: McGraw-Hill.

Selye, H. (1982). History and present status of the stress concept. In L. Goldberger & S. Breznitz (Eds.), *Handbook of stress: Theoretical and clinical aspects.* New York: Free Press.

Sewell, W. H., & Mussen, P. H. (1952). The effects of feeding, weaning, and scheduling procedures on childhood adjustment and the formation of oral symptoms. *Child Development, 23,* 185–191.

Shapiro, A. K., & Morris, L. A. (1978). The placebo effect in medical and psychological therapies. In S. L. Garfield & A. E. Bergin (Eds.), *Handbook of psychotherapy and behavior change* (2nd ed., pp. 369–410). New York: Wiley.

Shapiro, D. A., & Shapiro, D. (1982). Meta-analysis of comparative therapy outcome studies: A replication and refinement. *Psychological Bulletin, 92,* 581–604.

Shaw, L., & Sichel, H. S. (1971). *Accident proneness: Research in the occurrence, causation, and prevention of road accidents.* New York: Pergamon.

Sheldon, W. H., & Stevens, S. S. (1942). *The varieties of temperament.* New York: Harper & Row.

Sheldon, W. H., Stevens, S. S., & Tucker, W. B. (1940). *The varieties of human physique.* New York: Harper & Row.

Sherwin, I., & Geschwind, N. (1978). Neural substrates of behavior. In A. M. Nicholl (Ed.), *The Harvard guide to modern psychiatry* (pp. 59–80). Cambridge, MA: Harvard University Press.

Shostrom, E. L. (1974). *Manual for the Personal Orientation Inventory.* San Diego: Educational and Industrial Testing Service.

Shrauger, J. S., & Sorman, P. B. (1977). Self-evaluations, initial success and failure, and improvement as determinants of persistence. *Journal of Consulting and Clinical Psychology, 45,* 784–795.

Silverman, L. H. (1976). Psychoanalytic theory: "The reports of my death are greatly exaggerated." *American Psychologist, 31,* 621–637.

Silverman, L. H., Bronstein, A., & Mendelsohn, E. (1976). The further use of the subliminal psychodynamic activation method for the experimental study of the clinical theory of psychoanalysis: On the specificity of relationships between manifest psychopathology and unconscious conflict. *Psychotherapy: Theory, Research, and Practice, 13,* 2–16.

Silverman, L. H., & Fishel, A. K. (1981). The Oedipus complex: Studies in adult male behavior. In L. Wheeler (Ed.), *Review of personality and social psychology* (Vol. 2). Beverly Hills, CA: Sage.

Silverman, L. H., Klinger, H., Lustbader, L., Farrell, J., & Martin, A. D. (1972). The effects of subliminal drive stimulation on the speech of stutterers. *Journal of Nervous and Mental Disease, 155,* 14–21.

Silverman, L. H., & Weinberger, J. (1985). Mommy and I are one: Implications for psychotherapy. *American Psychologist, 40,* 1296–1308.

Simonton, D. K. (1990). Personality and politics. In L. A. Pervin (Ed.), *Handbook of personality theory and research* (pp. 670–692). New York: Guilford Press.

Simonton, O. C., Matthews-Simonton, S., & Creighton, J. (1978). *Getting well again.* Los Angeles: J. P. Tarper (Dist. by St. Martin's Press, New York).

Simpson, S. (producer). (aired February 7, 1987). *Freud under analysis.* Boston: Nova.

Skinner, B. F. (1948/1962). *Walden two.* New York: Macmillan.

Skinner, B. F. (1971). *Beyond freedom and dignity.* New York: Knopf.

Skurnik, N. (1988). Le syndrome de Stockholm: Essai d'étude de ses criteria (The Stockholm syndrome: An attempt to study the criteria). *Annales-Medico-Psychologiques, 146* (1–2), 174–178.

Smith, M., & Glass, J. (1977). Meta-analysis of psychotherapy outcome studies. *American Psychologist, 32,* 752–760.

Smith, M. L., Glass, G. V., & Miller, T. J. (1980). *The benefits of psychotherapy.* Baltimore: Johns Hopkins.

Snyder, M. (1974). Self-monitoring of expressive behavior. *Journal of Personality and Social Psychology, 30,* 526-537.

Snyder, M. (1979). Self-monitoring processes. *Advances in Experimental Social Psychology, 12,* 85–128.

Sonstroem, R. J. (1984). Exercise and self-esteem. *Exercise and Sport Sciences Reviews, 12,* 123–155.

Sostek, A. J., & Wyatt, R. J. (1981). The chemistry of crankiness. *Psychology Today, 15*(10), 120.

Spence, J. T., & Helmreich, R. L. (1978). *Masculinity and femininity: Their psychological dimensions, correlates, and antecedents.* Austin: University of Texas Press.

Spergel, P., Ehrlich, G. E., & Glass, D. (1978). The rheumatoid arthritic personality: A psychodiagnostic myth. *Psychosomatics, 19,* 79–86.

Spiro, M. E. (1982). *Oedipus in the Trobriands.* Chicago: Chicago University Press.

Spitz, R. R. (1953). Psychoanalytische Begriffsbildung und physiologisches Denkmodell. *Schweiz Psychologie Anwendung, 12,* 24–39.

Spitzer, R. L. (1976). More on pseudoscience in science and the case for psychiatric diagnosis: A critique of D. L. Rosenhan's "On Being Sane in Insane Places" and "The Contextual Nature of Psychiatric Diagnosis." *Archives of General Psychiatry, 33,* 459–470.

Sroufe, A., Fox, N., & Pancake, V. (1983). Attachment and dependency in developmental perspective. *Child Development, 54,* 1615–1627.

Sroufe, L. W. (1978). Emotional development in infancy. In J. Osofsky (Ed.), *Handbook of infancy.* New York: Wiley.

Sroufe, L. W. (1985). Attachment classification from the perspective of infant-caregiver relationship and infant temperament. *Child Development, 56,* 1–14.

Stewart, M. A., & Olds, S. W. (1973). *Raising a hyperactive child.* New York: Harper & Row.

Stoddart, T., & Turiel, E. (1985). Children's conception of cross-gender activities. *Child Development, 56,* 861–865.

Stress, burnout high among managers. (1988). *Administrative Management, 49*(3), 7.

Stricker, L. J., & Ross, J. (1964). Some correlates of Jungian personality inventory. *Psychological Reports, 14,* 623–643.

Sullivan, H. S. (1947). *Conceptions of modern psychiatry.* Washington, D.C.: William Alanson White Psychiatric Foundation.

Sullivan, H. S. (1953). *The interpersonal theory of psychiatry.* New York: Norton.

Sullivan, H. S. (1954). *The psychiatric interview.* New York: Norton.

Sullivan, H. S. (1956). *Clinical studies in psychiatry.* New York: Norton.

Sullivan, H. S. (1962). *Schizophrenia as a human process.* New York: Norton.

Sullivan, H. S. (1964). *The fusion of psychiatry and social science.* New York: Norton.

Sundberg, N. D. (1977). *Assessment of persons.* Englewood Cliffs, NJ: Prentice Hall.

Szasz, T. S. (1966, June 12). Mental illness is a myth. *New York Times Magazine.*

Szasz, T. S. (1987). *Insanity: The idea and its consequences.* New York: Wiley.

Takahashi, K. (1986). Examining the Strange Situation procedure with Japanese mothers and 12-month-old infants. *Development Psychology, 22,* 265–270.

Tavris, C. (1987, September 27). Old age is not what it used to be. *New York Times Magazine,* Pt. 2, pp. 25–26, 91–92.

Thigpen, C. H., & Cleckley, H. M. (1957). *The three faces of Eve.* New York: McGraw-Hill.

Thoman, E. B., Liederman, P. H., & Olson, J. P. (1972). Neonate-mother interaction during breast feeding. *Developmental Psychology, 110–118.*

Thomas, A., & Chess, S. (1977). *Temperament and development.* New York: Brunner/Mazel.

Thomas, A., Chess, S., & Birch, H. (1968). *Temperament and behavior disorders in children.* New York: New York University Press.

Thomas, C. B., Duszynski, K. R., & Schaffer, J. W. (1979). Family attitudes reported in youth as potential predictors of cancer. *Psychosomatic Medicine, 4,* 287–302.

Thompson, S. K. (1975). Gender labels and early sex role development. *Child Development, 46,* 339–347.

Thoreson, C. E., & Mahoney, M. J. (1974). *Behavioral self-control.* New York: Holt, Rinehart & Winston.

Tolman, E. C. (1932). *Purposive behavior in animals and men.* New York: Appleton-Century-Crofts. (Reprint ed.)

Torgerson, A. M. (1985). Temperamental differences in infants and 6-year-old children: A follow-up study of twins. In J. Strelau, F. Farley, & A. Gale (Eds.), *The biological bases of personality and behavior* (Vol. 1). New York: Hemisphere.

Tribich, D., & Messer, S. (1974). Psychoanalytic type and status of authority as determiners of suggestibility. *Journal of Consulting and Clinical Psychology, 42,* 842–848.

U.S. Department of Health and Human Services. (1992, January 7). Advance report on final mortality statistics, United States, 1990. *Monthly Vital Statistics Report,* Vol. 40, No. 8, Supplement 2.

Underwood, B., & Moore, B. S. (1981). Sources of behavioral consistency. *Journal of Personality and Social Psychology, 40,* 780–785.

Ungerleiter, S., & Golding, J. M. (1989). Mood profiles of masters track and field athletes. *Perceptual and Motor Skills, 68,* 607–617.

Vaihinger, H. (1911). *The philosophy of "as if."* New York: Harcourt, Brace.

Vaillant, G. E. (1979). Natural history of male psychologic health: Effects of mental health on physical health. *New England Journal of Medicine, 30,* 1249–1254.

Vaillant, G. E. (1984). The disadvantages of DSM-III outweigh its advantages. *American Journal of Psychiatry, 141,* 542–545.

Van Ijzendoorn, M. H., & Kroonenberg, P. M. (1988). Cross-cultural patterns of attachment: A meta-analysis of the strange situation. *Child Development, 59,* 147–156.

Vockell, E. L., Felker, D. W., & Miley, C. H. (1973). Birth order literature, 1967–1972. *Journal of Individual Psychology, 29,* 39–53.

Volpe, A., & Kastenbaum, R. (1967). Beer and TLC. *American Journal of Nursing, 67,* 100–103.

Walker, L. (1984). Sex differences in the development of moral reasoning: A critical review. *Child Development, 55,* 677–691.

Wallston, K. A., & Wallston, B. S. (1981). Health locus of control scales. In H. M. Lefcourt (Ed.), *Research with the locus of control construct* (Vol. 1, pp. 189–243). New York: Academic Press.

Ward, R. A. (1979). *The aging experience: An introduction to social gerontology.* Philadelphia: Lippincott.

Waters, E., Wippman, J., & Sroufe, L. A. (1979). Attachment, positive affect, and competence in the peer group: Two studies in construct validation. *Child Development, 50,* 821–829,.

Watson, J. B. (1913). Psychology as a behaviorist views it. *Psychological Review, 20,* 158–177.

Watson, J. B. (1924/1970). *Behaviorism.* New York: Norton.

Watson, J. B., & Rayner, R. (1920). Conditioned emotional reactions. *Journal of Experimental Psychology, 3,* 1–14.

Weary, G. B., (1978). Self-serving biases in the attribution process: A re-examination of the fact or fiction question. *Journal of Personality and Social Psychology, 36,* 56–71.

Weinberger, J. L., & Silverman, L. H. (1987). Subliminal psychodynamic activation: A method for studying psychoanalytic dynamic propositions. In R. Hogan & W. H. Jones (Eds.), *Perspectives on personality* (Vol. 2, pp. 251–287). Greenwich, CT: JAI Press.

Weiner, H. (1977). *Psychobiology and human disease.* New York: Elsevier.

Weiner, I. B. (1983). The future of psychodiagnosis revisited. *Journal of Personality Assessment, 47,* 451–461.

Weissman, M. M., Leckman, J. F., Merikangas, K. R., Gammon, G. D., & Prusoff, B. A. (1984). Depression and anxiety disorders in parents and children: Results from the Yale family study. *Archives of General Psychiatry, 41,* 845–852.

White, G. L., & La Barba, R. C. (1976). The effects of tactile and kinesthetic stimulation on neonatal development in the premature infant. *Journal of Developmental Psychology, 9,* 569–577.

Whiting, B. B., & Edwards, C. P. (1988). *Children of different worlds: The formation of social behavior.* Cambridge, MA: Harvard University Press.

Whiting, J.W.M., & Child, I. L. (1953). *Child-training and personality.* New Haven: Yale University Press.

Wiebe, D. J., & McCallum, D. M. (1986). Health practices and hardiness as mediators in the stress-illness relationship. *Health Psychology, 5,* 425–438.

Wildman, R., Batchelor, E., Thompson, L., Nelson, F., Moore, J., Patterson, M., & DeLaosa, M. (1980). *The Georgia Court Competency Test: An attempt to develop a rapid, quantitative measure of fitness for trial.* Unpublished manuscript, Forensic Services Division, Center State Hospital, Milledgeville, GA.

Willerman, L., & Cohen, D. B. (1990). *Psychopathology.* New York: McGraw-Hill.

Williams, C. D. (1959). Case report: Elimination of tantrum behavior by extinction procedures. *Journal of Abnormal and Social Psychology, 59,* 269.

Wilson, E. O. (1975). *Sociobiology: The new synthesis.* Cambridge, MA: Harvard University Press.

Wilson, E. O. (1978). *On human nature.* Cambridge, MA: Harvard University Press.

Wilson, J. Q., & Herrnstein, R. (1985). *Crime and human nature.* New York: Simon & Schuster.

Wilson, R. S. (1983). The Louisville Twin Study: Developmental synchronies in behavior. *Child Development, 42,* 1381–1398.

Winterbottom, M. R. (1953). The sources of achievement motivation in others' attitudes toward independence training. In D. C. McClelland et al., *The achievement motive* (pp. 297–304). New York: Appleton.

Witkin, H. A. (1973). The role of cognitive style in academic performance in teacher-student relations. *Educational Testing Service Research Bulletin* (No. RB–73–11). Princeton, NJ: Educational Testing Service.

Witkin, H. A., & Berry, J. W. (1975). Psychological differentiation in cross-cultural perspective. *Journal of Cross-Cultural Psychology, 6,* 4–87.

Witkin, H. A., Dyk, R. B., Faterson, H. F., Goodenough, D. R., & Karp, S. A. (1962). *Psychological differentiation.* New York: Wiley.

Witkin, H. A., & Goodenough, D. R. (1977). Field dependence and interpersonal behavior. *Psychological Bulletin, 84,* 661–689.

Witkin, H. A., Lewis, H. B., Hertzman, M., Machover, K., Meissner, P. B., & Wapner, S. (1954). *Personality through perception.* New York: Harper.

Witkin, H. A., Price-Williams, D., Bertini, M., Bjorn, C., Oltman, P. K., Ramirez, M., & Van Meel, J. (1973). *Social conformity and psychological differentiation.* Princeton, NJ: Educational Testing Service.

Witkin, H. A., et al. (1977). Field-dependent and field-independent cognitive styles and their educational implications. *Review of Educational Research, 47,* 1–64.

Wolcott, J. H., McNeekin, R. R., Burgin, R. E., & Yanowitch, R. E. (1977). Correlation of general aviation accidents with the biorhythm theory. *Human Factors, 19,* 283–293.

Wolf, S., & Wolff, H. G. (1942). Evidence on the genesis of peptic ulcer in man. *Journal of the American Medical Association, 120,* 670–675.

Wolpe, J. (1958). *Psychotherapy by reciprocal inhibition.* Stanford, CA: Stanford University Press.

Woodworth, R. S. (1920). *Personal Data Sheet.* Chicago: Stoelting.

Worobey, J. (1986). Convergence among assessments of temperament in the first month. *Child Development, 57,* 47–55.

Yarnold, P. R., Grimm, L. G., & Mueser, K. T. (1986). Social conformity and the Type A behavior pattern. *Perceptual and Motor Skills, 62,* 99–104.

Yochelson, S., & Samenow, S. E. (1976). *The criminal personality.* New York: Jason Aronson.

Zuckerman, M. (1983). *Biological bases of sensation seeking, impulsivity, and anxiety.* Hillsdale, NJ: Erlbaum.

Zuckerman, M., Koestner, R., DeBoy, T., Garcia, T., et al. (1988). To predict some of the people some of the time: A reexamination of the moderator variable approach in personality theory. *Journal of Personality and Social Psychology, 54,* 1006–1019.

Author Index

Subject Index